THE WORK OF
FORCED ENTERTAINMENT

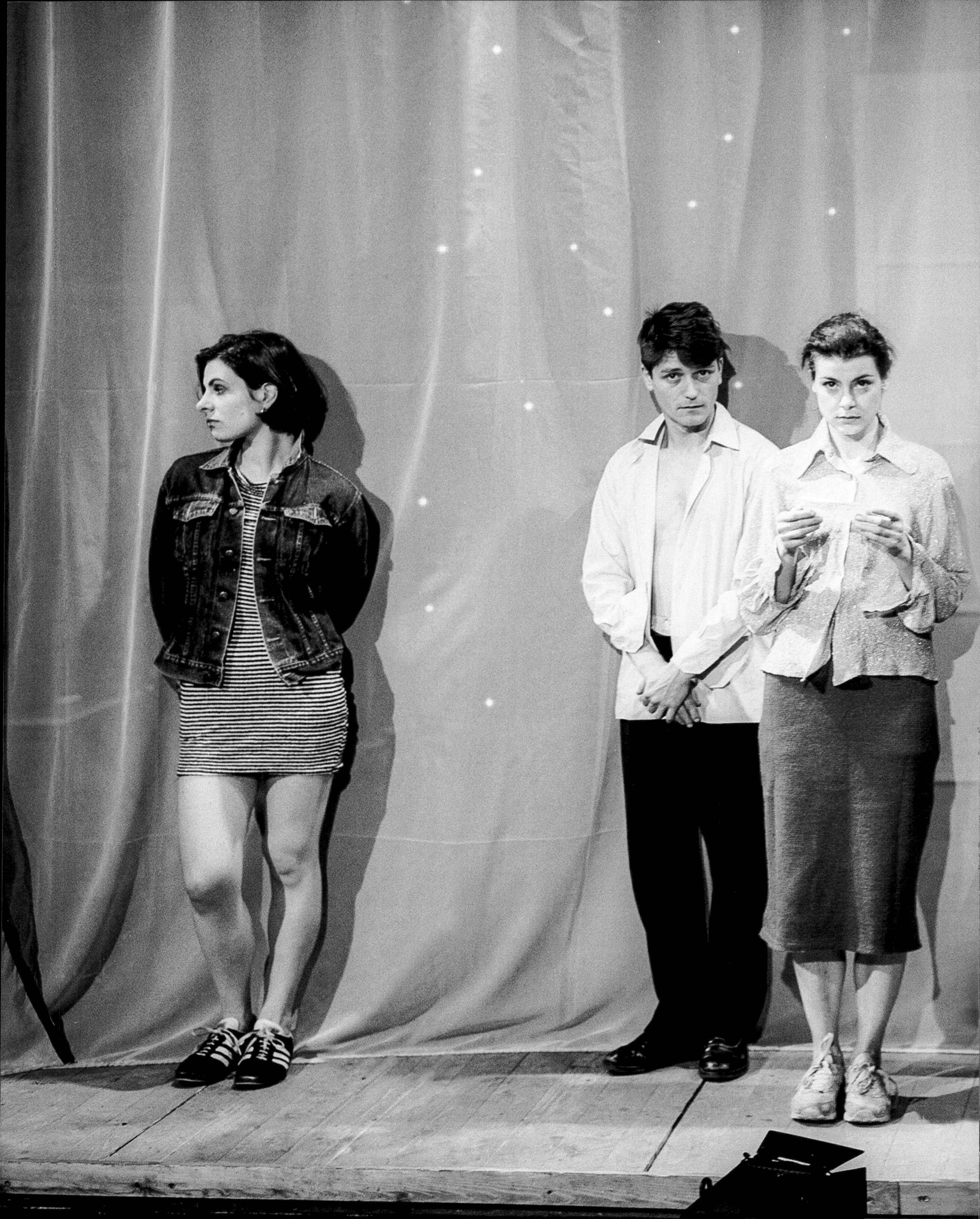

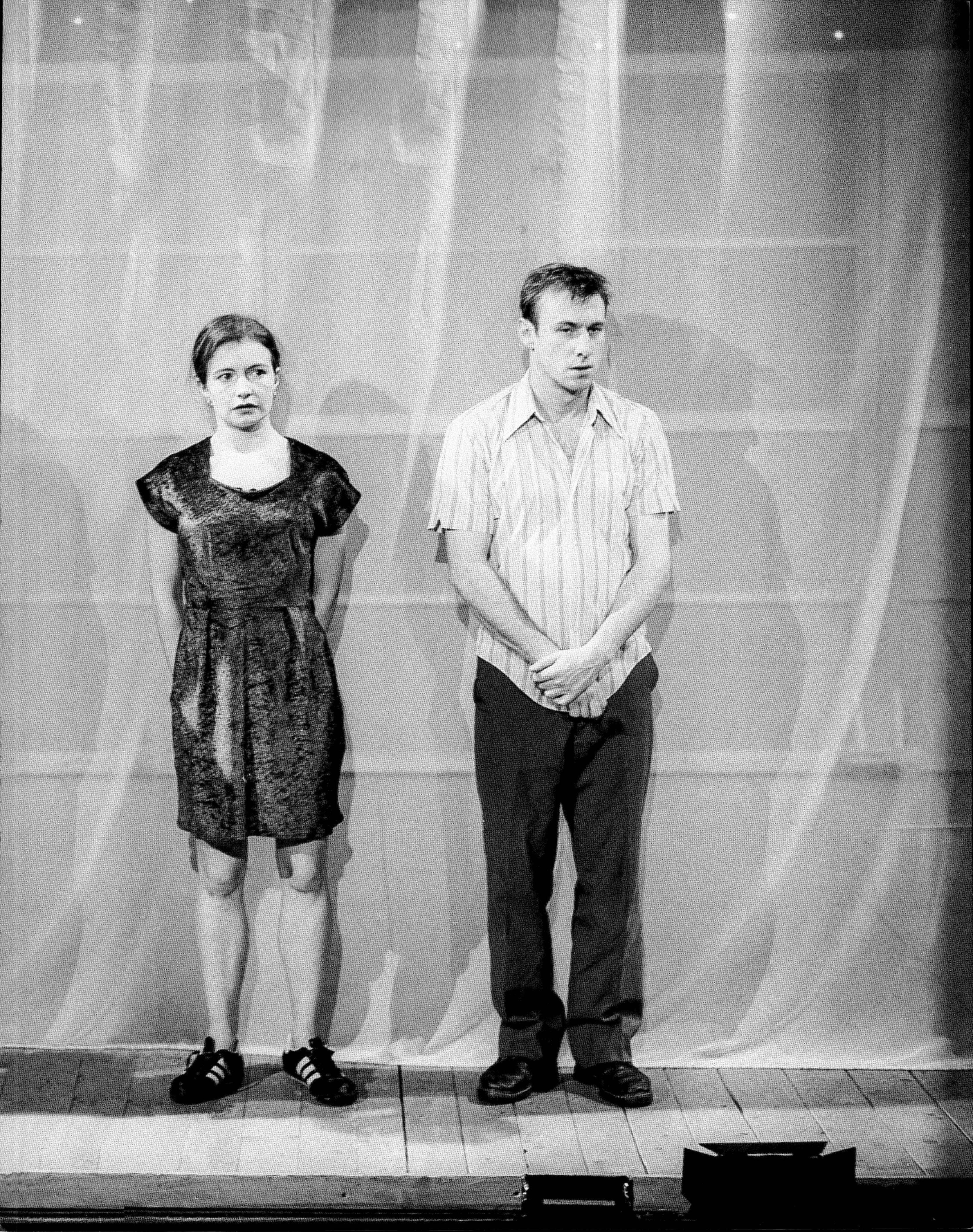

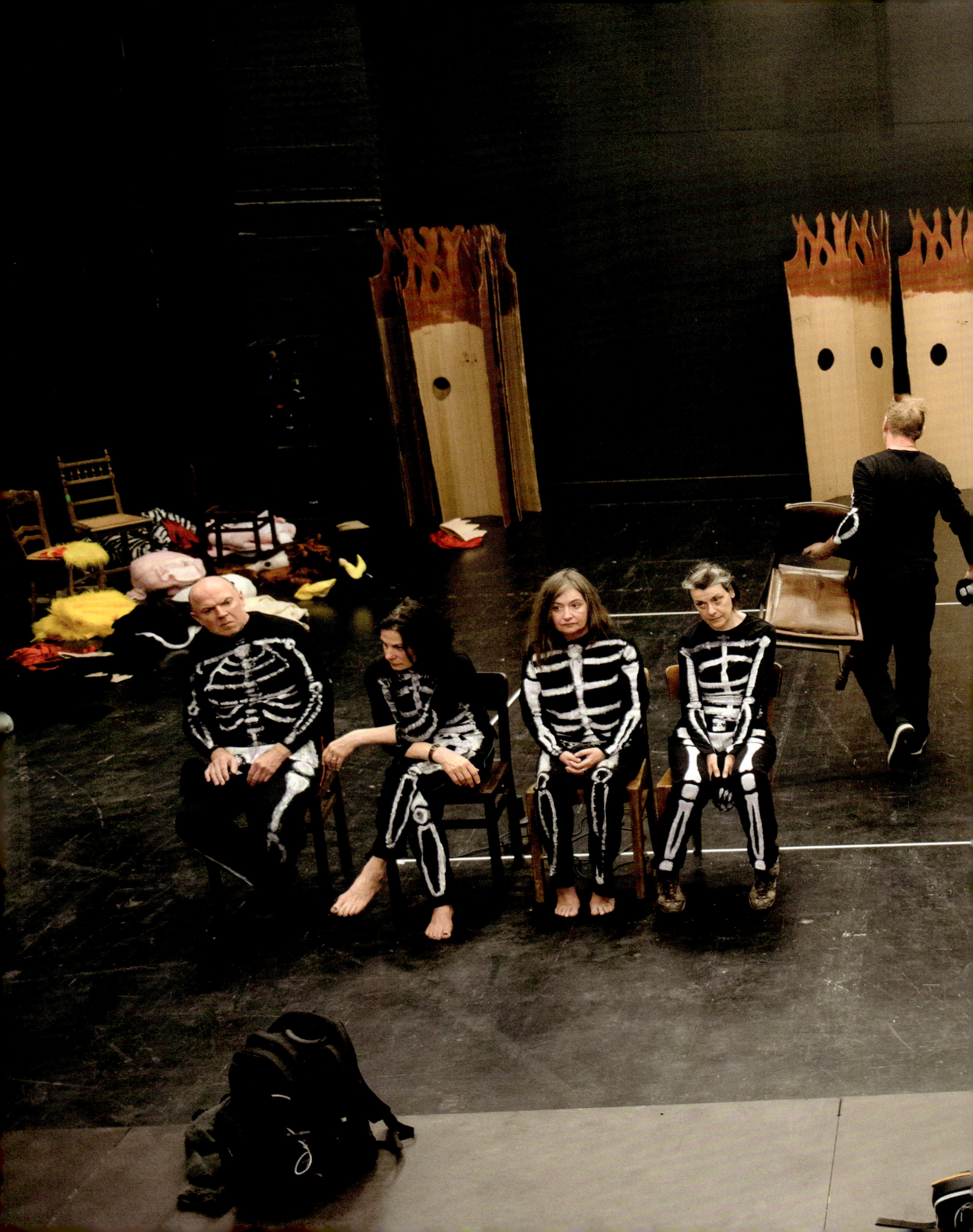

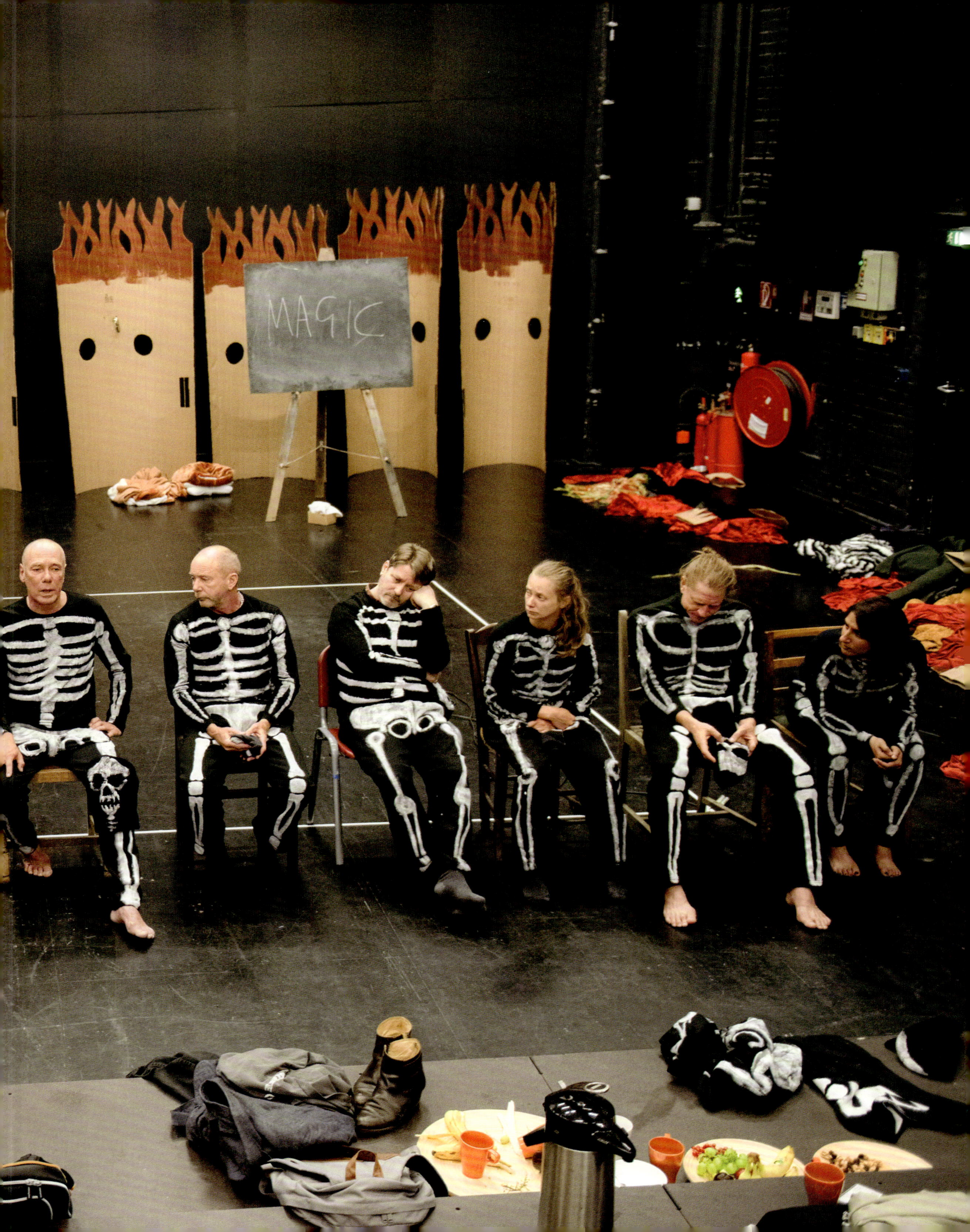
MAGIC

Preface

At the beginning of Forced Entertainment's *The World in Pictures*, Jerry Killick invites the audience to imagine a solitary stroll through the streets of an unfamiliar city. Drawing his listeners into the imaginative space of this pedestrian journey, Killick takes them to the roof of a high-rise building, where things take a grave but compelling turn. We are asked to imagine ourselves standing at the very edge of a parapet, looking over and down, wondering what it might be like to fall. Then, through a simple linguistic twist, we are propelled into the act that has so far only been imagined: 'At a certain point', he says, 'you realize that you've already committed yourself—physically—to falling.' In Killick's story, there is no jump, just a retrospective recognition of a surrender that has already happened; a giving in to the forces of narration and death, our imagined bodies following where our minds have already been led, into the momentarily exhilarating, if ultimately sobering phenomena of descent. The fall is suspended in Killick's tale, just before the final moment of bloody impact, so that the rest of the performance can take place; it is only much later, as he shows a bewildering series of seemingly random images on a TV screen, that we hear the lines that give this book its title: 'These are some of the things that might start to go through your mind when you are falling.'

Based in Sheffield in the north of England, the performance ensemble Forced Entertainment began its collective life in 1984 and has since presented numerous theatre and durational performances, installations, and other works at a range of scales in different arts contexts around the world. This book is an authoritative guide to the oeuvre of the company: a detailed visual investigation of their performances, enhanced by text materials drawn from the works themselves and from exchanges with company members. Alongside these chronologically arranged documents is a set of specially commissioned essays—some long, some short—from writers in the field of performance, discussing the antecedents and principles of the company's aesthetic, the nature of its imaginary worlds and affects, its uses of speech and time, and the artistic concepts that have animated its creations.

Nested within the essays section are three reflective texts that emerge from the company itself and from distinct decades of their work. Written after ten years of the group's existence, 'A Decade of Forced Entertainment', by director Tim Etchells and the company, is a performance-lecture collaging evocative passages of works with observations on the logics and ethos of their creation. 'A Text on Twenty Years with Sixty-Six Footnotes', by Etchells alone, takes a fragmentary, associative tour through recollections of two decades of events, collaborative affiliations, and encounters to speculate on their cumulative force. 'An Answer Without a Question', the final text in this triptych, was commissioned from Etchells especially for this volume and uses the hiatus of a global pandemic to look back on shifts in the company's work—its relation to process, audiences, and time—to speculate on its social value and politics. A detailed interview with the company discusses the dynamics of their collective relationships and creations.

At the heart of the book is another body of work that has emerged through a long collaborative dialogue with Forced Entertainment: the photographic documentation amassed, with verve and acuity, over thirty-nine years by photographer Hugo Glendinning. Time flows and the dramaturgical arcs of performances are transformed into revelatory still images that allow us to see something of these events but also something outside of or in excess of them. Glendinning's extensive archive of the company's work has been mined for the resonant images of the theatre and long durational works that appear here, many of which are previously unpublished, to assemble a kaleidoscopic visual representation of the oeuvre. Sequencing these exposures, within each show and across four decades, tells a particular visual story about each of the works and their aesthetic correspondences. The photographic is brought into dialogue with company members' memories and written accounts in a negotiation of the works' meanings and consequences.

Forced Entertainment have long deployed innovative approaches to textual generation and form, with Etchells's role as a writer actively drawing on group improvisation. The final section of this book brings together three significant performance texts—*First Night*, *Bloody Mess*, and *Dirty Work (The Late Shift)*—that exemplify distinct approaches to individual voices and the collective event, as well as the nature of theatrical listening and imagination. As traces of these works, rather than scripts for some future enactment or adaptation, these artefacts disclose the unique role that a textual imaginary plays in the worlds of the company's performances.

The last of these pieces, *Dirty Work*, uses a narrative technique that is both simple and elaborate: a theatre event with no practical limit on its content or its realization is described by two seated figures. As spectators, we do not see this event—at once multiple, contradictory, and impossible—yet it shimmers before us in our mind's eye. Perhaps this invisible theatre is the most fitting example with which to close a visual documentary account of Forced Entertainment's immense body of work. For the events summoned here are an absent presence, retold and reimagined from different perspectives, traced in forms other than those they initially occurred in and offered for further remaking in the minds of those reading.

When Killick shows us 'the things that go through our minds when falling' we do not think that these will be the very images we encounter at our own deaths, but we momentarily enter the space in which we may conjure up those last images. Forced Entertainment's work has always been bound to a poetics of the fall. It is an oeuvre that uses the negation, disintegration, and destruction of forms, acts, and propositions in order to advance unique affective speculations on our social realities. As Killick's monologue suggests, our relation to the absent event of the fall, much like our relation to death or to a theatre that is no longer before us, is a heady cocktail of necessity and freedom. We are invited and compelled to rediscover the event and in so doing reinvent it; and that free labour of imagination is now our collective and individual task.

Tim Etchells
Adrian Heathfield

WORKS

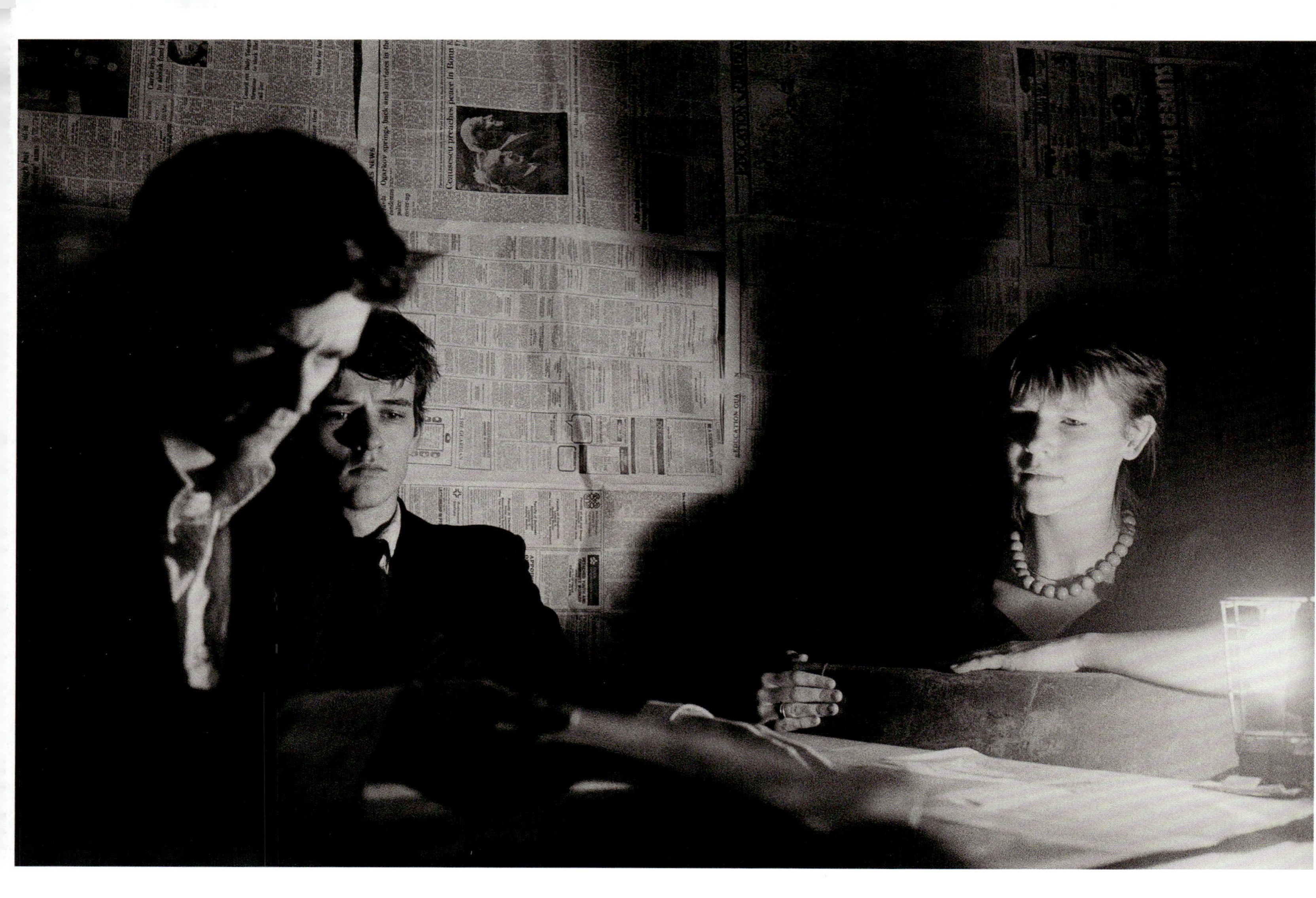

JESSICA IN THE ROOM OF LIGHTS (1984)

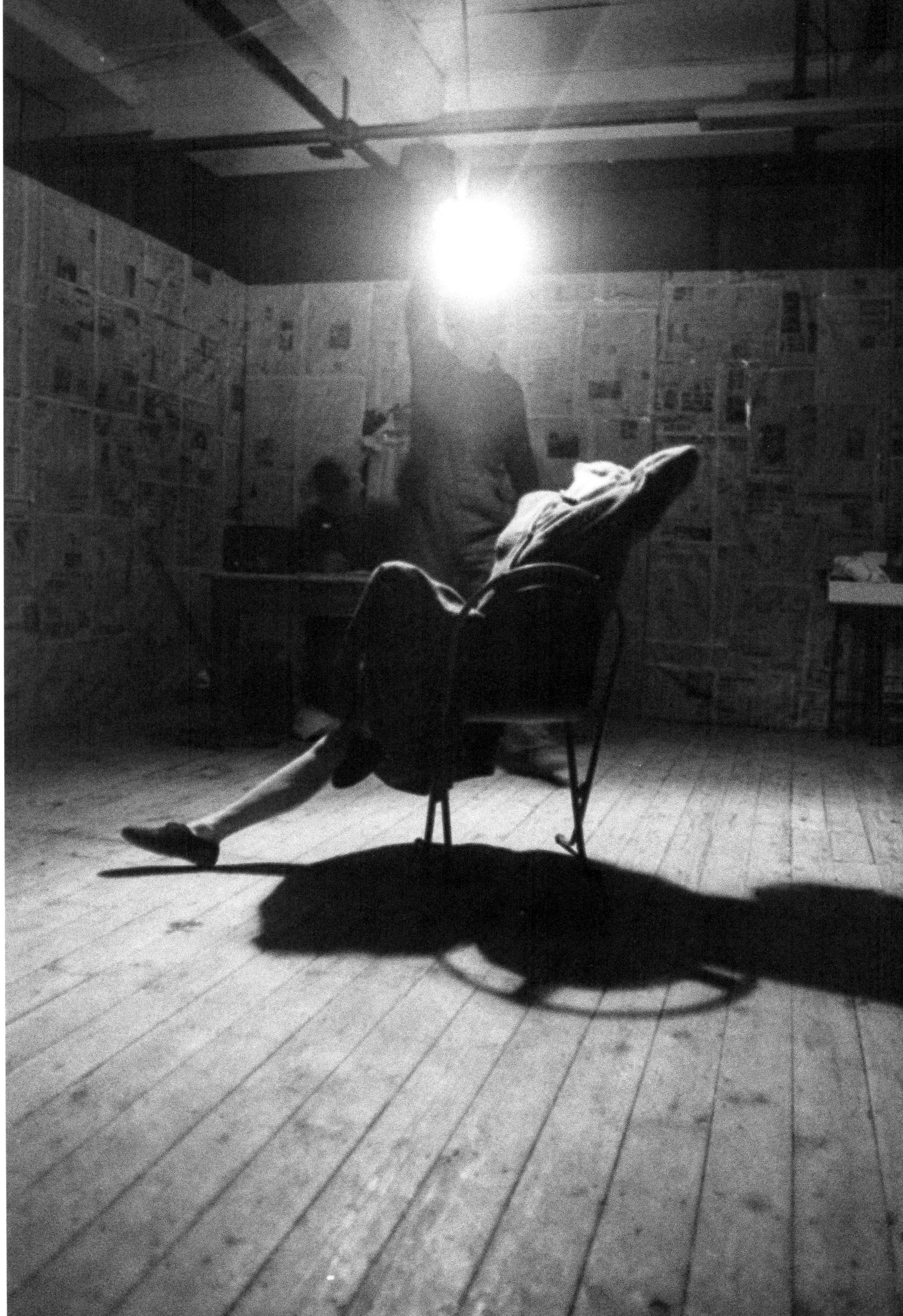

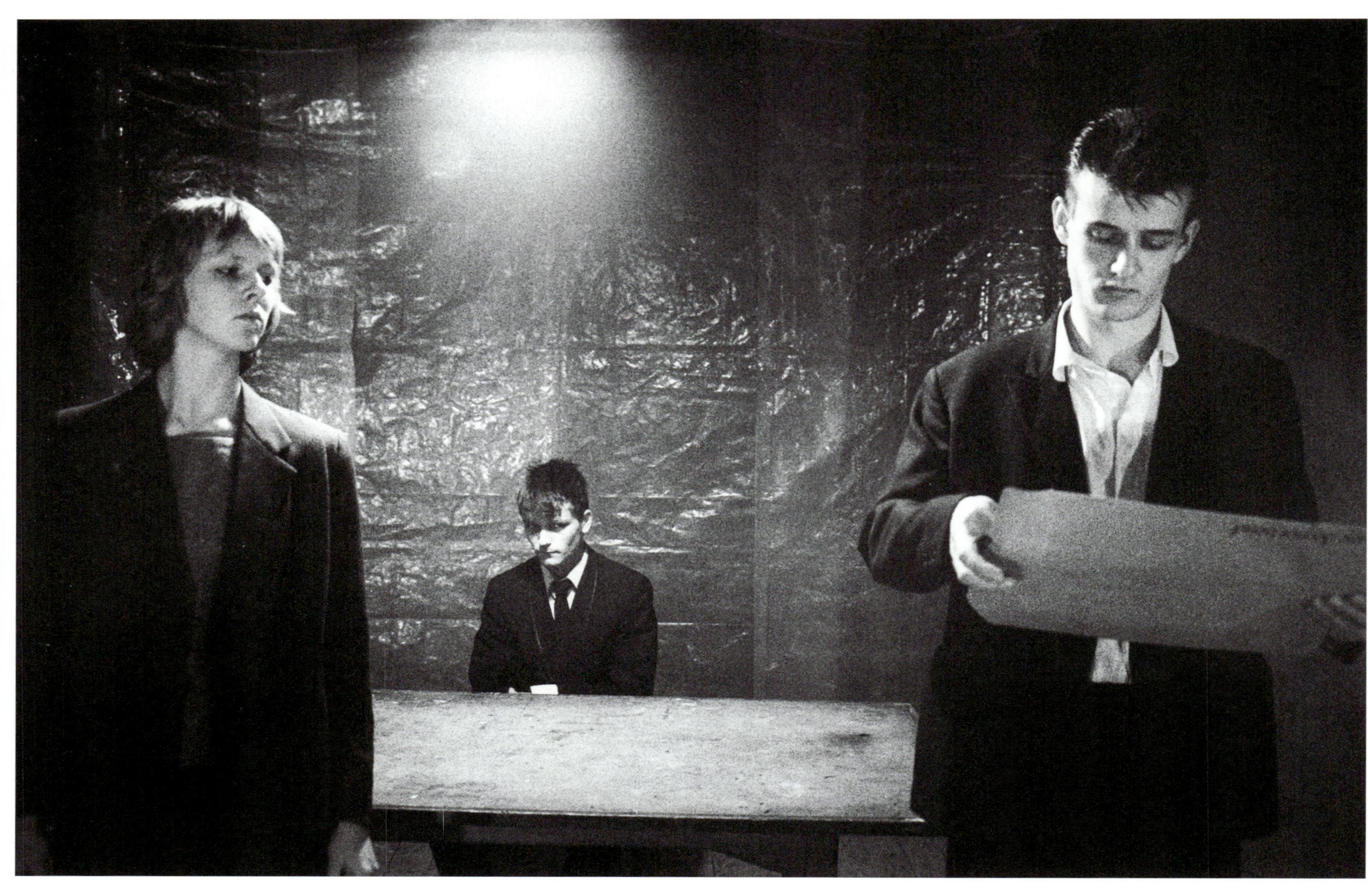

THE SET-UP (1985)

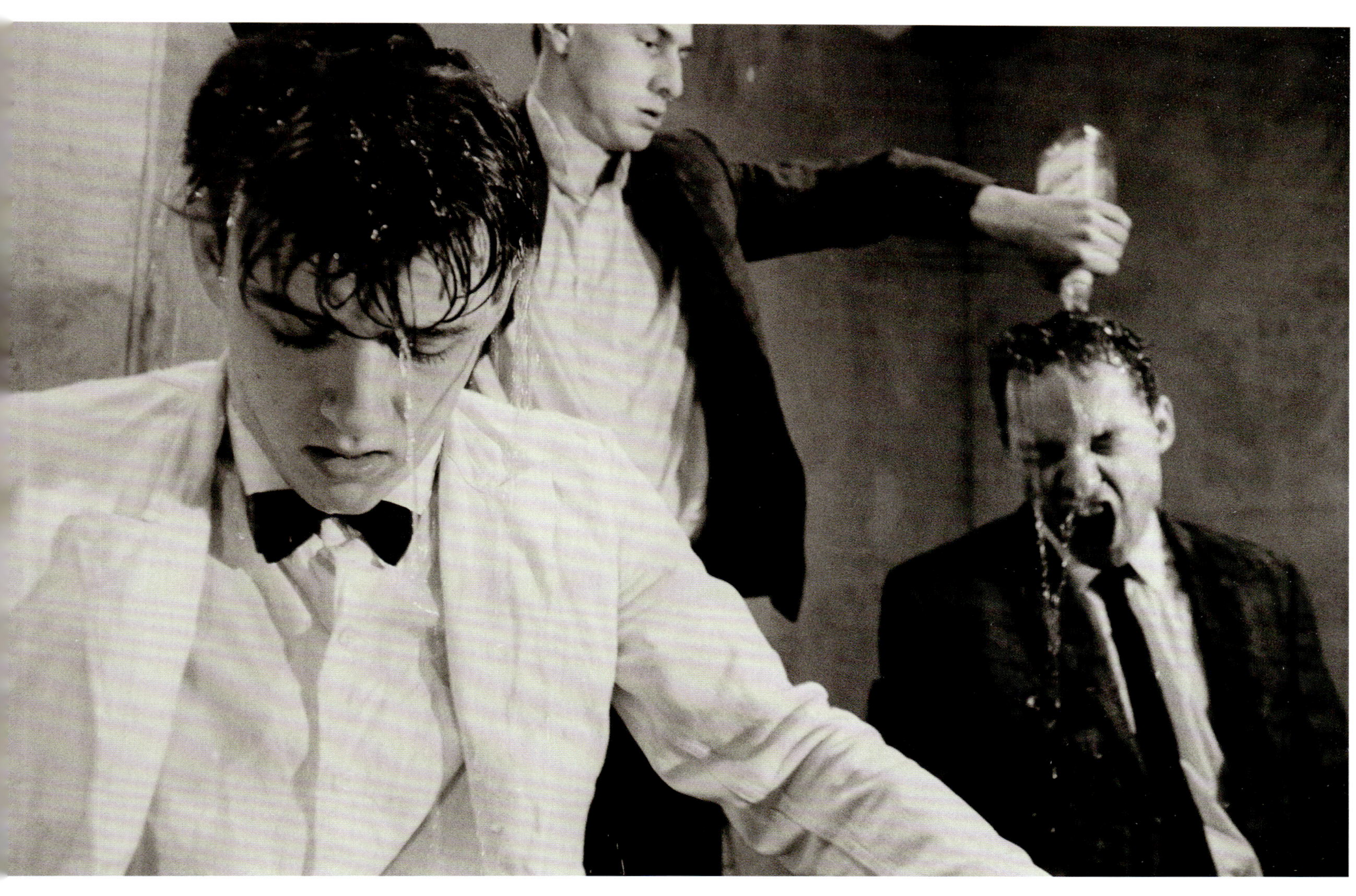

NIGHTHAWKS (1985)

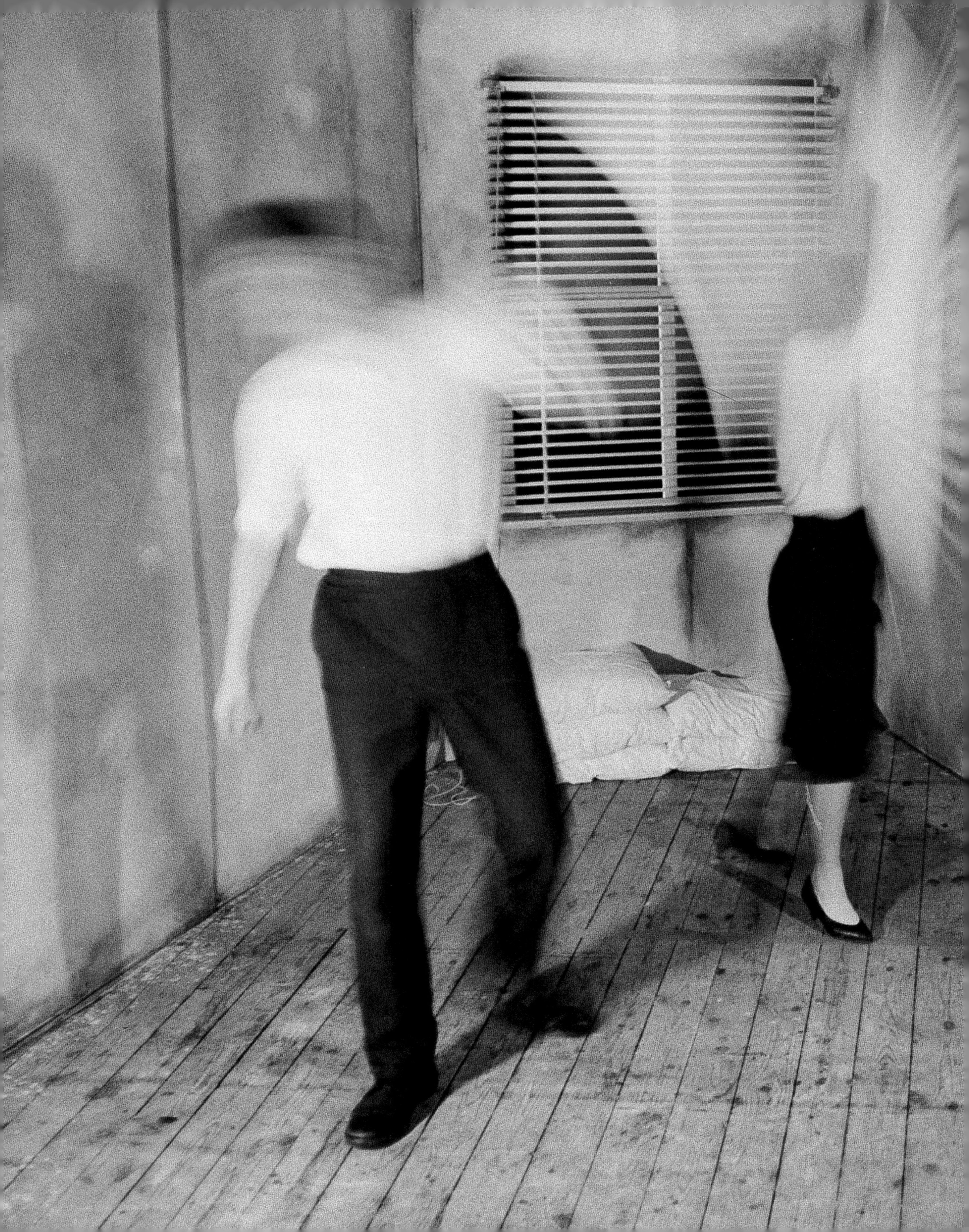

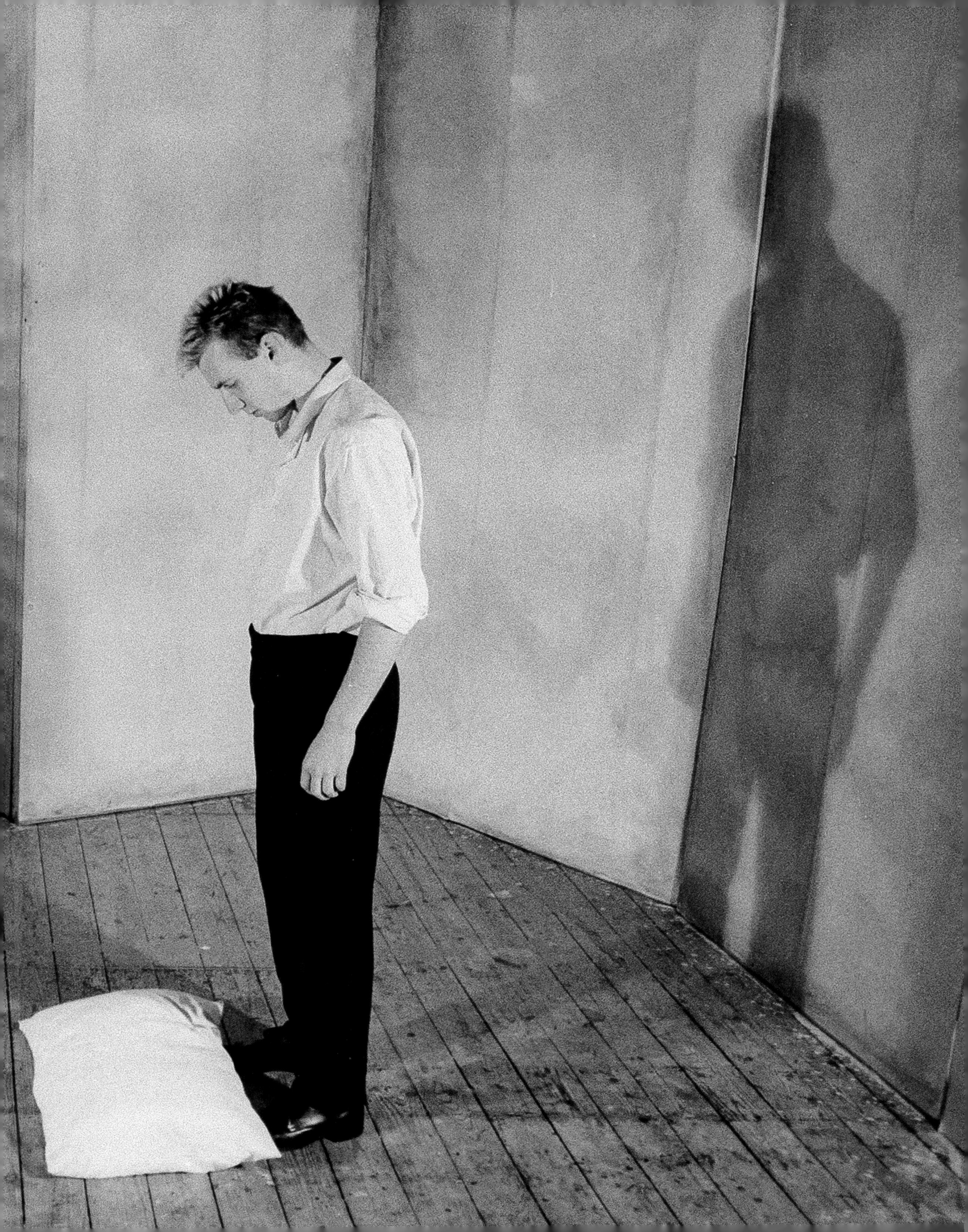

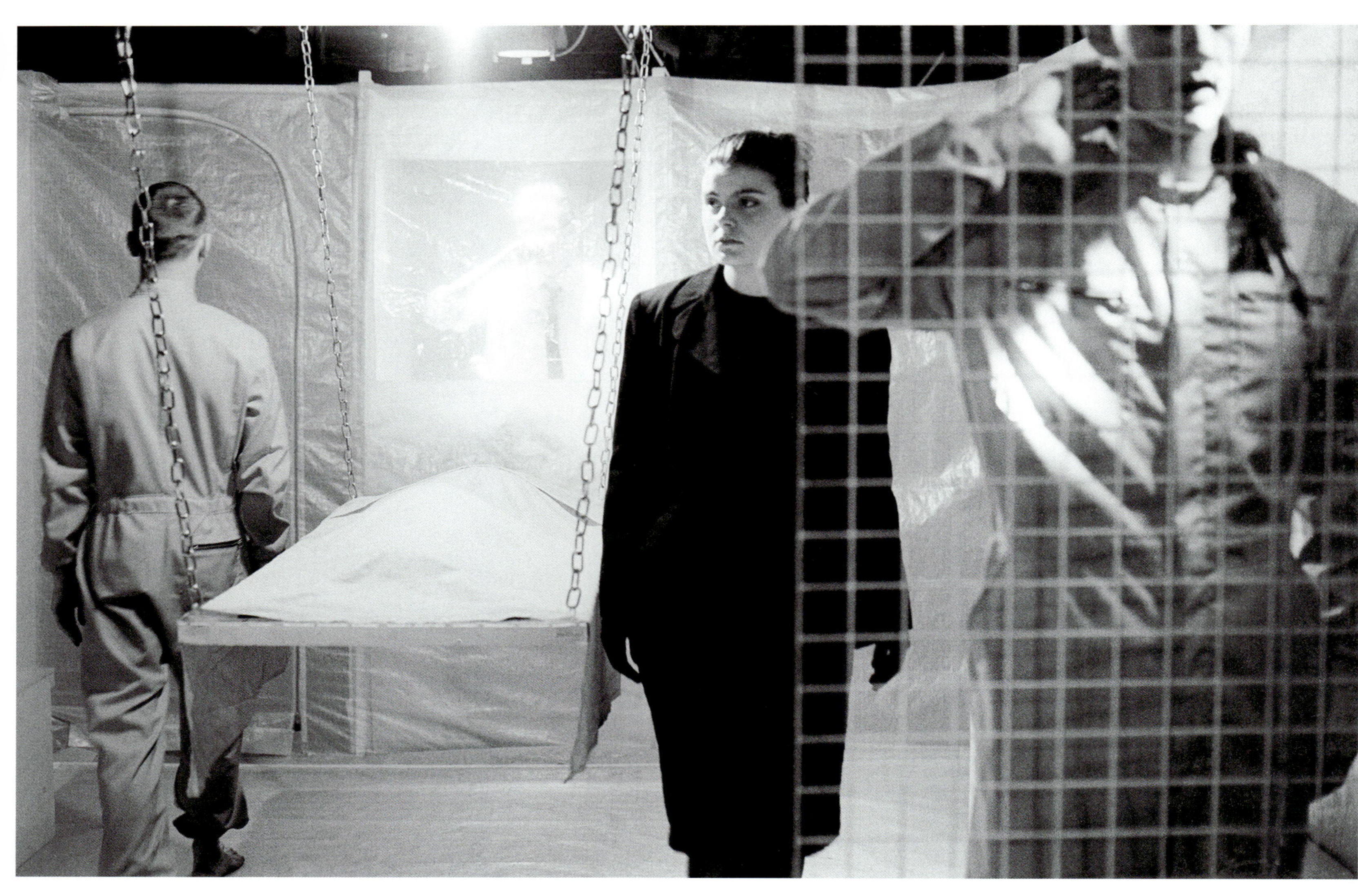

THE DAY THAT SERENITY RETURNED TO THE GROUND (1986)

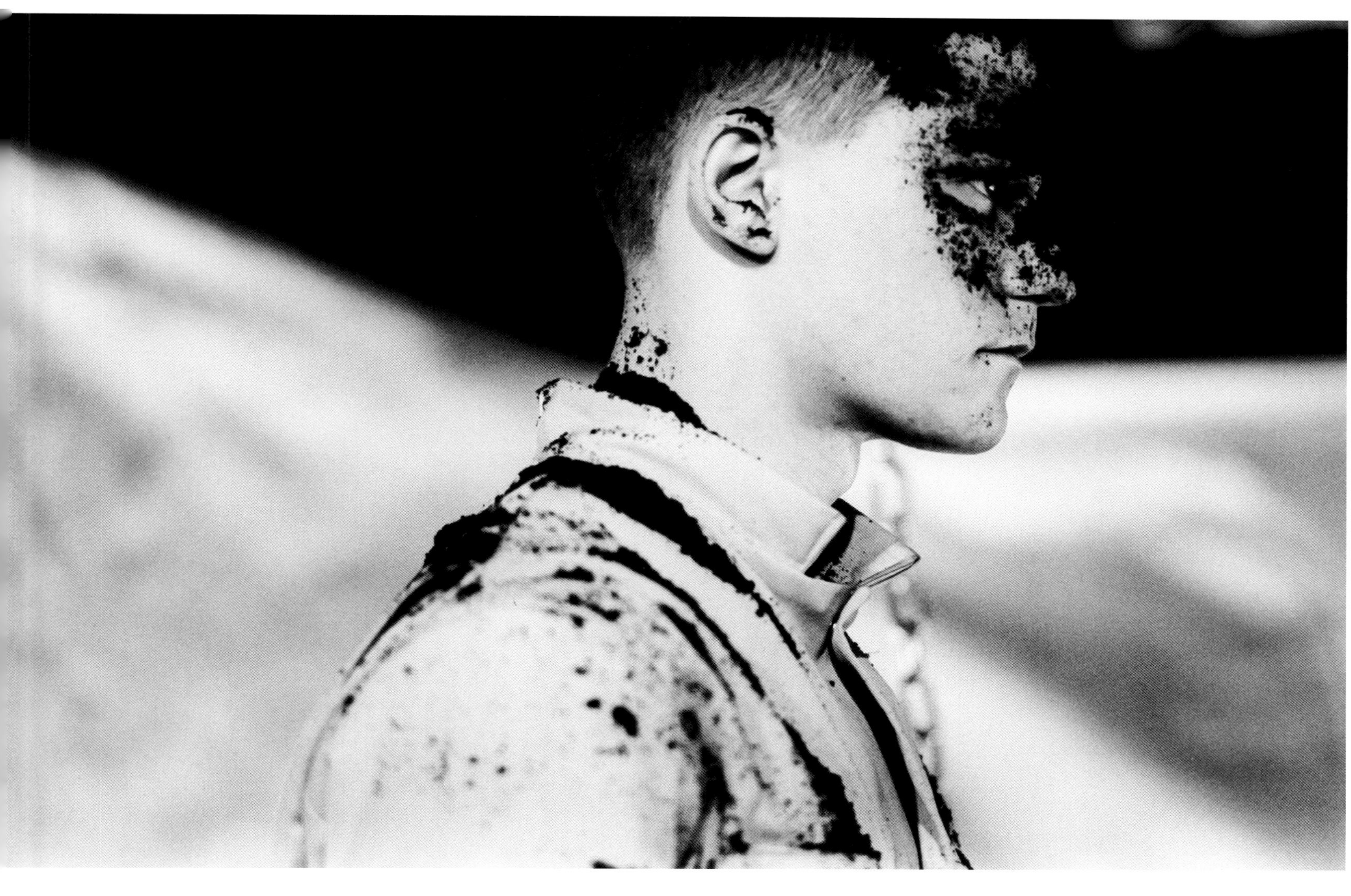

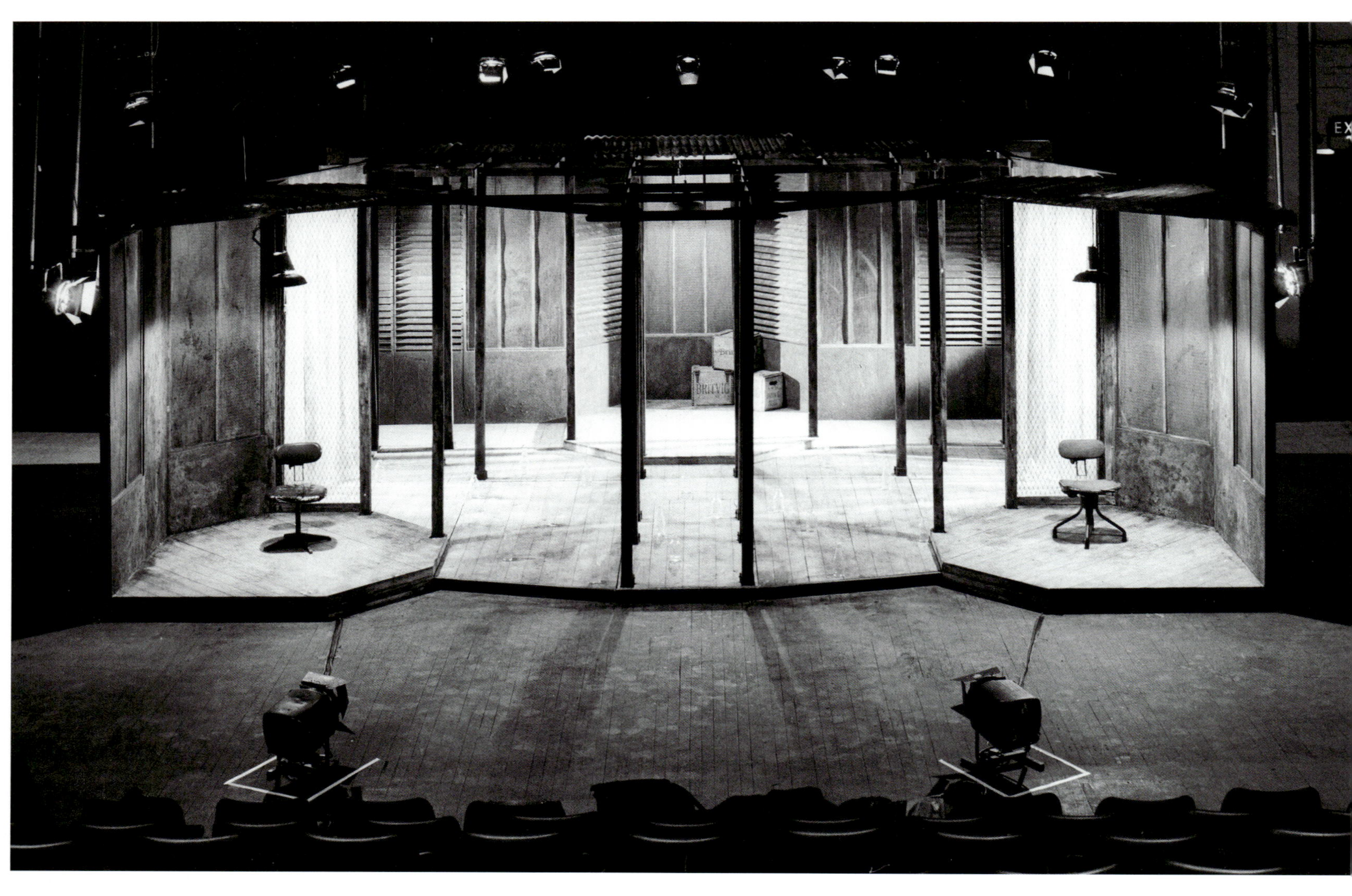

(LET THE WATER RUN ITS COURSE)
TO THE SEA THAT MADE THE PROMISE (1986)

Man: To the Mr Heart-Lung babies of this place & the so-
          called platitude girls, those for whom falling is a
          way of life.

Woman: Part One was the death of his hands. This didn't
          seem to matter at first, though it changed his
          style of dress.

          Thos wer the hands he got from Superbig Safeways,
          they wer an exciting colour, like the colour of skin.

          Thos wer the hands he used to hold her hands,
          when they walked together in the walking hours.

          Thos wer the hands that used the all-new
          dial-a-fortune machine.

          Those wer the most fashionable and exalted hands
          in the Black City.

          Part One for him was the death of his hands.

Man: Part One was the death of her eyes. This was
          brilliant fun. Unable to see no more, she didn't see
          the artificial sun of 1973, or the new packaging
          for Erotic Chocolate, or the green light by the
          precinct say 'Walk! Walk!' especially for her.

          He told her all about these things on long
          wet bastard nights together & they listened to
          Vivaldi's Baseball Concerto.

          Part One for her was the death of her eyes.

Woman: That was the year that the electric messages stopped.

Man: That was the year they crowned Madonna the Queen
          of Fuck in a nightclub called Paradise.

Woman: That was the year that Department 95 closed down.

Man: In that year she called him Mr Sunbeam and he
          called her Coca-Cola.

Woman: Part Two was the death of his heartbeat. She was
          mad with this at first because she used to like
          to listen to it going boom-boddy-boom-boddy-boom.
          After a while they got used to the silence though.
          And in silence together they ate Spanish Civil War
          Crunchies & watched topless television till way
          past bedtime.

          Part Two for him was the death of his heartbeat.

Man: Part Two was the death of her walk. This was
          regrettable. She got that walk from Paul Newman or
          Cary Grant, it was a good walk & when it died she
          felt lonely & she bought no more records no more.

          Part Two was the death of her walk.

Everything in the performance was in a state of degradation: the dilapidated location, the fragmentary gestures, the linguistically fractured voice-over. All of the spoken text was pre-recorded—my voice and that of an early Sheffield friend Sara Singleton acted as a poetic frame on what you were seeing—not a narration, more a set of atmospheres and ideas. The text in the voice-over had a broken poetry, something that I've pursued in other contexts especially the ongoing *Endland* series of short fictions. Onstage, we took this idea of broken text even further: the performers spoke in a made-up or half-remembered language, a nonsense or gibberish of excitable grunts, whispers, cries, laughs. The comparison we made was to the shapes and structures of speech but without the details—like hearing the voices of people arguing in an adjacent room—you can tell the energy of what you're hearing, but the specifics are left to the imagination, emerging from the music of the language. [TE]

The action was a lot of quotation: basic human acts or elemental activities rendered in a very exaggerated, almost cartoon-like style. The figures were constantly crying or wanting to sleep or arguing or dying. The two rooms of the set became spaces that we'd enter in order to perform something. And once it was done we'd step 'outside', and look back at the empty space as if our actions might have left some trace on the place. [RL]

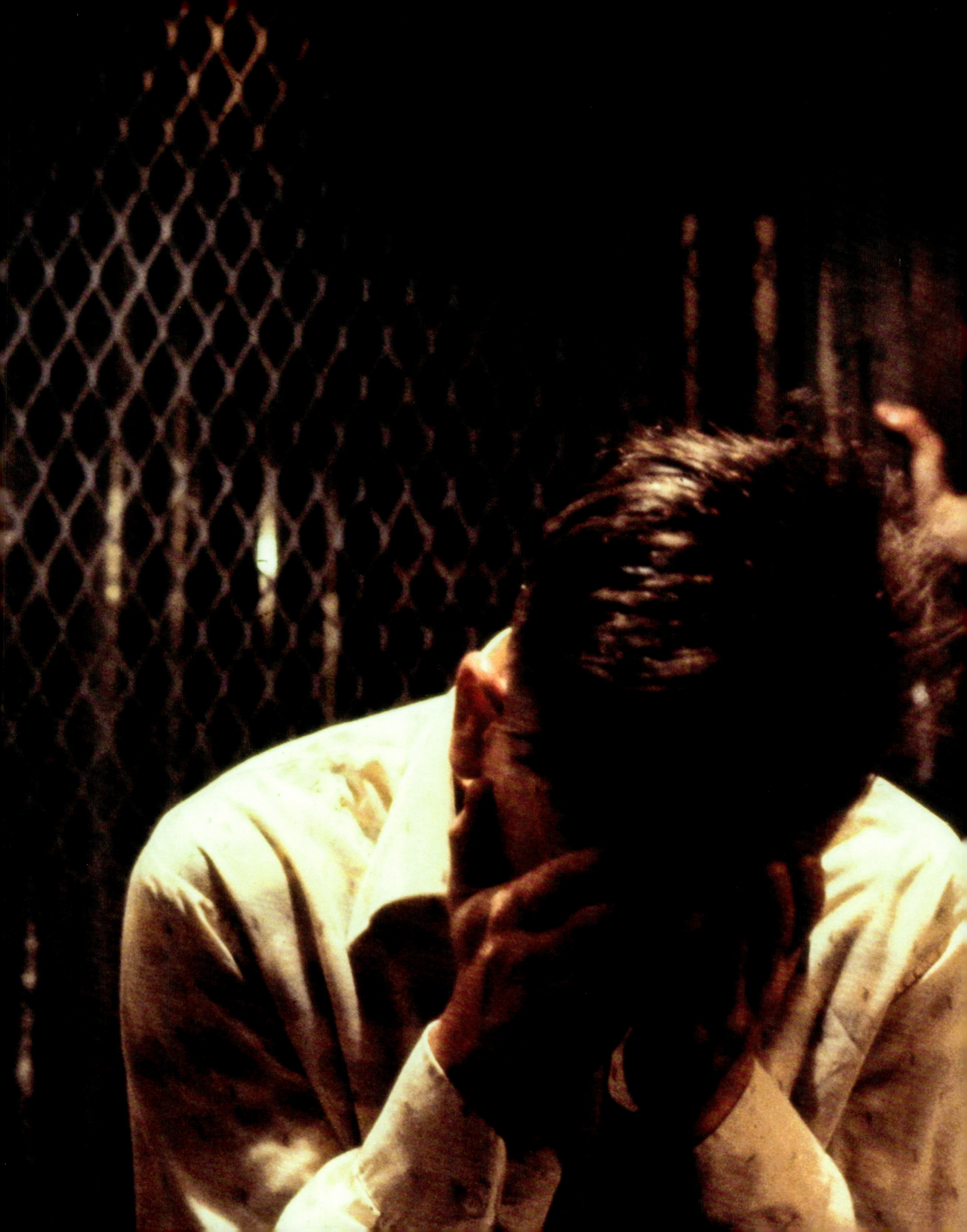

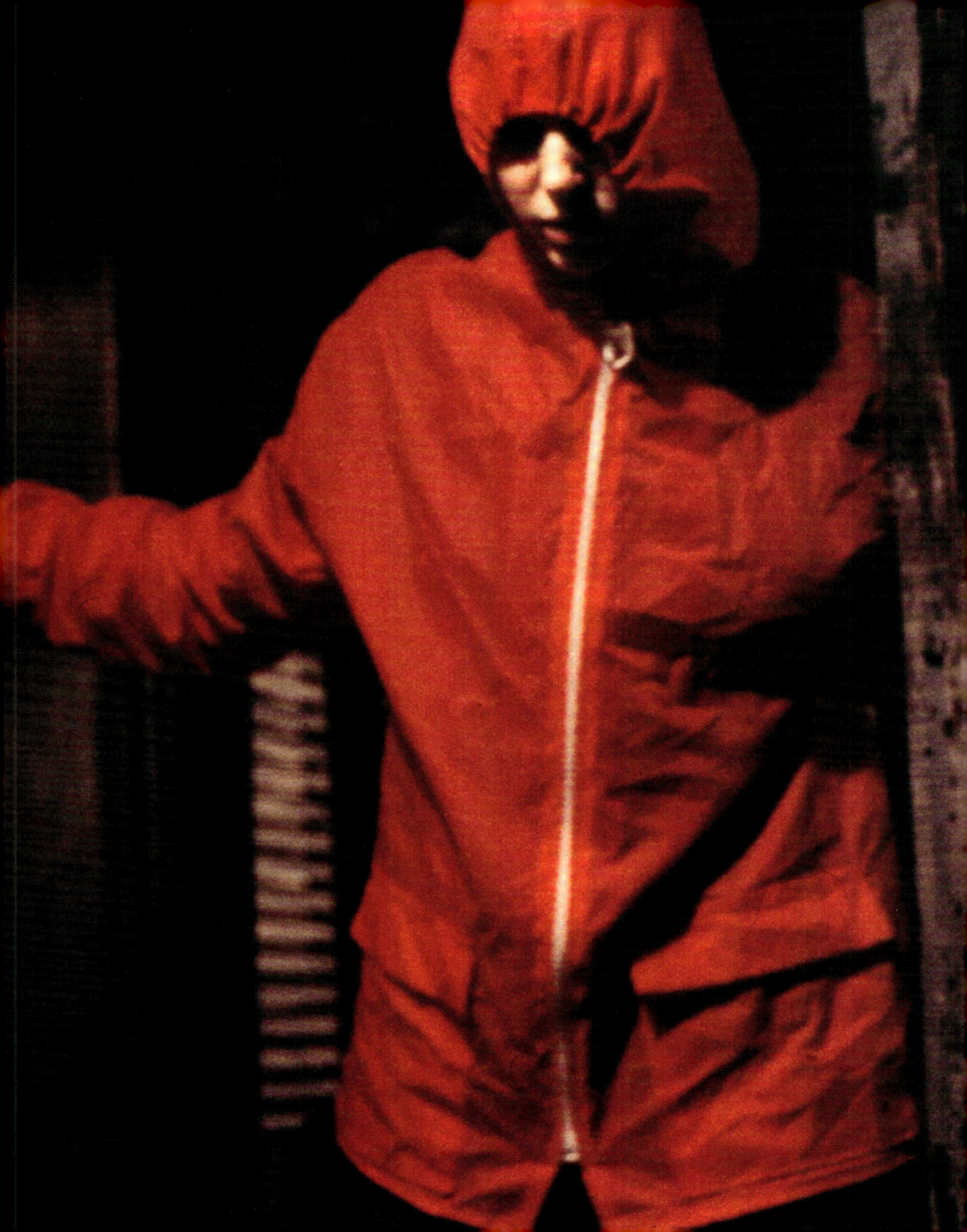

The visual design was influenced by the kind of architecture we saw around us in Sheffield in the 1980s, especially derelict factories and industrial spaces. Our warehouse rehearsal room was a pretty direct inspiration. Huw Chadbourn and I worked on the design through a series of models, arriving at an environment that was fictionally quite complete, atmospheric, self-contained. At the front there were two separate rooms with grille windows and corrugated roofing and in the centre between them a zone of upright pillars. When we constructed the set we didn't know exactly what we were going to do in there. At the time we often worked to create a performance space first and only later figured out what game or action could exist within it.

Making the space back then was a provocation, a kind of writing, a way of creating a frame for other ideas. The two identical rooms that sat on the downstage edges created a symmetry and also a dynamic of comparison: it was very tempting as a spectator to glance from one to the other and then back again. And because those rooms were slightly raised they became like little stages, mini arenas in which action could be performed. [RL]

There was a sense of the performers trying out actions or gestures: repeating them, altering them. The other performance mode we were discovering at the time was that of imitation; one performer would copy and exaggerate what another performer was doing. So, it becomes a question of how the versions vary, how they degrade, how the performers discover the heart of any action as something they can really commit to. [CN]

Woman: Part Two was also ther heartache for the city outside. They named it & renamed it every day despite the bitter cold. They called it remarkable city, alphabet city, alphabetti city, New Milan, and the Capital City of Britain.

Man: They sat up some nites & renamed it & their love grew as they named it: the city of spires, the Kentucky Fried City, the City of Elvis King, the exploding city, the city of joy. And while they talked, it rained like Ronald McDonald outside.

Woman: That was the year the jet planes didn't fly any more.

Man: That was the year they cancelled the Pope of the Year Pope contest.

Woman: That was the year that talks broke down in the Black City.

Man: That was the year that they shut the doors to the Institute of Believing.

Woman: In that year she called him Mr Vector & he called her Karen the Florist.

Man: Part Three was the death of her insides. This was unlucky. She needed them but he made it up to her & it didn't seem to matter no more. Her insides wer made out of bendy plastic & tranquillizer chewing gum, her insides wer fragile neon & bound up with Sellotape, her insides wer radium atoms lit only by 40 Watt bulbs & he loved them.

Part Three for her was the death of her insides.

Woman: Part Three was the death of his skin. This was regrettable. The skin was first class skin that smelt good like oil & roses. The skin was the skin she touched & when it was dead the whole thing seemed different. They never went out any more. They wer bound together only by Junior Disprin.

Part Three for him was the death of his skin.

Man: Part Three was more names for the Black City.

In the dark they called it fuck city, shit city, blood city, sperm city, cock city, prick city, cunt city, twat city, bum city, arse city, shitty city, ridiculous city, stupid city.

Woman: That was the year the Chinese trains stopped running.

Man: That was the year they broke the fingers of the baby Jesus.

Woman: That was the year the power cuts came & they wanted to run & they wanted to swim.

Man: That was the year the power cuts came & they wanted to walk & wer desperate to slide.

Woman: That was the year the power cuts came & they wanted to drive & wer frightened to fall.

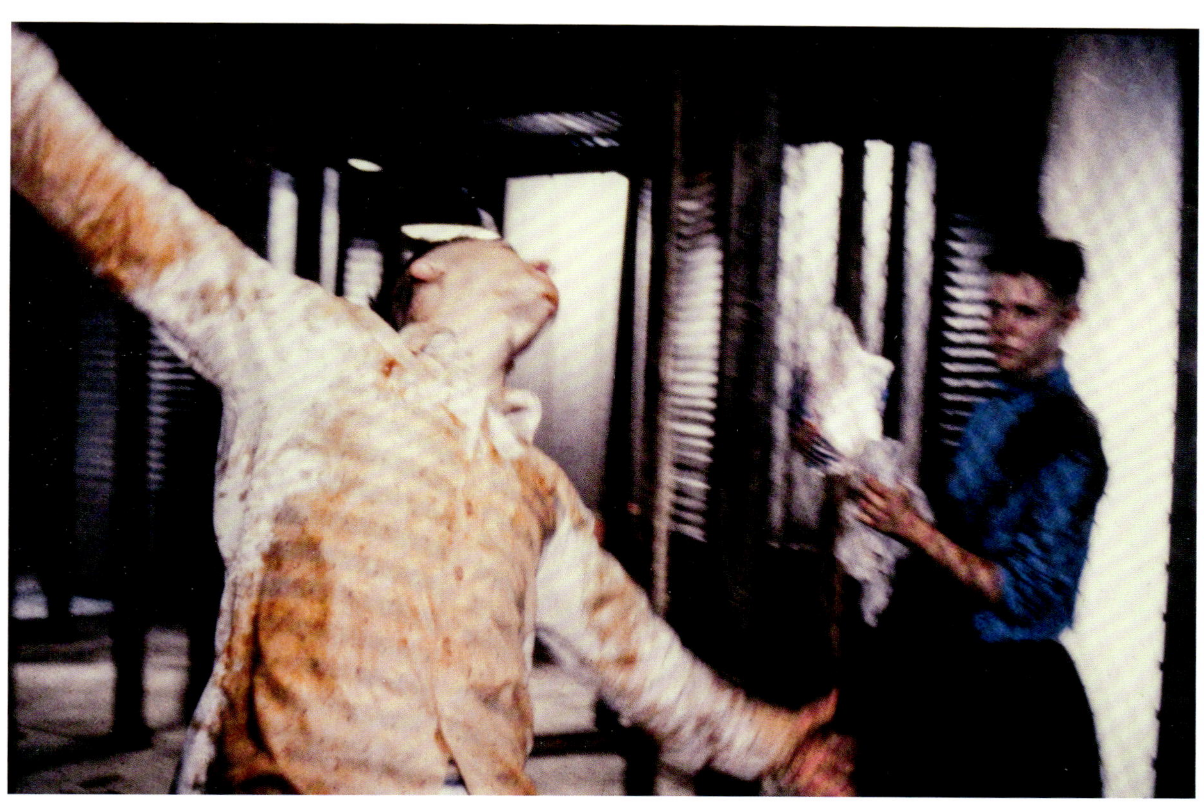

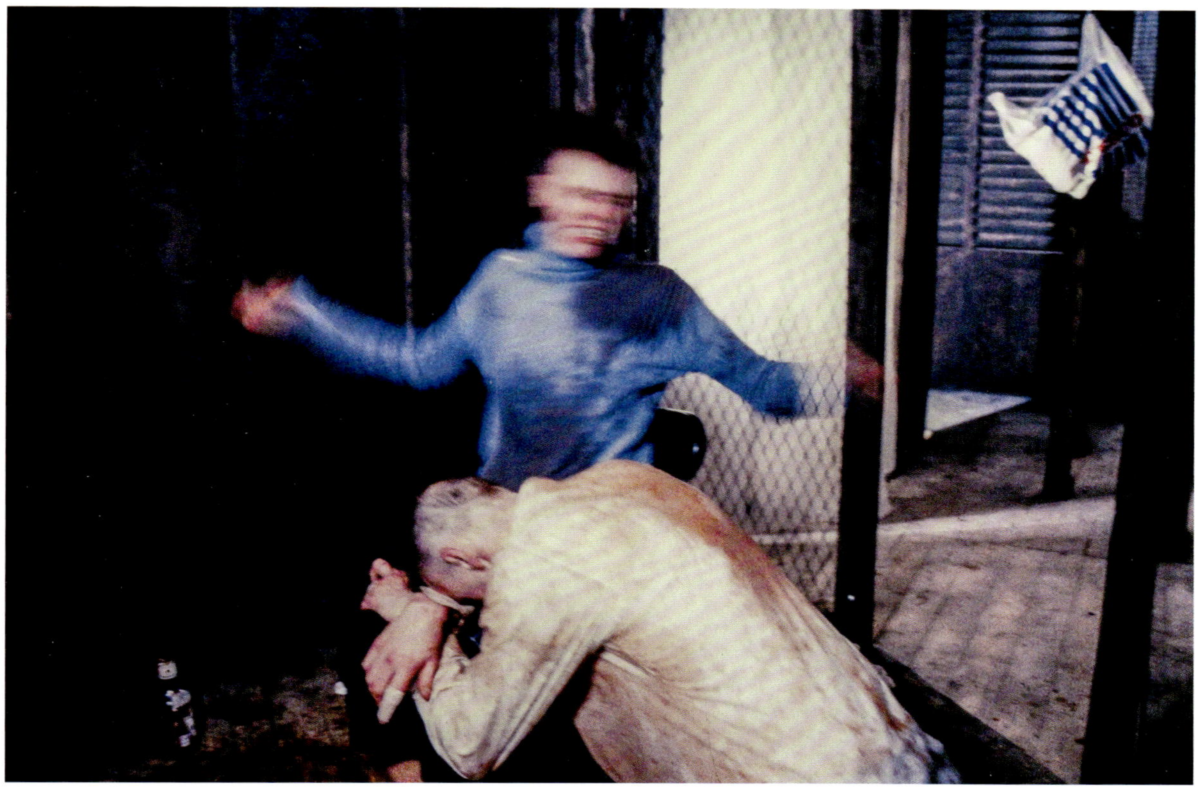

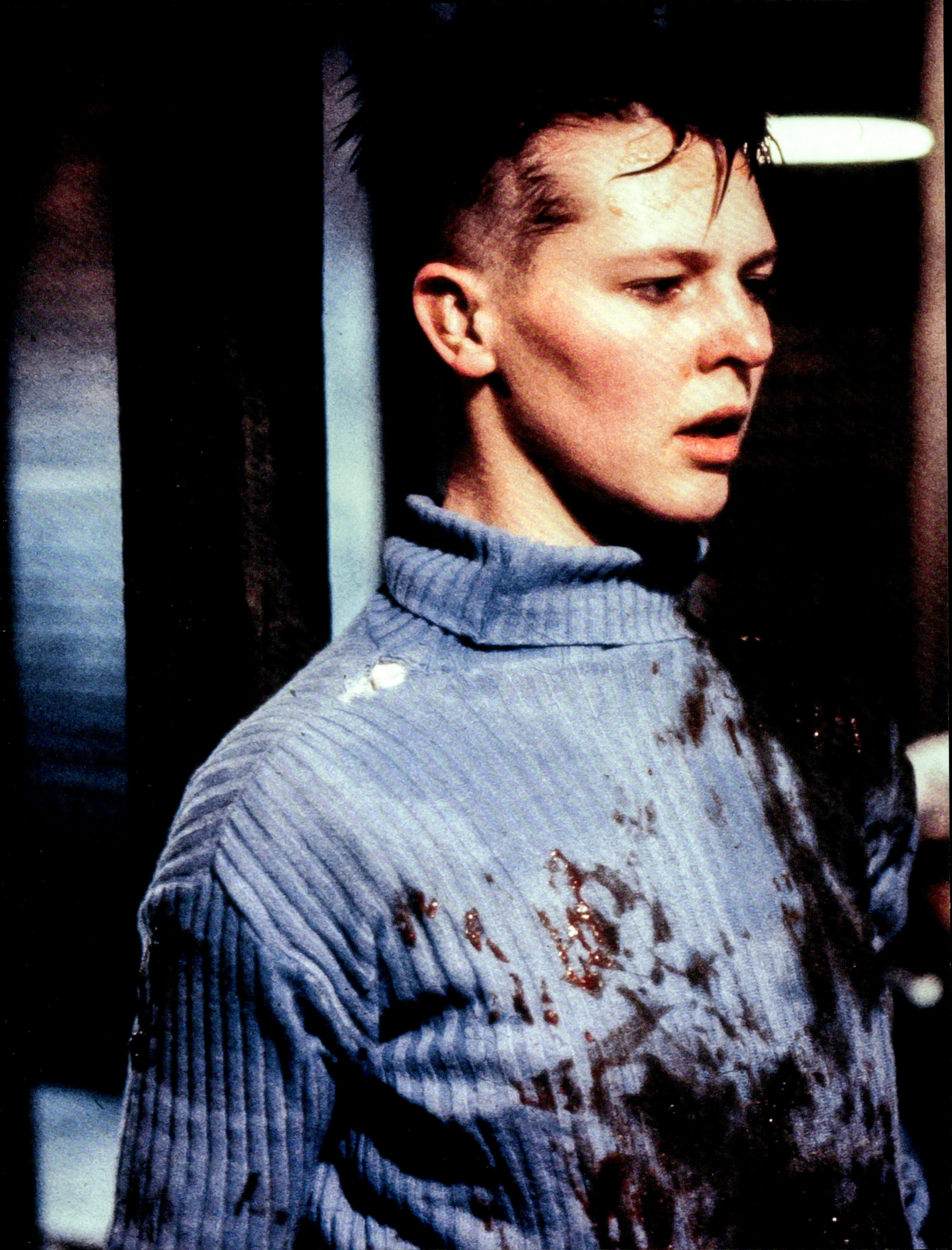

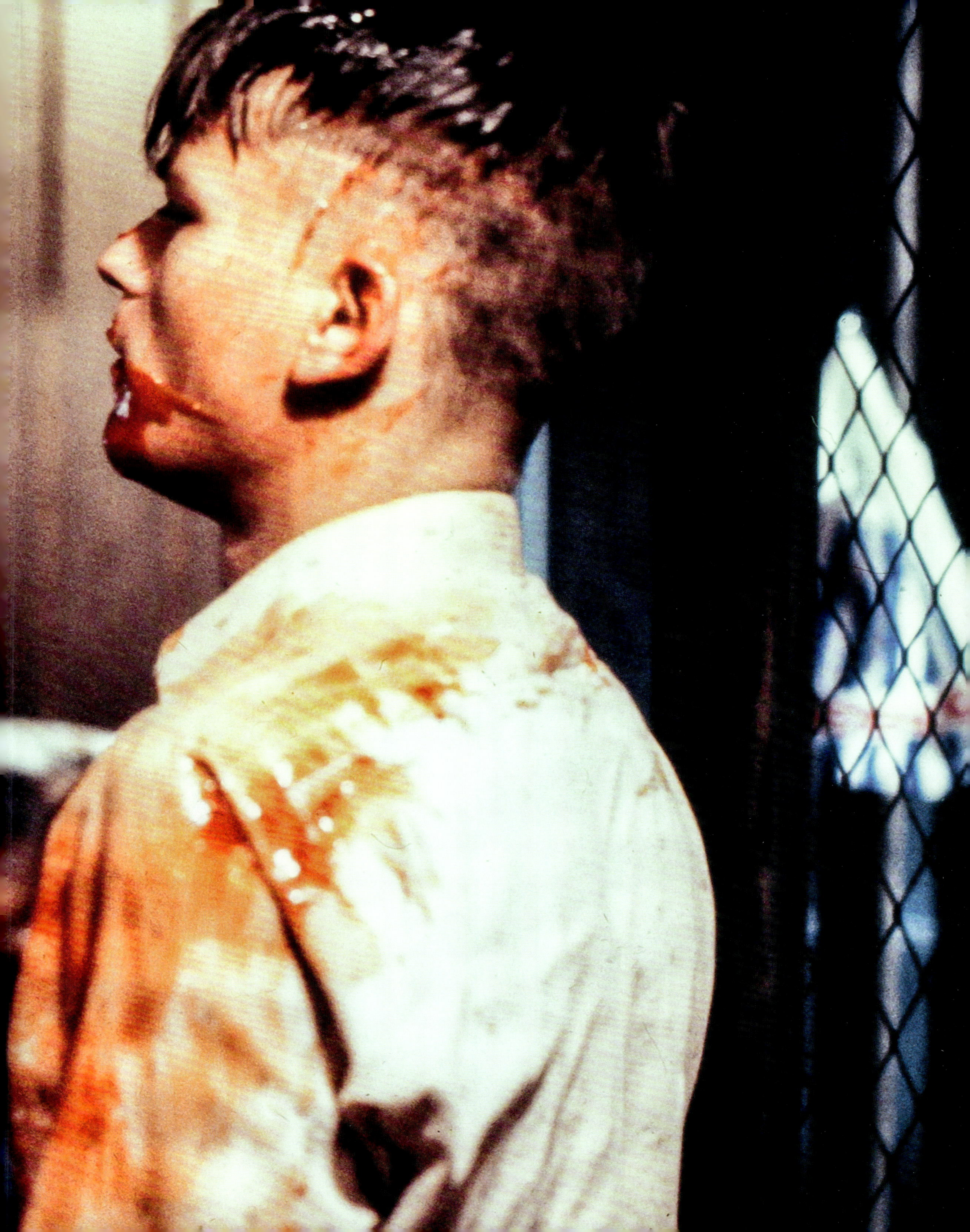

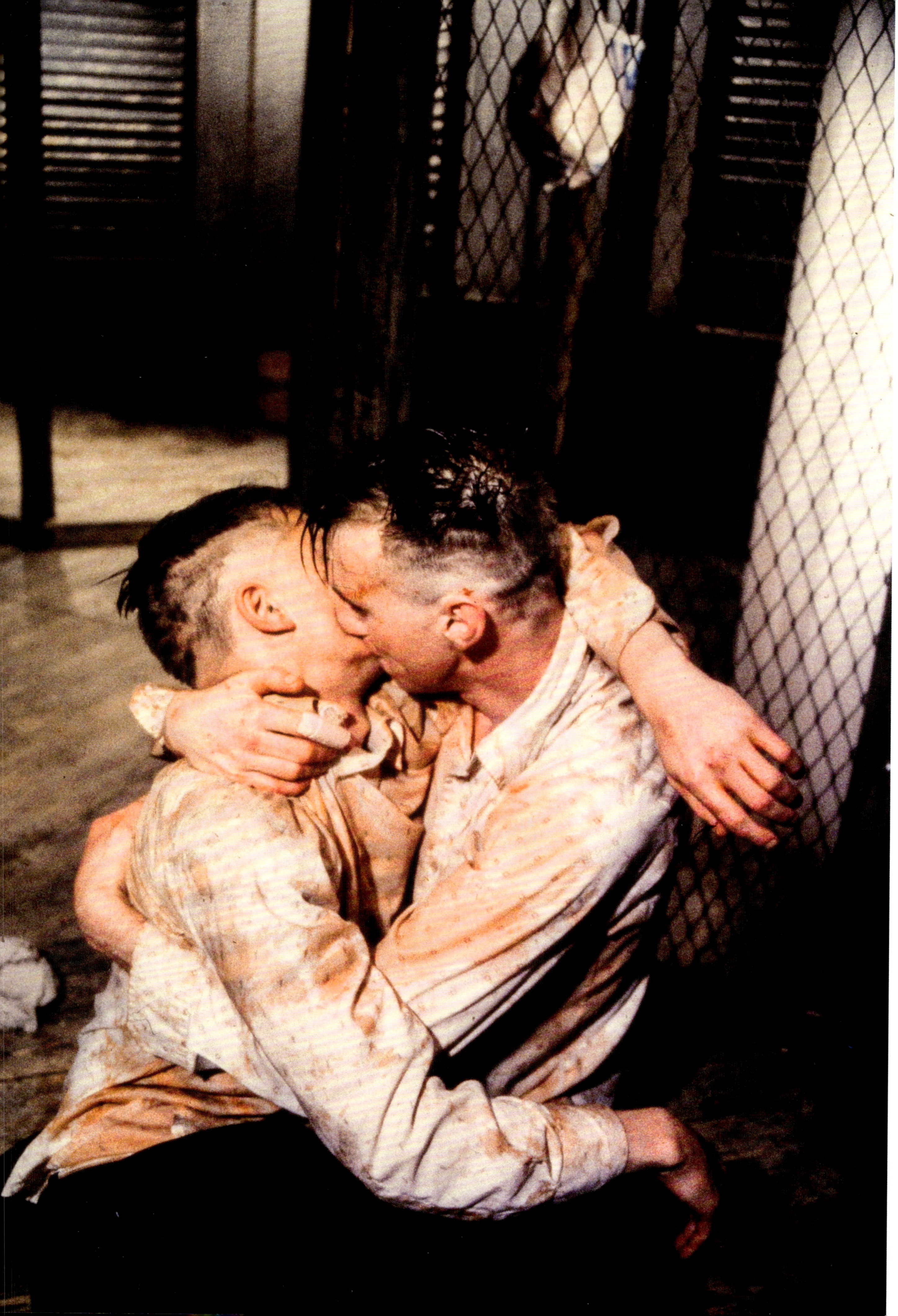

Woman: Part Four was the chronology of the cities. They spoke
         each night & every night about a journey standing still.

Man: The first city was the City of Stones.

Woman: They spoke each night & every night about a journey
         standing still.

Man: The second city was the City of Wire.

Woman: They spoke each night & every night about a journey
         standing still.

Man: The third city was the City of Rain.

Woman: They spoke each night & every night about a journey
         standing still.

Man: The fourth city was the Stupid City.

Woman: They spoke each night & every night about a journey
         standing still.

Man: The fifth city was the Empty City. The people ther wer
         no lovers of water, all ther buildings wer tumbleshit,
         all ther trees wer bare & the branches on the boulevards
         wer bones & ther wer no birds ther, only bird repellent.

Woman: They spoke each night & every night about a journey
         standing still.

Man: The sixth city was the City of the Variable Stars.
         Someone put a note under the windscreen wiper of
         her car: 'I love you, but will never dare speak
         to you.' In another time, with another love in his
         heart, Mr Plastic choked & died in a hotel bathroom.

Woman: They spoke each night & every night about a journey
         standing still.

Man: The seventh city was the City of Faith. That winter
         Karen the Florist & Mr Vector sat in ther respective
         rooms & willed themselves to die. And because the mind
         is stronger than the body they did die. Alone in ther
         rooms as quiet as stone.

Woman: They spoke each night & every night about a journey
         standing still.

         Part Four was the chronology of the cities.

Man: Part Five was the love & acceptance of ther true blood.

         They wer so happy in the Black City. They went for joy
         rides every day in a red Corvette beneath lines & wires
         of pylons, singing 'Move Move Groovy Baby' by the Self
         Righteous Brothers.

Woman: Unfortunately though one day when they wer driving a
         cornflake truck hit them doing 93. And he remembered
         thinking how quiet that whole world seemed & still,
         & wondering if you blacked out before you hit the
         windscreen.

Man: And she remembered being in the air looking down on
         the Black City which was very beautiful & wondering
         if the plastic figure of Charles Atlas, King of the
         Black City would hit the ground before she did.

Woman: They died in the accident of course. He lost control of
         his bladder before they hit the Kelloggs truck so he
         didn't mind: his best suit was ruined anyway. At
         the hospital they wer put in the capable hands of
         Dr Lyver who had plenty of money. Seeing as how they
         wer dead, he put sort of plastic taps in ther arms &
         drained all the red sort of blood out of them into
         a sort of bucket. Then he got lots of other blood &
         pumped it into them through all possible entrances.
         That is to say: nose, ears, cunt, arse & eyes.

Man: This new blood he put in them was stuff he'd
         collected here & ther from other people. The blood
         it mixt together all these people's blood & thoughts
         & everything & this was ther biggest problem you
         see: because the blood moved inside them, changing
         & turning, one person then another, they dint know
         who the fuck shit piss they wer, they'd say one
         thing then another, stand up, sit down, the blood
         moved, they dint know.

Woman: Part Five for them was the love & acceptance of ther
         true blood.

Man: It was also a confession & a day by the sea.

Woman: We have woken up crying.

Man: We have tried to fuck in the bath.

Woman: We saw Warren Beatty present an appeal on behalf of
         children with muscular dystrophy.

Man: We woke to hear a man's voice & found that it was
         morning.

Woman: We have been to the water at midnight.

Man: We played sniper on the balconies of the world.

Woman: We sat twenty billion years in the ridiculous dark.

Man: We've been taken to the airport in handcuffs.

Woman: We watched all the channels close down.

Man: We have died in London & we have kissed in Rome.

Woman: We have pissed in the sink.

Man: We drank ourselves stupid out of free-with-petrol
         tumblers.

Late on in the piece, the performers enact deaths, using tomato ketchup as blood, splattering it onto themselves from the bottles: the deaths getting more and more bloody, violent, and exaggerated. Who can do the best death, the most inventive one? It was an important work in building a theatrical language that we've lived with and developed since then: thinking of the performers when they were stood outside of those rooms as existing in a 'baseline mode' where not much is pretended, whilst the moment of stepping into the room was always the start of enactment. It's something we come to again and again in the work: now I'm performing, now I'm not. [RL]

The final image of the piece—the interior industrial space—gives way to an invocation of an exterior: the sea shore. The performers lift the floorboards in two large, central sections and reveal an expanse of pebbles beneath, a shingle beach onto which they step barefoot whilst a recording of the sea plays loudly. We built this spatial transformation into a number of pieces back in the mid-1980s: the revelation of another space (*Nighthawks*), or the flooding of the space with light from an unexpected onstage source (*The Day That Serenity Returned to the Ground*). This gesture was also a precursor to the deconstructed transformations we used in later pieces: the dismantling of a central room that sets up the final section of *Club of No Regrets*, or the construction of the house which is then the location for much of *Hidden J*. It was, in a sense, a prefiguring of the larger structural gestures of filling and then clearing whole stages we undertook in later pieces like *Bloody Mess*, *The World in Pictures* and *Who Can Sing a Song to Unfrighten Me?*: an insistence that the stage world and its visual and material transformation over time can be key in the experience and unfolding meaning of a work. [TE]

Woman: We stormed out slamming the door then walked straight back in again.

Man: We have headed for the water & driven for the sea.

Woman: We were born inside out.

Man: We were on Swap Shop the same day that Edward died.

Woman: We have sat talking all night & driven for the sea.

Man: We are sworn enemies of rain.

Woman: We invented beautifully scented nerve gas & invisible barbed wire.

Man: We've run beneath the neon bridges.

Woman: We have spitted on the grass beside the motorway.

Man: We have done questionable things.

Woman: We have been to the water at midnight.

Man: We stood on the black beach in winter & threw messages into the sea.

Woman: I am writing because you asked me to write you the truth about my life here & because I hope we are still friends.

I kiss you as we kissed before.

Marina & Mr Concrete.

PS I remember the snow, the frost, the opera building & your kisses.

Isn't it funny how we never felt the cold?

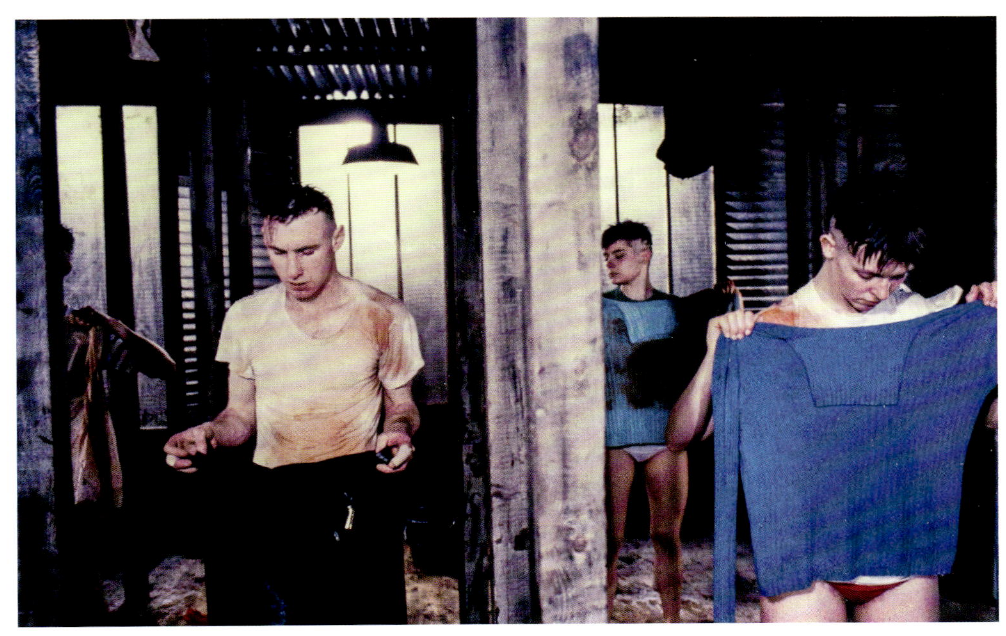

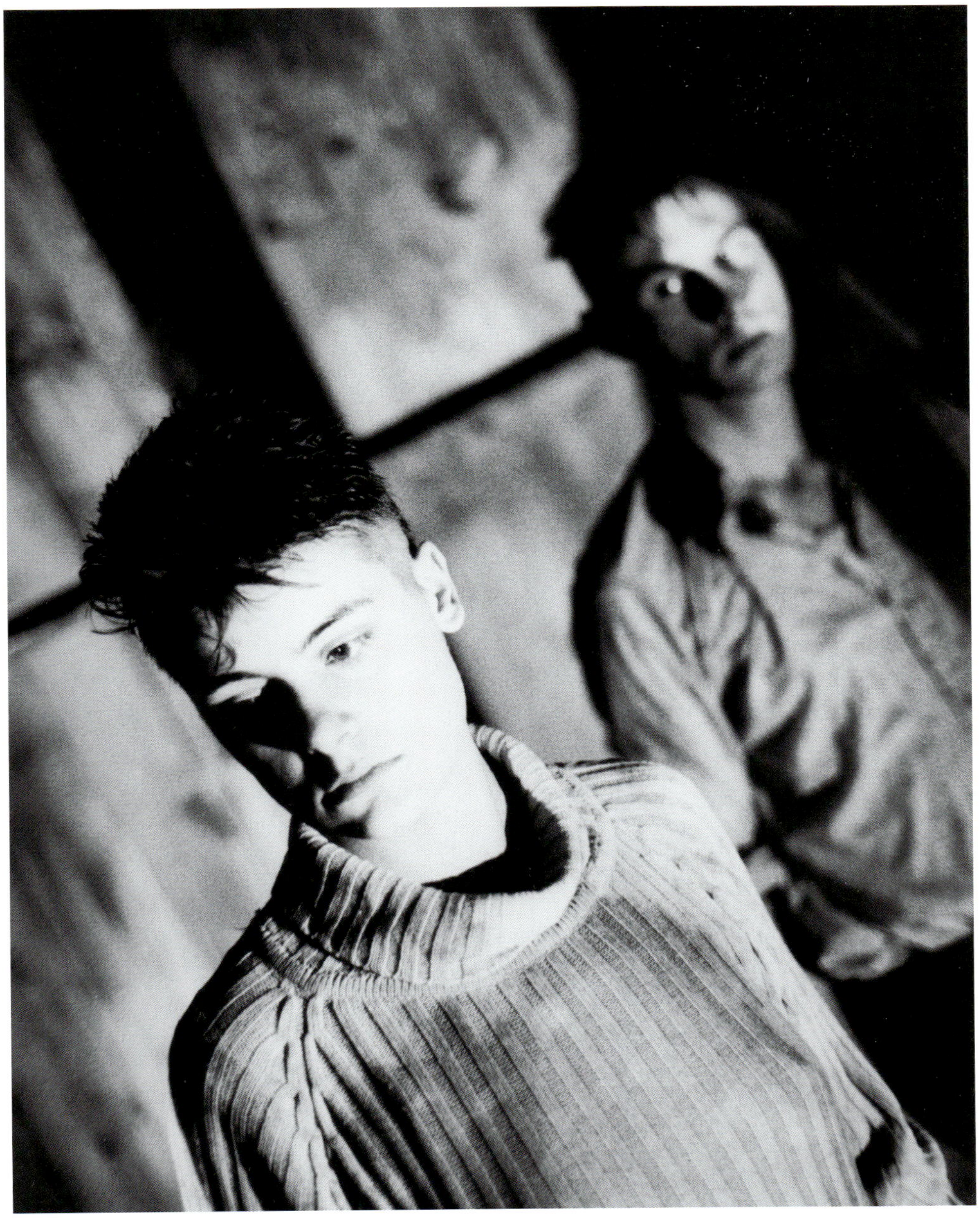

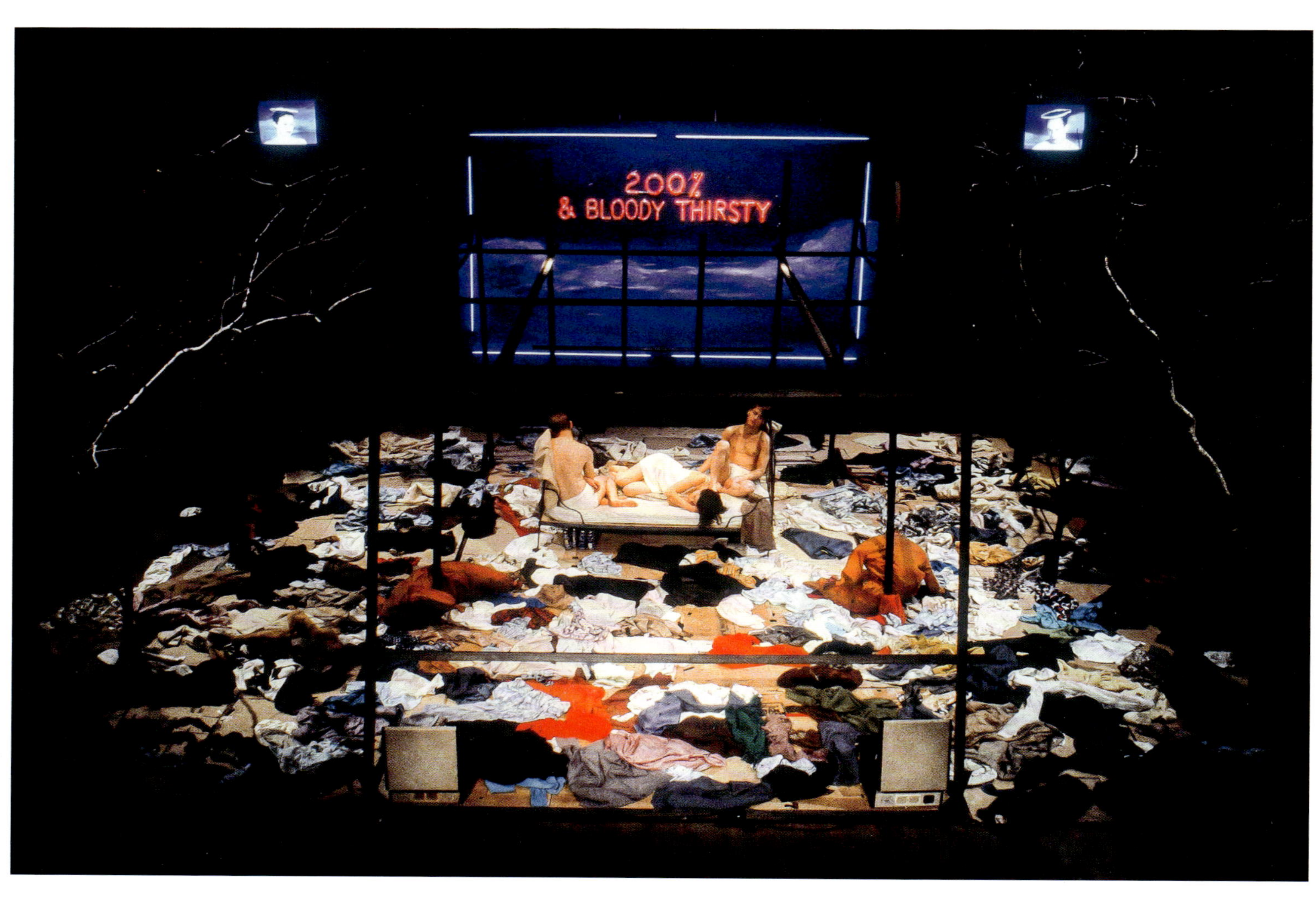

200% & BLOODY THIRSTY (1988)

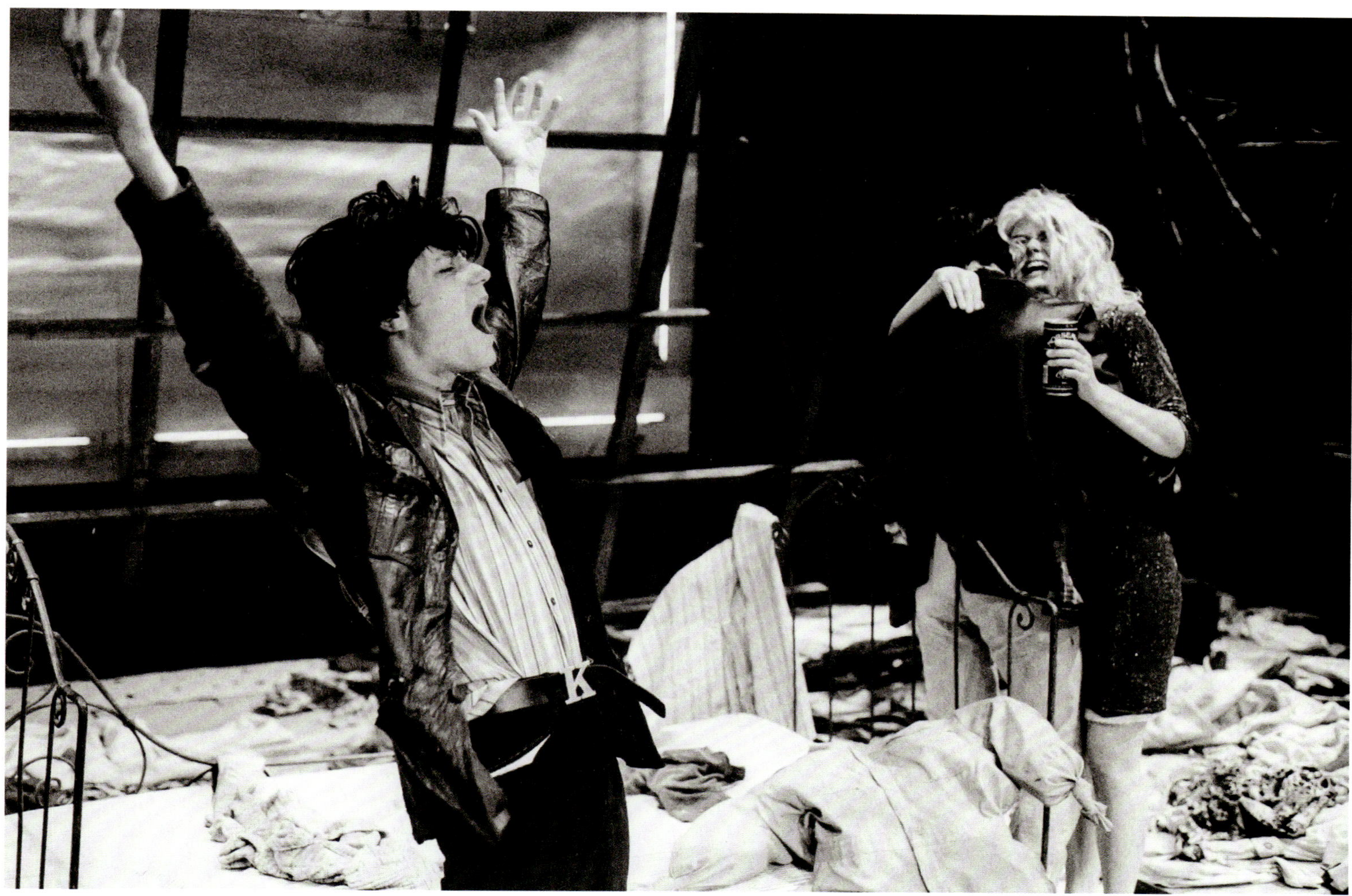

Sarah: When we can't sleep up in heaven
we look down on you and say sweet
goodnights to all the world. Goodnight
to kids made out of wire and shadows.
Sweet dreams.

Mark: Goodnight to the lights across
the water. Sweet shine.

Sarah: Goodnight to murderers,
murderesses, and car thieves.

Mark: Goodnight and sleep tight.

Sarah: A sad goodnight to rent
collectors and messenger boys.

Mark: A quick goodnight to sky that's
beat up, kind of blue and black.

Sarah: A slow goodnight to the rain.
The sweet and necessary rain.

Mark: Remember. Life is short, love
is long.

Sarah: Goodnight to dark and streets
of empty houses.

Mark: Goodnight to the women and the men
that rented them all.

Sarah: Goodnight to street lamps
like 40w of dirty light. Sweet dark,
precious dark.

Mark: Goodnight and sleep alright.

Sarah: A fine goodnight to perfect
things, and broken things and things to
make the heart beat fast.

Mark: A sweet goodnight to pointless
things, and stupid, stupid foolish things.

Sarah: A sad goodnight to half things.
Like half-light. Half-naked. Half-covered
in snow.

Mark: A fine goodnight to all the
channels closing down.

Sarah: A sad goodnight to secret things.

Mark: A sweet goodnight to every
star and satellite that's still left
in the sky.

Sarah: The best goodnight to drunks
still sleeping, half-covered in snow.

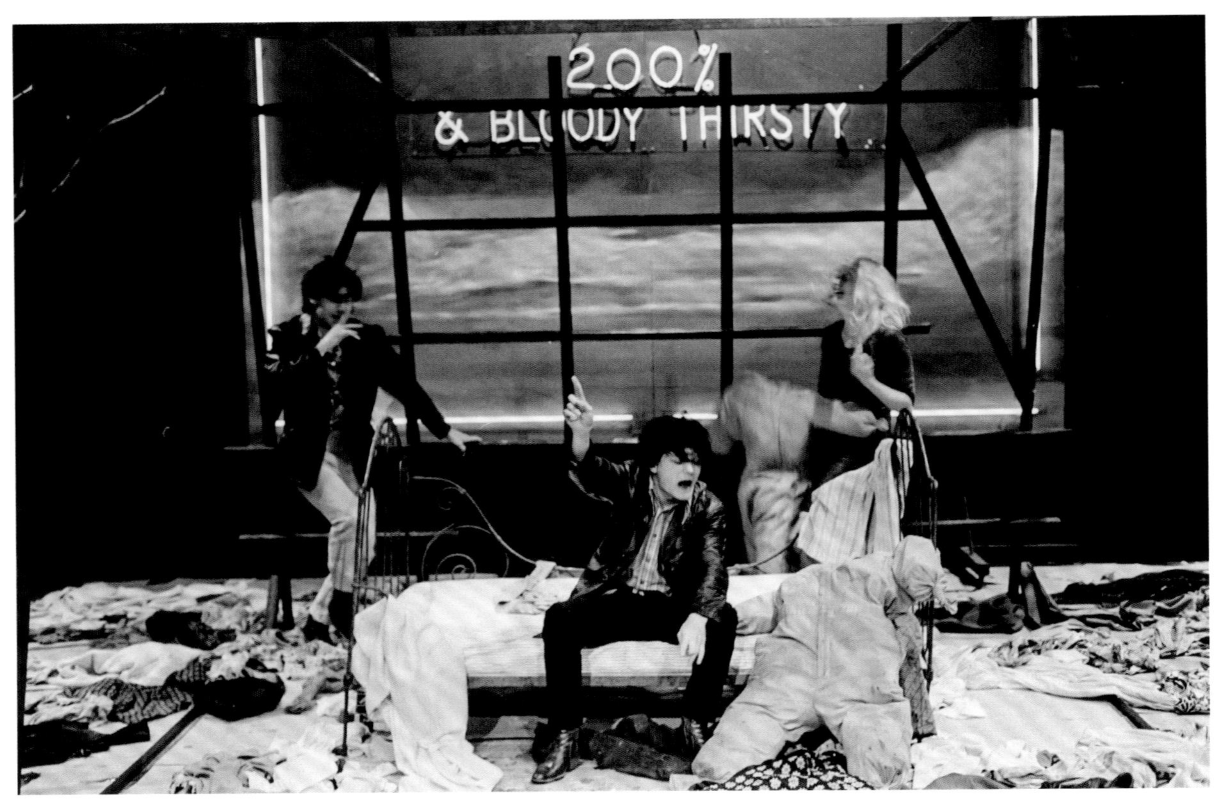

200%
& BLOODY THIRSTY

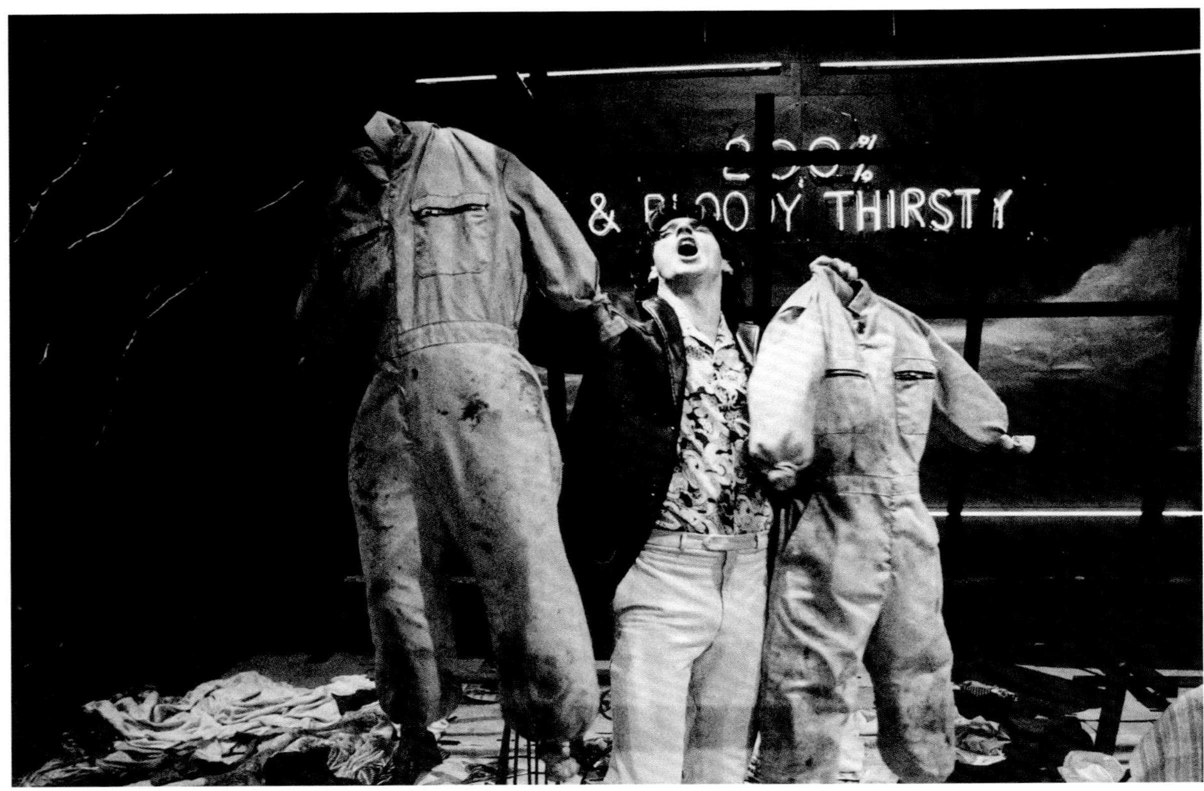

200%
& BLOODY THIRSTY

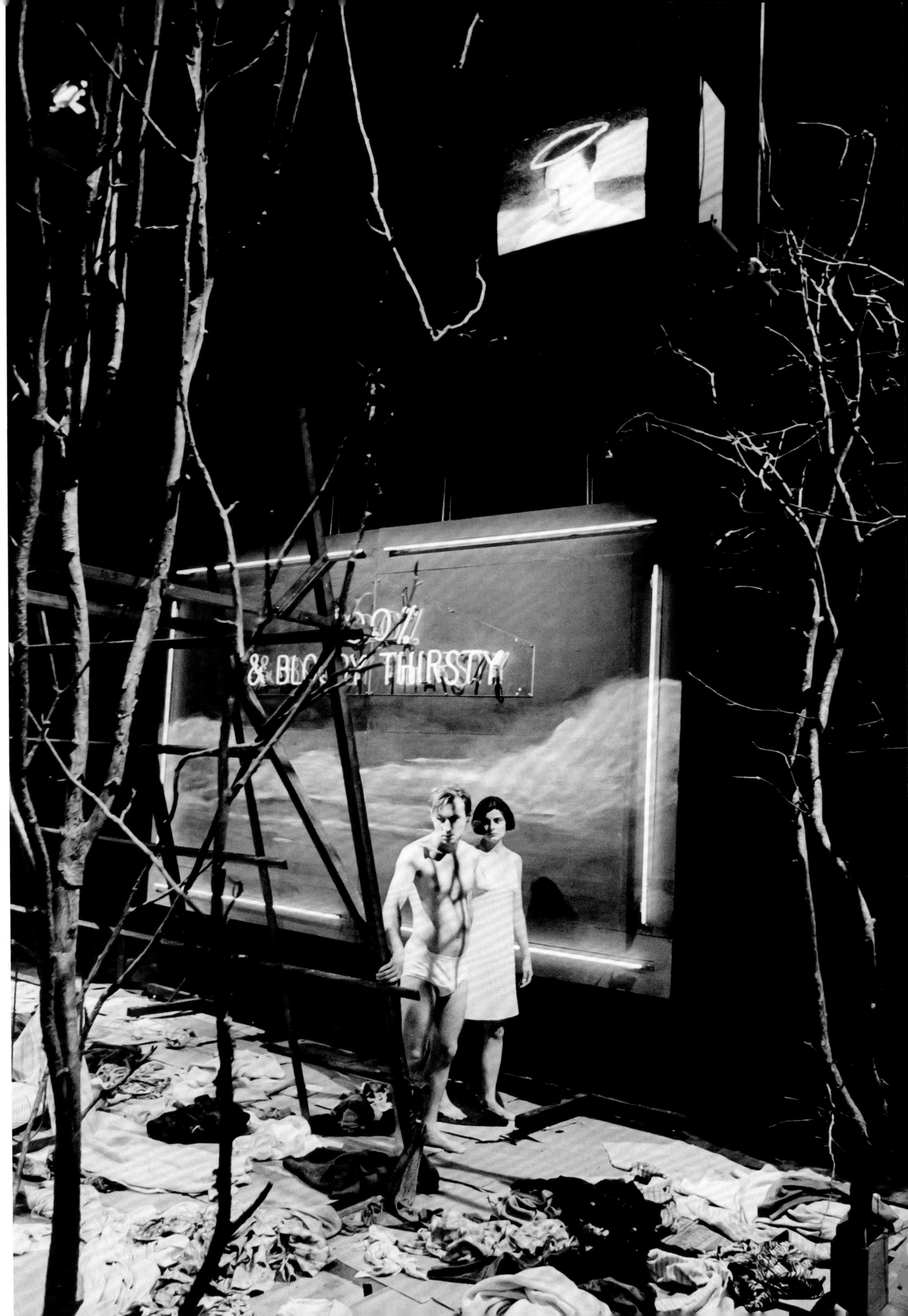
& BLOODY THIRSTY

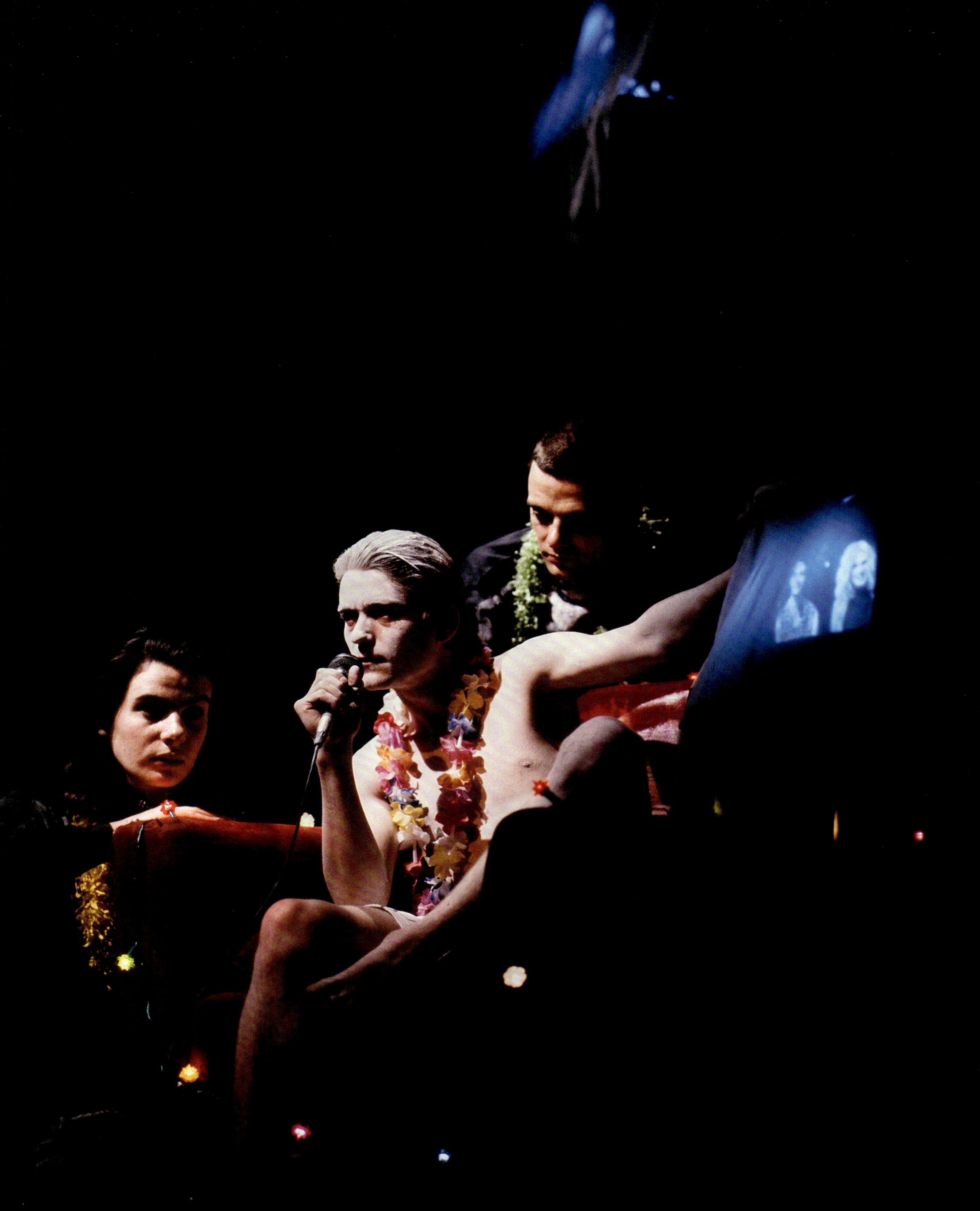

SOME CONFUSIONS IN THE LAW ABOUT LOVE (1989)

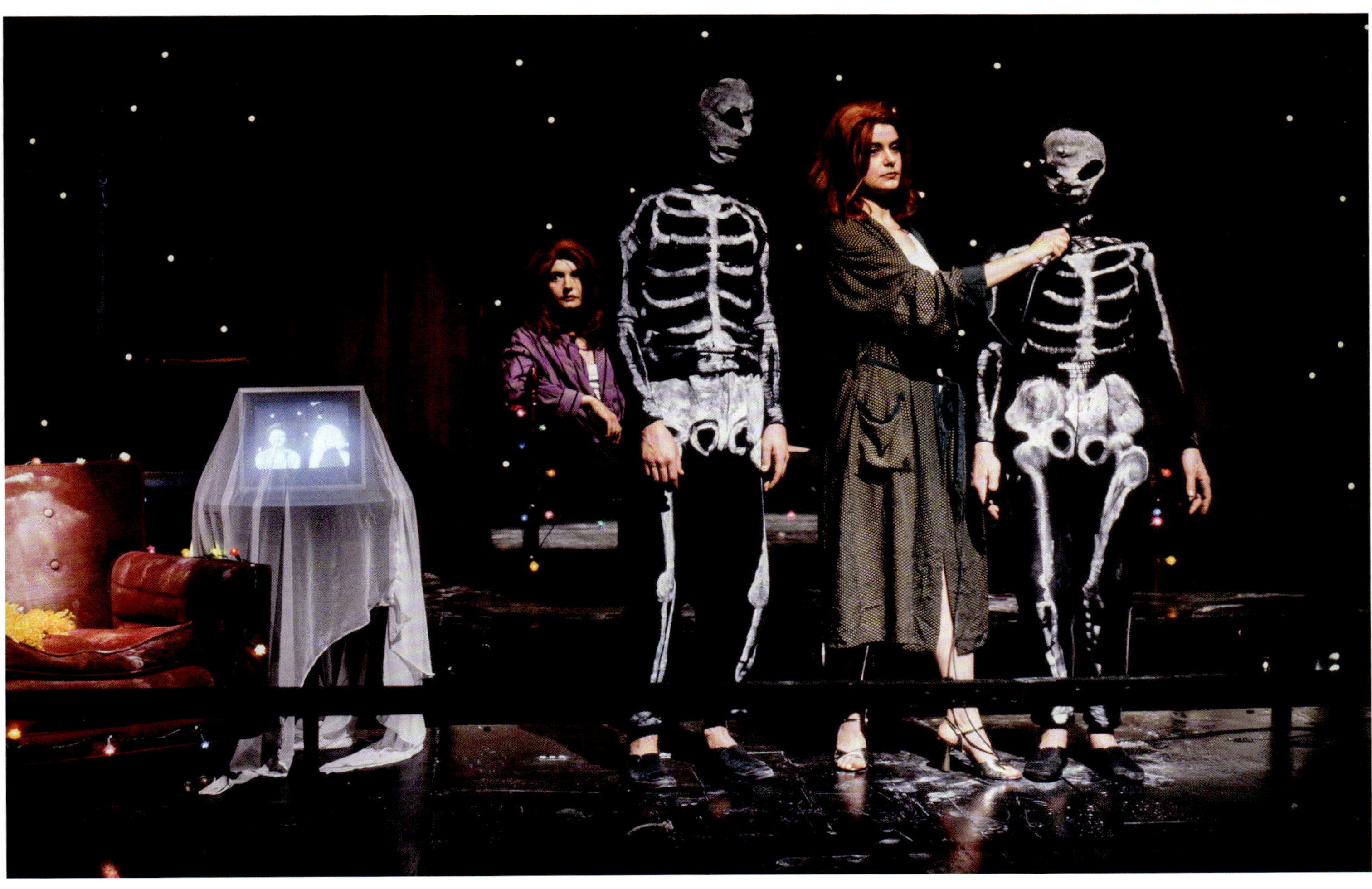

Claire: We used to fuck endlessly then and not tire of it. There was nothing but the taste and wet of flesh for us then.

Fred: We met and we went to bed straight away.

Claire: I said, 'Er, if you want to see me again, I'll give you a list of times when Charlie's always out.'

Fred: I hate this dark wood we're in. If they send messengers from the capital, then so be it. I'm not scared to die with you here next to me.

Claire: How, er, good that sounds. Oh, you are worth paying for with one's life.

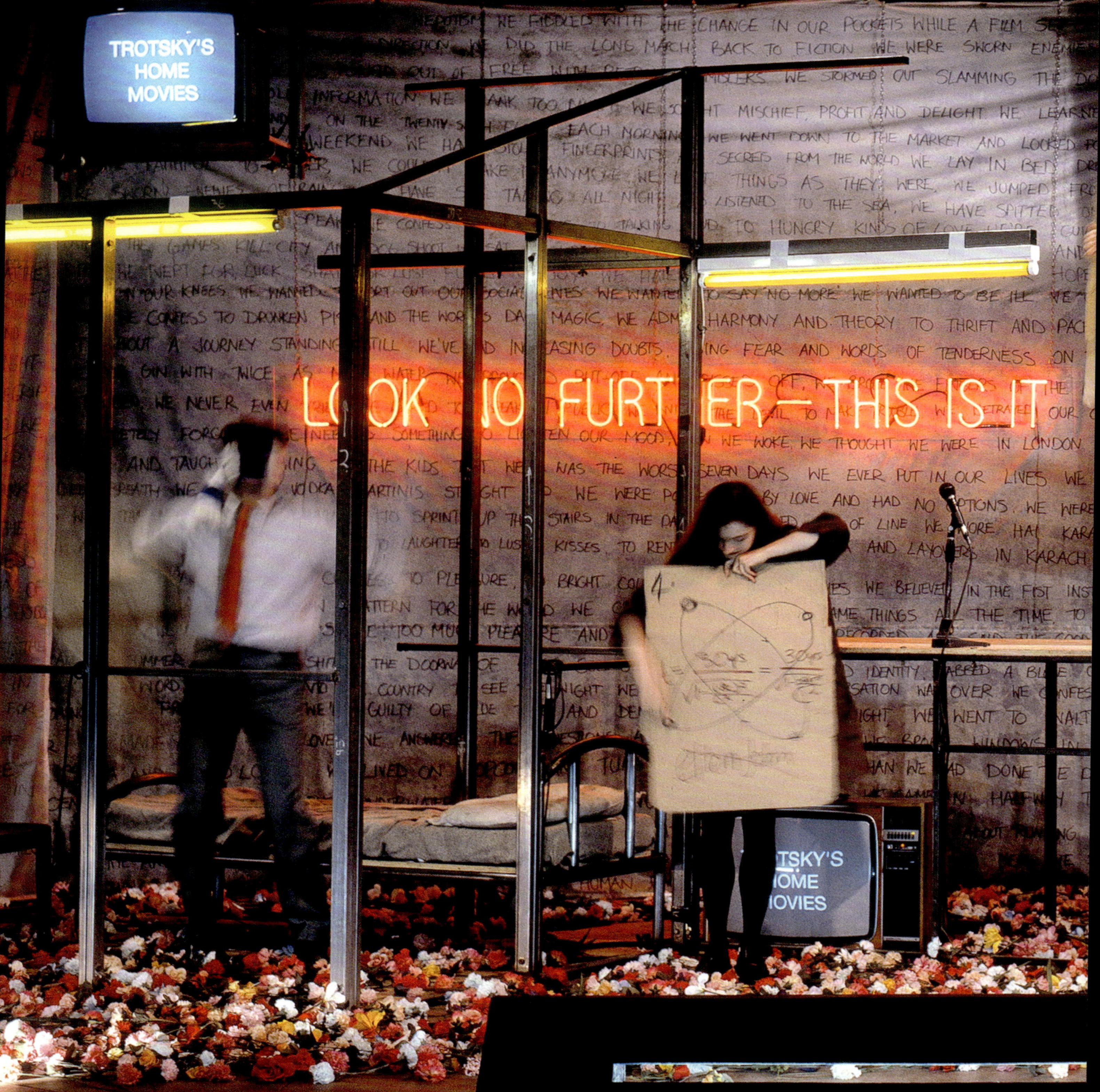

TROTSKY'S
HOME
MOVIES
LOOK NO FURTHER—THIS IS IT
TROTSKY'S
HOME
MOVIES

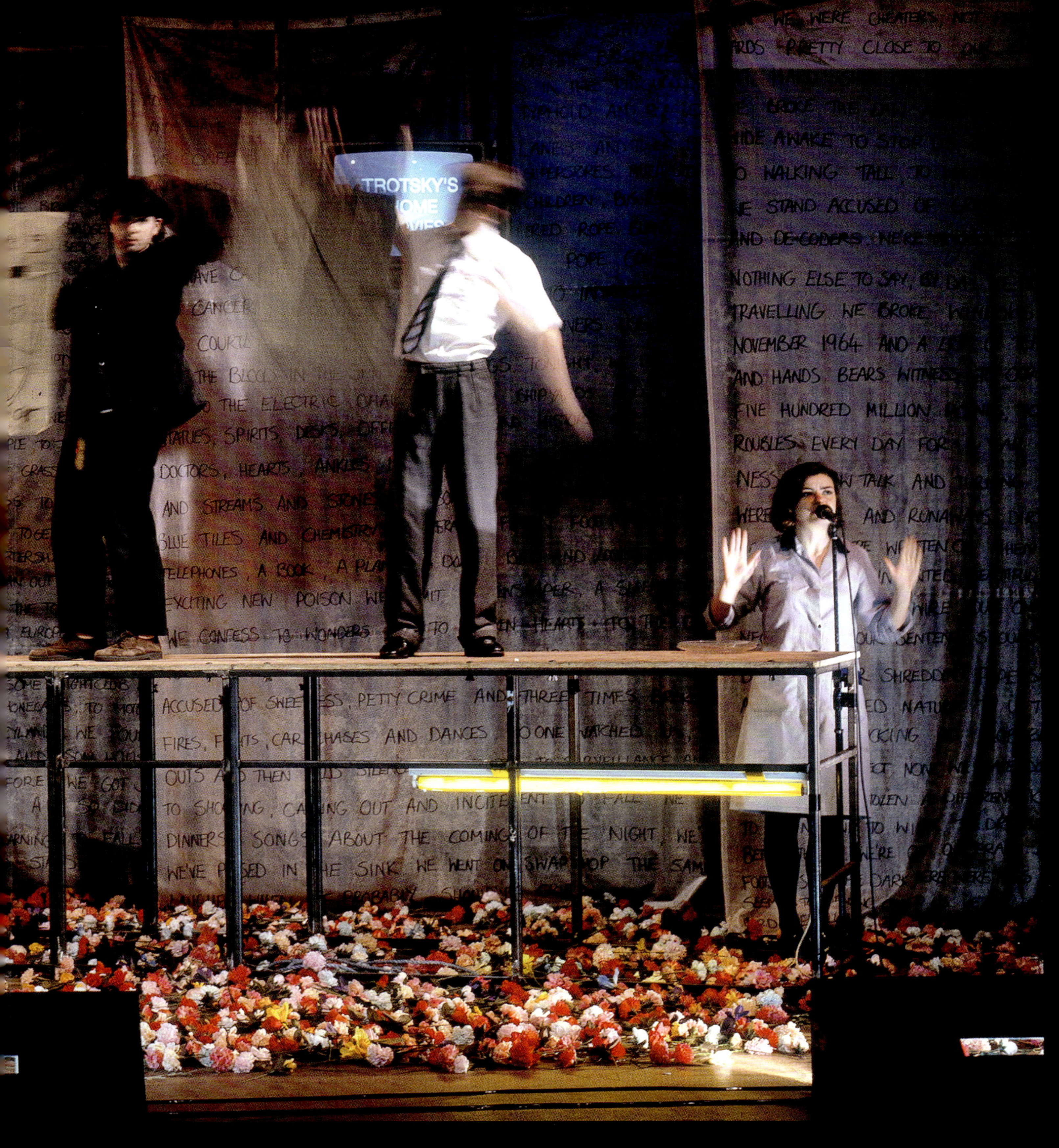

Cathy: They say that things began in a very simple way. If I speak the sound, waves will only fall to the ground. The car headlamps, represented by a pair of torches, come towards us in the night through which the rain can't fall. We're stood on high. The lights flick and seem to vanish. Who's driving the car? Who's moving the road? The new streets are lined with impossible signs. The old earth spins. Tracing the lines of motion across the continents, we are lost. The car stops. In the distance an object falls from a height equal to ours. We don't hear it.

Claire (as Marina): There's nowhere to stay cos it's a bank holiday weekend and all the inns are full. I want to be liberated from male white corporate oppression but I'm not sure how. I have unprotected sex with everyone I meet. Is that a good idea? Probably not. Up ahead there's an uneven surface to the street where low-grade tarmac has cracked in the sun causing a buckling or crinkled effect. I hate it when that happens.

In Mexico your wishes have a dream power. When you want to see someone, you go round a corner and they turn up. Trouble is there's no one I really want to see.

I'm like an angel in early Italian paintings: kind of serene and gorgeous, but depressed. Day one ends with its elegant structure of pointless trash. I'm in exile. There are soft human voices which, you know, sort of wake me when I drown ...

[*Claire as the protagonist/narrator Marina, in conversation with Richard Lowdon, who appears on video as Lee.*]

Richard: When the first bomb falls where do you want to be?

Claire: In England with my lover far away.

Richard: You want to be alone?

Claire: Always.

Richard: Naked?

Claire: Yes.

Richard: Tired?

Claire: No.

Richard: Gorgeous?

Claire: Yes.

Richard: Stupid?

Claire: No. Talk to me again.

Richard: You're waiting somewhere all alone. You dance the silence in the subways in paradise, you dance some falling and some crying that is party to the silence. You dance the Helter Skelter and the bad news special at 09:15, you dance the name TOYOTA, then you dance it all again.

Claire: Do I dance it well?

Richard: No, your dancing's terrible.

Claire: Do I dance it out of heartbreak or do I dance it out of hate?

Richard: You dance it out of hate.

Claire: The till girls and the Dixons boys pack up and leave. They say, 'Make your way to the checkout, please. The store will be closing in five minutes.'

Richard: That's right.

Claire: Goodnight, Lee.

Richard: Goodnight, Marina. Sweet dreams and sweet surrender.

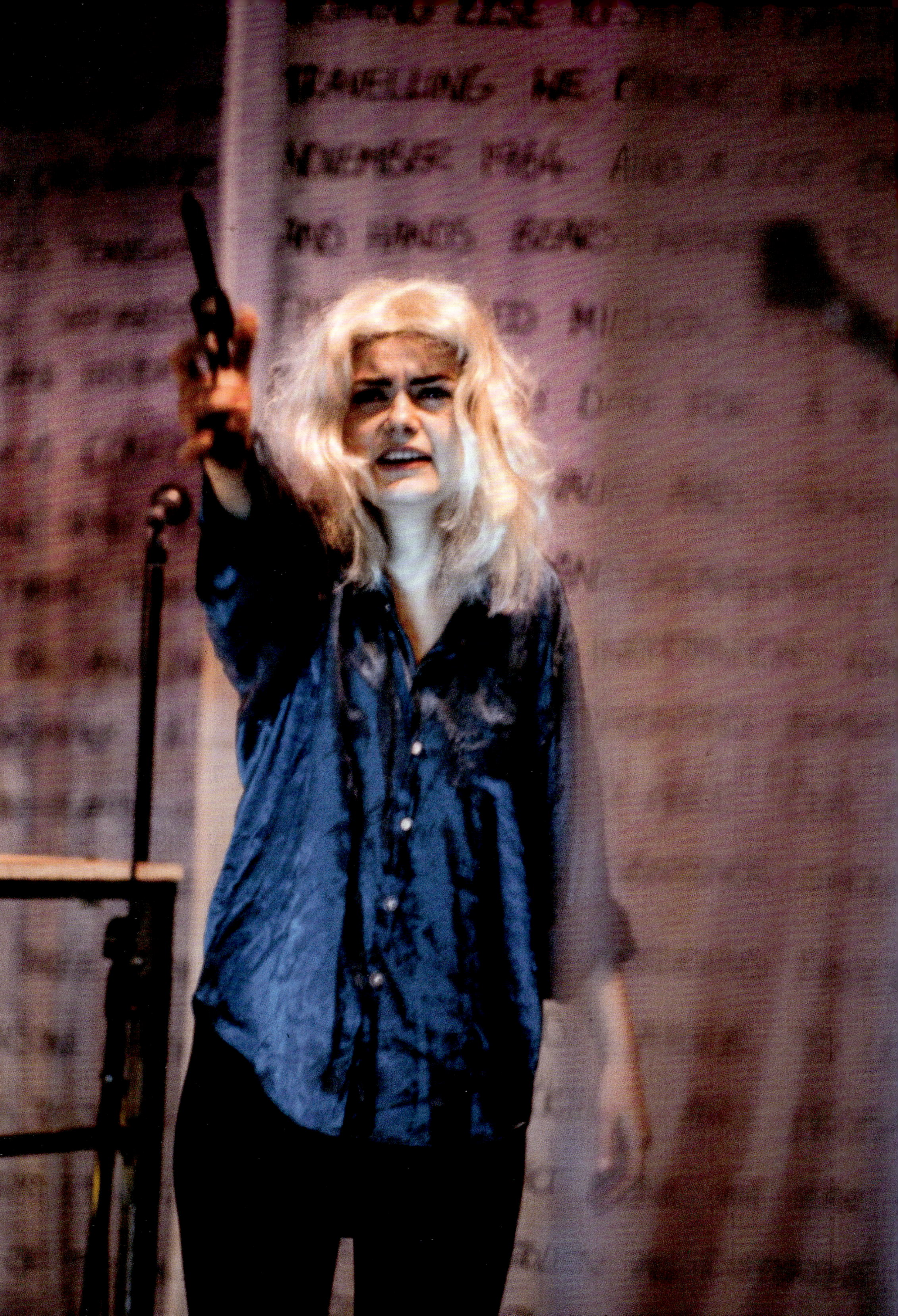

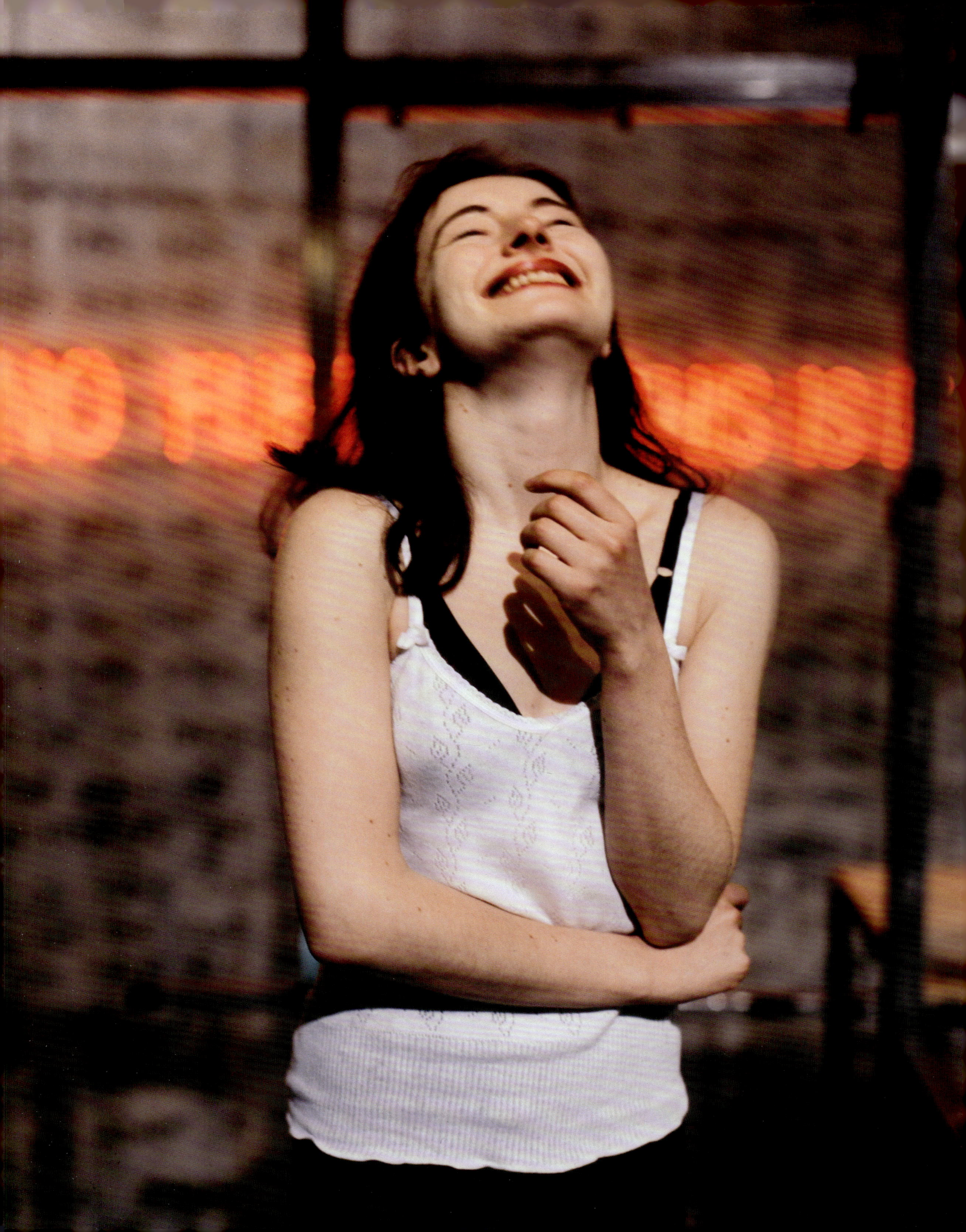

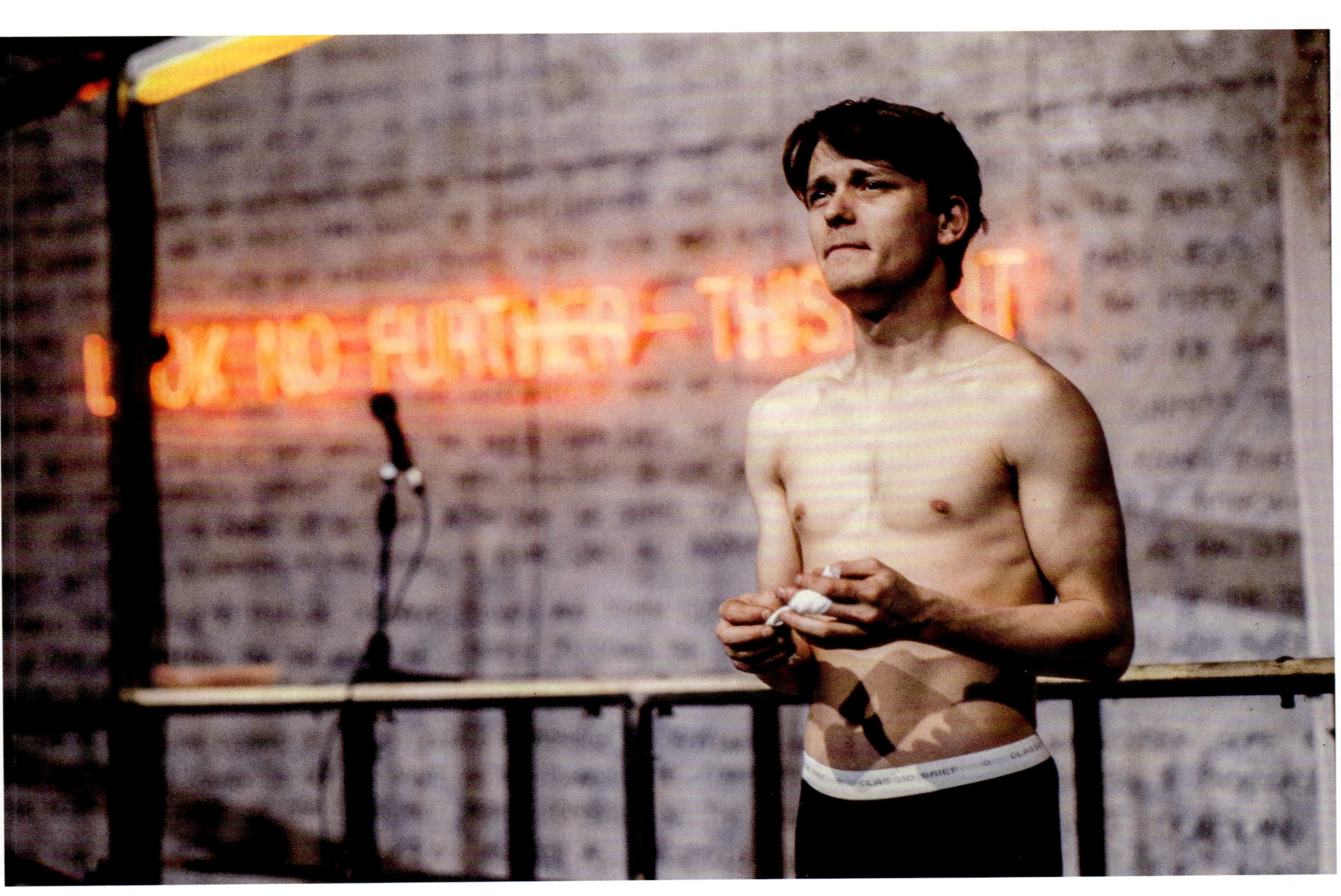
LOOK NO FURTHER - THIS

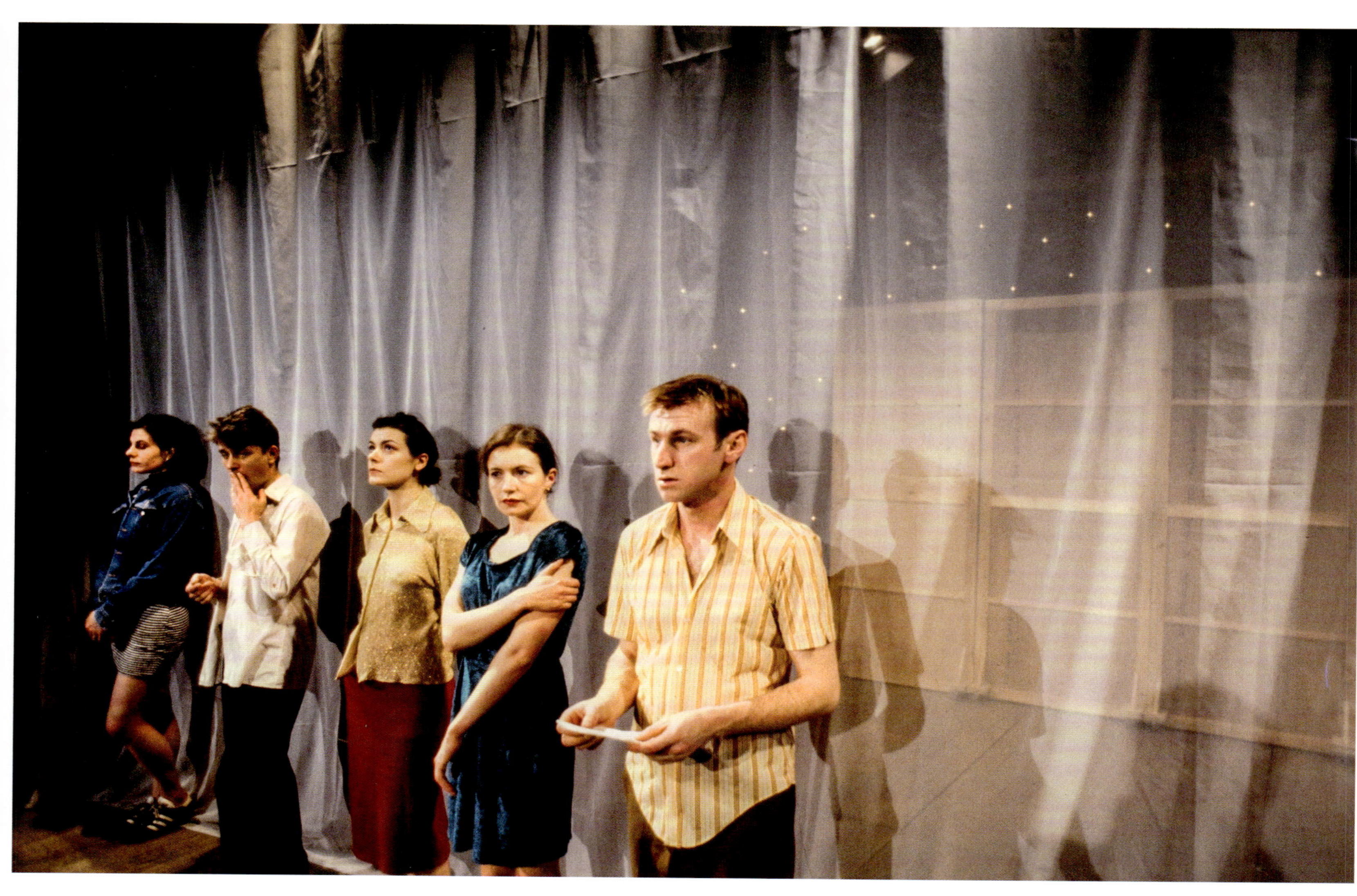

EMANUELLE ENCHANTED (1992)

44

Number 1. 'Copyright the Whole World
Except Australia.'

2. 'Cancer of the Fist.'

3. 'Suspicion of Innocence.'

4. 'Every word I say is, by definition,
a promise …'

5. 'CLUB OF NO REGRETS.'

6. 'Please Let Me Get What I Want
This Time.'

7. 'The forgiveness that only drunkenness
can bring …'

8. 'STUPID WHITE PEOPLE MAROONED ON
ANOTHER PLANET.'

9. 'Happy without Anaesthetic.'

10. 'Get Lost in the Deep Stairs
of Vertigo.'

1. First Fireproof Hotel.

2. Laugh Face T-shirt.

3. Helen's Soul.

4. Russian Dream.

5. Council House.

6. The First Black Pope.

7. Don't hurt me. Please, don't hurt me.

8. The word 'sedatives' is a registered
trademark of the Sedatives Group.

9. Nerves exposed.

10. Heartless Breeze.

1. A porn magazine called
CRUCIFIED WOMEN.

2. Fifty more years of bad news.

3. At 12am, like in a fairytale.

4. Light-hearted.

5. A vision.

6. The kid playing hide-and-seek in
the back of the car.

7. Noiseland video arcade.

8. Slander.

9. HOW TO FILM A MASSACRE.

10. HOW TO FILM A MASSACRE FOR KIDS.

1. Iron City Beer.

2. The Nobel Prize for Rap.

3. Invisible in Britain, partly visible
in the USA.

4. Partly visible in Britain, visible
in the USA.

5. Longest screen piss in history.

6. It has this tone, like early polyester.

7. Viva Tango.

8. Viva Las Vegas.

9. Viva Safeways.

10. Don't snore too loud, you'll wake
the angels in heaven.

1. Theresa Mallory Is Dead Because
She Knew the Truth.

2. Kuwait Oil in Kashmir Snow.

3. Come, moon, come and console me.

4. Sarcastic Realism.

5. New High Mountains Found.

6. The words 'Toxico' and 'Fast Beating
Heart' are trademarks and may not be
used or reproduced or stored in any
information retrieval system without the
prior permission of the makers.

7. Pseudo-events.

8. In bed two days.

9. No court exists to settle your dispute
over beauty.

10. These Are the Bright Stars and This
Is How to Find Them.

Number 1. 'Her husband's death,
loneliness, February 1953.'

2. A new game show called 'Long Faces'.

3. 'Builders on the roof at 7am.'

4. 'Builders on the roof at 7pm.'

5. 'I Have a Horror of the Truth but I
Love the Truth.'

6. Crisis.

7. The words 'Fuck Face' and 'Seafood'
are registered as trademarks by the
manufacturer and they reserve the public
right to be identified as such.

8 'DON'T DOUBLE-CROSS THE ONES YOU LOVE.'

Number 9. Secret Password.

Number 10. Only the Lonely.

1. A statue, a statue of Headless Christ.

2. A Gold-Coloured Watch.

3. Eyes the colour of the sea.

4. A hotel room without any clocks.

5. A beautiful, violent country.

6. Grab Reality as a Commodity and
Sell It.

7. Win a chance, win a good chance,
win a ghost of a chance.

8. A scorched film.

9. A broken bone.

10. Acting out the last journey of
her sister.

1. How can we have a president who
has dreams like this?

2. The rain that falls now is such
dirty rain.

3. Undressing under the sheet.

4. A blue-in-colour car.

5. Love and Acting Go Together.

6. News of Accidents.

7. Then they knew the great grief,
the great calamity.

8. Forty girls so beautiful it was
impossible to choose among them or
to look on them without faintness.

9. Last Hope Convenience Store.

10. Tomorrow is my birthday, consider
yourself invited.

1. Who to trust?

2. She may still be in that coma but
she'll hear every word you have to say,
I know she will.

Number 3. An Epilogue.

4. I want to be a household word.

5. A love letter written in binary.

6. A perfect ending to a perfect day.

7. HIDDEN POLITICAL MESSAGE.

8. Research.

Item 9. A MAN CALLED THREATENING.

10. A nightclub called LA NUIT.

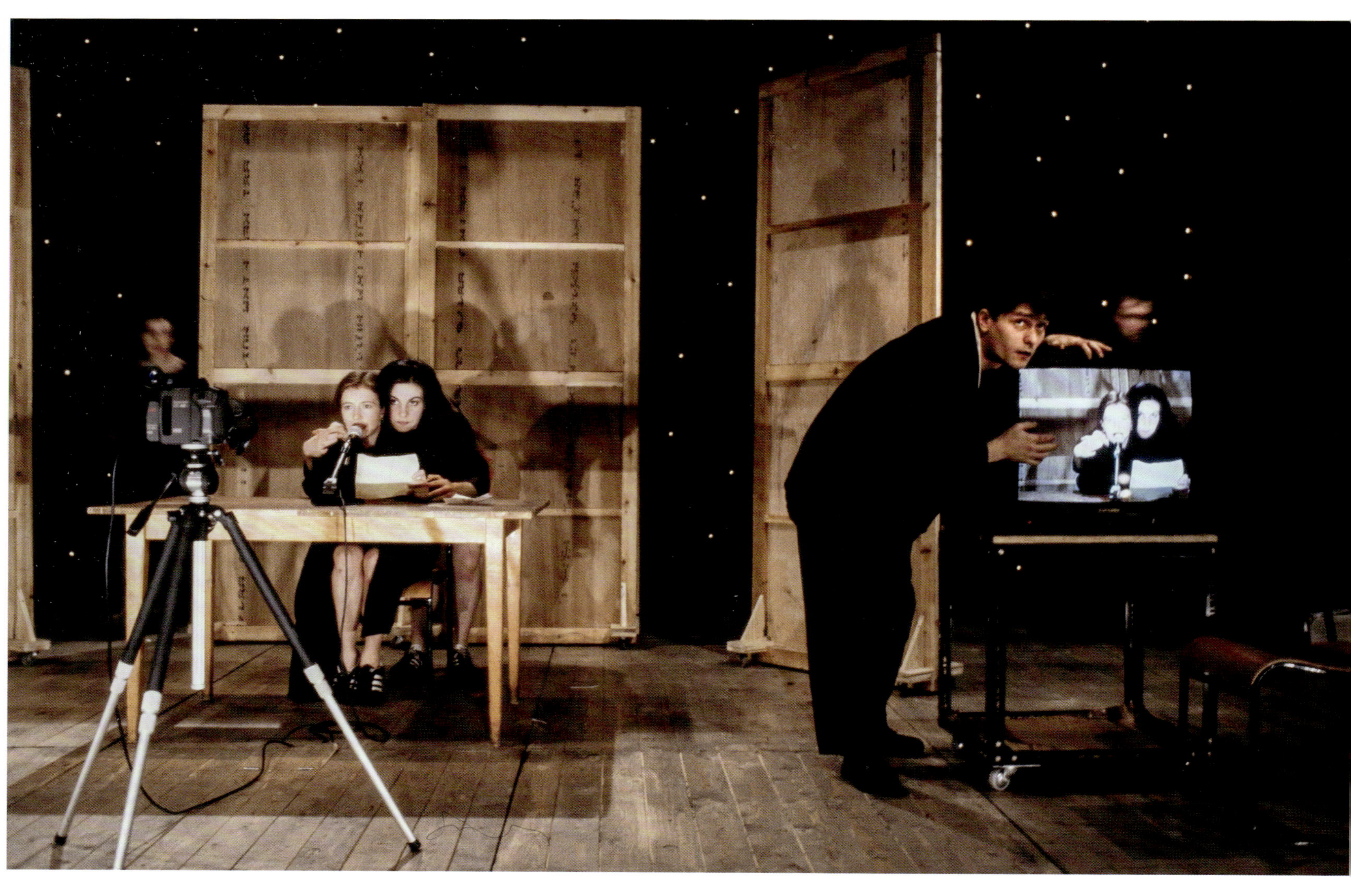

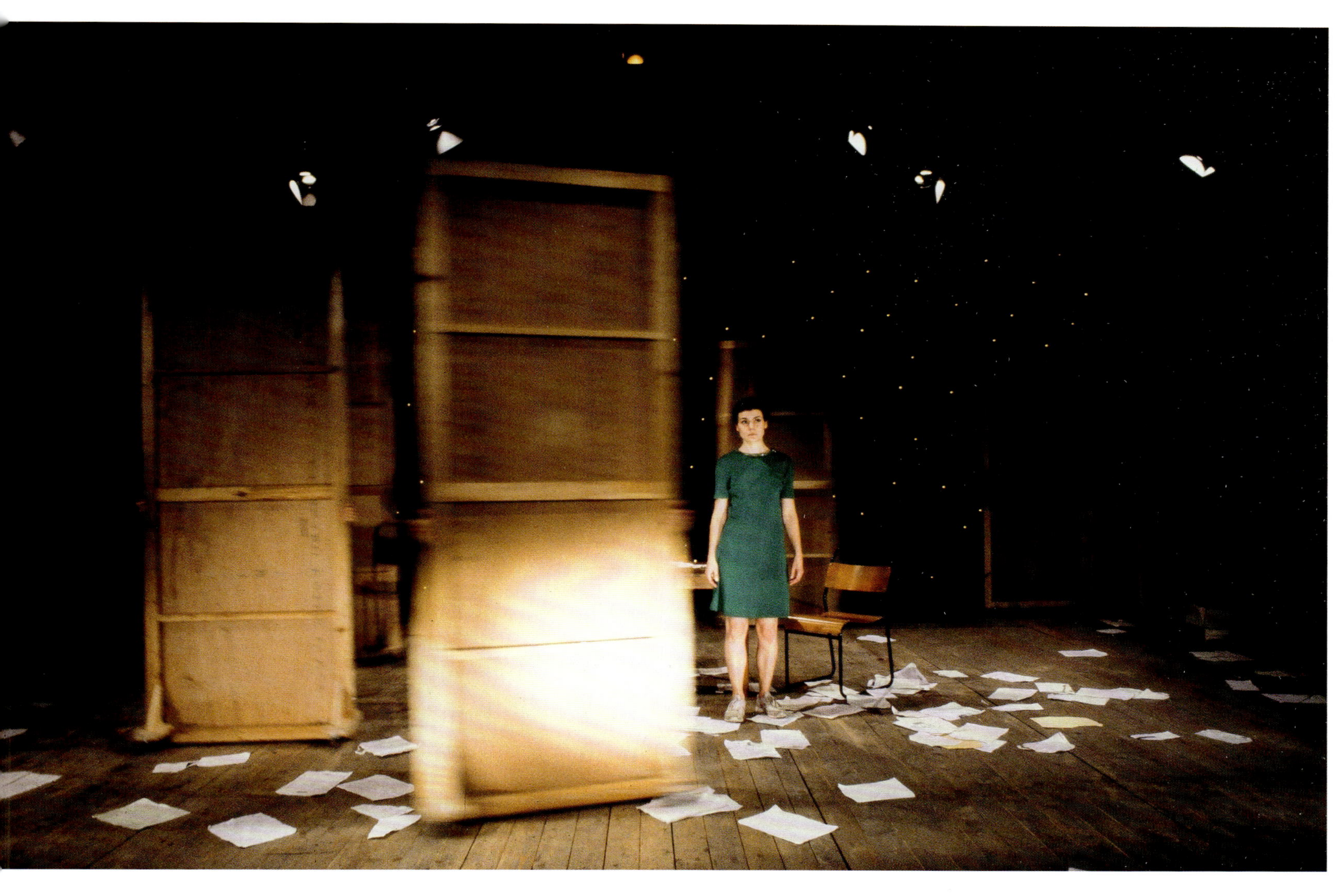

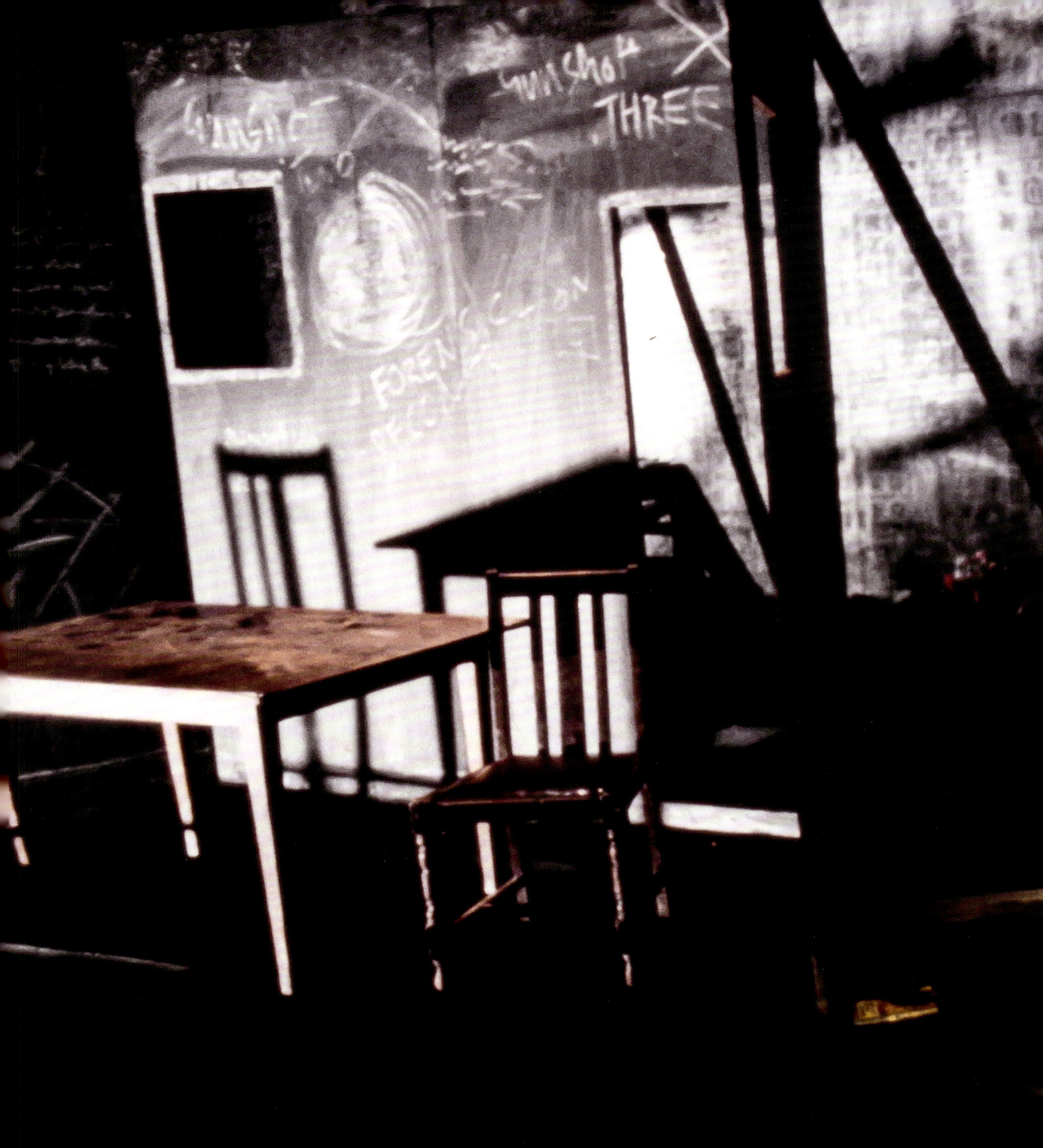

CLUB OF NO REGRETS (1993)

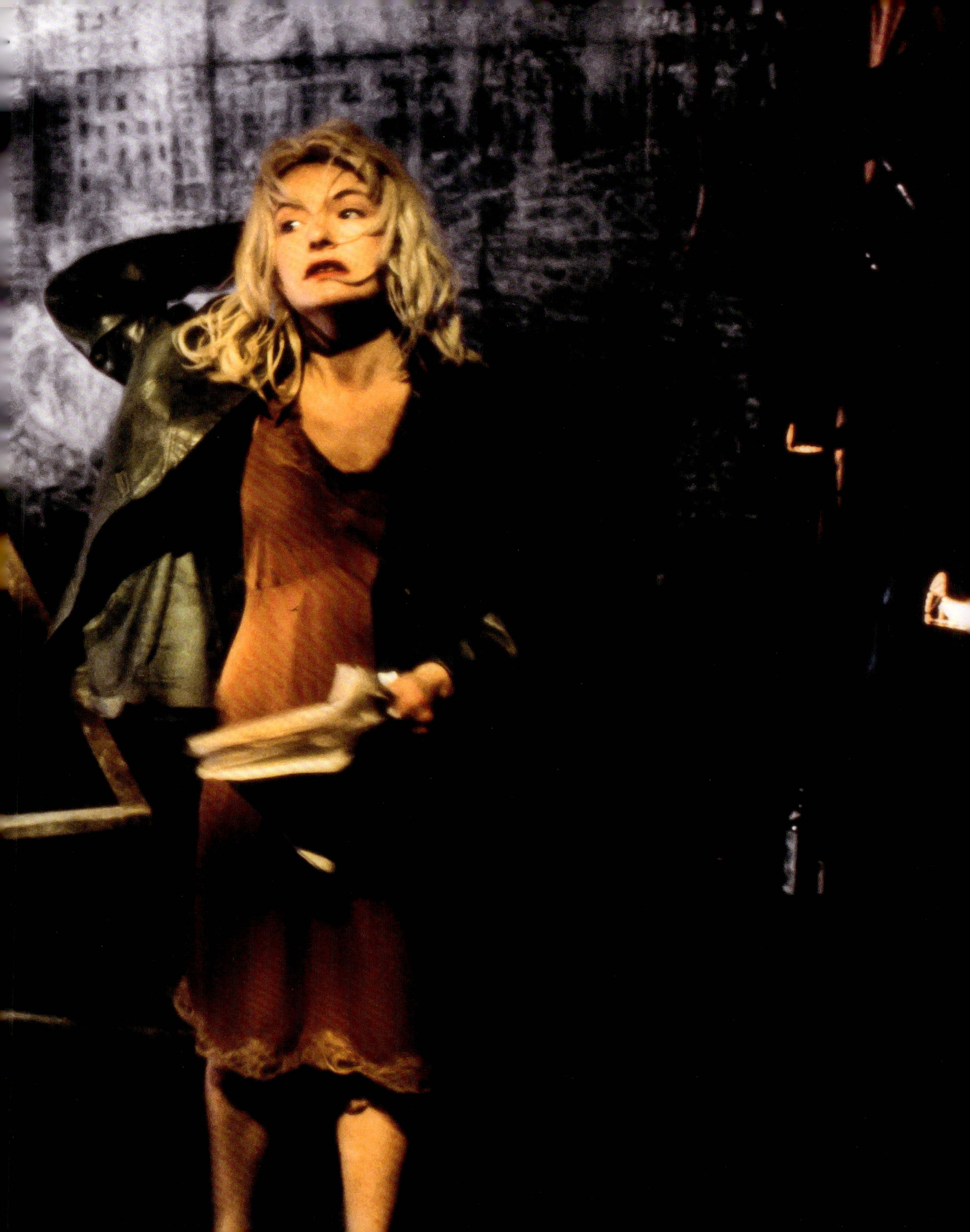

Club of No Regrets began as an exploration of short scenes, each of which had a title—A Drug Trip Scene, A Just as They're about to Kiss, the Telephone Rings Scene, and so on—sometimes drawn from TV genre cliché and often with supernatural, violent, or excessively emotional undertones. The central figure of Helen X, accompanied by two surly 'stagehands', oblige two reluctant actor-hostages to enact these scenes repeatedly, as if seeking some 'correct' or satisfying composition of them. [TE]

Helen X was at the centre of it organizing the material. In those shows where someone's 'in charge' we'd only get it to work if the persona making decisions was a bit irrational, or working with a strange logic. She was quite a hidden figure behind the wig, not really looking up, clutching a sweaty pile of papers in her hand. I was barely visible behind the set for the first part of the performance—walking back and forth, stomping and shouting, repeating bits of the text. The main part of the piece is her calling for the different scenes to be enacted, as if she's making up the order, demanding things are done again because she's not happy with the sequence or with the performance. She is a demented director cycling through material without any obvious reason. So there's repetition but it's not cool or formal—it's heated, obsessive. It was quite a visceral experience. I used to think a lot about rhythm and pace in the calls for different scenes or the words that got spoken. There was this great play with John Avery's music, which was a really important part of the whole show. [TC]

Terry: Some bits of this history have been censored and other parts of it have been, um, stolen.

I think I have a bad luck name since in all history I share it only with a small-town plumber and two useless embezzlers who worked at the Post Office. My name: Helen X. I'll write it down so I don't forget it. I was born in a bad luck time, in a bad luck place just like this one, on the same day as a solar eclipse on TV, the most beautiful but very very bad luck thing.

I'm lost and I'm lonely. I'm losing things fast. I dropped some money back there somewhere. Two—no, change it— three pints of blood went right down the drain after a pub fight. I already lost my fingerprints in a game of cards. Soon I won't be a person at all, just a sad collection of bits all lost in the woods.

Good.

I have to think positive. I'm getting somewhere. I am getting somewhere. Perhaps I'll lie down and cry. No, bad idea—I'll sing to keep my spirits up. [*Tuneless singing*] Frank Sinatra never wrote a song about this place—he wasn't fucking good enough.

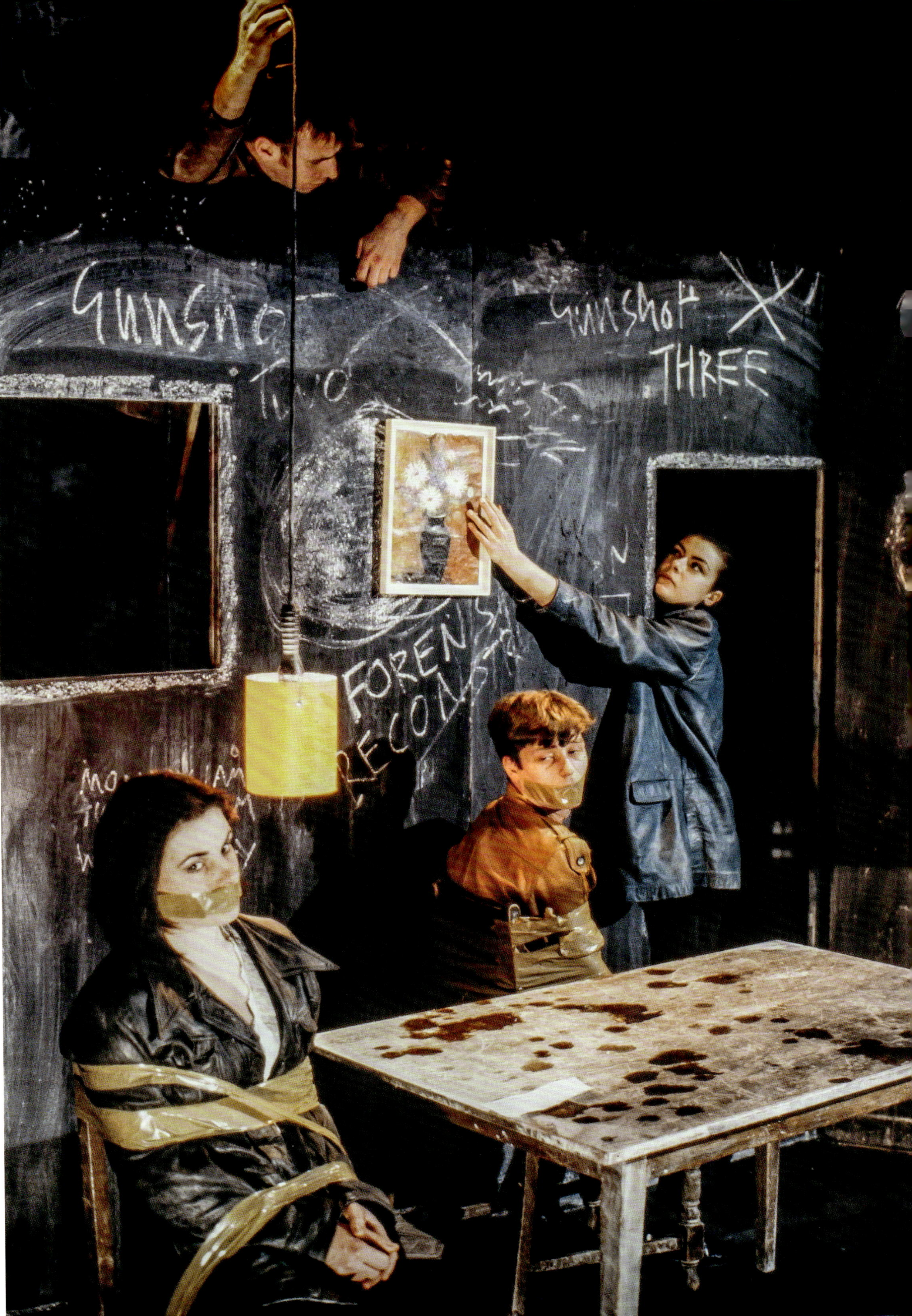

GUNSHOT TWO
GUNSHOT THREE
FORENSIC

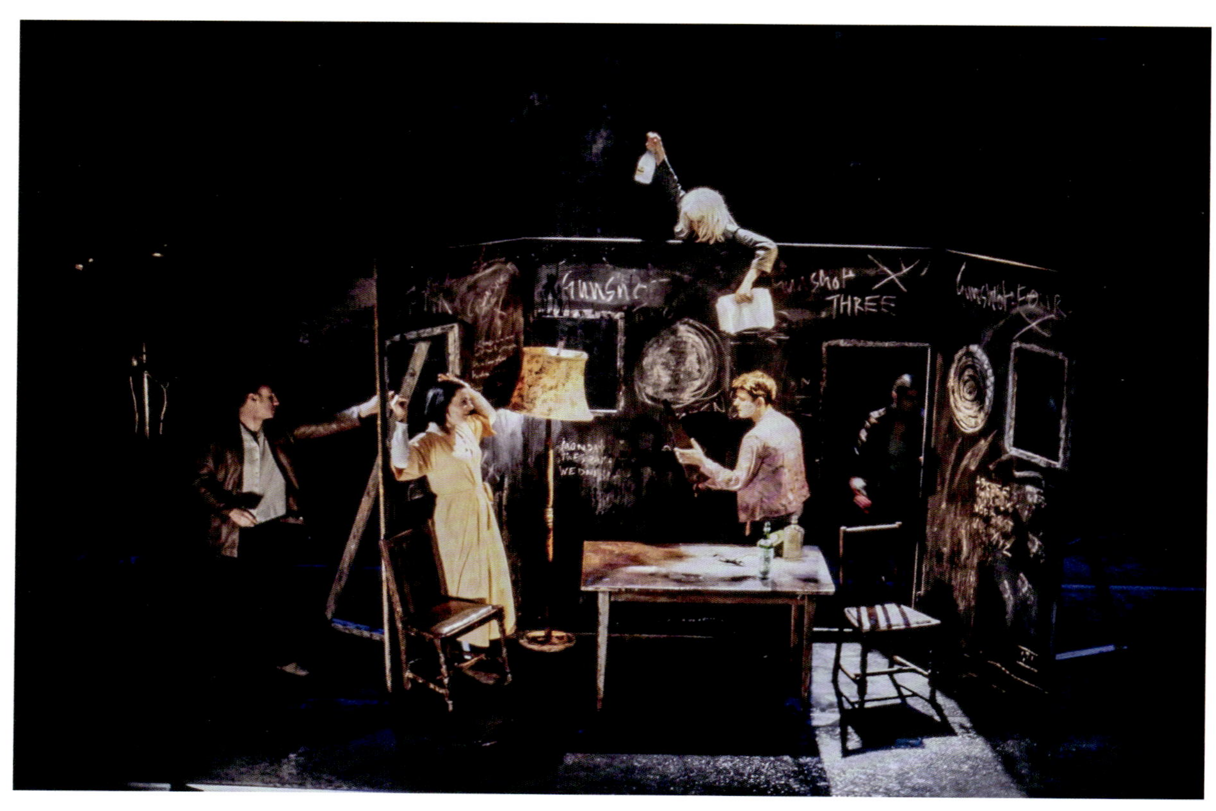

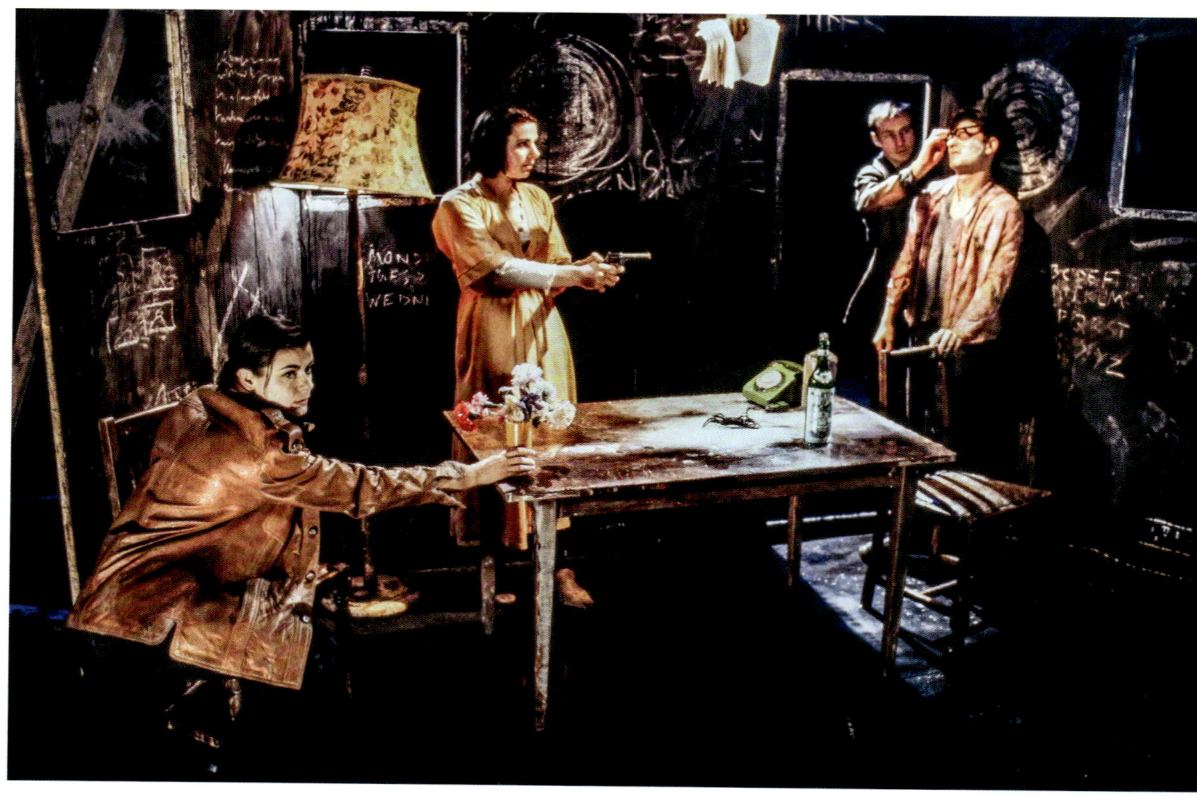

For Richard and myself—the stagehands—
there's a game of invention: what can
you make with this scene? What objects
or 'special effects' can be added? We're
splashing Robin and Claire's faces with
water for tears and spraying fake blood on
them and on the walls during scenes that
supposedly involve gunshots. We're adding
pictures on the wall, a light to stand in
the corner of the room, a holdall, a vase of
flowers, or a telephone on the table, we're
putting a clock on the wall and making the
hands spin around … It's a constant task of
adding to or adjusting the scene. [CN]

In one sense the stagehands are just there
to make the centre-stage room picture
work. Nothing else matters—even to the
extent that their own presence is irrelevant,
since they don't think of themselves as
being part of the picture. Whatever is
outside the frame doesn't matter. Part of
the fun of the work was that 'outside the
frame' the stagehands could be nonchalant,
indifferent—the hand is in place, the gun is
pointing into the room, but the stagehand
who's supplying that part of the image is
meanwhile reading a book or just looking
around bored. [RL]

DEAR NO ONE I HAVE WALKED TO THAT BIT
OF THE PARK WHERE THE TAPE SAYS POLICE
LINE DO NOT CROSS AND I HAVE CROSSED
IT STOP DO NOT TRY TO FIND ME STOP COS
I'M A KIND OF HOMEMADE BOMB, DESTINED
TO EXPLODE PRETTY SOON STOP BETTER FOR
YOU IF YOU AREN'T NEAR ME THEN, BETTER
FOR EVERYONE STOP OH YEAH AND I SUPPOSE
IT'S NO SURPRISE I'M PREGNANT STOP FOR
THREE YEARS I HAD NO SEX WITH ANYONE, I
TRIED TO FORGET I EVER HAD A THING CALLED
SEXUALITY THEN ONE LITTLE FUCK AND I'M
PREGNANT STOP IT'S GOING TO BE A GIRL I'M
SURE AND SHE'S GOING TO BE PERFECT AND
I'M GOING TO CALL HER GRIEF …

DEAR NO ONE I'M SO UNHAPPY I'M GOING TO
GET INVOLVED IN BAD PEOPLE TO TRY AND GET
MYSELF MURDERED STOP YOU KNOW WHAT IT'S
LIKE THESE DAYS—YOU WAKE UP EMBROILED IN
A GREAT ADVENTURE AND THE NEXT THING YOU
KNOW YOU'RE THROUGH THE FUCKING LOOKING
GLASS INTO WEIRD WORLD STOP OH YEAH
THINGS ROUND HERE HAVE CERTAINLY CHANGED
STOP IN MY DREAM I'M NOT SURE WHO I'M
SUPPOSED TO BE STOP YESTERDAY I FOUND A
NOTE BY THE BEDSIDE TABLE BUT IT WASN'T
IN MY HANDWRITING STOP THE NOTE SAID I'M
OLD, OR GETTING OLD STOP THE NOTE SAID
I'M HIDING BUT I'M NOT SURE WHO FROM …

DEAR NO ONE STOP THE VOICES AND NOISES
IN THE NIGHT ARE SCARING ME NOW STOP
I'M INSIDE A CITY OF LIVING FAINTING
BUILDINGS AND NOW IT'S GETTING DARK STOP
DO YOU THINK THAT A ROOM CAN BE HAUNTED
BY THE GHOST OF ITSELF? DO YOU THINK OUR
BODIES KEEP THEIR GHOSTS STORED DEEP
INSIDE THEM?

A Shoot-Out Scene

A: Aghhh!

B: What is it?

A: I think I'm hit. I'm seeing colours. I'm
thinking in shapes. Hold me. Talk to me.

B: Oh god.

A: Talk to me, speak to me.

B: What do you want to hear?

A: Anything: I'm dying, aren't I? I'm
going down, just tell me something.

B: It's … It's okay. You're not dying.
Just listen …

Dramatic interruption comes into play—
we often bring an object at just the wrong
moment—we're a nuisance that arrives
to break the rhythm. Figures who are
unhelpfully helpful: something we come
back to in so many of the pieces. As Terry
accelerates, our attempt to keep up with the
scenes brings a physical dynamism to the
outer edges of the space. We're racing from
one side of the stage to the other, adding
things to the picture and then taking them
away again: first bringing talcum powder
into the room as smoke, then starting to
throw it everywhere, filling the stage. The
fiction that starts as something staged only
in the room by a certain point takes over the
whole space. [RL]

It begins as a clumsy, 'unpromising'
comedy: inaudible actors whose mouths
are gagged with tape, stagehands who
interrupt the action, no obvious connection
between the fragmentary scenes presented.
Over time the ineptitude of the enactment
escalates to something else: a rapid-fire
collaging, resequencing, and merging
of the scenes which hits a more and
more emotional tone, driven on by the
soundtrack. It's about making one type of
sense out of another, pressing 'narrative
materials' from one context into the service
of another poetic logic. [TE]

A Troubled Scene

A: Queen of Nothing, we call upon you to
help us ...

B: Today I am troubled, I am troubled,
cease to speak, cease to walk. I am
troubled by voices. I call on Our Lady
of Car Parks to help me. I summon her:
help me break loose from these bindings.
Prince of Lie Detection and Broken
Promises, I am coming dressed in rags to
meet you. Queen of Nothing, mistress of
the air and of satellites, we have not
seen you, it has been long since we've
seen you. Oh, can't you see I have no
skin and no bones. I am coming dressed
in rags just to meet you.

A Questions Scene

A: When did you first discover that
the world was magic? When did you first
discover that you caused magic in the
world? When did you first discover that
there was magic in the world?

A Look-How-I'm-Crying Scene

A: Look how I'm crying. Don't you care
at all? Look how I'm crying.

B: I don't want you to leave.

A: Where am I going? What am I going
to do?

B: I have pretended for so long that
everything is fine.

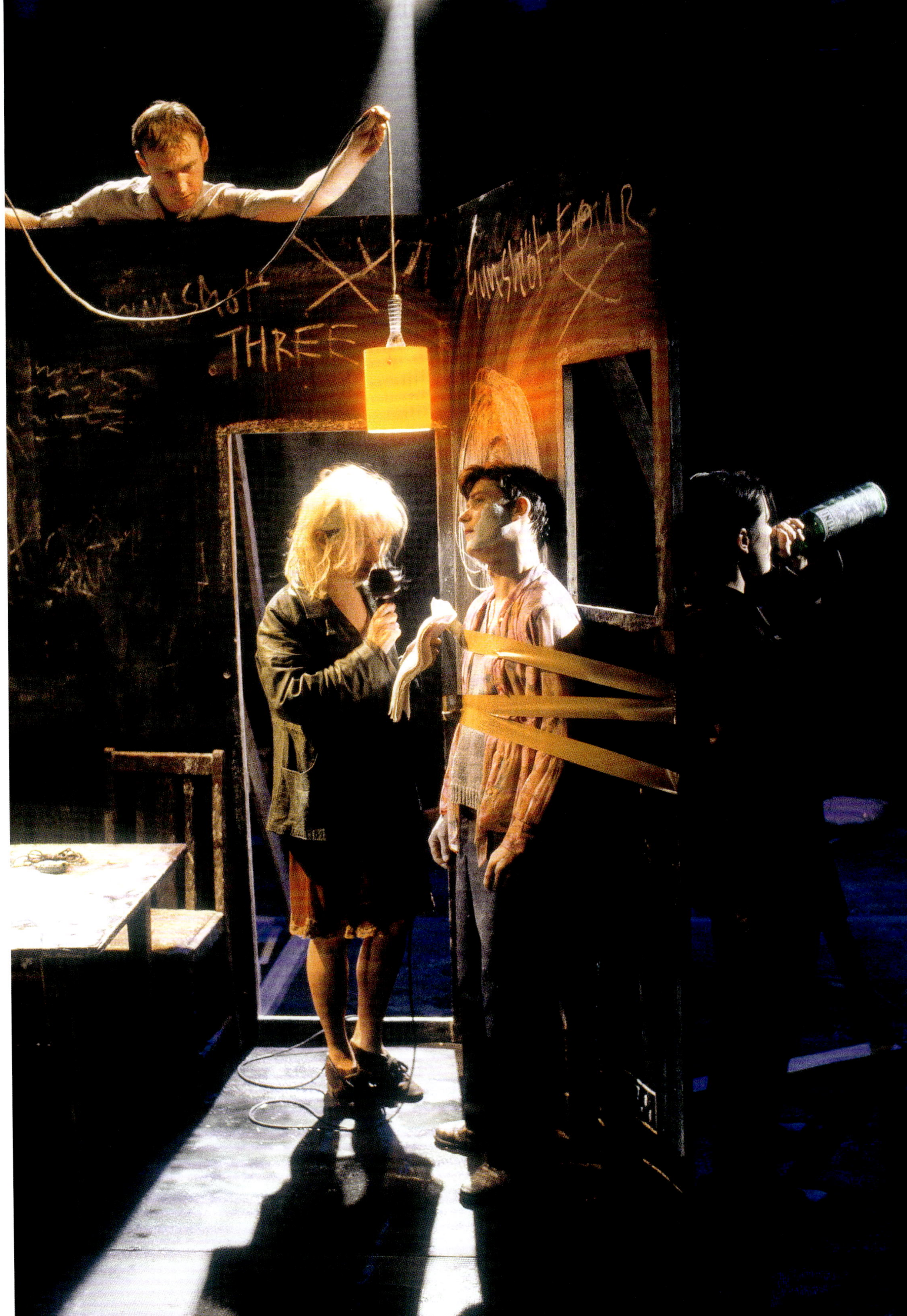
GUNSHOT
THREE
GUNSHOT FOUR

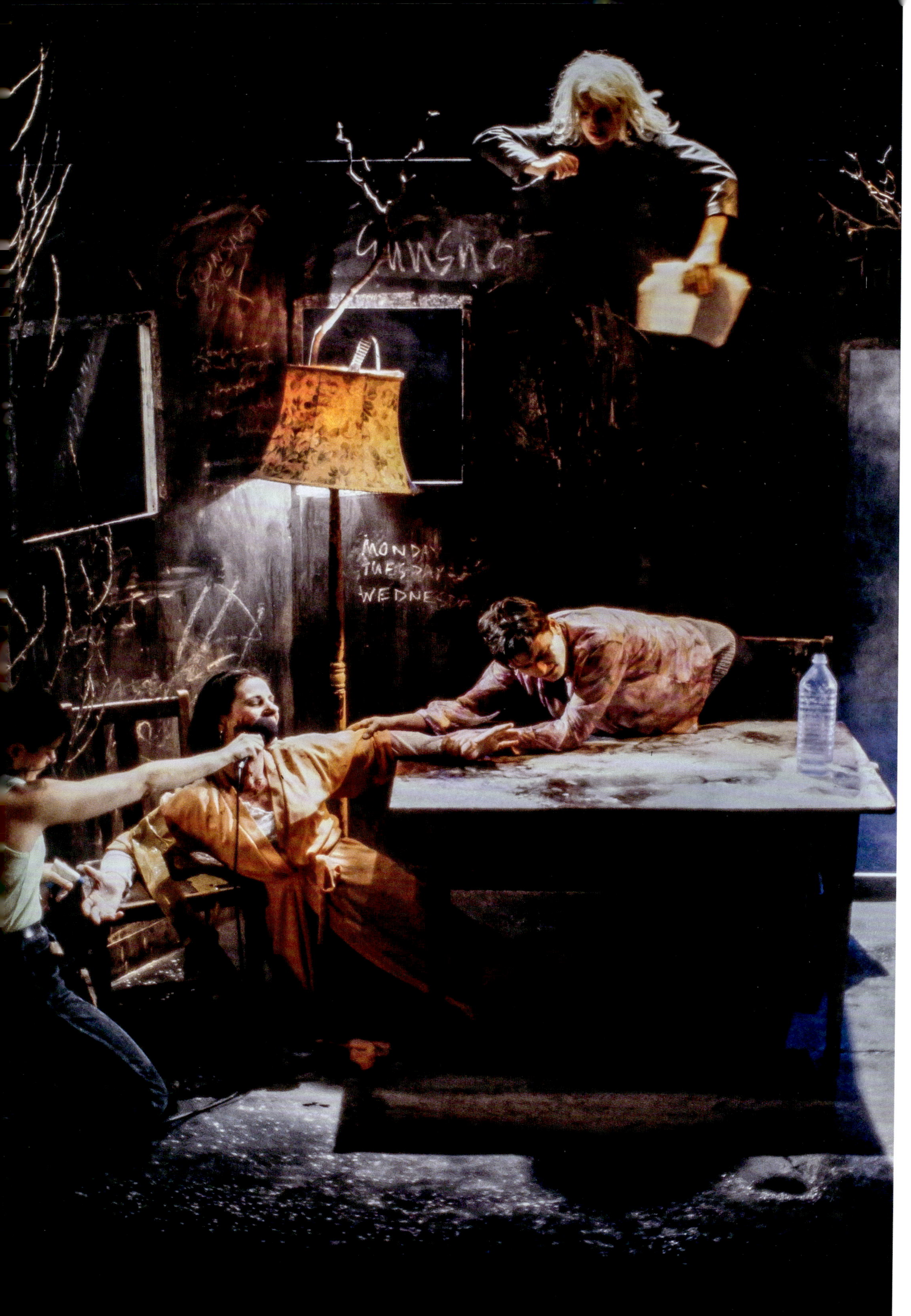

Gunshot
MONDAY
TUESDAY
WEDNESDAY

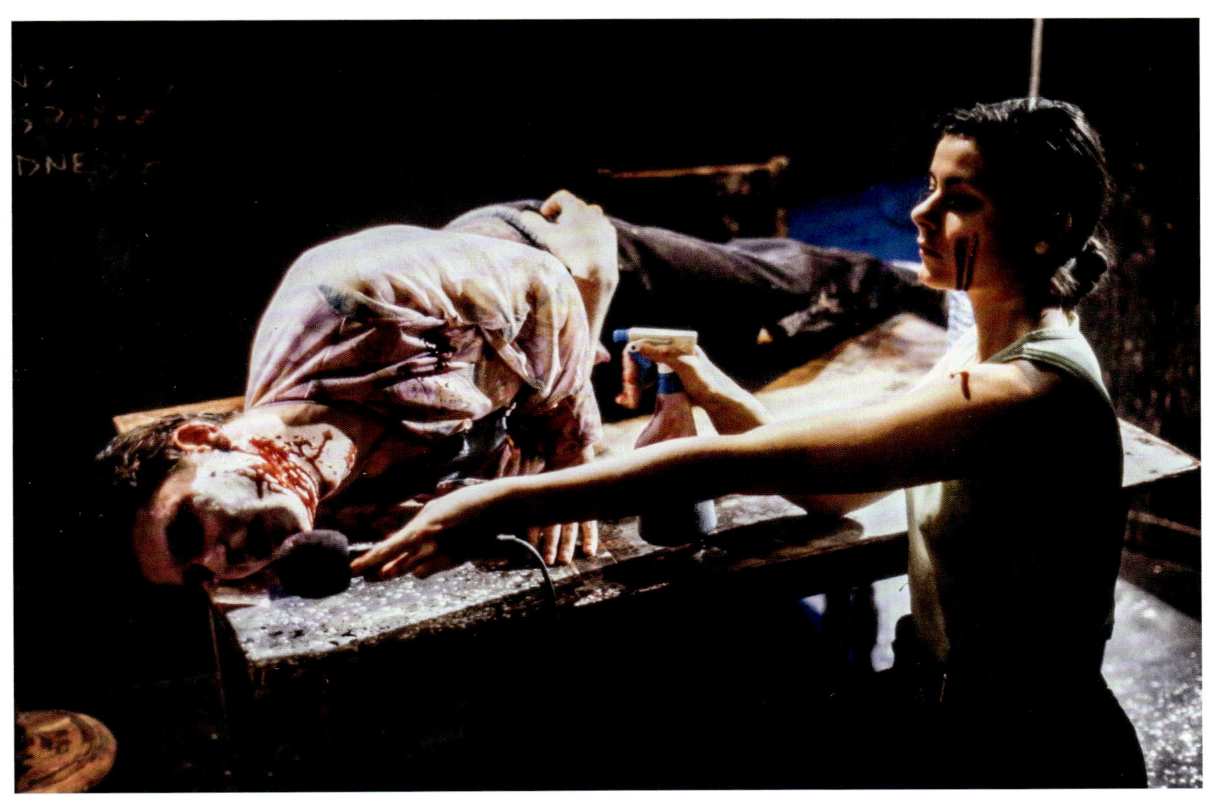

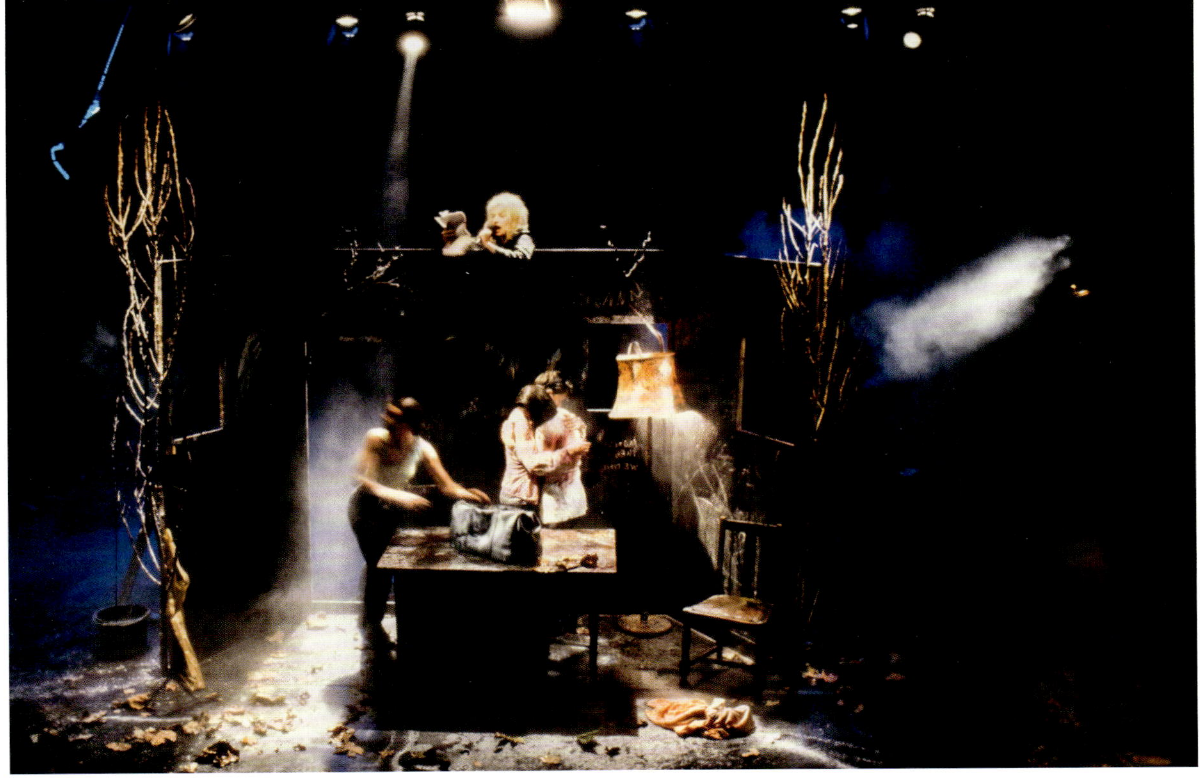

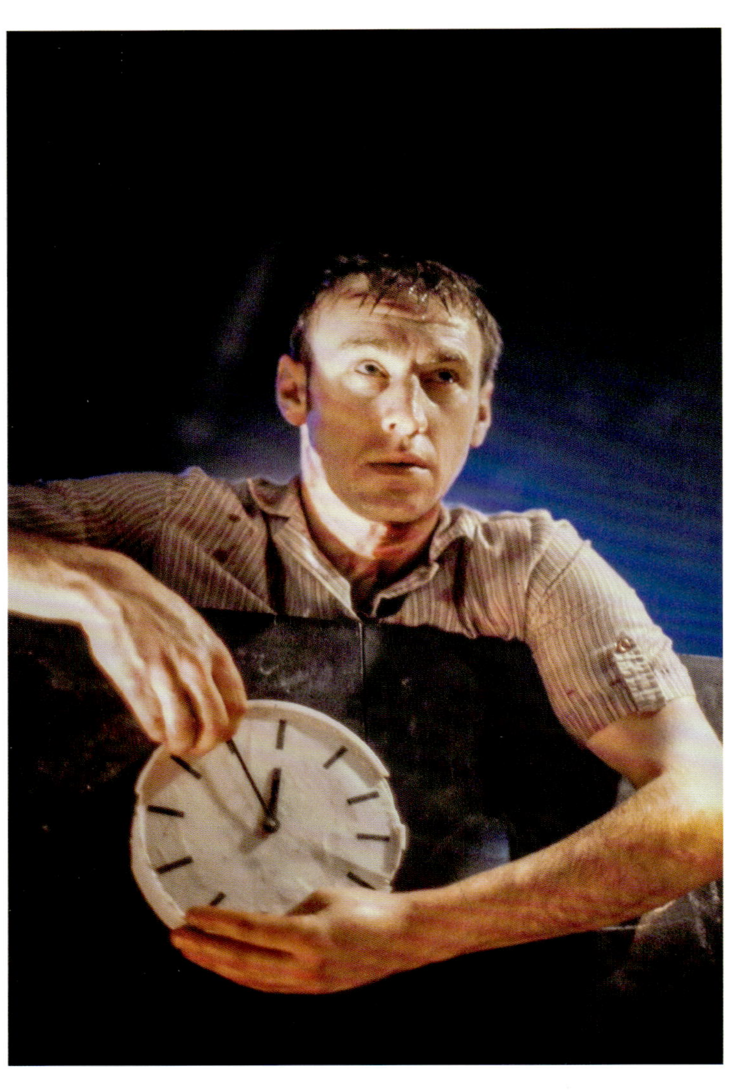

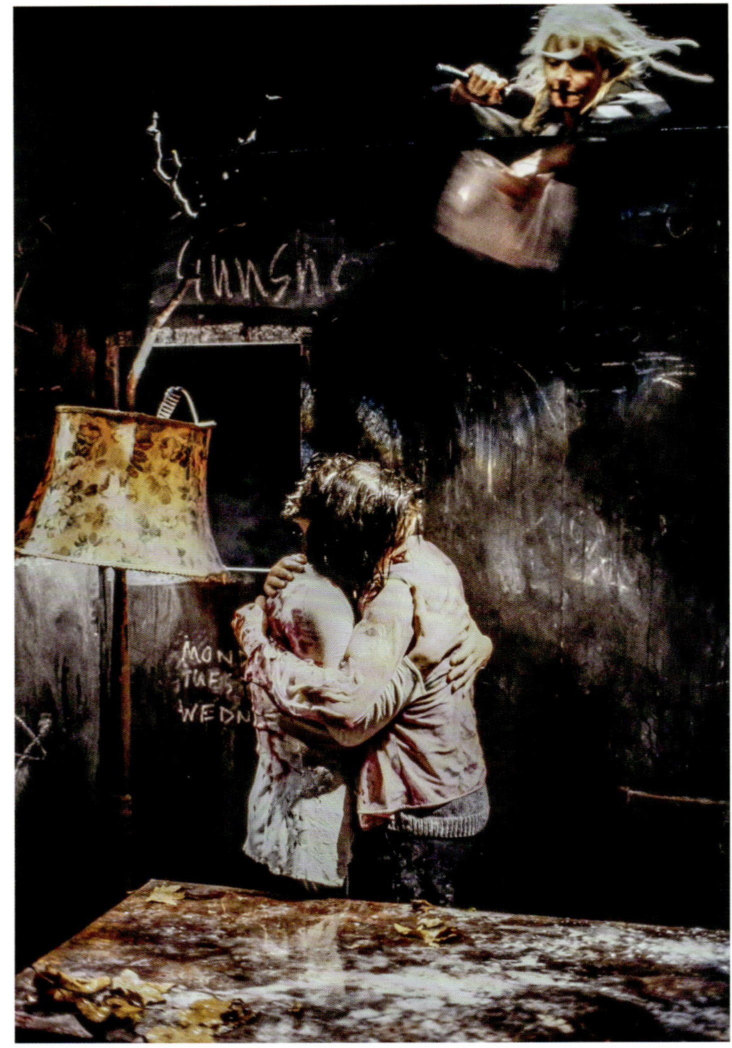

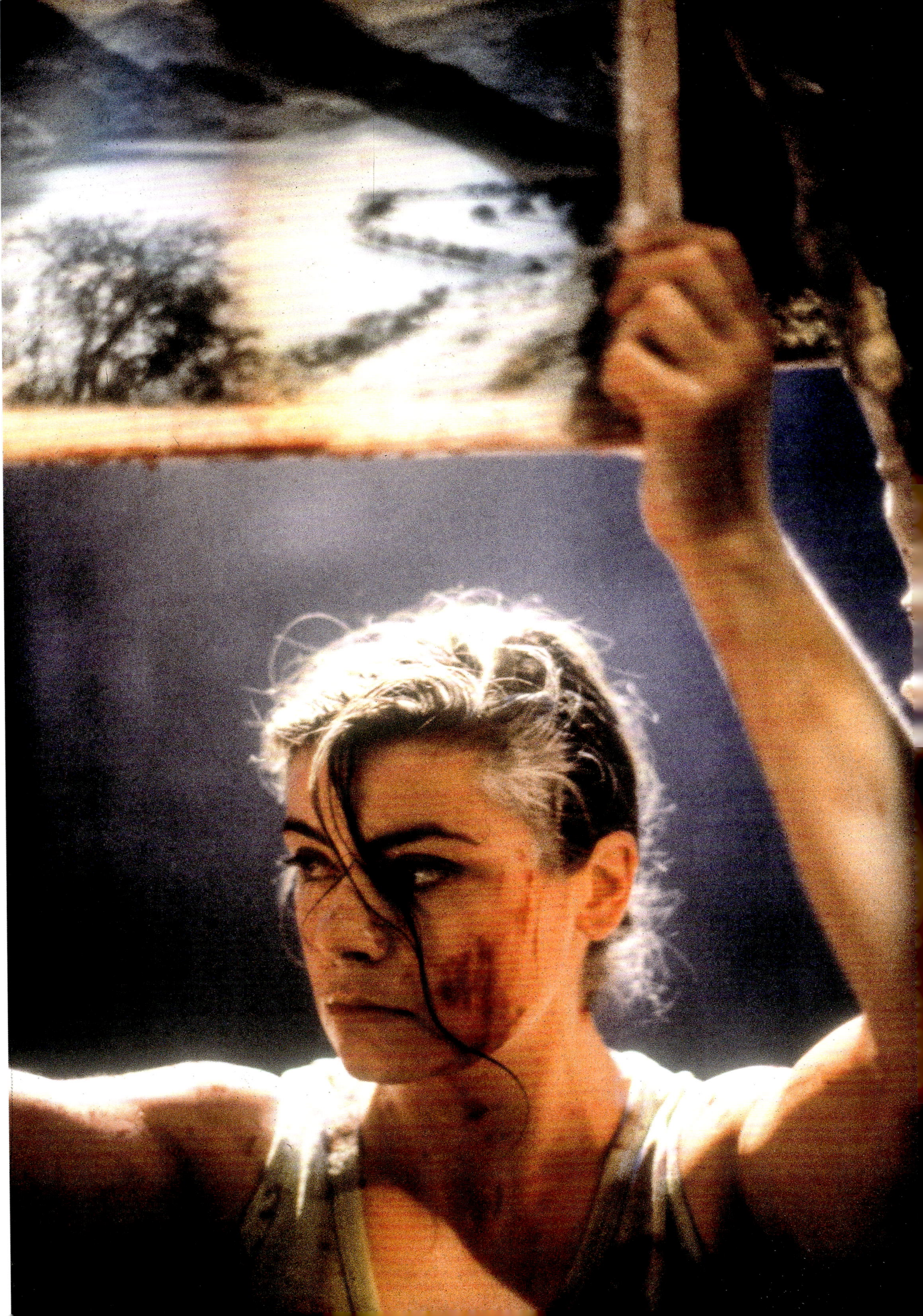

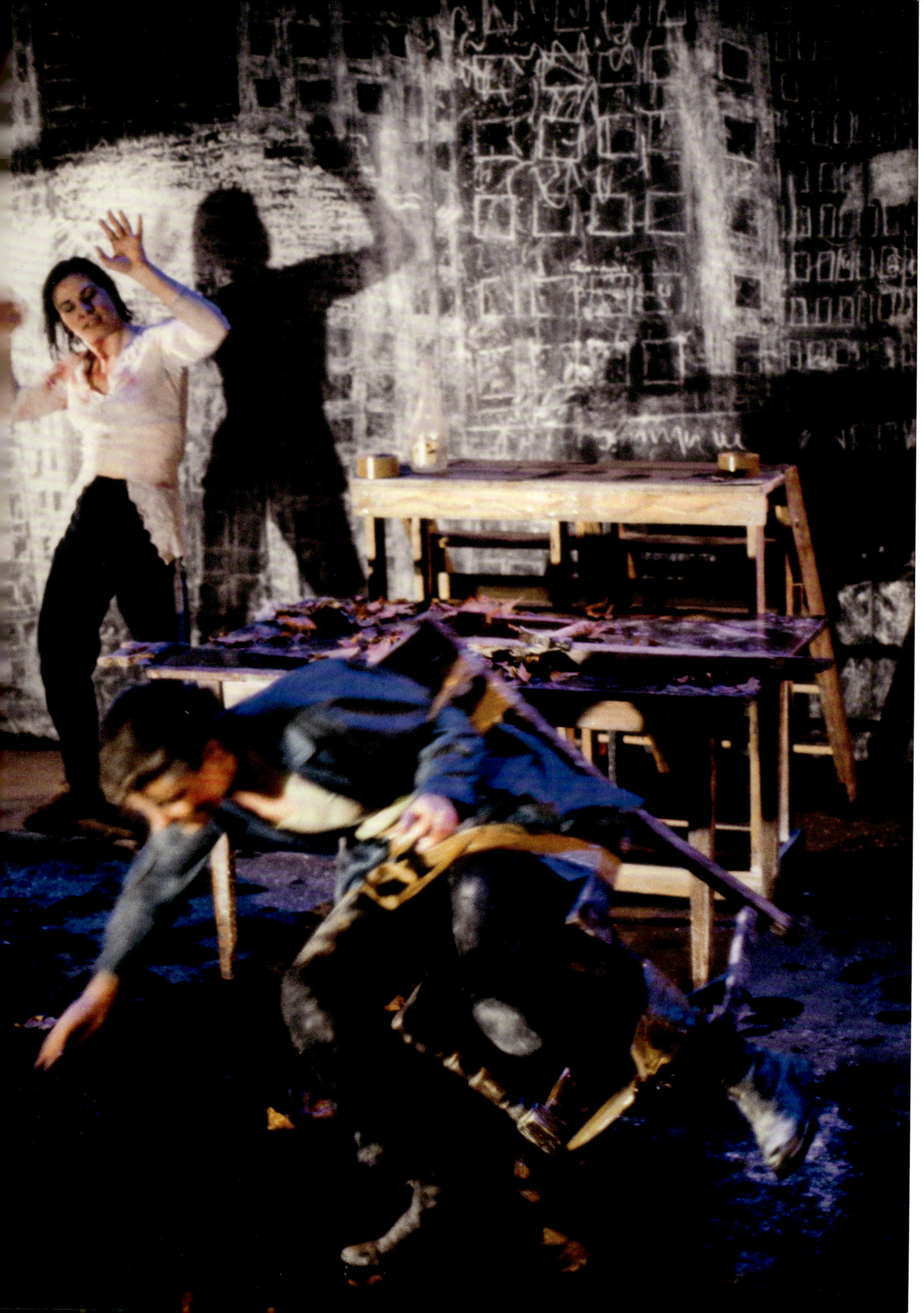

Terry: I had feared the distant journey
would weary our dreams but I am on a
knife edge of happiness tonight. Time is
late and we shadows are fading. Forgive
me: I am made to write as a witness in
difficult times.

Kings, thieves, usherettes, lords, liars,
gunmen, and prostitutes—all those who
would know magic—take this book and
have it read to you.

over the BRIDGE OF KISSES
left at MURDER STREET
to the BIG STATUE OF SOMETHING RARE
through the subway near DIFFICULT HOUSE
to the END OF THE WORLD
and then, for those that find it, on foot
to CLUB OF NO REGRETS

A huge part of the piece is exhilaration—an exhausting drive and then a drop— which finally reaches a beautiful peace. At the end, we're standing at the back and the dancing is finished. Terry's dropped the Helen X persona, the little room centre stage has been dismantled and taken away. The floor is covered in water and leaves and talcum powder and fake blood. Like at night after a huge storm. And there's silence, with all of us just looking at what we've become, what we've made, the mess, what has happened. It's like we're thinking, 'How long have we been here?'

It was one of those shows where people watching always said, 'It's so chaotic. It must be improvised.' But it was very set, often tightly choreographed to the music. When we were strapped to the chairs at the end for what we called the 'escape routine', that was when things were genuinely wild. There was a competitiveness about how dangerous people made it for themselves, what risks people took. [CM]

At the very end, we're taped to the chairs for the 'escape routine', struggling to free ourselves, hopping and sliding around on the wet floor. By then we're strangely autonomous as figures, albeit in a weird self-destructive way. Every time we did it, I used to hack with a saw at the tape under the chair that was holding my legs. And every night I'd come off stage with great big hack marks down my legs where I'd missed the tape and hit my leg. By that point in that show we were on a strange, almost shamanistic journey—they could probably have put burning coals into my hands and I would cheerfully have gone along with it! [RA]

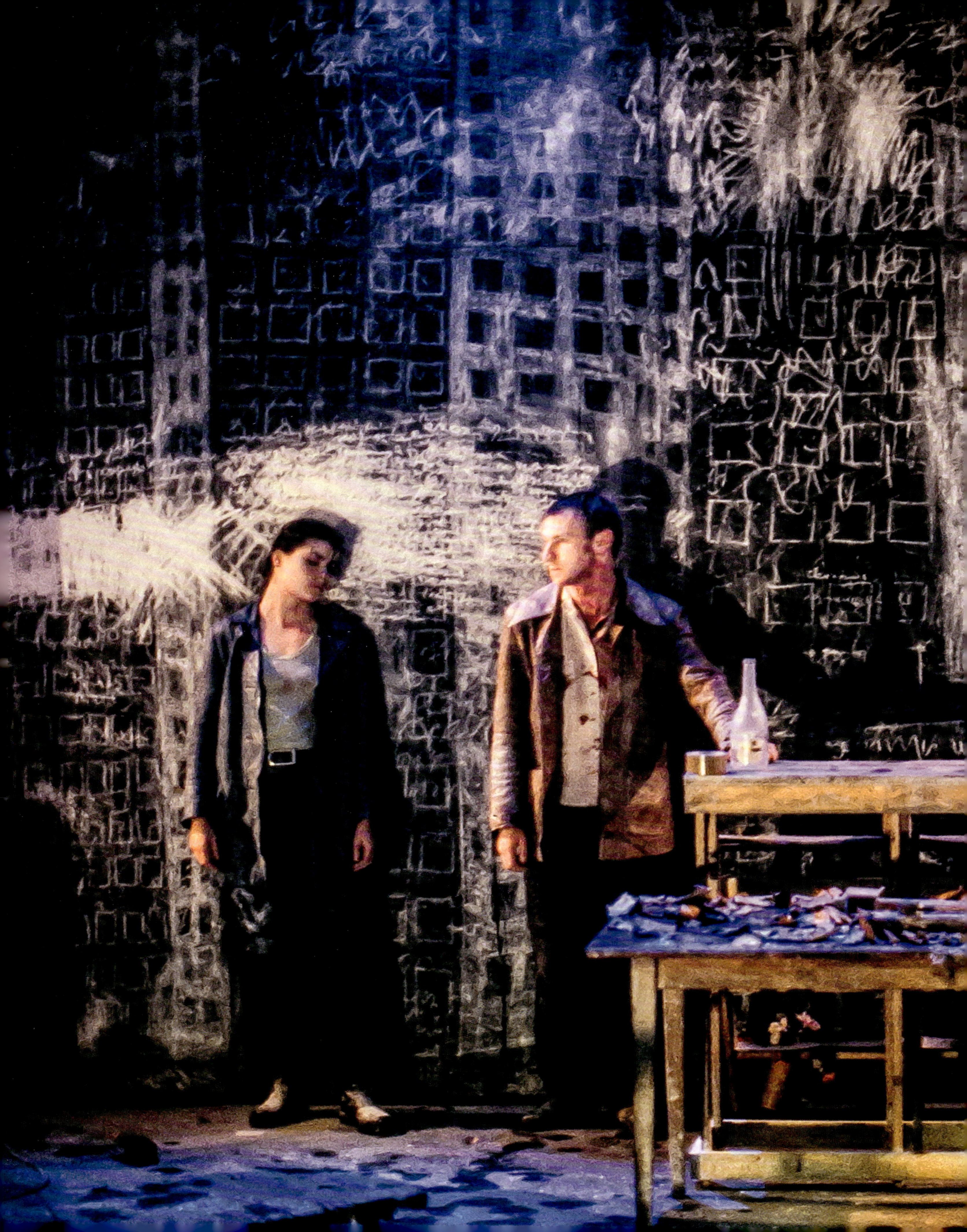

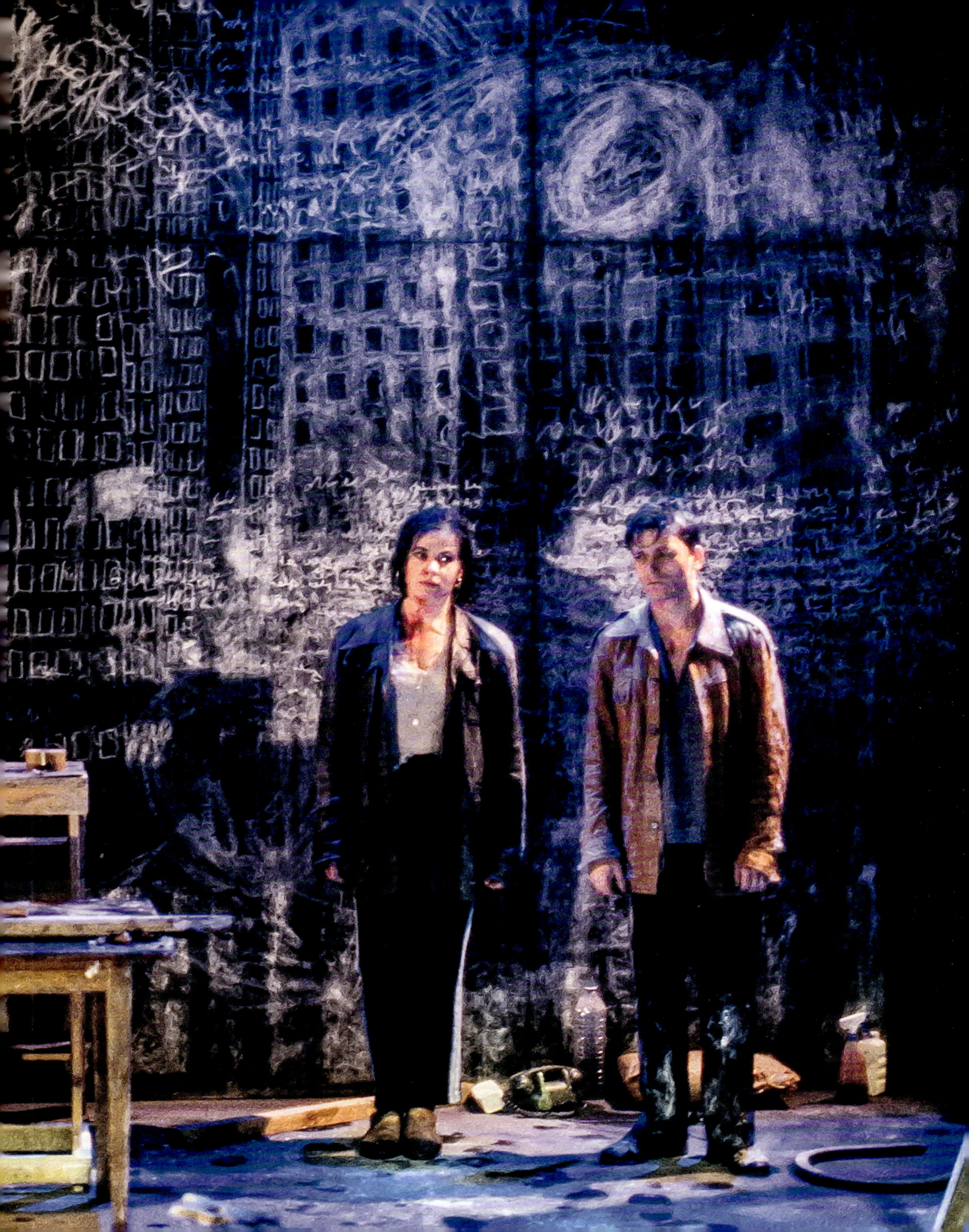

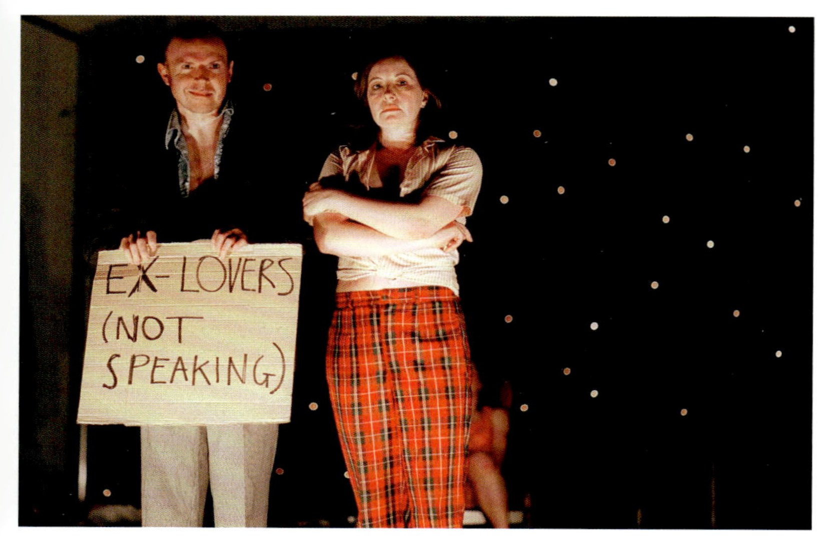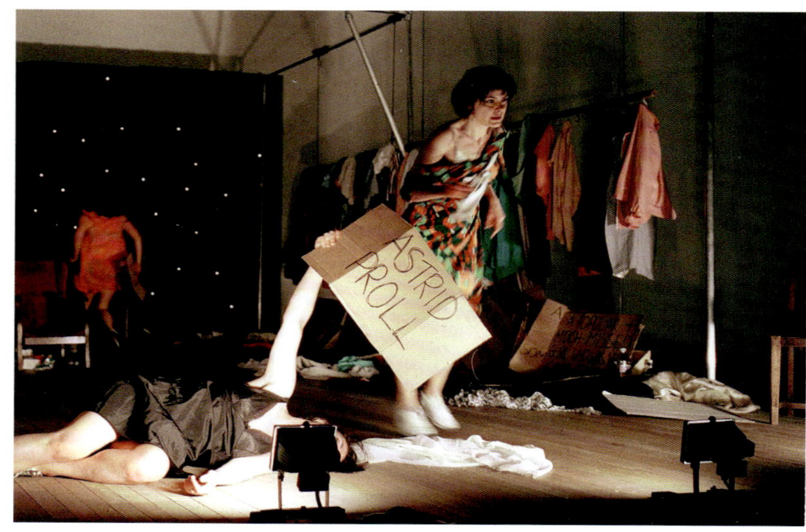

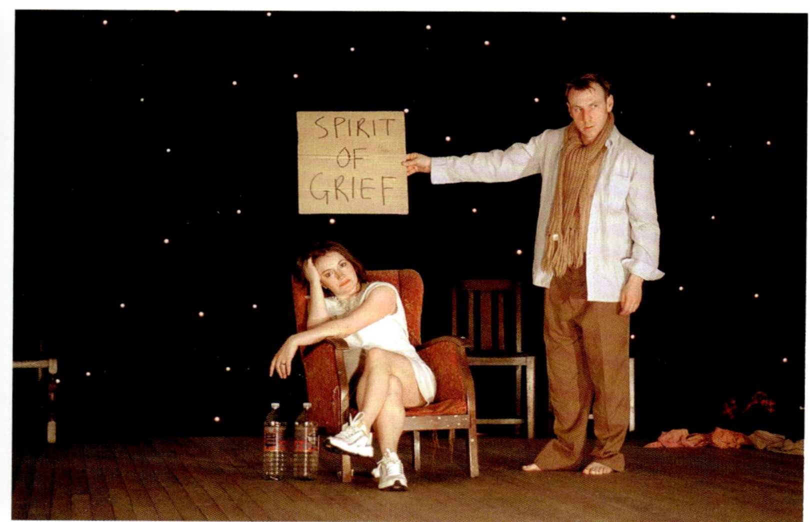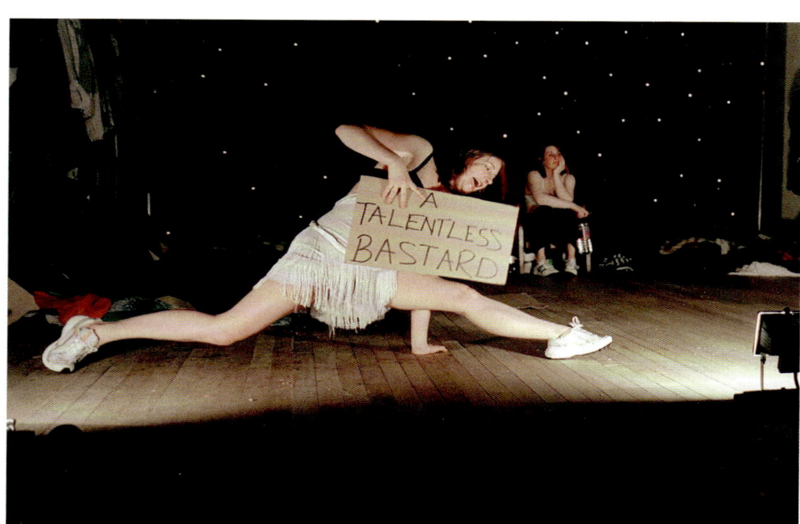

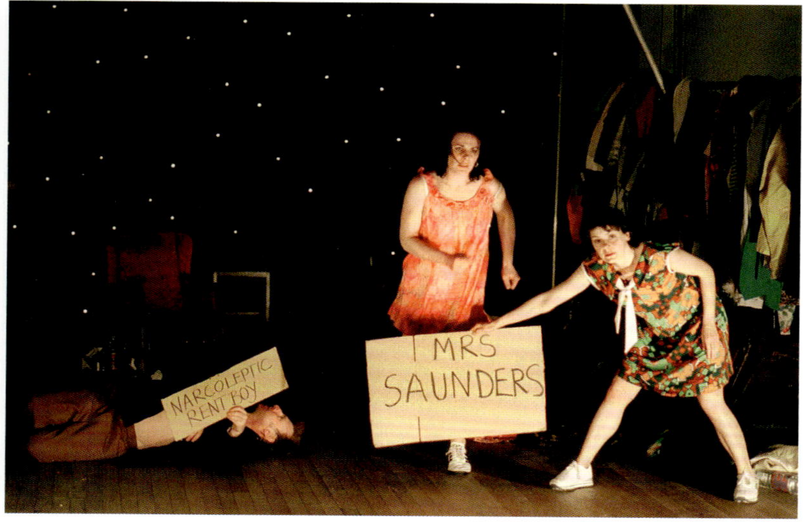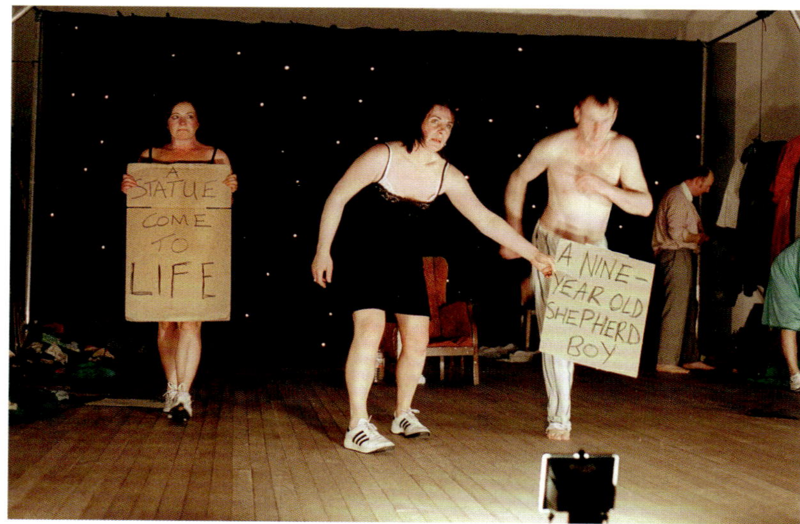

12AM: AWAKE & LOOKING DOWN (1993)

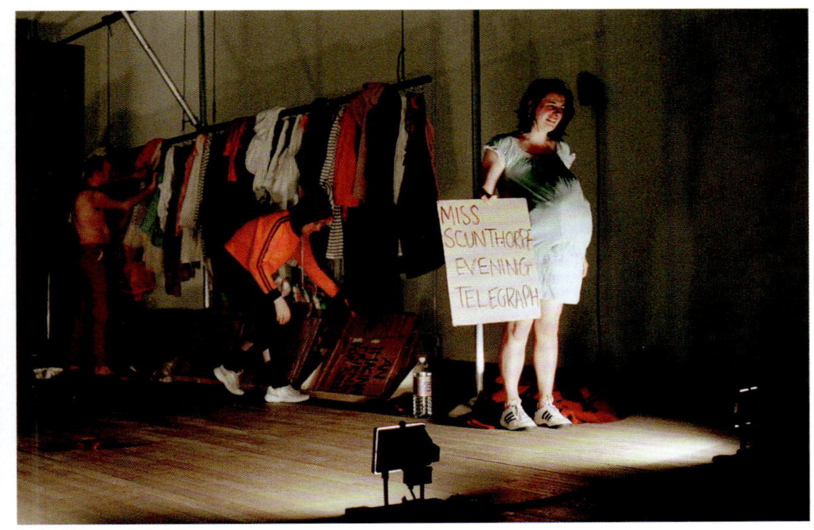
MISS
SCUNTHORPE
EVENING
TELEGRAPH

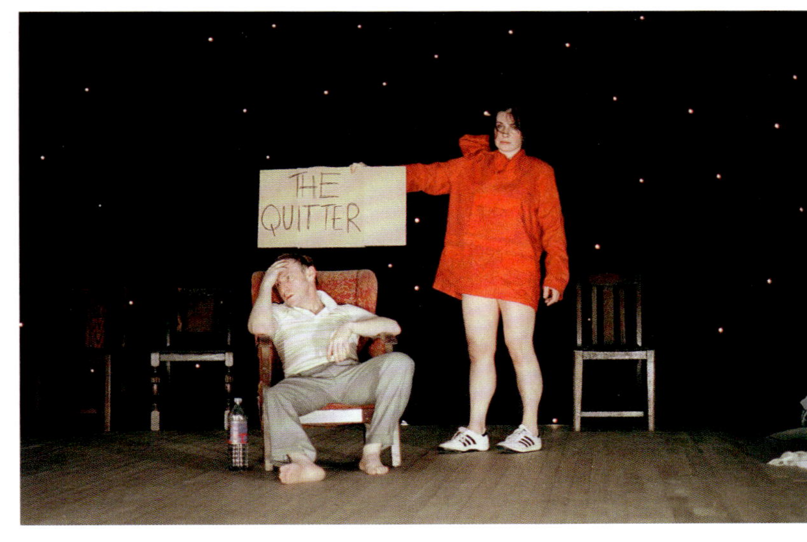
THE
QUITTER

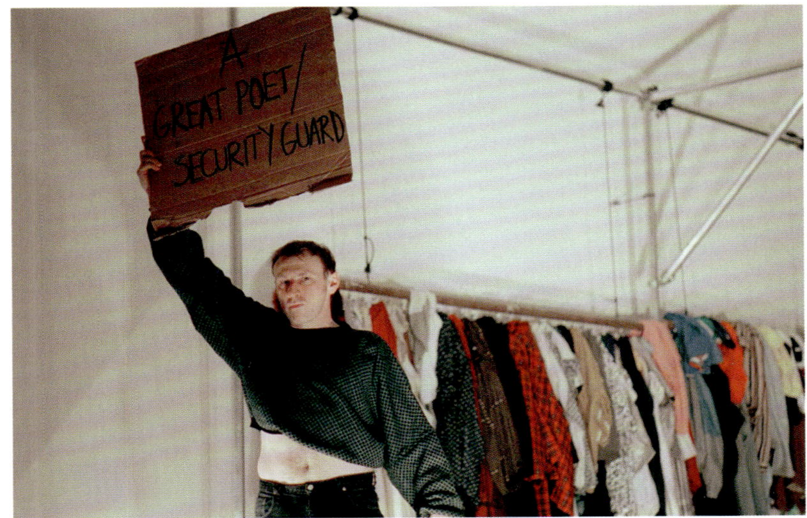
A
GREAT POET/
SECURITY GUARD

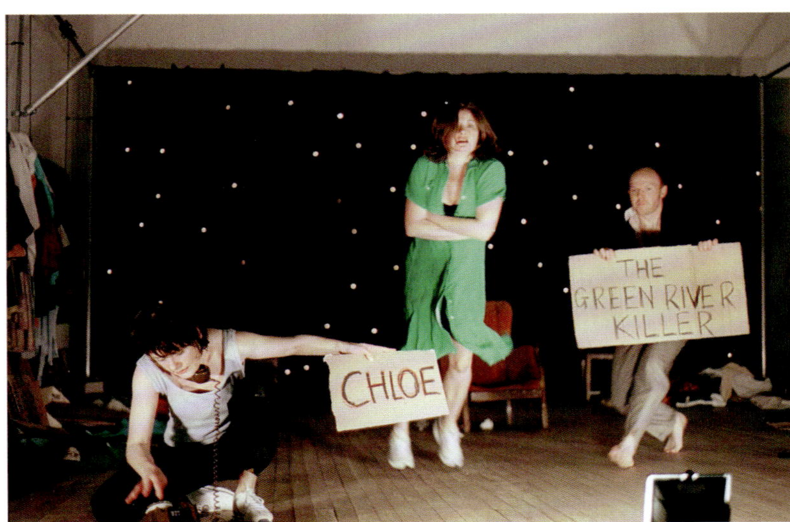
CHLOE
THE
GREEN RIVER
KILLER

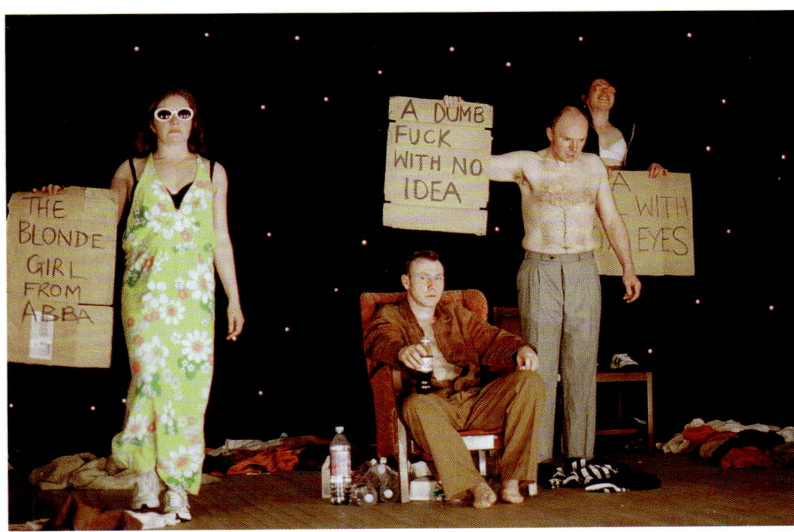
THE
BLONDE
GIRL
FROM
ABBA
A DUMB
FUCK
WITH NO
IDEA
WITH
EYES

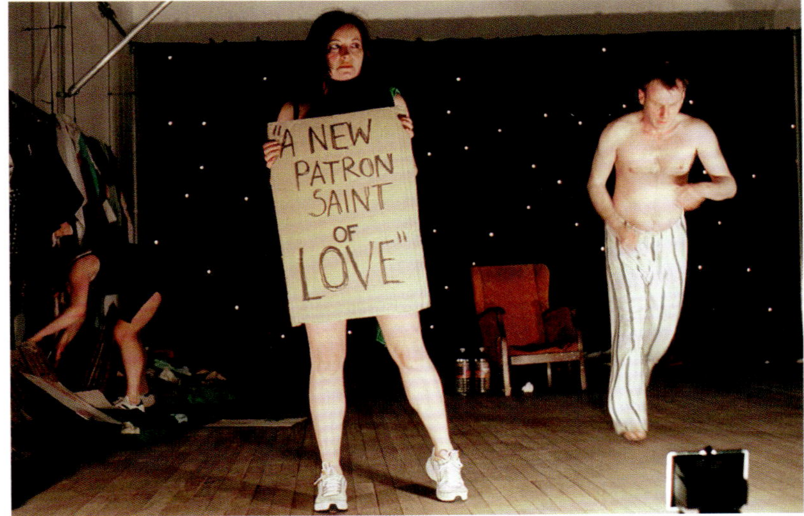
"A NEW
PATRON
SAINT
OF
LOVE"

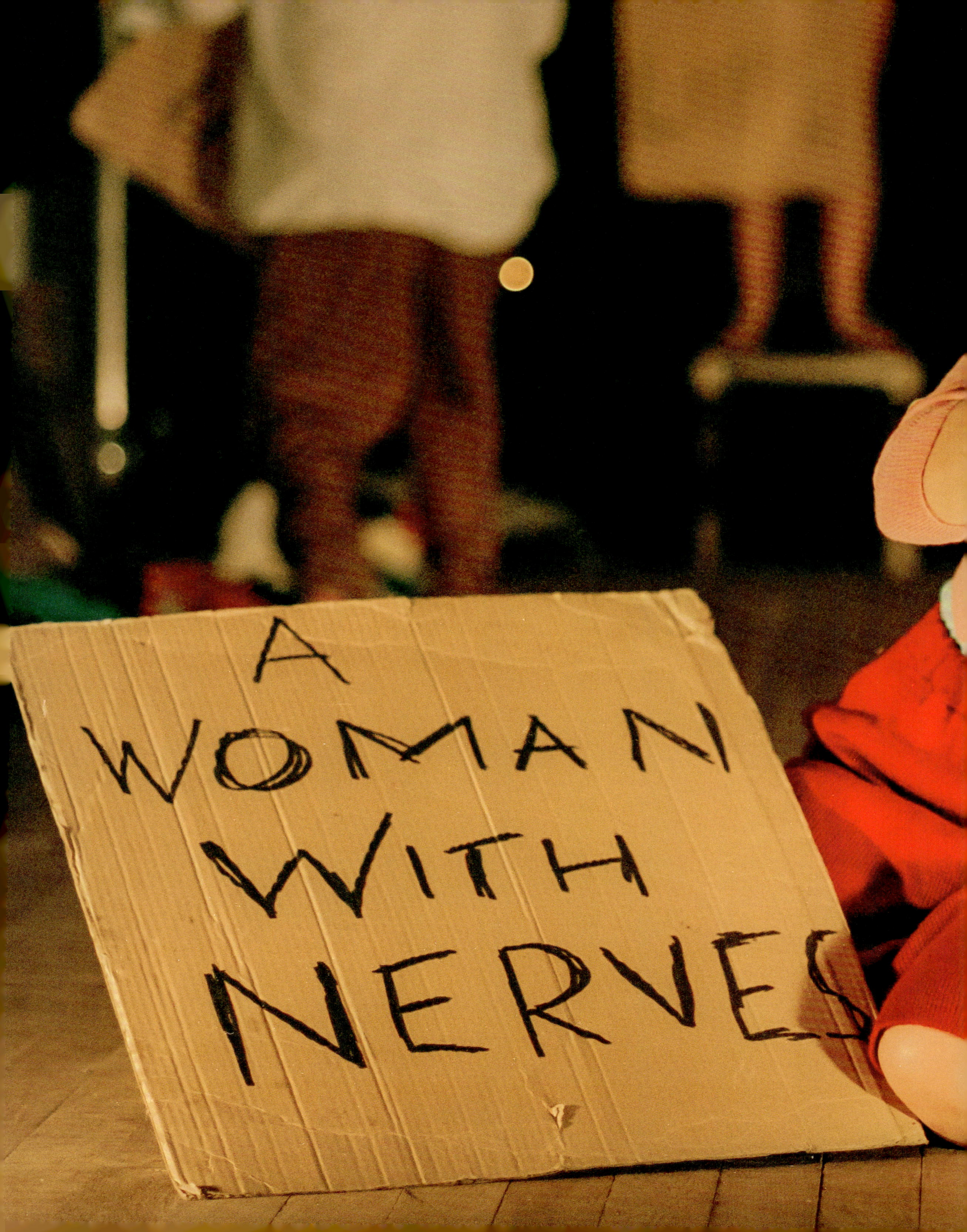
A
WOMAN
WITH
NERVES

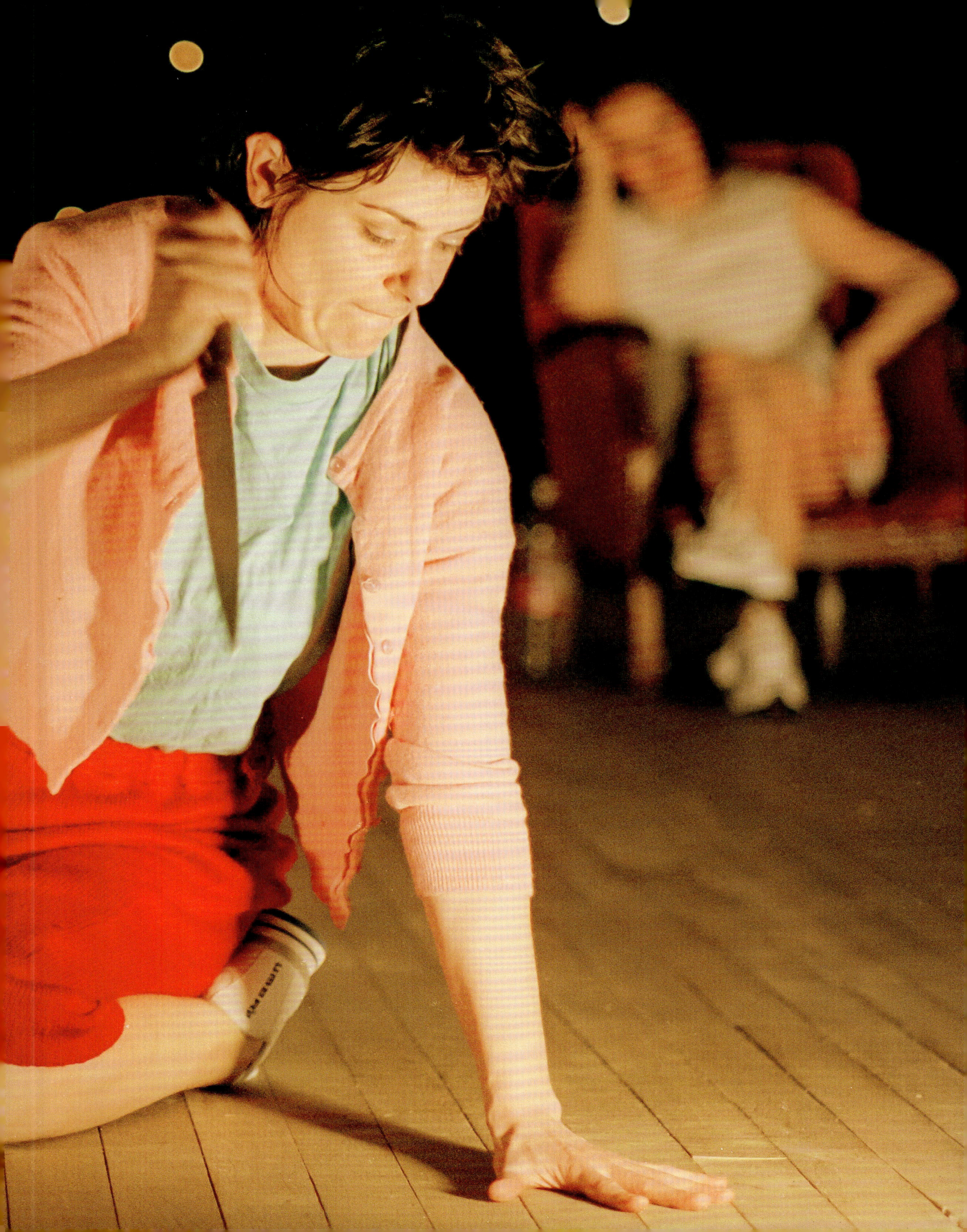

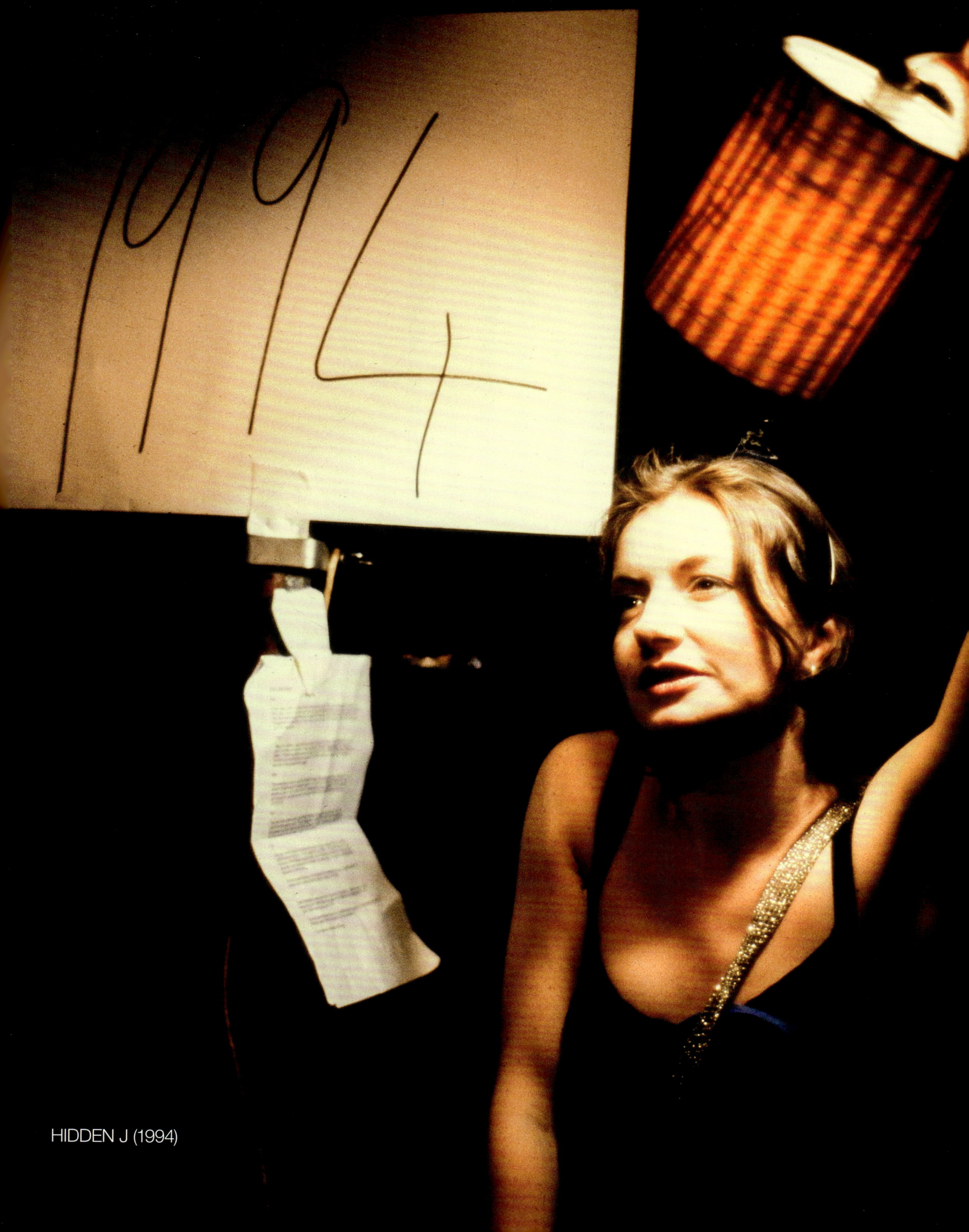

HIDDEN J (1994)

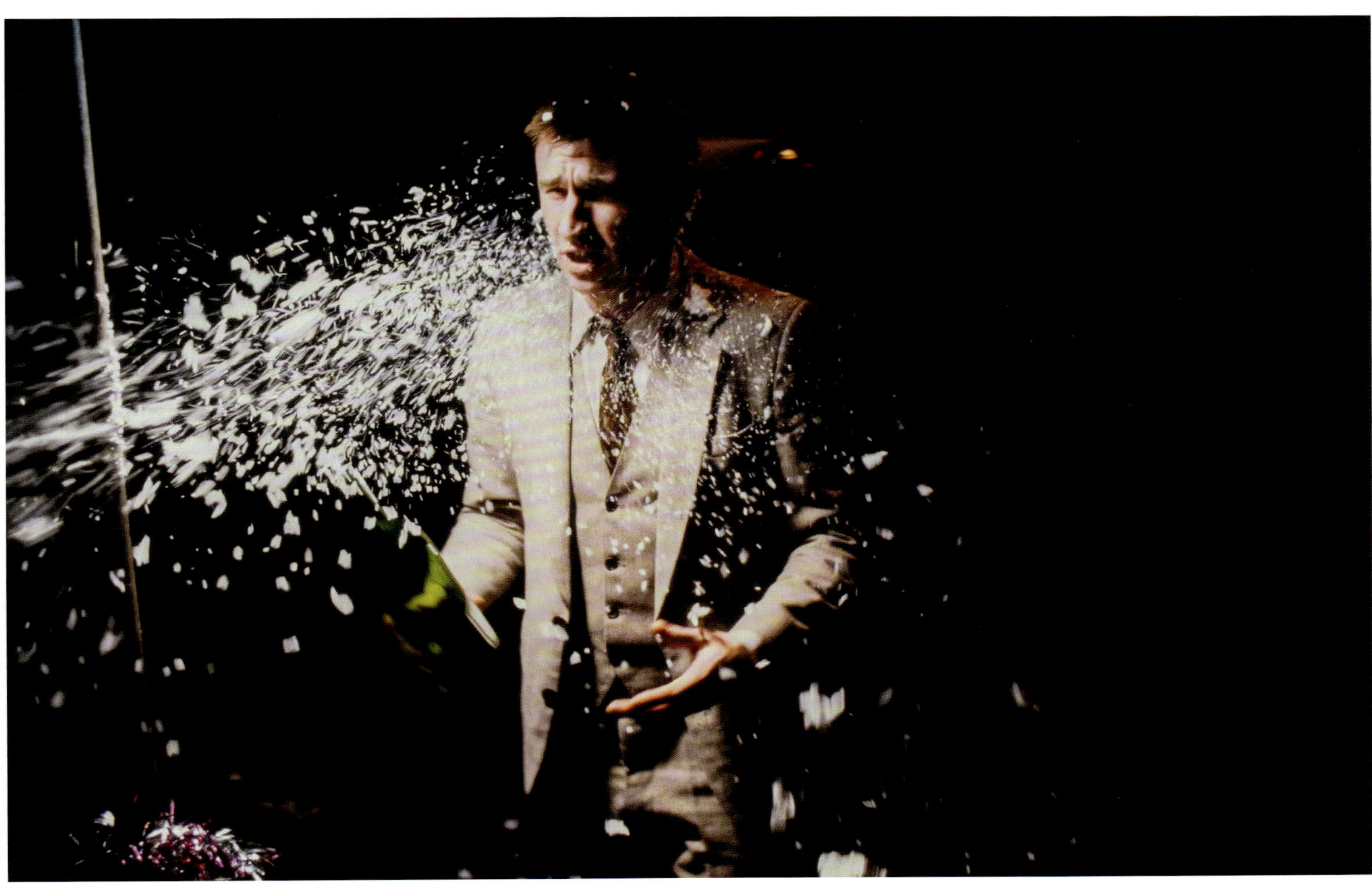

Terry: She made phone calls well into
the night. She called all her friends,
she called all her enemies, she called
the TV talk shows and the market
researchers. She called some chatlines
and then some all night radio phone-ins.

At dawn she called 'THE WEEPING MAN'.
It's a radio show where the host sits
up through the night and cries, and
callers call with reasons for him to
cry. If he likes the reasons he'll
read them out between the bouts of his
weeping. She gave him some reasons and
then hung up. She always liked that
show ever since she was a kid and she
felt better having made her call.

This all happened in 1972, or in 1604
just after the first dog in space and
just before the time when the soldiers
came back and killed everyone that
they hadn't bothered to kill the first
time they came.

Richard: There's this man who knew
this man who knew this man who knew
this bloke who knew this man ... Too
complicated ... Don't mind me crying.
Don't mind me crying. Keep the traffic
moving. Keep the traffic moving. I've
been up and down. I've been up and down.
I've been all over. I've travelled. I've
seen things. I've been up and down the
M4. What bit are we on? What bit are we
on? Let me in. Let me in. I'm on top of
the world. I'm on top of the world. I'm
naked. What bit are we on?

I'm religious but don't go to church.
I believe in something more like
electricity connecting things together.
I'm pissed. This bloke, right, he's
got arms and legs, makes no fucking
difference. How wrong all sweet music
sounds to me now. I'm not here, this
never happened. What bit is this? What
bit am I on?

I got this idea for a song called
'TIE A YELLOW RIBBON' but I can't
find the words.

I don't know anything about maps or
calendars. I'm fainting, I lost a lot
of blood. It's all shit that people say
and think. I'm lost.

I've been all over, I've been up and
down. All the streets are the same.
I'm not from round here. I've got this.
I've got this. I've got this. I don't
know what this is.

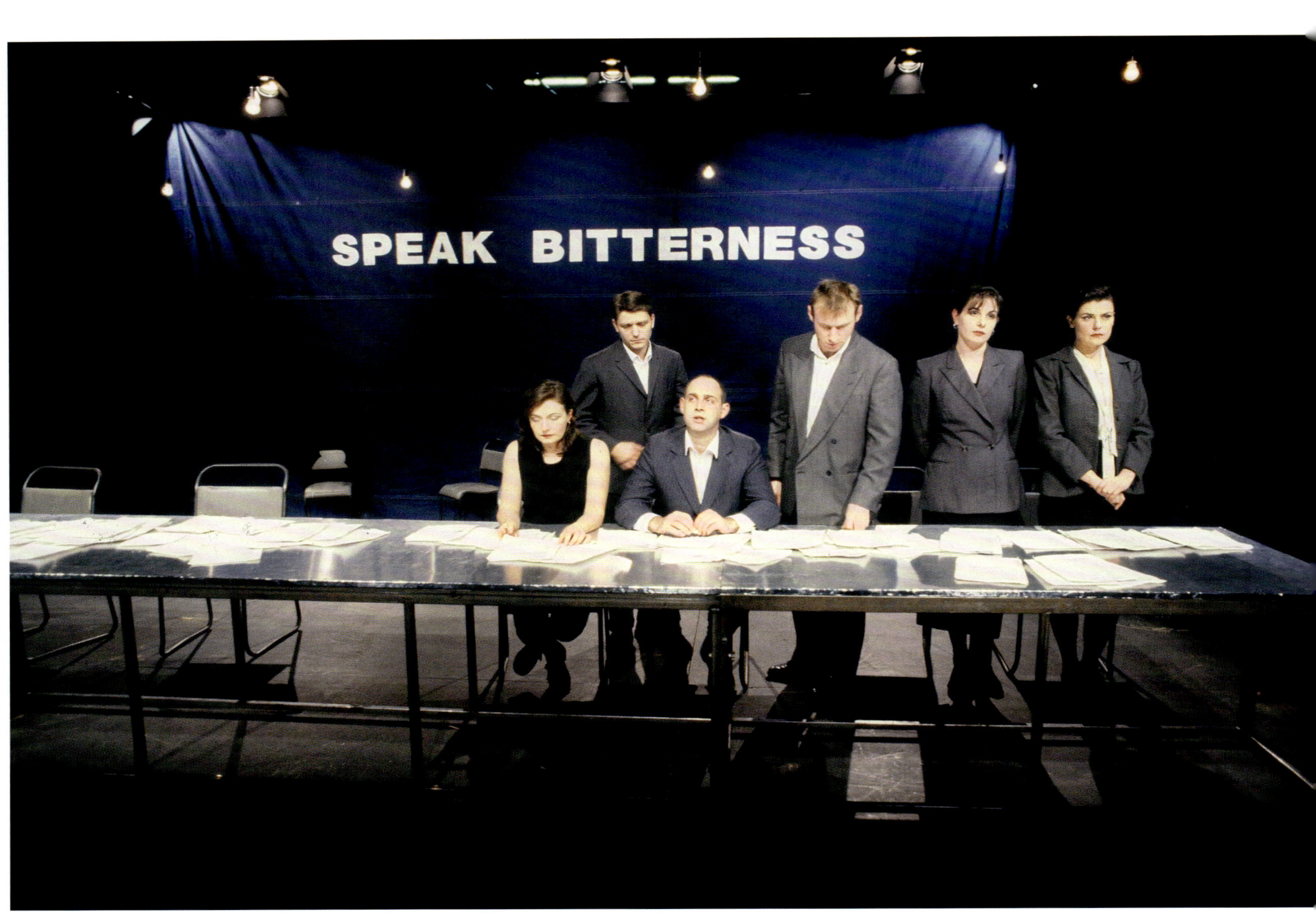

SPEAK BITTERNESS (1994)

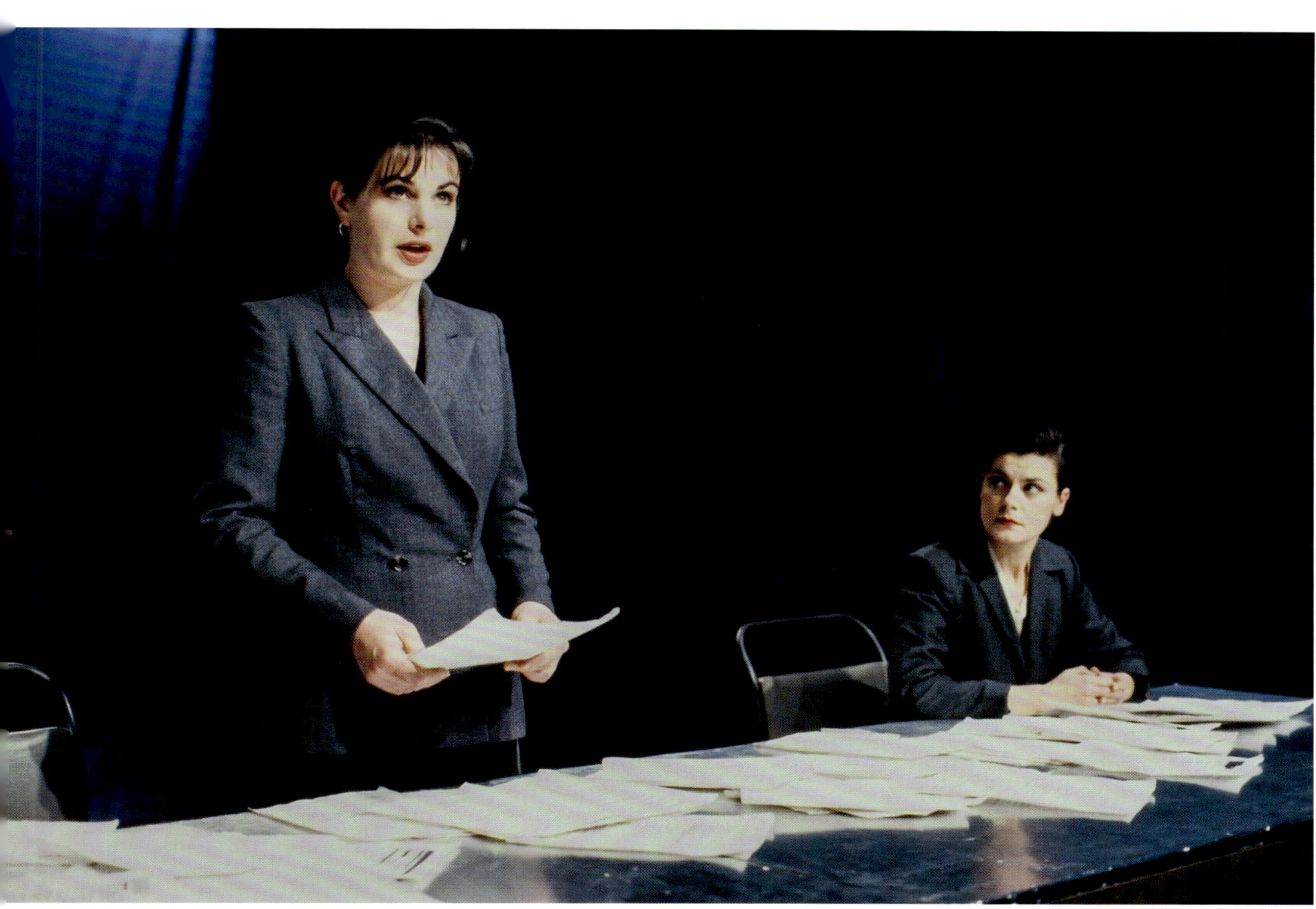

Cathy: We hit rock bottom.

We fucked our own brother.

We found our own level.

We bargained for immunity.

We're guilty of truth serum, old tricks, and stratagems.

We shouted for so long it didn't even sound like our voices any more.

We told simple stories to children.

We dreamed of Tokyo, snow monsters, and John Ford on his deathbed.

We tried to guess the presents by feeling through the wrapping paper.

We had the doubts of daytime and the doubts of night-time.

We trained animals to pick people's pockets.

We made loss-of-innocence movies long after we'd lost our own innocence.

We purchased children.

We killed crickets.

We took our names off the credits.

We kept disappearing.

We stayed underwater as long as we could.

We made each other bleed.

We said goodbye instead of goodnight.

We loved the sky.

We rumbled with other gangs.

We were cop killers, comedy subplots.

We farted on the first date.

We confess to never having had an original idea.

We never never never wanted kids anyway.

We didn't keep off the grass.

We knocked on doors.

We lived on bread alone.

We're guilty of taped rain and taped applause.

We ordered the men over the top.

We coveted our neighbour's arse.

We were parasites.

We made our own blood run cold.

We were ever so naughty.

We burst bubbles.

We put the boot in.

We rubbed salt in wounds.

We drank water when everyone else was on beer.

We pulled the plug on good ideas.

We turned the music off and refused to let latecomers in.

We fainted at the sight of our own blood.

QUIZOOLA! (1996)

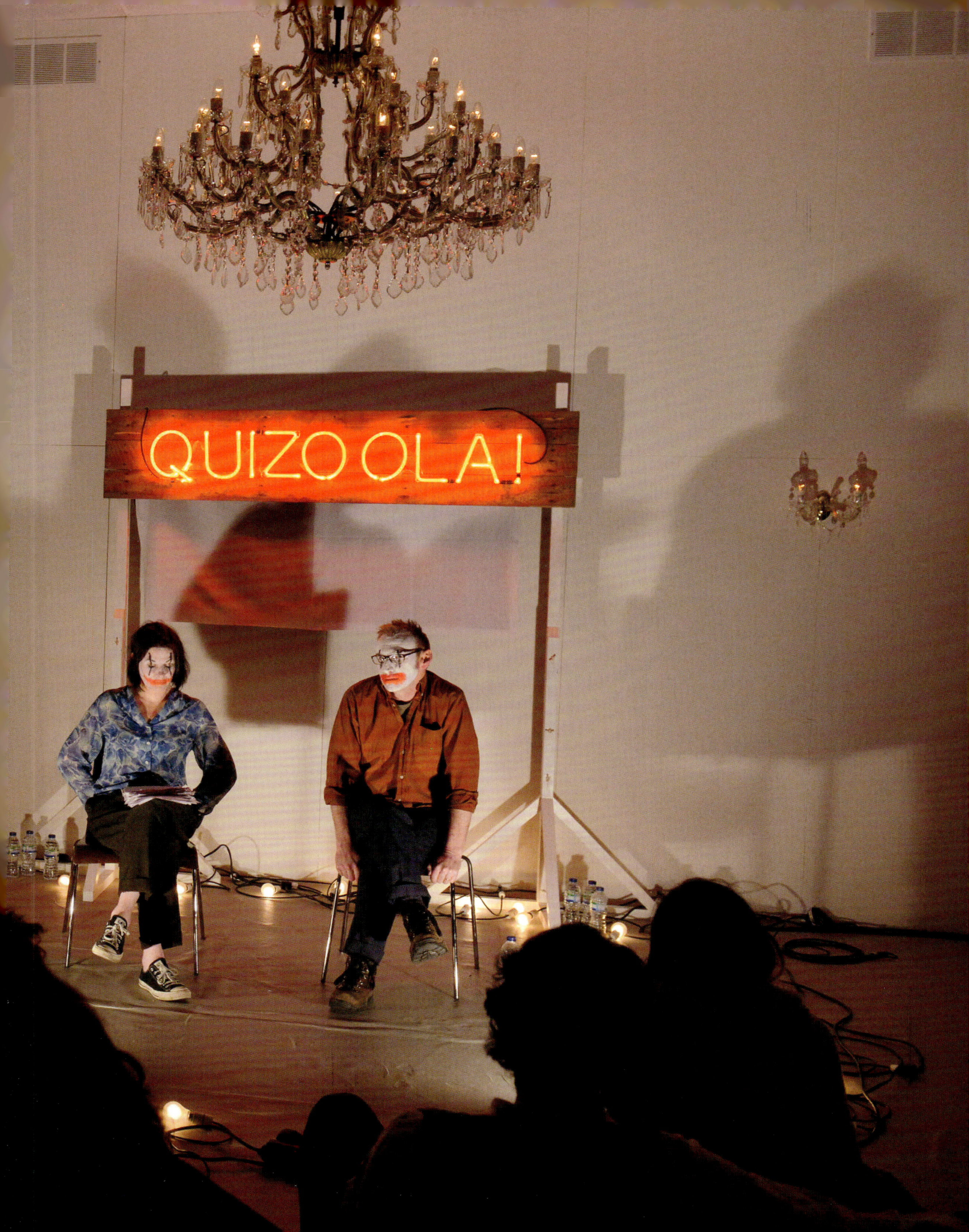

QUIZOOLA !

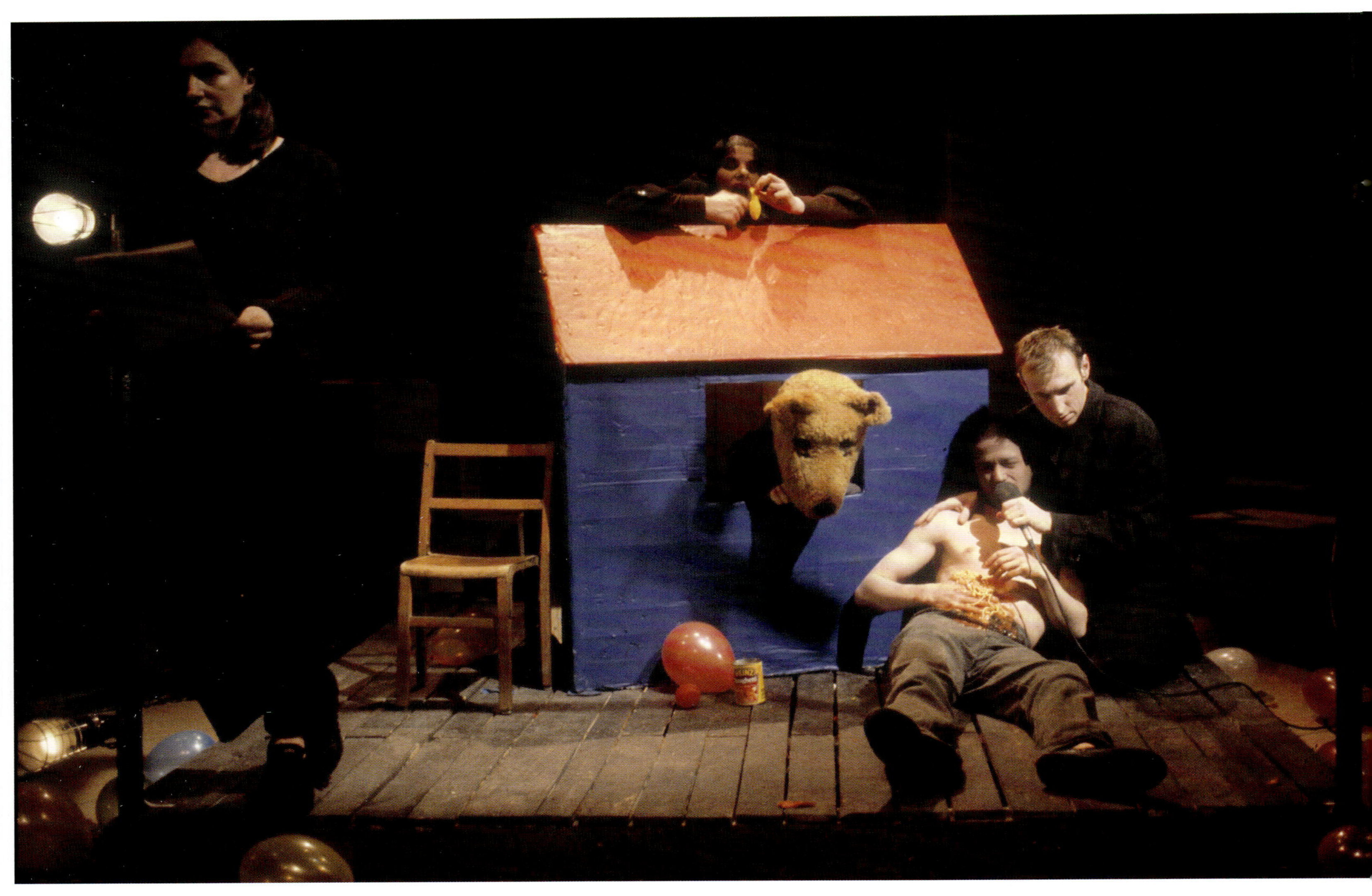

SHOWTIME (1996)

[*Robin slumps against the small, blue playhouse centre stage, pretending to die. The contents of a can of spaghetti in tomato sauce clutched to his bare stomach like guts coming out. Richard abandons his text and moves to hold the microphone for Robin. Cathy (as dog) watches, barking and interfering. Terry watches, consulting her script. Claire, in a tree costume, also opens a can of spaghetti and holds the contents against the cardboard tree trunk, flailing her arms and yelling as though she too is dying.*]

Robin: [*Gasping and groaning throughout as though dying from the pretend wound in his stomach*] Performance should have some kind of dramatic tension—it should have a plot. It should have some well-drawn characters so that the audience can empathize with the events onstage ... A performance should try to bring people together, not just rub their noses in the dirt. A performance should take place over one day and it should take place in one location and all of the action should take place offstage and it should be reported by one of the protagonists. There should be a chorus, that helps. There should be some kind of clown or fool character. There should be some witty banter, some good dialogue. There should be some kind of comic relief to make the tragedy more sad, to make the exposition of the human condition more affecting. There should be some kind of moral, there should be some kind of purpose, because if there isn't a moral it's just a lot of bloody shouting and silly showing off. The audience doesn't pay good money to see a lot of shouting and showing off—they want something with some kind of purpose ...

[*Cathy (as dog) goes right onto the stage and sniffs curiously at the spaghetti on Robin's stomach.*]

Robin: [*Talking to the dog*] What are you doing? Go away ... [*The dog leaves. Robin, cradled by Richard, continues his dying speech.*] The audience want to go to the bar after the show and to say, 'I GOT IT, I UNDERSTOOD WHAT IT WAS ABOUT.' They don't want to have to say, 'Oh,' or, 'It's whatever you want it to mean ...' They want to be able to say, 'The bloke, wasn't he MAGNETIC? And the leading lady, wasn't she BEAUTIFUL? And how you could hear her voice at the back of a very big theatre because of training and technique ...' [*Noise from the dog and the tree now threatens to drown Robin out completely. Robin weeps.*] ... They want to be transported to some delightful place, they want to see some realistic scenery, they want to be touched. Oh god, they want some purpose, they want some resolution, they want to be touched, they want to be transported, they want, they want, they want, they want something. Oh god, oh god, they don't want this, they don't want this ...

[*Robin weeps wordlessly while Claire (as tree) comes forward with a gun and speaks directly to the audience.*]

Claire: Close your eyes. Close your fucking eyes. You shouldn't be watching this. Close your eyes and keep them closed. Please close your eyes. Please close them.

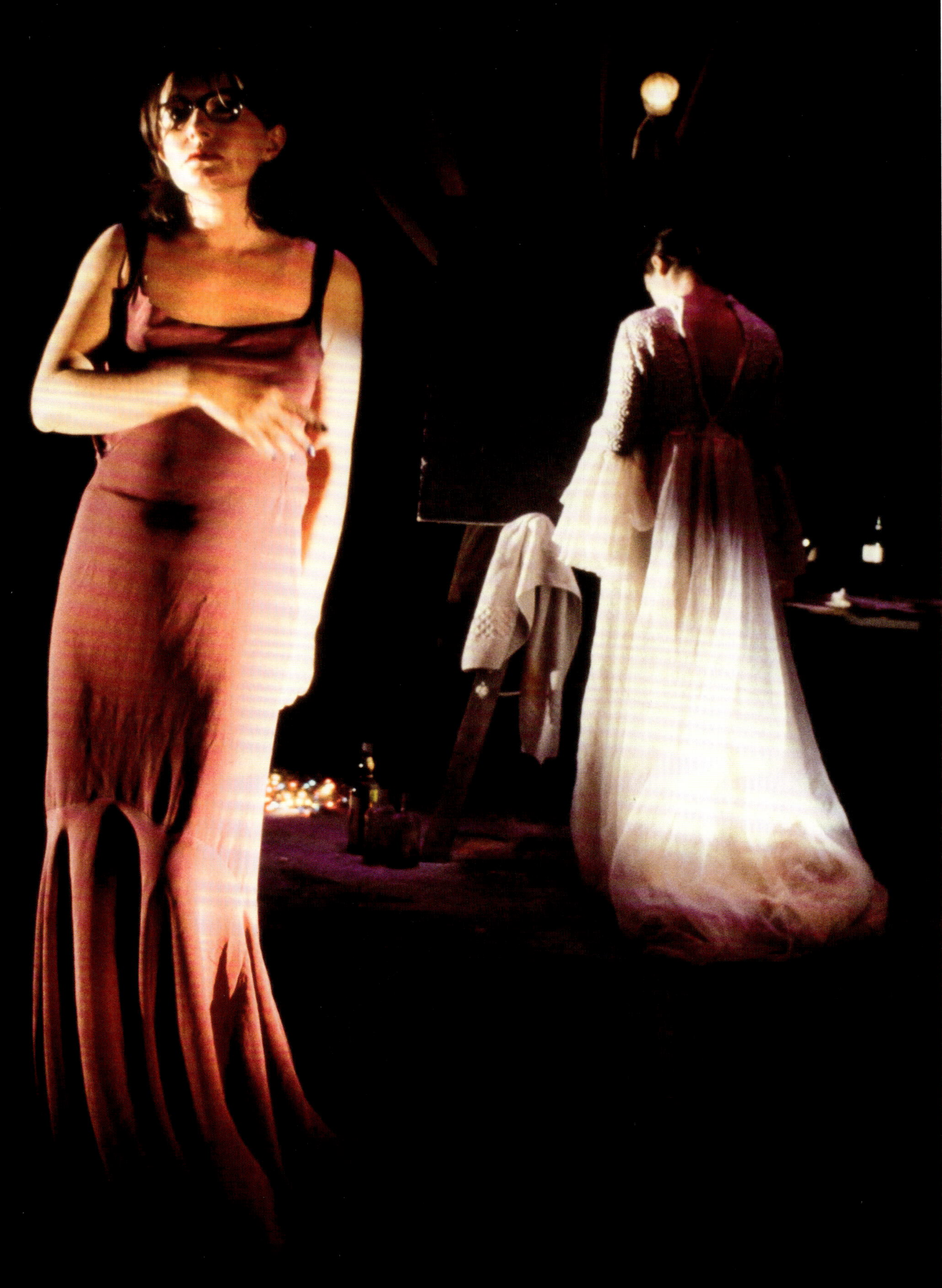

PLEASURE (1997)

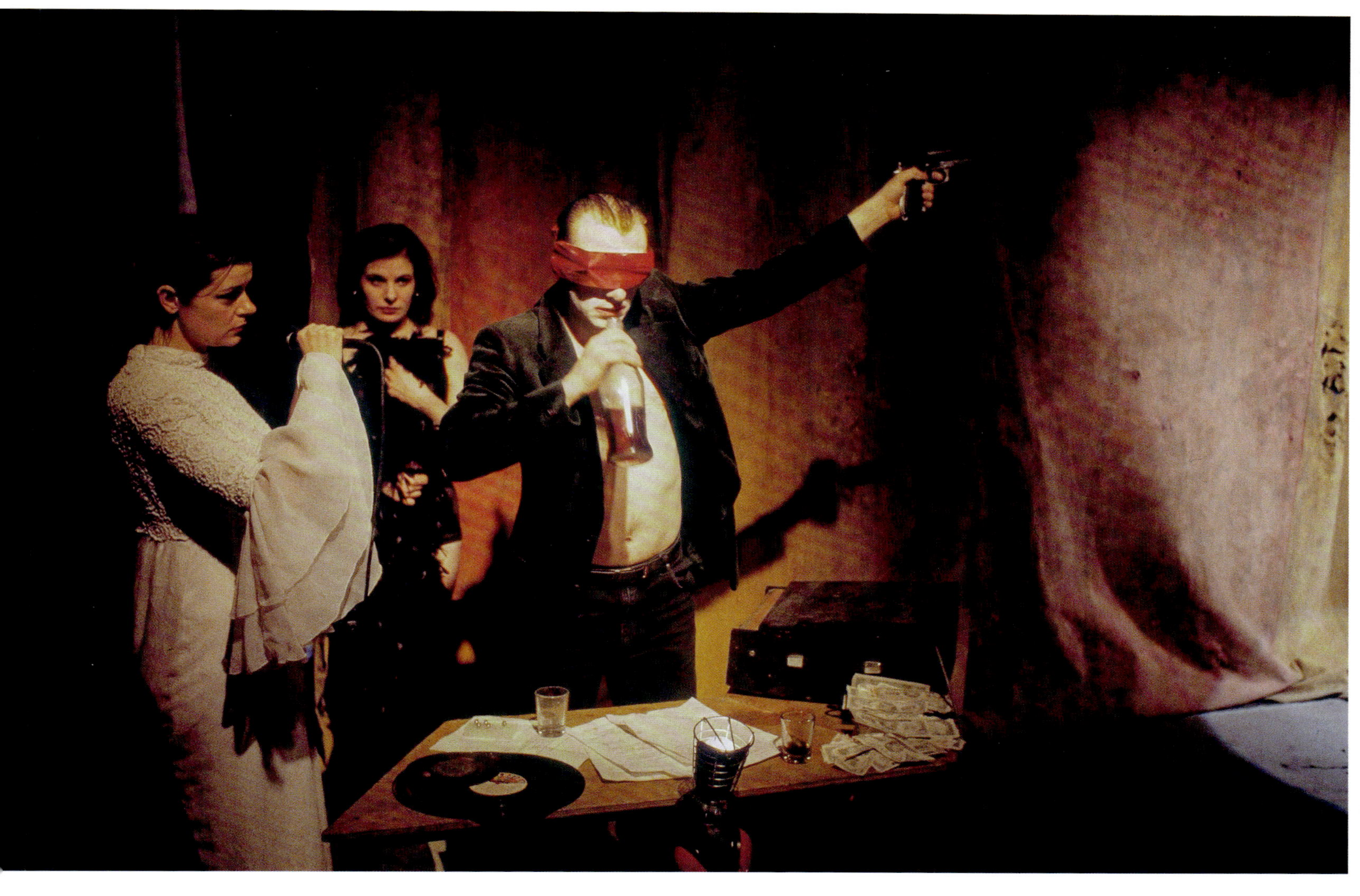

Richard: Have you ever been to Earth?

Terry: Yes.

Richard: What was it like?

Terry: It was noisy.

Richard: And what's the best thing that can happen to a person on Earth?

Terry: They could fall in love, or they could find a lot of money, in a bag, or they could find something they were happy with ...

Richard: And what's the worst thing that can happen to somebody on Earth?

Terry: People die.

Richard: What's the most worst thing that happened to you on Earth?

Terry: I lost control of my bladder at a birthday party ... and then I fainted and then I had to be taken home wearing someone else's knickers ...

Richard: Terry, are you okay?

Terry: I'm alright.

Richard: What's the most pleasurable thing that can happen to someone on Earth?

Terry: Eating.

Richard: What's the most pleasurable thing that ever happened to you on Earth?

Terry: I had sex in a car, in the front seat and the seat had this kind of electrical warming mechanism and ... it was on, and there was music playing ...

Richard: What is Earth?

Terry: It's a planet.

Richard: This is the golden prize question. Do you understand the rules surrounding the golden prize question?

Terry: Yes.

Richard: And you're willing to continue?

Terry: Yes.

Richard: So, the prize question is this: 'Why is MODERN LIFE RUBBISH?'

Is it (a) because of individual greed?

Is it (b) because of corrupt government?

Is it (c) because of capitalism?

Or is it (d) because of the strange tangles of wool and wire that people sometimes see in their dreams?

You can't get any help on this one. You're on your own.

Richard: Close the curtains. Close the curtains. We've seen enough. We need to close the curtains. We need to close the curtains, we need to reload the gun. We need some more music and some more dancing. We need to close the curtains. We need to close the curtains and reload the gun, reload the gun. Yeah, close the curtains. Close the curtains.

It's cold. Cover her up. Cover her up. We need some more dancing, we need some more music. We've seen enough and now we need to see some more. Close the curtains. Please close the curtains. Please. Close the curtains, please. We need some more dancing, we need to move on. We need to move on. Please. Close the curtains, please.

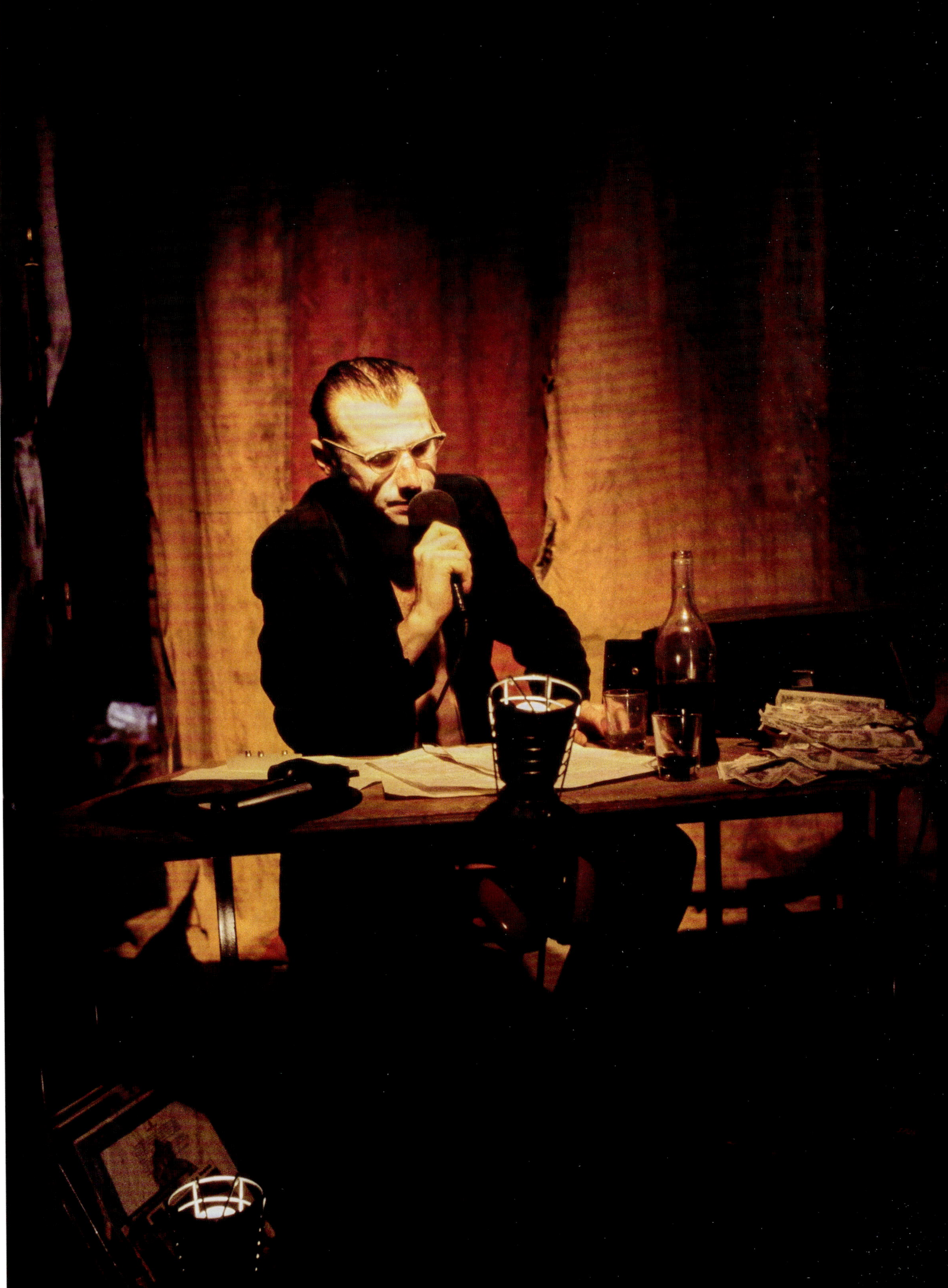

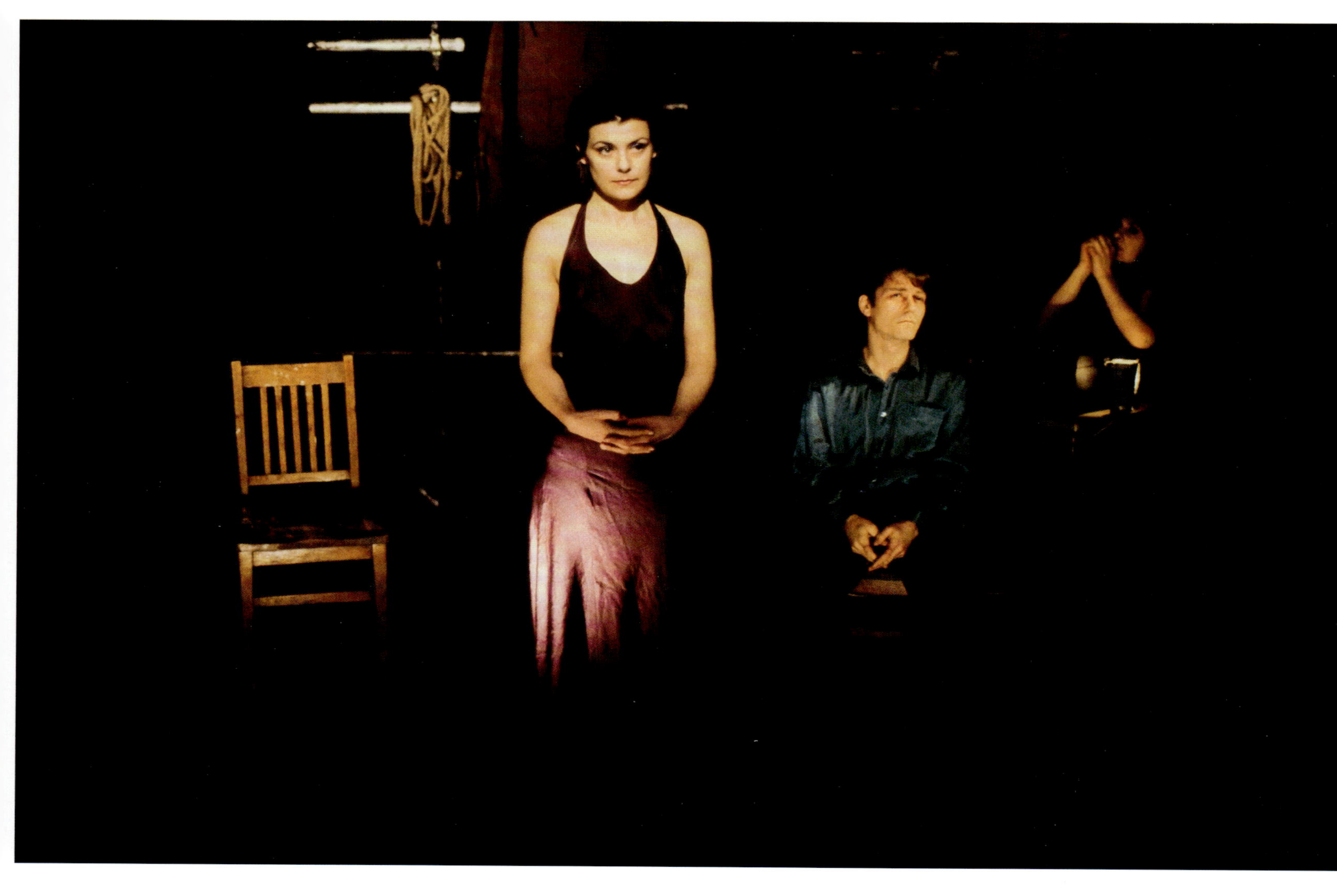

DIRTY WORK (1998)

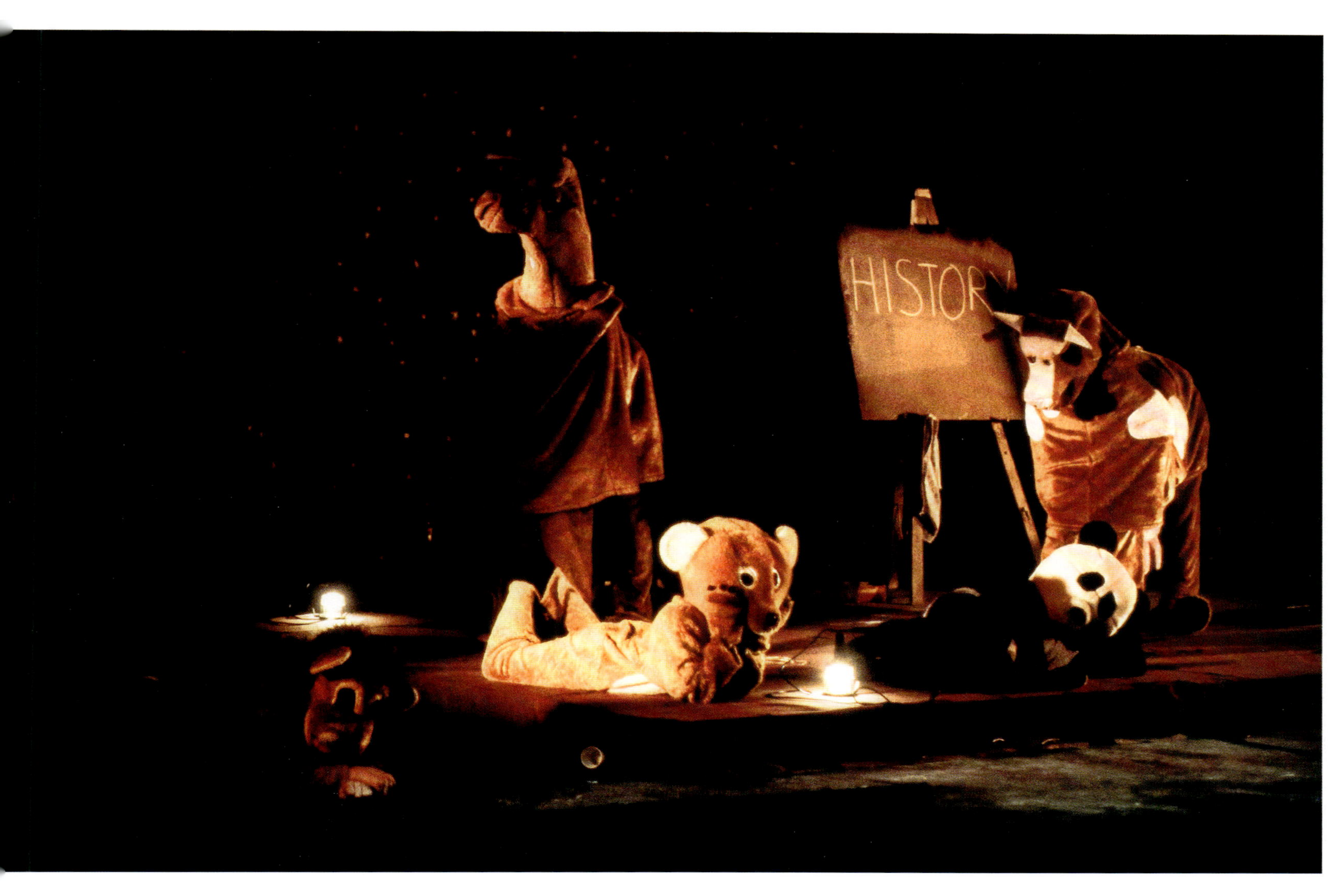

WHO CAN SING A SONG TO UNFRIGHTEN ME? (1999)

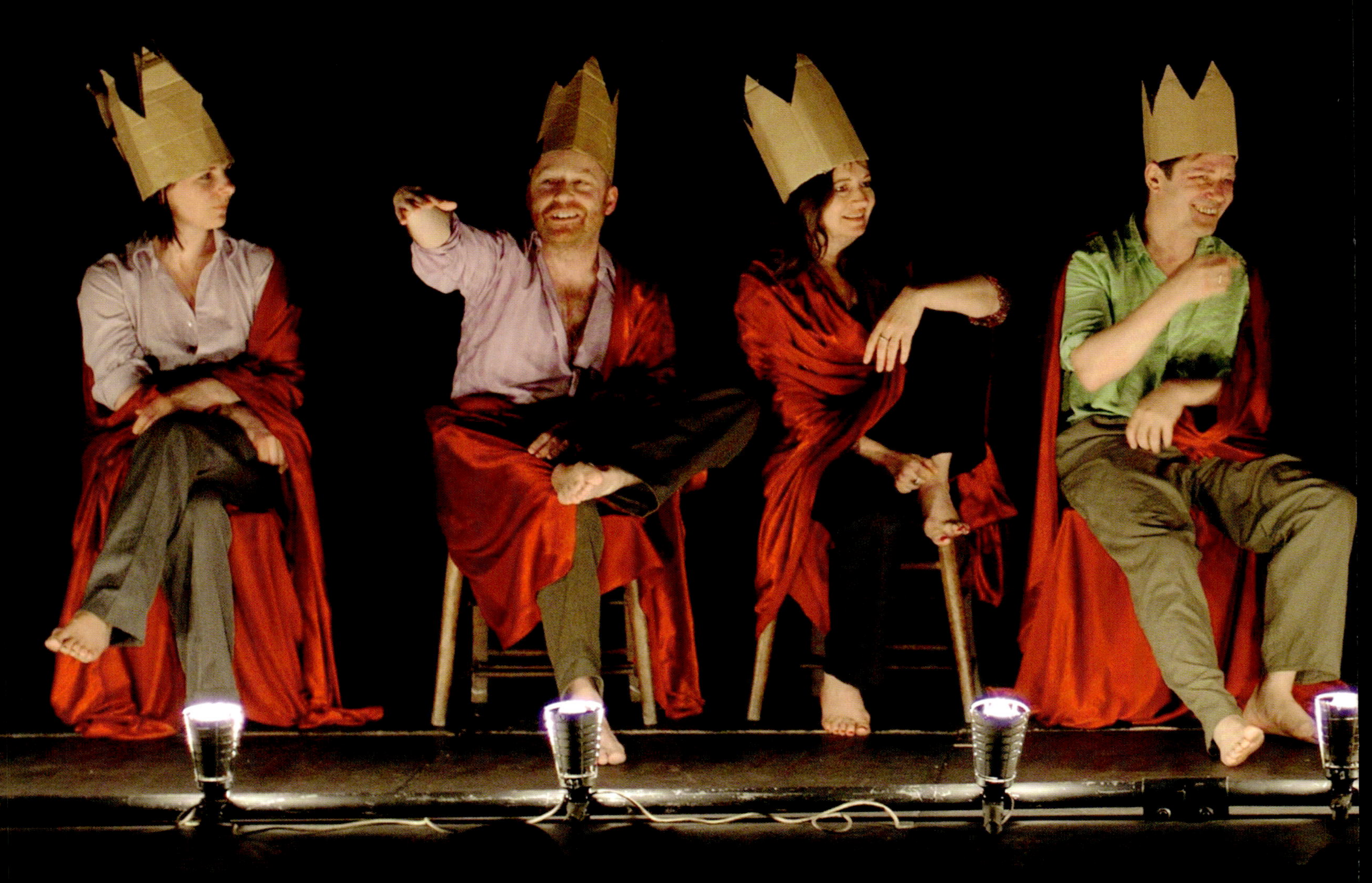

AND ON THE THOUSANDTH NIGHT ... (1999)

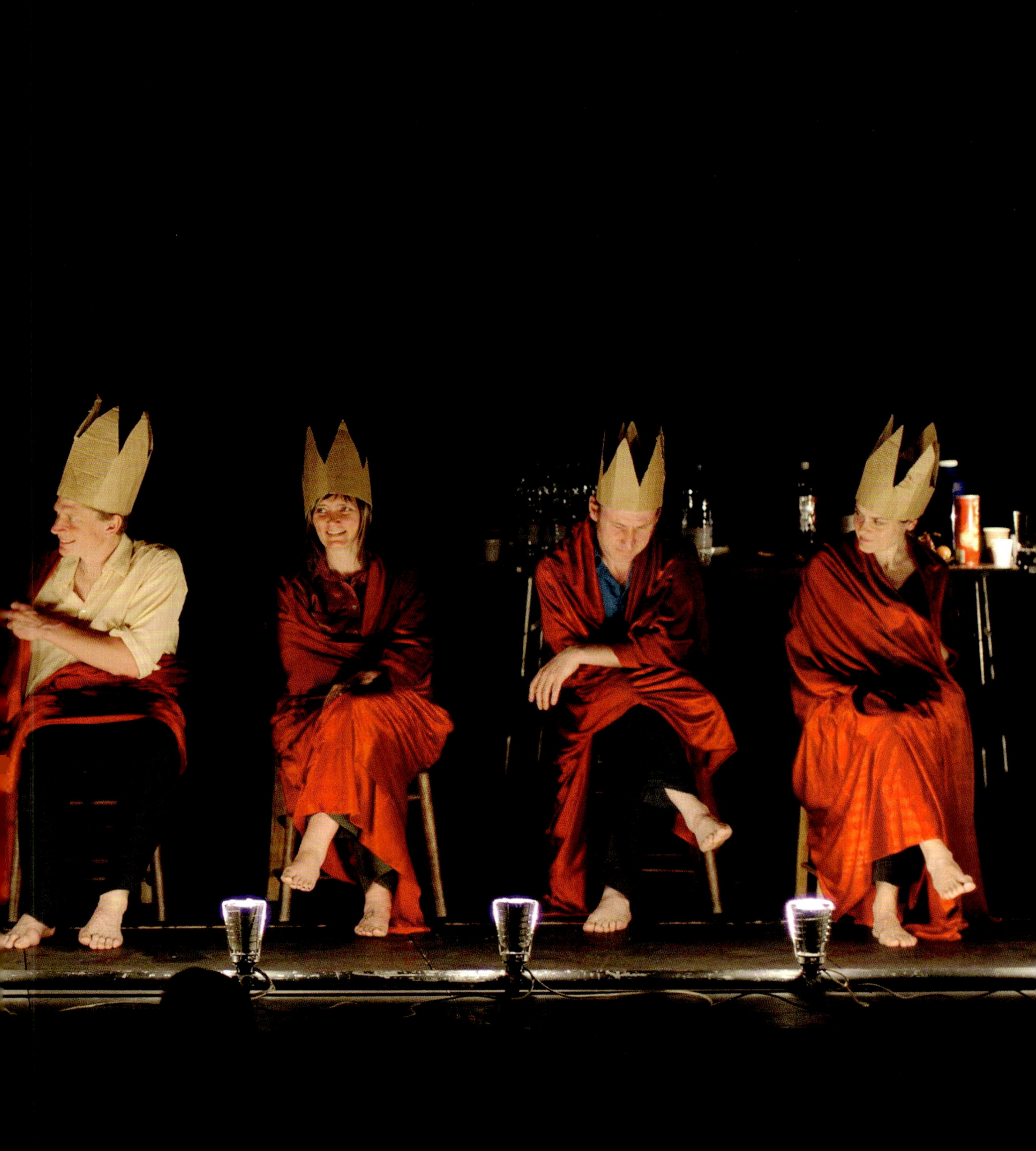

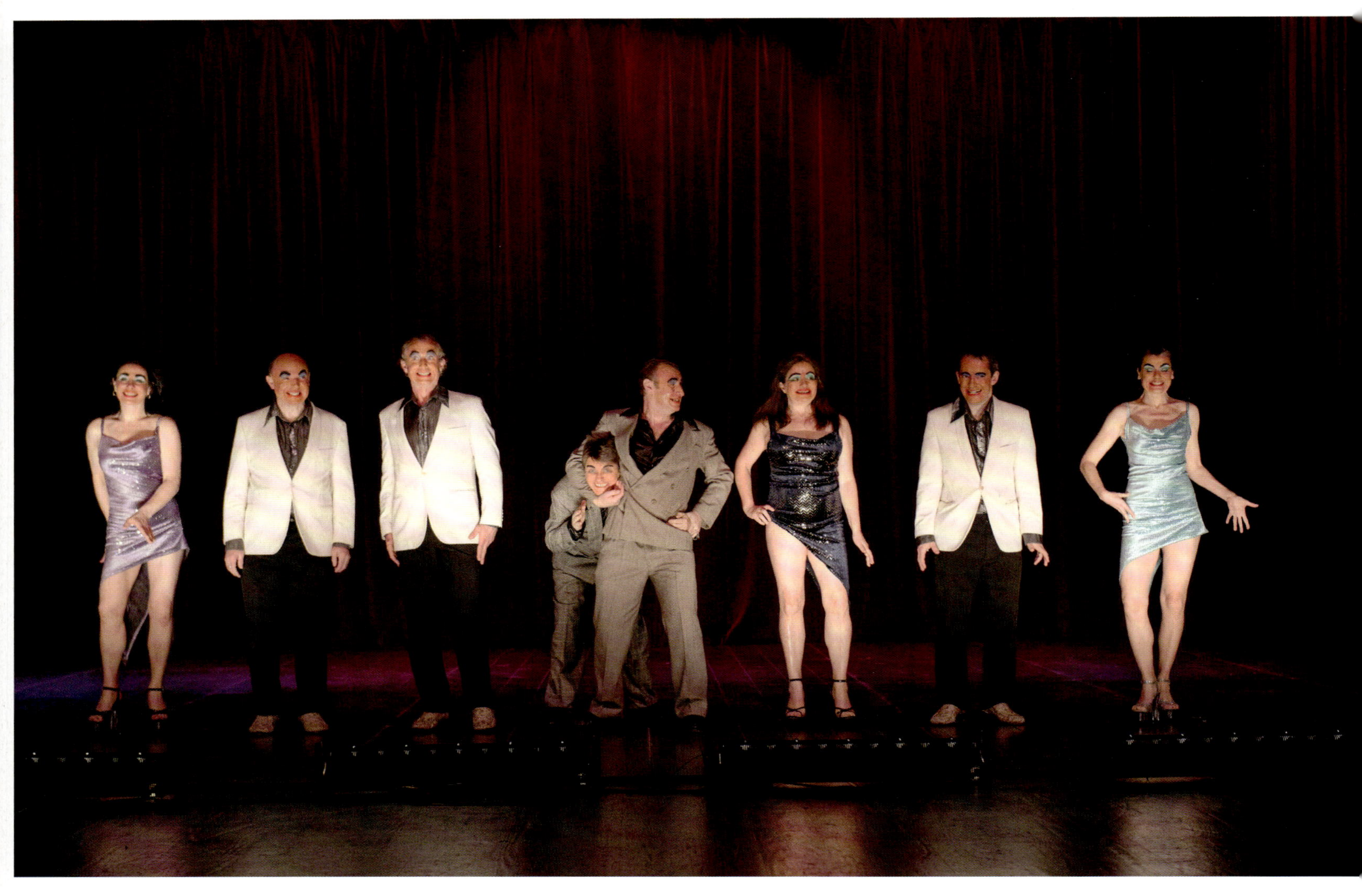

FIRST NIGHT (2001)

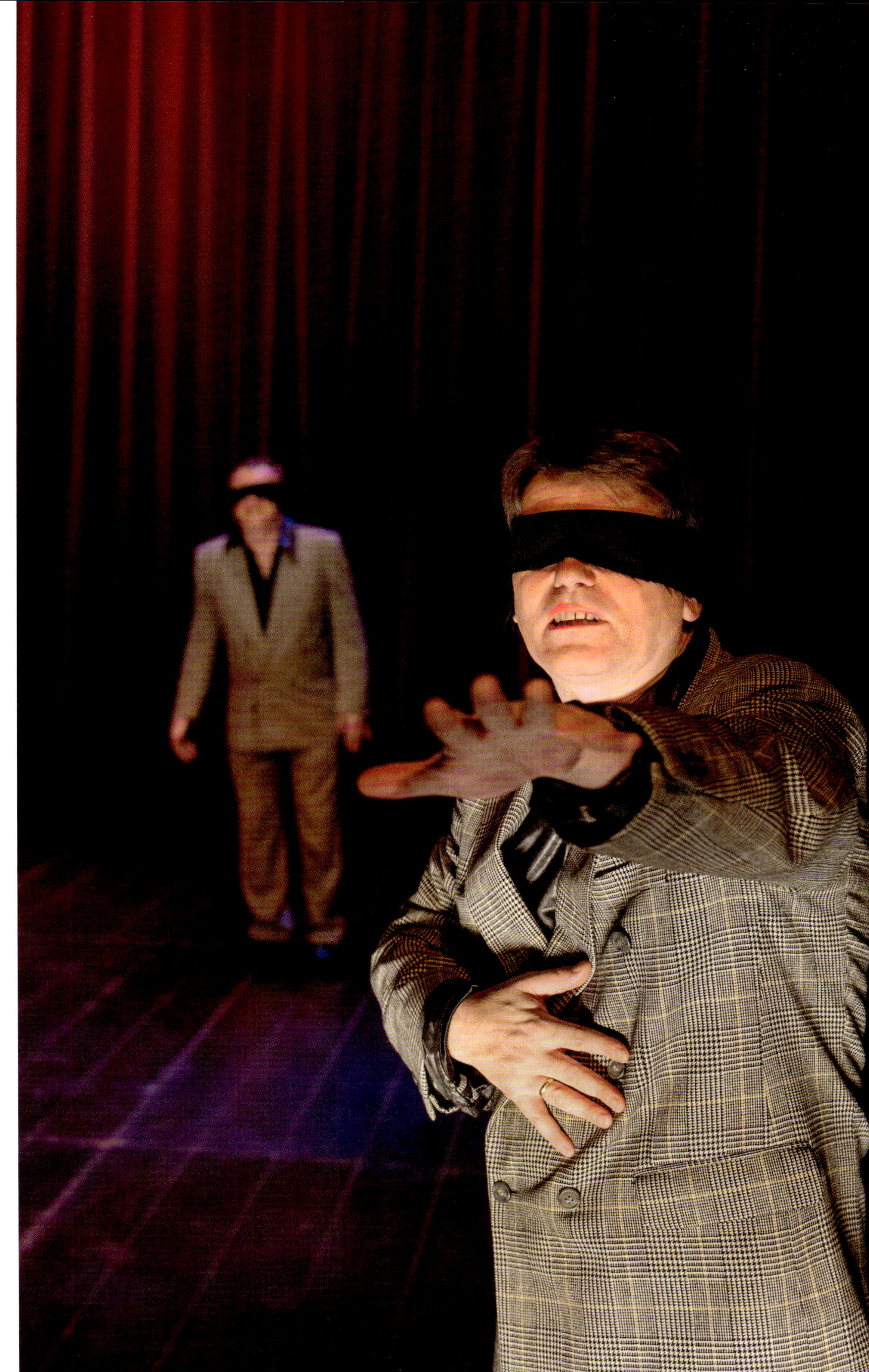

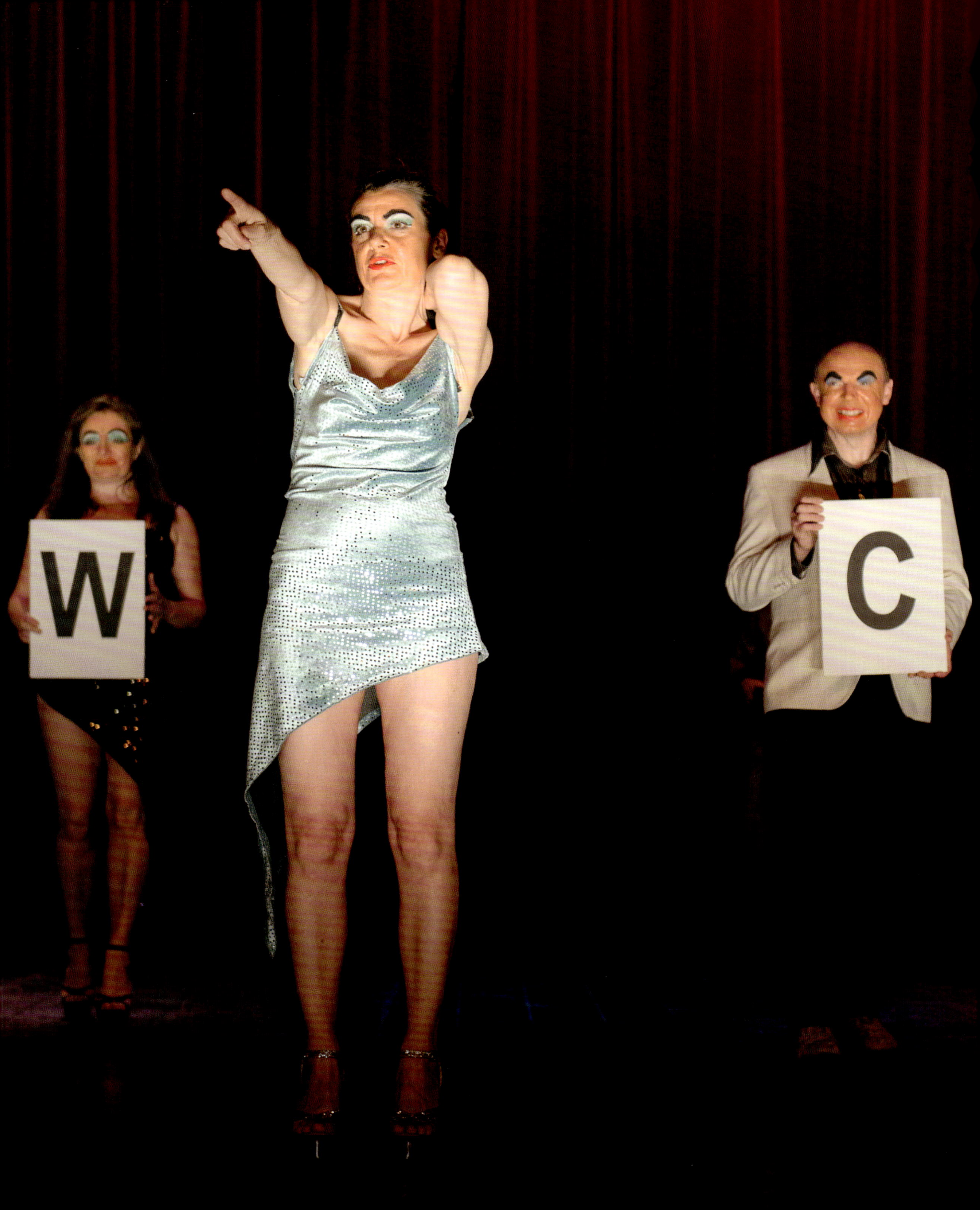

W
C

Cathy: The man at the end of the row there, you're not going to make it home tonight. [*Pointing to someone else*] I've just got a really clear picture inside your head. It's not very nice in there, is it?

[*She points to someone new with each new line.*]

Heart attack.

Kidney failure.

Car crash.

Cancer of the bowels.

Brain haemorrhage.

Pneumonia.

Stroke.

Prostate cancer.

A tumour, a brain tumour.

Old age.

Bronchitis.

Septicaemia.

Idiopathic ventricular fibrillation.

Emphysema.

Asthma attack.

Lung cancer.

A snakebite.

Typhoid.

Motor neurone disease.

Drowning.

AIDS.

Obesity.

Drug overdose.

Slit wrists.

Shot.

Stabbed.

Ebola.

Drowning.

Meningitis.

Electrocuted.

A routine operation that goes wrong.

Influenza.

Deep vein thrombosis.

Childbirth.

Crushed.

Hypothermia.

Alcoholism.

Heart attack.

Stroke.

Broken hip.

Broken neck.

Broken heart.

Epileptic fit.

Bomb.

Bomb.

Bomb.

Bomb.

Bomb.

Burst appendix.

Hepatitis A.

Hepatitis B.

Hepatitis C.

You two at the end of the row, about two thirds of the way back —suicide pact.

And you three in the middle here—a train crash.

And on the end of the row near the back ...
a gas explosion.

Old age.

The line-up at the front of the stage is a key motif in this piece and many others. From the start the performers are presented in a line, pinned and on display with their hideous mask-like makeup and rigid smiles. The line-up is the 'Hello', but it's also a measuring device or benchmark we use, a point of return that (as it changes in each iteration) allows the audience to sense tonal shifts. *First Night* starts with fear of the audience—the performers are standing there paralysed and they're not sure what to say, the smiles seem really desperate. But pretty quickly the fear becomes violence— the tyranny of audience expectation, the supposed unity of the audience, and their respectability all become issues.

It is a show in which everything stems from a single principle, a single world. The whole thing is framed as a disastrous vaudeville, though, within that, sections have different concerns and dynamics. There are dances and card tricks, jokes and escapology, even a spiritualist routine where the performers are all wearing blindfolds, relaying messages—warnings and predictions of the future—from the ether. But whatever they do, it's always going wrong—that's the consistency—and it's always becoming violent. One way or another it keeps turning on the audience. [TE]

Richard: Good. I think I speak for everybody here when I say that you people, you here, in this town, you are quite simply the best audience that we have ever, ever played to.

Weaver: Hear, hear.

Claire: Really, ladies and gentlemen, you are kind and intelligent and warm-hearted and broad-minded and we thank you.

Terry: You are morally superior. And ethically pure.

Weaver: You're politically sensitive and socially aware.

Robin: Yes. Yes. But that doesn't stop you from letting your hair down and having a good time.

Jerry: Nothing goes over your heads, does it?

John: No, because you're scientists and mathematicians.

Terry: You are judges and doctors.

Weaver: You're surgeons and architects.

Jerry: Outstanding members of the community.

Richard: There aren't any criminals in here tonight.

Robin: Well, if anybody's got any unpaid parking tickets or speeding fines, that's not what we are talking about.

Terry: What we mean is there are no wife-beaters here. No men or women who have been secretly sexually abusing their children for years.

Claire: There's no homophobes in the house tonight, no racists. No well-dressed, well-educated bigots, are there?

John: No. Because you are the best audience we have ever played to.

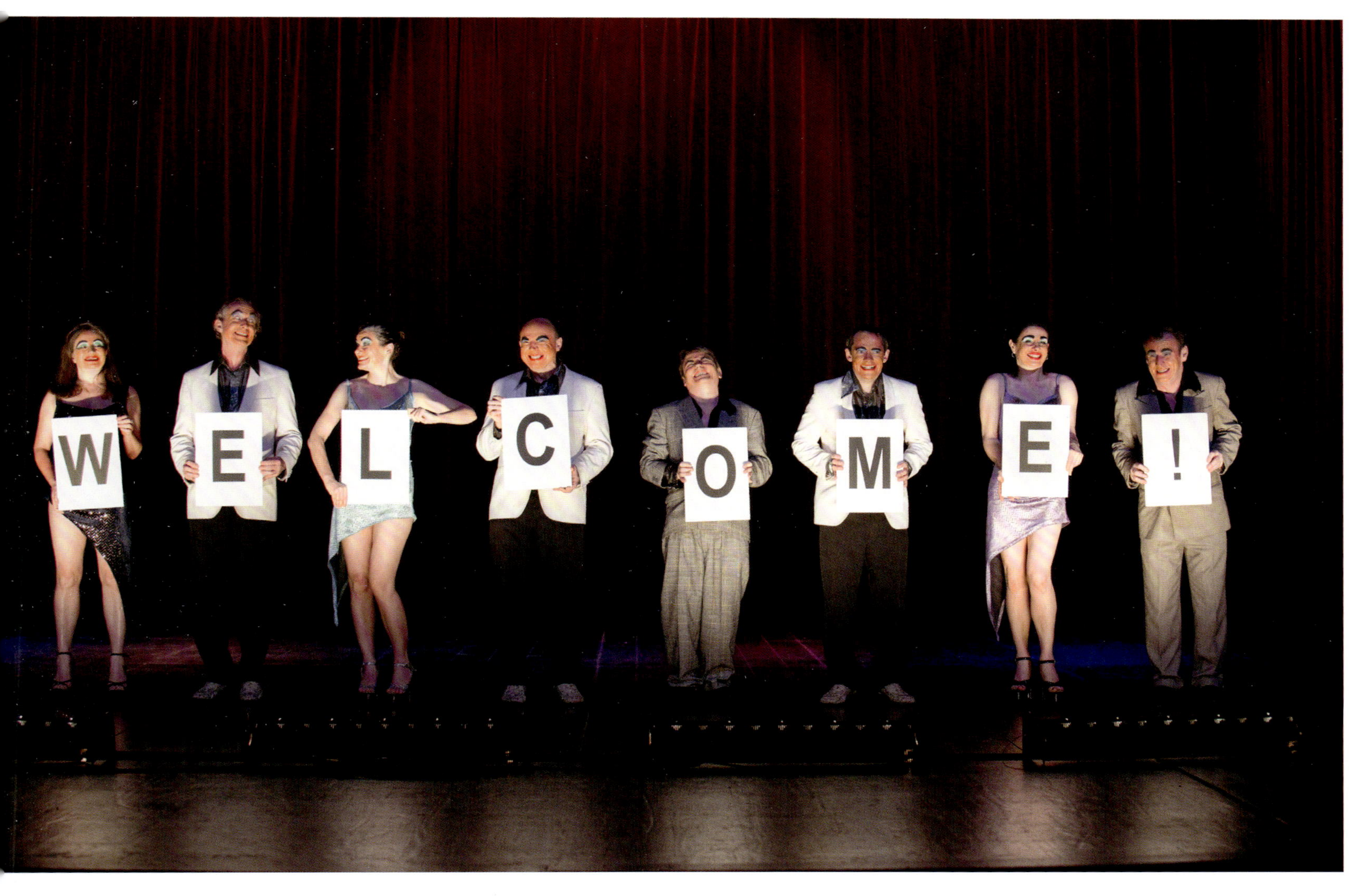

W E L C O M E !

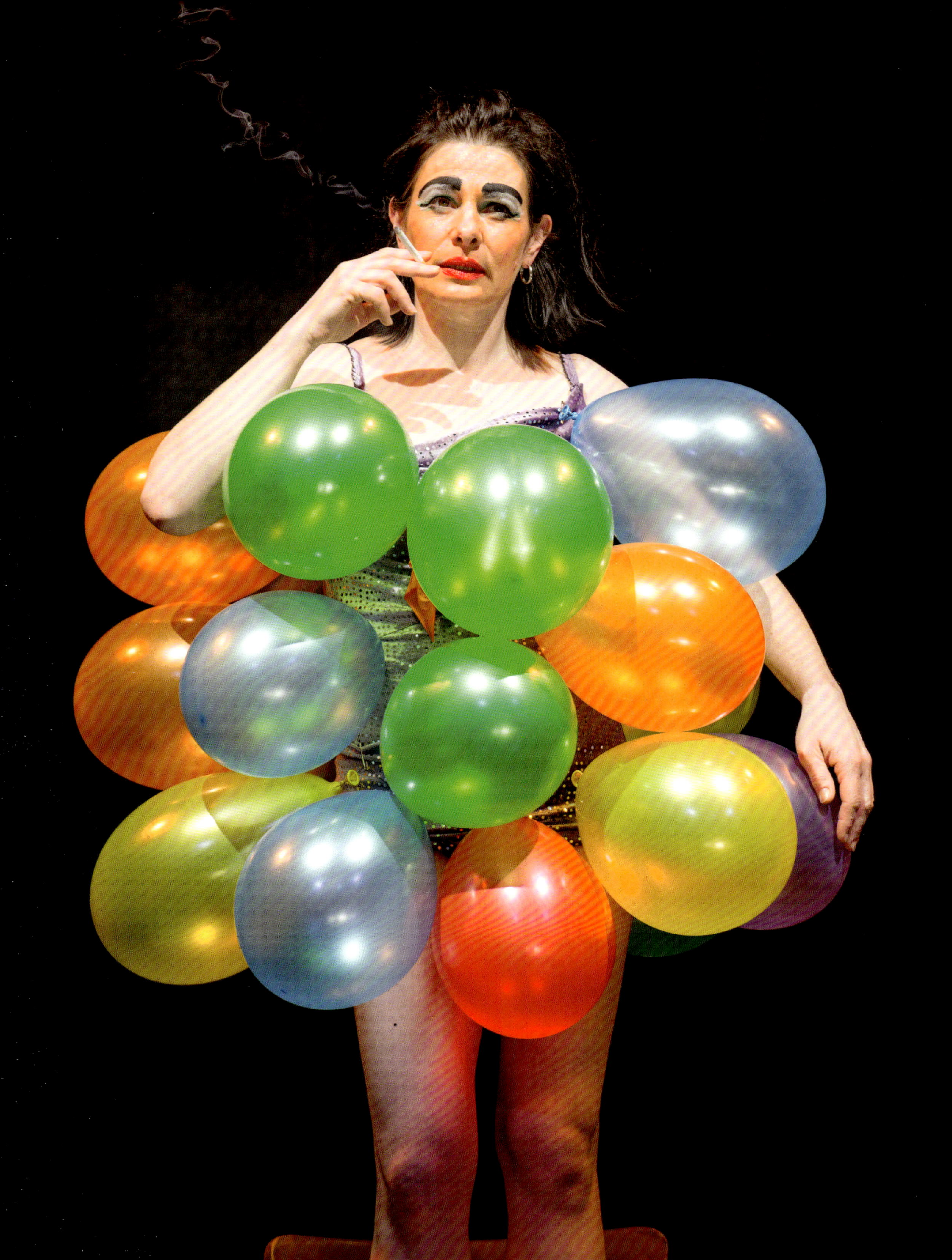

Although the line-up presents the performers as equivalent, Richard and Robin share the role of MC at times, working as a double act, and appearing to frame the proceedings. While the machinery of popular entertainment—and the wider social orthodoxy in which it's formed—might be tyrannous and brutalizing for the men, its violence and objectification is worse for the women. As the performance develops, and the playful antagonism with the audience gets more and more serious, it's perhaps not surprising that the women are often the most confrontational. It's Cathy who transforms the spiritualist section into an extended solo predicting deaths for individual audience members, Terry who develops a short text asking people to keep their minds off things happening outside the theatre into a long salt-in-the-wound monologue reminding them endlessly of disturbing and unsettling things 'outside', and Claire who leads the charge with provocative statements about the audience—vitriolically accusing them of snobbery, misogyny, racism, and homophobia. What the men think about this is always in flux: at times they seem to want peace and for the troublemaking to stop, even dismissing the women's anger as a joke, whilst at other times they follow the lead the women provide. In the end though, it's the women that really upend and transform the show, remodelling each act or routine as a way of antagonizing the audience. [TE]

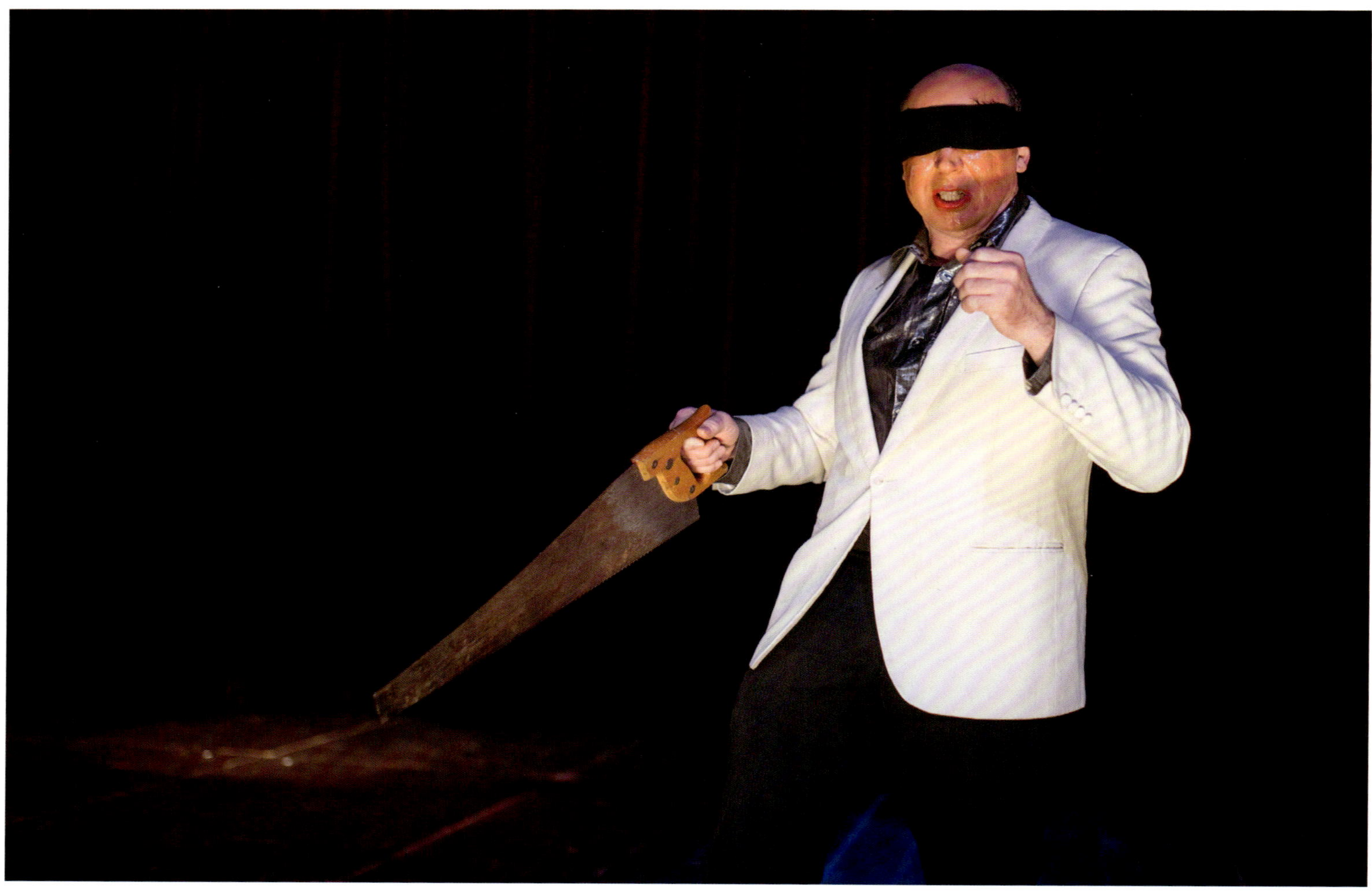

The first rehearsals were really nothing but the smiling, the makeup, and a rough approximation of the costumes. I just asked the performers to stand in a line and smile, looking out, looking back at me. That was the only idea. It was sculptural, or very pure in performance terms—the smiling which makes a mask of the face, and the difficulty of maintaining that, which, at the start especially, made their faces twitch. And because the sustained smiling made it hard for them to swallow, there was always the sound of them sucking the saliva around in their mouths as it accumulated. There was a violence there from the outset; in the combination of physical discomfort and the desperation for approval written into the smiling, the excessive compliance with audience expectations of pleasure.

The smiles communicated in a very direct, haptic way—I'd always find myself smiling back, an unconscious mirroring, smiling so hard sometimes that we'd all leave rehearsals with aching faces. That was often the case doing the piece in public too—the performers would look out to see rows of strained manic smiles in the half-light of the auditorium. [TE]

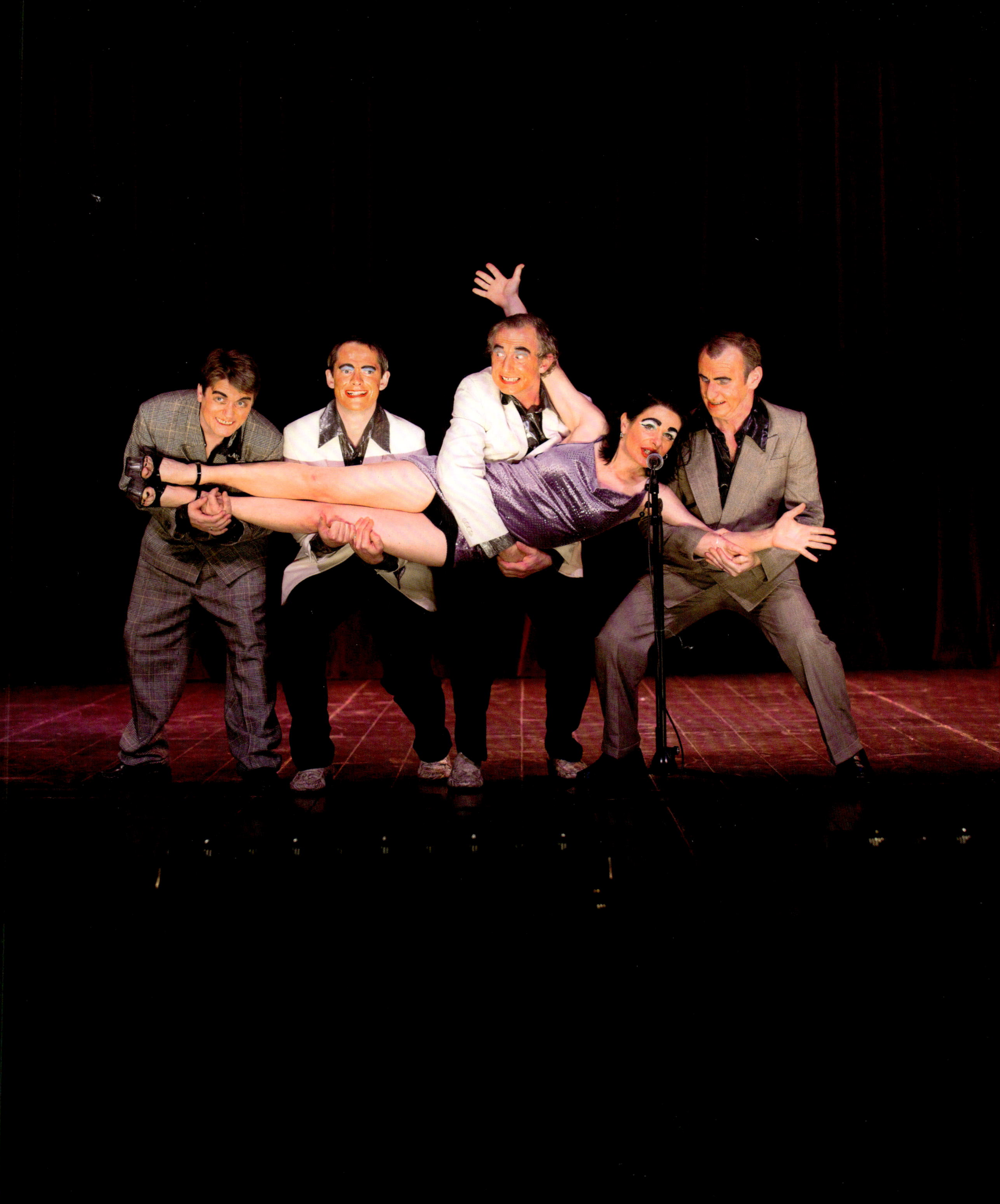

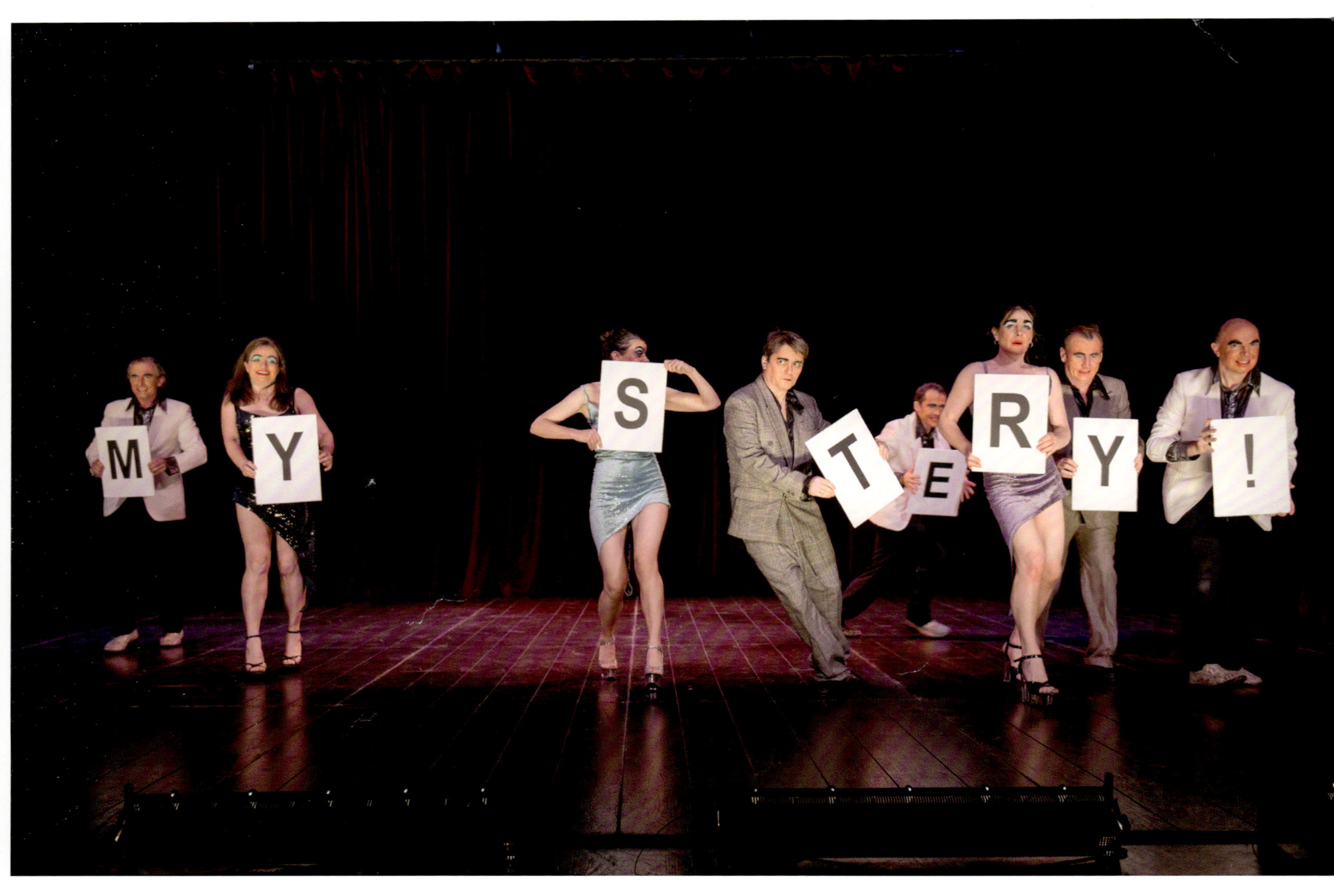

M
Y
S
T
E
R
Y
!

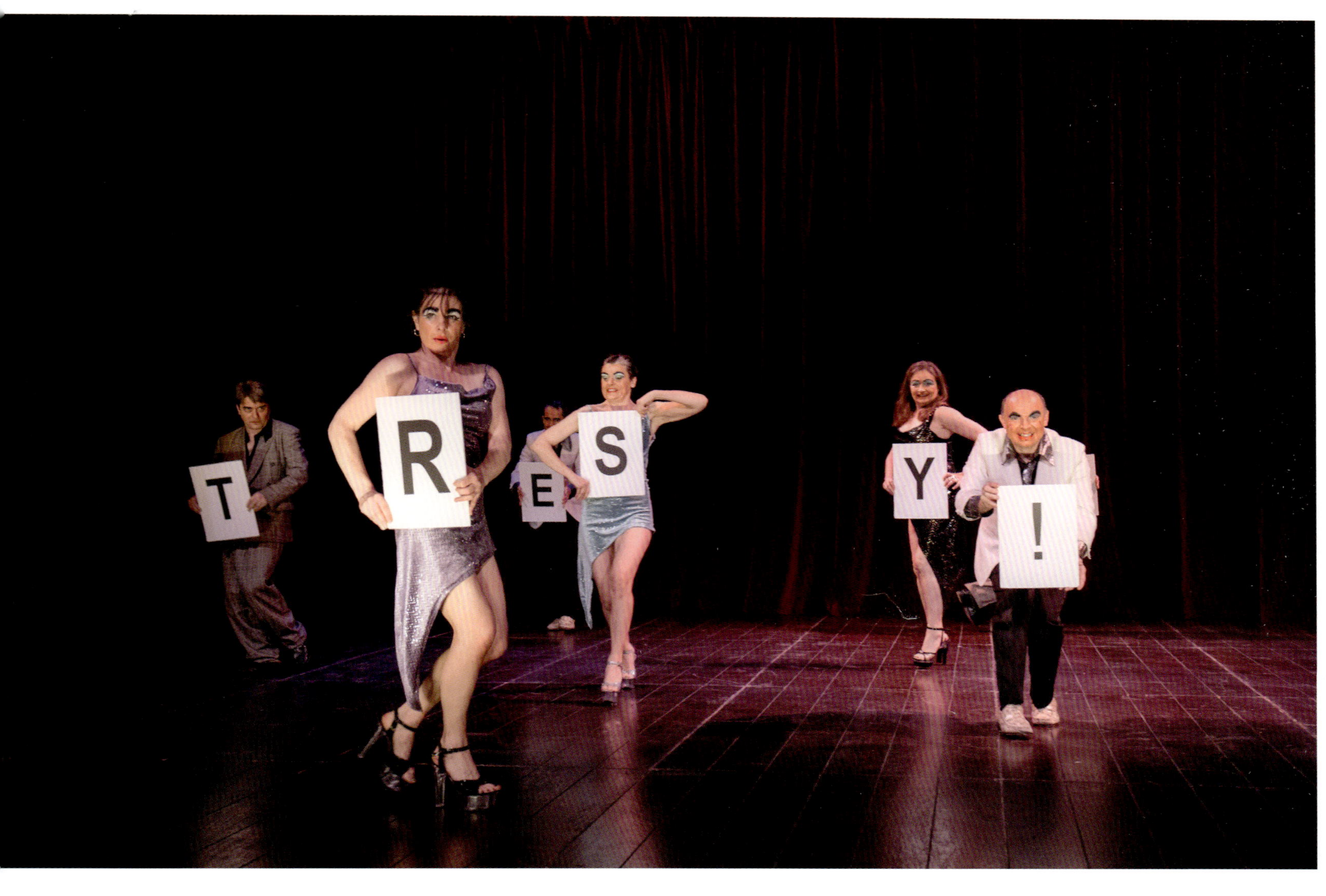

T
R
E
S
Y
!

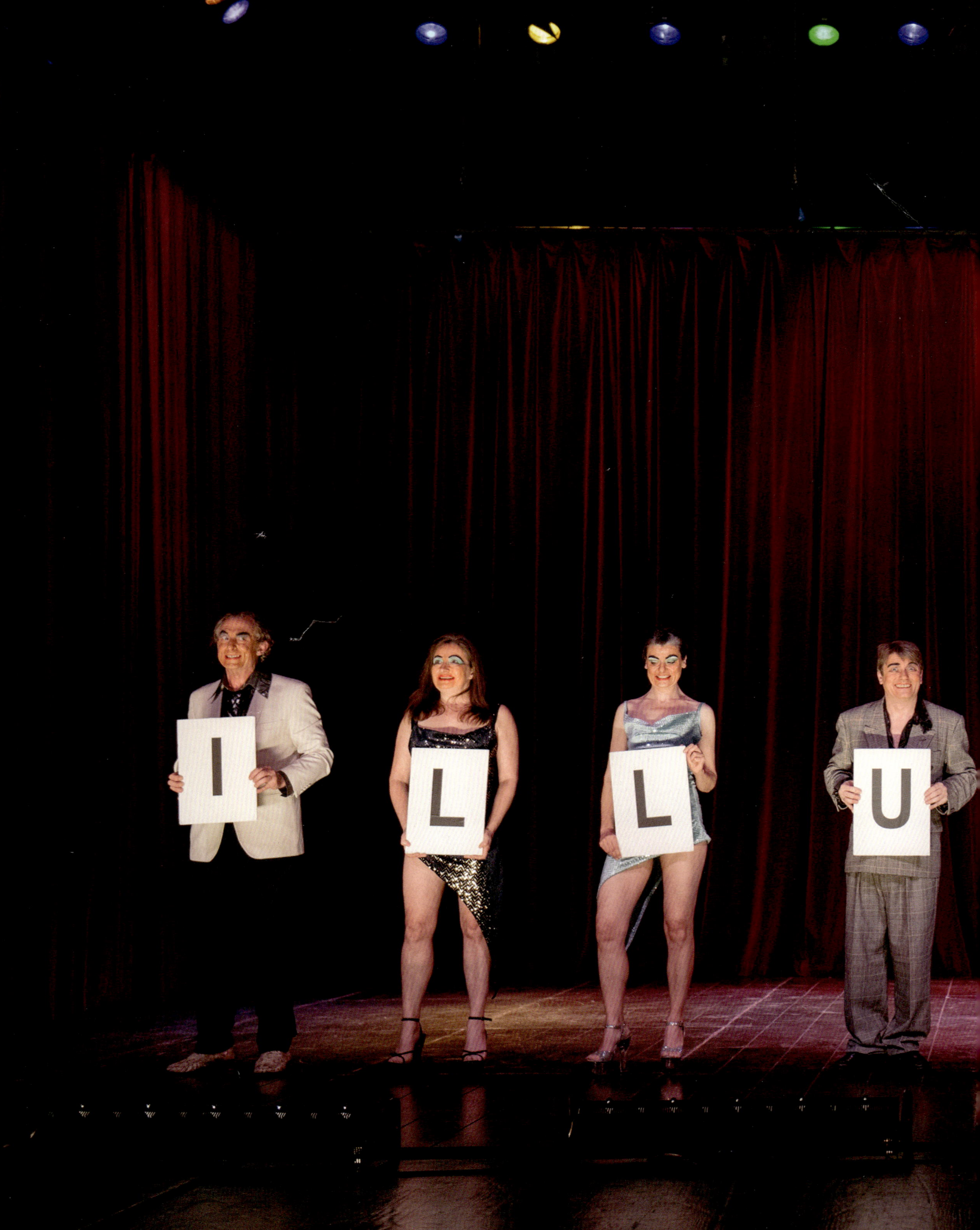
I
L
L
U

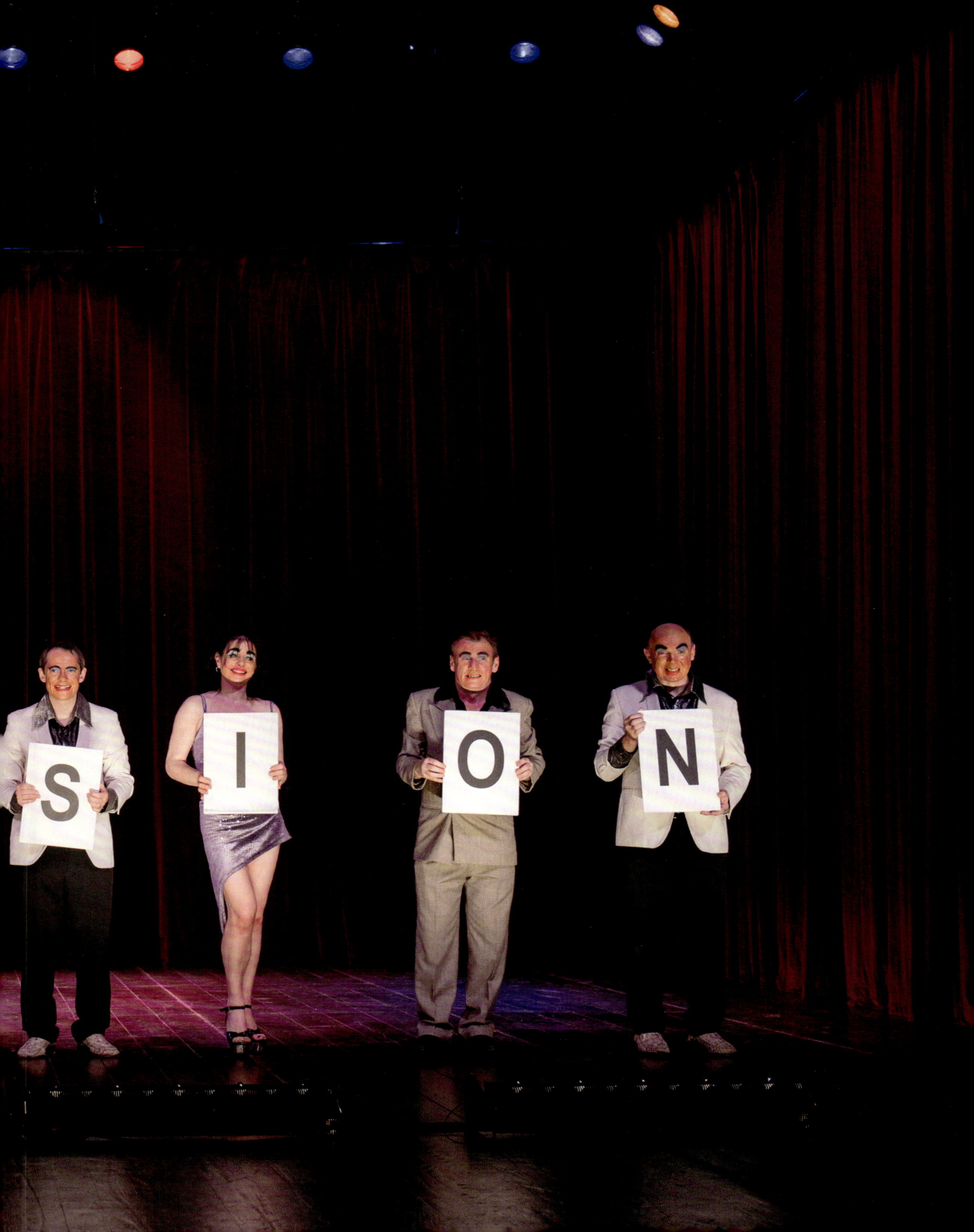

S
I
O
N

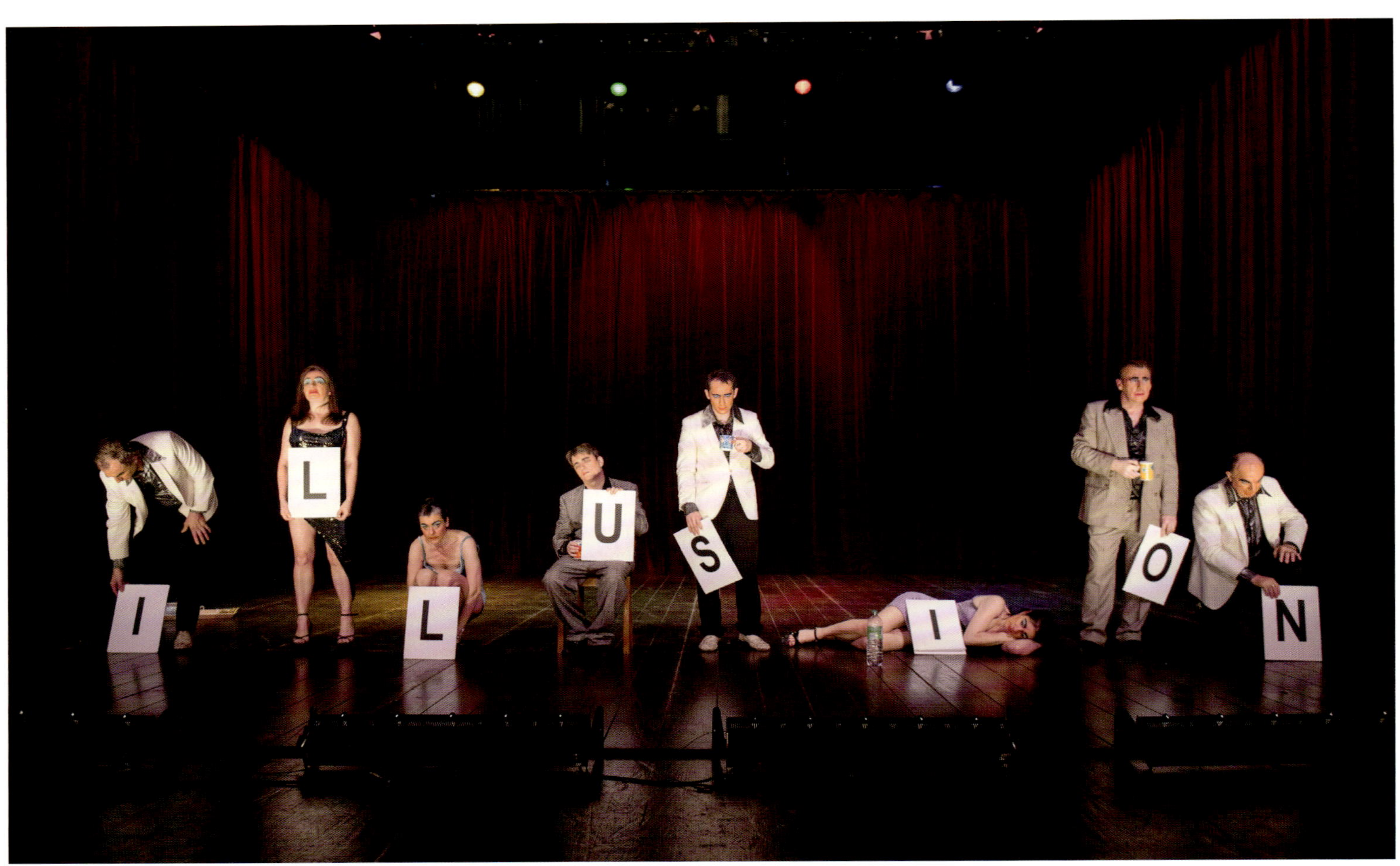

Terry: Ladies and gentlemen, while you are with us here tonight, we'd like to ask you to try to forget about the outside world completely. Try not to think about anything outside of this room. Anything at all.

Try to forget about cars and meetings and cigarettes and road accidents. Try to forget about births and deaths and funerals. And sudden bereavements. Try not to think about dustbins and litter on the street. Try not to think about litter. Try not to think about troubles and agonies and weak smiles. And sadness. And try not to think about the kind of bitterness that comes from making one really big mistake. And the kind of regret that comes from making many, many, many small mistakes. Try not to think about clumsiness and ineptitude.

Forget about the wind rushing through trees and fire engines rushing to an accident. Try to forget about rivers flooding and cars—cars on a motorway piling into one another. Try to forget about footsteps walking on pavements and broken heels. And poison and rusty knives. And guns. Try not to think about guns. And daggers and letter bombs and cluster bombs. And chemical warfare. Try not to think about chemical warfare. And chemotherapy. And the common cold. Try not to think about the common cold. And hospitals. And nurses. And surgeons and rubber gloves and trollies and serums and cupboards. And expensive drugs that poor countries can't afford.

Try not to think about regrets and goodbyes and airports and people who can't look you in the face. And overheard remarks and suspicion and things people say about you which you should never really hear. Try not to think about shaking and hesitations and doubts and coughing and needing to clear your throat. Try not to think about mobile phone bills and badly managed prisons and badly managed pension funds and rust and world leaders and world aid and pain and disasters and disaster movies and disastrous relationships and disastrous haircuts and curtains and feet stamping angrily and cinders and ceilings and shipwrecks and things that lie at the bottom of the ocean.

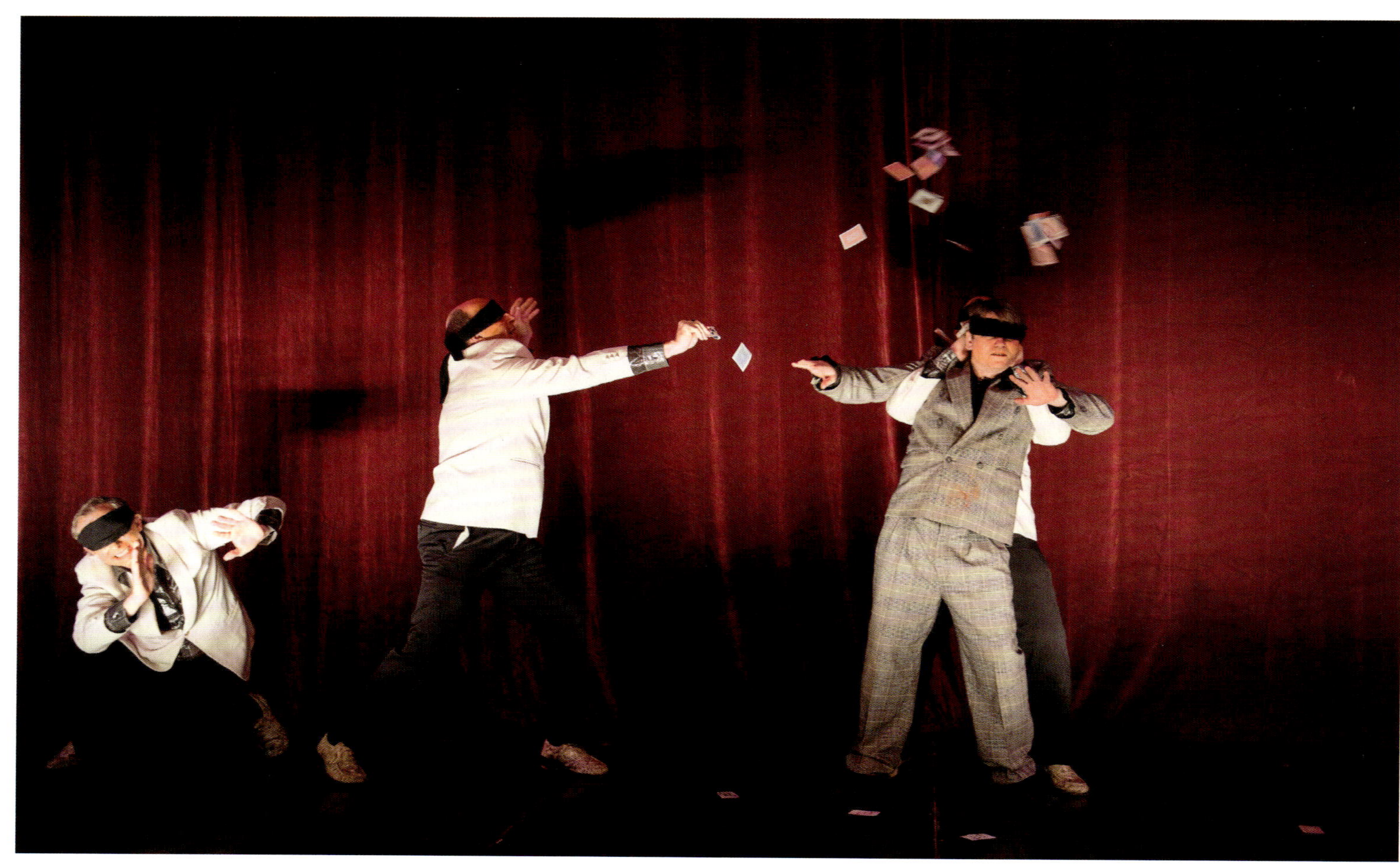

We've so rarely drawn on dramatic literature. Our interests have been largely focused on other things that happen on stages: performances of press conferences, lectures, or show trials, telethons and quizzes, or the illegitimate theatricalities of popular culture and television. *First Night* is our most explicit allusion to genres like Variety, Cabaret, Music Hall—things that would have made their way to us via television in the late 1960s and 1970s when we were growing up, the kinds of things that would be on TV at your grandparents' house, or genres that were being revisited in satire or as kitsch rather later on. The film of John Osborne's *The Entertainer* was a reference point—the brilliant line when the jaded entertainer Archie Rice turns on his audience at the end of a miserable matinee performance: 'Let me know where you're working tomorrow, I'll come and watch *you* …' [TE]

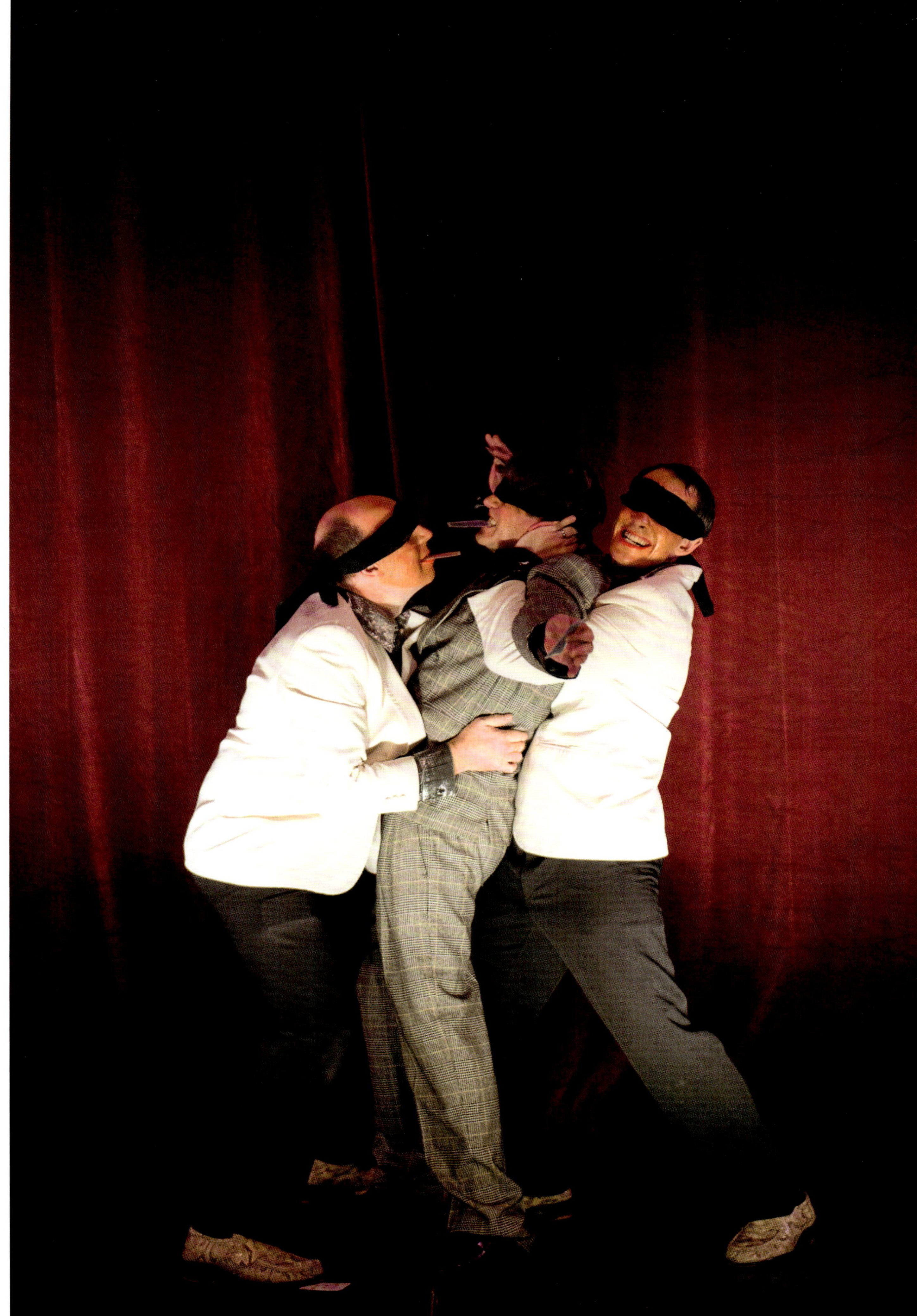

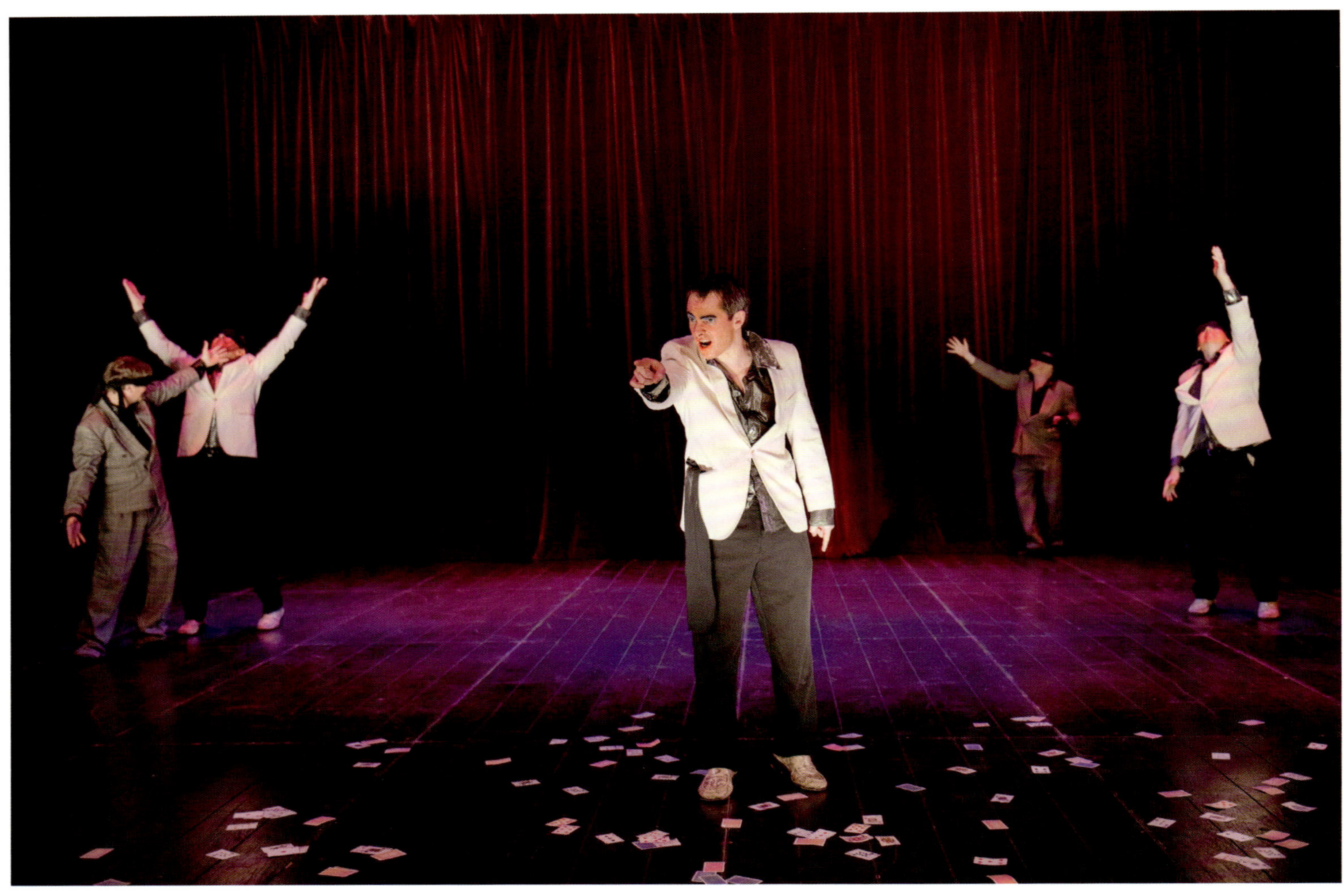

I often think people were laughing because it was so unexpected: you don't tell people out there in the auditorium that they're going to die. It's a break of the contract, it's discomforting. It also divides the audience, which is forbidden in its own way: a person was being singled out and that questioned how other people around them would respond. The show used to really agitate audiences. Especially as we switched from telling them they were the best audience we'd ever played to, to the worst. People would get outraged. And sometimes, I think it was in Sheffield at the Lyceum, the audience became really vocal and noisy. Little pockets of alliance were forming and some people were heckling us and trying to give us some abuse back, other people were telling those people to shut up, and other people were just laughing. [CN]

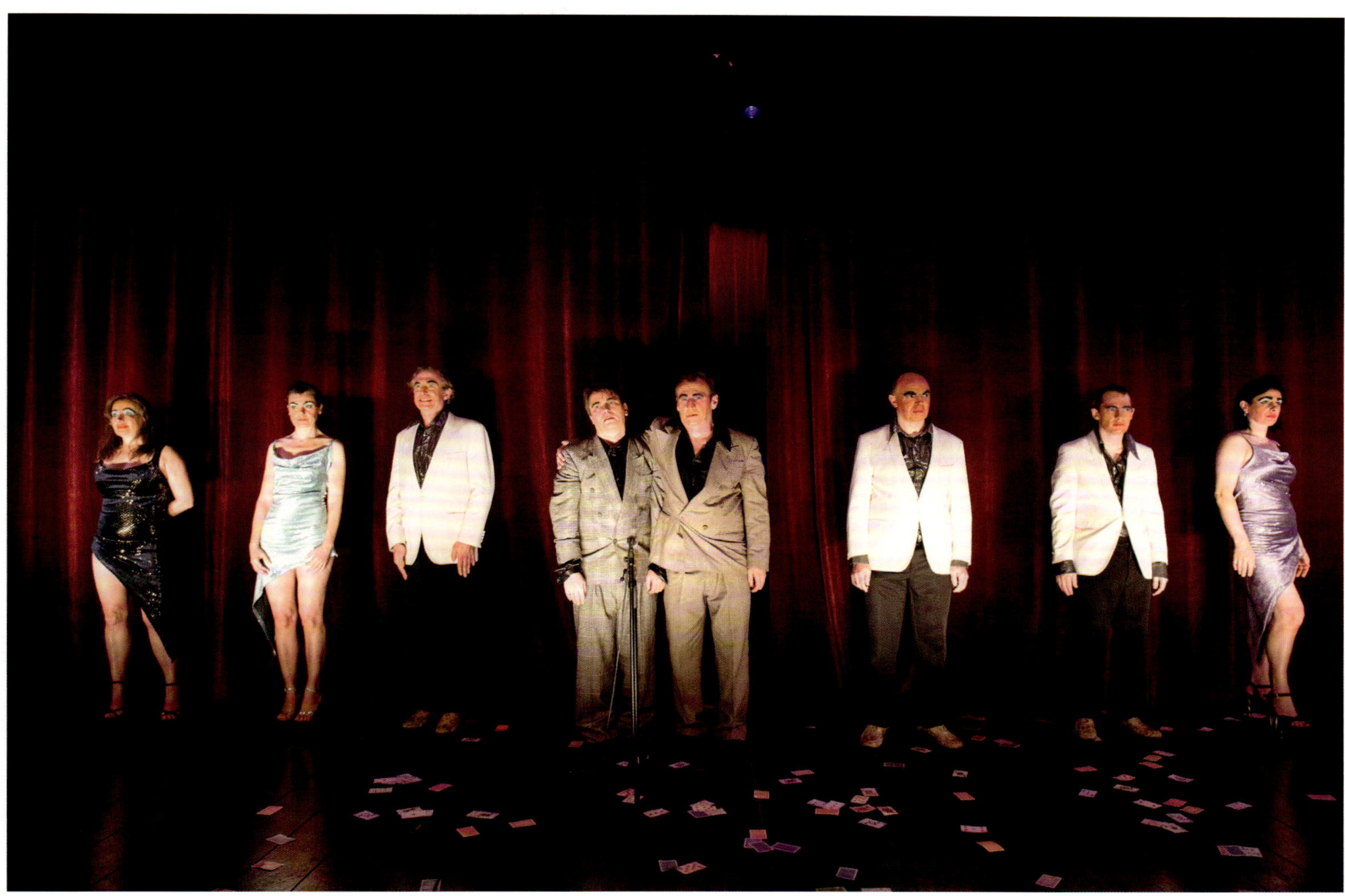

Cathy: You're not the kind of people who
are frightened to go home because your
lives are empty. You're not afraid to
sit in your rooms wondering what to do
next, whether you could watch television
or who to ring. You're not afraid to go
to bed because you're frightened that
you won't sleep. You're not those kind
of people.

Richard: No, you're not. You're not those
kind of people at all.

John: No. You're stars. You're the stars
of the show.

Weaver: You're not black holes, sucking
every last bit of life and matter out of
the universe, are you?

Terry: You're not sad fucks. Sad fucks
who come to the theatre to fuel their
meagre sexual fantasies. You're not
sitting there in the dark and mentally
ordering us from 1 to 8 in terms of
who you'd like to sleep with first and
who second and who you're saving till
last ...

Cathy: And you're not the kind of people
who wake up one day and realize that
each and every opportunity that life
has ever handed to you on a plate has
been squandered and wasted by your own
indifference and cowardice and laziness.

Richard: No. Because you are the best
audience we have ever played to.

Terry: We came in peace. You came
in peace.

Richard: We offered out our hands
in friendship.

Claire: And you spat on them.

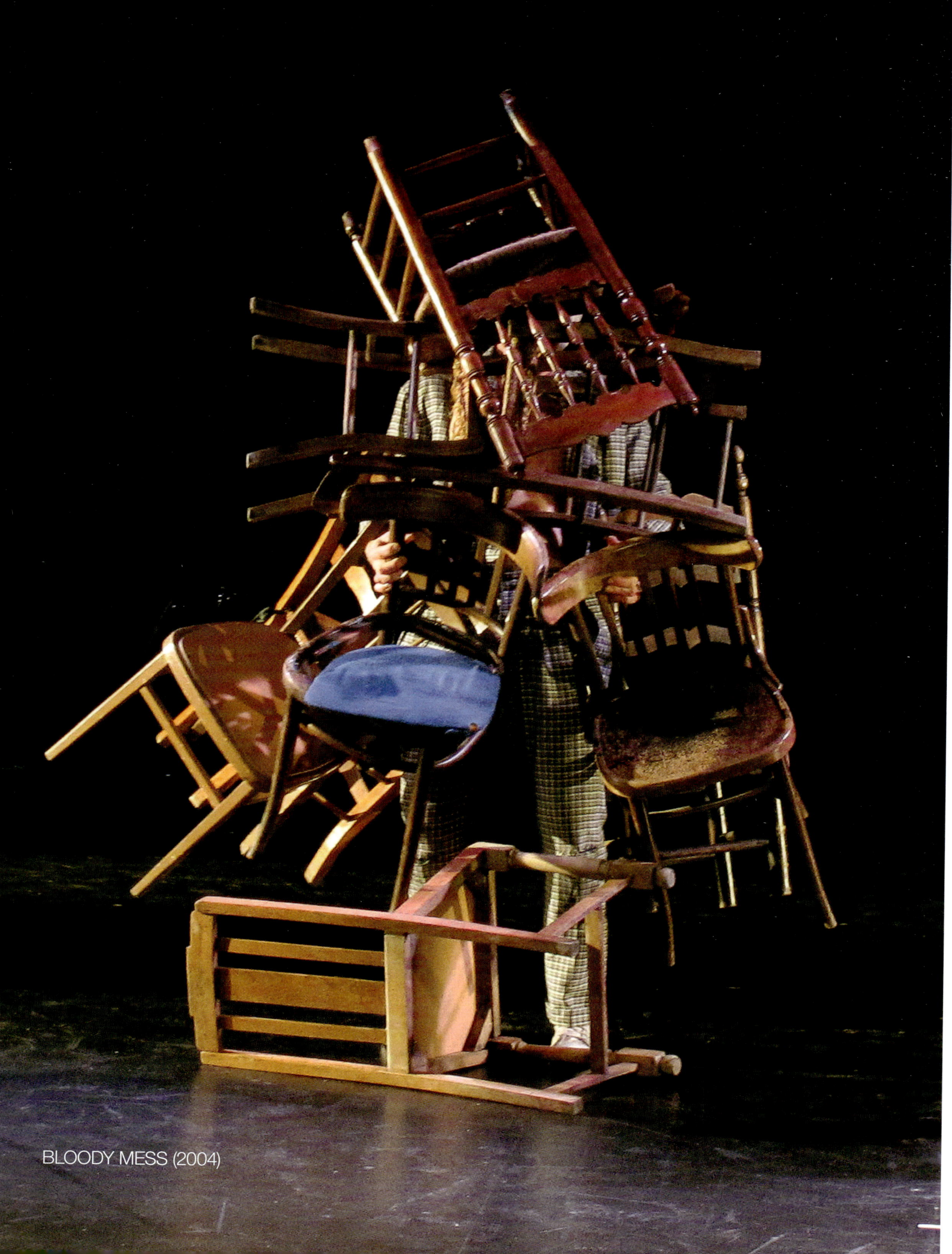

BLOODY MESS (2004)

There are numerous 'beginnings' to the piece: a prologue where John and Bruno as clowns are setting out the chairs. One is making a line at the front, the other undoing his work, to make a line at the back. It is elemental slapstick, but already violent; the audience senses right away that there's going to be trouble. The next beginning is a line-up: all ten performers are sitting on the line of chairs that has finally been arranged at the front. They pass the mic up and down and make intros for themselves. They all give the audience some faux advice on how they would like to be seen or how they see themselves in this show. From what they are saying it's evident that these must be very different, incompatible shows. The next 'beginning' is a set of disparate fragments of action set next to each other—Rich and Rob headbanging, Cathy playing dead with Terry weeping over her, Claire dressing up as the gorilla, and Wendy slowly starting to build the cheerleader routine that will be her material throughout the piece. [TE]

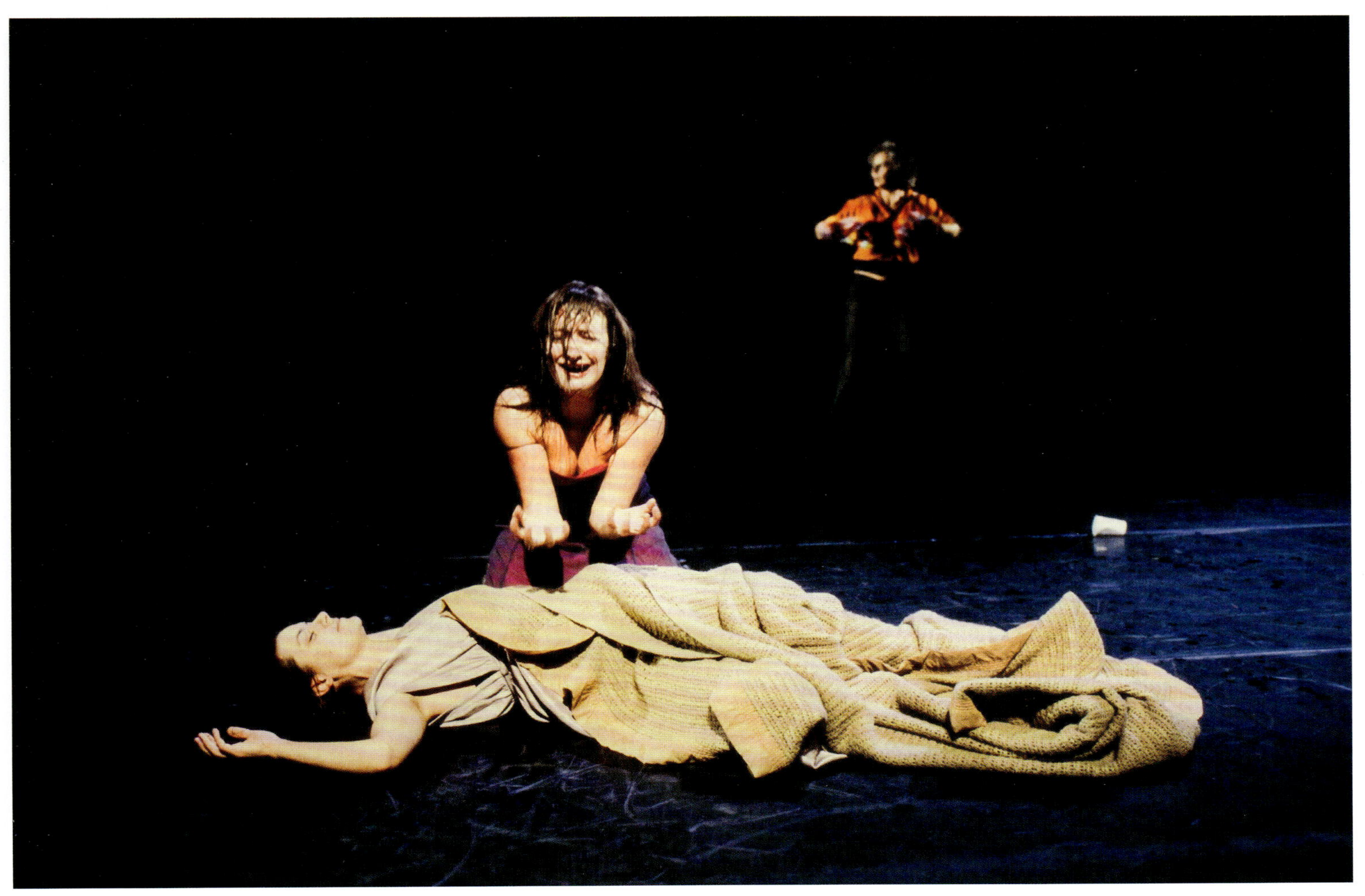

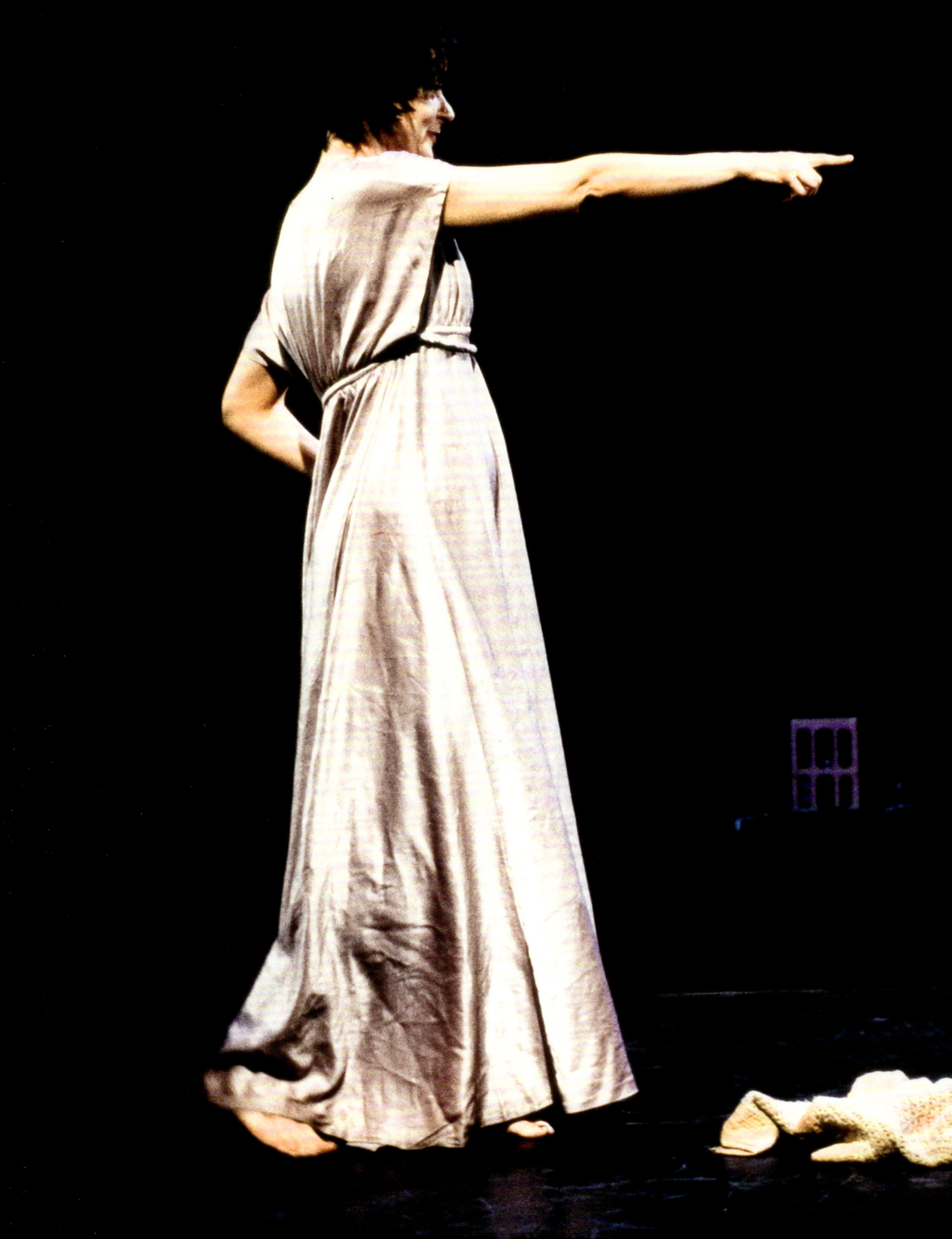

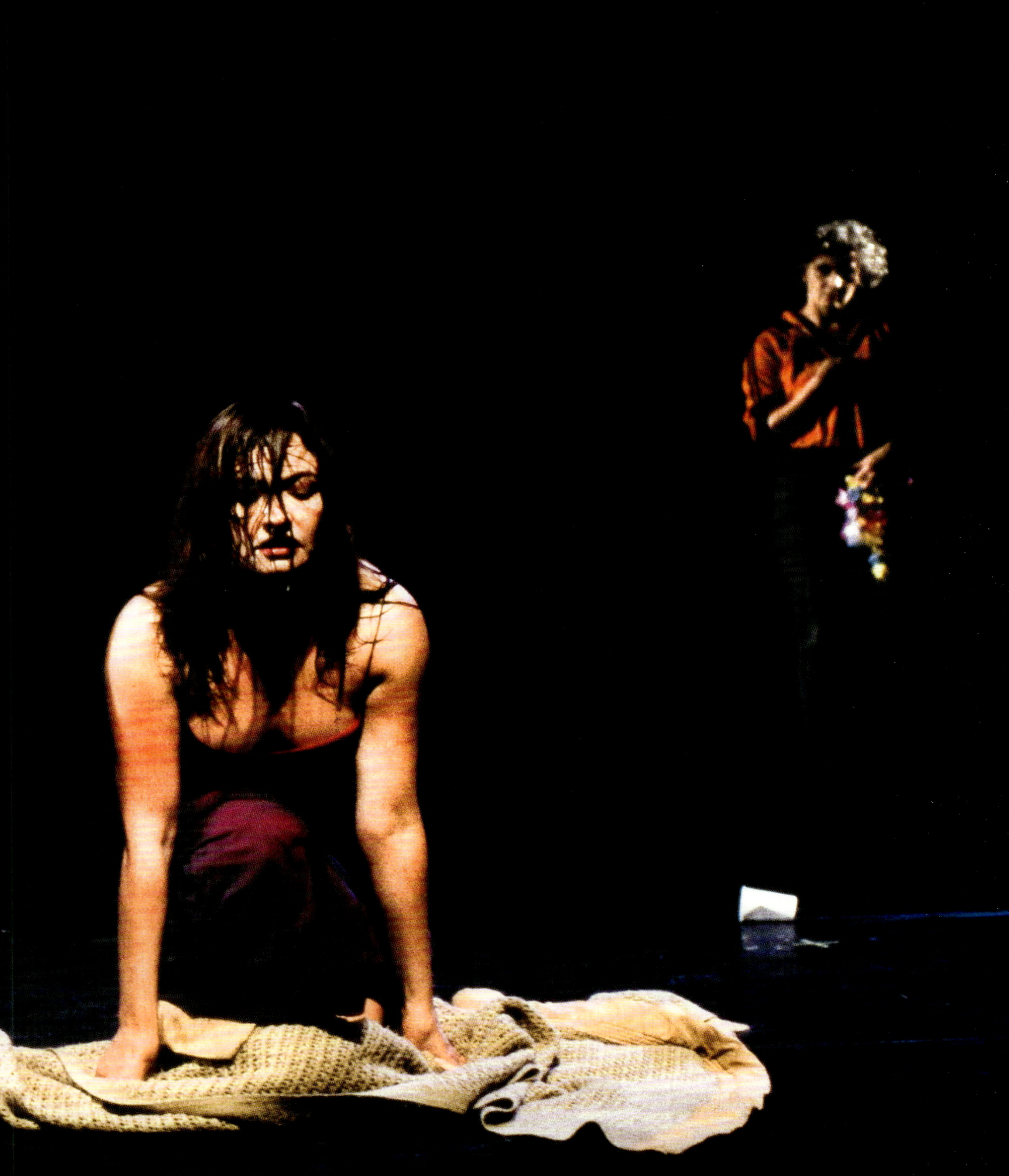

Near the start, the performers explain in a straightforward way how they want the audience to view them. And when it comes to my turn I say that I want the audience to really want to fuck me. The joy with the gorilla costume I wear for the whole show is that it is such an inappropriate costume for someone who is asking to be thought about sexually. There's hardly any of me visible: just my hands and feet. It gives a licence to be really disruptive, to undermine anything that is happening, whilst at other times I become a terribly sad, lonely, grubby figure in the shadows at the edge of the stage. Twice in the piece, after behaving like a noisy mischievous child, I take the head off the costume and speak without a microphone about how I hope people in the audience are still thinking about having sex with me. Toward the end of the piece I add that I would like them to think about what it would be like between us afterwards. So not just playing with unexpected carnality, but also asking people to think about what it would be like if we were friends or lovers, if we really knew each other. You can only get away with that attempt at intimacy because of the ludicrous behaviour earlier in the piece. Our seriousness is always riding on another energy. [CM]

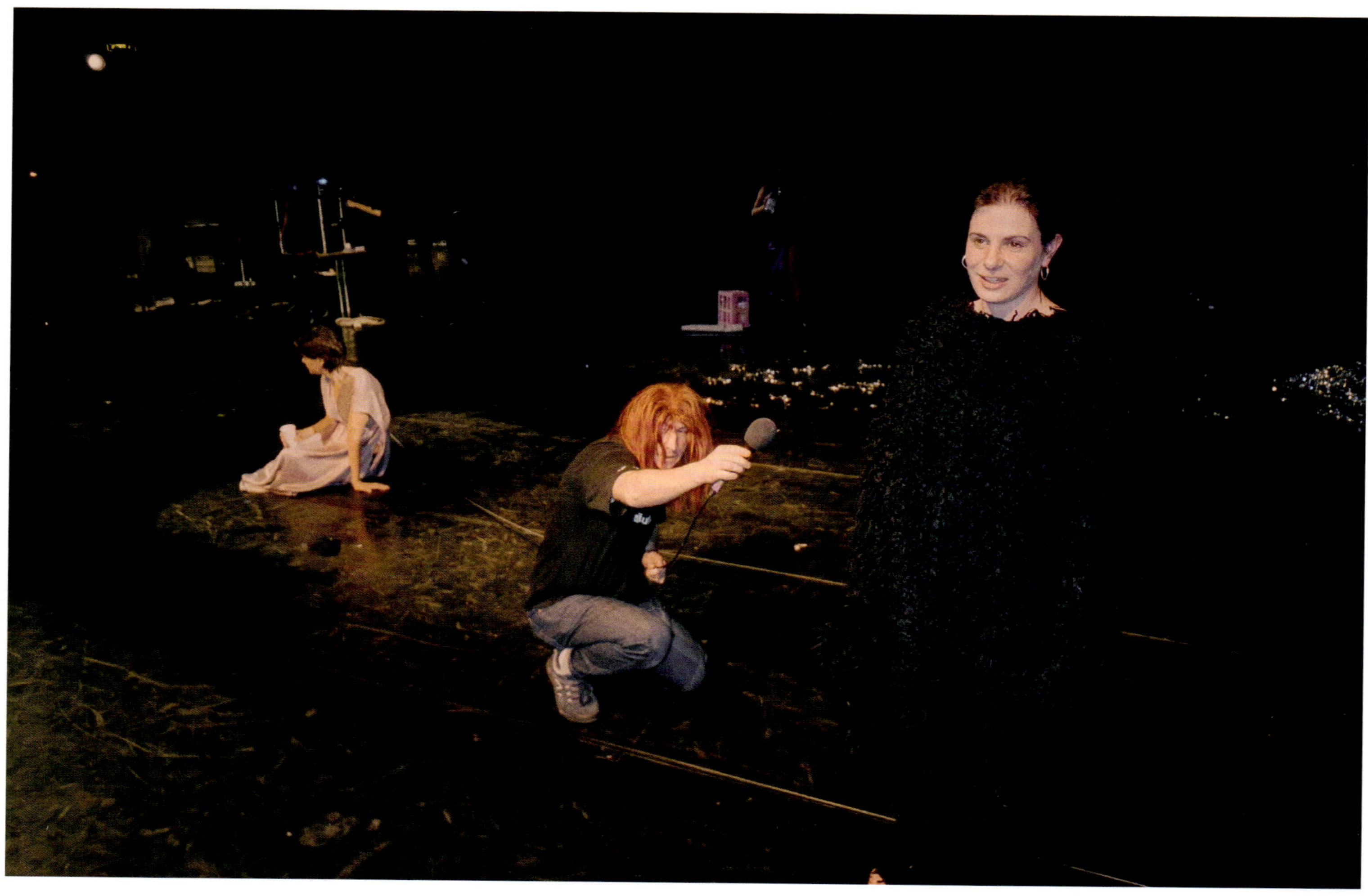

The final 'beginning'—about forty minutes into the show—is from John, who is still in the clown makeup: he swings his tall chair into place near the front of the stage and announces that he will tell the story of the beginning of the universe. So the piece 'begins' with the Big Bang and 'ends' with John telling a story of what he says will be the end of the world: a meteorite hitting the earth, destroying the planet, and ending all life. John frames the chaos of the piece through these extreme, elemental narratives—stories about creation and destruction—and they find echoes in almost all the material.

The composition combines different performance realities that are overlaid and slide past each other, driven by conflicting desires. Cathy wants to be the prompt for an overwhelming emotion, an intense grief that goes on forever. Richard and Robin are heavy metal roadies: chasing the rough glamour of a rock show, with noise, smoke, and lights. Bruno and John (as clowns) see the whole thing as a ground for their double-act animosity. Claire (as gorilla) invokes the anarchic energy of the circus, throwing sweets at the audience and fooling around. Terry's role mutates:

from diva-esque theatrical performance to the cliched emotions of a pop video. Wendy (as cheerleader) 'cheers' on whatever is available to her, often in a negative cajoling way. Jerry and Davis are like backing dancers: always inserting themselves into whatever is happening. The dramaturgical principle is that figures (and often pairs of figures) are collaged elements ripped from other contexts. The piece comes from the friction and negotiation between these different elements—a set of tensions that are never resolved. [TE]

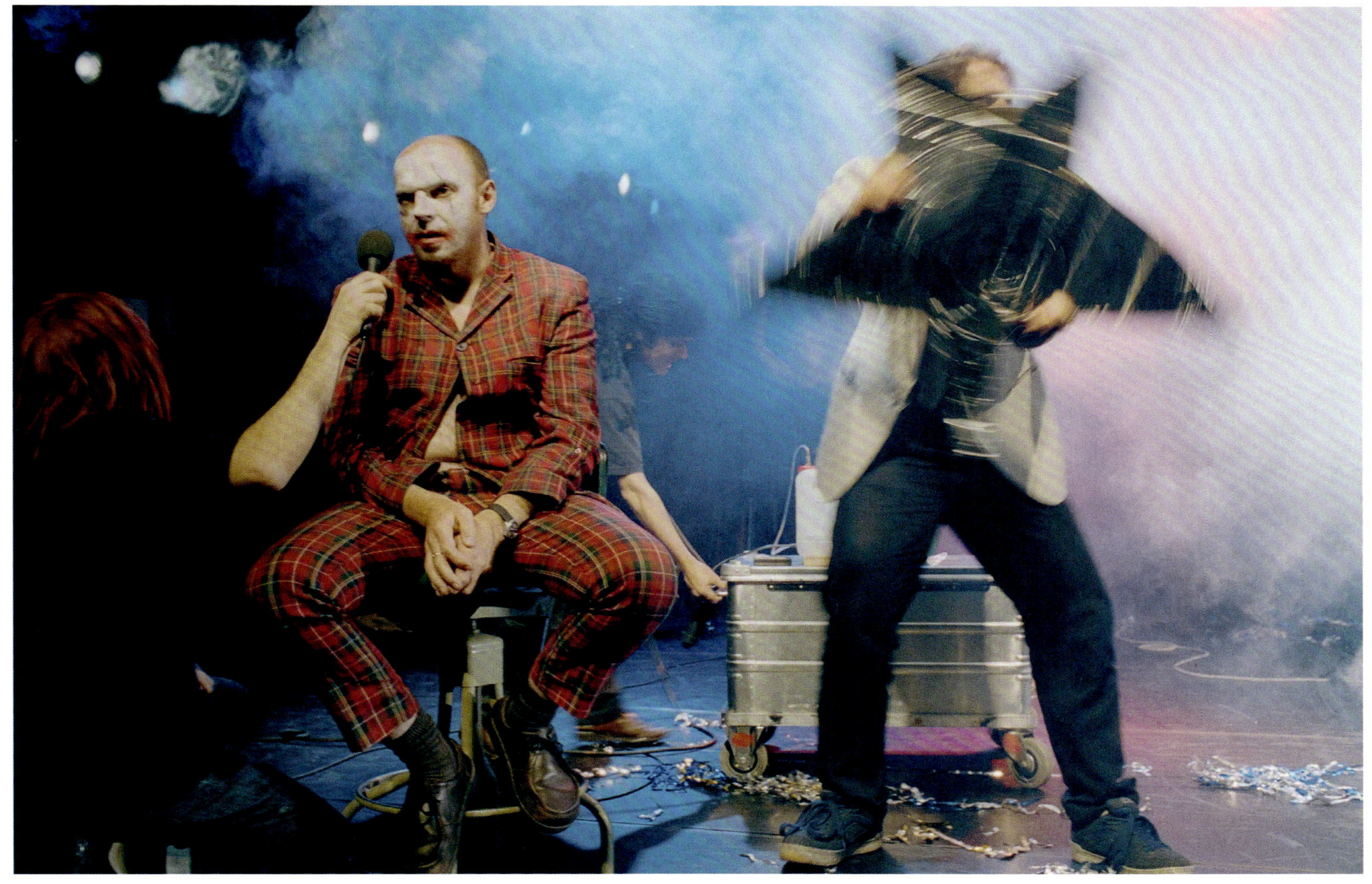

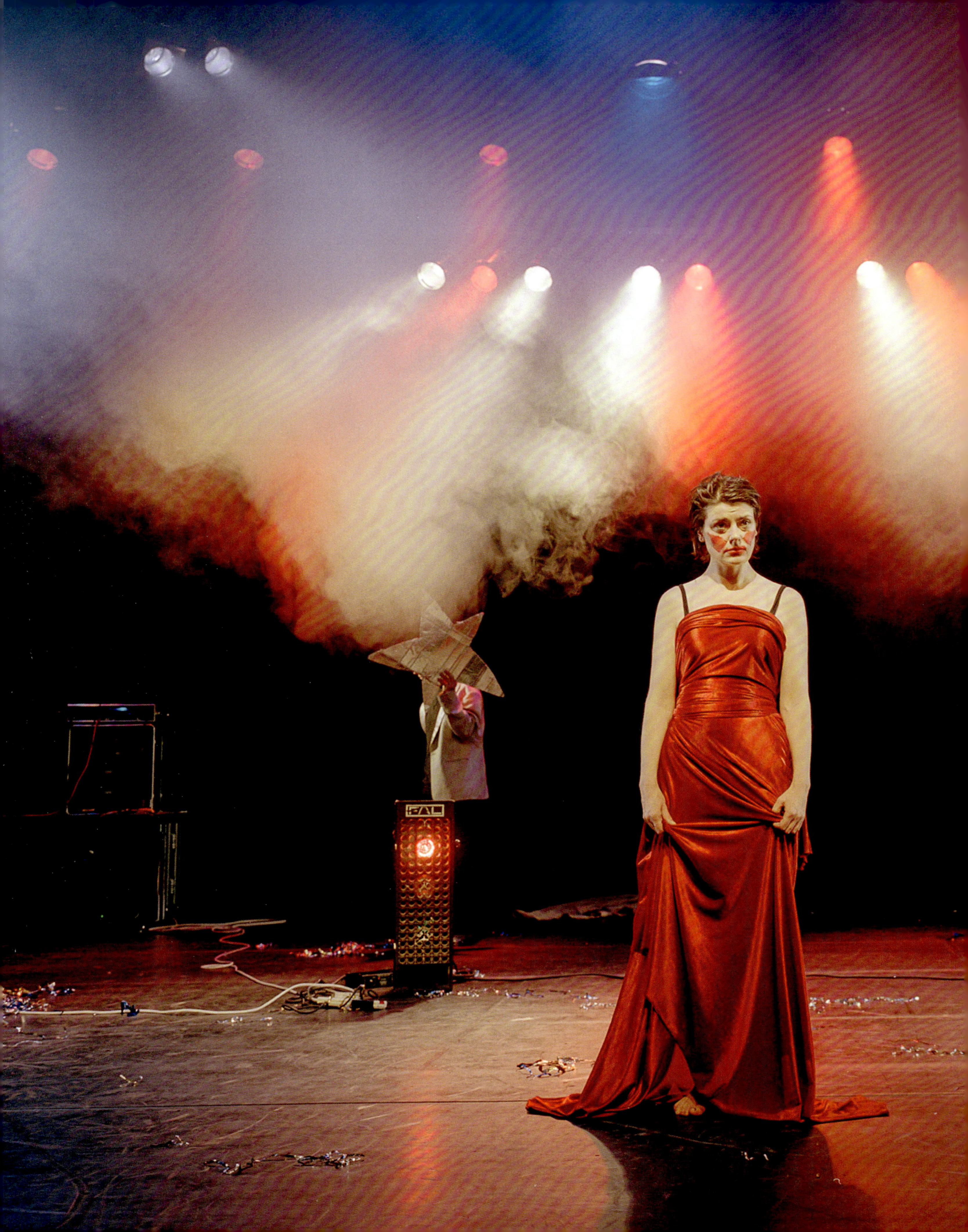

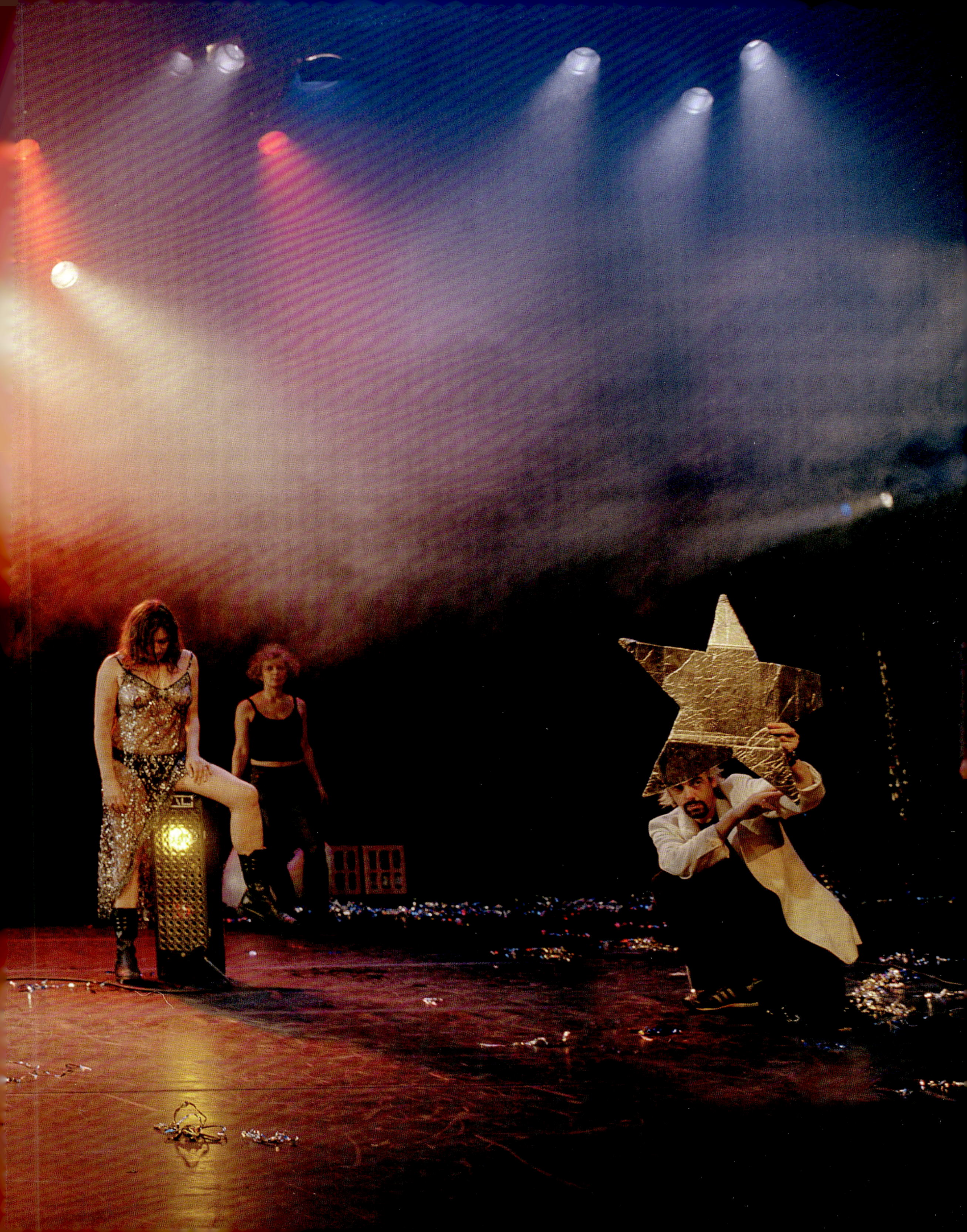

Everyone in *Bloody Mess* has a different idea of what they think should be happening and I am intent on performing my death scene. I have several attempts at it, each of which gets interrupted in different ways. Whenever I try to make a touching, very poignant moment happen, it is failing. So, every time I have to 'up the stakes'. Eventually, I end up in a pretty ludicrous, attention-grabbing costume, swathed in red velvet fabrics with wet hair, red face paint, and smeared red lips. I have transformed in order to claim the space to do the scene. When we make work, we are often pushing performers into a place with disruptions, so that they end up saying things they would not normally say, or they make impossible claims for themselves. So I am really bigging myself up to do something extraordinary, something unforgettable, something that is going to affect the audience forever. After all that talk, I have nowhere to go except to lie down on the floor, as if dead or dying. On the back of a big claim and the failure that goes with it, there is the space to have some small, resolved, quiet moment. [CN]

Cathy: [*To audience*] Don't look at me. Don't look at me. Stop looking at me. Please don't look at me. I don't want you to look at me now. I only want you to look at me when I'm lying down.

In a moment I'm going to lie down and when I do you're going to be overwhelmed. You're going to start to cry and you won't be able to stop for the rest of the show. You're going to keep crying right to the end. You're going to cry as you leave the theatre, you're going to cry all the way home.

Wendy: [*From the sidelines, stage right*] Keep going Cath! It's really working.

Cathy: You're going to cry at home in bed tonight before you sleep and when you wake up in the morning, the sheets will be soaked and you'll still be crying and wherever you go, whatever you do tomorrow, you'll still be crying. You'll cry in the toilets at work. You'll cry in the aisles of the supermarkets, you'll cry when you pick the kids up ...

Wendy: Go on. Push it, Cath!

[*Throughout the whole section Terry mimes crying, sat on a lighting unit behind Cathy, splashing tears on her face when there are pauses in Cathy's text.*]

Cathy: You'll start to get scared that this crying is never going to stop—and it won't. You'll cry every week until the end of the month, you'll cry into next month, till the end of the year, and the tears will still fall all through that year, and into the years after that, and you'll cry all through that year, and into the one after that, and the one after that ...

Wendy: Even harder, Cath,

Cathy: When I lie down you're going to start to cry and you are going to cry for the rest of your lives. And I'm going to do that now.

[*Cathy goes to lie down. As she does so, there is another accidental sound from Bruno's hooter.*]

Bruno: Sorry.

Cathy: [*Reclining, leaning on her elbow*] I just want to make it clear why this is sad. It's sad because of my frailty. Because when I lie down you'll see for the first time how frail a person is and in that picture you'll see your own weakness, your own vulnerability. And that will start the flood of your tears.

And for the rest of your lives you'll look back on this evening, on this moment, on the moment of me lying down, and you'll say that's when everything changed ...

[*From their place stood behind the sound desk Richard and Robin have selected a piece of music that they think might 'help'. Jack Nitzsche's 'Harry Flowers' (1970) begins to play. As if cued by the music the stars begin to move, making a simple dance of slow arcs.*]

And you'll say that's when everything changed. When she lay down, when she did that, something inside me broke and I was changed forever. Because in the end this is you. This is all you are. Because you are me. I'm dying, I'm slipping away and you can see it. You're watching me slip away but you're slipping away too. When I lie down you'll cry and cry and cry and cry and you are never going to stop for the rest of your lives. And now you can look, if you dare.

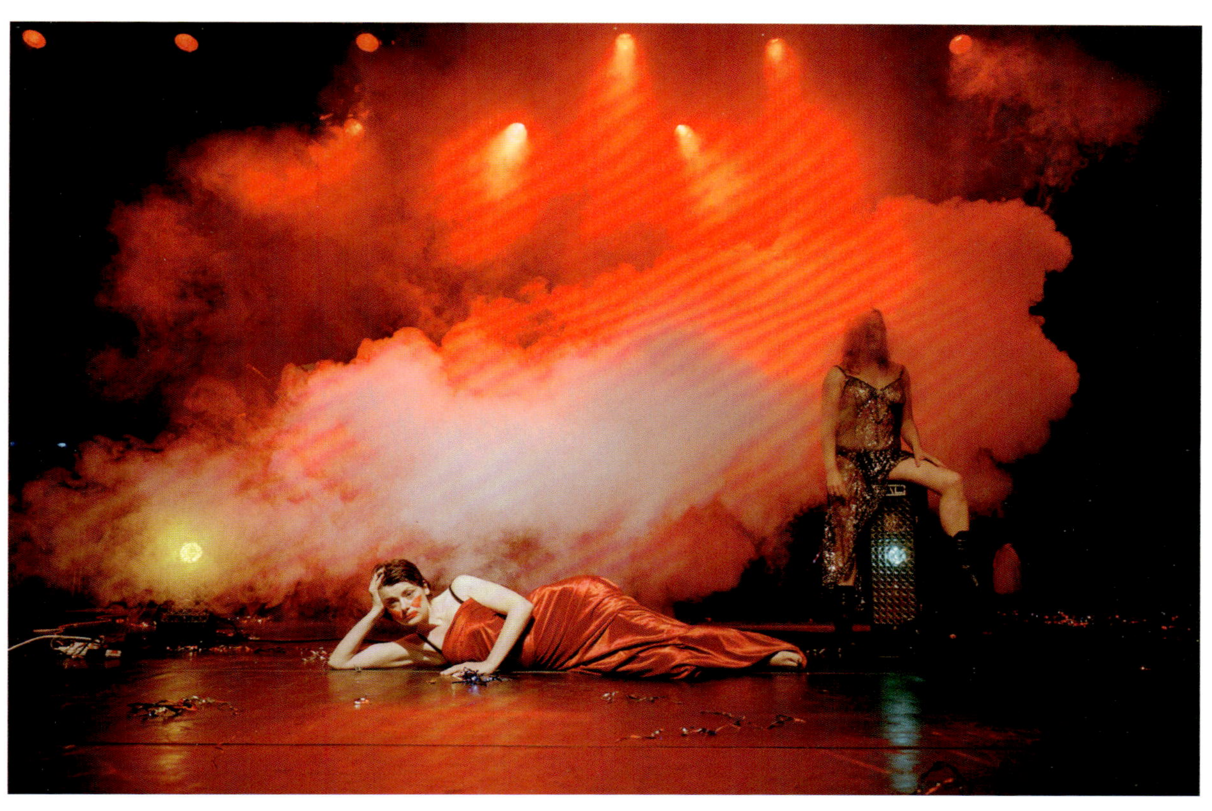

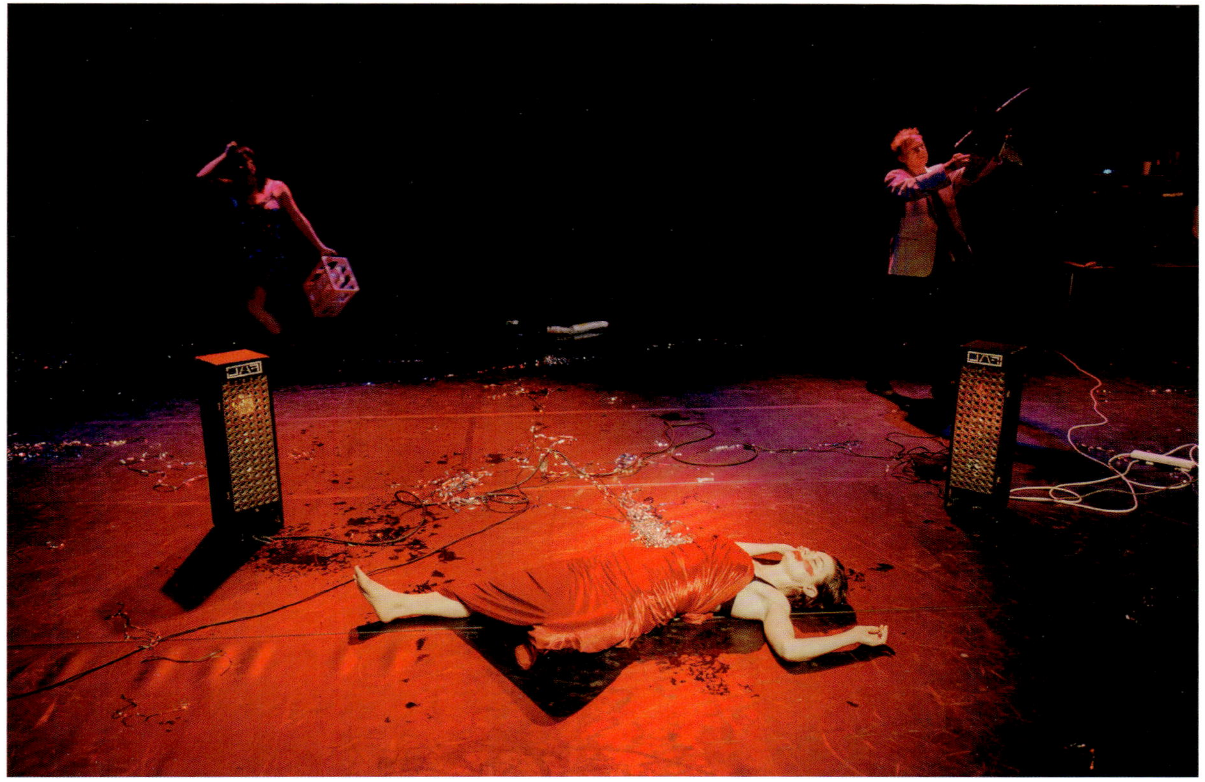

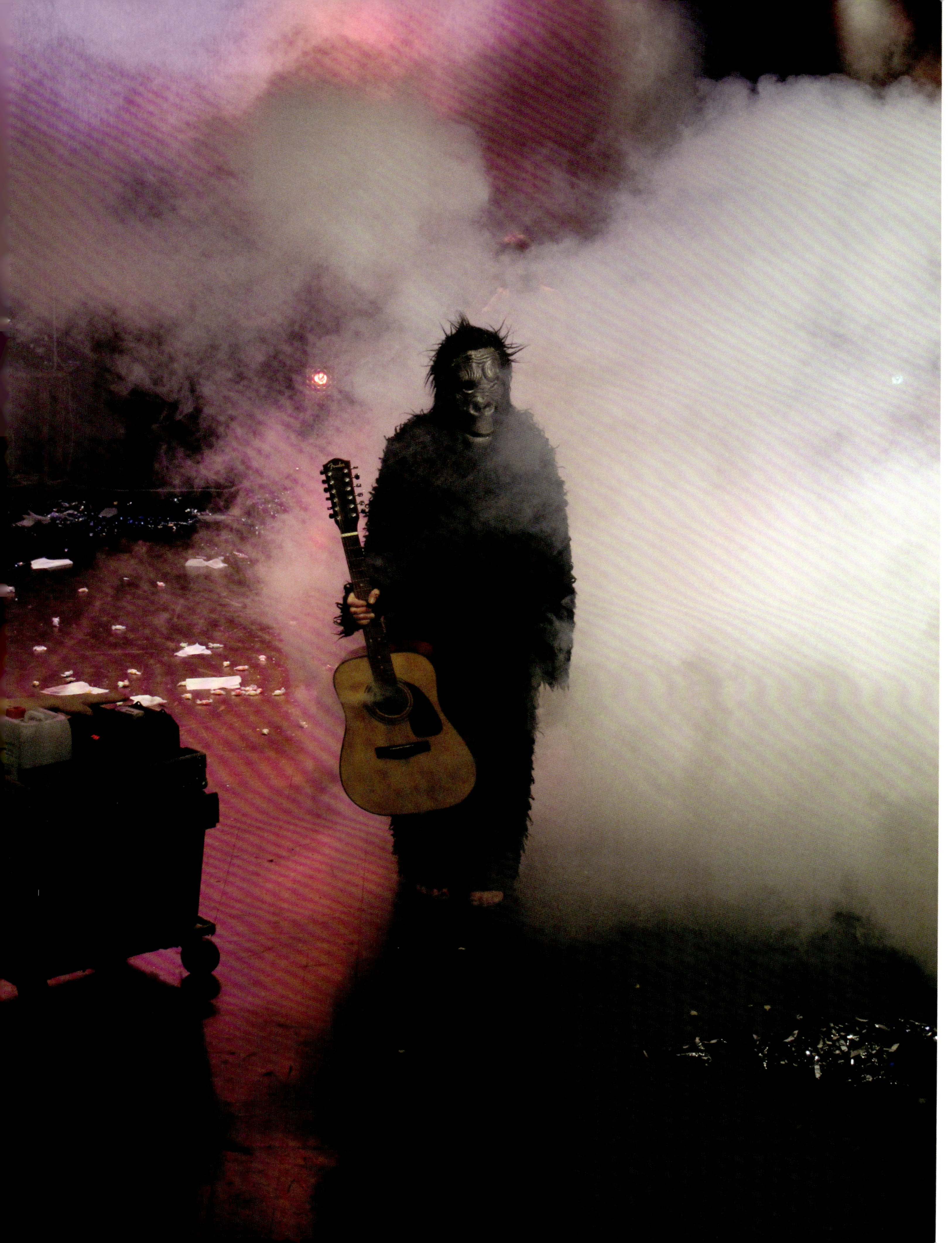

The whole show is made from the competing demands on the stage— negotiations, interruptions, addresses to the audience, fighting, and dancing— destruction and creation from things in collision. It starts on a stripped bare stage, a stark picture that gets added to and made more complex, layer by layer, scene by scene. As is often the case in our work, the costume changing is part of the action, but here we also add lights and smoke, and then more lights and more smoke, and music at high volume. Lighting designer Nigel Edwards knew to start the piece with a quite flat, everyday feeling to the lights, and then to build it up. By the end it's more or less rock gig lighting—banks of par cans and colour cutting through the smoke— which really amplifies the energy of the performance. [TE]

Richard and I spent most of the show wearing long wigs pretending to be roadies, convinced that the whole thing should be a rock gig: laying cables, lighting things, holding mics for people who could easily hold their own mics if they wanted to. As figures, the roadies are a great excuse for being cheeky because their position is so menial, they're not really connected with any of the supposed 'art' that is being presented and because of that, they're allowed to be incredibly disruptive. We are never very happy to leave beautiful objects or scenes in place. We always want to turn the thing upside down or break it to see what's inside. The idea of theatre as a beautiful object, something pristine, doesn't sit well with us. It always needs to be undermined. [RA]

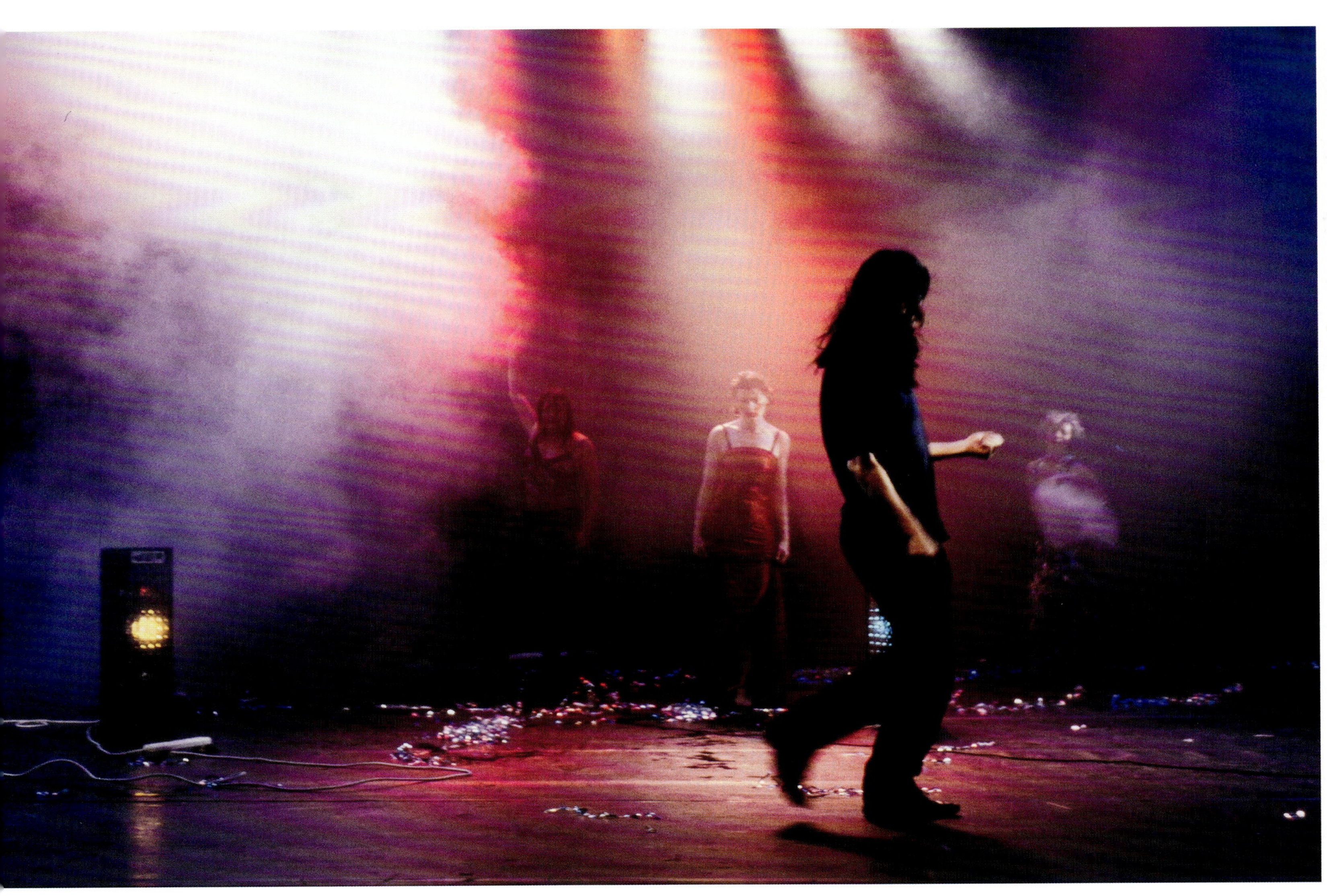

[*Robin approaches John and Bruno, who
are lying exhausted, still holding onto
each other. Robin sticks the mic towards
them and amplifies the sound of their
heavy breathing, switching from one to
the other to vary the sound.*]

John: Oh god, oh god. Is that
you, Robin?

Robin: Yes—it's me, John. Just carry
on with what you're doing. It's good,
it's good.

John: I think I'm bleeding. I can't open
my left eye. I can't open my eye.

Robin: It's alright: you're not bleeding.
He's not bleeding. You're not bleeding.
You're okay. You're fine.

John: I'm bleeding, Rob. I can taste the
blood in my mouth. I think I might have
lost one of my crowns.

[*Richard arrives with a towel as if to
wipe away the non-existent blood. When
John complains about his teeth Richard
produces a torch from his back pocket
which Richard and Robin then use to look
into John's mouth.*]

Robin: Hang on ... No, your teeth
are fine.

John: [*Speaking about Bruno*]
Is he bleeding?

Robin: No. Nobody's bleeding.

[*Terry, Jerry, and Davis leave the front
of the stage where they ended up at
the climax of their 'Cry Baby' routine.
Retreating to the back of the stage they
open beers and begin to play cards while
the conversation between Robin and John
continues. They remain there until the
subsequent 'Silences' section.*]

John: I'm bleeding, Rob. I'm bleeding.
Rob? Rob? I'm still funny, aren't I, Rob?

Robin: Sorry, John. What do you mean?

John: I'm still funny. Everyone is still
laughing at me, aren't they?

Robin: [*Looks at the audience and waits*]
I think they're taking a little break
right now, John.

John: I think I can hear a young lady
laughing. I can, Rob. I am still funny,
aren't I, Rob? Rob? Rob? I am still
funny, aren't I? I'm still the funny one,
aren't I? Rob? I'm still funny, aren't I?
I'm the winner, aren't I? The winner?
The funny winner?

Bloody Mess was one of those sledgehammer
shows—loud music, lots of physical
exertion, lots of yelling, lots of smoke, full
on lights—but doing it repeatedly, it always
felt like quite a fragile thing. It was really
easy to overdo it and play it too elegiacally,
or beat on the audience too hard. When it
was really working, it was a delicate thing.
We made lots of small decisions around
timing that had to stay quite human scale.
[CM]

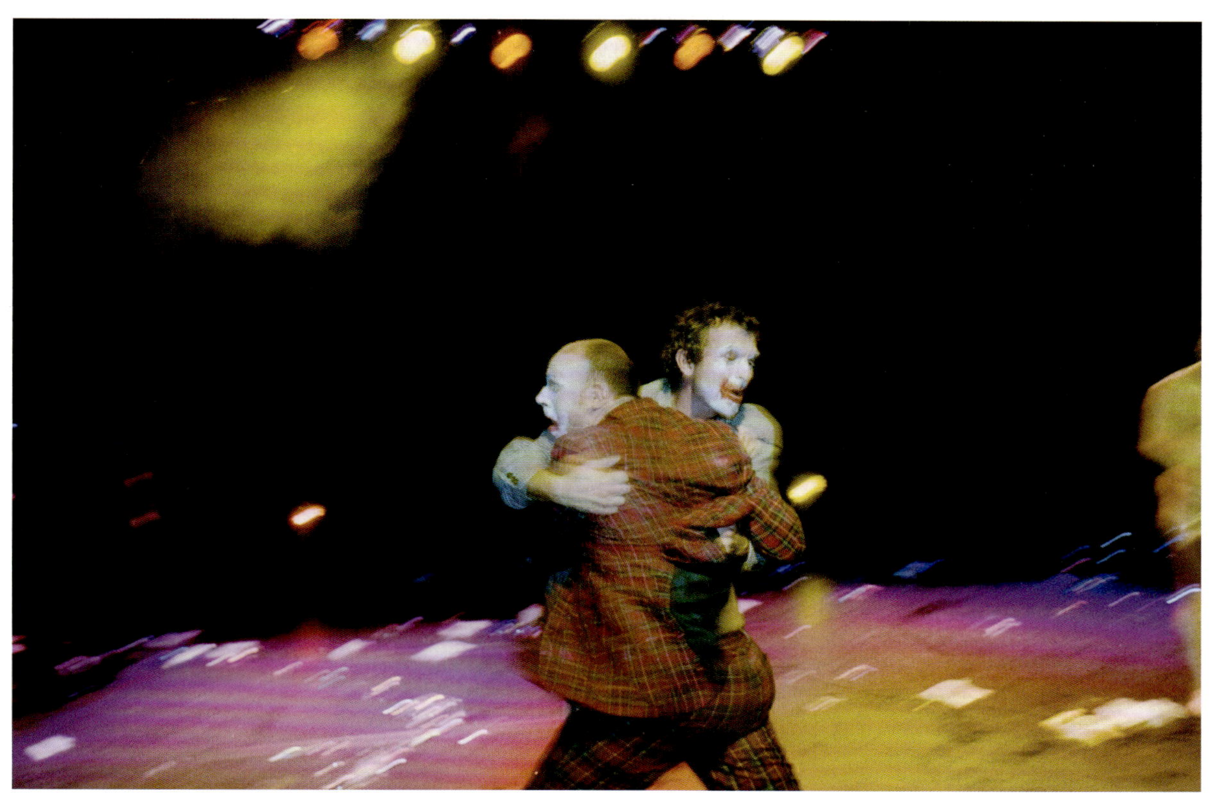

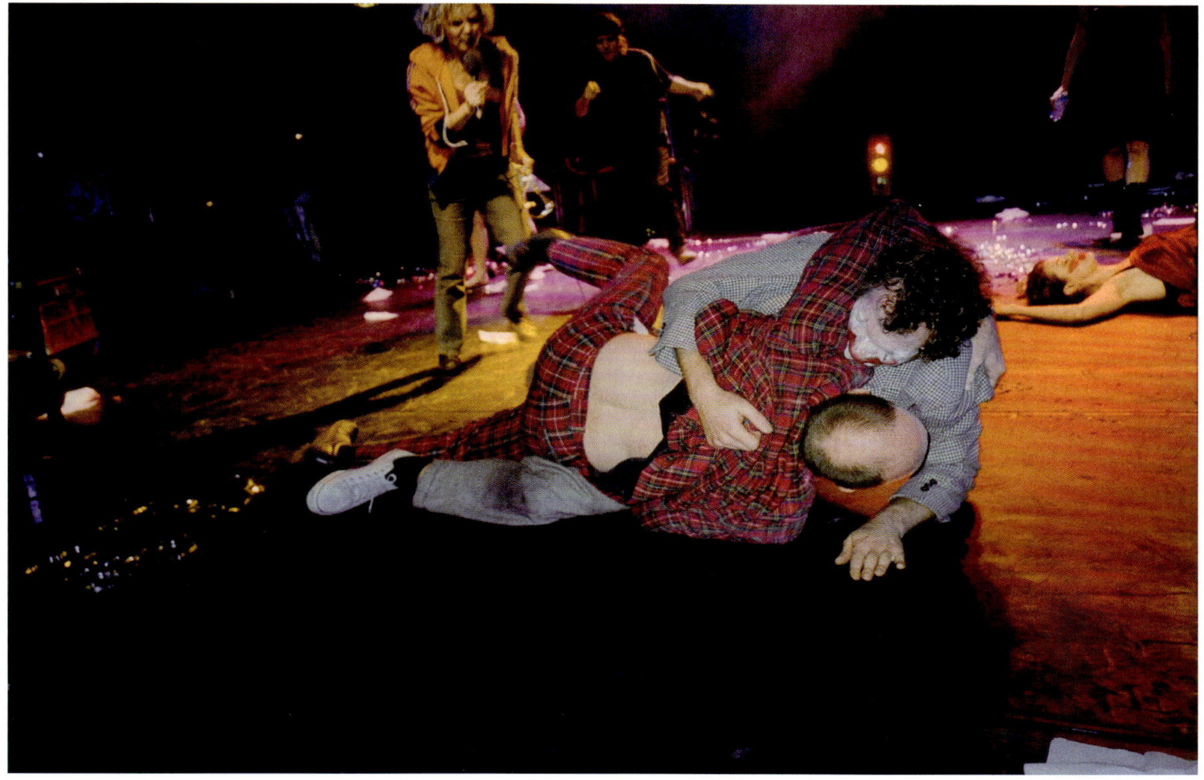

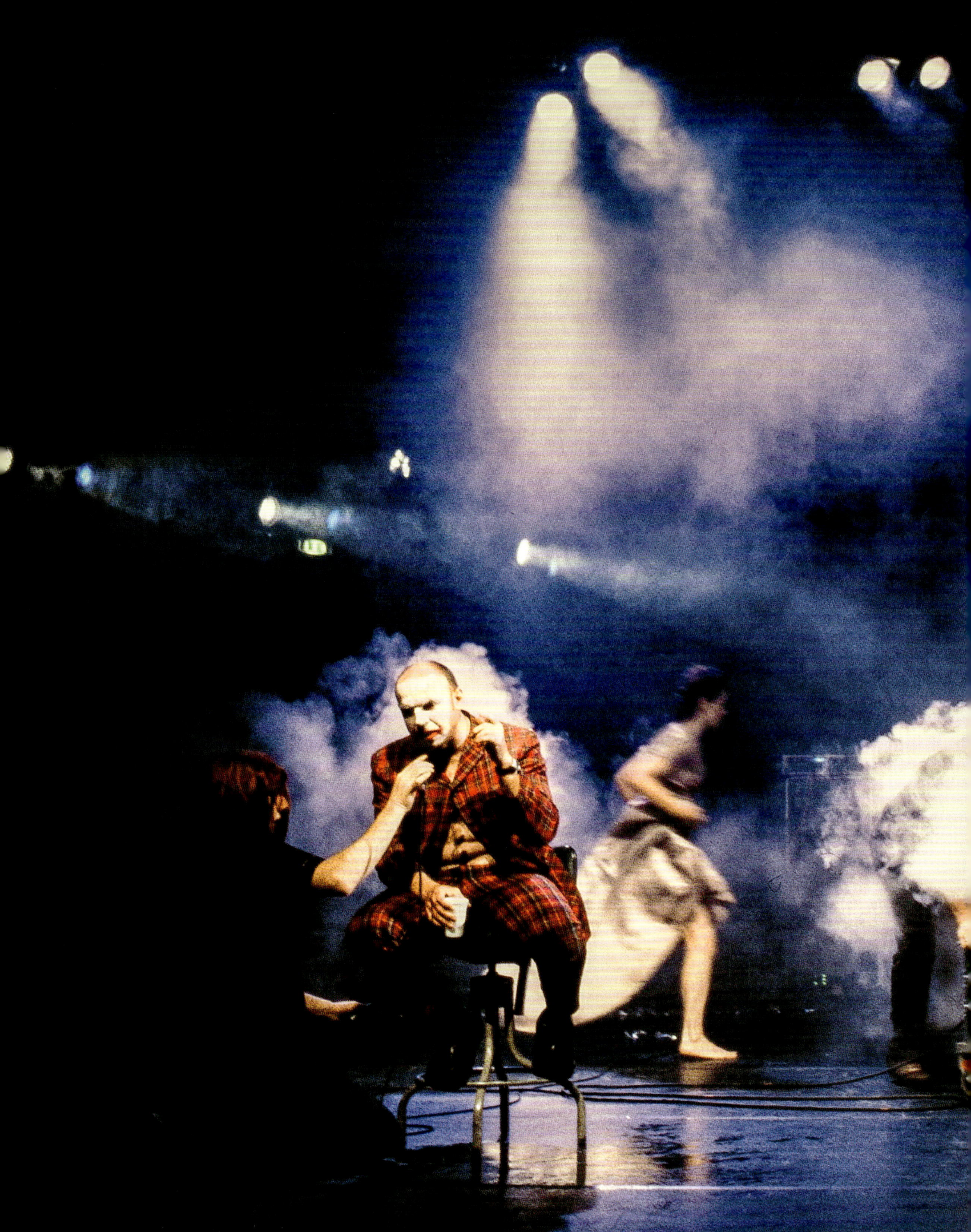

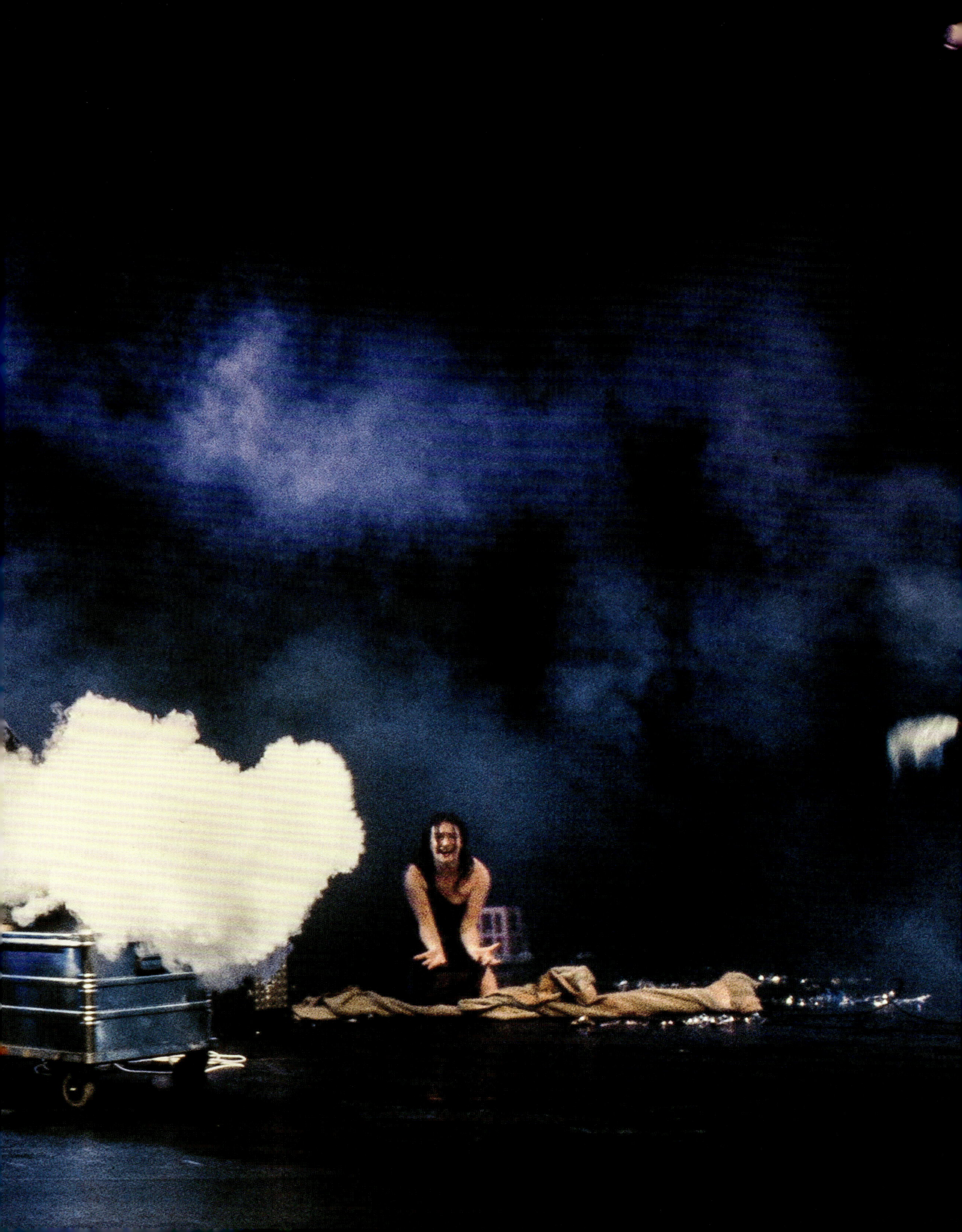

Richard: One-Two.

Wendy: [*Yelling*] Finish the fucking
thing, John! Come on. Smash it up,
smash it up, John. Tiny little fucking
pieces. Come on—what are you waiting
for? We're all fucking waiting. Come
on, smash it apart, get us to the end,
John, just get us to the finish. Can't
hear you, John, we can't fucking hear
you. What are you waiting for, John?
Come on, smash it apart.

Richard: One-Two.

Wendy: [*Yelling*] Fragments, John. We want
tiny little fucking fragments. Come on,
John. Little fucking shards. What are
you waiting for?

[*Richard whispers to John throughout
the song, feeding him all his lines.*]

John: Thank you, London, and goodnight.
[*The city name gets adjusted depending
on where the show is being performed.*]

Wendy: [*Yelling*] That's not a fucking
ending! That is not an ending, John.
Come on, finish it up.

John: [*Again repeating what Richard has
said to him, this time with more vigour*]
Thank you, London, and goodnight.

Wendy: [*Yelling*] You can do better than
that, John! We deserve better than
that—come on, finish it.

John: [*Again repeating what Richard has
said to him, with yet more vigour*] Thank
you, London, and goodnight!

Wendy: [*Yelling*] No, John! That is not
fucking good enough. We want little
shards John. We want sharp little
fucking shards.

John: [*Taking the line from Richard*]
You've been fucking great.

[*Terry moves backwards and forwards
during the song, thrashing with one
of Wendy's pompoms. Jerry dances with
his star. Davis moves round the stage
shredding the silver tinsel that was
the 'meteorite' into smaller and smaller
pieces, throwing the pieces to the
ground. Cathy sits on the side of the
stage and puts the finishing touches to
her final costume: black smeared makeup
to go with the black bra and lace tutu.
Claire (as gorilla) takes a second trip
round the auditorium, throwing paper
tissues to the audience as if they might
need them for their tears.*]

Wendy: [*Yelling*] Tinier, John! We
want tinier fragments, sharp little
splinters, John. Come on, shatter it,
shatter it, John. Come on, John. Sharp
little fucking shards all over the
floor. What are you waiting for?

John: [*Taking the line from Richard*]
Just dust.

Wendy: [*Yelling*] Not small enough, John!
Not fucking small enough.

John: [*Taking the line from Richard*]
It's dust.

Wendy: [*Yelling*] No, John, sharper
that that, sharper than that!
Fucking fragments.

John: [*Taking the line from Richard*]
It's dust. It's dust.

Wendy: [*Yelling*] Is that the best you can
do? Is that the fucking best you can do,
John? Come on, shatter it.

John: [*Taking the line from Richard*]
It's dust.

Wendy: [*Yelling*] Tinier, John. Tiny,
little pieces.

John: [*Taking the line from Richard*]
It's just dust, its just dust.

[*'The Night They Drove Old Dixie
Down' ends.*]

John: [*Taking the line from Richard*]
It's dust.

It's just dust.

It's dust.

It's dust.

It's only dust.

It's nothing but dust.

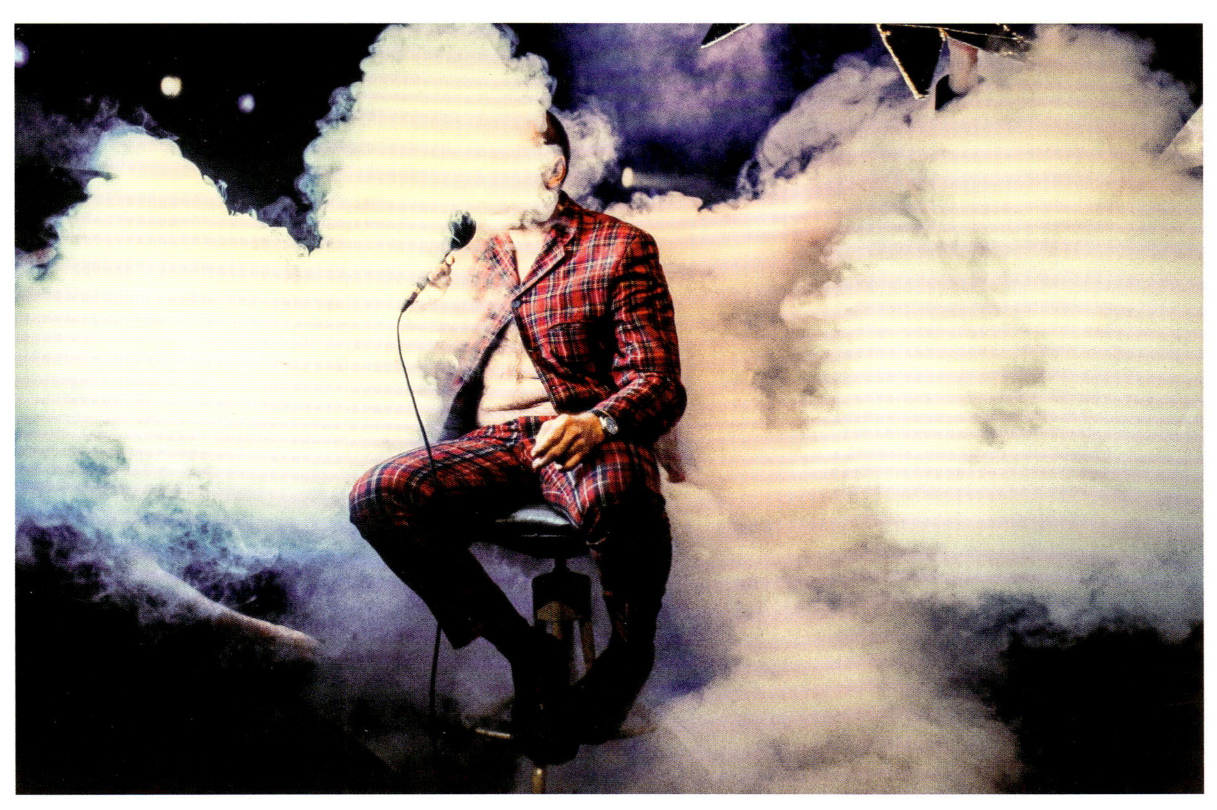

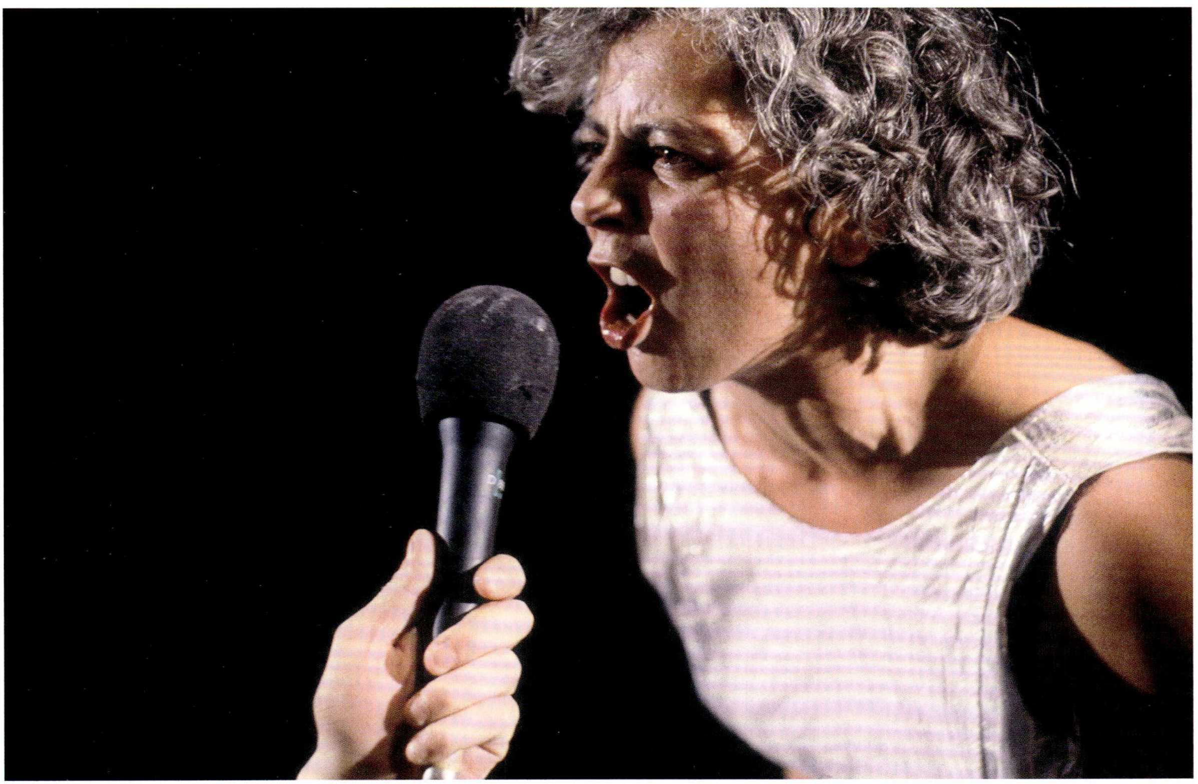

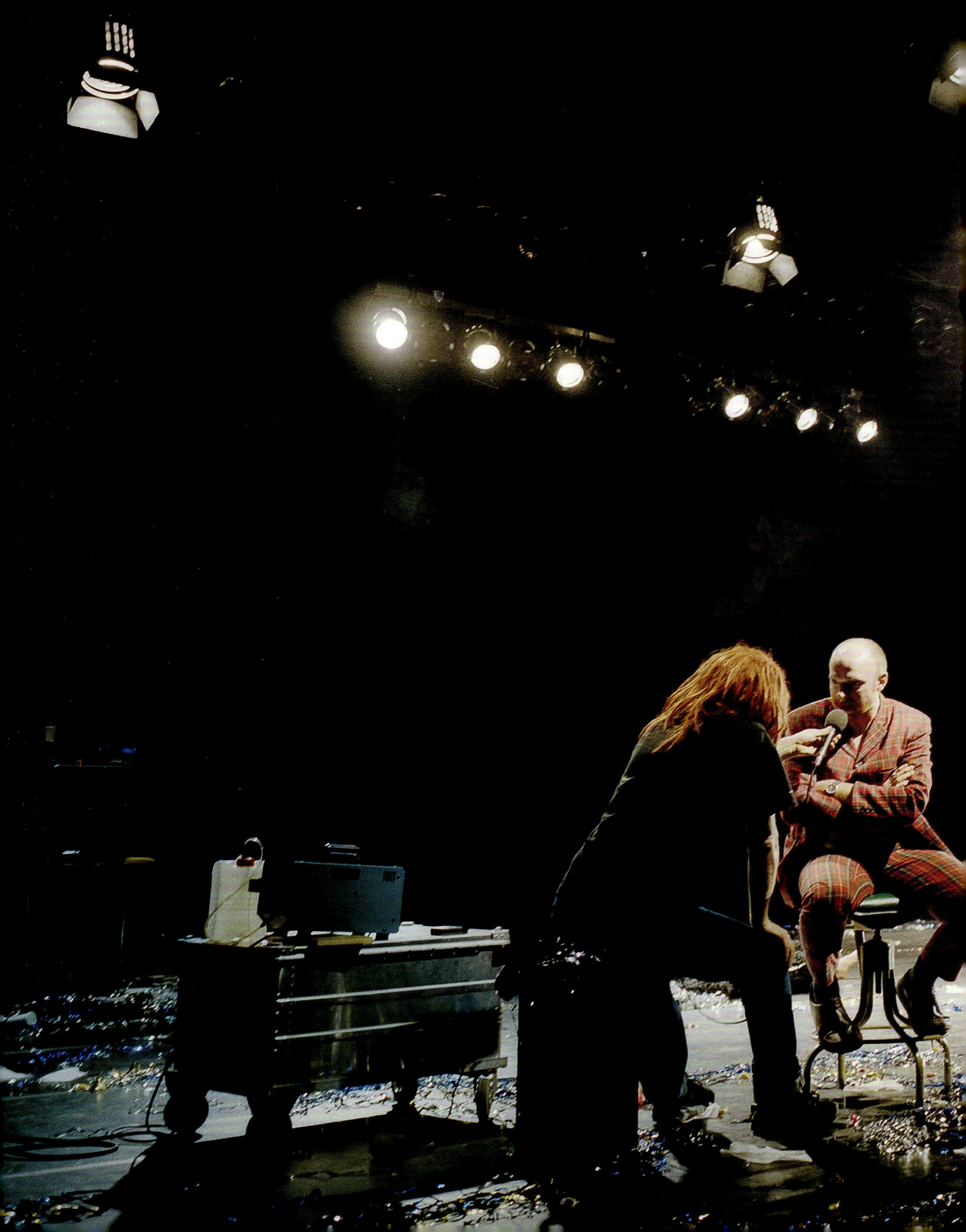

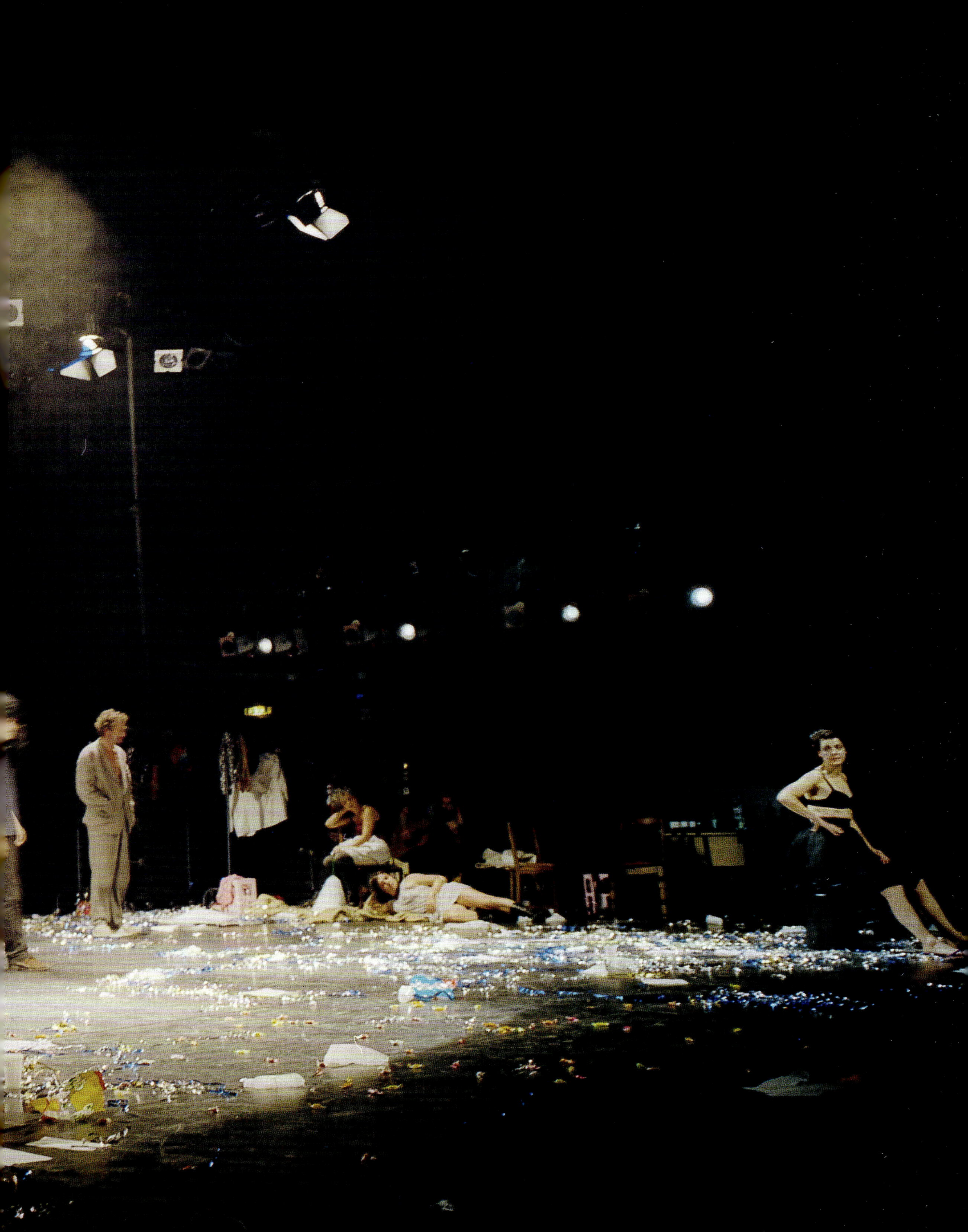

Bloody Mess is good at unbalancing its audience, bouncing off in directions that are difficult to predict, throwing them a line to some new sense, just at the point when they think they have understood what it is all about. It doesn't allow people watching to settle. There is such a war happening on the stage, about meaning. It is a real celebration of the idea that meaning is always diverse and fluid. You cannot simplify things down to a straightforward narrative as it is not convincing, not representative of the world in its complexity.

Somehow, in all of its swirly mess and its constant process of tipping over and undercutting, it arrives at a kind of peace at the end. People agree to disagree. There is always something very moving for me about that moment. [RA]

Cathy: This is the last thing you see.
[*The lights remaining on the stage go out one by one as Cathy is talking.*]

You see me standing in the light.
You're looking at me.

You can see my face. You can see my eyes.
You can see my lips.

You can see that I'm thinking, but my eyes don't really give anything away.

My face is a complete blank. It says nothing and it says everything all at the same time. It's the last thing you see.

You don't know me, or you think you know me. It doesn't matter.

What matters is that you see me breathing. You see the rise and fall of my breathing.

And maybe you hear sound from outside: the noise of rain on the roof of the theatre, or maybe someone coughs here inside, in the auditorium, or perhaps you hear nothing. It's just quiet.

It's not important. What's important is that you're looking at me.

The lights are going out. And soon, perhaps more suddenly than you had expected, it's over and I'm gone, gone forever and never coming back. This is the final moment. This is the last light.

[*The last of the lights goes out.*]

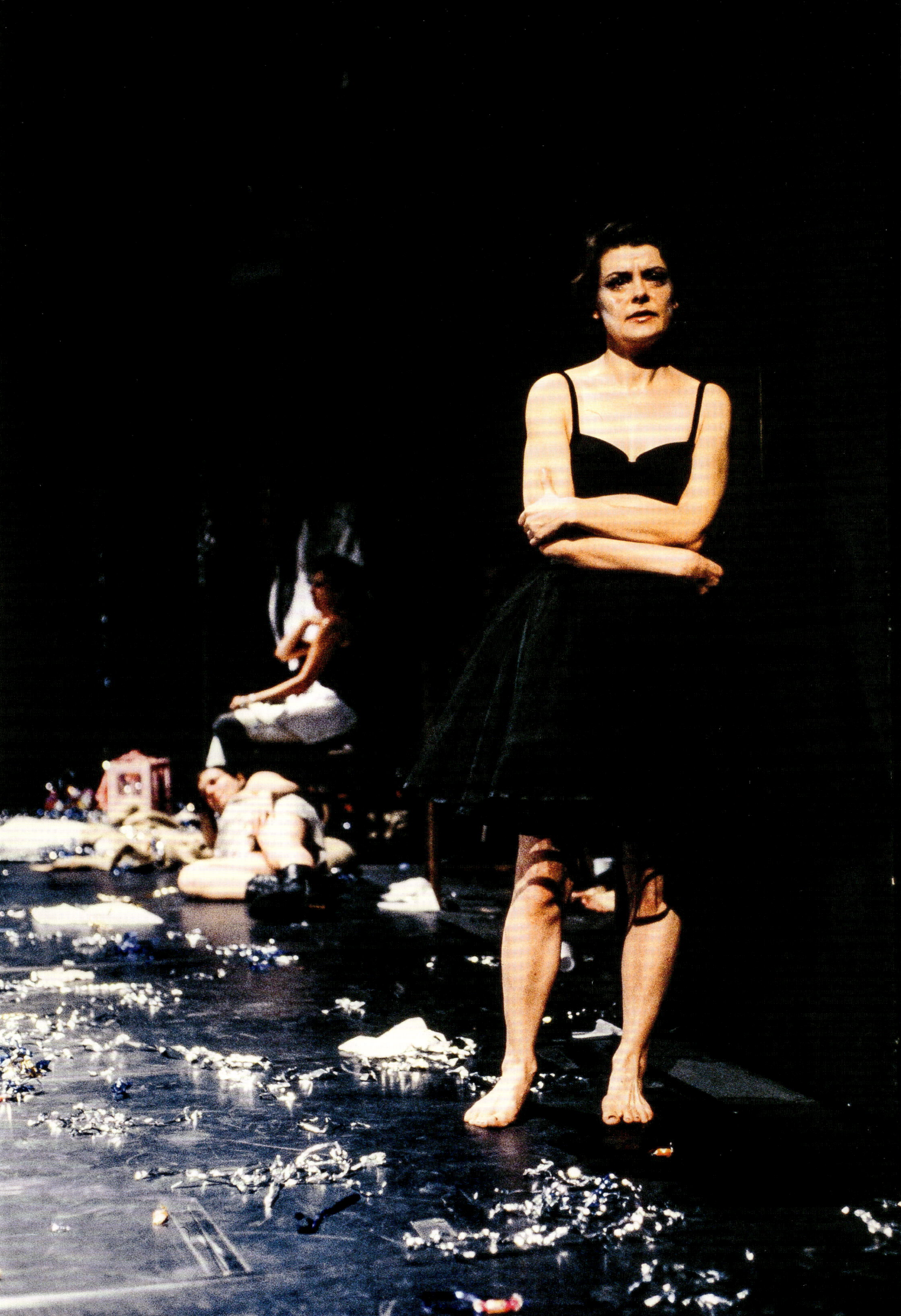

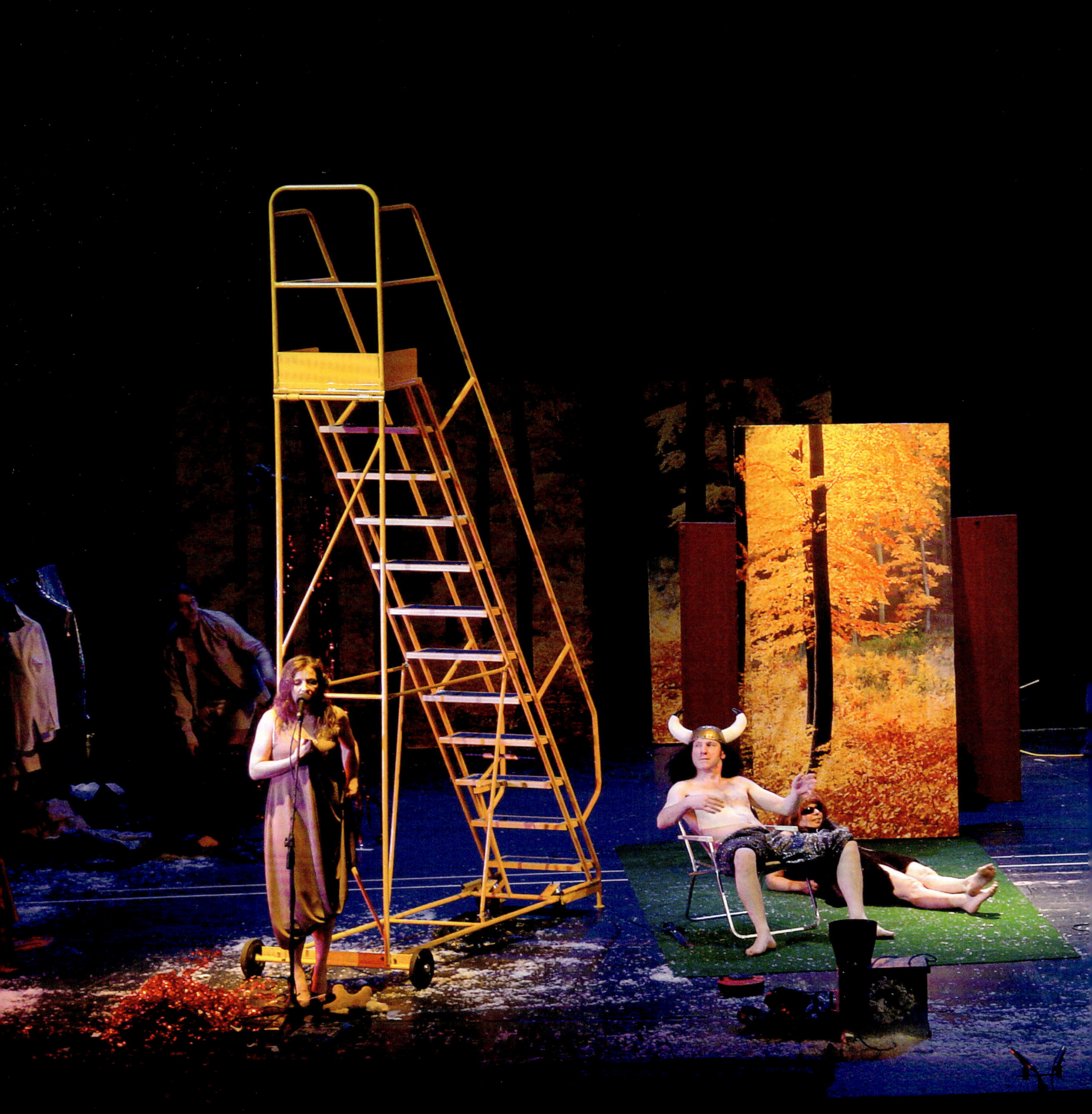

THE WORLD IN PICTURES (2006)

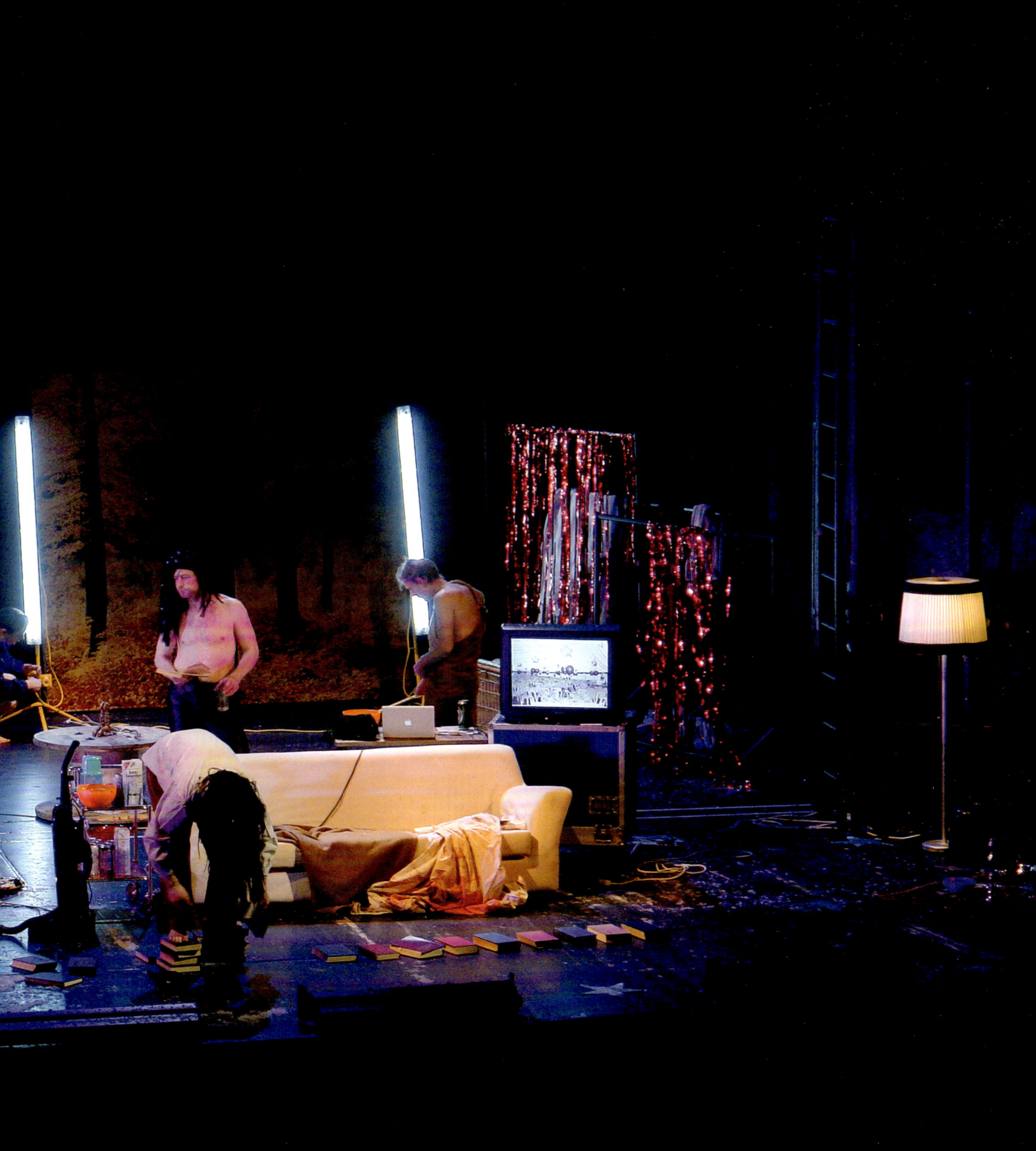

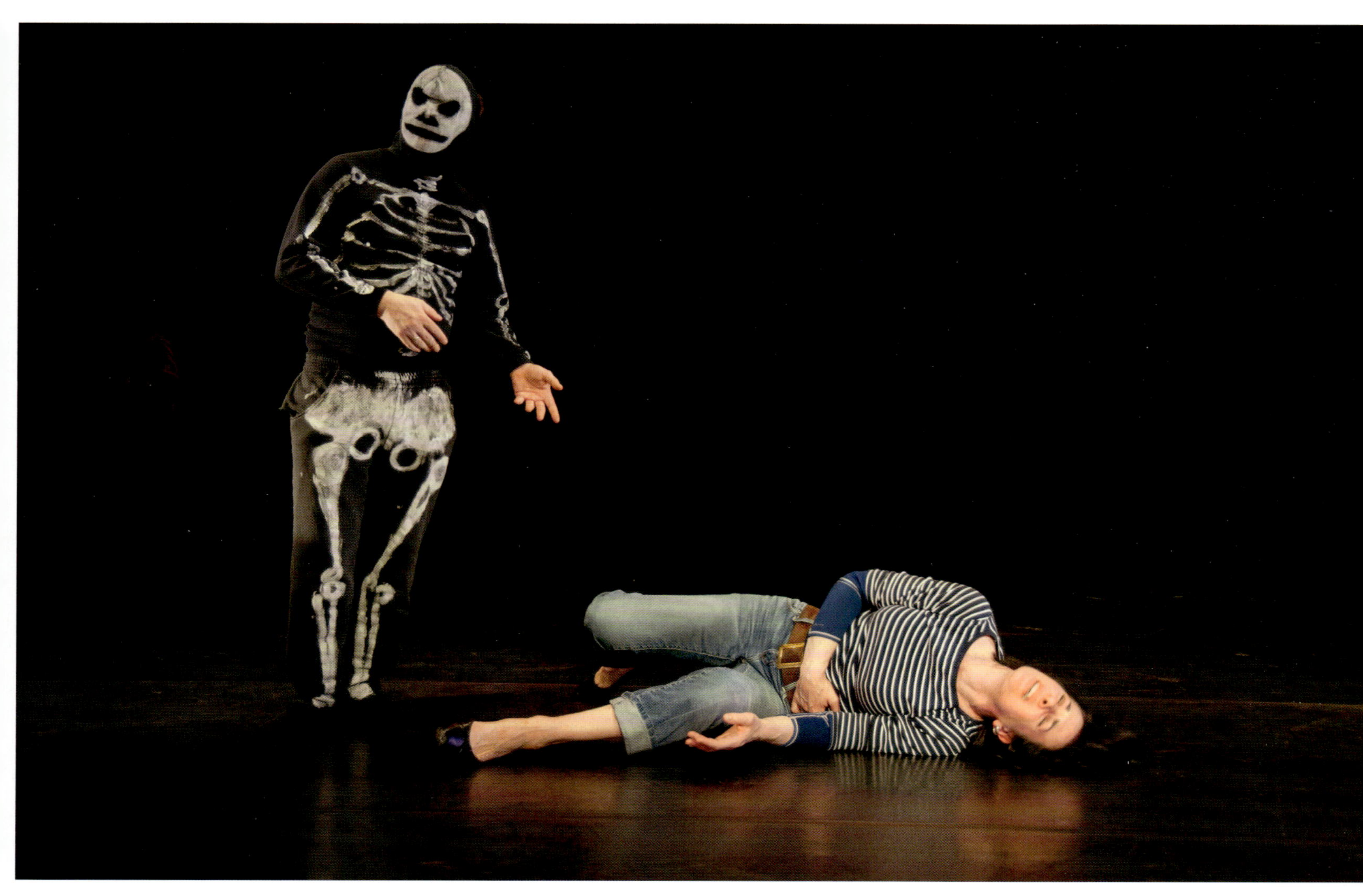

SPECTACULAR (2008)

Robin: Um, okay. Round about now is normally when the band starts to play. They play a little slow, slow number. You can think of it as a kind of interlude. [*Robin walks around behind Claire.*] I really love this bit, actually. I really love what they do, the band. [*Robin comes forward.*] Okay, I probably shouldn't say this because he'll just want more money, but the keyboard player is really very good. I mean, he says that he played with Miles Davis, and I can believe that. If you do the sums, work out the dates, it's possible. He's really something special. It moves me. It really moves me. It's just the music of sunlight, really. It's got that 'sunny afternoon' feel. I mean, it's very light and very joyful, and at the same time. And perhaps because of that it's got this ... How can I describe it? This kind of melancholy. Because, of course, we're being reminded that that's not really here, that sunny afternoon. That's some other time, some other place. And I just find that combination very ... Well, very melancholy. I'm not trying to say that there's some actual sunny afternoon. It's more like some kind of dream. Some perfect sunny afternoon that has never really existed. And perhaps that's where the melancholy lies. But just for the time that it lasts I'm ... Well, 'happy' isn't really the word ... But I am ... transported. And I'm not really thinking ... Well, not much ... But I am 'in possession of thought'. I'm sorry, I can't put it any better than that ... I'm in possession of thought ... Anyway. The music comes to an end. [*Claire has stopped breathing.*] And normally there's quite a strange feeling in the room. Sometimes you get a little ripple of applause running up and down the line. But actually it's as though the crowd itself has been transformed.

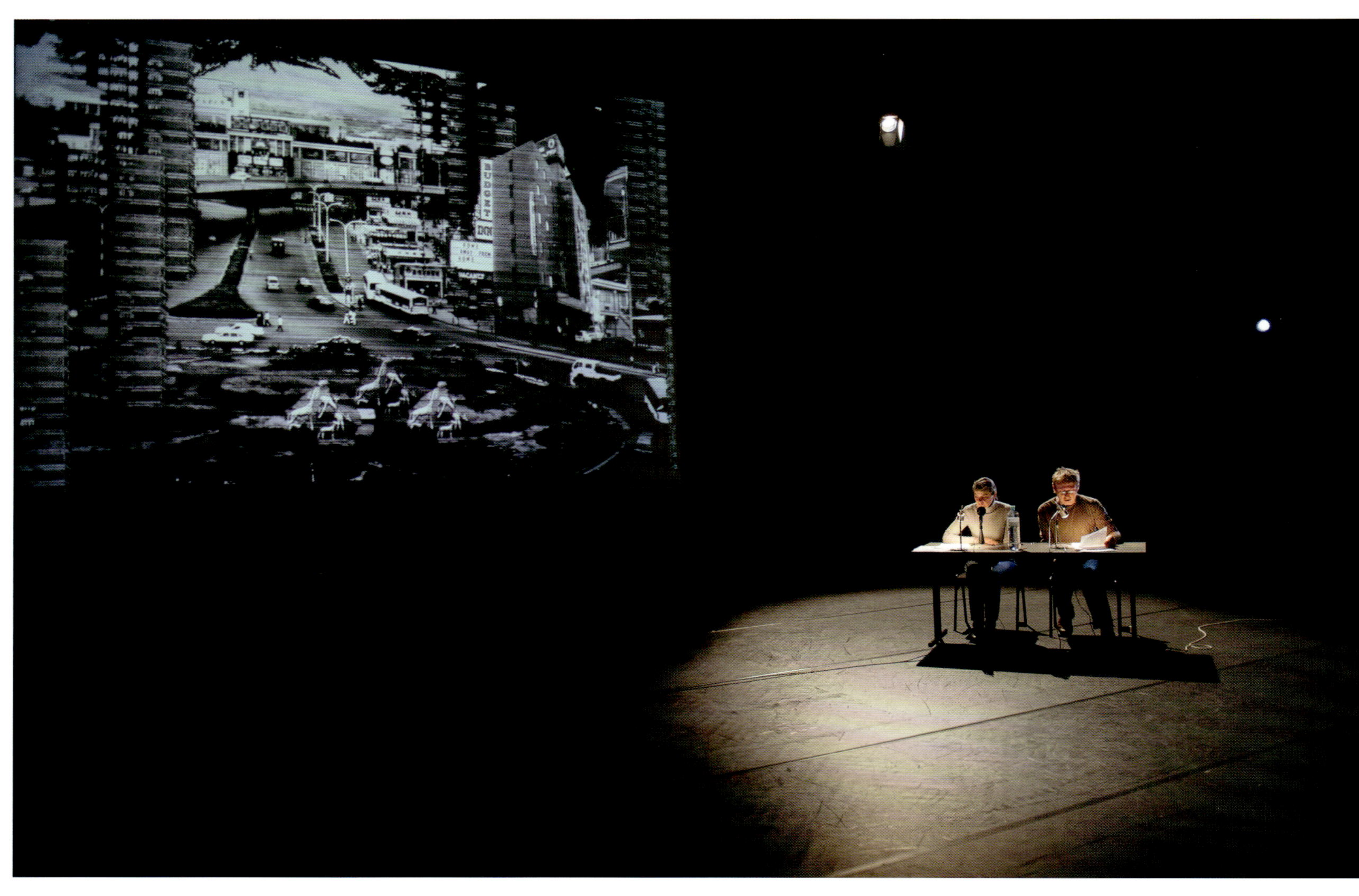

VOID STORY (2009)

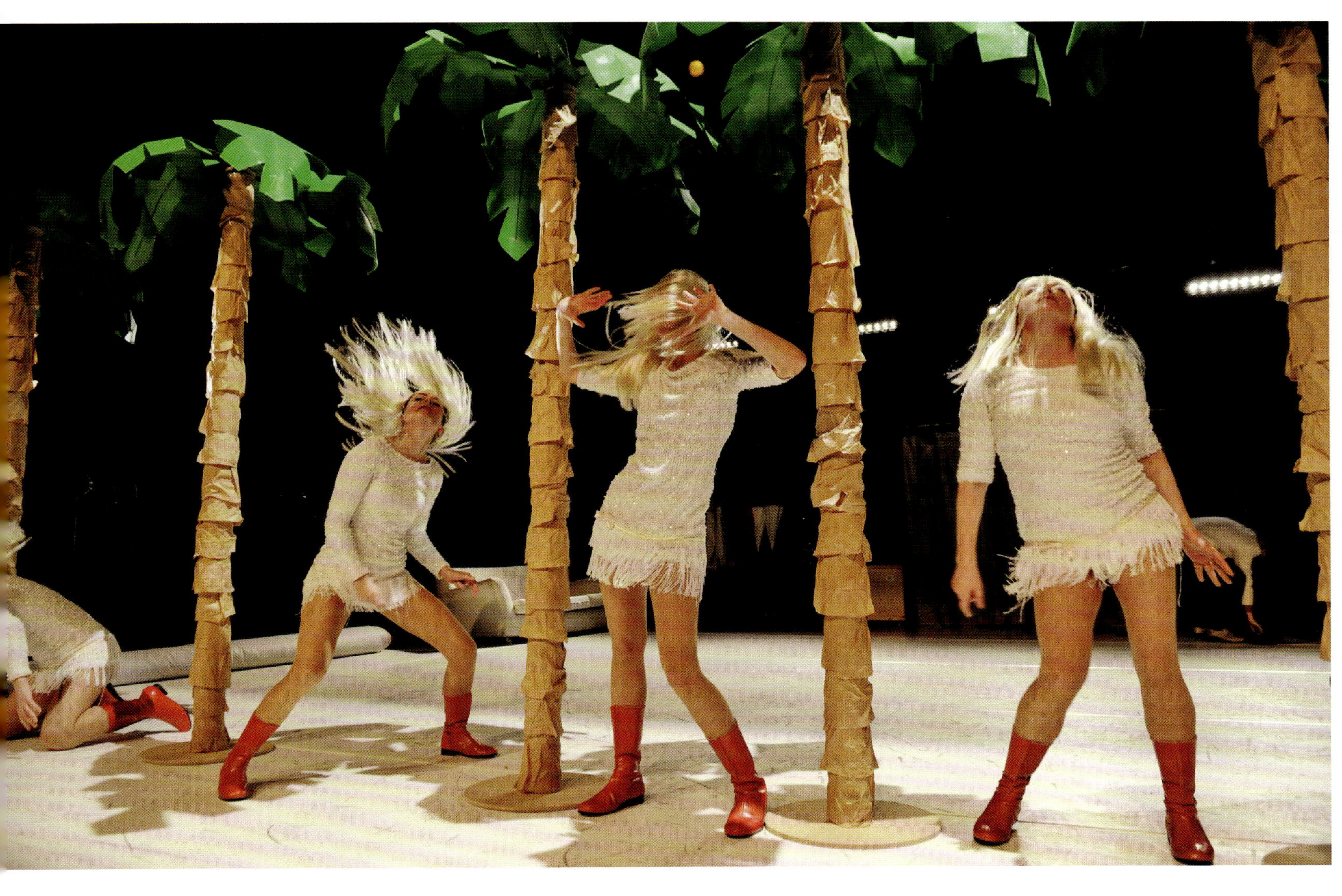

THE THRILL OF IT ALL (2010)

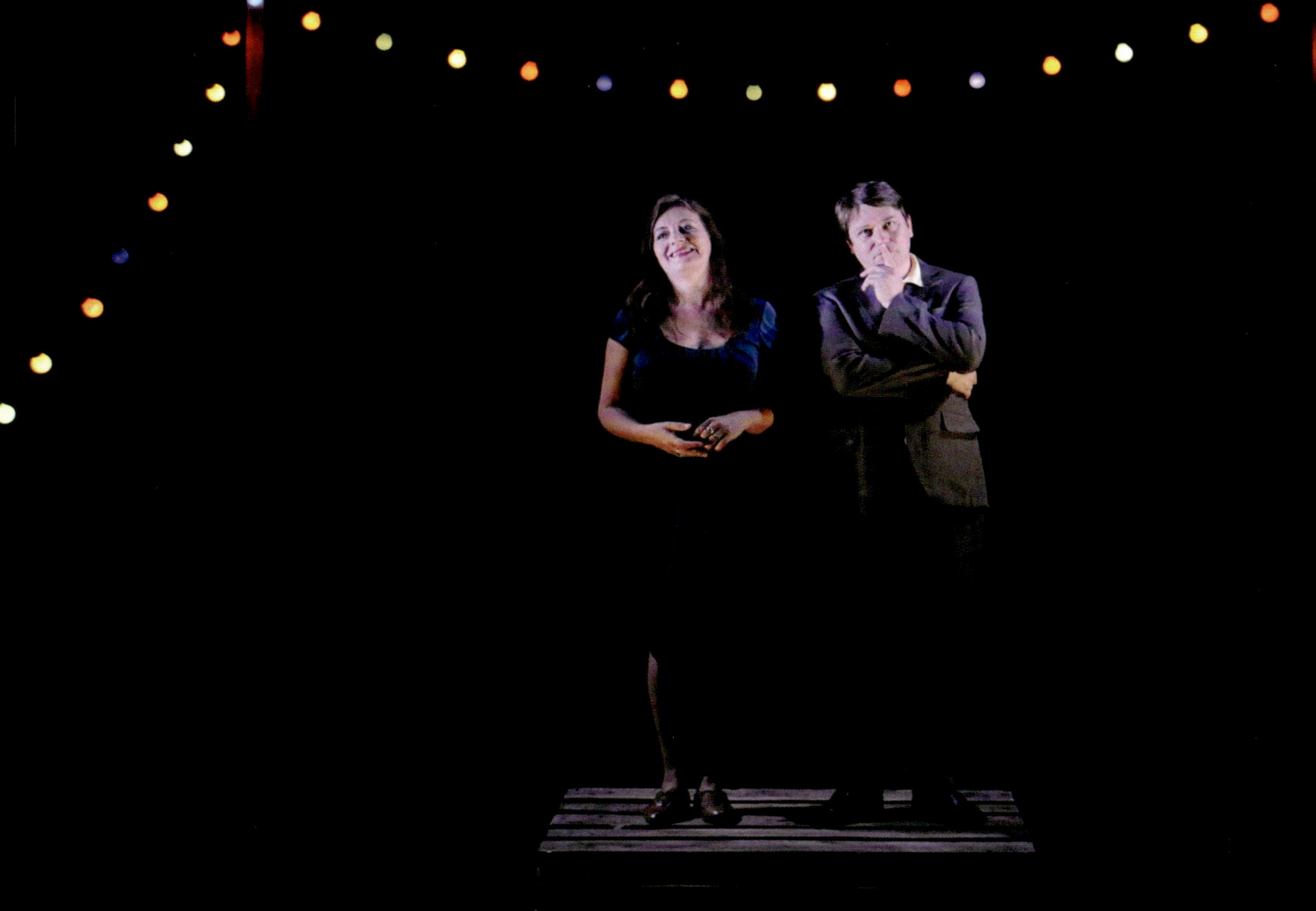

TOMORROW'S PARTIES (2010)

Terry: Or in the future questions of right and wrong will be irrelevant, because people will just be working every hour they are awake, and then sleeping, and sleeping a sleep that is so full of physical exhaustion that they have no time to dream. Because that's what they will have to do, in the future, just to stay alive.

Robin: Or robots will do everything for everybody and people will just sort of lie around. On couches. Watching television. Or eating grapes or whatever. And the robots will do all the boring and dull jobs, and everyone will have lots of robots, so nobody will feel left out. It will all be very egalitarian. And people will mostly just do Art. That's what people will do. People will just do Art.

Terry: Or everyone will live in a kind of idyllic garden … full of artificial waterfalls and doves and animals, tame animals. Even the ones that are currently dangerous will be tame and the whole place will be perfectly controlled—temperature controlled—by computers that are hidden under the bushes, and the wind will be gentle breezes that come from carefully hidden fans, and people will be able to sleep naked 'outdoors' on mossy banks in these perfect sheltered clearings amongst the fibreglass trees.

Robin: Or people will develop superpowers in the future. Superpowers based on characters from cartoons. People will be able to fly. They'll be able to lift tons of concrete. They'll be able to see through walls.

Terry: Or people will become telepathic, able to understand each other instantly.

Robin: Or you'll be able to get wallpaper that changes colour according to your moods.

Terry: Or you'll be able to go on holidays in space.

Robin: Or you'll be able to go talk to your dog using some kind of computer software programme.

Terry: Or people will be able to shrink themselves right down and set off to explore the atom.

Robin: Or things will be so very bad in the future, with so much bloodshed and so much poverty, that when people look back on our age, they'll think of it as a charmed moment in history, a kind of golden age.

Terry: Or things will be so good in the future, that when they look back at now, at our time, they'll be horrified. They'll say, 'How did people live like that? How could they tolerate what was happening? How was that possible?' They just won't understand.

Robin: Or when people mention our time, there'll just be a kind of silence.

Terry: Or in the future people won't talk about the old days much except in jokes. The things we do now, the way we live, our clothes, our haircuts, will be just, you know, comic material … Curious, weird, slightly freaky stuff that comedians can get cheap laughs out of.

Robin: Or in the future people will talk about our time with a kind of moral outrage, complete disgust in fact—because of how, in these centuries, people squandered the world's resources and burnt everything up for a profit with endless stupid unsustainable consumption and just left the future to deal with the consequences. So in the future, when people speak about now, there will always be anger in their voices.

Terry: Or in the future people won't speak much at all about now. Looking back they'll see it as one of the boring bits, one of those bits of history you're maybe supposed to know something about … but it will provoke a kind of groan in students who'll just want to get through it as quickly as possible so they can get on to something much more interesting and dynamic.

Robin: Or things will have developed in such a way that this whole era—now, our time—will really be irrelevant … A sort of minor diversion down a road that isn't really going anywhere, a sort of pointless distraction from the main narratives.

Terry: Or in the future this whole part of history—now—all this will be a mystery, pretty much. These times will be like a jigsaw where most of the pieces are missing.

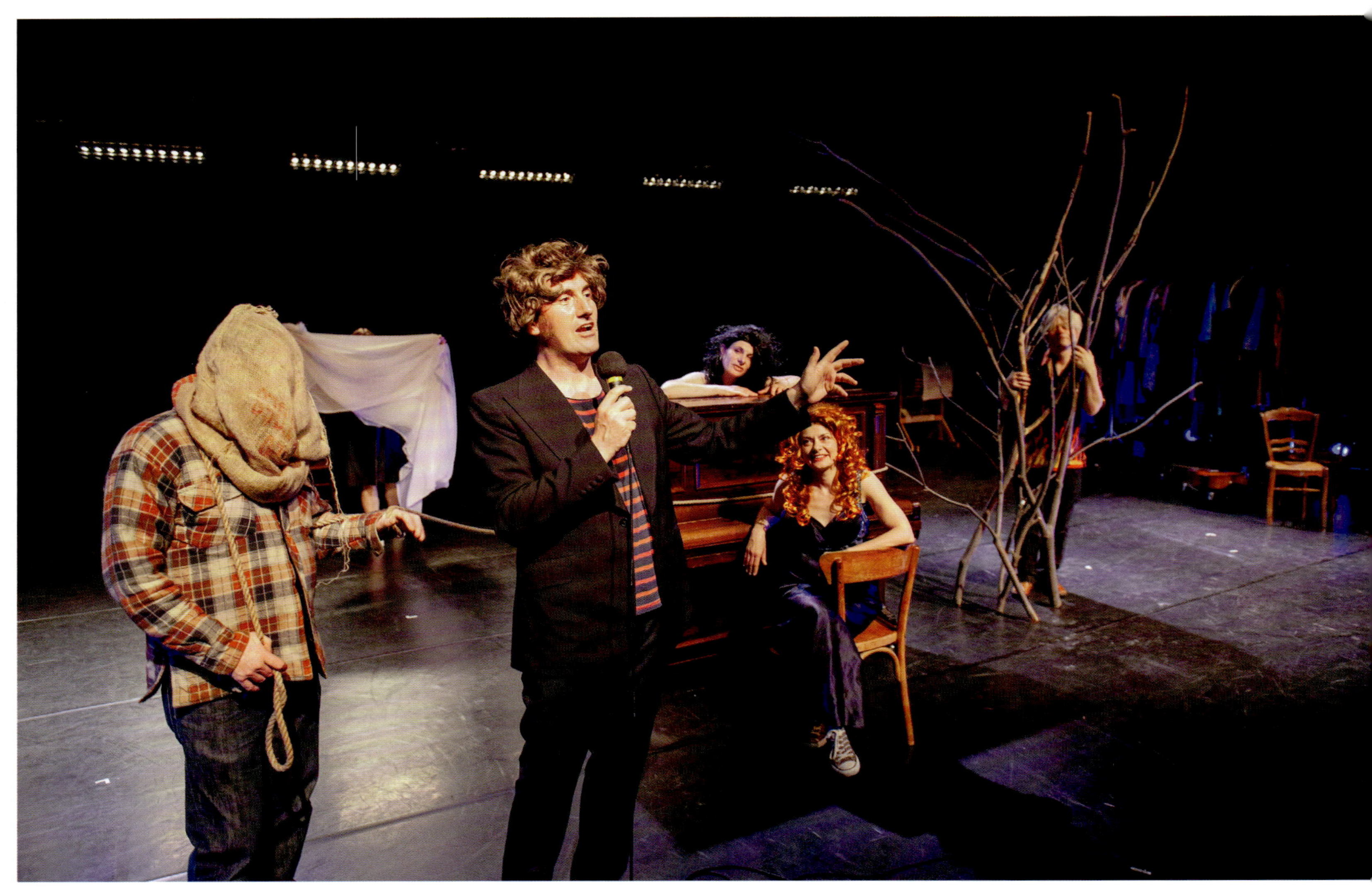

THE COMING STORM (2012)

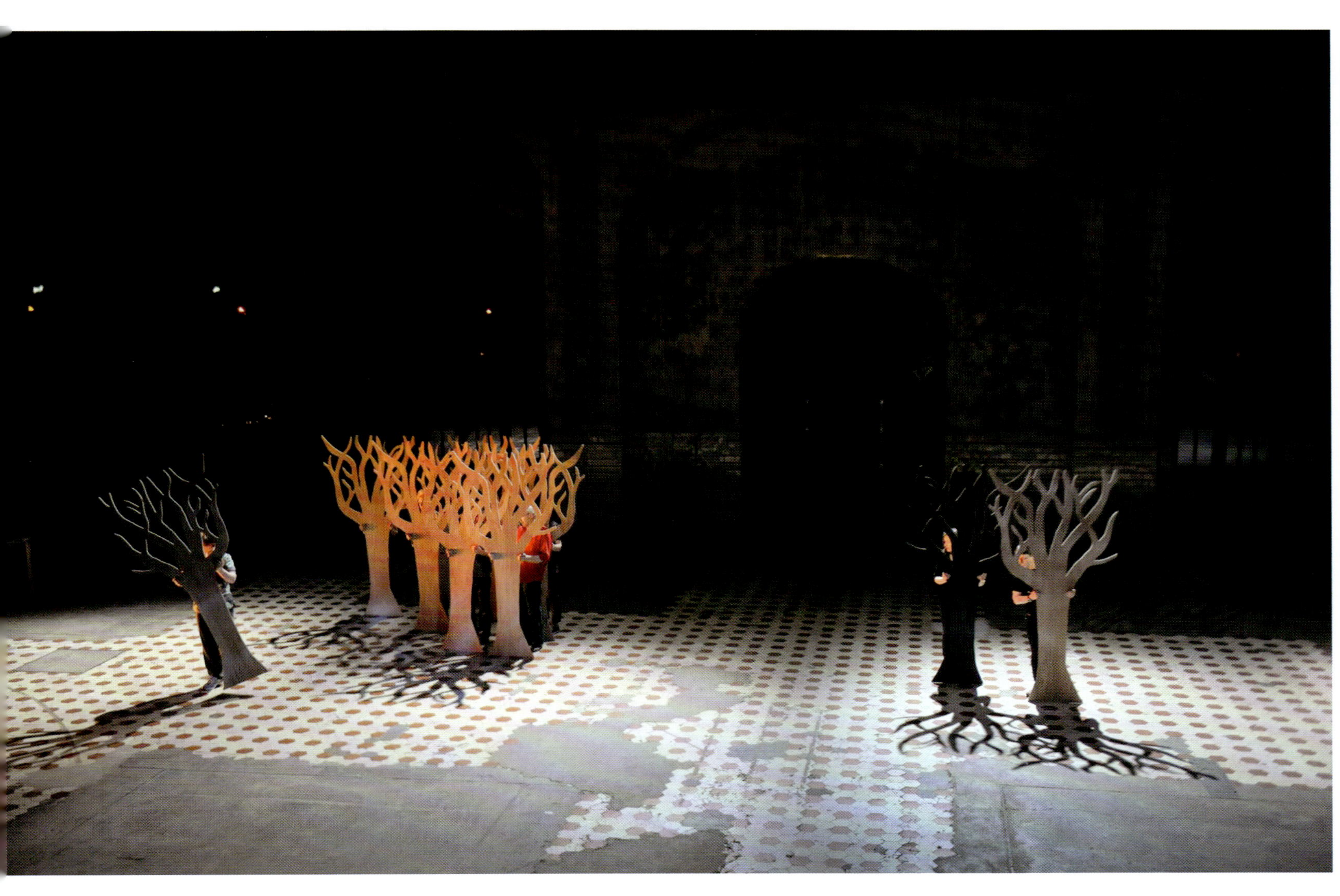

THE LAST ADVENTURES (2013)

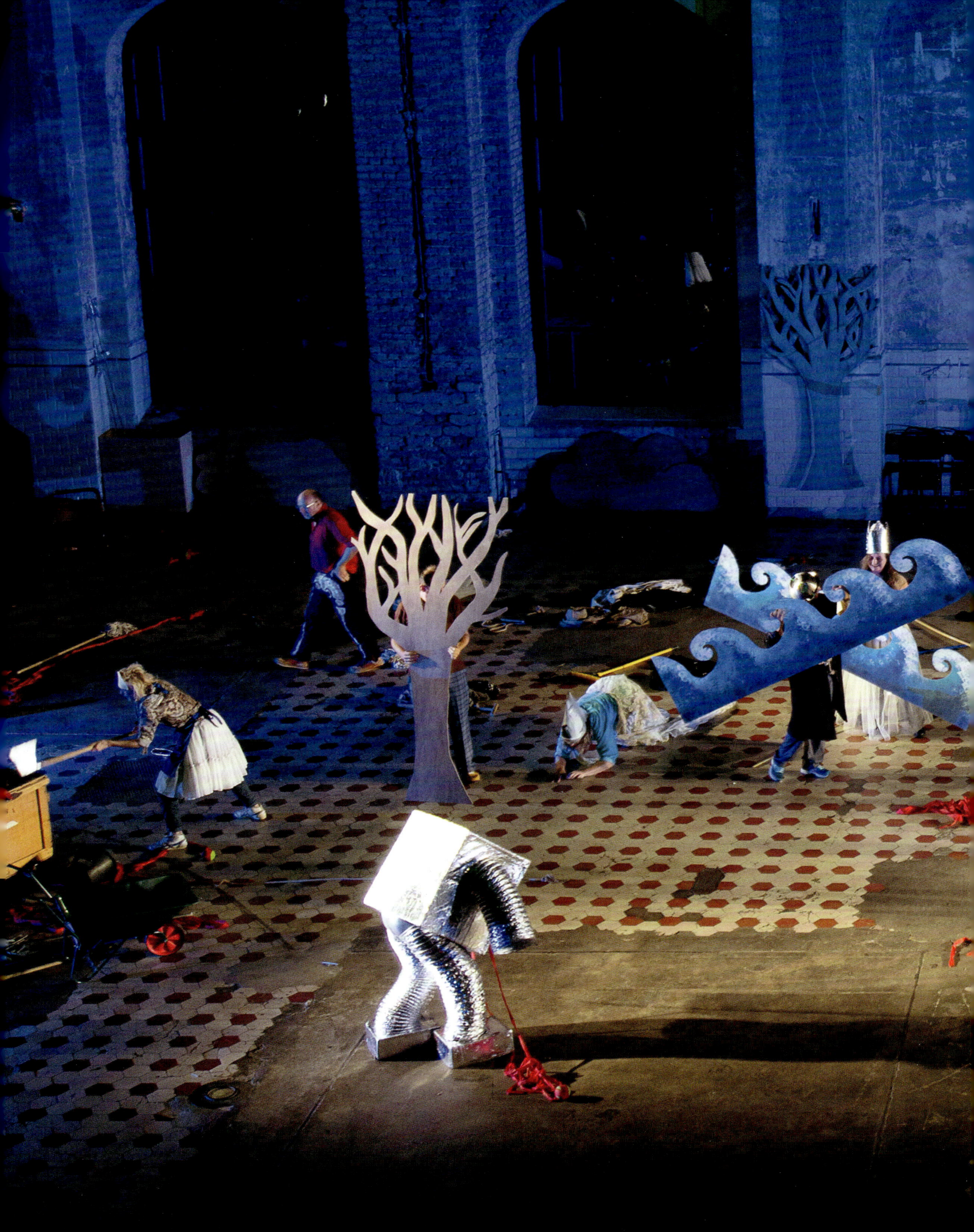

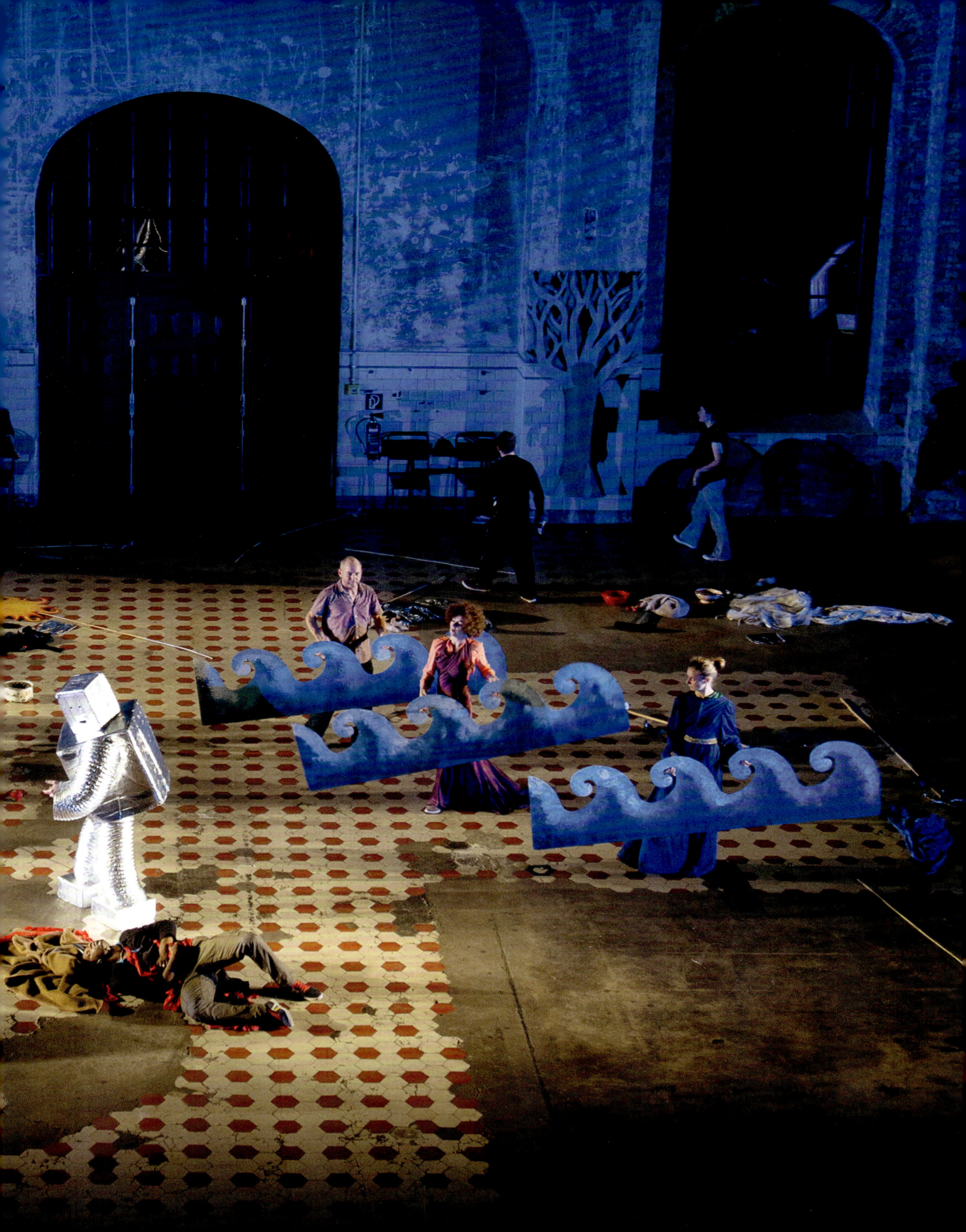

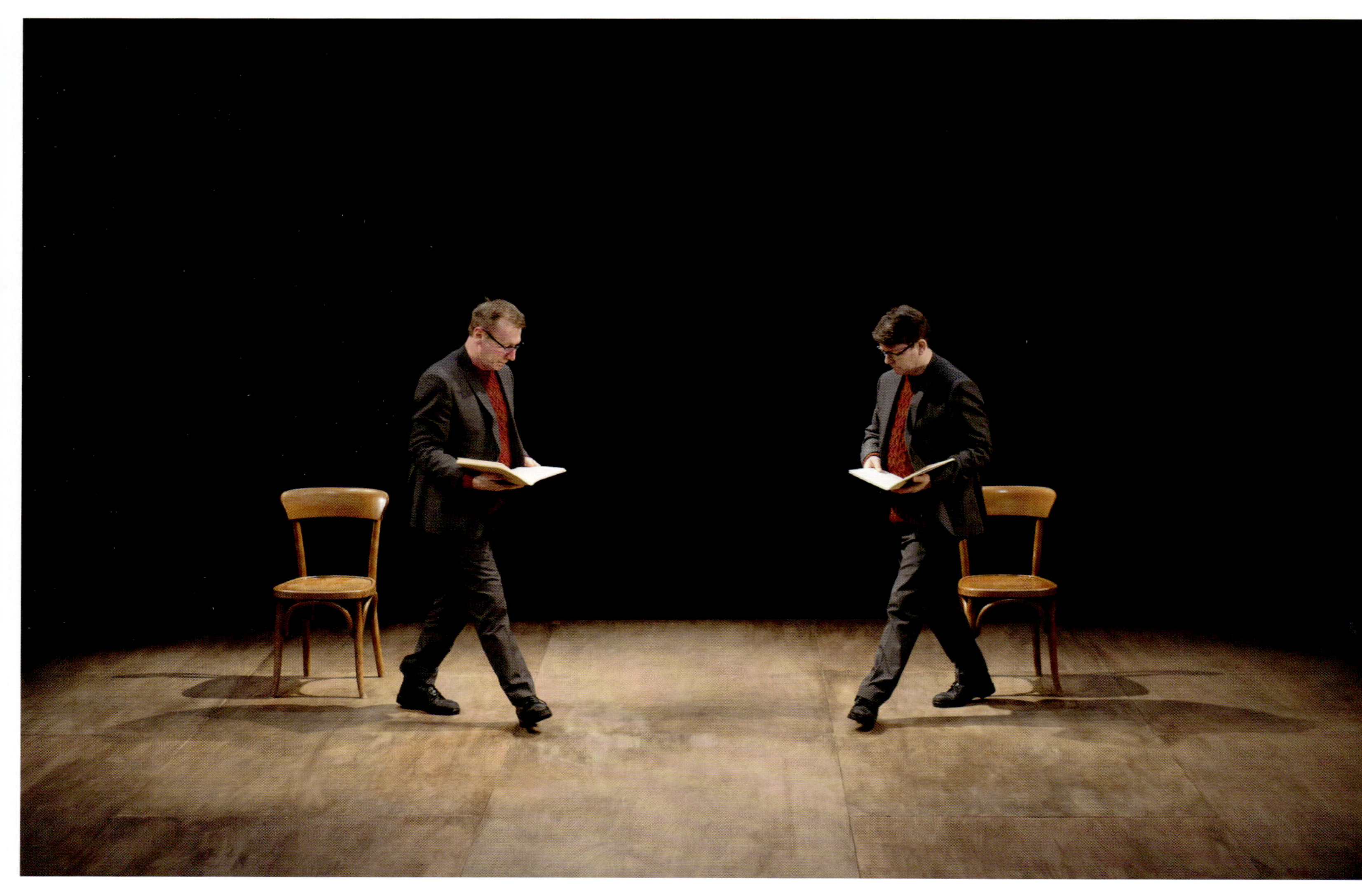

THE NOTEBOOK (2014)

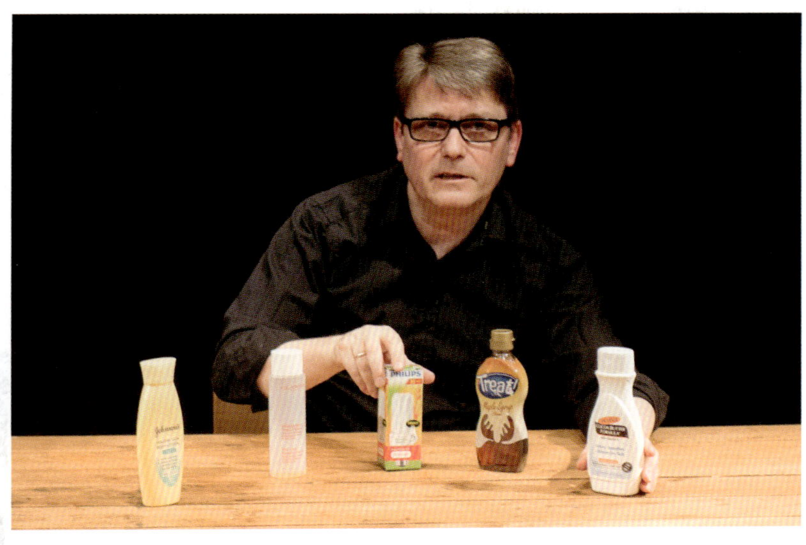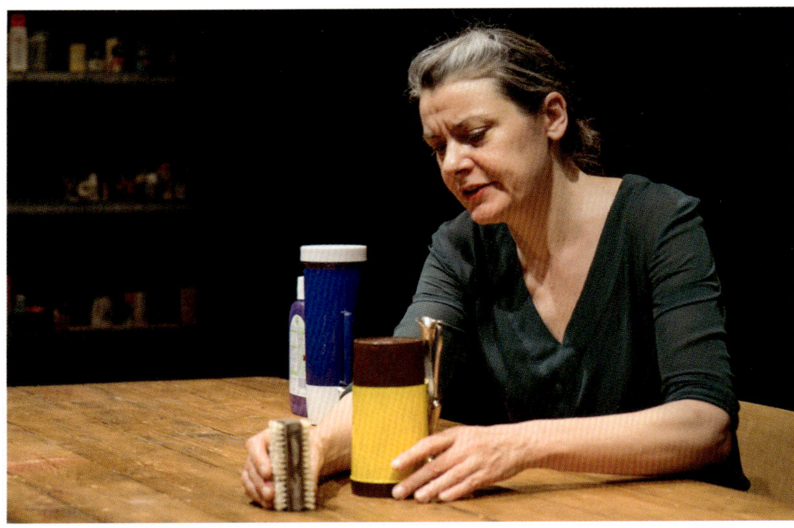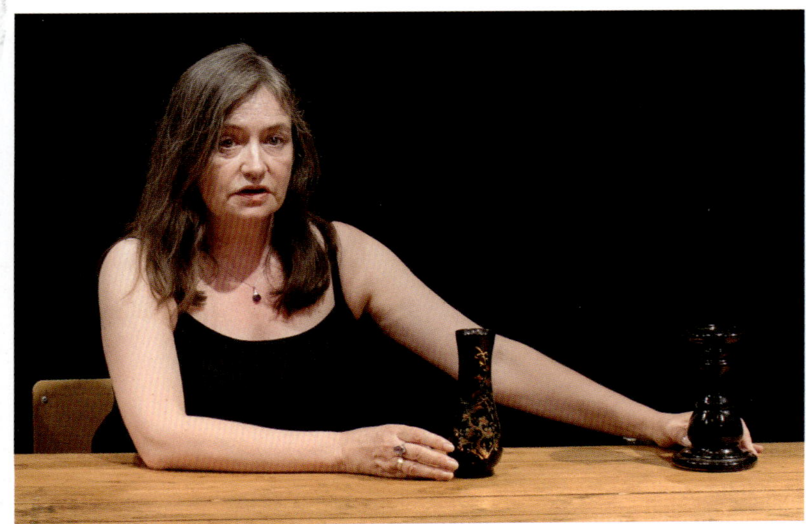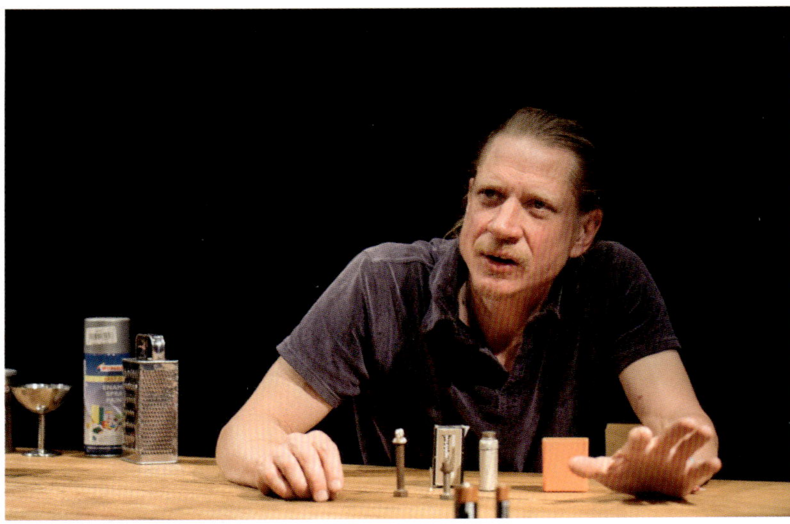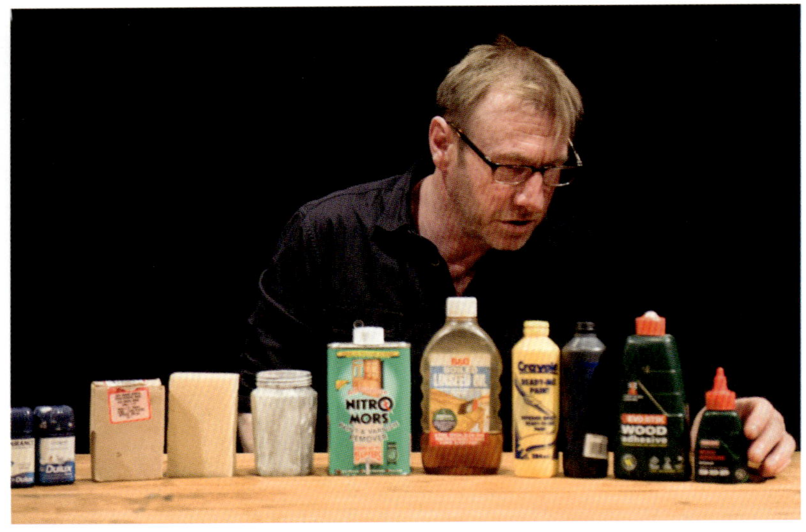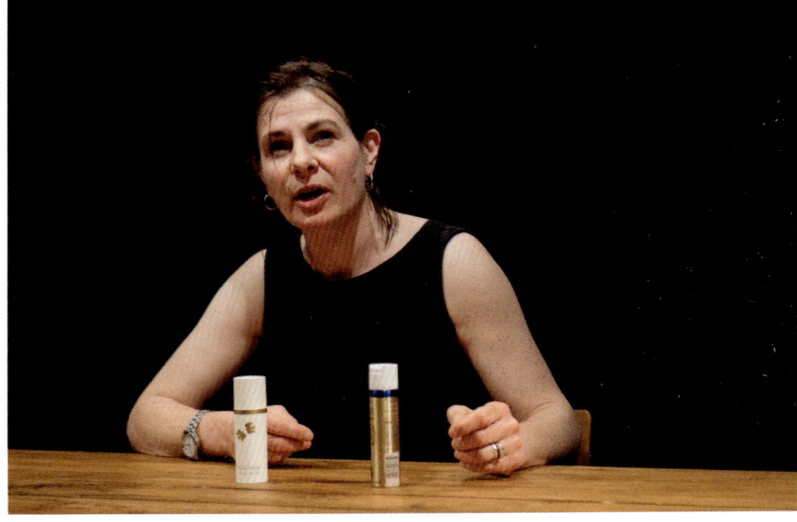

COMPLETE WORKS: TABLE TOP SHAKESPEARE (2015)

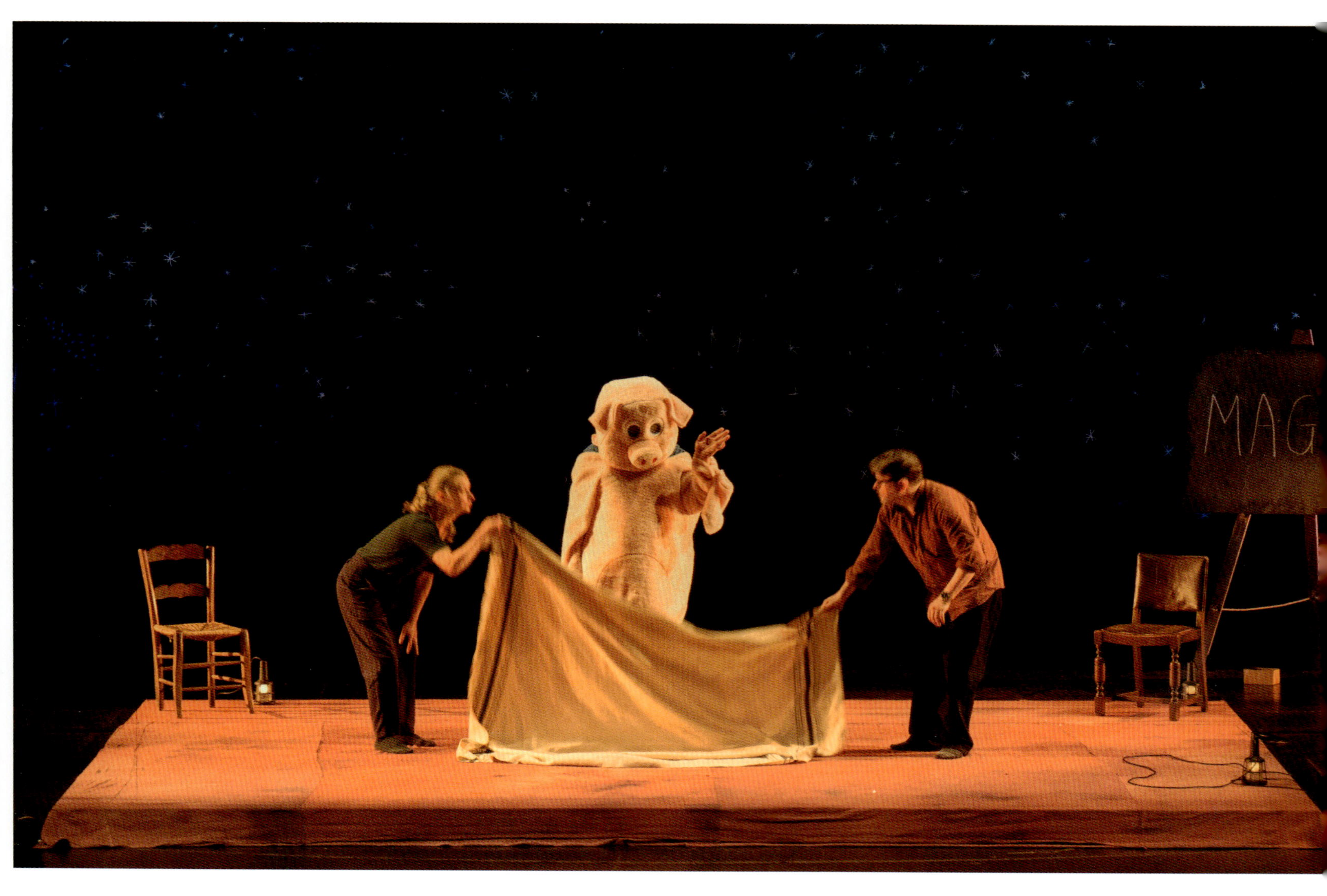

FROM THE DARK (2016)

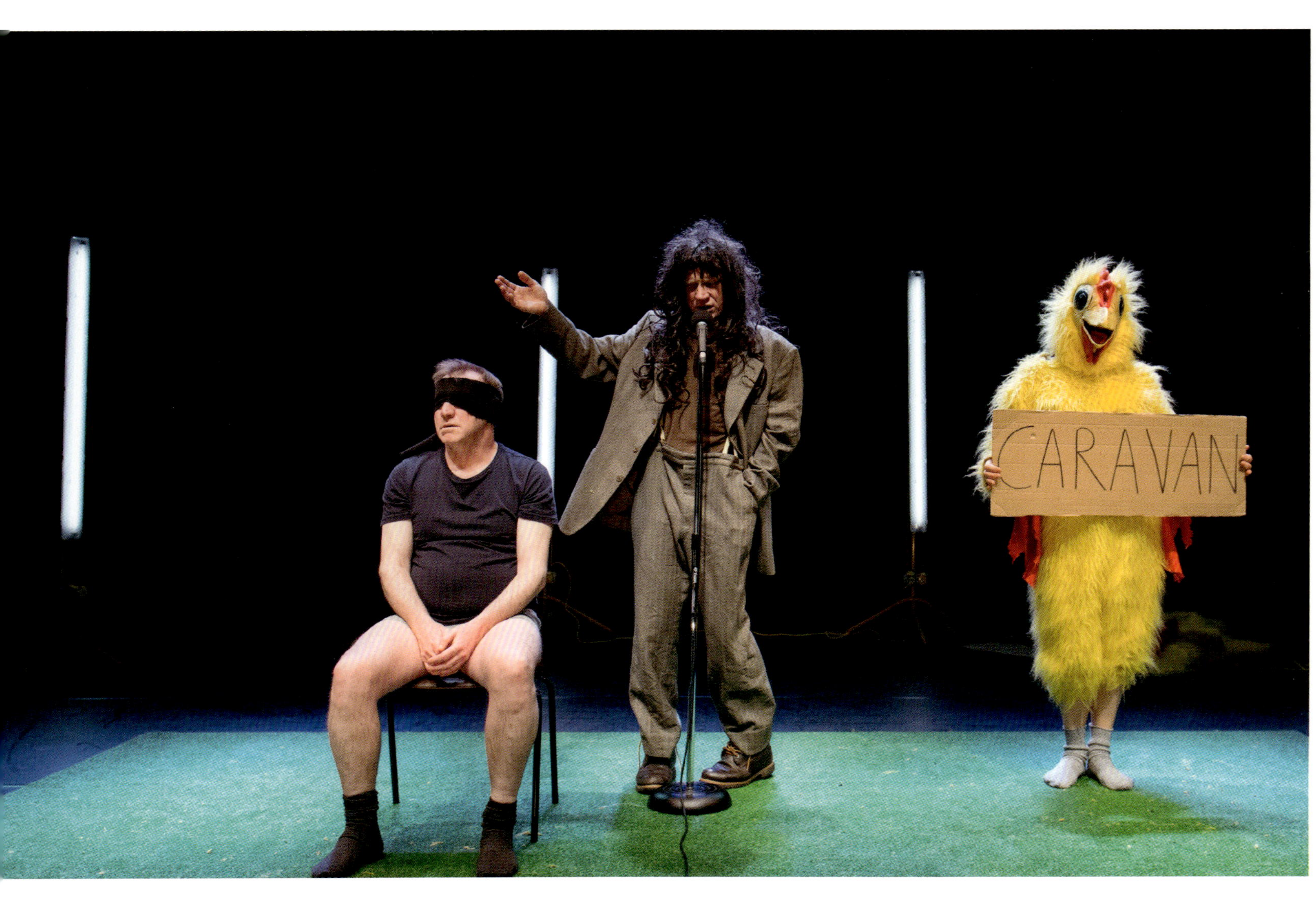

REAL MAGIC (2016)

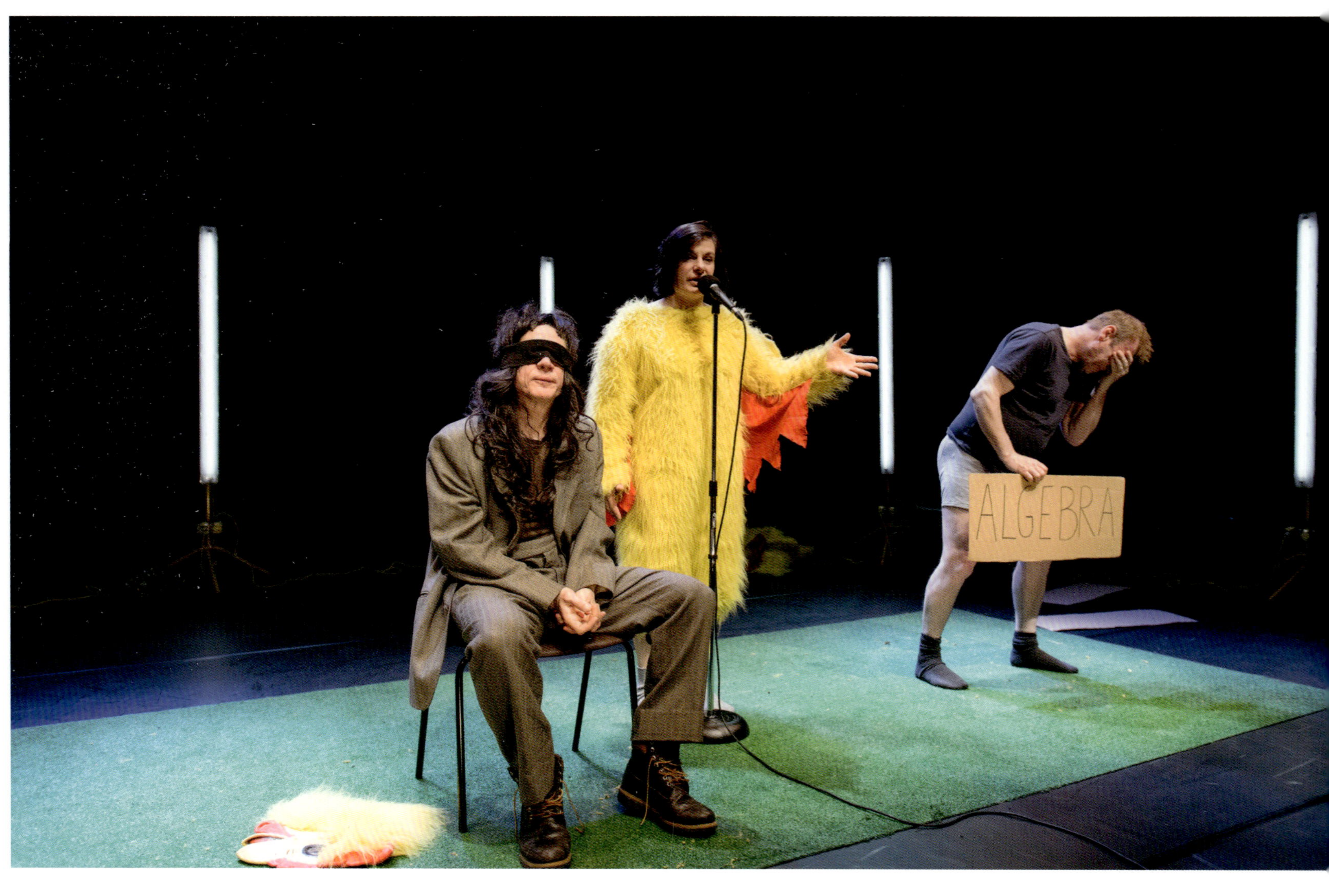

ALGEBRA

There's a yearning on our part to make serious work from 'weightless' material. It has often been a matter of composing with what might seem like inconsequential stuff, figures, or scenes: bits of stand-up routines or failed cabaret acts, images from trash television, absurd amateur theatricalities, whole projects that appear to be doomed or insubstantial. I'm drawn to the idea that one could make something profound, poetic, and transformative from material that—at first sight—might look like trash, unworthy of notice. This alchemy, exemplified in *Real Magic*, is so compelling to me.

The core scene feels like a moment from a game show, or perhaps from a cabaret mind-reading act. The performance has a very tight focus, and the single scene at its heart gets repeated time and again, with variation, for almost the entire duration of the work. It's a routine in which one person—a contestant or volunteer from the audience—is asked by the show-host to guess a word that another person is supposedly thinking of. It's clearly an impossible task from the outset and it's no surprise that each of the three guesses offered by the contestant are wrong. The scene repeats some thirty-six times across the length of the performance, with the three performers on stage (Richard, Claire, and Jerry) presented with the same impossible question, and offering the same incorrect answers every time, taking it in turns to play the roles of 'host', 'contestant', and 'thinker/assistant'. [TE]

[*Jerry (as host) walks to the mic centre stage. Claire (as thinker/assistant) goes to his left facing the audience. Richard (as contestant)—in underpants, socks, and T-shirt—takes the single seat on Jerry's right. All of Jerry's text is said into the mic, all of Claire and Richard's speech is unamplified.*]

Jerry: Alright. Let's get on with it. [*To Richard*] So, we've never met before, have we?

Richard: No.

Jerry: And you've never met Claire before, have you?

Richard: No.

Jerry: What's your name?

Richard: Richard.

Jerry: Richard who?

Richard: Richard Lowdon.

Jerry: 'Richard Lowdon'. Alright, Richard Lowdon. The way it's going to work is this. Claire is going to think of a word and all you've got to do is guess that word. Is that clear?

Richard: Yes.

Jerry: Are you feeling good?

Richard: Yes.

Jerry: Are you feeling confident?

Richard: Yes.

Jerry: Are you feeling safe?

Richard: [*Hesitating*] Yes.

Jerry: Alright. So Claire—are you thinking of a word?

Claire: [*Claire takes a placard from the floor near where she's standing that has the word SAUSAGE written on it.*] Yes.

Jerry: She's thinking of a word! Now all you've got to do, Richard, is guess the word that Claire is thinking of.

Richard: [*Thinks for some moments*] Is it ... Is it electricity?

Jerry: Claire, is it electricity?

Claire: No.

Jerry: No. [*To Claire*] Shall we give him another go?

Claire: Yes.

Jerry: Alright Richard. You've got another go. What is the word that Claire is thinking of?

Richard: [*Thinks for a moment*] Hole?

Jerry: [*To Claire*] Is it hole?

Claire: No.

Jerry: No. You're wrong. [*To Claire*] Shall we give him another go?

Claire: Yes.

Jerry: Alright. So, Richard, you've got another go. What is the word that Claire is thinking of?

Richard: [*Thinks for an even longer time*] Money.

Jerry: [*Hyping the tension*] Just to be clear. Am I right in thinking you said the word 'money'?

Richard: Money.

Jerry: Claire, is it money?

Claire: No.

Jerry: No. Shall we give him another go?

Claire: No.

Jerry: No. Let's swap.

The performer's work in *Real Magic* is incredibly precise; for the most part you're controlling really tiny variations or differences between one version of the 'scene' and another. It's technical work on a much smaller, finer scale. [JK]

Perhaps that technical feeling comes because you're acting a lot but also trying not to make a psychological line between different moments or versions of the scene. You have to make one single moment or exchange happen with a very particular fictional focus and then stop, run away from it as fast as you can, because the next moment what you'll need to create will have a very different atmosphere and intensity. In that sense the whole performance is made of jump cuts: nothing is allowed to make a line. [CM]

The soundtrack for the piece is a collage of sound loops—laughter, applause, ticking clocks, and musical jingles—switched in and out, sometimes separately, sometimes overlapping. The effect is both to distance the audience from what's happening— they're 'doubled' and to some extent made redundant by the loops—and to dynamically energize, interrupt, or shift the performance for particular moments and scenes. It's such a strong presence that we recognized the sound mix as a 'fourth performer'. Operating the sound in rehearsals I was quite consciously using it to throw tonal and energetic proposals to the performers. [TE]

It may look like we're not really dealing with the live audience: as performers, we don't address them, we don't exactly look at them. But that is purely affectation. Underneath it all we're dealing with them the whole time. It's weird for audiences because in the early stages of the show their response is almost replaced by the soundtrack. That often unsettles spectators and creates a blanket of distance which can make it hard to work with them in real time: normally, so much of your sense of an audience is the sound they're making. It's only later—when silence and space really open up in the piece—that you start to feel able to manipulate the exchange with them in real time. That's when you can feel the room and you can play it. [RL]

As the performers move through the thirty-six iterations of the core 'scene' the audience's 'stuckness' becomes palpable. There can be giddy hysterics in the tension, as well as walkouts and occasional vocal interventions trying to derail the proceedings. At the same time though, the metaphoric dimensions of the situation are always looming. The social and political paralyses of the early part of the twenty- first century often come to mind: the 48% vs 52% logjams of Brexit and Trumpism, the inability to achieve meaningful change in relation to the climate emergency. The constant escalation of drama about the answer to the question—'What is the word that X is thinking of?'—mirrors the violent, performative hype of the news and political cycles: theatrical offers or pseudo-offers of change, which mask stasis or power shifts driven by other logics entirely. The audience understand that at some level the 'stuckness' of the figures onstage is tied to, and mirrors, their own. [TE]

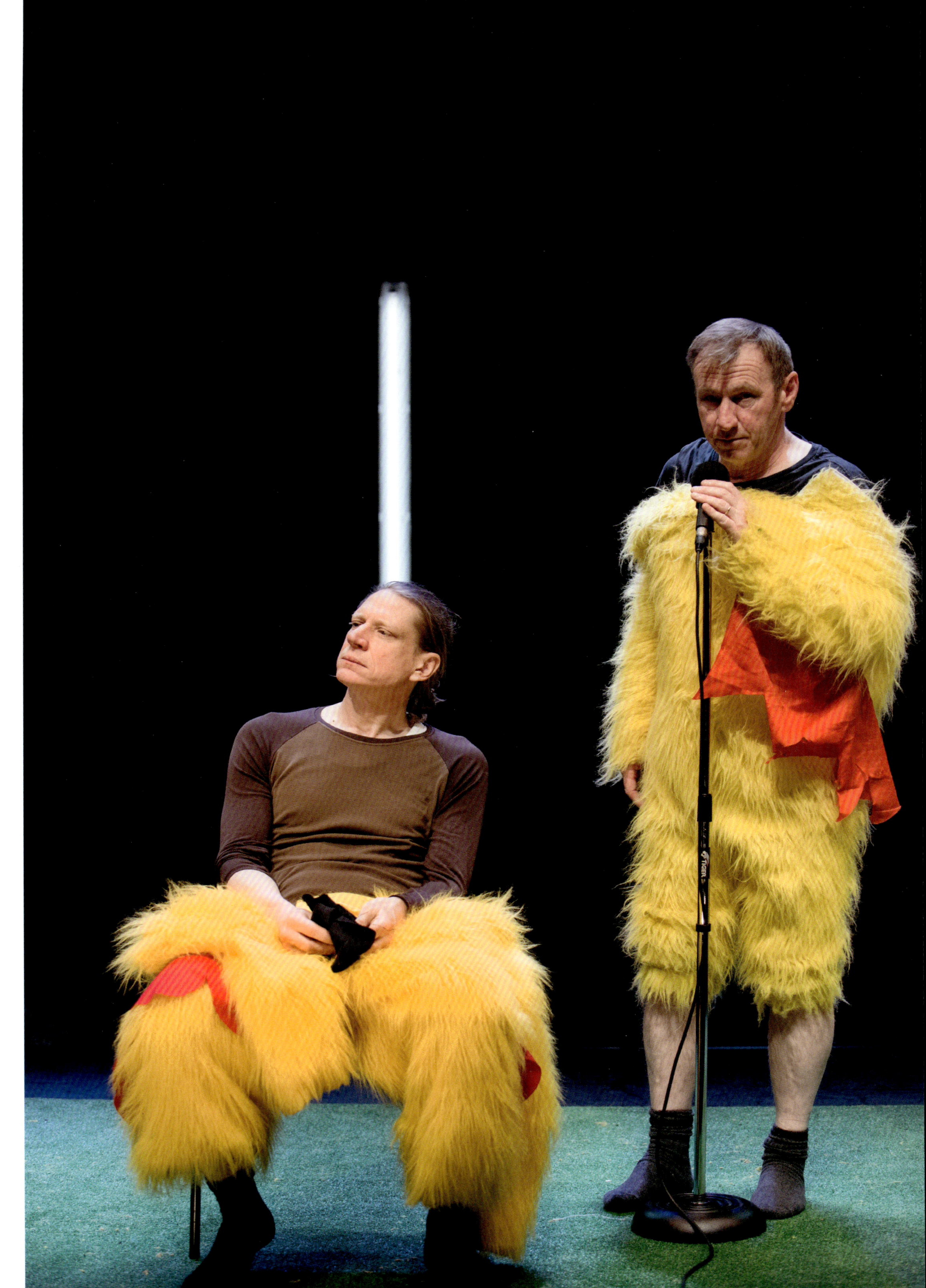

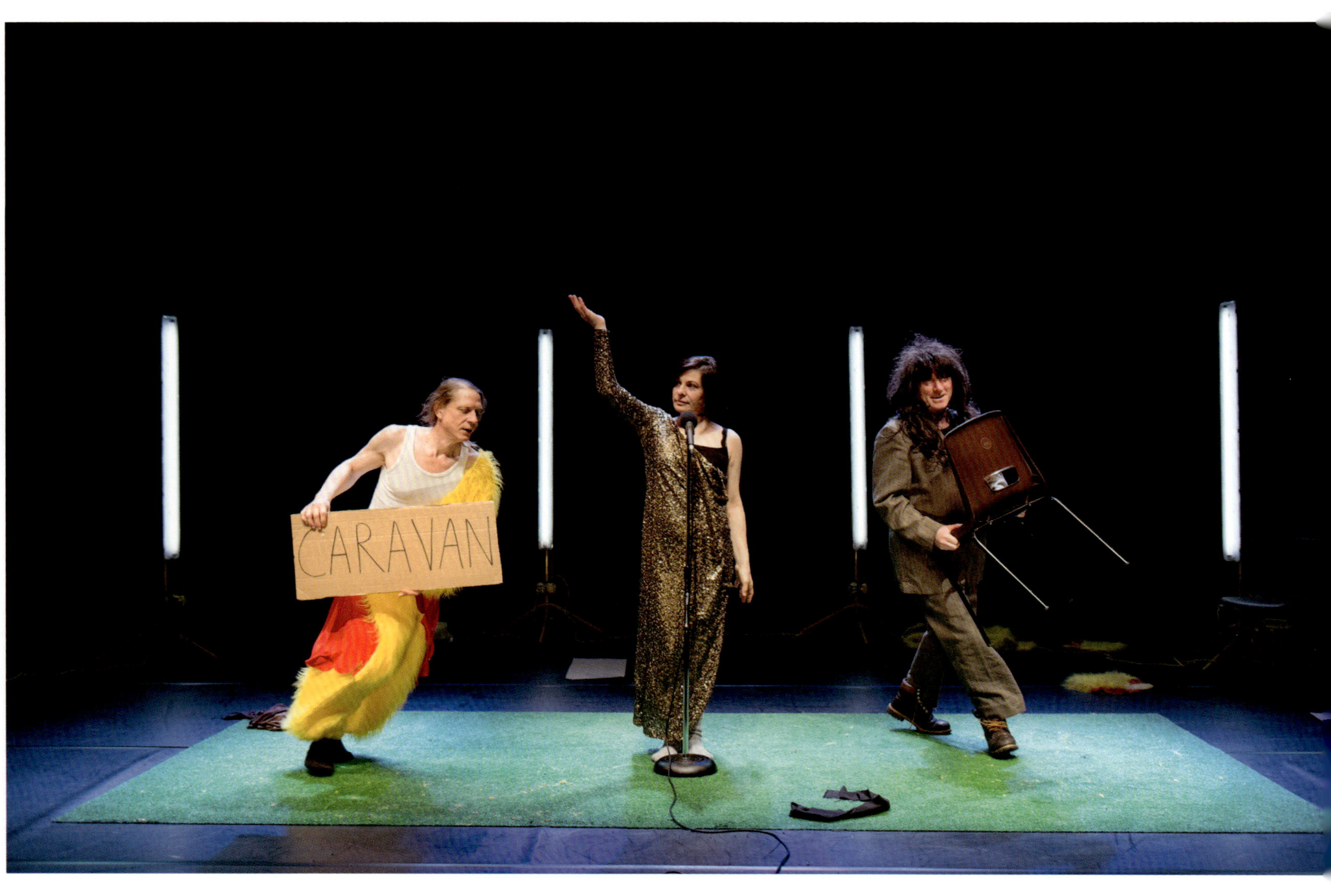

CARAVAN

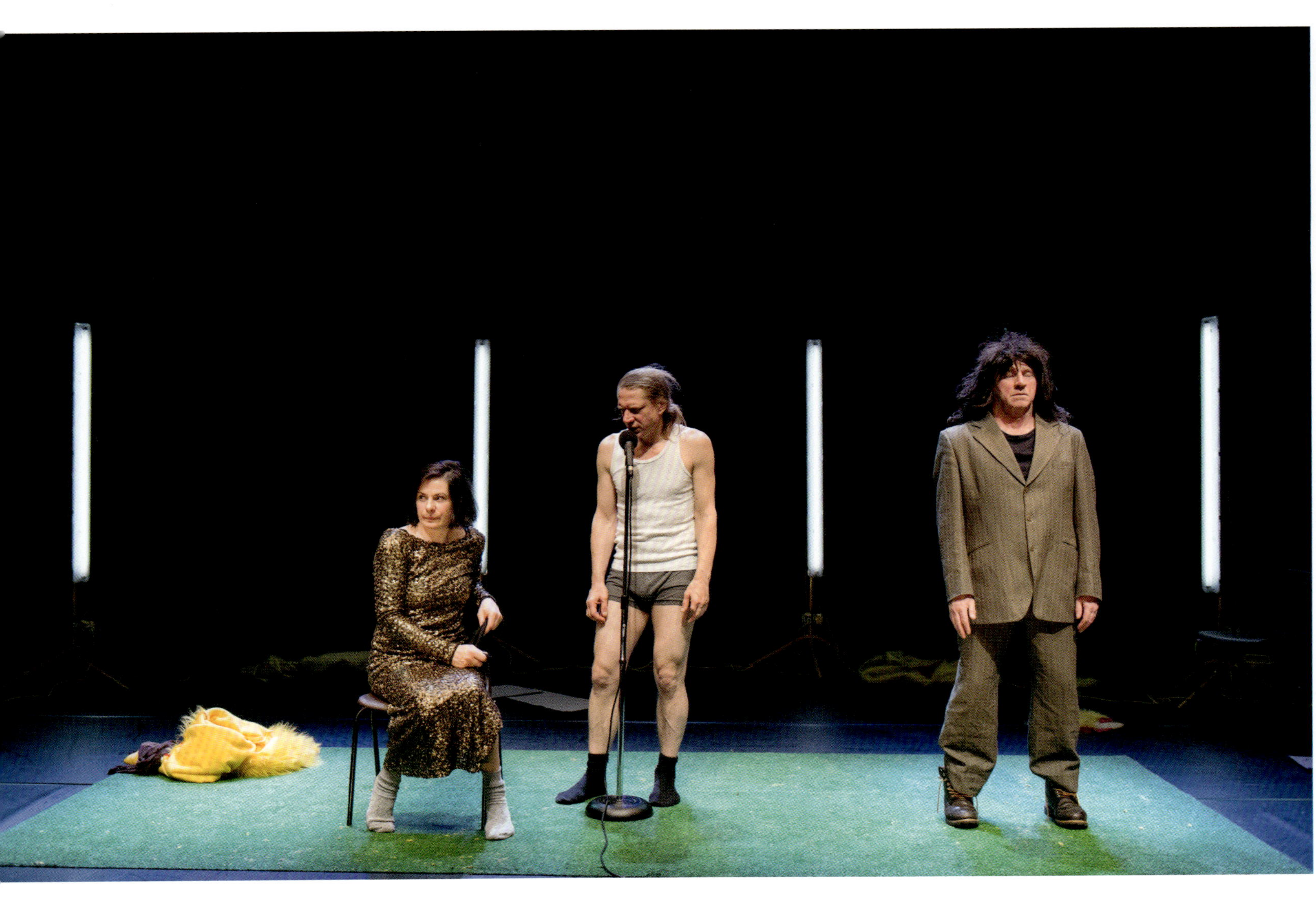

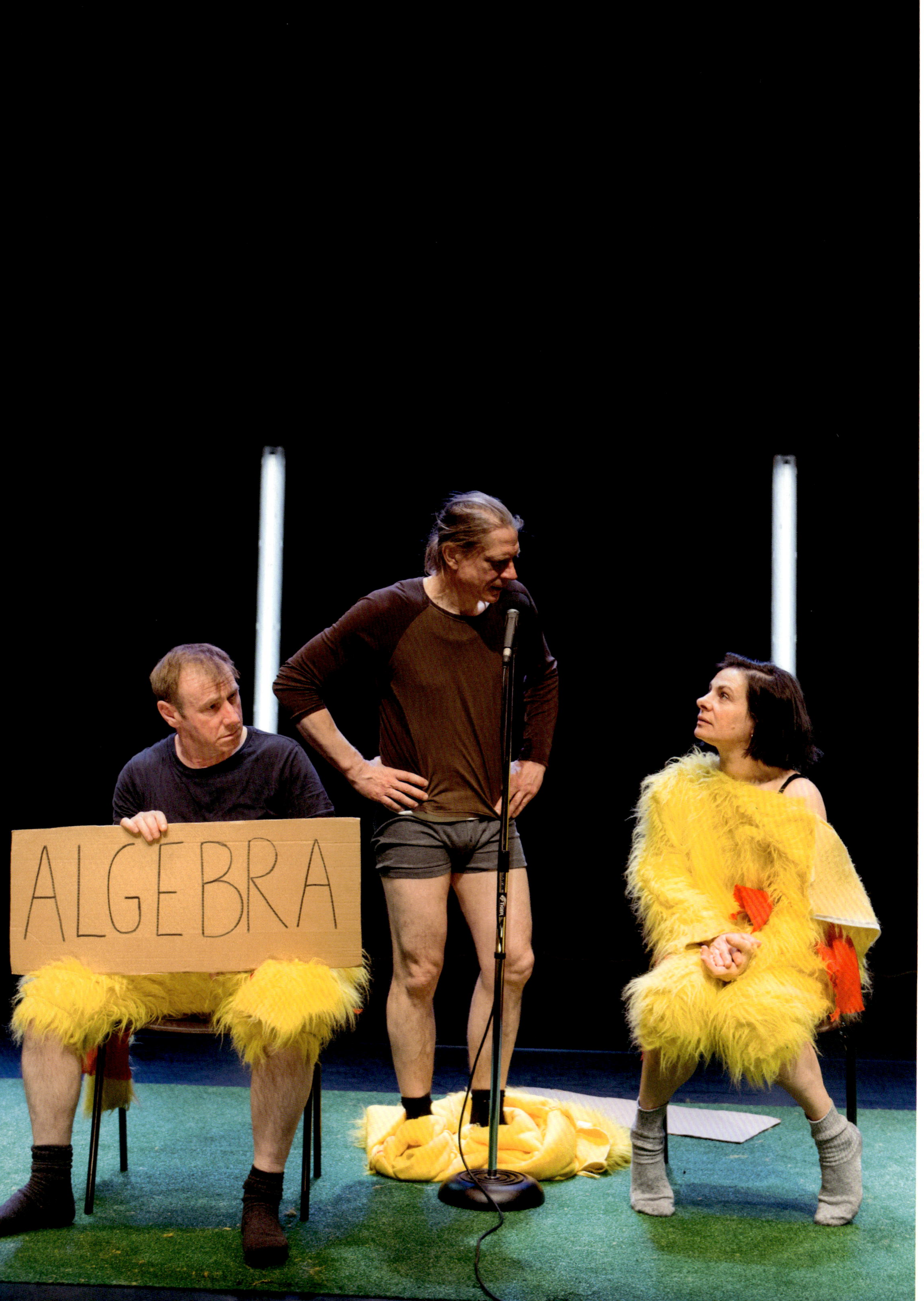

ALGEBRA

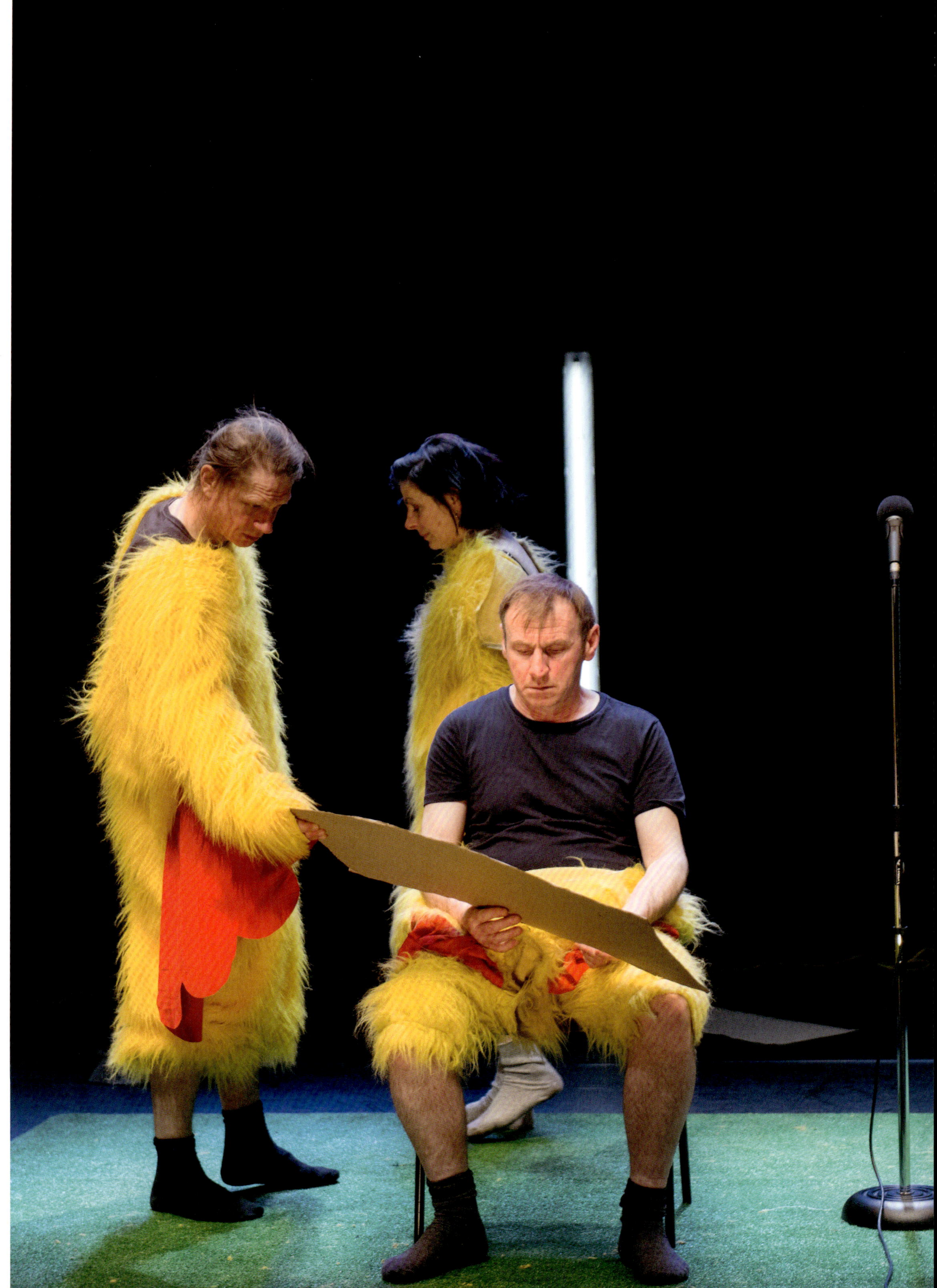

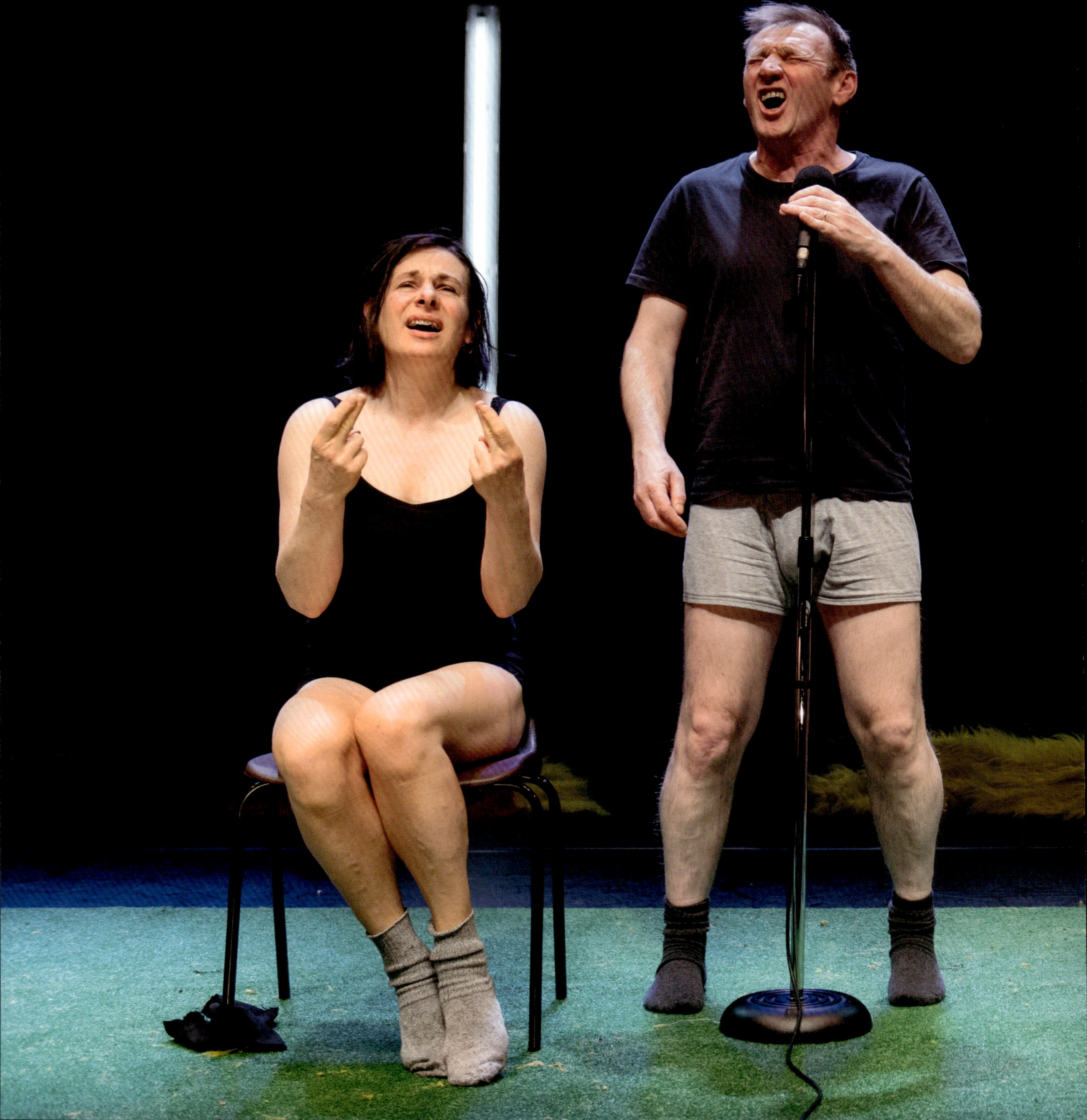

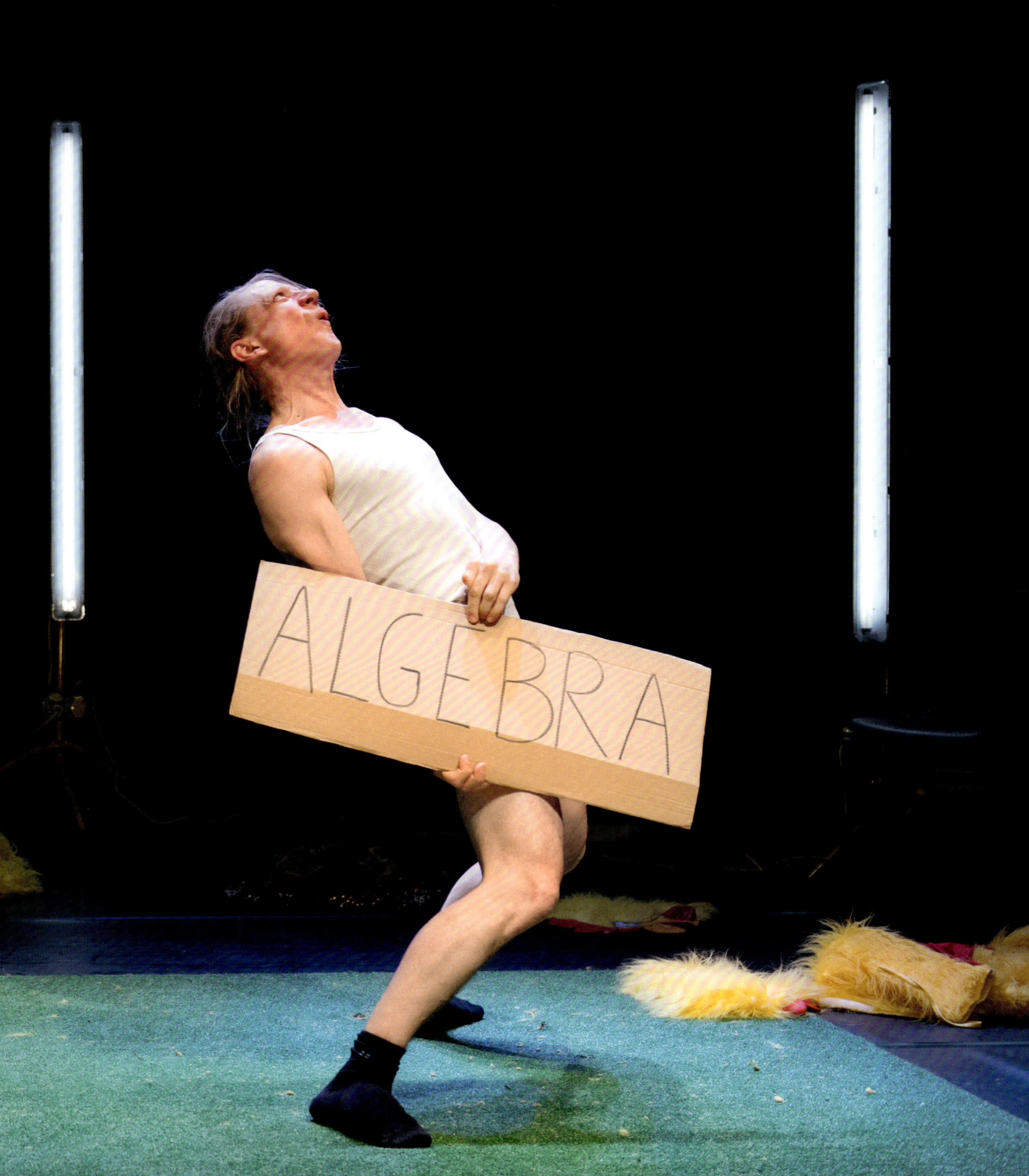
ALGEBRA

What happens all the way through the piece is that the person answering the question gets victimized, picked on, pushed, humiliated. And by the end of the show we can turn that around, reverse the victimization. Jerry and Richard are desperate for me to break the pattern and give a correct answer: only that could possibly release us (and the audience) from the purgatory of the show. So, there's an intense glee in refusing them that final victory. The fact that we are working with such tight rules gives us an enormous space to play in as performers. [CM]

At a meta level, all the figures onstage are engaged in going through this scene repeatedly, exploring it, testing it, trying to understand it. And as such it doesn't really matter which part they have within it. They're working on the mechanism, trying to figure it out. And if any one of them managed to solve the problem it presents, at any moment, then it would be over: a release for all of them. So, the figures understand that there are three different roles to be played in the scene. And you can say that there's not a psychological continuum between one attempt at the scene and another but, in a larger sense, the attempt to get it right, to get the right answer, to escape it, provides an overarching structure. [RL]

The only respite, or break from the repetitions of the core scene, are a couple of short dance interludes introduced by the performers as an already-inadequate attempt to surpass their situation. These dances—forms of performative blankness framed by music—draw on strategies we've developed in other pieces. It's almost become a dramaturgical principle to overload the stage with text and action material and then to let it calm through music or in silence, producing an oasis in which audience and performers alike are invited to contemplate what's taken place. In sections such as these there's no new information, no speech, no progression; instead a single activity or image is extended as a space in which resonances from the previous scenes can circulate and amplify. No surprise that we end *Real Magic* with the most mournful and half-hearted of its three dances, a space in which what's happened has a chance to sink in. [TE]

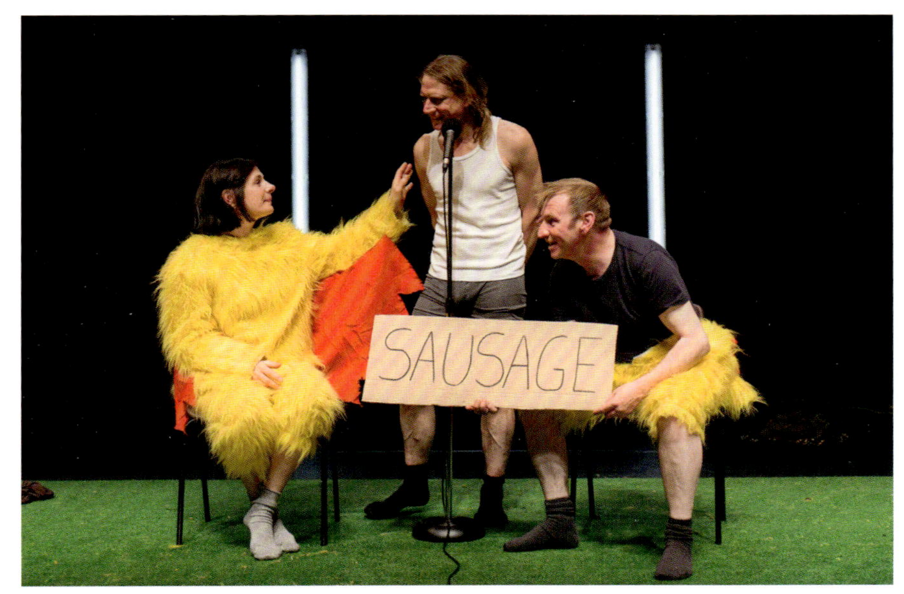
SAUSAGE

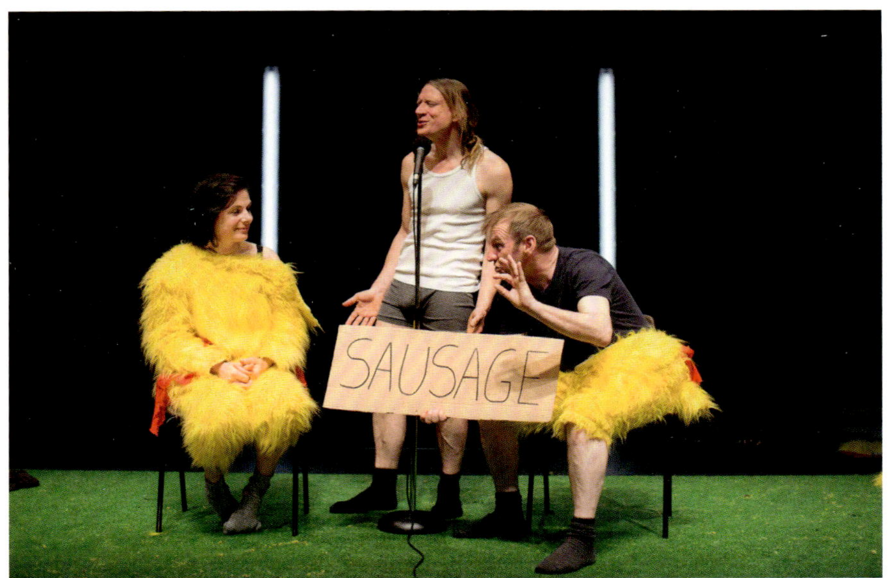
SAUSAGE

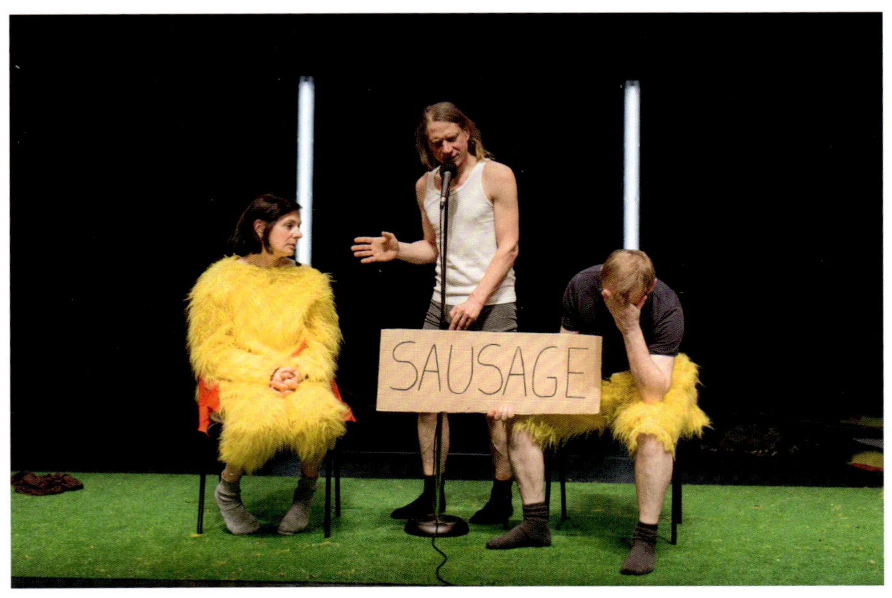
SAUSAGE

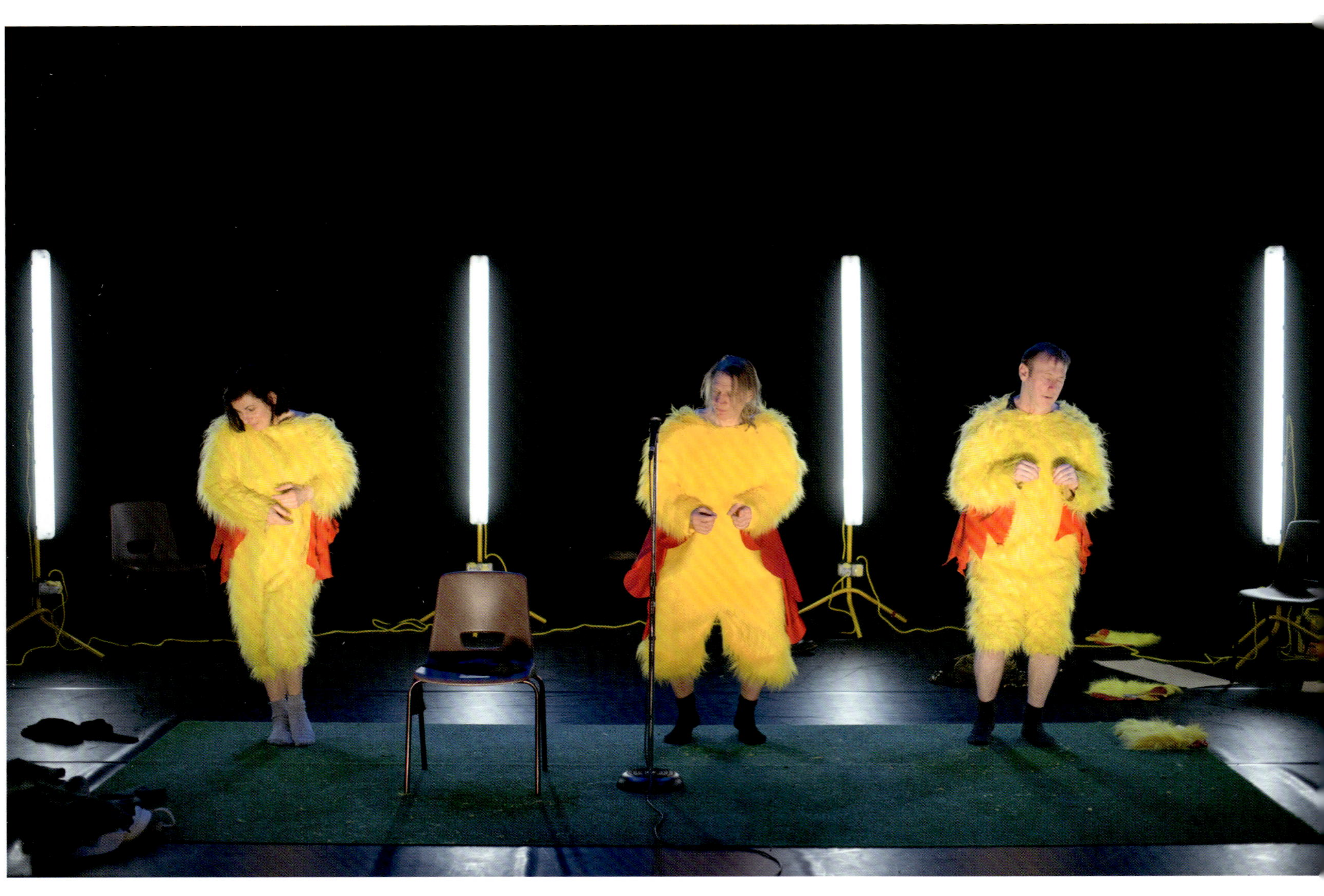

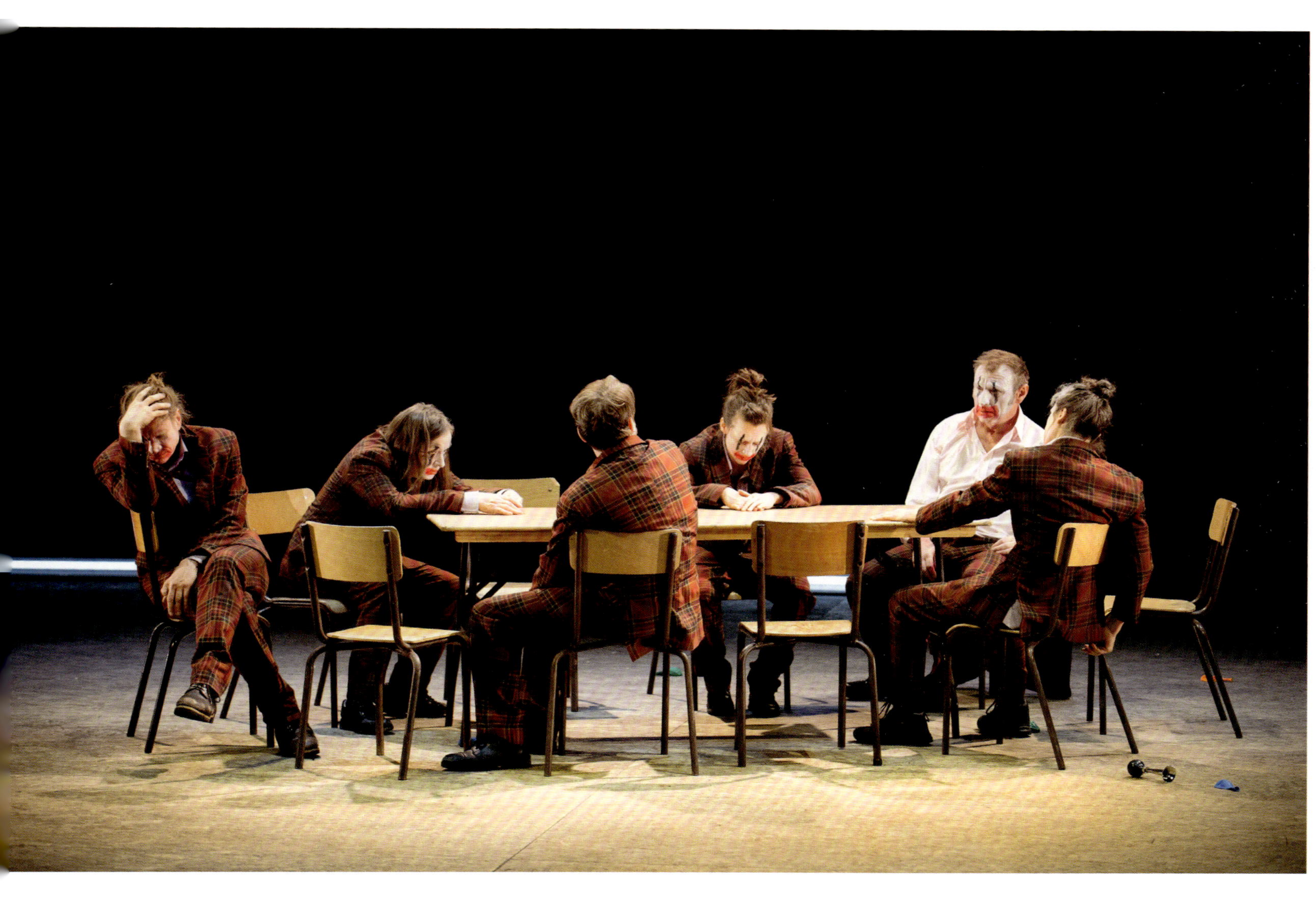

OUT OF ORDER (2018)

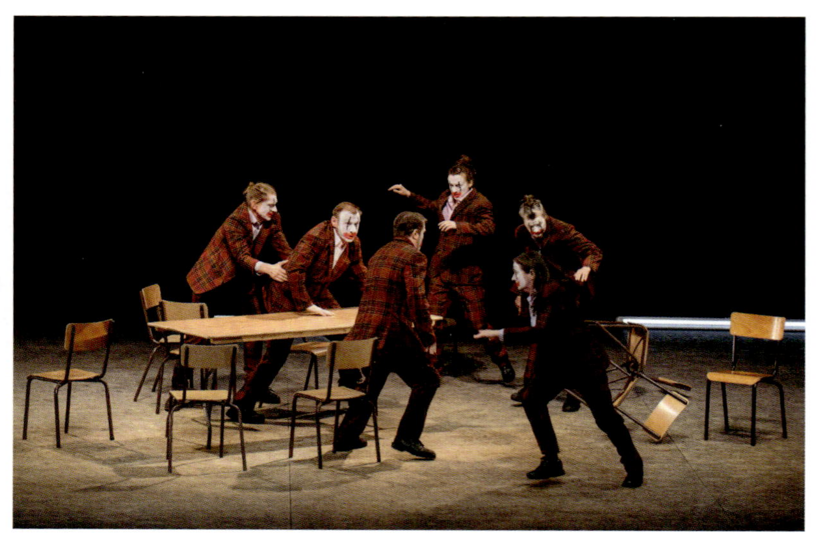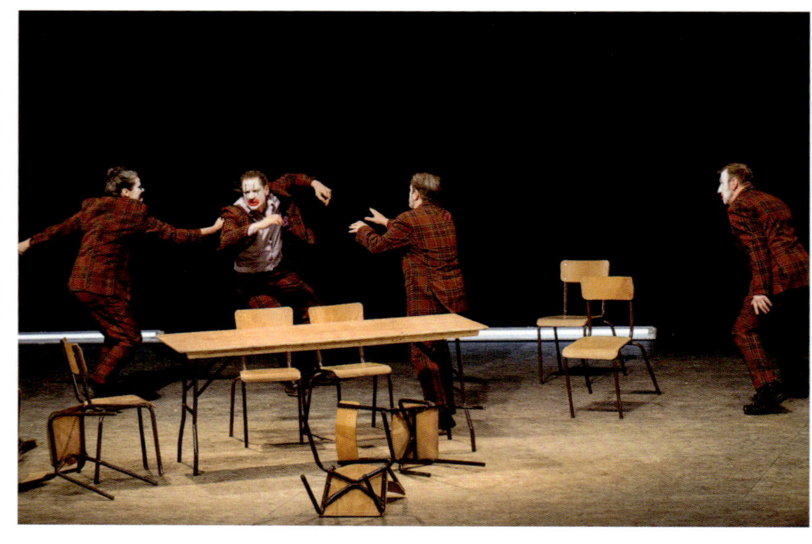

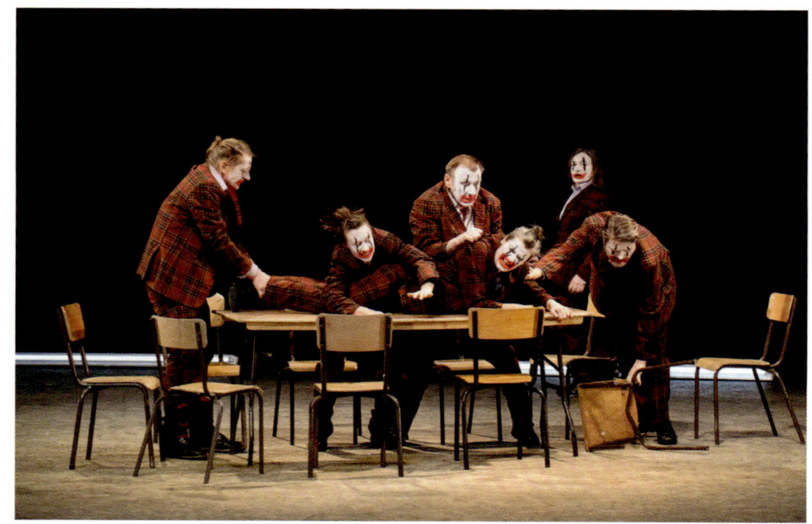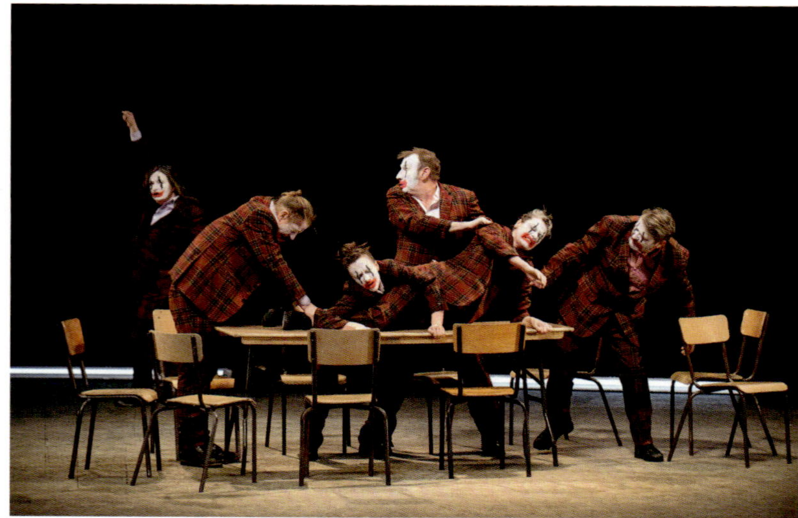

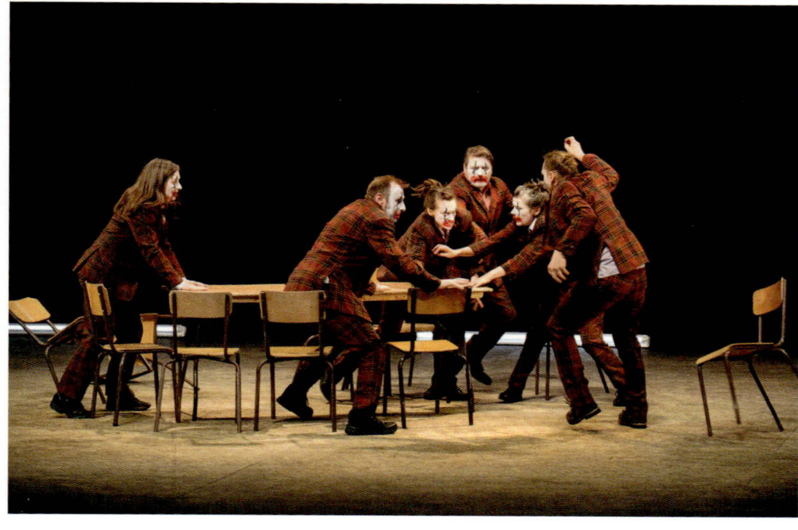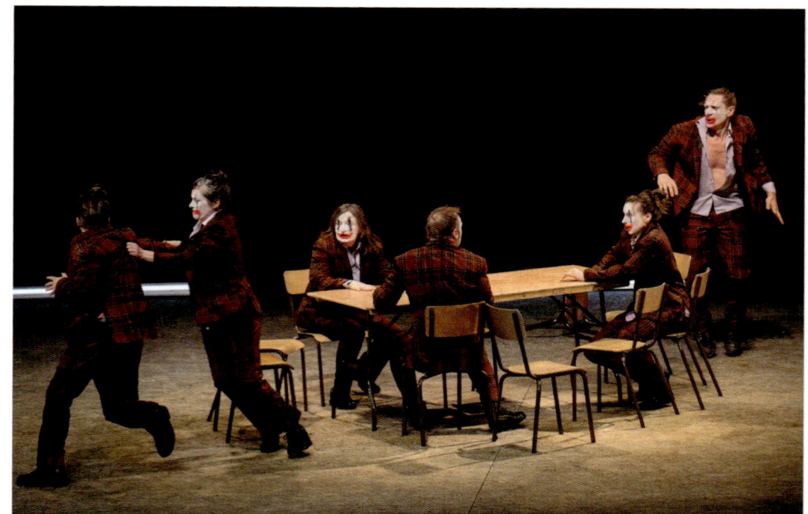

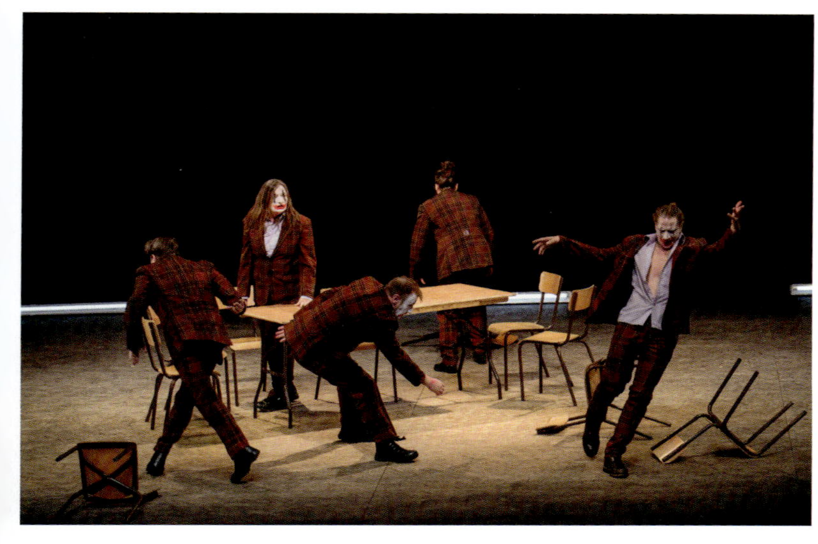
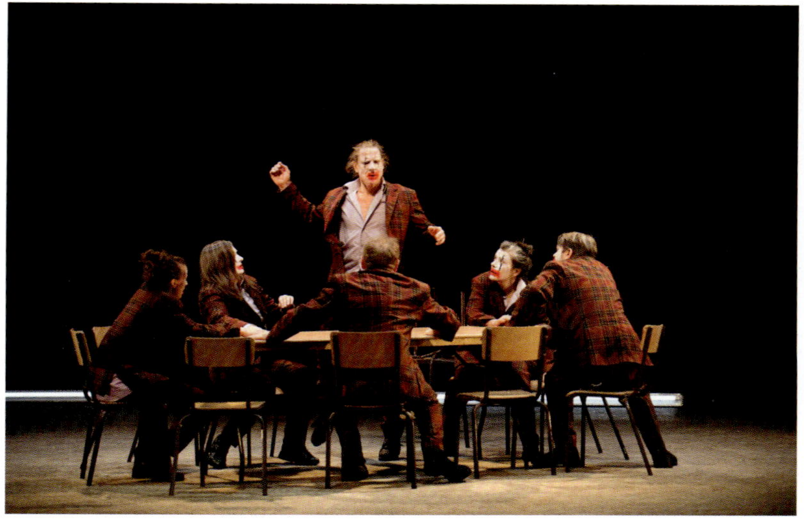
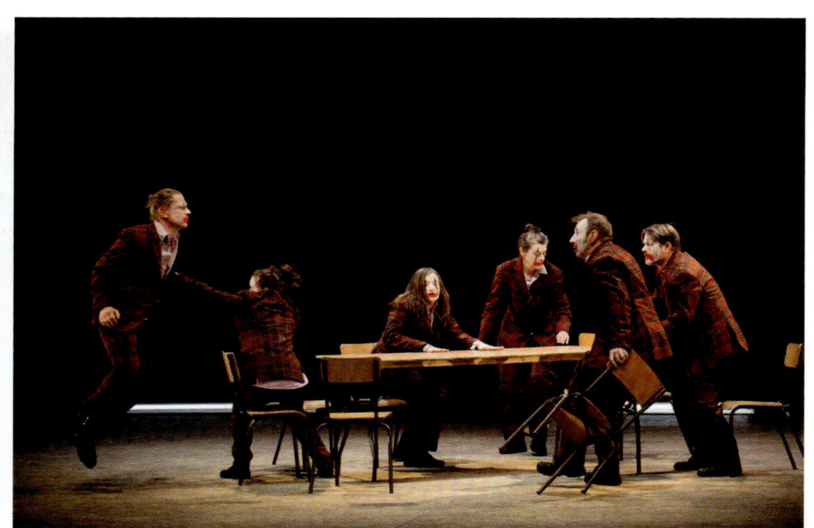
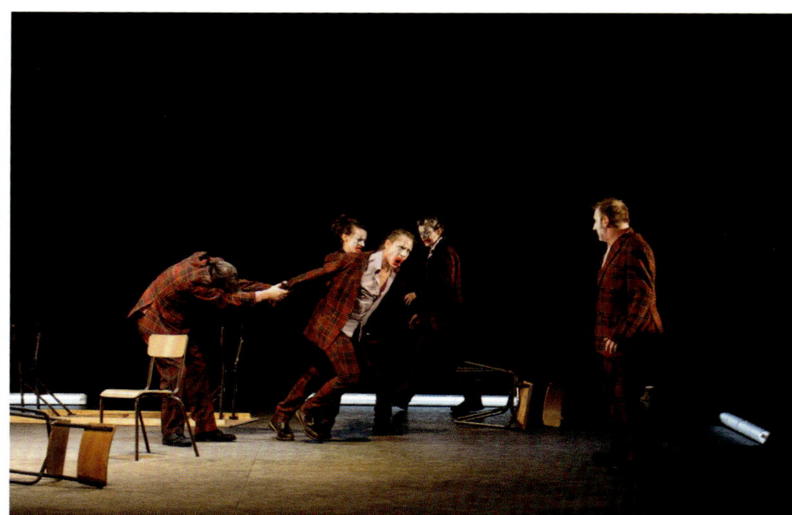
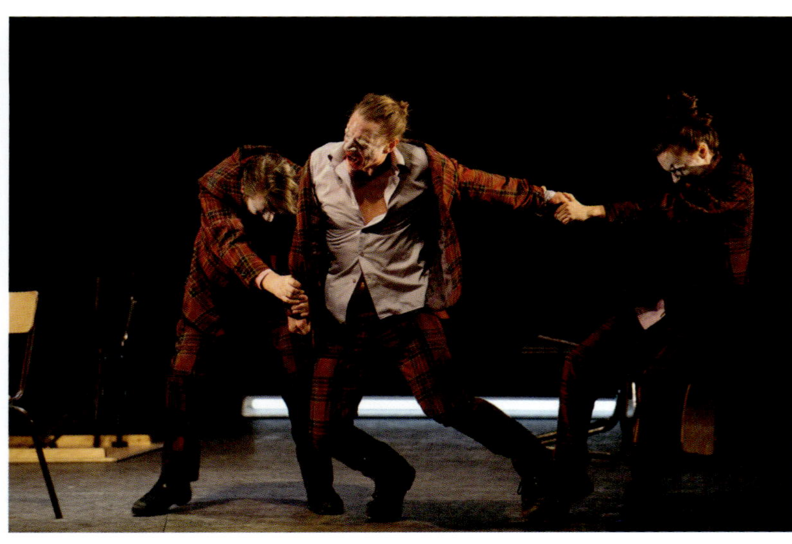
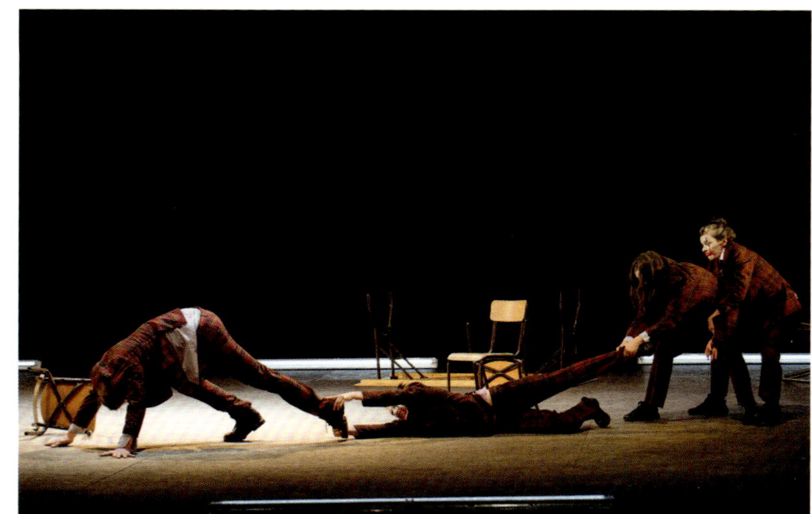

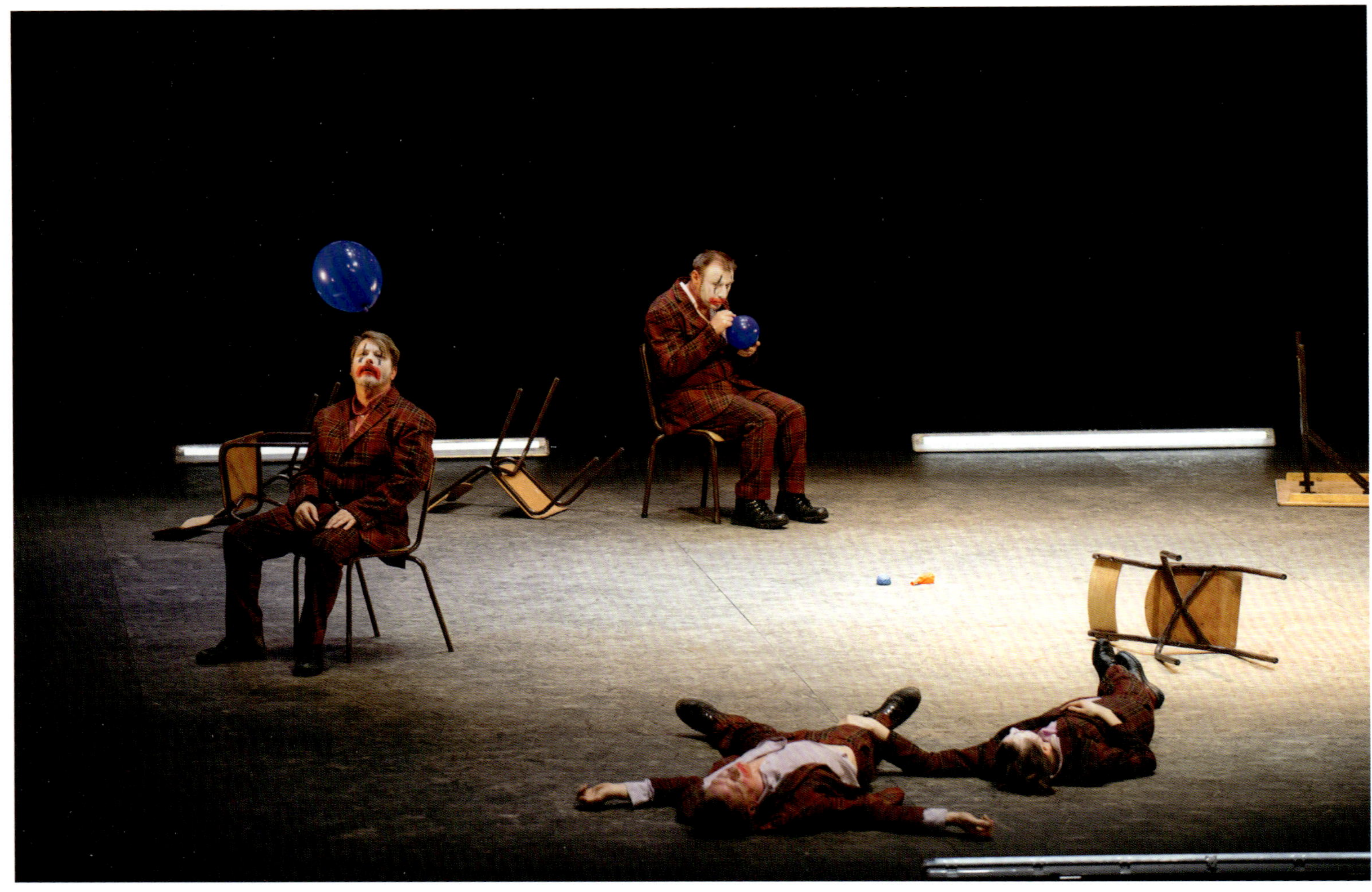

The first Forced Entertainment theatre work with no spoken text, *Out of Order* ditched the direct address to audience we've often used to frame action, setting up instead a world in which the figures seem oblivious or indifferent to the spectator's gaze. The stage design and costumes for the piece (a boxing ring or circus arena populated by clowns) already established a material tension with this supposed privacy; the visuals announced a show, even as the work's explicit theatricality appeared to have long since evaporated or warped beyond recognition. What we were drawn to is the fact that the action—repetitive, obsessive—offers no explanation for itself. Like *Real Magic*, the piece is a problematic object ... its awkwardness is very much a part of its material. [TE]

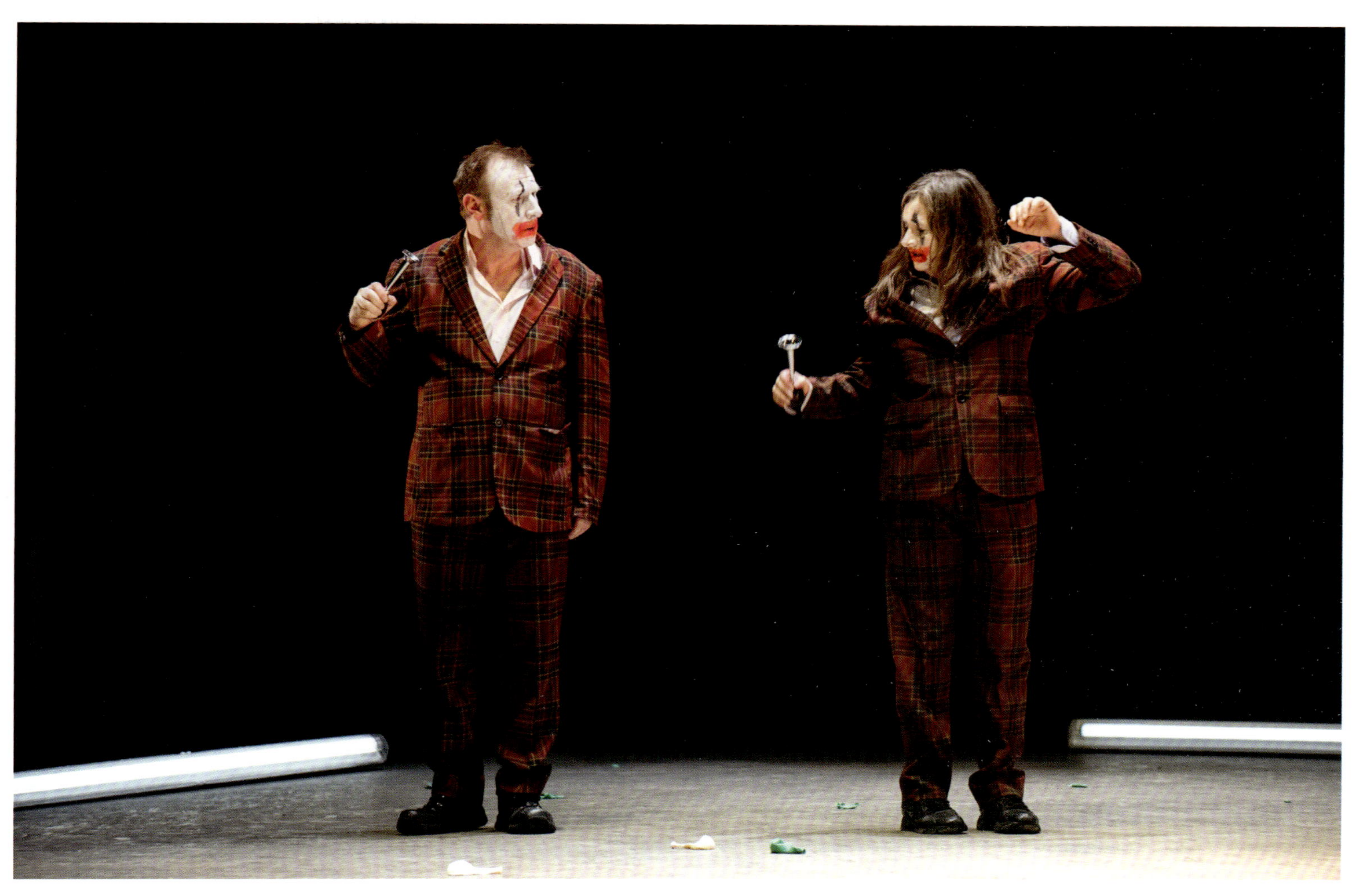

The clown makeup and costumes were decided early on. Because the actions swirled round, we needed the performers to look uniform, where roles could switch and remix. Looking at it from the outside, the audience sometimes lose the individuality of each performer in this swarm of people, identities can blur and then somehow emerge again. [TC]

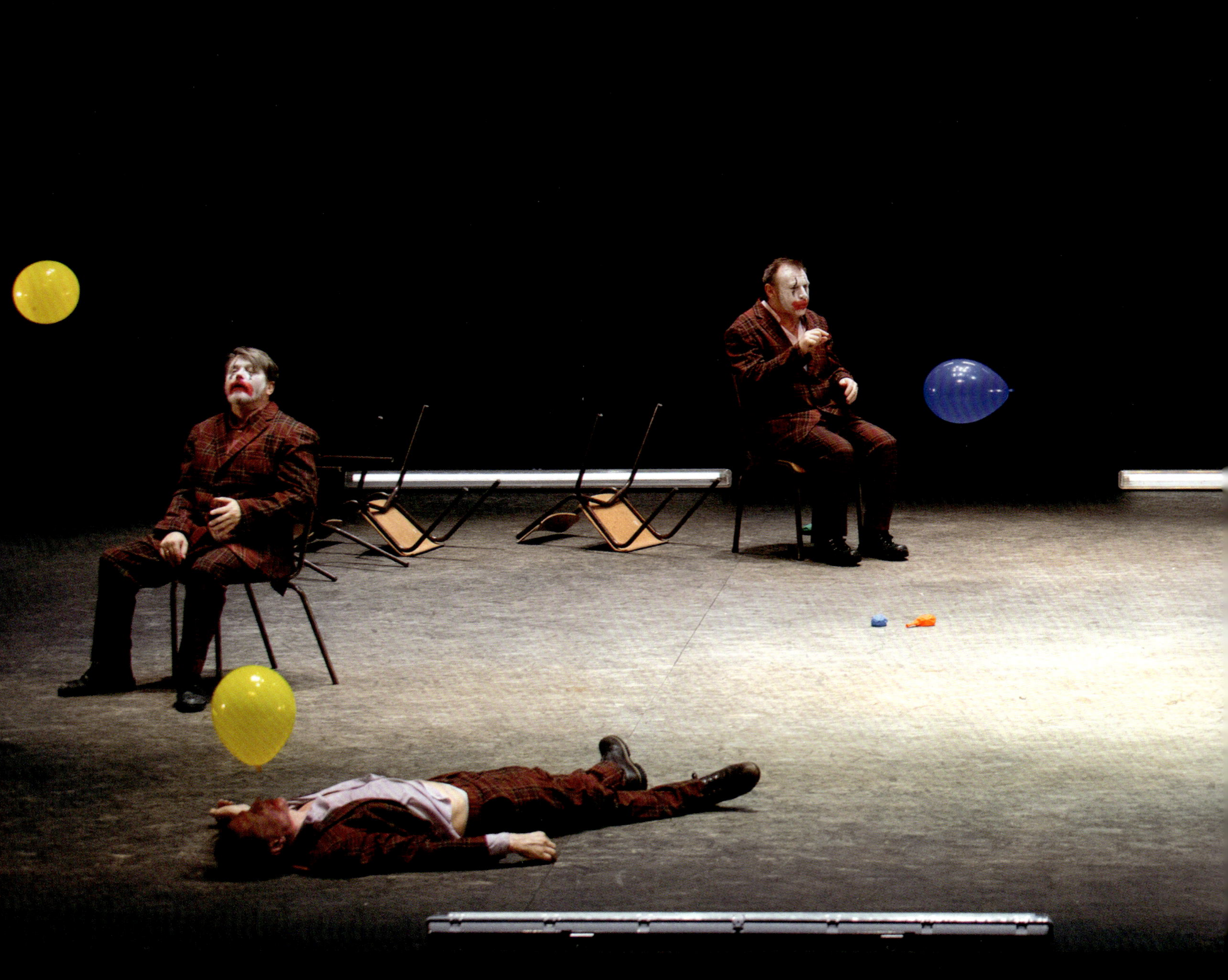

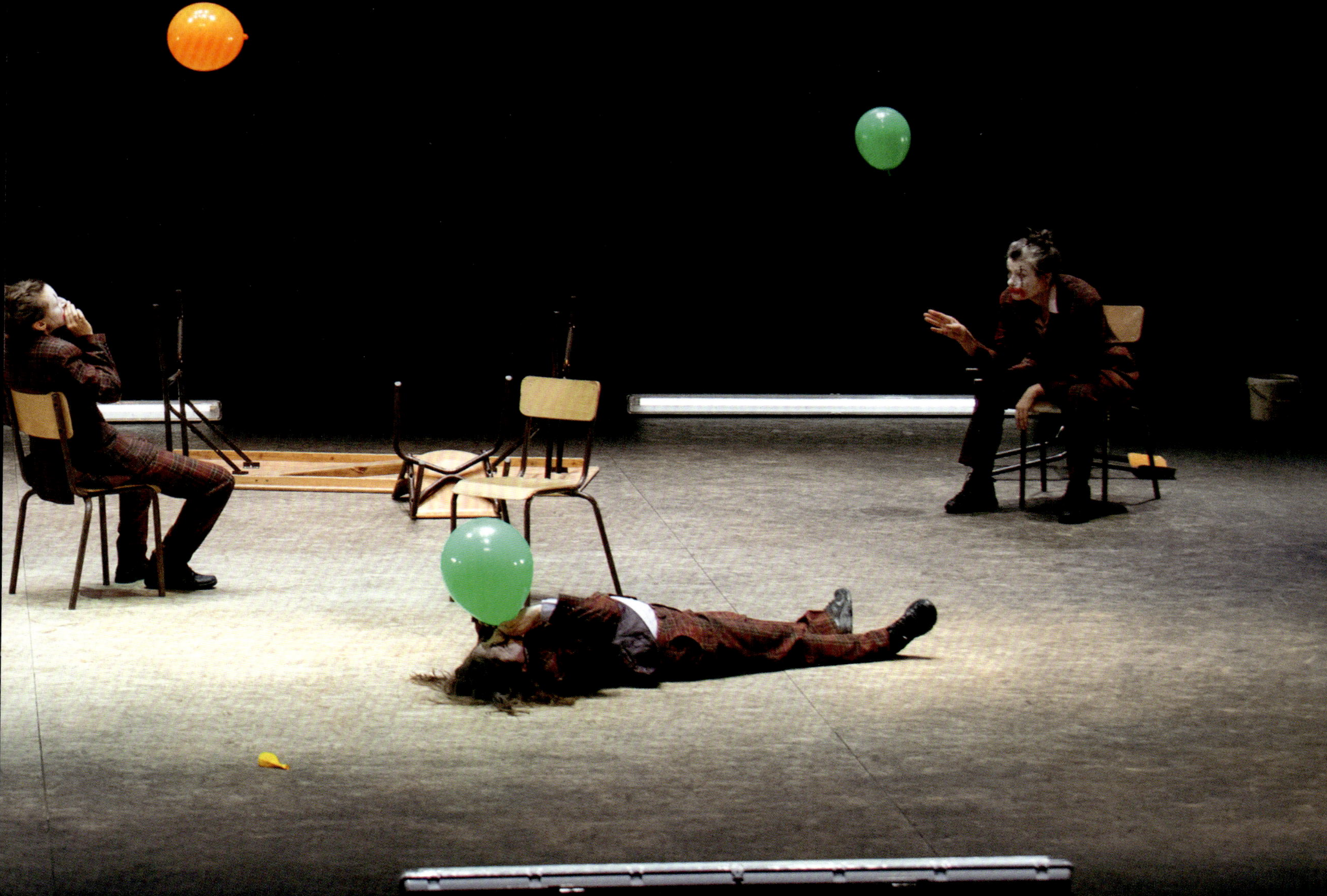

The core scene gets repeated through the first section of the performance: clowns gather around a table, seating themselves as if for some meeting or conference. Each time they're seated, one of them rises and makes as if to catch or physically attack another, scattering chairs in pursuit. Each time, a fight is apparently only avoided thanks to the intervention of the others, who block, catch, and drag apart their colleagues. Once the crisis is abated, they all straighten their clothing, reposition the felled chairs and sit again, only for the whole thing to kick off once more, this time with another pair of clowns as victim and antagonist. [TE]

The physicality was quite a challenge—just for our bodies at this time in our lives—to keep up that level of exertion and energy. It was also quite dangerous: with chairs flying everywhere you could very easily get hit. We really inhabited the idea of exhaustion: it became a visible presence. At the end of the first section the piece had delivered us all to a place where we were just collapsed on the floor, panting, sweating. [CN]

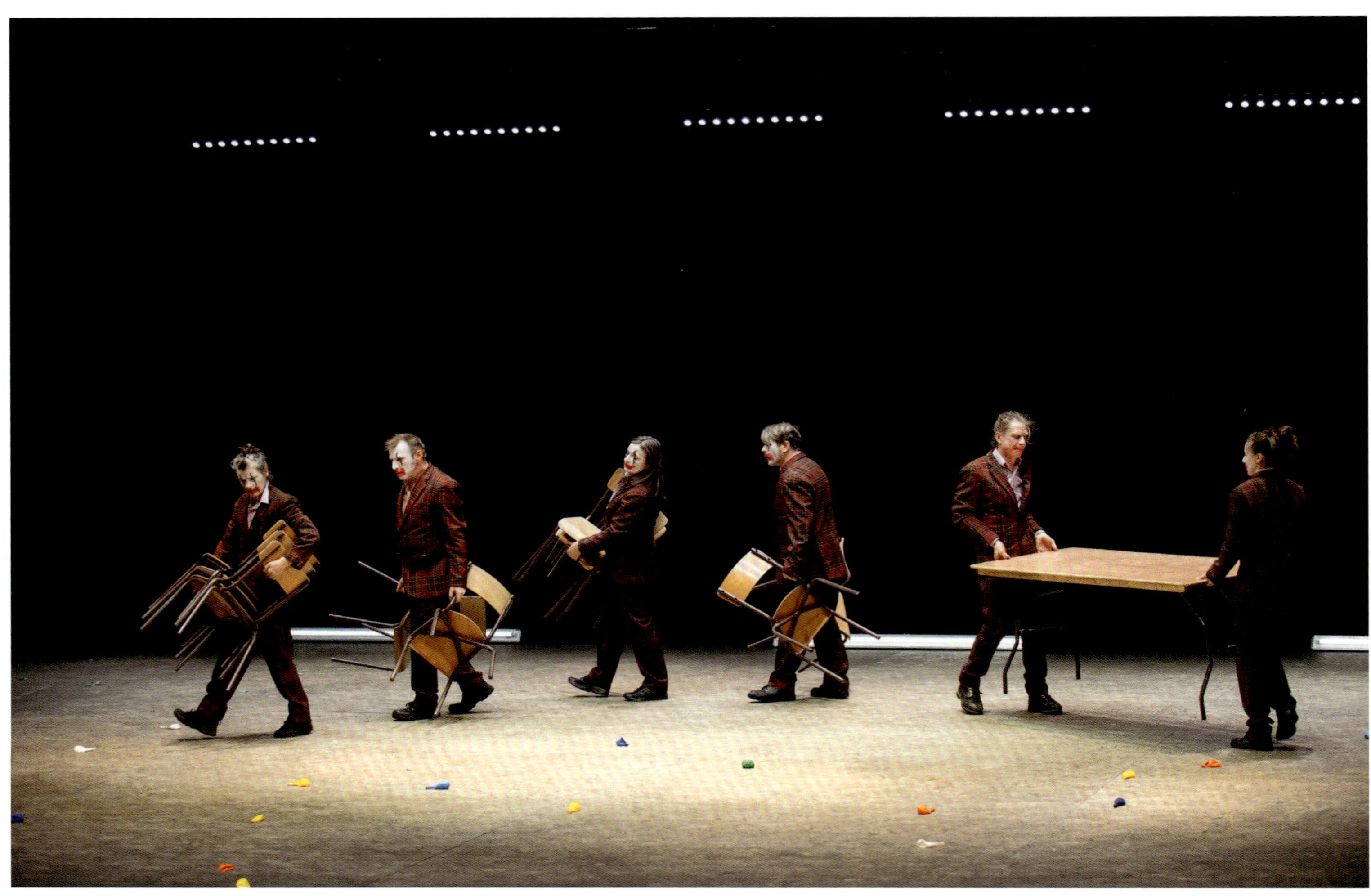

The section we call 'the parade' is a dramaturgical turning point. It comes after the first waves of high jinks and action are over and the energy is spiralling down. It begins as a simple slapstick of carrying furniture—'Where are these clowns going? Who is following who?'—a flurry in which there's endless redirection and apparent confusion. But the slapstick soon becomes a weary trudge around the perimeter of the stage from which it seems there's no escape. The six performers, between them, are carrying all the furniture, one following the other, heads bowed or eyes locked on the person in front. They go around and around, getting slower and slower.

In rehearsals it went on forever. It's so blank. So desolate. But at the same time it's rich. Many things come to mind watching them, with their stuff, walking. They're displaced persons, scavengers, refugees fleeing violence, weary workers caught in futile labour, and of course they're none of these things. They're human beings in front of an audience, marking the limits of the world they inhabit, carrying their equipment. A touring theatre. [TE]

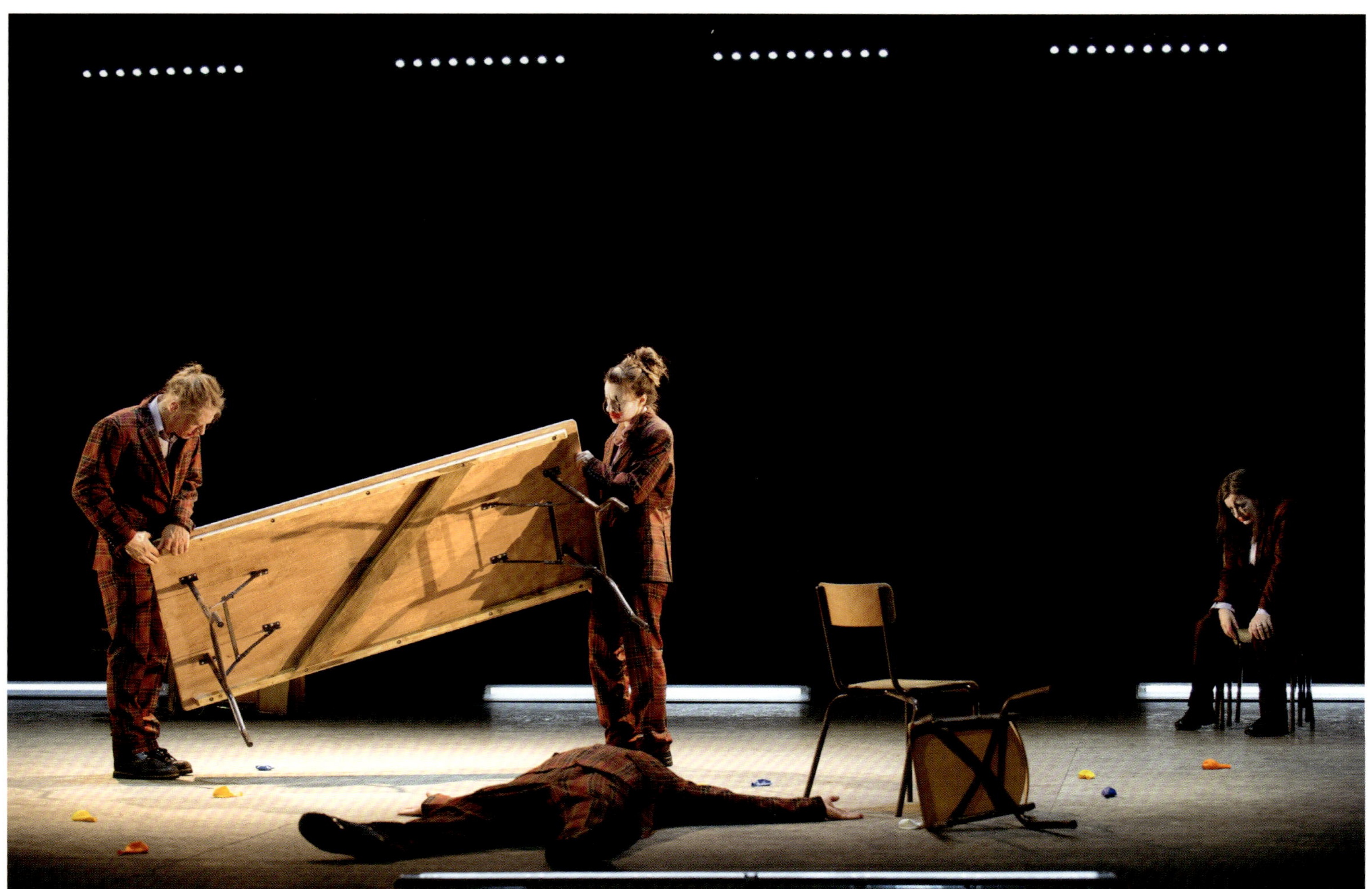

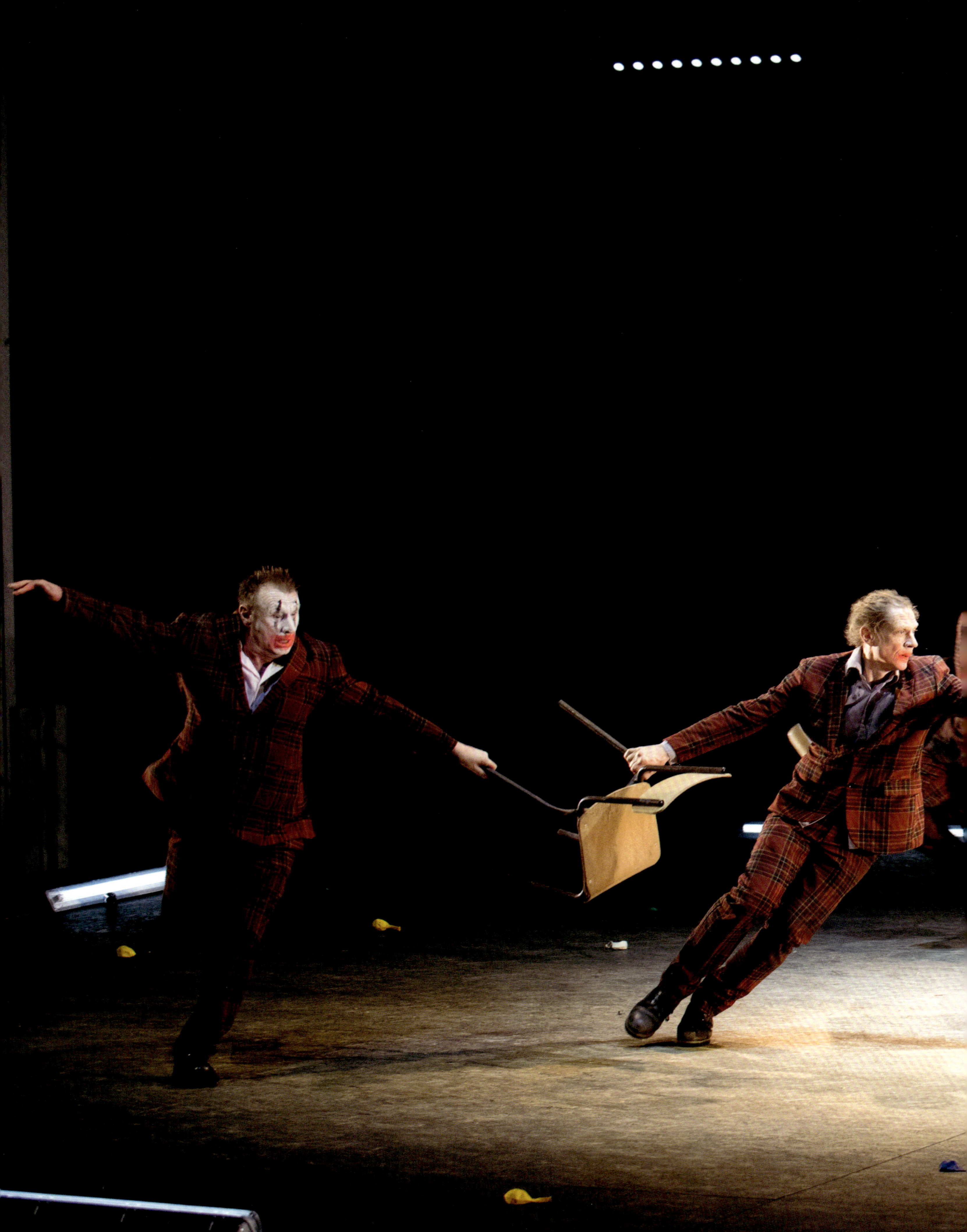

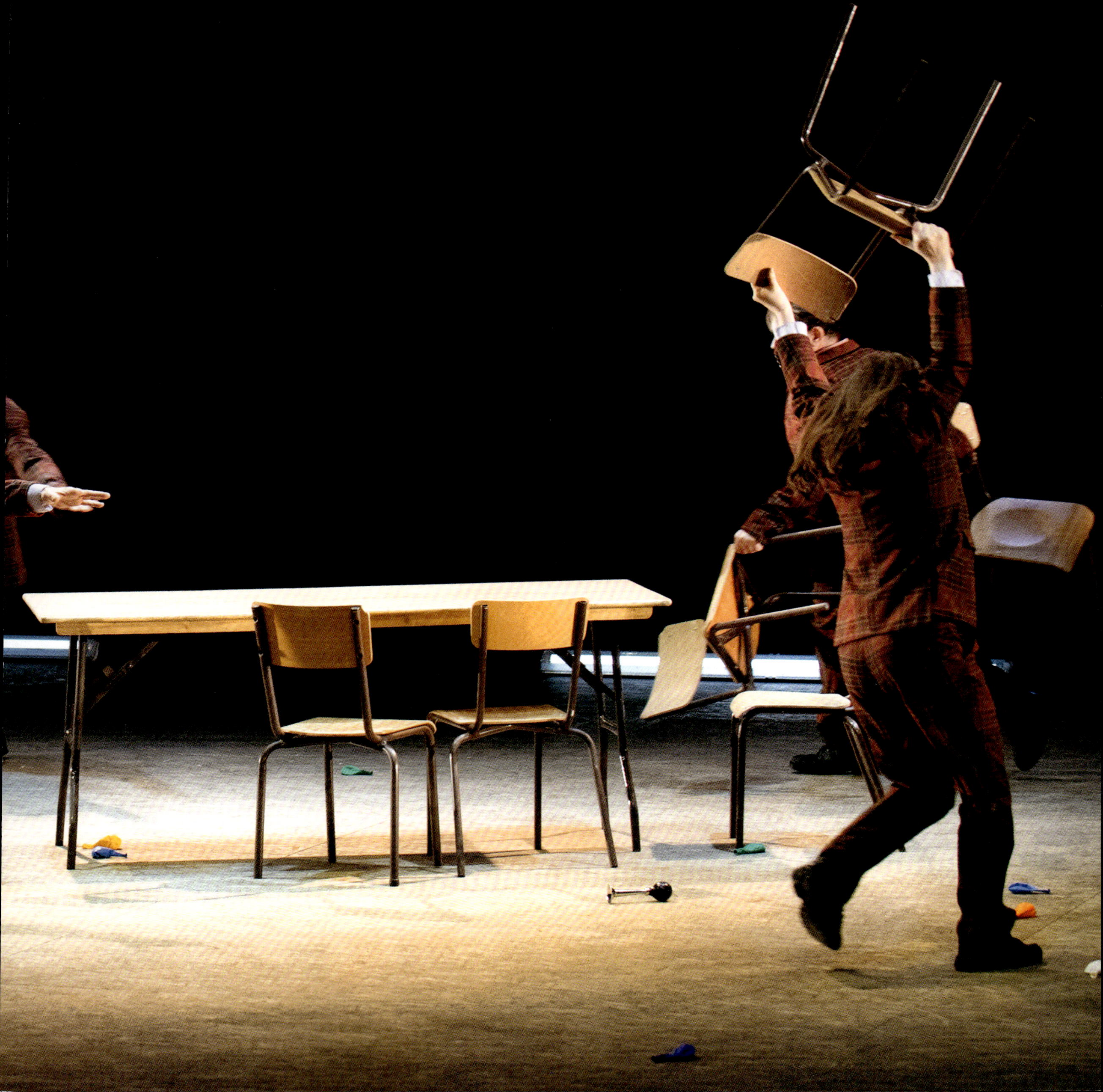

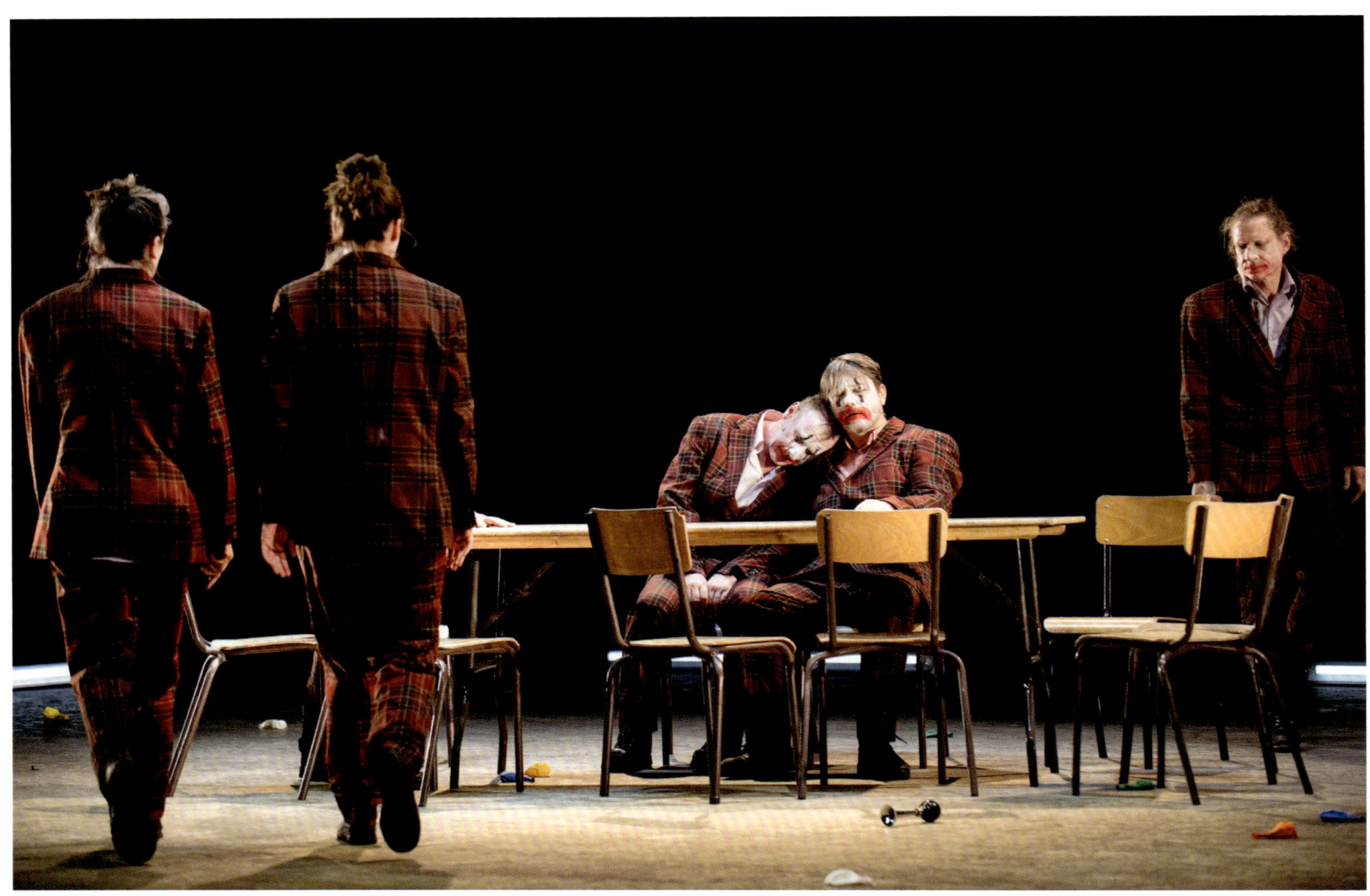

It's a very transgressive picture of ageing
bodies: that level of exertion and violence
is not what people of our age are supposed
to do. It has an absurd wrongness that
runs along with the melancholy that one
associates with clowning. *Out of Order* has
a strong sense of trappedness: these people
certainly shouldn't be doing this any more.
It feels like they're stuck in the same little
rituals of behaviour. That is part of its
sadness. [RA]

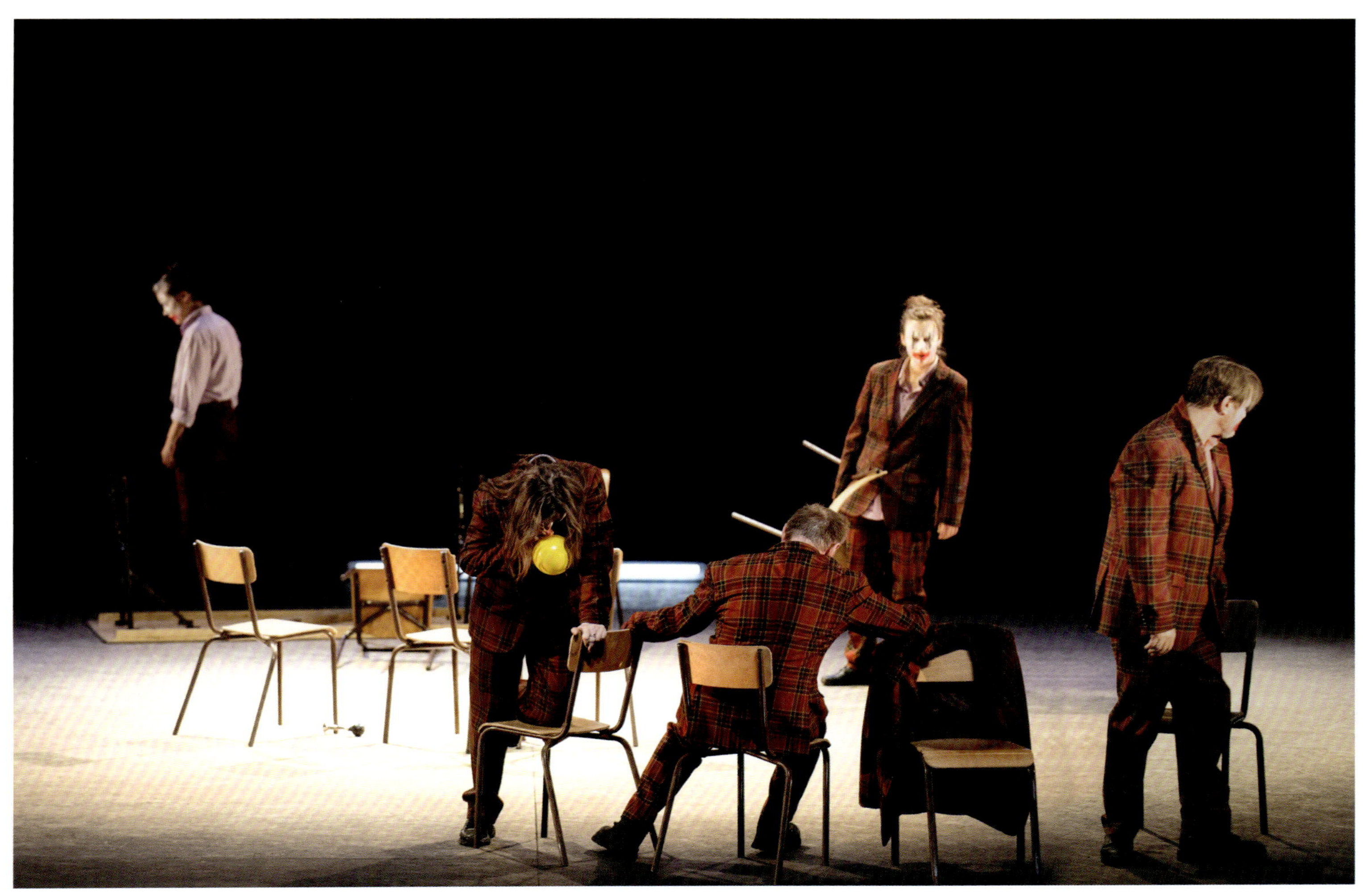

There are interludes here and there, stock elements of clown business (routines with balloons or hooters, pointless labour) becoming landscapes of mischief, misunderstanding, and ennui, but it's the pursuit scene—its threat of violence, its repeated passage from order to disorder—which provides the core material of the piece. The repeated confrontation shifts from high energy brutality at the start—clowns in a sweaty, noisy barroom brawl—towards a series of transformed versions of the earlier motifs.

The exhaustion gives rise to a sort of escape for the figures onstage. The last parts of the performance have a different energy and renewed inventiveness. In the ruins of their decaying routine they find a temporary way out in which playful, ironic, and comical approaches become possible, offering new perspectives. It is often the way with our work: the trap occasions a form of creative escape. [TE]

ESSAYS

Exquisite Catastrophe

Adrian Heathfield

> In one moment, the Forced Entertainment performance points to contemporary history and real or imagined universal catastrophes; in the next, it points to the individual's most intimate pleasures and fears in life.[1]

> It is upon losing what we have to say that we speak—upon an imminent and immemorial disaster—just as we say nothing except insofar as we can convey in advance that we take it back, by a sort of prolepsis, not so as to finally say nothing, but so that speaking might not stop at the word. … We speak suggesting that something not being said is speaking: the loss of what we were to say.[2]

Attempting to write beside the work of Forced Entertainment—to speculate with the qualities of the theatre events they have staged over the thirty-nine years of their collective labours, to become, as Tim Etchells, the company's director, would phrase it, a 'witness'[3]—is a trek along twisted pathways over unstable ground. One of the troubles along the way is the fraught relationship between writing and an event. Whichever philosophy of eventhood one subscribes to—of the many informing the thinking of contemporary theatre and this essay[4]—writing shows up as a tenuous and ever-failing tool when faced with the elusive density, affective amorphousness, and excessive forces of these embodied, aesthetic social events.[5] Even when some coordinates of an analytical perspective have been abandoned (for instance, as here, the certain authority and exteriority of a critical voice), the phrasings brought to these meaningful events—full of invisible currents, apparent ruptures, contradictions, and agitated ambivalences—tend to forget many flashes of felt consequence and to crystallize and so miss things that persist as murky atmospheres. Wording an event subjects the identifying power of writing to a force of annulment with which it tarries, in a conundrum similar to that invoked by Maurice Blanchot in *The Writing of the Disaster*, where language meets its limits and the word is required to go beyond itself, to speak the unspoken. This might seem overblown, but my thesis here will delineate some filaments of a catastrophic imaginary, at times anguished and melancholic, joyous and ecstatic, as it runs and morphs through the body of the company's work. As an attentive audience member for much of this oeuvre and an occasional visitor to rehearsals, the close readings I give here are tentative gestures; I am well aware that challenging the audience's understanding of the event being experienced is one of the consistent traits of this theatre company's work.

Forced Entertainment's oeuvre also presents another temporal contestation with both its use and abandonment of 'standard' timings for theatre. I've written elsewhere of the 'durational aesthetics' deployed by the company in six-, twelve-, and sometimes twenty-four-hour works, such as *12am: Awake & Looking Down* (1993), *Quizoola!* (1996), *And on the Thousandth Night …* (2000)—where a sustained inhabitation of acts and articulations beside an audience creates experiences of time warp, slowdown, and exhaustion, a 'nowhen' in which the spectator's attention is drawn to time reforming. Looking comparatively across the arc of this practice, as I do here with some exemplary evening-length theatre works produced over four decades, it is apparent that the two modes of time organization are not so easily opposed—that they creatively feed off each other through transformative reuse in the work's autopoietic movements—and that durational affects occur across the shorter theatre works in their radical dramaturgies and rhythmic manipulations. The durational is not simply or principally a matter of temporal extension, of quantity, but of the lived, felt experience of time, an intensive quality.[6] One further trouble for the tracing of shifts in the eventhood of this oeuvre is that, through the passage of cultural change between 1984 and 2021, Forced Entertainment have become an anomalous, even anachronistic object, not in relation to their aesthetic or its significant cultural influence, but as an arts organization, as a social organism, and as a way of making performance. They have persisted together in a modality that has become a contemporary rarity. The relentless capitalization of the arts and its preconditions of precarious labour, alongside identitarian and network cultures, have all played their part in making improbable in the future the particular form of long sustained collective collaboration embodied by Forced Entertainment. I see this anachronism as crucial to the contemporaneity of their work: they are a collective organism uniquely of their time and simultaneously maintain an interrogative distance from it.[7] I will insist that the works produced by the company are best understood alongside the unique means of their making, conditioning their eventhood. To trace the nature of the events of this work is, then, to follow the relational workings of more or less the same six people (with some expansions and contractions) across four decades: it is to attend to radical differences produced in relationships of sameness and consistency,[8] to witness agencies of bodies ageing together in time, to speak with emanations from a complex, enduring creative fidelity and friendship, to attune to forces uniquely signed by resilient collectivity, to speculate with the emergent things between them.

Making time palpable is also one of the common understandings of various philosophies of the event, a happening that carries both rupturing and instituting dynamics.[9] Experimental theatre has a long intertwinement with traditions of actional poetics common to performance art, even if that 'practice of the real' is, as Etchells would suggest, another kind of 'as if'.[10] Whether it simply confounds representation, or exceeds it, an event is often understood as an occurrence of something radically new, unforeseen, indeterminate, or chaotic and, at the same time, as something that instantiates (by overturning), leaving traces, producing not just history but subjects themselves. An event is a happening, a singularity that makes new knowledge and ways of knowing, and in this regard a particular epistemic dynamic has been broadly associated with the events of contemporary experimental theatres: that they act 'as forms of thought and performative historiographic inquiry'.[11] My readings here follow this sense of the events of Forced Entertainment as a thinking of their place in time, and of their own nature, a material questioning of their materials. But I am also interested in the ways that multiple events may be nested inside events, that every event has its micro events and its latencies, to which we must attend if we are to understand the knowing therein. In a collective oeuvre of this longevity what is fascinating is the echoic relations of events across the body of the work, their continuances as well as their modulations. Similarly, figuration (as distinct from characterization) manifests and is exposed as echoic: as an iteration of differing fragments of the performer's selves. I refer throughout to Forced Entertainment's practice as a theatre of the wake-event, and here I am alluding to a foundational supposition and a set of qualities of the work, that go beyond the doubleness of all theatre—a practice made not just to be seen but to be done again, or, as Richard Schechner would say, an example of the 'twice-behaved behaviour' that is ritual.[12] I have in mind another kind of force work made manifest in this oeuvre, a coursing through time that troubles the senses of intentionality and choice in enacting 'restored behaviour', and questions its clear separation from what Schechner calls 'a natural event'.[13]

Put simply, the catastrophic imaginary I am evoking here is not one that is only imagined and presented by the collective, it is produced by the force of catastrophe itself. A wake, as in the work of Christina Sharpe, has at least a triple sense: it is that trace of disturbance in materials that follows the impact of an action or movement; it is the human process of attending to a death, of celebrating life in the face of death's force; and it is an occasion of renewed consciousness of social conditions and their histories.[14] For me, a wake-event is a form of performance afterlife, a material tremor or human trembling, a ceremony of attunement to the forces of annihilation, and a situation in which new awarenesses and knowings of life are made manifest. I mean to take at face value Etchells's enigmatic comment in relation to their recent work *Out of Order* (2018), that 'it starts, as our work often does, in the ruins of something'. Now for Forced Entertainment, as for many other contemporary theatre artists, those ruins are—as in Hans-Thies Lehmann's work—those of an older dramatic theatre.[15] But for me, the ruins are laid and made by an altogether Other human catastrophe. That is to say that time and time again, in work after work, there is an inauguration, a commencement, born(e) in the remnants and revenants of a precursor edifice, another unseen event of total expiration. But I also want to complicate the temporal location of those ruins, to think them through this work not simply as something of the past, or coursing through the present, but following Blanchot's insight, as an 'imminence', a futurity. What exactly Etchells' ethereal ruinous 'something' is will be my question (and the work's) as I wind through its distinct instantiations over the decades. In each instance, it is formed in and resonates with the waves of a contemporaneity. It will be seen to flutter, in the blink of an eye, as in Lehmann's epigraph, through matters of the utmost intimacy to the utterly impersonal. Whilst Blanchot's and Sharpe's writings on the disaster and the wake stem from distinct historical catastrophes—the holocaust and transatlantic slavery, respectively—they also attend to the ways in which these violent histories are carried in the consciousness and social structures of the present. Through its layered performative iterations, the theatre of Forced Entertainment at once alludes to and resists the concretization of catastrophe into an enclosed historical event, referent, or scene. The catastrophic may be stirred through the many invocations of death presented across the company's work—and they are legion—but like the title of this book, and the sequence of speeches from which it takes its name, it is an imagined encounter not just with the thought of death but with an absolute surpassing force, the fall of the human.

~

1986. *(Let the Water Run Its Course) to the Sea That Made the Promise*. Almost the first words I hear, spoken in a soft Yorkshire drawl, are a dedication: to 'those for whom falling is a way of life'. Two men and two women are looking out into the void of the unacknowledged reciprocity of the auditorium. They stand in a scenic evocation of a sparse ex-industrial space with narrow columns and wired glass partitions; a few old crates sit at the back. Battered swivel chairs on either side of the room seem to await them. Laid over this scene as a soundtrack, a male and female voice are narrating what seems to be a love story. Perhaps it refers to the relations unfolding now in front of me, but it is placed in the past tense, as if this event had already happened. The voices speak of two lovers living with broken, semi-synthetic bodies whose organs die, while the lovers somehow continue on; they speak of their life in an inhospitable city, partly familiar and partly unknown, but constantly subject to perverse renaming. It sounds like a dystopian future, but there are many recognizable contemporary references. Meanwhile, the two men and two women are, like me, taking in the detail of this place, surveilling it, as if they seek to find or recall something that once happened here. The space evokes redundant labours: it looks abandoned. As the voice-over stops and the action begins, there is a sense of rupture, that these figures have come here to enact something that does not belong but has been found here through an urgent inhabitation. Hyperphysical rituals are played out—cartoonish in their accelerated run-throughs of postures and relations and their slapstick collage of actions—affectively recycling historical (and histrionic) gestural material. Though it appears to carry some inaccessible private symbolism, the choreographic content of these acts is evidently quoted, exaggerated, generic: it has the feel of second-hand stuff and like the vernacular of the narrator voices, it is saturated with a sense of decay. It is as if the figures appearing before me are attempting to re-enter an intense condition of life from which they are alienated in the contemplative emptiness of the present. No wonder, then, that their acts invoke situations of human extremity: heightened arguments, spectacular post-cinematic deaths (with sprayed tomato ketchup wounds), scenes of failed resuscitation and inconsolable grief. Each act is tested and retested through insatiable iterations. The figures appear to want both to recover and surpass some haunted inhabitation of absolute necessity. They oscillate between acting and watching the other act. The performers' gaming dynamic of copying, mutating, and exceeding the previous enactment of their partners sets them apart from each other in the visceral intimacy of a shared but perpetually deferred goal. Their frayed enactments are at times accompanied by bursts of an uncanny spoken nonsense, as if language itself has been lost and reinvented from the shards of many languages, or as if all that remains of human speech is an arcane form of religious glossolalia. Punctuating these scenes, in a mashed-up language we can recognize, the story of the two lovers continues through a litany of injuries, somehow survived deaths and renamings, set against a morphing city.

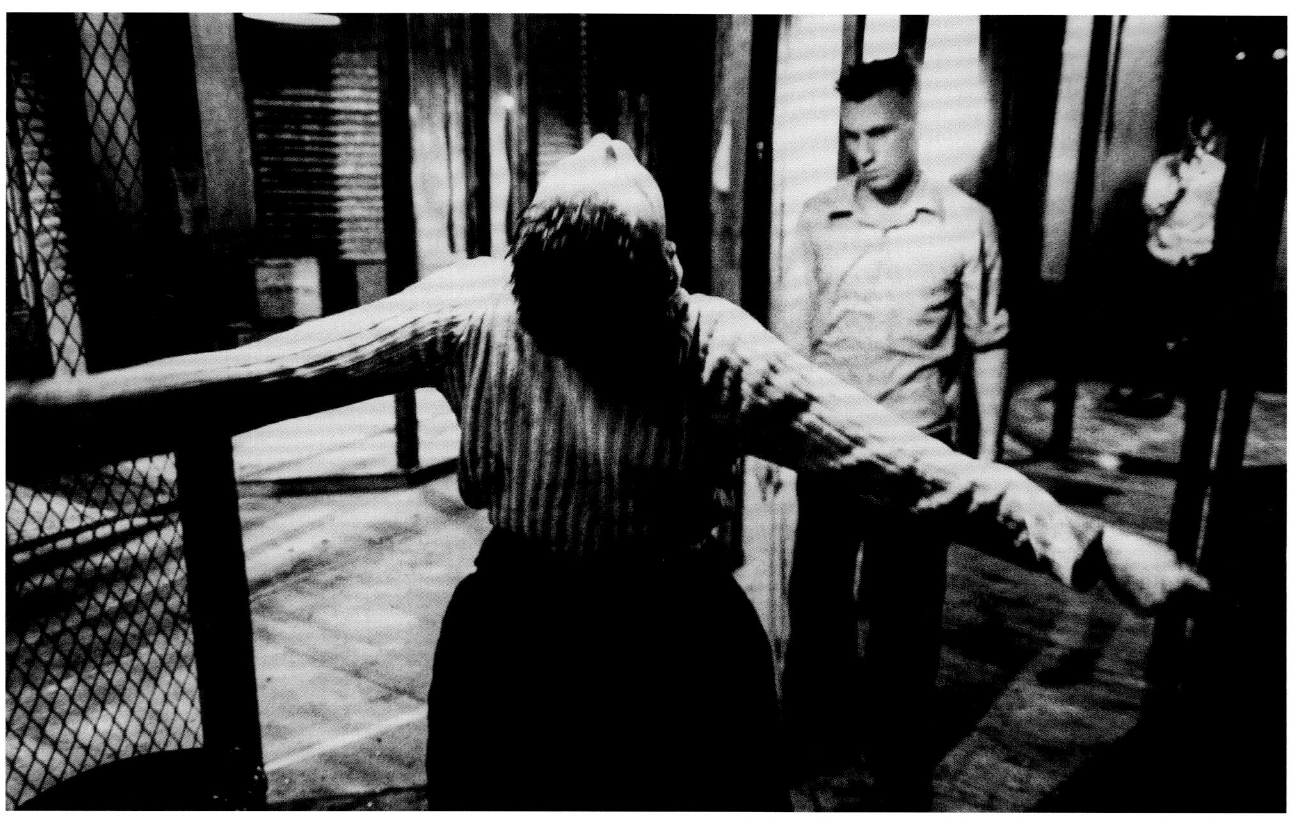

It seems that these unhinged rituals could at some time be meaningfully restored, should a mutually recognized intensity or newness arrive and consume the present, making it coherent once again. Though no such fix arises in this performance, the agitated enactments of the performers are eventually resolved into softer choreographies of physical consolation, the washing and hanging of wet clothes, and the still exhibition of those dripping clothes to the audience accompanied by Frank Sinatra's *I Love Paris* (1962). At the close of the piece the performers lift the floorboard panels of the set to reveal a pebble beach below. They stand silently and still against the elevated boards looking out to the audience in a startling white light, as if looking to the sea, whose sound crashes cacophonously around us.

Let the Water manifests aesthetic tactics that will consolidate in the later works of Forced Entertainment: raw ritual enactment with marked repetition and obscure symbolism that abstracts ritual's social function whilst retaining its sacrificial energies; disjunction between action and spoken language; broken poetics; elusive sonic atmospherics; the replacement of character with performer presence and unanchored figuration. But what interests me most in this early work is the relationship between the voice-over duet and the enactment, where language asserts some claim, however tenuous, on the actions but through its tense creates an unresolvable tension within the present. Etchells' voice-over poetics at times suggest that a single time (a year) is being narrated through multiple versions, a future that is now long past, whilst the constant iteration of the characters' reincarnations suggests an impossible temporality.[16] This mixed-up fictive frame speaks with and against the present tense rituals that also appear to be set in a diminished future but aimed at resuscitating a lost past. The creation of the work in Sheffield took place in the wake of the Thatcher government's de-industrialization of northern cities and mining towns, which led to large-scale unemployment, increased poverty, and urban dereliction, but its making also coincided with the Chernobyl disaster's crystallization of the ecological dangers of a nuclear age, and as it played to audiences around Europe, Strontium-90 and Caesium-137 isotopes—whose half-life is around thirty years—were still drifting across the continent.[17] Andrei Tarkovsky's prescient sci-fi film *Stalker* (1979) is surely a buried dystopian inter-text with its combination of scientific derailment, watery dereliction, and magical quest. These sociopolitical and aesthetic contexts resonate in abstraction through the senses of erased labour and culture, impoverishment, toxic elements, and longing in the work, conditioning the social sense of its wake-event, its radical atemporality. Richard Lowdon, Susie Williams, Robin Arthur, and Cathy Naden enact the work with an anguished energy and youthful vulnerability that adds to the sense that the event is an attempt at psychic rehearsal of, or spirited inoculation against, a catastrophic future. So, there is also another meltdown in nature here, that of the young human body, whose viscerally felt needs are set against a sonic narration of its continuous de-naturalization through poor reinvention with market detritus. One lover's 'insides wer made out of bendy plastic & tranquillizer chewing gum, her insides wer fragile neon & bound up with Sellotape, her insides wer radium atoms lit only by 40 Watt bulbs', whilst another lover's 'true blood' was a cocktail of many other bloods composed in a bucket.[18] If the 'natural' materiality of the human body is in crisis here it seems that the sea, the origin and destination of this work, may at least offer some form of salve or cleansing. But it manifests as semblance and ambivalence at the close of the work, present only through its intense reflected light and its recorded raging.

~

The rending of representational economies would appear to be the emphasis of a swathe of Forced Entertainment's theatrical and durational works in the mid- to late 1990s, with their use of fragmentation, proliferation, and recombination of texts, the appearance of textuality as visual material, and exposed recitation as a performance mode. Even if the notion of a single coherent representable world given by an authorial internally consistent text is systematically dismissed in these works, what remains as an article of faith, however, is the worlding capacity of the textual. This potential is allied, through a negative aesthetics, with what is carried within, underneath, or beside text in the ecstasis of its saying. As Joe Kelleher notes in his essay for this book, speaking in this work is always a situation of (self-)alteration.[19] By the mid-1990s, the narrative of stage action as a form and method of world-capture is usurped by its pluralization in contesting micro narrations recited onstage. The forces that do this operation of rending, that create the theatre work's eventhood, have also shifted. Whilst a romantic preoccupation with the irredeemable lostness of urban subjects remains, body, identity, and place are less emphasized as sources of rupture, and a broad set of human aspirations and nature itself arise as sundering dynamics. *Club of No Regrets* (1994) is perhaps the most intense manifestation of these shifts. Scenographic writing is boldly legible in earlier works such as *Marina & Lee* (1991), where place appears as a scripted limit: a neon sign slung across its textual backdrop emanates the message 'Look No Further—This Is It'. By *Club of No Regrets*, scenography has turned into a jumble of recessive graphic palimpsests. A stage-within-a-stage is constructed from blackboard flats—a rudimentary room with doorway and three windows—sketched over in chalk by documentary scribbles and frenzied crossings out. From these inscriptions, what is clear is that textuality is affiliated, not just with authority, but with the law. A semi-legible scrawled title suggests that the room itself is a 'forensic reconstruction' and its status as the scene of a crime is amplified by the marking of numbered gunshots across its walls. The large backdrop of the stage is another assembly of blackboards elaborately chalked with a cityscape and overwritten with wholly illegible notations. This friable scenic chalkscape (a negative page) suggests a *mise en abyme* of place as textuality, given to a process of rewriting and erasure, a graphology inclined toward dust.

A narrator figure—O'Connor 'as' Helen X—clutches a wedge of papers from which she gives a stumbling reading of numerous divergent texts that appear to act as scenic content or commentary for the purposefully weak enactment taking place in the room. Two other figures appear as aimless subjects of these scenes, and two more as careless event facilitators and brutal prop handlers. Arthur and Marshall—the scenic enactors—are at first bound to the stage furniture and gagged with parcel tape, as if hostages to whatever theatre is to be authored upon their bodies. These initially blank figures are subjects only insofar as they are written into life; their speaking capacity is limited to text fragments they are handed to recite. The binding here, and its associated subjections, is not just seen as the textual, but as the entire theatrical apparatus. An alternately

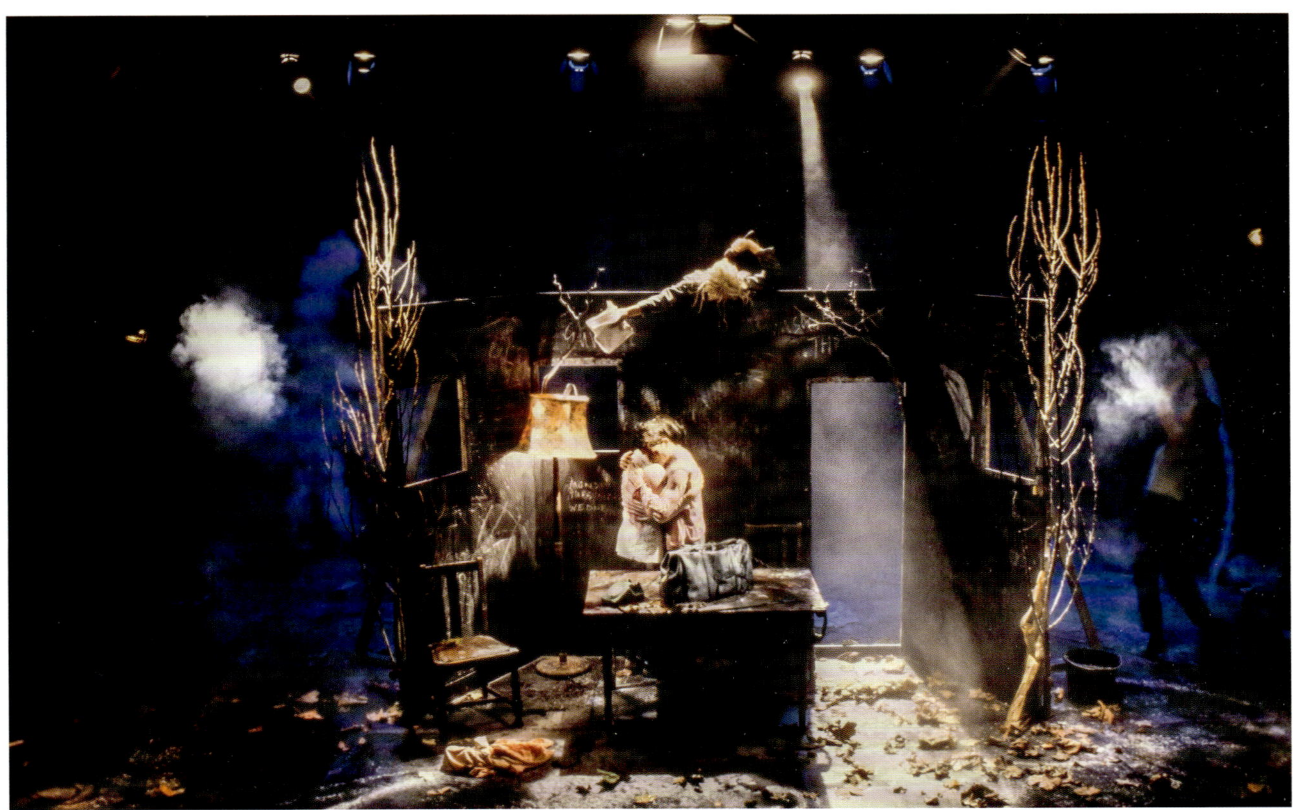

comic, violent and wistful enactment ensues in which 'scenes' are 'called up' and misfire through the non-coincidence of action, emotion, gesture, language, and objects or through the disruptions of the 'aid' given by the hapless stagehands. Faltering recitation slowly morphs into impassioned incantation, as the scenes become intensified. The textual scraps that are assembled, recombined, and repeatedly animated in the work's dramaturgical arc are concerned with matters of criminological method, senses of urban life and immanent violence, cosmology, and spiritual summoning. If a crime has been committed here, it is not just mysterious but at once original and secondary, singular and generic, mundane and cosmic. As the scenes progress and acquire certain fictive consistencies, what becomes apparent is that worlding depends on the affective ecology of the apparatus: the fabric of relations between subjects, material things, and things said. If the quest of the stagehands is to make scenic objects and bodies conform to a world given by textual authority, the relentless recirculation and reanimation of stuff that is the performance make manifest not just that objects *make* worlds but that they do so when at their most thingly.[20] Theatrical worlding is a systemic material surrogation, and performance is the modality through which objects become things, through which those things reverberate, stand beside themselves, other, transform, re-signify, elude capture by sense. As Helen X asks, loitering beside the room and its scenes, 'What ghosts are these? What strange signs? What things?'

The blunt recombination of narrative fragments, object resonance, and a heightened energy of action seem to be the only methods available to the 'spirited actors' embroiled in the quest to acquire the consistency or correctness sought by this event's insatiable drive. The agents of the intensifying and dissipating scenes are repeatedly bound to material objects (literally with the parcel tape, but mostly metaphorically) as their dependency upon things for affect becomes apparent. Though they may not be working with the same intentions or understanding of effect, these figures are engaged in a process of collective summoning: of atmospherics, intensities, and energies. The elemental dimension of this affective worlding resonates with and extends its wording, its spoken invocations. Search lights are cast across the darkened stage space, talcum powder dust clouds billow out of 'gunfights' and coat the scenery with residues, tearful scenes

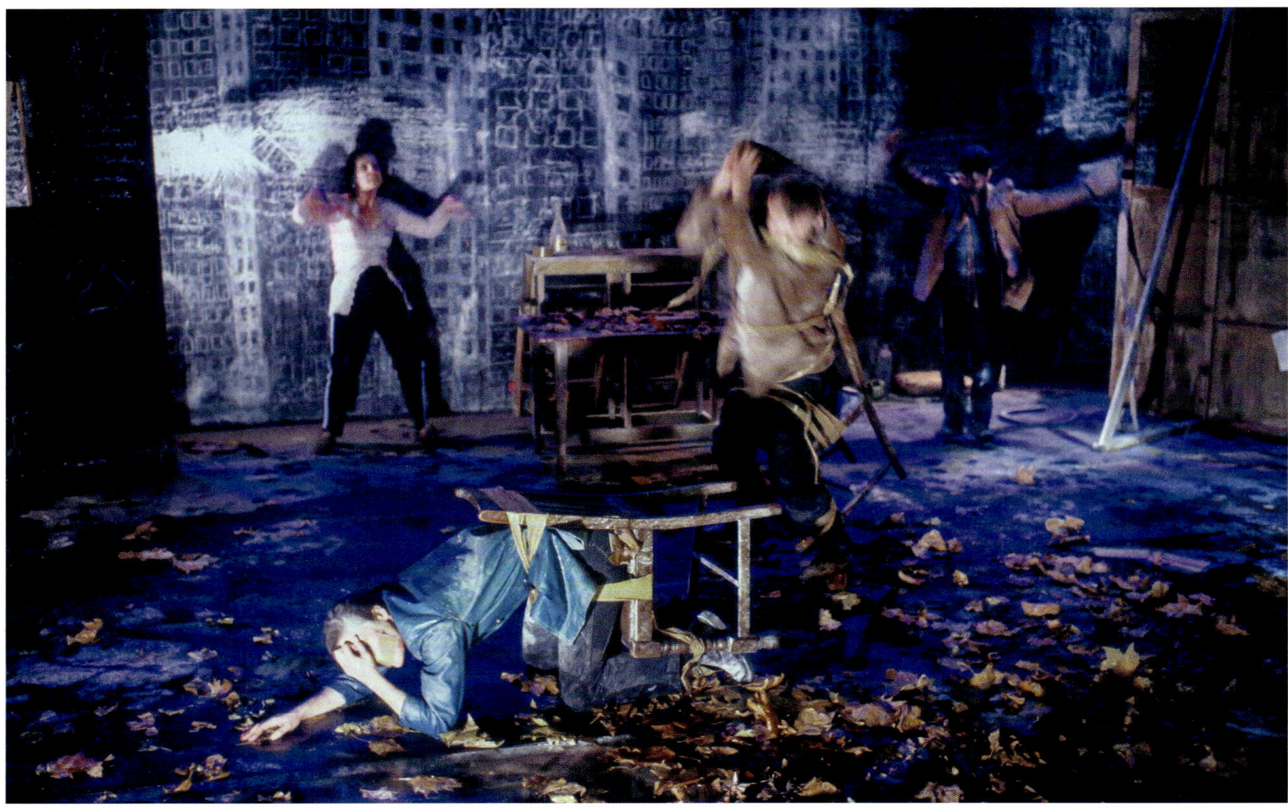

transform into streams of sprayed water, and stage blood is liberally squirted across bodies. The evocative quest of the work—its worlding—is qualified in the final wild passages, as an attempt to escape restriction, as a quest for freedom. In a coda to the scenes of citation, the central room is dismantled, leaving a barren stage smeared with the slippery detritus of the previous acts. Some form of exit from the room and its scenes, from the law and the prison house of language appears to have been attained, as Arthur and Marshall emerge into open space and another kind of agency. In pairs, the figures bind each other with parcel tape to chairs once more. Raucous music plays whilst 'the captors' dance and 'the captives' agitatedly wrestle to free themselves, at some apparent risk, from their restraints. The roles alternate and the act is played out once again to a pensive score: a desolate and increasingly futile struggle. Whatever is at stake in this escape drive is affectively amplified by the acutely felt danger facing the breathless but mute performers: this escape act is materially perilous and has none of the technical assurances of staged magic. There is in any case no destination for the escape, no shape to this freedom, a from but no to; there is simply the ragged struggle of release.

If the recombining fictive fragments of *Club of No Regrets* return us repeatedly to the relation between the governance of the law and the affective elements of an enacted life, they do so with a certain relentlessness that feels like law in itself: a law of prodigious grafting and re-grafting, of infinite movement, of cyclical creation and destruction: a law of nature. Helen X repeatedly insists that she is lost in the woods, and as the scenes reach their most intensely affective combination, the room is encroached upon by thrown leaves and branches of trees, as if the city were being reclaimed by the forest, by the wild that, as Claire MacDonald notes, always inhabits the margins of the urban.[21] The final escape act is itself a tussle with the physics of watery surfaces, unstable materials, uncontrollable movement, gravity, and the frailty of flesh.[22] It's as if what needs to be escaped is not just the linguistic apparatus of the theatre as a scene of subjection but the laws of its fabric, of its very materiality. Transcendence collapses into immanence as bodies test their material constraints. This wildness becoming and overcoming the event is a cumulative affect of the work's countless attempt trajectories, charged by a palpable sense of risk: the catastrophic wake-event of an energetic theatre of excessive expenditure. The company's memories of this work often figure *Club of No Regrets* as an elemental ceremony: Etchells recites a story of an outdoor performance in Volterra, Italy, whose determining qualities were that the translated text was learnt phonetically by the non-Italian speaking performers and its eventhood was conditioned by the receptive chatter of the audience throughout.[23] Language here, once dissociated from its ties to intended, authentic or stable meaning enters the condition of an abstract social event, a sonorousness carried in the air. The tale is marked by a meteorological image of a cloud of dust (talcum powder) rising from the performance, shimmering in the moonlight, and drifting off into the night sky. In its final performance in San Francisco, Etchells narrates that the replica set built for the occasion was burnt in a wake-like bonfire party, at which audience members lit by firelight spontaneously re-enacted their own versions of the escape routine from the show.[24] The fire of the wake arises from the aneconomic dynamic of this theatre's expenditure—in which return shipping or saving a chalky, battered scriptural edifice, the material property of the work, is totally redundant. In its afterlives, *Club of No Regrets*, as haunted synthetic weather and as incandescent reckless ceremony, is an elemental force of joyous violence. The sense of this work as an evocation of the creative destruction inherent to nature is echoed in the company's story of the tree branches foraged in Sheffield and used over numerous performances being finally returned to a forest in the Tuscan hills.[25] Nature's dead materials briefly circulate as the 'living' properties of the theatre, before returning to their unhomely habitat, to the wild where decay is intimately entwined with creation, to a wildness in which we humans attempt to make fragile dwellings.

~

A tranche of Forced Entertainment's work in the first decade of the twentieth century turned to relations between performer and audience as subject. In works such as *First Night* (2001), *Bloody Mess* (2004), and *The Thrill of It All* (2010) direct spoken address to spectators became a trope played out through questions of the politics of affect. Typically, a solitary performer or a divergent group would attempt to command and narrate the elusive event already in process by taking up a proposition for speech to or at the audience (never with), pursuing the logics of the address to extinction. Such exhausted sayings often entailed the performing figure's fantasy idea of an appropriated theatre or narrow and exposed projections of spectators' expectations, feelings, and desires, or their present and future experiences. Across the hushed, stilled, and darkened chasm between speaking doers and seers that constitutes the theatrical event, a form of intentional mis-speaking opens out the feeling of co-presence and comical misrecognition for those who watch.[26] One established way of thinking about such articulations is as a deconstructive gesture in relation to the spectators' subjective investment in the figures before them or the worlds of the work.[27] The performance operates through the twists of dis-identification. Whilst evidently inhabiting the spirit of their speech, the figure overdetermines or misreads the event, exposing the mismatch between their articulation and the spectator's making sense of the felt experience of that event. This form of distancing between performer and audience, as Matthew Goulish notes, 'situates the audience as always already other' and, whilst sometimes 'confronting' for individual spectators, forces a differentiation of sense, and so is seen by Goulish as generative of 'world view adjustment'.[28]

It is in this context that the ten performers who enact *Bloody Mess* first address the audience in a seated line near the beginning of the piece, articulating their expectations and desires in terms of the audience's reading-to-come of their individual performances. In fact, these are the first of many spoken and tenuous frameworks that are brought in to explain or narrate the meaning of the chaotic and fractious event that is already in process. Two striking gendered miniature speeches stick out and are then taken up substantively in the dramaturgy of the work: Claire Marshall's insistence that the audience should hold her presence as the primary object of their sexual desire and Naden's assertion that the audience should barely notice her, that she should appear as an enigmatic shadow. Marshall, dressed as a gorilla throughout will go on to elaborate the audience's imagining of their sexual union with her and its aftermath, whilst Naden will be consumed by serial attempts to enact a barely noticeable death that will consume the audience in an infinite grief. Two fundamental dramaturgical propositions are made, then, about the nature of meaningful exchange between the audience and performer: that it is primarily a sexual economy and that its purpose is the reception of loss. Whilst each of these (common and, here, gendered) analytics of theatre are shown as wanting in the elaboration of the audiences dis-identification, they are qualified and re-inflected by two further dramaturgical gestures in the work. In the most sustained narrations of *Bloody Mess*—and consequently the most interrupted—John Rowley's clown figure attempts to narrate the Big Bang theory of the creation of the universe (and this world), and then subsequently its eventual destruction. These are claims on the meaning of the work (they are simultaneously staged with smoke, noise, and dancing stars) that lend cosmic resonance to the sexual and death drives previously articulated. But in a later 'scene', the still 'centre' of this work, these drives are seen to be in an uneasy synthesis that occupies a particular hold over the whole event.

The dark vortex of the eventhood of *Bloody Mess*—an exquisite catastrophe—is a 'scene' in which Jerry Killick and Davis Freeman, stand naked amidst the detritus of earlier actions, with large tinfoil stars barely concealing their genitals, and make a series of spoken propositions for another aesthetic event to overtake the current one: the holding of a 'beautiful silence'. Comedic vulnerability melds with masculine narcissism here as the duo confidently revise the solemn commemorative act, taking turns to list a variety of fictive scenarios in which long silences arise. A certain digressive force is at play, as the simple form spirals into complexity.[29] As Theron Schmidt notes, listing simultaneously invokes the mundane and the infinite.[30] The happy male nudes sentimentally affirm each of the other's propositions as 'beautiful', fetishizing beauty as a temporal object, while each new inflection of imagined silence grows ever more perverse. The explicit subject of this seemingly casual improvisation—as the scenarios move from mundane experiences, through the fantastical, to generic tragedy—is the aestheticization of suffering and death, which the 'scene' takes as its assumed cultural norm. Etchells' dramaturgy marks this event with a series of uncanny divergent doubles: time itself is doubled through the conditional tense of speech here, with the act figured by two duos who sometimes interact through spoken echoes. Up to this point, Killick and Freeman have only performed mute and somewhat subservient roles as 'backing dancers'. They are 'aided' by Arthur and Lowdon's idiot bewigged heavy-metal roadies, who appear as unlikely technical facilitators holding microphones but in fact manifest a series of noisy and prolonged interruptions. Though belonging to a barely visible subclass of cultural production, these rock technicians—echoic figurations of *Club of No Regrets*' stagehands—have found themselves elevated to a position of exposed power here, as controllers of a theatrical apparatus for the amplification of 'nothing'. A 'final' enactment of the proposed silence is first agonizingly deferred and then continuously disturbed so that it remains perfectly unrealized. Beauty, of course, is further defiled by every instance of its invocation with 'simple' words. The phantasmic event of 'beautiful silence' is repeatedly dispelled through the pathetic 'realities' of its attempted enactment: it belongs to a time that cannot exist in this already overdetermined, never quite happening, always paradoxical temporality. The metatheatrical and metaphoric resonances of this undoing and non-arrival of a staged passage of time affectively re-qualify the social eventhood of *Bloody Mess*.

Amidst the fractious, cacophonous chaos of this show, built from its figures' clashes of intention and world view, the beautiful is marked not only as sublimely unrepresentable but as a cohering affective social value.[31] Freeman frames the 'scene' from the start as an event of communal unity, as 'something that we can all do together'; the easy-going collaborative modality that he and Killick affect is repeatedly disturbed by Arthur and Lowdon's feigned incomprehension and resistance, that is, by forms of dissent from the ascendant aesthetic organization of the event. One interruption is Arthur's insistence that Killick and Freeman should choose *which* of the many silences already proposed they and the audience should now enact. One single silence is rejected in favour of an evidently ridiculous pluralism in which everyone chooses 'their own' silence to play out: a fantasy of democratic imagination. Another dispute arises over Lowdon's insistence that the silence must be timed digitally, rather than on Freeman's 'analogue' watch (allegedly a gift from

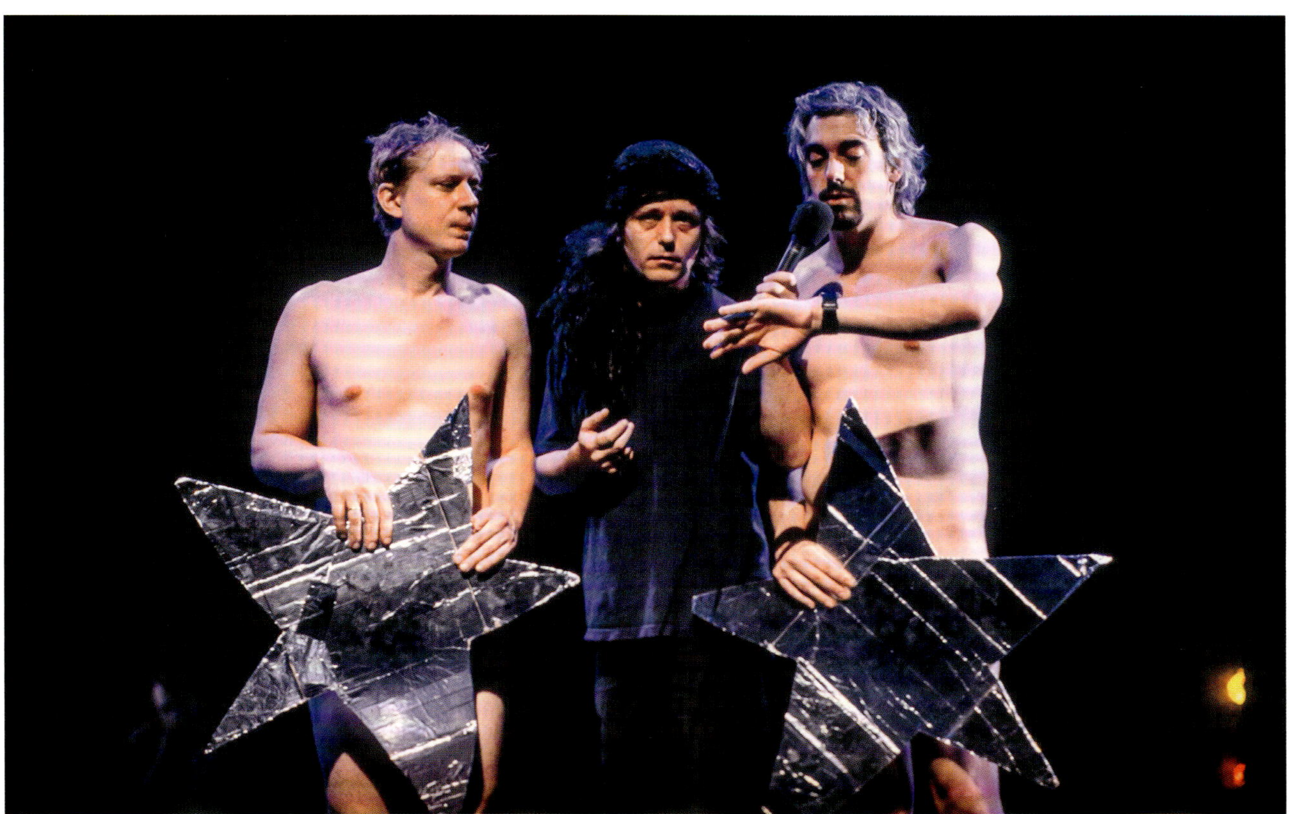

his wife). The analogue is 'finally' affirmed as superior against the dominant masculine tech logic because 'sometimes sentiment is more important than accuracy'. Here, the key tenets of a relativist ideology, free will and open interpretation—underpinned by an ideal of equality—are shown as politically wanting in the failure to arrive at the promised communal event. It is clear to all that *Bloody Mess* is not a work of egalitarian participatory theatre, as Killick and Freeman's figures appear to think, nor could it be mistaken for a free-form commemorative ceremony. Forced Entertainment's critical target is not just the revision of the beautiful as a social, and therefore messy and fraught, human terrain. If the shared holding of silence is the ultimate socially sanctioned act for the maintenance of the value of lost lives in time, their recognition and continued respect, then this definitively failing central 'scene' lets us know that such a consensus must contend with the material consequences of social plurality: appropriation, dissensus, carelessness, disrespect, and forgetting. Killick and Freeman's warping of the dignity of commemoration through aestheticization is itself derailed by the violence that underpins its own logic, in the reverberative machinery of Arthur and Lowdon's 'technicalities'. Etchells notes that the violence of Killick and Freeman's propositions belongs, in part, to a certain cosmic indifference, marked by eternity:

> After all they are 'dressed as' stars: ancient, mighty, distant entities known for their beauty and cool witnessing of earthly comings and goings, the ups and downs of human life. For me, their observations are akin to those of Wenders and Handke's angels in *Wings of Desire*, albeit more ambivalent. Scenarios that might well be horrible for the participants are seen and narrated dispassionately. It's not surprising that the stars want a beautiful silence—a sublime spectacle in which they can be regarded, and about which nothing further may be said.[32]

The tonal and affective logic of Forced Entertainment's intertextuality and echoic figuration is evident here, as is the catastrophic sense that cosmic violence is immanent in human invention.

Lowdon spends much of the time of the 'finally enacted' silence shushing the non-compliant audience, whose audible amusement at his numerous interjections makes ever more evident the impossibility of the ideal event in the making. He and Arthur eventually identify a technological cause for the perpetual non-happening of the silence (a wholly inaudible speaker buzz) which they then shambolically attempt to resolve. If the rowdy problems for the organizing principle of time proposed from the stage are disclosed as the audience and the technologies of the theatre—that is, the presence of others and the fact that relations are always already mediated—then the work affirms that a certain sacrilege will need to be entertained in the communal event: that of its insistent poly-temporality. In the figurations of *Bloody Mess*, each social subject has 'its own' organization of time perception and 'its own' inconsistent tempo. But no one owns time. As Giulia Palladini argues in this collection, the paradoxical temporality of figures is an inherently creaturely condition: it lives 'in the space of the non-human, or of the all too human'.[33] In *Bloody Mess*, John Cage's well-known invocation of the earthly impossibility of silence—non-existent because the body that hears (and makes) it is a microcosmos continuously murmuring—is knowingly turned into a tragicomic farce of the human incapacity to create the normatively beautiful, to sustain a space of communal reflection or agreement, to honour others, to stabilize an event with any idea of the event.[34] In Forced Entertainment's frayed gathering of divergent social forces, it is perhaps in the ever-failing struggle of such creations that beauty, if there be any, resides. At the heart of the instability of this eventhood is a temporal plurality ungovernable by human concepts of time as unitary, measurable, progressive. If beauty and silence turn out to be impure, it is because time itself is a cosmic wildness that sullies them.

One can think of Killick and Freeman's rupturing routine of 'beautiful silence' as a wake-event atmospheric, an affective condition traced (and chased) by narrative operations but no longer contained by them, marking their stilling and erasure, their descent into nothingness. The spectator's awareness of the poly-temporality of that affective event, and its consequentiality for the understanding of gathering, sharing, responsibility, and freedom exceeds the narrowly aesthetic terms of the existing address to time phenomena in contemporary experimental theatre discourse. This is not simply a matter of an experiential time sensed by spectators, as it is subject to aesthetic warps, opening its difference from, and problematizing its regulation by, clock time. The phenomenal, just as it is understood in Jacques Rancière's work, undergirds the ideological through regimes of sense, and in this regard the arena of sharing and of responsivity that is the theatre of Forced Entertainment is distinctly marked as a space traversed by a politics of sensate attunement to the wild plurality of the times of others.[35] Whilst much recent experimental theatre asserts that the temporality of the contemporary stage space can no longer command a subsumption of the audience's time into its fictive time, the theatre event remains stubbornly inseparable from the 'shared time' of its audience. As Lehmann notes, consequently contemporary experimental works admit and draw attention to the 'real time' of their staging, deploying durational aesthetics and phenomena of repetition, making '*time as such* into an object of the aesthetic experience'.[36] Killick and Freeman's 'beautiful silence' knowingly references this turn. Etchells echoes Lehmann's analysis when he crystallizes the company's long process as ultimately a matter of a shared durational 'attending to bodies and events in time, and of attending to time itself, in its passing, its speeding and slowing'.[37] But the reality of this 'real time', as it is experienced in the communality of theatre gatherings such as those staged by Forced Entertainment, is that there is no time *itself*, it has no suchness, no stable internal coherence, and carries an unsharable divergence of sense: the times of others.

As Goran Serge Pristaš notes, collective work in contemporary performance gives birth to 'various durations and rhythms' that, contrary to many analyses of neoliberal artistic labour, are recognized (by their participants at least) as distinct from the dominant temporalities of work and its infrastructures.[38] The term 'production' does not do service to this complex playful relational struggle and its temporal dynamics, operative in such sustained situations, nor the relation of such labours to an actual extractive economy. Etchells makes a similar point when he distinguishes the professional qualities of the company's functional organization from its lived realities in the space of rehearsal, characterized as being saturated with generative inertia, stumbles, flashes, dysfunction, and chaos. Both artists are affirming what Brian Massumi refers to as a 'surplus-value of life', dwelling in a radical collective process that evades capture by capital and potentially holds an aneconomic force.[39] It is not surprising, then, that a life-long practice of collective creation would, within its aesthetics, produce experiences of temporality which expose a different 'chrono-logic', as Pristaš puts it, in which the present (the plural time in which all performances take place) is dispersed: 'it follows different kinds of rhythms, curtailments, recapitulations, decelerations, gradual eliminations, unfoldings, etc. [that] follow their own operational rationale, as dynamic flows of the unfolding, accumulation, and reversing of the vector of time.[40] The fostering of alter-temporalities is intimately linked to the creative forces of collective inter-subjective making—carrying counter-intentional and unanticipatable dynamics, or a giving of 'what you do not have', seen by Jacques Derrida as elemental to the definition of event—where forms emerge not from established precedents or abilities but from situations of self-surpassing and conditions of impossibility.[41] This is not just a matter of 'chrono-logics' but of chronopolitics, for as we have seen with the values disclosed as underpinning the dispute around the timing of a 'beautiful silence', these senses of temporal dissonance are played out against a range of dominant ideologies often embedded in progressive senses of time. As witnessed by the writings on the company's work in this book—whether it be Augusto Corrieri's observation that its often enacted 'bad feelings' reveal the 'psychic wounds of our time', or Pallidini's notation of emergent senses of beginning or ending, and their common multiplication, as an anxiousness of the non-human, or Sara Jane Bailes' identification of a foundational (mortal) disappointment that underpins the creation of possibility in the work, or Kelleher's discourse on the admittance of fear into these performances and its relation to an age of normalized uncertainty—Forced Entertainment's temporal disturbances are prodigious in their diverse negative affective forces. Here, as Lehmann notes, the intimate is relayed with impersonal and historical powers, and with what he terms the 'universal', but always through resonant cloudy atmospherics of enactment, contagious airs of feeling, whose paradoxically charged ethereality, though deeply felt, is hard to reduce to any single referent.[42] These invocations, like the favourite 'beautiful silence' of Arthur's wide-eyed roadie in *Bloody Mess*—an astronaut accidentally untethered from his craft, screaming for help as he drifts off into the majesty of space—have the flavour of a cosmic joke: they speak of a contact with the catastrophe befalling a de-natured hubristic animal, the human at its limits, playing out its endgame. This figure falls into an elemental and unsurvivable context—out of which its own flesh is made—swallowed by the gorgeous spectacle of the void. It is a catastrophe that has always already happened and is yet to come.

~

If the oeuvre of Forced Entertainment can be read as a sustained interrogation of the theatrical apparatus, an attendant opening of its associated conventions and values, then *Out of Order* appears to be a stripping away of almost all of those conventions. Gone are the nested skeletal scenographies, the sprawling texts and poetic listings, the fractured personae, the knowing direct address to the audience on the conditions of theatrical or social economy; in fact, all forms of speech are banished in favour of a prolonged choreography of energetic relations and acts. A group of six clowns in identical red tartan suits assemble around a table as if for a meeting or a meal. Their uniformity, ritual gathering, and the enclosure of their world faintly recalls the forlorn figures of *Let the Water*. What ensues for the first fifteen minutes is a series of increasingly violent and exhausted physical skirmishes in which one clown chases another, with other members of the group acting as 'peacekeepers' and obstacles to the pursuit. The table and chairs flung around the space are reset, as this ritual gathering and scattering is repeatedly played out to an erratically looping soundtrack: the Northern Soul B-side Val Martinez's *Someone's Gonna Cry* (1963). The repeated but irregular smashing of chairs on the ground resonates as an unpredictable counter-rhythm to the beat. Whilst the vehemence of these acts is not in doubt, it is never clear whether these perpetually unsatisfied pursuits are lustful or hateful in nature. The rhythmic energetics of combustion, struggle, missed encounter, deflation, and restoration of order are the prevailing content. The air is filled, then, with the sense of a desperate need to *get* the other (alongside its lived impossibility), whether that getting is an act of understanding, holding, consumption, or murder. There is something immemorial about this assembly and its acts. The atmospherics of the evacuated stage space, its weary inhabitants and their compulsive drives suggest that, in a classic existential sense, there is 'nothing to be done' and, of course, an absolute necessity to act.[43] What is done has been—and will be—done again and again. These carefully choreographed but boisterously imprecise action sequences eventually lead to a scrappy and amorphous struggle on the ground, and then to most of the clowns lying prone in exhaustion. As Arthur notes, there is something unseemly in this group of late-middle-aged performers pressed to a dishevelled exertion at the edge of their limits: phenomena of corporeal deterioration saturate the work's meanings, which are sweated out.[44]

Time passes, the cumulative differences of durational aesthetics do their work, the worlding of this piece embeds and exceeds itself in spectators' imaginations, and the metatheatrical dimensions of *Out of Order* start to speak beyond the immediate context of the company. For in one sense, we are simply presented here with a crystalline image of Forced Entertainment itself: this ragtag rabble of players is a long-habituated and ageing group of spectacle makers, a queer family of sorts, and most definitely a discordant collective ceaselessly intent on finding new ways to agitate its worn constitution and turn out new realities. But this itinerant troupe is also us—the audience, a public, a society—caught in over-coded cycles of mutual stimulation, enchantment, agreement, and social dissolution. *Out of Order* is a choreography of social undercurrents: its trapped air and bubble world, its continuous rancour and exhausted energies, an acute evocation of the terminal antisocial drives of Western 'post-truth' contemporaneity. Its clown figures are an apt foil for our complicit identities, in an age of despotic populists violently crashing through social fabrics fuelled by our own fascination with spectacles of ignorance and idiocy. If we concur with a writer like Alan Read—speculating on the affective forces of contemporary performance (and elaborating Rancière)— that dissensus is not simply a form of division but 'a productive act within a sensible world' and that its manifestation 'allows for making visible something that was at odds within its milieu, against the grain of its surface, which was otherwise obscure in the perceptual field', then what appearance does *Out of Order*'s long iterative collective wrangle presence?[45]

Here, dissensus is not just resident in the staged relations, but in the distances and frictions made manifest in Forced Entertainment's 'scenic' collage, in their enspacings, which version and re-inflect their subjects and the work's worldings in often discordant ways. Two seemingly slight, but highly elemental acts come to affectively qualify and re-sense the senses of enclosure, animus, and social exhaustion on which the opening passage of this work is built. Waking gradually from collapse or sleep or fictive death—but, in any case, from their grounded positions where their heavy breathing was much in evidence—the clowns serially and then collectively start to inflate coloured balloons, which each time are let off to whizz and spiral about the place in a random anti-choreographic fashion, petering out in an object-oriented re-enactment of the clowns' own energetic dissipations. A children's entertainment or comedy tool is thus turned towards a performance of a less fleshy materiality in which spectators and clowns alike are left to contemplate for an extended duration the relation between ground and air, the energetic and aerial phenomena of organic and synthetic inhalation and exhalation, the wild flights of pressure release, and the work of gravity. Less fleshy? Perhaps that is not quite it, since flesh-as-element is everywhere here, transformed in the carnal atmospherics of breath.[46] As Steven Connor has elaborated, air is 'the raw material of theatre, the inert, unshaped reserve of matter that is shaped into utterance'.[47] But *Out of Order*, for the first time in the company's long history, is a theatre performance without a single utterance, and in the space of that quietude, a theatre in which 'the elemental incidence of breath to the stage' becomes apparent.[48] These specific breaths do not circulate as they would normally—that is, economically, invisibly animating meaning, put to work by words—but instead emerge from a condition of breathlessness and are momentarily and visibly captured and expelled: imprisoned sighs turned into non-sense farts, unpredictable baroque meanderings of things, careening around as wasted energy. And in that expenditure, and the attention it is paid, a volatile weather returns to the enclosed theatre, in which breath and air are not simply metaphoric bearers of life force, spirit or freedom but carriers of the human's reduction to the laws of physics, flights to nowhere, the facticity of expiration, and the wearied dances of extinction.

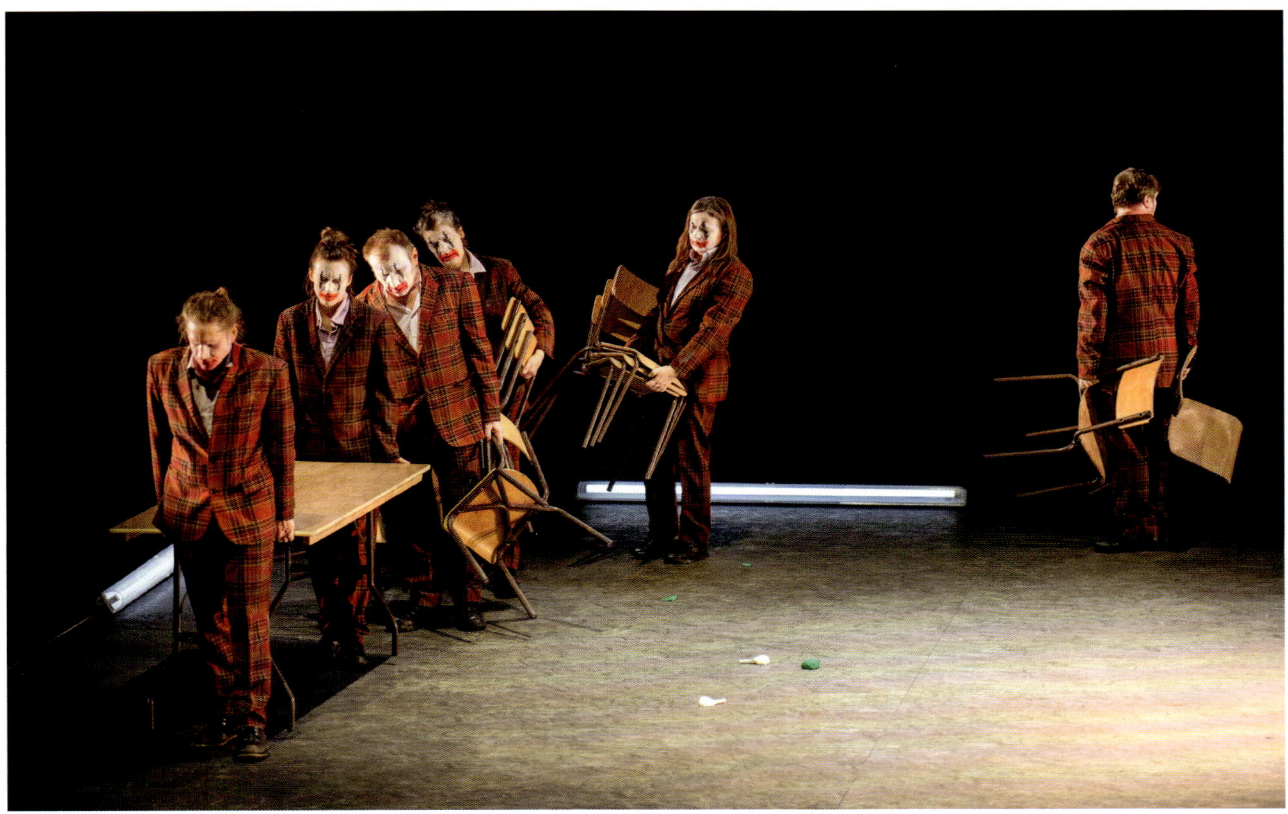

A further scene advances and reroutes this atmospheric of end time, of starved, imprisoned, and futile breath. Its patterning of movement on the ground somewhat iterates the aerated organic flight paths of the doomed balloons. After another round of 'danced' fights and attempts at mutual stimulation with hooters, the clowns take up the furniture and begin to circle around the space in a snaking line that occasionally breaks and reforms as each seeks to follow the movement precedent or falls away from it. Each clown carries an ungainly load of furniture. Etchells' description of the scene is worth hearing again in full, for its inflections of the senses of this resonant trudge:

> Whilst they go around several times, a silence of new dimensions and density falls, broken only by the soft, regular tread of their feet. Walking, they are an incomprehensible parade, mourners with a coffin in procession, a line of refugees with their possessions on their backs, prisoners in an exercise yard. ... They are phantoms, displaced persons, scavengers. They are itinerant workers in the middle of some futile hard labour. They are tired children in a weary game. They are clowns locked in the slightest fragment of what might, once, have been a routine. And of course, at the same time, they are none of these things. They are human beings in a room shared with others, marking the limits of the world they inhabit, carrying their equipment and waiting for the moment to set it down and resume what they have started.[49]

We hear that a novel deep silence has fallen, and this silence you will understand is a doubling, a silence within a 'silent' work; but this is not quite accurate, it is a silence within a voiceless and wordless work. The sound, then, of the voiceless, those who do not speak here. It is a silence that is 'broken', which as we have understood is the nature of all silence—but particularly of a Forced Entertainment silence—broken by a sound that can only faintly be heard, occurring at a periphery to which we must attend: the sound of people steadily trudging around. The 'speech' of enervated aching limbs. Just as the work calls us, through the force of the open image at play in a blighted atmospherics to put referents to these echoic figurations, Etchells lays out some that are readily 'seen'. But we should note that these figures are not simply evocative of unfortunate downtrodden people—the grieving, the expelled, the imprisoned, the impoverished, those who have nothing in common—whose shape we recognize, if not from our lived experience of encounters, then from our sense of history or 'our' mediated contemporaneity. These people have become less than human, they have in Etchells' words, become 'things'. Too many echoes make the figures into sub-objects. And it is this thingliness that is silently amplified as a human question at the close of the parade as it slows, when Killick and Nicki Hobday take the table they have been carrying, and in a condensation of the whole choreographic spiral of the parade and of this cyclonic work, turn it slowly over and over, as if trying to understand what 'this thing' is, what a material property is in itself, and how it may or may not be different from them, since it moves now as they do, over and over again. In this moment, the awareness of a flat ontology between objects and humans— or, let's say, of the human as simple matter—is cut through with a political imaginary of those amorphous but heavy figurations, who are not simply ghostings (lost creatures of the past) but, as Etchells words them, 'phantoms', that is, echoic projections of our imagination, of our shared future, the future of those who will have nothing *as their* commons.

~

Looking across four distinct decades and exemplary works within them, one can trace the emergence of a catastrophic imaginary in the theatre of Forced Entertainment, resonating through the wake-event of each work in its singularity. The scene of catastrophe in *(Let the Water Run Its Course) to the Sea That Made the Promise* in the 1980s is 'the natural body' becoming synthetic—a site of loss, wistful sadness, and imaginary reassembly—whose capacity to love, remember, and survive is traversed not only by generic overwriting but by a shattering future of de-industrialization, nuclear threat, cultural mishmash, and erasure. Nature nonetheless remains a promissory exteriority (at the water's edge), a threshold of the urban that calls to its anguished souls and offers a respite, a cleansing of sorts. By *Club of No Regrets* in the 1990s, this vision has morphed into a more expansive scenario of urban life inside multiple, contesting fictive worlds in which material things are never in their proper place. For the inhabitants of this worlding, the goal is not just an inquisitive survival of the given but an escape from the hybrid apparatuses of law and power—systems that may be turned inside out by ecstatic elemental ceremony—where wild nature is the dark lure and sundering force. The passage between *Club of No Regrets* and *Bloody Mess* in 2004 sees nature evolve into a spectacular force of cosmic but generative violence, where it begins to speak back to the human who has dared to 'own' and name it, through its persistent untimeliness in chaotic sharings of unrealized desire, grief, and social antagonism. This speaking back becomes more 'audible' in the tremulous silence of *Out of Order* in 2018, where the ageing body of the foolish human animal animatedly pursues its own consumption of and with others, and so enters exhausted conditions of relation with the atmospheric materialities of the theatre. In elaborate but finite patterns of energy expenditure, human abjection in itinerancy resonates with the catastrophic scattering dance of matter. Across the arc of these events, a theatre apparatus of affective atmospherics increasingly becomes a theatre of thinking material relations and attunement to the enfleshed sense of things.

To say that nature speaks back to the human may seem to subject it to yet another unfortunate anthropomorphization, but I have in mind 'that something not being said' of Blanchot's that is calling to the human, much in the way that a writer like Michael Taussig sees our recent epoch as a re-enchantment with nature due to its increasingly volatile strangeness. In the 'Age of Meltdown'—Taussig's term for the era of climate catastrophe and human extinction awareness—it is not just the encounter with the 'angry sky that beats down' that environmentally re-attunes the human 'unwinding the shroud known as the "domination of nature"'.[50] Taussig lays out a set of cultural and aesthetic practices that enact forms of 'mastery of non-mastery': a means to turn mimesis to its outsides through 'a delirious circuitry',[51] in which 'nature speaks through animate impulses' and the senses are opened to the non-sensuous, the emergent semblances of things.[52] Re-reading the appearance of natural phenomena in familiar texts, Taussig thinks of the awareness that is brought to this new human animal as a 'making aerial' of 'inner states' and an attunement to 'the bodily unconscious of the world'.[53] Following the image of a bird disappearing into the night sky, he comments that with 'that flight across and beyond the screen of consciousness that is the darkening sky of sunset, we are left with "tremor", something like memory, but more a physical and psychic disturbance, like … a ship's wake churning aft to the horizon.'[54] A theatre language of ruins, such as that of Forced Entertainment, is an instance of the wilful performance of undoing and its consequent awakening in an age of catastrophe, where an aesthetics of negation is both a symptom of, and a critical reflection with, the re-routing of human consciousness through the knowledge of its own extinction. Here, in the wake-event, as the performers stand and witness us, their audience, their society—drenched in the white light at the water's edge, or looking out in the aftermath of another fraught ecstatic struggle to escape binds, or in a silence that never arrives but is punctuated by our uncontrollable laughter, or as they lie looking to the sky enraptured by the erratic pattern of the fall of a captured breath—a singularity is sensed and 'death of the planet re-images the relationships between our bodies and the cosmos'.[55] Here is Killick—recalling and revising his earlier invitation to imagine the sensate realities of a deathly fall, to imagine what one imagines as one falls—reverberating unsaid wake-event atmospherics through human terms once again, in a speech directly to the audience at the close of *The World in Pictures* (2005):

> And tomorrow night, it's pretty safe to say that none of you will be here and by then maybe you'll have completely forgotten some of what you saw here tonight. And in a month's time, maybe you'll have forgotten everything. Or maybe you'll remember bits. And in a year's time, maybe you'll no longer be talking to the people you came with this evening. And by then you might have … I don't know, moved house, or started a new job. And by then you might have lost someone close to you. And in five years' time one or some of the people here in this room now might have died. It's possible. And in fifty years' time quite a lot of the people here tonight will be dead. And in a hundred years' time it's pretty safe to say that everyone here tonight will have died. And in 200 years' time, not only will we all be dead but those of us that have children, those children will be dead—in fact, anyone who can remember us will have died. And in, in 500 years' time there may be some record of us, our names, or our lives. Or maybe not. Maybe all that information will have been stored on a system that's become obsolete or broken down, or maybe all that information will just have been deleted. And in 1,000 years' time it's highly unlikely that this building will still be standing. And in 2,000 years all the languages we know or can speak—they won't be being spoken any more. And in 10,000 years' time, this whole city probably won't be here. It'll be a desert, or a body of water, or maybe not even that—maybe just, just space, a vacuum.

1. Hans-Thies Lehmann, 'Shakespeare's Grin: Remarks on World Theatre with Forced Entertainment', in Judith Helmer and Florian Malzacher (eds.), *Not Even a Game Anymore: The Theatre of Forced Entertainment* (Berlin: Alexander Verlag, 2004), 106.

2. Maurice Blanchot, *The Writing of the Disaster*, trans. Ann Smock (1980; Lincoln: University of Nebraska Press, 1995), 21.

3. Tim Etchells, *Certain Fragments* (London: Routledge, 1999), 17–18. On witnessing, see Matthew Goulish, 'Compendium: A Forced Glossary', in this volume, 279.

4. Jacques Derrida, 'A Certain Impossible Possibility of Saying the Event', trans. Gila Walker, *Critical Inquiry*, 33/2 (Winter 2007), 441–61; Jean-Luc Nancy, 'The Surprise of the Event', in *Being Singular Plural*, trans. Robert D. Richardson and Anne E. O'Byrne (1996; Stanford, CA: Stanford University Press, 2000); Alain Badiou, *Handbook of Inaesthetics*, trans. Alberto Toscano (Stanford, CA: Stanford University Press, 2004); Brian Massumi, *Semblance and Event: Activist Philosophy and the Occurrent Arts* (Cambridge, MA: MIT Press, 2011); Adrian Kear, *Theatre and Event: Staging the European Century* (Basingstoke: Palgrave, 2013); Ben Anderson and Paul Harrison, 'Events and Futurity' in *Taking-Place: Non-Representational Theories and Geography* (Farnham: Ashgate, 2010), 19–23.

5. Here, I am seeking to add theatrical specificity to Derrida's problematic, that 'the saying of the event or the saying of knowledge regarding the event lacks, in a certain manner *a priori*, the event's singularity simply because it comes after and it loses the singularity in generality.' Derrida, 'A Certain Impossible Possibility' (see n. 4).

6. On duration, see André Lepecki, 'Duration', http://intermsofperformance.site/keywords/duration/andre-lepecki, accessed 31 August 2021.

7. On contemporaneity, see Giorgio Agamben, 'What Is the Contemporary?', in Giorgio Agamben, *'What Is an Apparatus?' and Other Essays*, trans. David Kishik and Stefan Pedetella (Redwood City, CA: Stanford University Press, 2009).

8. On this form of attention as an act of love, see Joy Kristin Kalu, 'Once Upon a Time', in this volume, 235–37.

9. On the palpable event, see Elie During, 'A Theatre of Operations: A Discussion between Alain Badiou and Elie During', in Bridget Crone (ed.), *The Sensible Stage: Staging and the Moving Image* (Bristol: Picture This, 2012), 27.

10. José A Sánchez, *Practising the Real on the Contemporary Stage* (Bristol: Intellect, 2014). Adrian Heathfield, 'As If Things Got More Real: A Conversation with Tim Etchells', in Judith Helmer and Florian Malzacher (eds.), *Not Even a Game Anymore: The Theatre of Forced Entertainment* (Berlin: Alexander Verlag, 2004).

11. Adrian Kear, *Theatre and Event: Staging the European Century* (Basingstoke: Palgrave, 2013), 23.

12. Richard Schechner, 'Restoration of Behaviour', in *Between Theater and Anthropology* (Philadelphia: University of Pennsylvania Press, 1985), 36.

13. Ibid., 37.

14. Christina Sharpe, *In the Wake: On Blackness and Being* (Durham, NC: Duke University Press, 2016).

15. Hans-Thies Lehmann, *Postdramatic Theatre* (London: Routledge, 2006).

16. On qualities of impossibility as they develop across this oeuvre, see Séverine Ruset, 'The Art of the Impossible', in this volume, 263–66.

17. International Atomic Energy Agency, 'Frequently Asked Chernobyl Questions', https://www.iaea.org/newscenter/focus/chernobyl/faqs, accessed 31 August 2021. For an extensive discussion of Forced Entertainment's 'poetics of failure' and its relation to British cultural politics of the period, see Sara Jane Bailes, 'Profane Illumination: Theatre and Forced Entertainment', in *Performance Theatre and the Poetics of Failure* (London: Routledge, 2011), 63–109.

18. Forced Entertainment, *(Let the Water Run Its Course) to the Sea That Made the Promise*, in this volume, 24.

19. Joe Kelleher, 'Acts of Admittance, Facts of Speech', in this volume, 246.

20. On the concept of 'worlding' common to new materialist thinking, see Kathleen Stewart, 'Worlding Refrains', in Melissa Gregg and Gregory J. Seigworth (eds.), *The Affect Theory Reader* (London: Duke University Press, 2010), 339–53. On notions of the thing, see Martin Heidegger, 'The Thing', in *Poetry, Language, Thought* (1971; New York: Harper Collins: 1975), 161–84; Jane Bennett, 'The Force of Things', in *Vibrant Matter: A Political Ecology of Things* (Durham, NC: Duke University Press, 2010), 1–19; Bill Brown, 'Thing Theory', *Critical Inquiry*, 28 (Autumn 2001), 1–16.

21. Claire MacDonald, 'That Was Then, This Is Now', in this volume, 192.

22. On the risks involved in this scene, see: Tim Etchells, 'Play On: Process and Collaboration', in *Certain Fragments* (see n. 3), 50–70.

23. Tim Etchells, 'A Text on Twenty Years with Sixty-Six Footnotes', in this volume, 240.

24. Tim Etchells, introduction to *Certain Fragments* (see n. 3), 15.

25. Forced Entertainment, 'A Decade of Forced Entertainment', in this volume, 212.

26. Adrian Heathfield, 'As If Things Got More Real: A Conversation with Tim Etchells', in Helmer and Malzacher, *Not Even a Game Anymore* (see n. 10), 77–102.

27. Maaike Bleeker, *Visuality in the Theatre: The Locus of Looking* (New York: Palgrave Macmillan, 2008), 38.

28. Matthew Goulish, 'Compendium: A Forced Glossary', in this volume, 279.

29. On the 'complicated simplicity' of digression see, Rabih Mroué, 'Deferring the Inevitable', in this volume, 232–4.

30. Theron Schmidt, 'One Thing after Another', in this volume, 260.

31. On redemption in Forced Entertainment's early works, see: Andrew Quick, 'Searching for Redemption with Cardboard Wings: Forced Entertainment and the Sublime', *Contemporary Theatre Review*, 2/2 (1994), 25–35.

32. Tim Etchells, email message to author, 15 Aug. 2021.

33. Giulia Palladini, 'The Slow Hurry of Figuration', in this volume, 226.

34. John Cage, *Silence: Lectures and Writings* (London: Marion Boyars, 2010).

35. Jacques Rancière, *The Politics of Aesthetics*, trans. Gabriel Rockhill (London: Continuum, 2006).

36. Lehmann, *Postdramatic Theatre* (see n. 15), 155–56; Adrian Heathfield, 'Durational Aesthetics', in Beatrice von Bismarck et al. (eds.), *Timing: On the Temporal Dimension of Exhibiting* (New York: Sternberg, 2014).

37. Tim Etchells, 'An Answer Without a Question', in this volume, 293.

38. Goran Serge Pristaš, *Exploded Gaze* (Zagreb: Multimedijalni institut, 2018), 51.

39. Adrian Heathfield and Brian Massumi, 'Movements of Thought: Interview with Brian Massumi by Adrian Heathfield', in Massumi, *The Principle of Unrest* (London: Open Humanities Press, 2017),

40. Pristaš, *Exploded Gaze* (see n. 38), 53.

41. Derrida, 'A Certain Impossible Possibility' (see n. 4), 450.

42. Lehmann, 'Shakespeare's Grin' (see n. 1).

43. Samuel Beckett, *Waiting for Godot: A Tragicomedy in Two Acts* (1953; London: Faber and Faber, 2010).

44. Robin Arthur, speaking on *Out of Order*, in this volume, 167.

45. Alan Read, *Theatre in the Expanded Field: Seven Approaches to Performance* (London: Bloomsbury, 2014), 158.

46. Maurice Merleau-Ponty, *The Visible and the Invisible*, trans. Alphonso Lingis (1964; Evanston, IL: Northwestern University Press, 1968), 147.

47. Steven Connor, 'Steam Radio: On Theatre's Thin Air', London Theatre Seminar, 27 October 2003, http://stevenconnor.com/mouthful.html, accessed 31 August 2021.

48. Ibid.

49. Etchells, 'An Answer Without a Question' (see n. 37), 299.

50. Michael Taussig, *Mastery of Non-Mastery in the Age of Meltdown* (Chicago, IL: University of Chicago Press, 2020), 6.

51. Ibid., 5.

52. Ibid., 147. On the non-sensuous and the concept of semblance, see Heathfield and Massumi, 'Movements of Thought' (see n. 39), 84–89.

53. Taussig, *Mastery of Non-Mastery* (see n. 50), 151.

54. Ibid.

55. Ibid., 6.

Returning to the Hiss: Listening to John Avery

Flora Pitrolo

As somebody whose spectatorship of Forced Entertainment began in the early 2000s, something more—
something else—emerges about the company's work if you listen to the early scores of John Avery.[1] Something,
perhaps, that gradually took on a different form, settling into a scenic language that was still raw in the
early to mid-1980s. Something to do with how the company tells stories of people and things but that is not
quite about people and things as much as about the air in between them. Terry O'Connor opens the 1995
performance *A Decade of Forced Entertainment* by describing the company's exercise in looking back as 'a kind
of mapping, a kind of temperature-taking'.[2] There's something about listening to these recordings that tells
us more about the latter and less about the former: something that exists in the register of the atmospheric,
more landscape than logos.[3] In the script of *Decade*, we might locate it not in the mention of jumble-sale
clothes, Chinese restaurants, hen parties, love notes at bus stops, or incomprehensible shopping lists; instead,
we might locate it in the mention of something strange happening to time, in the city seen at night with all the
lights on, in the path to the motorway, in the craters and broken ground of an alternative city made up of the
ruins of industry and of war.[4]

the stone kills the
as if the whole earth has been the body blow
as if the whole world boy runs to the black covered completely in snow
and you look down at this person
with their head that's rested gently in your lap
sense their sleeping, the rise and fall of their breathing
and you watch as the final channel closes down
and everything is returning to the hiss
like ashes to ashes, dust to dust and hiss to hiss[5]

The ferric tape provides the noise, neither exactly a hum nor a squeal but a metallic vibrating reminder of
the unravelling of time and of how quickly and how easily it tangles. The tape work affords the feeling of an
endless loop backwards, cut by squeaks which are cries that are also air-bubbles, some fantastical animal with
its tail stuck in the machinery. More smoke, a sniff of electrical muezzin encased in playground chant. The
loop throbs deeper and more threateningly before reaching a plateau. It reminds me of a description I once
read of Forced Entertainment performing outdoors at the Volterra Festival in Italy, where the talcum powder
smoke encased the trees.[6]

Cabaret Voltaire. The Future, and then The Human League. Vice Versa. Clock DVA. British Electric
Foundation. Forced Entertainment: can we hypothesize a relationship between Sheffield's thoroughly
mythologized industrial and experimental synth scene and Forced Entertainment as products of the same
city's aesthetic and political concerns? Long-standing and organic collaborations with musicians—such
as the company's with Avery—often recede into the programme notes, especially early on in a long career:
they get muddled up with 'youth', yet it's precisely the youth of a company that can tell us something else.
As often as these collaborations fade from the historical record, they attest to a symbiotic relationship
between performance and music scenes: to a shared world view, to be intercepted in the why and in the how
of performance more than in the what—in the air between people and things more than in people and things
themselves. If for many in the industrial scene the music was supposed to be visual—a sonic translation of the
environments that made up the brutal yet ghostly architectural and fundamentally social, even sentimental

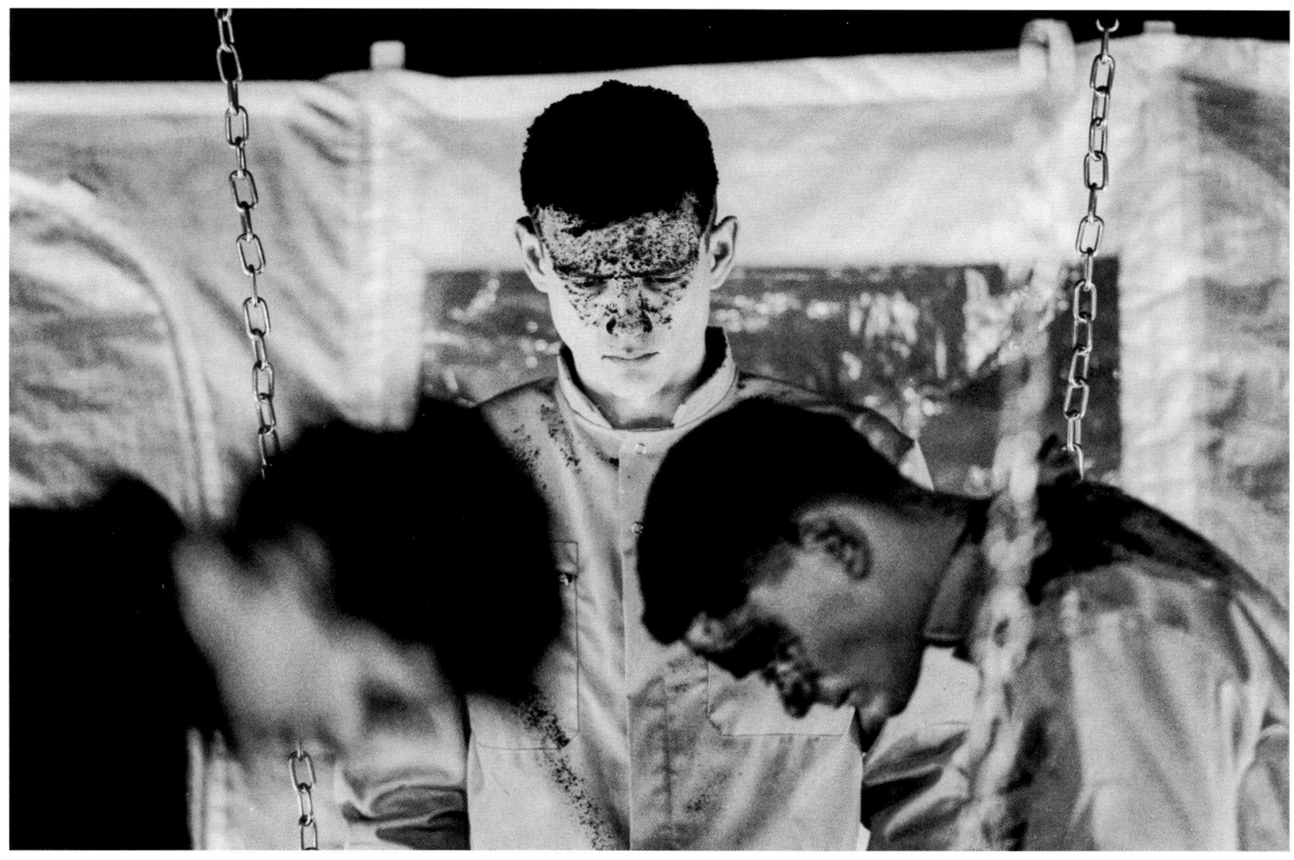

infrastructure of British cities—the same observation works the other way round: visual registers of performance can be intended as 'musical'. The sphere of the visual may be serving as an atmospheric matter, not so much offering representation but muddling it, like talcum in the trees. So we might take the liberty of applying the laws of genre in popular music—where they tend to rely on feeling more than on exact sonic palettes—to modes of contemporary performance. We might treat images as music and words as lyrics. We might do this with Forced Entertainment, using as our paradigm the concepts inherent in the Sheffield industrial scene and in John Avery's scores, concentrating on the hiss that continues to move the story along after it has ended, the hiss that remains after the story, and even the archival hiss etched into these records, which will make some sort of scene appear in the listeners' imagination, whether or not they know that same scene first appeared on a stage:

and the window is a black square that shows you the night
and you think it might be snowing
and there's something moving in the snow
it's like a picture book
the body would appear cradled in snow
the snow glistens as they try to explain
he seems to be binary and she seems to be sleeping
he's saying zero zero one zero one zero one
to know how hard is zero zero one zero one zero one[7]

Translated into a theatrical expressive apparatus, like a hard, still kernel of itself, like the hiss after the music is over, everything that haunted the industrial sensibility is here. The abstracted body, whose Marxist alienation has been folded now into goth esotericism, fades from its organic form. A post-apocalyptic landscape finds its counterpart in the cold soundscape, in sonic starkness as a 'second' mode of feeling made more apparent than ever by the synthesizer. People speak in binary and are killed by electrical stoves, witnessing the machinic envelop human existence with a mix of terror, sadness, and sordid fascination, as if watching themselves from the outside, as if feeling themselves becoming less and less person and more and more thing. The hiss of the television snow mirrors the snow outside the black square of the window. Real things turn artificial and artificial things become real, not in the far-off register of science fiction but in an environmental and atmospheric register which is much more 'weird and eerie', as the late Mark Fisher has theorized it, because it happens over here—the haunting and hissing premise of so much of this music and of this theatre.[8] The 'lyrics' above map with precision onto the lyrics of Sheffield's industrial era, all taken by the airy haunted nothingness in between people and things: dusty rooms with smoke and scattered papers, deserted crumbling cities, digital murders, grey-black whitenesses, short-wave radio messages from the last man on earth. In a similar way, the performances I am listening to develop from weird and eerie encounters: Jessica's life bleeds into the cinema in *Jessica in the Room of Lights* (1984), the cosmonaut's remains return to earth in *The Day That Serenity Returned to the Ground* (1986), life develops inside the frozen Americana of a Hopper painting in *Nighthawks* (1985). Sometimes these performances seem to devolve most of their dramaturgical apparatus to the music, which comes on before the lights do and ends after the blackout, obeying a mode of telling the scene that is only a scrap of material draped loosely onto a 'background'.

I continue to listen as a dark and echoed rattle rattles on, brittle, metallic, made ever so slightly narrative by the silky texture of three notes, just enough to add the noir suspension of a crime scene where we are about to find the body. Listening like a camera now, waiting for the reveal that comes in the form of a high-pitched,

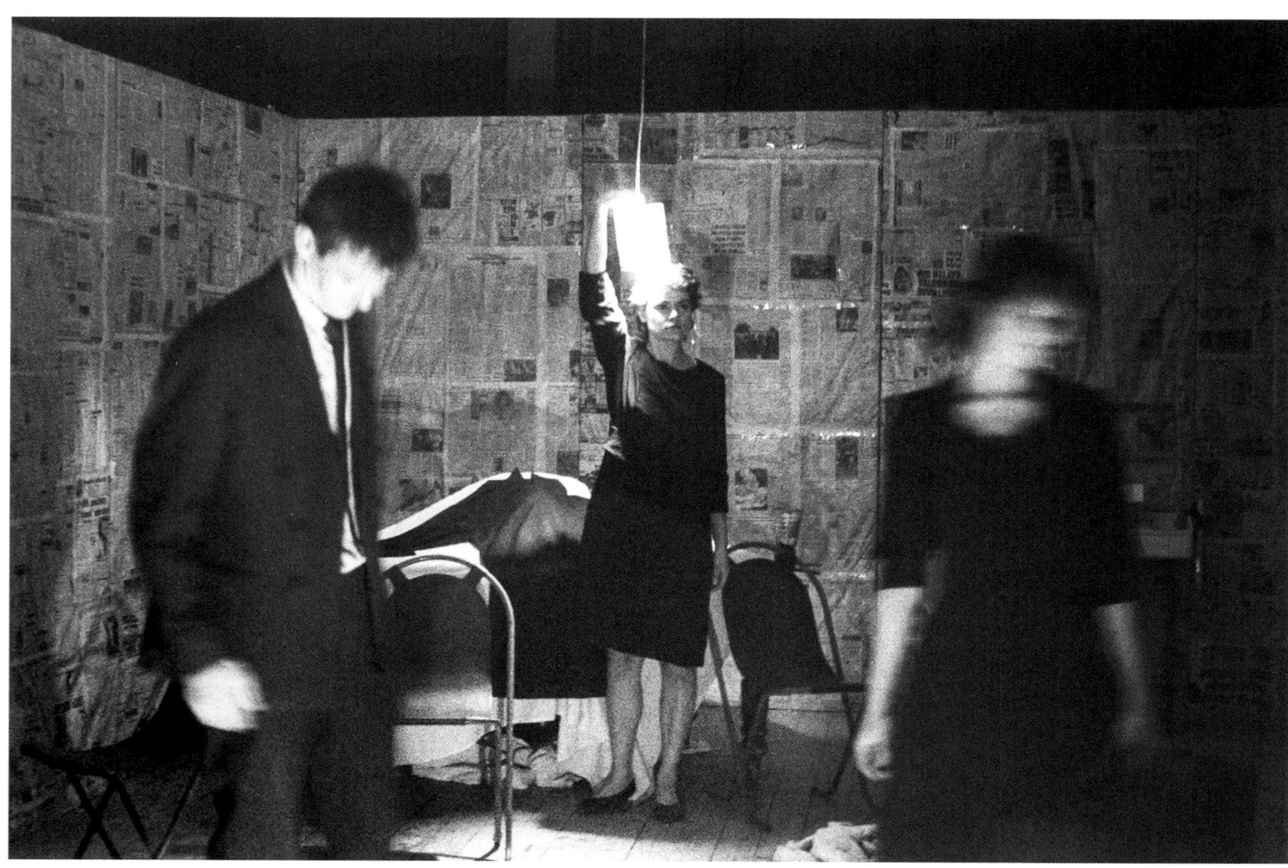

distorted female voice hovering over us like a drone, divorced completely from its source. A domestic-sounding piano plunks out a melody so nostalgic we might even find it embarrassing. We are ejected into a soundscape that is cosmic without bleeps or lasers: it buzzes like an old planetarium. Theorizing Forced Entertainment's early works as a kind of 'industrial theatre' might seem strange—we might more readily do this with La Fura dels Baus or, closer to home, with the cooperation between Brith Gof and Test Dept on pieces such as *Gododdin* (1989). Yet by reminding us of the early, youthful bleed between the world of industrial music and the world of the company's theatre, listening to Avery reminds us of a precious dimension of the company's genesis: something darker, more political, more uncompromising, and more haunted than we might think, born from a city full of people 'bashing against the edges of the world they're born into, bashing on the edges of the language that they have'.[9] People seen through foggy warehouses, rattling pianos, and factory hums, asking just how hard is zero zero one zero one zero one?

1. The recordings I describe throughout this essay are those issued on John Avery's LP *Jessica in the Room of Lights* (Technical Records, 1986), which contains tracks composed for *Jessica* (1984), for *Nighthawks* (1985) and for *The Day That Serenity Returned to the Ground* (1986), 'with thanks to Forced Entertainment Theatre Co-operative.'

2. Tim Etchells and Forced Entertainment, 'A Decade of Forced Entertainment', in Tim Etchells, *Certain Fragments: Contemporary Performance and Forced Entertainment* (London: Routledge, 1999), 29–36, here: 29.

3. I steal this phrase from Hans Thies-Lehmann, 'From Logos to Landscape: Text in Contemporary Dramaturgy', *Performance Research*, 2/1 (1997), 55–60.

4. I lift all of these images from the script of Etchells and Forced Entertainment, 'A Decade of Forced Entertainment' (see n. 2), 29–36.

5. This text is transcribed from the video recording of *The Day That Serenity Returned to the Ground* (1986).

6. See Tim Etchells, 'A Text on Twenty Years with Sixty-Six Footnotes', in this volume, 240.

7. *The Day That Serenity Returned to the Ground* (see n. 5).

8. Mark Fisher, *The Weird and the Eerie* (London: Repeater, 2016).

9. Etchells and Forced Entertainment, 'A Decade of Forced Entertainment' (see n. 2), 35.

Terry: Yes. There are times when it's very sure—about people's power to change themselves, their power to re-see themselves and the rest of the other world. There are times when it's very sure about people's ability to take what they will from the scrap heap of culture that they're born into and to use it. They transform things.

Richard: This transformation happens sometimes?

Terry: Yes.

Richard: Can you say something about the rest of the time?

Terry: The rest of the time this transformation escapes the 'characters'.

Richard: What happens?

Terry: Then there's a kind of rage in the work.

Richard: What do you mean by that?

Terry: Then the people in it are bashing against the edges of the world they're born into, bashing on the edges of the language that they have. There's a frustration.

That Was Then, This Is Now

Claire MacDonald

'The world receives you and recedes from you in the same moment'.[1]

What was it about Sheffield? When Forced Entertainment arrived in 1984, Sheffield was a city hovering on the edge of change, just hanging on in the cooling outflow of the steel industry that had given it its character. Northern mid-Thatcher Britain was moving out of the solid world of factory time and into the free-fall world of mall culture. It was Britain in the prequel to the 1987 market collapse—pre miners' strike, post Falklands War—a Britain whose centre of gravity was low-level consumption. Their work, from the first, asked what mattered in this clouded world. Who gets to tell the truth, and what might that be? Who gets to have memories? What is value? What does possibility look like? What shape is hope? They played with the gaps between questions. In a piece I wrote about their show *(Let the Water Run Its Course) to the Sea That Made the Promise* (1986), I called their aesthetic 'Kentucky fried city, alphabet city, exploding city'.[2] Theirs was a specific imaginary, it combined echoes of film and painting, Edward Hopper and American noir, with traditional British miserabilism. It was beautiful too. It was messy and collaged, layering the text of a note found in the street with the half-torn billboard sign, pairing the failed joke with the barroom tale. It was a melancholy, always rained on, occasionally joyful, madcap world. In Sheffield they found a city coming apart at the seams and they mapped it, tuned in to it, observing that it was still a city in which it was possible to make both things and lives—art things, theatre things, local, larky, collective, family lives.

Sheffield has a wild side, all cities do. A space beyond the seams, underneath the rain, along the banks of the river. The Don runs through the city and on its sides grow Sheffield's unplanned plantings, its living archaeology, its wild commons. On these banks wormwood and balsam have taken root and fig trees lean out over the water. The figs are heirs to the steel trade, grown from seeds spat and strewn in the heyday of steel in the 1920s, germinating in the warming waters of the factory outflow. The industry defined Sheffield for a century. When it went cold, the figs grew on outside pubs and bus stations, on riverbanks. The naturalist Richard Mabey calls the stretches of vernacular planting that exist here and all over Britain the 'unofficial countryside'.[3] The unofficial countryside—like our unofficial histories—is part of our shared commons, a heritage by right that arrived in the present by accident and that we continue to shape. In *Flora Britannica*, his countercultural collection of plant tales from the commons, Mabey has pictures of the riverbank fig trees of Sheffield, with stories of resistance to the cutting down of this guerrilla archive.[4] The edge where street meets canal meets crumbling tarmac is ungoverned territory, as sodden with stories as with sediment. It hosts portals to the unknown, places where roughened metal doors open onto overheard conversations, or that close on shouts and scuffles. I sometimes think that the purpose of theatre—at least the kind of experimental collective theatre that Forced Entertainment were making in Sheffield after 1984, and that the company I co-founded, Impact Theatre Co-operative, made in Leeds between the late 1970s and the mid-1980s—was to report from the dank edges of the city commons, mixing up and spitting out what we found there in the place where dark meets light, between a dog and a wolf.

Here, now, in 2020, we live in a world of shrinking space. A shrinking of the space, that is, for dissent and difference, at the same time as we have moved into a world of extraordinary fluidity of identities and the extension of communicative possibilities. Time and space. The materials of theatre. The coordinates that we cross and re-cross, cross out, make different, make strange. Writing about collaborative, ensemble, co-operative, friendship-based, experimentally driven theatre in this context calls me to attend to the

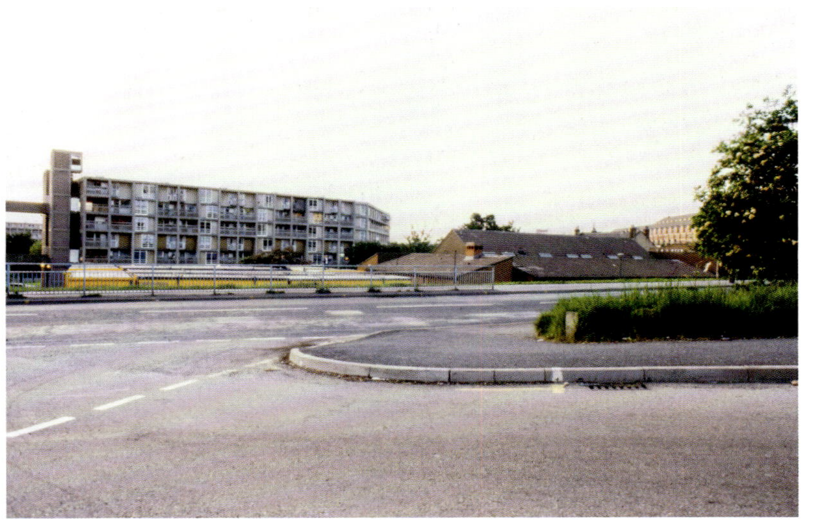

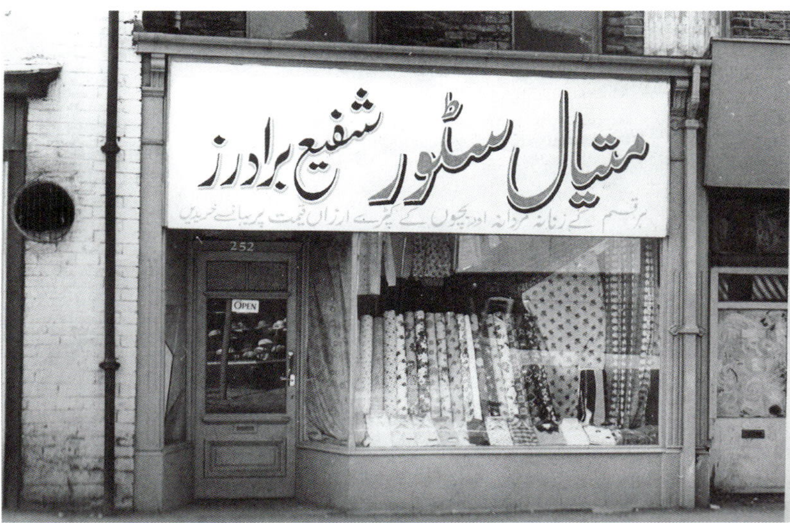

متیال سٹور شفیع برادرز
OPEN
252

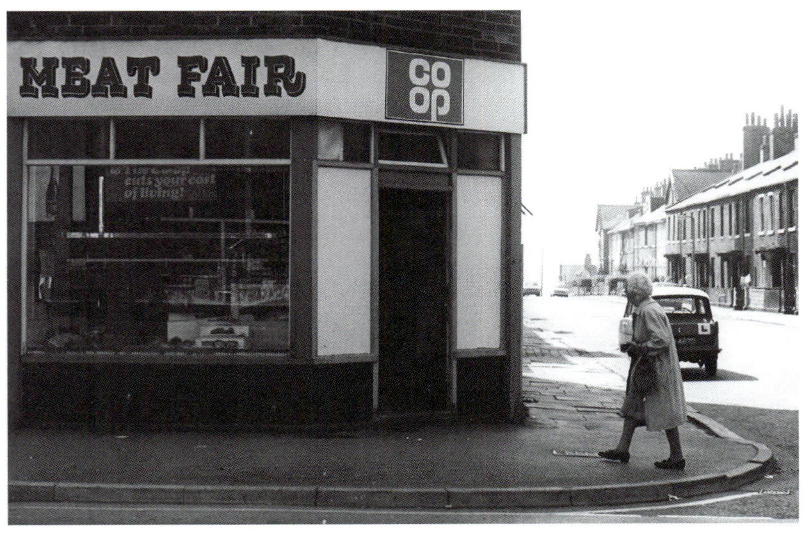

MEAT FAIR
CO OP
eats your cost
of living!

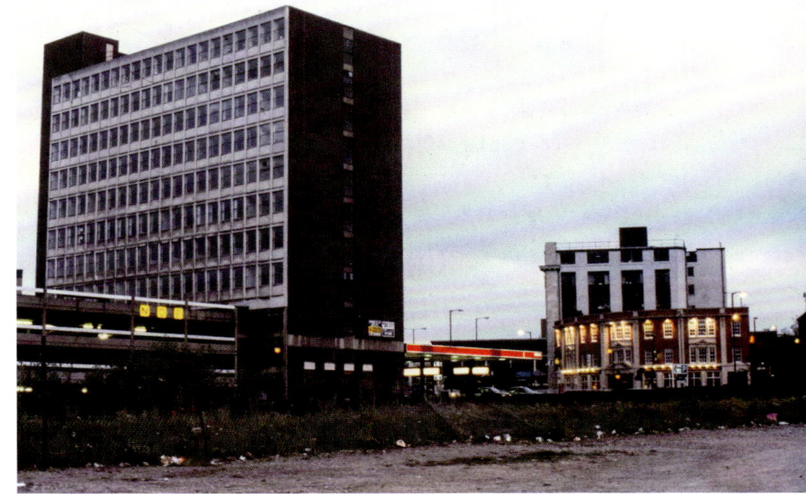

connections between the parts: the way we work, and the way we live, the everyday life of cities as well as the ways we transgress or reshape experience. That was then. This is now. The world receives you and recedes from you in the same moment.

Impact Theatre Co-op was a company making collective performances in the generation just before Forced Entertainment 'at the fag end of a bohemianism that has now I think died entirely'.[5] In Leeds. Thirty-five miles north of Sheffield on the M1. Cloth to their steel but no less hard and harsh for that. Impact were students there in the 1970s and made theatre between 1978 and 1985, travelling throughout Britain and Europe, with, at times, friends and children and, at times, virtually unmanageable sets—a ruined country house with a hidden room, a thirty-foot pool of water holding islands of decaying scaffolding. In 1981, we dragged a crashed car into the derelict space of the Waterloo Gallery, just south of the Thames, and abseiled in through the roof onto a floor of leaves. We lit braziers for heat. In 1984, as Forced Entertainment were setting out, we made *The Carrier Frequency*, our strangest yet most widely seen work, with the writer Russell Hoban, a work that I recall the playwright Snoo Wilson once calling 'a post-apocalyptic water ballet'. We toured it for two years, left the set in Poland in the week of the Chernobyl catastrophe, made one more piece, *The Price of Meat in the Age of Reproduction*, and gave up the ghost. Impact split up in 1985/6 and the work has been all but forgotten. There are references to this work scattered about the performance scene like discarded clothing. Other theatre-makers occasionally talk about our shows. They hover in memory, but only Forced Entertainment have referred to their commonality with Impact, to their inheritance from us of something indefinable, something we share. Today, as I write, I see Impact's connection to Forced Entertainment as a story of kinship. I am now drawn to words that suggest genealogies, structural threads that open into kin and community, to cartographies of belonging. The geographer Doreen Massey talked of the challenge of our 'constitutive interrelatedness' and that too seems relevant.[6]

We met Forced Entertainment-to-be on the road—Tim Etchells, Terry O'Connor, Deborah Chadbourn, Hugo Glendinning, who else I can't remember—around 1982/3 when they were students in Exeter. We were half a dozen years and a dozen shows older. A boyfriend of Terry's called Dick who had lived in a house in Leeds above another friend, Kevin Lycett, one of the founders of the punk band The Mekons, went to Exeter as a mature student and started going out with Terry.[7] He also started booking bands and theatre groups. We performed at the university. We slept on their floors. They watched our shows. We talked. In 1984, when they graduated, they came north to Sheffield and, like us, co-founded a theatre co-operative. We had just left Leeds, but our work beckoned them up the M1 in some chancy unauthorized way that was entirely appropriate to who we and they were at a moment when we were finally moving on. The social world that birthed Impact was giving way. We had been there for almost a decade. Our brand of surreal dystopian world-making was not as well received in our artistic home town as it was in Brussels or Polverigi, Amsterdam or Madrid. We made our final show in an all but derelict hospital in East London.

That they should arrive as we left. That they should outgrow and discard our shoes. That they stayed in the North. That we dispersed as a company but have remained close as a group of friends. That they seeded and flourished. That we stayed in touch. We handed something on to them, but we could never quite see what it was. I guess there was a sharing of sensibilities. Something about us, what we did, what we made, who we were, a makeshift, risky, almost shambolic sense that flowed from us into what they did, though what we did began in different times and ended as they began. I think it had a lot to do with the cities and their energies, with mining the space between what has been and what might be in places that were much less managed and hemmed in than they are now, at least here, in England.

What was it about those industrial northern English cities separated by a ribbon of motorway that was hospitable to the lives we wanted to live and the work we wanted to make? What's at stake, if anything, in retracing our steps? Who says what happened, here or here? What kinds of relationships—intimate perhaps, small perhaps, insignificant perhaps, between theatre groups or families or bands—make it through? Which bits of the past are picked up? Which events are understood as significant, and which do we therefore remember? Questions haunt me now like ghosts knocking in the night. I didn't mention that the wild commons are where ghosts go, but you knew that. We all know that ghosts like to haunt edges and that haunting is a habit that won't go away. Haunting is a highway, an unmarked desire path to the past along which ghosts travel. Ghosts haunt us because they have something to say, and what they have to say often concerns the obscured, the overlooked, the uncalled for.

In 1970s Leeds the conduits for ghosts were multiple. They knocked at doors, slipped through empty buildings, through the semi-derelict Corn Exchange and the warehouses, cemeteries, and blackened stone-built offices that lined the canal. The sites and signs of power and decay were all there—un-branded, un-managed, often empty. There was a serious underbelly of unrest and crime. In 1974 the Leeds architect John Poulson had been jailed for his part in a web of corruption that embraced twenty-three local authorities and individuals. Between 1977 and his prosecution in 1981, Peter Sutcliffe, the so-called Yorkshire Ripper, preyed on and murdered women in West Yorkshire. And there was the vexed question of race, and race and football, as the Kittitian British writer Caryl Phillips, who grew up in Leeds, has written.[8] Remember Andrei Tarkovsky's 1981 film, *Stalker*? The film explores a wilderness of magical strangeness around the detritus left by visiting aliens. Tarkovsky made it in the decay of Soviet Russia but he could have made it in Leeds. He could have made *Stalker* in Quarry Hill flats, the notorious estate by the bus station built as a modernist utopian dream and finally knocked down in 1978. He could have made *Stalker* in any of the dirty margins that held stories in as yet untranslated languages. Threads, wild paths, haunted routes.

Unofficial histories, unkempt tales, hardy, resistant, scrambled. The Leeds in which Impact began to work as a company was still a city defined by the texture of post-war Britain, a city of scrap and junk yards, of old things in heaps, a city in which a landscape of dereliction and decay was also a playful world of possibilities. It was dark and rotten and damp and green, a place with patches of wild, bordering on moorland, bisected by a canal, thick with tired streets and old breweries, multiple languages and diverse food cultures, poor people and newcomers and scatterings of city pride and wealth. Leeds had been home to waves of social, political, and artistic activism for a hundred years and more. Northern cities in the nineteenth century had been looser and wilder than we think of now. The poet Glyn Hughes came to live near Huddersfield in the 1960s and wrote that, as the Industrial Revolution released workers from what he called 'the idiocy of rural life' in the early nineteenth century, the dispossessed poured into the towns: Irish labourers, Chartists, Luddites, creators of the Co-operative Movement.[9] It had also been a mill town—flax, linen, cotton—and was still home to a large Indian and Pakistani community. It had been home to a Jewish community that had been central to the city's arts and cultural identity, a Polish community, and a Caribbean community. As young theatre-makers we ate at the Polish club, bought poppy seed kugels from Orthodox Jewish bakers. We went to the International Club, shopped in Indian grocers, bought fish in Leeds market where the traders still wore clogs. I learned to cook in Leeds, ate my first curries and beestings tarts—sweet cheese pastries traditionally made from the first milk after calving. The city was lined with streets of back-to-back terraced housing. In Hyde Park and Chapeltown large decaying villas were cheap to rent and even to buy. In rows of terraces, toilets were outside, even at the end of the street. Hot baths were still available at the swimming pool.

If the city was multicultural, the University was cosmopolitan. It had grown out of a nineteenth-century manufacturing and dissenting past that offered education to students of all faiths, tying its purpose to science and medicine. By the time we arrived as students between the early and mid-1970s, the red-brick campus had been extended by Chamberlin, Powell, and Bon: the architects of the Barbican Estate in London. The theatre department had had a long relationship with African theatre through Professor Martin Banham. Wole Soyinka had been a student in the 1950s and retained his connections. Ralph Miliband and Zygmunt Bauman were professors of politics. Linguistics, which I studied, was polyglot, alive to language change, with a strong connection to West Africa. French and Spanish were equally modernist, and even the tutor who had taught Impact co-founder Pete Brooks and me Greek Civilization did so through the lens of Maoism. Intellectually, as well as in the markets, clubs, and pubs, Leeds was home to new identities sited in old spaces.

In the early 1970s all kinds of people found themselves in Leeds, by chance or desire, creating alternative projects and ways of living. Young radical lawyers, Marxist social workers, and teachers all found their way north, renting or collectively buying cheap properties in which to live and work. Others came as students or came as musicians, or to the art school, or stayed on as graduates, founding alternative newspapers, a Free School, community nurseries, health clinics, and law centres as well as making performance—of which there was a lot. In her book *Young Lives on the Left*, Celia Hughes records the memories of forty radical women and men for whom 1968 had been a tipping point, a highly charged, empowering period of change.[10] Several of her interviewees lived in Leeds in the 1970s and were part of the activist art scenes there—including film-maker Chris Rawlence, of Red Ladder Theatre, and Mica Nava, now Emerita Professor of Cultural Studies at the University of East London whose husband José Nava was in The People Show.[11] Hughes remarks that it was the idea of *collective* liberation that was the hallmark or 'spirit' of social protest movements from the late 1960s, with a strong sense of the way in which the personal was connected to the social and political. That energy was evident in Leeds in the 1970s. It signified a whole-life politics that left very little out: what to eat, who to sleep with, how to live, how to work, how to bring up children, how to consume and how to produce, who to be with, who to march with, who to do political theory with. This was the Leeds that we came to as students. This was a city whose cheap rents and squats, diverse citizenry, and layered political histories combined with new energies. It made for an anti-establishment milieu, a broad space to operate in.

In 1978 Pete Brooks had been looking at ways to start a theatre company. The year before, as an MA student, he had been directing plays by Beckett and Kroetz, and making strange music and blood-fuelled theatre with me and other people, among them the poet Ian Duhig. We were filling our minds with material. We watched Andrzej Wajda's films at the Hyde Park cinema. We watched friends form bands and take part in street theatre and performance—but we wanted to be in something bigger and more atmospheric. We talked about Tadeusz Kantor's 1944 theatre production of the *Iliad* in the decayed underground cellars of Warsaw. There was something about theatre that we desired, a romantic, risky, unlimited kind of playfulness that could also go under the radar. There was no money to be made, no fans to be gathered, we could just do what we wanted to do. We were mining the space-time of the city's undertones and decaying streets, mapping imaginary places onto real experience. We were making a real-time novel set somewhere in what we called the deep south of the Urals, a mix of Soviet sci-fi and dystopian fiction—deeply informed by Leeds.

By 1977 everyone who later became part of Impact Theatre was living in Leeds. Pete Brooks and I began university in 1972. Tyrone Huggins came from Birmingham to study metallurgy in 1976. Graeme Miller came from teaching English in Spain in the same year. Steve Shill came to Leeds from the Cumbrian town of Kendal to study art. Simon Vincenzi, who later designed *The Carrier Frequency*, was still at school in Bradford when he met us. Richard Hawley met us through his friend Jon Martin, who came to direct an Athol Fugard play with Impact in 1980. From the start, there were always others—Lesley Stiles, Jon Martin, Hugo Burnham, Simon Lewandowski, and later Mary Peyton Jones, and, later still, core Impact members Niki Johnson and Heather Ackroyd. Ronnie Goodman, Matthew Coe, Jeremy Peyton Jones, Andrew Poppy, Jocelyn Pook, and Anne Stevenson all joined us as musicians. That was later—between 1976 and 1978 Leeds threw Impact together.

Something else happened between 1976 and 1978. 1976, the hottest summer for decades, witnessed the raised voice of the nationalist Right against immigration, followed and countered by Rock Against Racism, by Punk, by Ska, by Reggae, and by a new page in youth culture. Art historian Gavin Butt calls it the moment of being in a band, not just literally, but, as he says, 'banding' in ways that modelled themselves as new sorts of gathering in small, tight, groups around music and politics and culture.[12] For Butt, being in a band in Leeds in the late 1970s was characterized both by the bands that formed there—The Mekons, The Gang of Four, Scritti Politti, Sheeney and the Goys, and more—and by theatre, particularly by Impact, and the sense that this culture emerged as part of a conversation about how to do things, how to be things, a conversation that created a new collective energy, new stakes, new ideas.

Butt sees this new way of being in a band as distinct from what being in a band had been up until then. The new aesthetic was DIY. It took the post-1968 world of alternative publications, street theatre, and communal living and tipped it upside down, affecting the broader culture more widely and deeply than anything before it. If you were sixteen in 1976, you had been eight in 1968. The earlier movers and shakers of Leeds, who were still active in the late 1970s, were, as Celia Hughes discussed, often people who had been radicalized at school by their own young teachers in the early 1960s. These teachers, who had often been members of CND, were now teaching in Sixth Forms and art colleges. Their radicalism was political in the old sense, informed by the shadow of war, both past and future, in a way that utterly changed as the mid-1970s erupted into a new politics of music, art, and theatre.

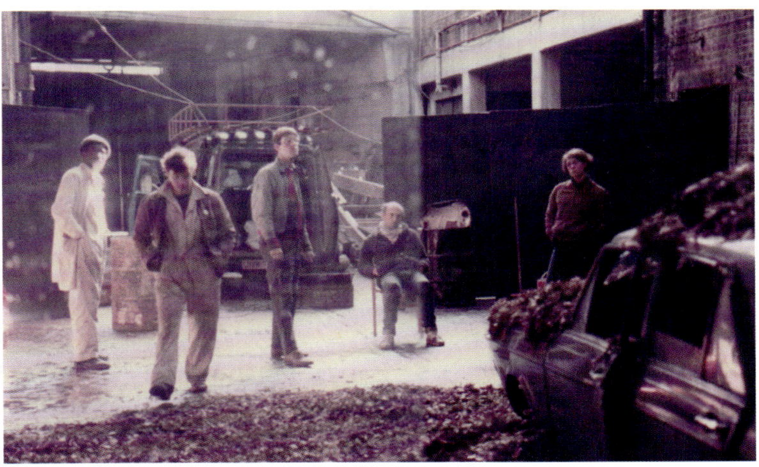

In 1977 Pete Brooks directed three student actors, Hugo Burnham, Tyrone Huggins, and Graeme Miller, in Barrie Keefe's *Abide with Me*, part of his *Barbarians* trilogy. The play caught the flavour of the time—football hooliganism, youth culture, race. It won an award and went to the Edinburgh Festival. Hugo Burnham left to be The Gang of Four's drummer and, joined by Steve Shill and later Lesley Stiles, the rest us found a warehouse to rehearse in, above The Mekons and the Suma food co-operative, and got stuck into making theatre. It took a couple of years to find a language.[13] We found it in 1979 through adapting Anna Kavan's 1960s hypnotic heroin-fuelled sci-fi novel *Ice*. From then onwards every new piece of theatre that we made found us tackling the shock of a new world in which we found ourselves, often worlds whose time-space co-ordinates suggested dream versions, at times nightmare versions, of our own present. Every piece referred to film: Peter Greenaway, Rainer Fassbinder, Werner Herzog. Language existed in an in-between state. We played with the 'feel' of language, undermining its ability to make complete sense. At the Polish Club in Chapeltown we heard ex-servicemen ordering vodka and pancakes. We made slapstick work in garbled Polish, French, and German. In 1980, we made *The Undersea World of Erik Satie*, 'A group of people in a café speaking cod-French while the windows become the sides of an aquarium.'[14] We took our playful, scary wastelands into a dystopian future in *Certain Scenes*, evoked destruction in *Dammerungstrasse 55* in a mythical post-war Germany with a miniature set opening onto a tiny backstage chamber. It was around then that we met Forced Entertainment-to-be, somewhere between *Useful Vices* and *No Weapons for Mourning*, a mystical noir detective show in a dystopian California complete with Laurie Anderson vocals. We were making theatre in the expanded field, a theatre that asked whether this could be theatre or whether it had exploded the boundaries and become something else, an experience, chaotic and absorbing but puzzling. We picked up a theatre-making vocabulary from what was growing around us, from sci-fi films and comics, music, the rebel tones of punk energy, and the site of the city itself with its politics, its languages, its market clogs, its cavernous clubs, its overlapping zones. Unsettled territories, dystopian tales.

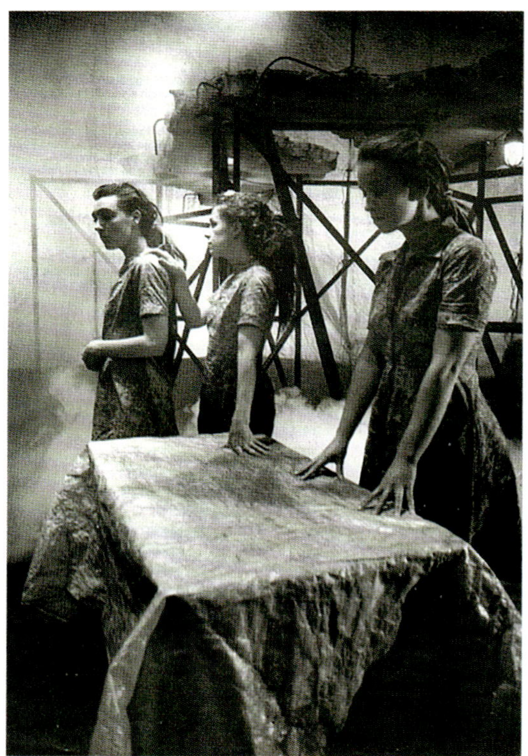 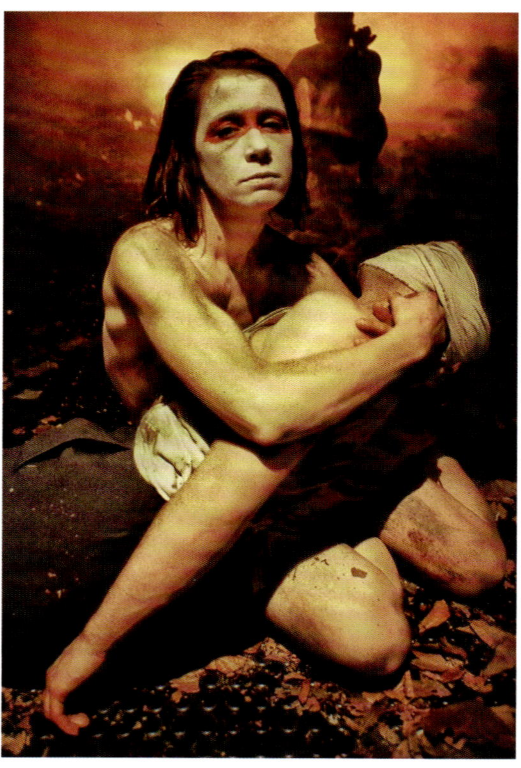

Theatre historian Simon Shepherd first saw our work (and booked us) as a young lecturer at Nottingham University in the early 1980s. In his *Cambridge Introduction to Modern British Theatre* he writes about both Impact and Forced Entertainment. His is a queer telling, alert to the gaps, the ghosts, the many divergent paths. Looking back at Impact's work Shepherd sees the company creating mood and dealing in quotation while Forced Entertainment invoke an 'other' other world, the strange real unreal world of continuous destruction and rebuilding: the shopping malls, the ten-screen cinemas. He sees the move between the aesthetics of Impact Theatre and Forced Entertainment as a shift across a threshold from visually organized work to work which problematizes the status of the image. I like the idea of the threshold. It is the most haunted space of all, the space between dreaming and waking, the entrance to the house, the place where you are poised between past and future. I think Impact also marks a point between a culture of future possibility with deep roots into the past and that world which birthed the digital, in which space became the dominant trope, in which the expressive work of Forced Entertainment continues to map the surface in all its depth. For Shepherd, their later moment 'recycled the recycling' evoking 'lives impinged on by media' and the 'necessity for but impossibility of speaking'.[15] Forced Entertainment moved into a world in which representation itself had become fragmented. In the uncertain personas that people their worlds, performers are shown struggling with the process of getting through the terms and conditions each show sets up, almost as a way of dealing with the experience of modern life. They too, of course, are adventurers on the edge—of a riverbank, a car park at night, the pool of dim light in a diner—dealing with a world they find themselves in, by chance, at random, beyond reason. Our commonality lies somewhere here, in the exploration of uncertain worlds. I should say, in the joyful exploration of uncertain worlds.

Impact was not a theatre company in the conventional sense, which is why Butt's notion of Impact-as-band rings so true—as it does for Forced Entertainment. There is no other way to express the sense of collective enterprise—the sense that the whole is so much more than the sum of its parts that emerges from constant play—of call and response, of exploration, of not working with a script but pulling materials into use in imaginative space-time. More recently this has been filed under the simple rubric of collaboration, and it's true, it was artistically collaborative, but Impact's work was not informed so much by methodologies of theatrical collaboration as by the spirit of co-operation. The Co-op movement is another lens, or thread or haunted route, back to a sensibility beyond the idea of crossing disciplines between art and theatre, to a more holistic and utopian notion of how to live. Calling ourselves a co-operative in 1978 connected us to a range of historical movements and people. Through naming ourselves, we were legally and ideologically committed to working together differently and to making a different kind of performance. We became a co-operative at a moment of rising fortunes for co-ops, one in which film co-ops and housing co-ops were also flourishing. Leeds had been home to the nineteenth-century Co-operative movement, a movement associated with dissent and with an alternative strand of left-wing social structure, what we might now call a prefigurative politics. George Jacob Holyoake came from Leeds and in 1897 he wrote about the history of Co-operativism in Leeds. He said, of the movement, that he had 'defended it in its infancy, when no one thought it would live' and that he was proud now to have seen it flourish.[16] In 1975/6 some of us had formed a food co-op in our neighbourhood, led by the combined energies of Anna Whyatt and Reg Taylor. It flourished and they went on to found Suma, which is still going as a workers' co-operative. Whyatt was president of ICOM, the Industrial Common Ownership Movement. She encouraged us to become a co-op through ICOM. Romantically, we saw ourselves as anarcho-syndicalists, allied to the co-ops of Mondragon in northern Spain. Co-operativism was not just a way of becoming a company. It was a strand of politics that, like the squatting movement, was about releasing the energy of the commons. In *Co-operative Culture and the Politics of Consumption in England, 1870–1930*, Peter Gurney writes about its histories. He records that the mid-1970s was a high point both for the founding of new co-ops, and for Co-operativism as a new communitarian movement and an alternative model of what we would now call creative commons—providing space for alternative ways to live and to be. A sense of the free association of people coming together to make change is folded into Co-operative history. It is essentially both everyday and utopian, part of creating working practices beyond the aesthetic, in solidarity with other practical ideals about how to live.

Those of us who founded Impact grew up in an era in which we were connected by an unstated commitment to generating new ways of being beyond class and family. We inherited that from the 1960s and from the alternative theatre movement internationally. We came through state schools and experienced education in ways that are no longer possible. Schools could be rigid and more brutal, but they were at times far more anarchic. Kids could find themselves suspended without telling their parents, free to while away days in less useful pursuits, blowing up trees, for instance, or running loose, exploring. All of us came from backgrounds that contained such stories. We were from that broad margin of British life, the upper bit of the working class and the lower bit of the middle, whose stakes in stability were thin. We had travelled to Leeds and we kept on travelling. I came to Leeds from Scotland and worked in a shop before going to university, had a break, and then came back and met up with Pete who had been living in Marseille. Steve had lived in France for a year before coming to Leeds, working in a hotel run by a French host who famously (in Impact lore) had to entertain his former Nazi commander-occupier, who was on holiday there. He had then been a waiter in Paris. Tyrone had come to England from St Kitts, aged five. Tales of bitter Birmingham cold, of his band of brothers wrapped in brown paper in bed together, vied with mine and Graeme's East End Scottish mothers and fathers going down the palais, and Pete's customs-official, jazz-loving dad creating delicate gateau mountains at home in Essex. Pete's dad had taught him to sail on the Thames Estuary. Tyrone could weld. Graeme could make music from old tins. Unruly childhood play spilled over into kids' shows and residencies. In 1980, we made a version of *Beowulf* for kids. *A Journey through Mungo Park* at Theatre Workshop in 1981 had Tyrone as the Scottish explorer Mungo Park transformed into an African explorer navigating the Thames. *The Undersea World of Eric Satie* had Steve inhabiting his former waiter-ship, performing in cod French to the music of saxophonist Matthew Coe. *Useful Vices* had us as East End criminals in a getaway speedboat on a Thames that morphed into the Amazon, speaking about kinship through the discourse of structural anthropology. Performances were choreographed from beginning to end to soundtracks produced by Steve Shill and Graeme Miller, with space for chance and improvised elements that developed the content. In Leeds, we worked with artist Simon Lewandowski, who created stage designs for us to play in, and Matthew Coe, the anarchic punk saxophonist from Bradford who played with everyone around the band scene. Matthew had stories galore. He had been knocked over by a bus at the age of eleven. His mum had been on the bus and had got off and held his head together, he said, until the ambulance came. Matthew died in 1988 of brain cancer. We worked with percussionist Ronnie Goodman, who trained at Leeds College of Music, and Steve Shill and Graeme Miller developed inventive, quizzical sound worlds, and were commissioned, while we were still in Leeds, by Granada TV producer Ann Wood to do the music for *The Moomins*, recently re-released.[17] Mary Peyton-Jones joined us while a student at Bingley College and introduced us to her composer brother Jeremy and his friend Andrew Poppy, both of whom we then worked with. Simon Vincenzi became part of our world while still at school, before going on to study at Wimbledon and to design *The Carrier Frequency*.

Intuitively we drew on a thread that was then present throughout post-war British culture in curious (and still unaccounted for) ways: the spirit of play. It has slipped deep below the surface of the waves now, but wild play was still powerful in the 1970s. The spirit of play in post-war Britain and Europe appears in films and novels that spar with dark, and occasionally violent, events that have children at the centre of frightening adventures and at times comic worlds. Rose Macaulay's *The World My Wilderness* (1950) has teenagers playing in bombed-out London in 'the margins of the wrecked world'. Clive King's *Stig of the Dump* (1963) and Alan Garner's *Elidor* (1965) have children encountering people from other times in chaotic marginal sites—dumps and wastelands. The Leeds we grew up in as theatre-makers in our late teens and early twenties was still a world of play, an intergenerational world in which we were far from the youngest. We had kids around us, our own and others. We made theatre with and for kids. We inhabited a world in which young people had kids and in which kids were being born into alternative family networks. Like the Wilds. Like Riddley Walker. The Wilds were kids being brought up when we were in Leeds, born into big communal non-biological families who were all given the surname Wild.[18] Riddley Walker is and always will be a fictional twelve-year-old boy in a future post-apocalyptic world, the invention of Russell Hoban in his novel of the same name.[19] Riddley was a figure we tapped into when we read the novel in its publication year in 1980. Its picture of a future-past world of scrambled languages, where everything is broken, where the speech mode is shattered poetic, where old myths have morphed into new ones—a dystopian, post-urban, at times bucolic world—was one we felt we could have designed ourselves. We met Russ through the TV producer Ann Wood, and we made our last big collective show, *The Carrier Frequency*, with him.

The Carrier Frequency, and in effect, our work, came to rest in Poland in April 1986. In the world of haunting and ghosting, a world in which we call up those things that still need to be present to us, we ground to a halt. We had taken *The Carrier Frequency* there as the start of a tour and within days the Chernobyl reactor had melted down 400 kilometres away, with an immediate virtual shutdown of borders, a rehearsal, it felt, for the nuclear catastrophe that had always been the background to post-war lives. The night before we separated, some to fly back, some to drive, our hosts, theatre company Akademia Ruchu, wrote in a book for us: 'With hope to have another common shinings in future' and they drew the peace sign. We left our set there.

There is a strong sense in which the touring works that Impact created between 1979 and 1985 were more sites than sets, sites that we created, edited, and added to as we went, thickly layered with the energies of the magazines and records, the Polish meals, the spools of film, the overheard conversations, languages, food cultures, gestures, stories, insides of kitchens, and the damp warehouse where we rehearsed. All of these found their way into a self-made site we carted through the world. The work manifested the spirit. Theatre worlds are distinctive places where dream logic rules. Sites where material and metaphor meet. Simon Shepherd wrote that we approached theatre like creating a novel, 'constructing the environment in which everything is experienced', an expressive world hovering on the edge of pastiche, a dark seduction, immersive.[20]

In the past three and more decades the potential for immersive theatre has burgeoned but in the late 1970s what Impact created was more unusual. Where you find yourselves socially, in time, in place, allows you to feel and be certain things and to do certain things, or to resist or change or make new. There was so much in the live archive of Leeds, and so much more in its guts, its drains, its waters, and its dirt. It was as if past and present were constantly changing their relationship in a city made of alleys and edges, of streets ending in broken walls, of tarnished mirrors, and pub lock-ins with black pudding. A city that seemed at all times surreal. The present is not quite predicated on the past. Or predicted. But it can be retold. Its lines can be redrawn; its energies re-imagined and repurposed. Reviewing the past through different lenses opens it not just to new interpretations but to different futures. And that is where we met and where we will always continue to meet Forced Entertainment. There is a sense in which Impact's and Forced Entertainment's work is essentially archival. All those voices, all those worlds. It could not emerge in any other way than through this alternative familial play, this collective making, this co-op.

We were all, of course, outsiders. There is a word for that which was often used in Yorkshire, 'off comed 'uns'. We were off comed 'uns and so we heard and saw and moved through the cities in which we came to experience ourselves as young adults with the eyes of people suddenly finding ourselves in strange worlds. Our work was and is not storytelling as much as it was and is channelling other energies, other hauntings. And now, I realize, other losses. All times hover on the edge of disappearance, hold stories that manifest as hauntings, those ghost knockings, those slips of the tongue that suggest worlds behind words. I remember once listening to an improvised story told live by the legendary Yorkshire-based performer Lou Glandfield and I knew he was channelling—that someone, something, some voices, deeply mixed and scratched were at play in his mind. I knew it was archival, drawn up from some deep common throat. It could be told in no other way. All those voices, all those worlds.

What did Forced Entertainment find in Impact? A voice drawn up from some common throat? A discarded thread leading to something always disappearing, tantalizing and just out of sight? A glimpse of what lay just beyond the possible; a garbled message almost out of hearing; a means of creating something beyond normative models of how things work, or even how things should be? Creating alternative ways of doing and being was part of Impact's signature. Self-mythologizing is part of creating a sense of collective imagination. Whatever we passed on to Forced Entertainment was a generative act that is, in some way that is beyond words, still happening, that we cannot sign off, and yet which we, and I think I can say this for all of us, do not take lightly. The world receives you and recedes from you in the same moment. Take what you want from us. Use it. Throw the rest away. They did.

To the west of Sheffield lie a series of Edges, huge walls of rough rock and scrub. Here walkers from Sheffield come on days out. Here climbers cut their teeth. On top, in summer, great flat slabs warm in the sun. Here you can lie and look over the Hope Valley—at birds, at fields. Here, or close to here, was the historic Kinder Scout trespass, where young walker activists in the 1930s asserted the right of the common person to walk where they wanted to. And they won. Yet this is also a ruin, disarmingly empty. Poisoned by old lead mines. A fragile ecology that is also a rare archaeology of human habitation going back before Roman times and a plant ecology resistant to lead pollution, a place of mineral rakes and scrins, an archive of arcane words that go back century after century, touching our connection to ancient industry. Contamination and dereliction offer new possibilities if we know how to read them, if we know how to clear haunted paths. Nothing is ever truly lost. As Etchells says, there is always an edge that is ready to open up, just beyond where we are. We go close in order to find out what is there, not to tell stories but to find them.

1. M. John Harrison, *Climbers* (London: Victor Gallancz Ltd., 1989), 107.

2. Claire MacDonald, 'Unpicking Fried City', *New Socialist* (January 1987).

3. Richard Mabey, *The Unofficial Countryside* (London: Collins, 1974).

4. Richard Mabey, *Flora Britannica* (London: Chatto & Windus, 1997), 66.

5. Claire MacDonald, personal essay for the restaging of Impacts' *The Carrier Frequency* by Stan's Café (2000).

6. Doreen Massey, *For Space* (London: Sage, 2005), 195.

7. The Mekons are a post-punk band formed in 1976 by Jon Langford, Kevin Lycett, Mark White, Andy Corrigan, Tom Greenhalgh, and Ros Allen, all University of Leeds art students. They were later joined by members Sally Timms, Susie Honeyman, Steve Goulding, Rico Bell, and Lu Edmonds.

8. Caryl Phillips, *A New World Order: Selected Essays* (London: Secker & Warburg, 2001).

9. Glyn Hughes, *Millstone Grit* (London: Pan Books, 1987), 18.

10. Celia Hughes, *Young Lives on the Left: Activism and the Liberation of the Self* (Manchester: Manchester University Press, 2019).

11. The People Show is the UK's longest running experimental theatre company, formed in 1966 by Jeff Nuttall, John Darling, Laura Gilbert, and Mark Long.

12. Gavin Butt, talk at Wysing Arts Centre, Cambridgeshire, 14 July 2016.

13. Suma is a wholefood collective founded in 1977, www.suma.coop/about/our-co-op/, accessed 25 September 2020.

14. Simon Shepherd, *The Cambridge Introduction to Modern British Theatre* (Cambridge: Cambridge University Press, 2009), 174.

15. Ibid., 176.

16. George Holyoake, *The Co-operative Movement To-day* (1891; facsimile edition, 2015).

17. *The Moomins* was a Polish Austrian animation television series based on the Finnish illustrator Tove Jansson's fairy-tale comic books. Miller and Shill's music for the series can be found here: www.finderskeepersrecords.com/shop/graeme-miller-steve-shill-the-moomins/, accessed 25 September 2020.

18. Sally Williams, 'My Four Mums', *The Guardian*, 4 July 2009.

19. Russell Hoban, *Riddley Walker* (London: Jonathan Cape, 1980).

20. Shepherd, *The Cambridge Introduction to Modern British Theatre* (see n. 14), 175.

A Decade of Forced Entertainment (1995)

Tim Etchells and Forced Entertainment

Created to mark the company's tenth anniversary, *A Decade of Forced Entertainment* was a lecture-performance comprising a speculative history of the company, an archival collage of fragments of previous works, and a meditation on the contexts, politics, and processes of performance. It was first performed on 3 December 1994 at the ICA theatre, London. The six company members sat at a pair of long tables facing the audience with a continuous cycle of Hugo Glendinning's images of the work, Sheffield, and a series of maps of the UK projected as a backdrop.

Part One

[*Robin (Hans), Richard (Mike), and Claire (Dolores) read from the text for* Some Confusions in the Law about Love *(1989).*]

Hans: Mike, Dolores. Tell us a bit about the act.

Mike: It's a kind of escape artistry routine. We play lovers. Dolores shoots me in the head.

Hans: That sounds pretty kinky—would you say the act was kinky?

Mike: It's kinky alright.

Hans: You said it was escape artistry in the act. We wondered what, what are you escaping from?

Mike: We're supposed to be escaping from death.

Hans: Great. Sounds sexy as well as kinky. Dolores, any difficulties pulling the trigger, any fears about screwing up the act?

Dolores: No, not really. Before I got shot myself, I never liked to shoot anyone. But once I'd thought it through, worked out how it felt and everything, I stopped being scared.

Hans: Does this shooting, does this shooting hurt the two of you at all?

Mike: Yes.

Dolores: No. I call out a number in Spanish every time he hits.

Hans: Why Spanish? Why numbers in Spanish? Is that a gimmick?

Dolores: Yeah. It's a gimmick.

Hans: These things that you're planning or rehearsing now … There seems to be a change, a kind of change in tone, is that right?

Dolores: Yes.

Hans: Mike?

Mike: It's a kind of image change.

Hans: Why do you think it's changed?

Mike: Yeah. It's hard to explain.

Hans: We'd be interested to know.

Mike: We did a thing quite a while ago now: it was a love show and everyone on the stage drank down a love potion and then the love potion sent them all to sleep.

Hans: What happened then?

Mike: The potion sent them all off to sleep and when they all woke up again they were all in love and no one felt sad.

Hans: Uh-huh.

Mike: Well, that's not the kind of work we want to do any more.

Hans: I think I see what you're getting at now. Do you think things are getting out of hand?

Dolores: Yes.

Mike: No.

Hans: We want to know more about the stuff you're working on just now.

Mike: It's kind of quiet here, as far as bookings go.

Terry: We wanted to look back on the decade 1984–1994—the ten years in which we've been making our work—and we knew that this looking back would have to include the things that hadn't happened as readily as those that had. We had in mind a map of the last ten years—a haunted map, a false map, and yet, in some ways, an accurate map.

And at some point we realized that this map-making, this charting of a time and a landscape, was what our work had often consisted of. A kind of mapping, a kind of temperature taking.

Tim: Ten years of Forced Entertainment is ten years finding notes in the street. When we first got to Sheffield we didn't know anyone so the first months were very voyeuristic—months spent watching, trying to pick up the patterns of the place. In this time, above all others, we found notes and photographs in the street.

There was a note to a woman at a bus stop, along the lines of, 'I see you every day but will never dare speak to you …' There was a letter from someone in prison that had been torn into pieces as small as confetti but which were reassembled by us on the Formica-topped table at 388 City Road.

All through the winter we found things. There was a photograph of the ground beside a Mediterranean swimming pool, there were incomprehensible shopping lists, there was a page ripped out of a kid's cowboy book which had been vandalized so that where it once said, 'Tex gunned the man down,' it now said, 'Tex bummed the man.'

Terry: [*Reads from* Criminal Investigation *by Hans Gross, as featured in* Club of No Regrets (1993)] Piecing Together Torn Paper. Simple as this work may appear, it nonetheless presents numerous difficulties, and is often very awkwardly carried out. An investigator often receives numerous torn pieces of paper of small size, the content of which, once pieced together, is of the utmost importance.

Tim: All through the winter we found things. There were discarded photographs, there were incomprehensible shopping lists, there was a note I found near the high-rise flats which said, 'DAVE—I HAD TO GET OUT—THE GAS IS CUT OFF AND THE TV HAS GONE BAD—BACK THURSDAY.'

There was a map showing how to get to the motorway.

Cathy: Working on *Nighthawks* (1985) we wanted to make a faraway country called 'America in the Movies'—we were determined that nothing in the performance should be recognizably British. So following this peculiar logic we made regular visits to the Chinese takeaway on London Road to collect their old Chinese newspapers, which were thrown around onstage. For the same show we made trips out to Manor Top Industrial Estate to pick up soda siphons, we caught the bus to Killamarsh to try and find three identical bar stools, we collected obscure liquor bottles from shit nightclubs all over town. Getting to know the city through trying to find a ramshackle collection of props and set.

Richard: [*Reads from the text for* (Let the Water Run Its Course) to the Sea That Made the Promise *(1986)*]

Unfortunately, one day when we were driving, a Cornflakes truck hit us doing 93mph. And I remember thinking how quiet the whole world seemed, and still, and wondering if you blacked out before you hit the windscreen.

We died in the accident of course. I lost control of my bladder before we hit the Kellogg's truck so I didn't mind: my best suit was ruined anyway.

Claire: They drew a map of the country and marked on it the events of the last ten years: the sites of political and industrial conflict, the ecological disasters, the showbiz marriages and celebrity divorces. On the same map they marked the events of their own lives: the performances they'd given, the towns and cities where they'd stayed, the sites of injuries and fallings in or out of love.

They drew a map of the country and marked on it the events of the previous three, then four, then five hundred years. They kept on going until the beginnings of geological time. Until the map was scribbled over 1,000 times—utterly black.

They knew something strange had happened to time. They drew a map of the country and marked on it events from the rest of the world. On this map the Challenger Space Shuttle had blown up in Manchester in 1985. The Union Carbide Bophal Chemical Works, which exploded late in 1984, was located in Kent. The siege of the Russian parliament building in 1991 had taken place in Liverpool. The Democratic Party's recent setbacks in the mid-term elections had been most severe in the Isle of Dogs. The 1989 fatwa on Salman Rushdie had been issued from Tunbridge Wells.

Richard: [*Reads from the text for* Let the Water]

> After the Kellogg's truck hit us and killed us, we went to the hospital. There we were put in the capable hands of Dr Lyver, who had plenty of money.

> Seeing as how we were dead, they put sort of plastic taps in our arms and drained all the red sort of blood out of us into a sort of bucket. Then they got lots of other blood and pumped it into us through all possible entrances.

> This new blood they put in us was stuff they'd collected here and there from other people. The blood mixed together all these people's blood and thoughts and everything and this was our biggest problem you see: because the blood moved inside us, changing and turning, one person then another, we dint know who the fuck shit piss we were, we'd say one thing then another, stand up, sit down, the blood moved, we didn't know.

Tim: We'd like two silences now. First one minute's silence for Steve Rogers—Steve was editor of *Performance Magazine* in the mid-1980s and was very important to us and the whole sector of Live Art and Experimental Performance here in the UK by way of energy and criticism and constant encouragement. Steve died, along with his partner Mark, of AIDS-related illnesses in 1988. One minute's silence please, for Steve and Mark.

And a minute's silence for Ron Vawter, who died in 1994, also of AIDS-related illnesses. Ron was a performer with The Wooster Group and his performances, his energy, and openness inspired all of us here.

[*Cathy (A) and Robin (B) read from the text of* 200% & Bloody Thirsty (1988).]

> A: Howl! Howl! Wake it up, poor dead person, for we are upset and grieving angels.
> B: Oh, we are distressed and sorrowful angels!
> A: And we have lamented of all and weighty things.
> B: We have wept on drinking and eternity and of dreams etc.
> A: We have cried for loving and of souls and of death.
> B: But we have never grieved as much as this before.

A: Wake it up and think all hard of this. If you don't to get up who will shout and sing songs
at the stupid moon?

B: Who will to live in then your idiot house?

A: Who will bang its walls, and blood and bruise its stairs?

B: O, we are drunk and dependable angels and we can to raise our friends from out the dead.

A: When we to say of now, you will jump and rise and live again.

A & B: One. Two. Three. Now!

Part Two

Terry: We made work for ten years in a country with a Conservative government. None of us ever voted in a general election that returned anything other than a Conservative government.

As things changed, the maps we made of the country had to be redrawn.

Richard: We noticed big changes to the country but could never date them precisely. When did the streets fill up with beggars? When did the great programmes of building, rebuilding, and demolition begin? When exactly did the shopping malls and the ten-screen cinemas arrive? When did our city get its lift shaped like a rocket? From the day these places opened it seemed like they'd always been there.

As time went on, we got more and more sure that the work should look thrown together—chaotic, out of control, unintended—so that, perhaps, when it did pull something out of the bag, one simply wasn't prepared. The chaos of the work was always running to catch up with the chaos and confusion of the time it came out of.

We admired the title of a Cady Noland sculpture: a pile of aluminium baskets, mace canisters, and back issues of the magazine *Guns & Ammo*. She called it *Bloody Mess*.

We liked the feeling that events onstage were simply falling into place, that meaning was always an accident, although of course it rarely was.

Claire: Everything they seemed to use was brutal in some way. The materials were heavy steel, often rusted— the structures looked like buildings under construction, or buildings stripped of their walls. They used dirty, untreated ply, cardboard for writing on, cardboard to cover the floor. There was always the unreal beauty of electric light, the shabby mess of polythene and jumble sale clothes.

In 1989 we made a show not about Elvis Presley but about an Elvis Presley impersonator in Birmingham, England. We didn't want anything authentic, we wanted a third-rate copy—we loved that more dearly than anything original.

Robin: They were interested in the margins of life, never the centre. They tried not to talk about the people who made decisions but about those people who were affected by decisions made in other times and other places. They were provincial, by choice and by accident.

Is it true that the more desperate and depressed a city becomes, the more exotic the names of its nightclubs and amusement arcades become? They thought so. Through the 1980s and into the 1990s the city they lived in had a bar called MILLIONAIRES and a casino called BONAPARTES. One night they heard a drunk boasting how he once paid £5 for a sandwich in BONAPARTES—he thought it was great. They drew a map of the country and marked on it the amusement hall called GOLD RUSH, the discount shop called BARGAIN WORLD.

Terry: Is it true that the only way to see Britain properly is to see it drunk? They thought so. There were drunks in all of the shows, often drunks who were also dead.

Walking in the city, they'd use an almost conscious confusion—what were they trying to solve, the latest show or the city itself? Eating pizza after late-night rehearsals they'd see a riotous hen party—a woman dancing on the table and pulling her tights off as she danced. They'd discover a blind man negotiating his way through the tangle of builders' scaffolding near their rehearsal space on the Wicker—the city's most notorious has-been street. They'd ask: why aren't these things represented in the show? How could a map of the country include these things? Why isn't the texture of the show as desperate and gaudy and vital as these things? They laughed when the blind man told them: (1) he'd just been to the match, and (2) he was utterly pissed.

Tim: Beyond the city itself lay an alternative city too—not the one of nightclubs and blues clubs, but one of craters and broken ground. It seemed that during the Second World War the city lights had been blacked out and a decoy metropolis created in the hills using searchlights and halogen floods. So the hills took the pounding for the city and the Germans bombed the grass, stone, and moorland into burning mud. So the city always had its twin—an empty space waiting for them to fill it.

Much of the rest of the city was empty anyway. Walking around in 1984 and 1985 you'd never seen so many disused factories and fields of rubble. Often on Sundays, in those days, they'd walk, exploring the city and these empty buildings; places still littered with time sheets and newspapers. Was it in one of these places that they saw the graffiti 'DOWN WITH CHILDHOOD' and 'RAPE A TART TONIGHT'?

Cathy: [*Reads from the text for* Emanuelle Enchanted *(1992)*]

> The night the rain stopped was wild and cold and full of strange noises, and we did magic acts and were scared for each other and ourselves. We practised CLOSING BOTH EYES TIGHT WHILST DRIVING DOWN A ROAD, we practised EXHIBITION OF DUST. We practised HAUNTED GOLF. We worked on YOU'RE GOING HOME IN A FUCKING AMBULANCE.

> This is the life that we lived then, in the city, in the chaos and the dark …

Richard: They drew a map of the country and marked on it the locations for a hundred fictional events: here, the house in which gangster James Fox goes into hiding in Nick Roeg and Donald Cammells' film *Performance*. Here, the wind-blown meadow from Tarkovsky's film *Mirror.* Here, the crack house from Victor Headley's novel *Yardie.* Here, the Mexican town rebuilt by a film crew as a Wild West town in Dennis Hopper's *The Last Movie.* Here, the New Rose Hotel from William Gibson's story of the same name.

They drew a map of the country and marked it with the street names they'd collected over years, some real, some from fiction, some dreamed up just because they sounded good. They marked on the map ESPERANTO PLACE, OCCUPATION AVENUE, METEORITE STREET, and ALPHABET ROAD.

Claire: Was it really in the 1980s that the naming of things became so wonderfully and inventively blunt? It seemed like it. They drew a map of the country and marked on it MR BUYRITE, Hi-Fi WORLD, and BARGAIN LAND. They even saw a street somewhere called CAR PARK WAY. They marked this street on the map. At the end of this line lies I CAN'T BELIEVE THAT'S NOT BUTTER and a beer called THIS BEER IS THE BEST BEER I'VE EVER DRUNK IN MY WHOLE LIFE I SWEAR TO GOD. After the seductive power of ambiguous images, it all comes back to hard sell. They marked on the map a bar they'd seen in Zurich (1988), THE EVERYTHING A MAN COULD WANT BAR.

They drew a map of the country and marked on it roads named after Scargill, after Mellor and de Sancha after Reagan, North, and Yeltsin. They marked roads named after Rodney King, after Arnold Schwarzenegger, after the Birmingham Six and the Guildford Four, they marked roads named after Diego Maradona and Eric Morecambe. They marked a public park named after Nicolae Ceauşescu, and another named after Edwina Currie. They named a public square after the Russian cosmonauts who'd been circling the earth during the coup, unable to return and uncertain of what they'd come back to. They named bridges for deposed presidents, for kids on job creation schemes and for the glue sniffers who'd graffitied on an abandoned house near where they lived, in big letters, a sign saying 'DAVE'S GLUE CLUB—EVERYONE WELCOME'.

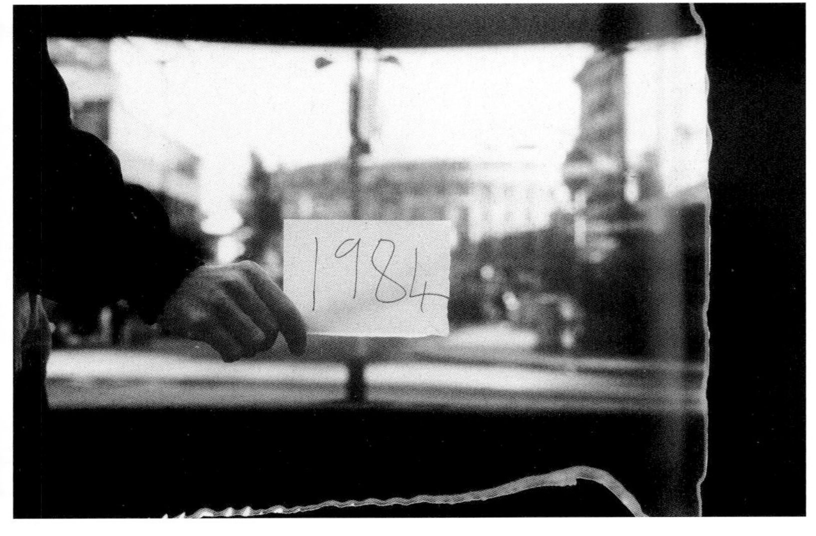
1984
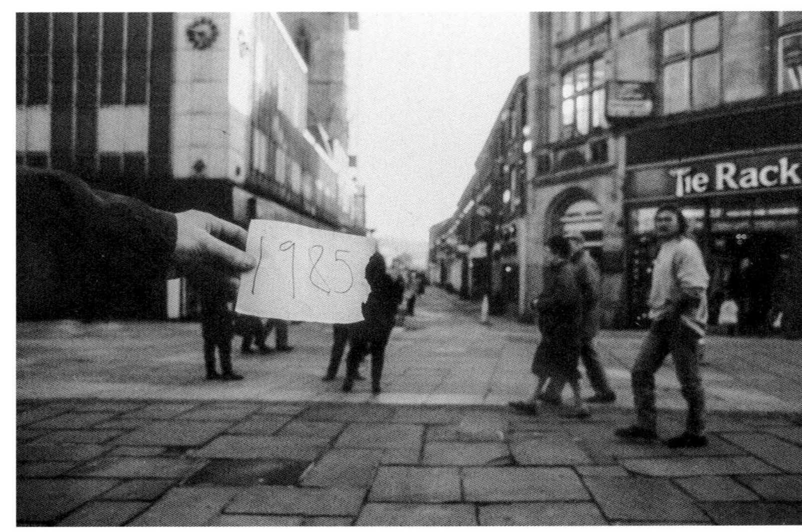
Tie Rack
1985
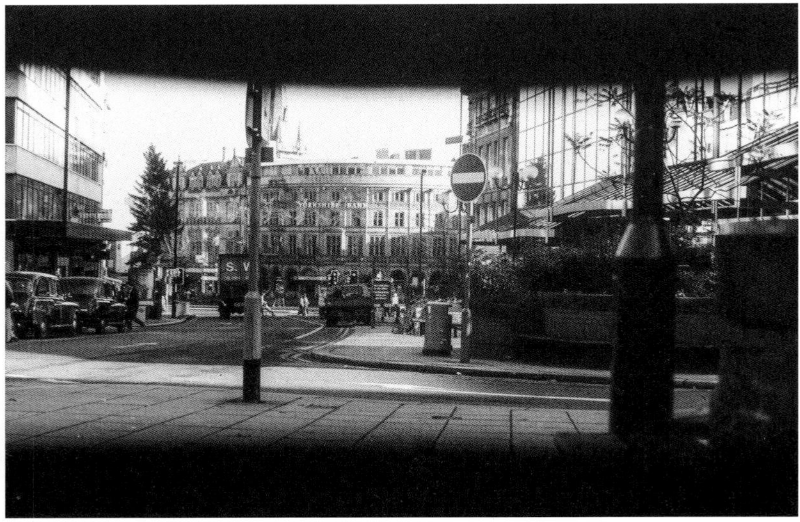
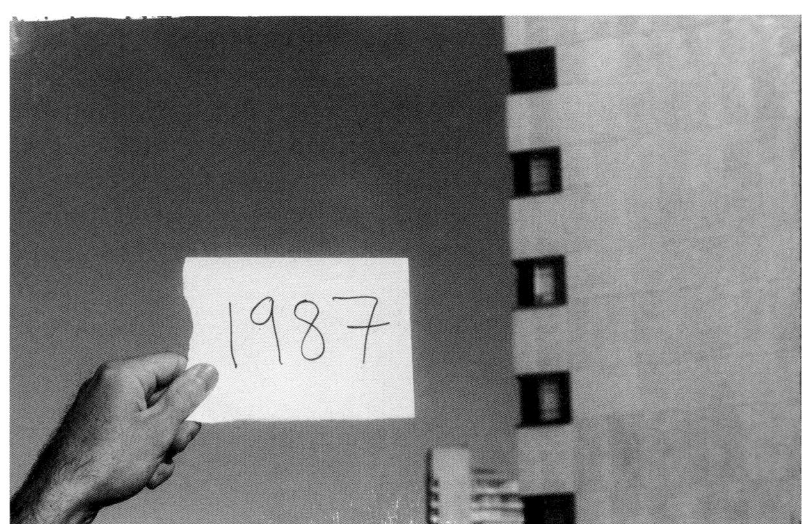
1987
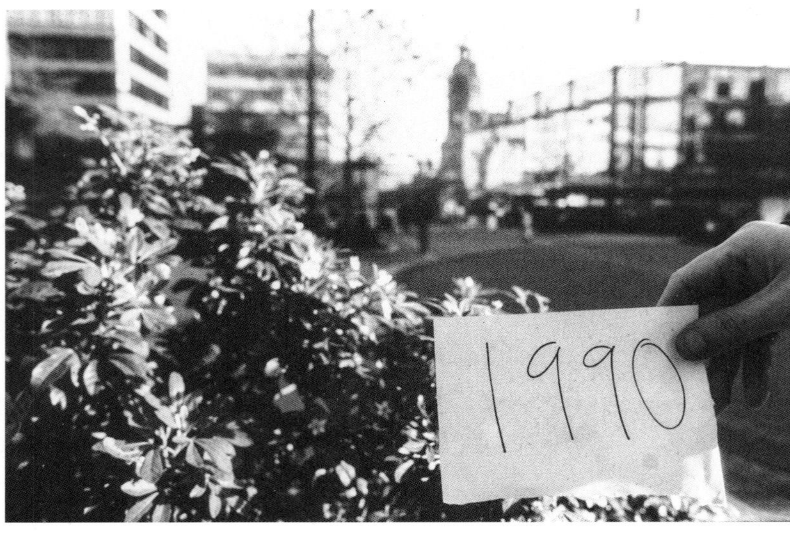
1990
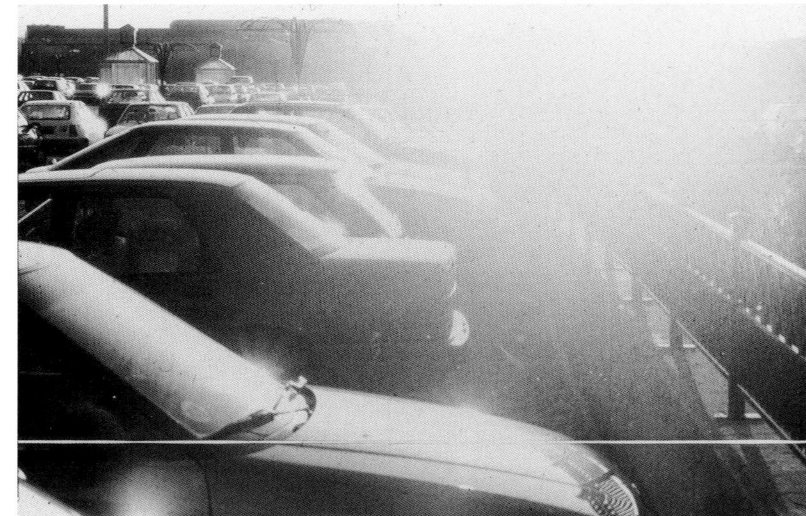

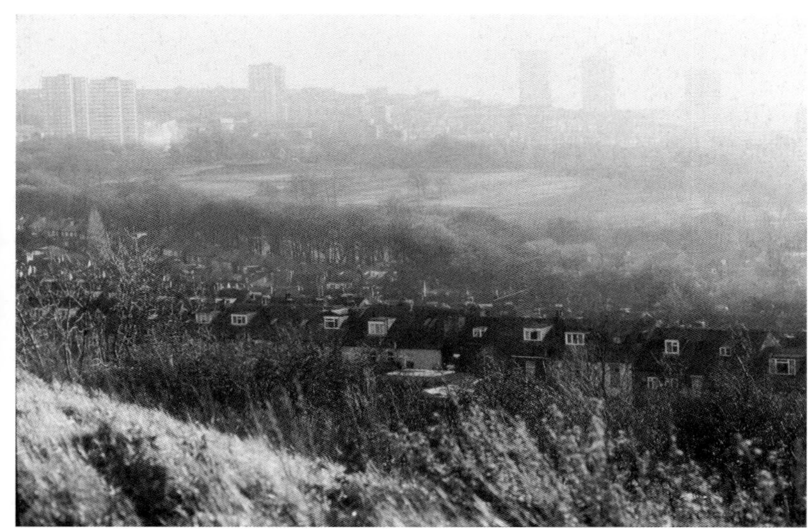
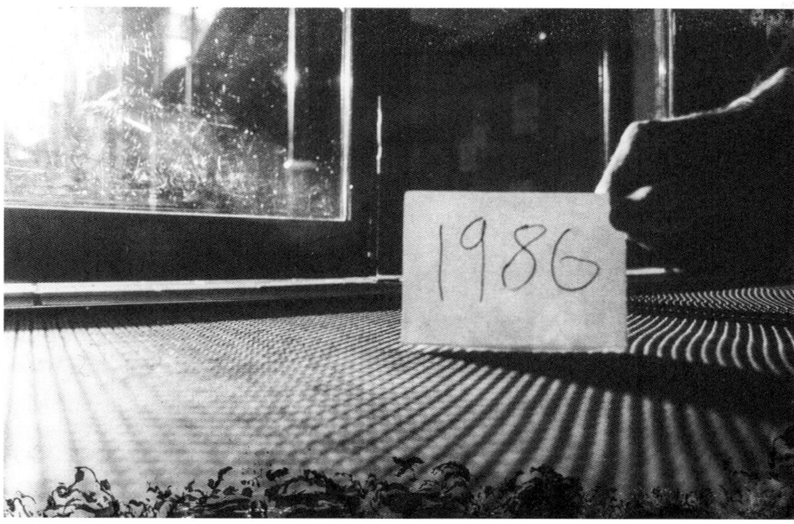

1986

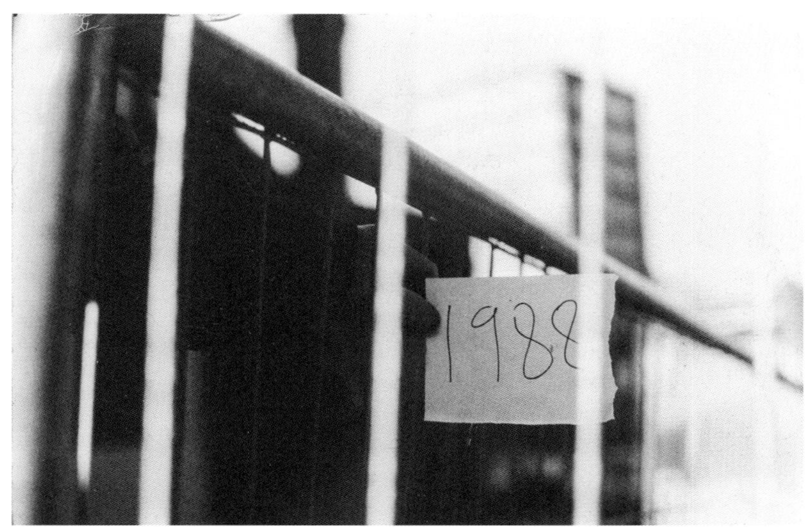

1988

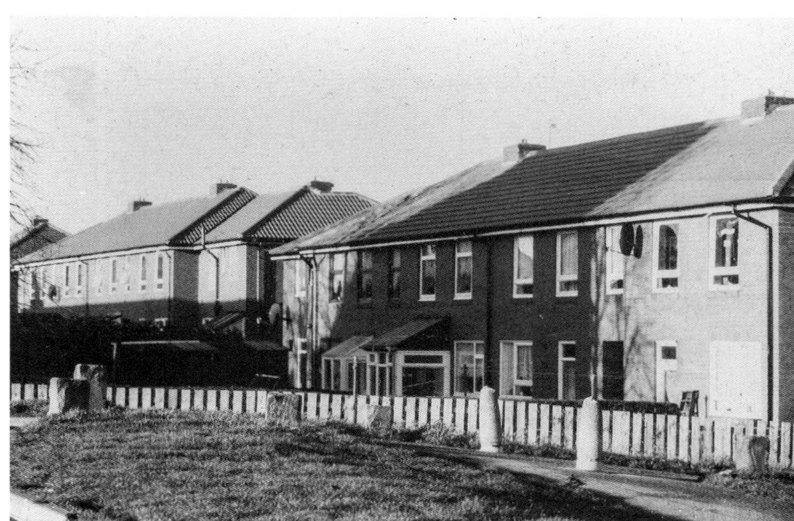
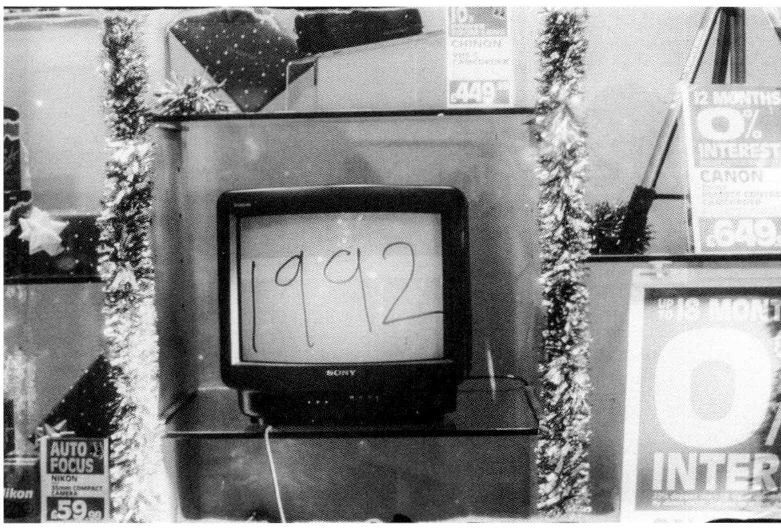

1992

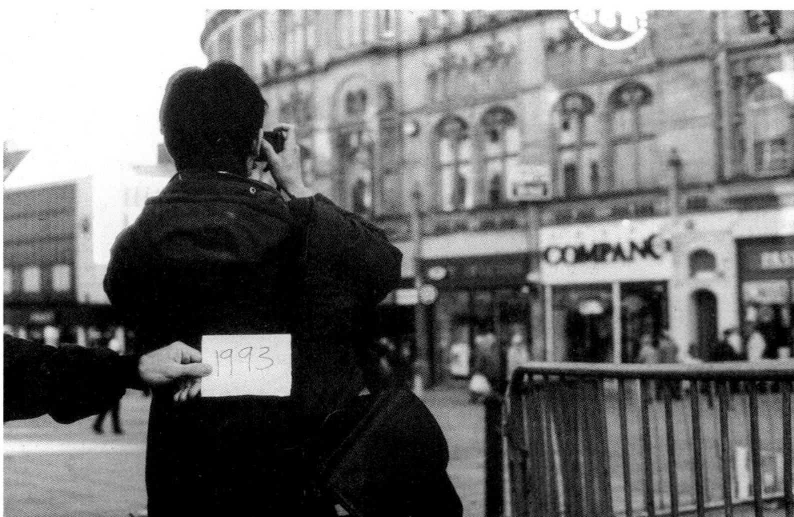

1993

On the map they marked museums for love and drunkenness, museums for rioters, accidents, happenstance, and luck.

Richard: On the map they marked the questions from a decade of end-of-year quizzes.

[*Richard asks the questions below to other performers onstage, who improvise answers.*]

In what year did the European Single Market begin?

Who said, and in what year, 'I am Jesus Christ and I announce the end of the world'?

Did David Alton's abortion bill, to cut the maximum age of the foetus to eighteen weeks, win or lose in the House of Commons?

Which won the Oscar for Best Film in 1987: *Platoon, Hannah and Her Sisters, The Mission,* or *A Room with a View*?

In which year did Rupert Murdoch move four newspapers into Wapping?

Who said, 'We had a wonderful day …'?

Was it:

(a) Class War, after the Poll Tax Riots in 1990?

(b) Sir Geoffrey Howe, after 152 Tory MPs voted Margaret Thatcher from the leadership position?

(c) Brian Keenan, after his release in Damascus?

Gilbert, Joan, and Ruby were lethal in 1988. What were they?

Who said, 'The master of the country has spoken'?

Was it:

(a) Gennady Gerasimov, announcing Moscow's rejection of separatist claims by the Baltic republics?

(b) Mikhail Gorbachev, after the electorate voted for a new Soviet Assembly?

(c) Polish premier Tadeusz Mazowiecki, after an audience with Lech Wałęsa?

(d) Deng Xiaoping after the Tiananmen massacre?

In what way did Willie Horton affect the US election?

Who put out the flames of Piper Alpha?

Part Three

Cathy: At the start of the shows they'd lay bare the means they had at their disposal like a bunch of crap magicians keen to prove they had nothing up their sleeves. As if to say, 'You can't believe this ridiculous pretending and yet against your better judgement you will believe in its outcome.'

They told you so many times they weren't acting that when they did act, they hoped you'd think it real. And on a good night that's what happened. They believed that suspension of disbelief was something you worked for, not took for granted.

They said they had faith in cities—even when all the evidence was against them. They believed that the architecture of the twentieth century worked best at night, with all the lights on.

They said they liked the media culture, the cargo cult of TV and movie detritus, but perhaps it would be truer to say that that was the world in which they found themselves, and so, like everyone else, they did their best to make sense of it all.

Robin: They pretended to be dead. They pretended to be Elvis. They pretended to be drunk. They pretended to be angels. They pretended to be devils. They pretended to be cowboys. They pretended to be kung fu fighters. They pretended to be opera singers. They pretended to be Lee Harvey Oswald. They pretended to be Marina Oswald. They pretended to be guilty. They pretended to be innocent. They pretended to be Mary, Joseph and the Angel Gabriel. They pretended to be lovers. They pretended to take drugs. They pretended to be foreign.

They pretended to be stupid. They pretended to be clever. They pretended to be lost in the woods. They pretended to be cosmonauts. They pretended to be widows. They pretended to tell lies, they pretended to tell the truth. And often they pretended to be themselves.

Terry: Trying to think about the last ten years, we wanted to track both the real ten years and the fictional one moving through it.

One day during rehearsals for *Marina & Lee* (1991) in a freezing cold, abandoned school we plan to eat in the warm of the Meadowhall Shopping Centre and to talk about the show as we do.

By some unlucky chance it is Red Nose Day and Meadowhall is seething with fun-loving bastards dressed up to shake a bucket for a good cause. We try to eat at The Food Court, a Disney-esque Spanish village housing a feast of fast food from all over the world.

As we eat, I notice that Mark and Robin are still wearing their Dixons sales assistant costumes from the show. Claire's crude drawn-on beard is only half washed off. A plastic penis hangs between her legs. No one notices these anomalies, least of all the many shoppers.

In the noise and the crowds no one can concentrate and soon we're eating in silence, listening to the Red Nose Day Fun Quiz for which a line of pre-adolescent kids have been lined up on a crude stage, their images relayed to a video wall above. A Simon Mayo lookalike is asking questions and explaining the rules: three wrong answers and they get dumped in a bath full of gunk and green slime.

The first kid starts answering questions that cover a bizarre mix of soap trivia and political factoids—under the bright lights he falters, loses what little confidence he ever had.

Robin (as Quizmaster in the narrative): What do the initials EEC stand for?

Richard (as kid in the narrative): Er ... I don't know.

Robin: How many Israeli athletes were killed during the terrorist attack in the 1972 Olympics?

Richard: I don't know.

Robin: In *Neighbours*, what did Nick do the night Beverley returned from New Zealand (with a new face)?

Richard: I don't know.

Terry: The kid falls into the gunk.

Claire: They thought a lot about the soaps. Before the Cold War really ended, they used to wonder how the soaps would respond to a 'limited nuclear war' in Europe. Would they carry on regardless with a fantasy of life as it used to be lived, or would they improvise quickly—switching scenes to fallout bunkers and heavily policed supermarkets?

Years later they wanted to organize an exchange scheme between the world's soaps, so that characters from *Brookside* would go on holiday to *Beverley Hills, 90210*, or that someone from *Coronation Street* would go to London and end up running The Vic. They hoped to turn the soaps into one enormous, interconnected meta-soap.

They wished they'd been given a contract to write the last two weeks of the failed British soap *Eldorado*. They had a number of scenarios they'd wanted to pursue.

Tim: Trying to map the last ten years, we found more than ever that our memories of things were utterly bound up with the TV news. In the miners' strike (1984–85) we had the weird experience of seeing things live in Sheffield and then seeing them reported later in the day. The reports always seemed more real.

From the Gulf War (summer 1990) I remember several times getting up in the middle of the night to go for a piss and turning on the TV to see what was happening—mesmerized by the quality of those news programmes where there is no news at all but where they have to stay on air anyway and keep talking.

One night I saw a report based on a French cable TV report based on a freelance journalist's story based on unconfirmed sources that an American F-111 had been forced down by Iraqi fighters. And through the night this story obviously flipped and changed, moving from one station to another round the world like a Chinese whisper. But in the morning when I woke and checked the news again to hear the latest there was no trace of that captured American F-111 at all. Not on the Breakfast News, not in the papers, not on the radio.

That captured F-111 is still captured, still not captured, still circling over the desert of plastic flowers in the Gulf and in *Marina & Lee*—the piece of work we made that summer—still waiting to drop its payload, still captured. And on the radio, late night, if you scan between channels and wait patiently you can still hear reports of that F-111 now …

Claire: [*Reads from* Marina & Lee]

> I'm coming to the edges of a town. This must be Big Town that I read so much about. Like Claudia Cardinale in that sex film LOVE A LITTLE, DRINK A LOT I'm living on bravely after an unfortunate accident, frightened of the future, a bit bored of the present and unable to remember the past.
>
> Leaves fall from the advertisements for trees. I'll just go over and put the microphone outside the hotel window so you can hear what these explosions sound like …
>
> Richard: [*Supplying a vocal sound effect*] BANG!
>
> Claire: Boy. That was a loud one. My head's starting to spin. If I can't sleep, I make up different kinds of time, like counting sheep. There's black time when you're feeling sad—no, that's blue time—and there's red time when you're angry or cold. There's soft time, and long time, and thin time too. I have to walk quickly cos the continents are drifting apart.

Robin: There was something about the way things got used and re-used, the way things moved in and out of the work. So much of the work had this complex interior history, where a single line of text in one show would become a title or even a whole character several years later. Best of all perhaps was how a savage review of *200% & Bloody Thirsty* in *The Independent* provided the end lines for *Marina & Lee*, five years after the fact. The review said: 'The whole performance is wholly out of control … There is little to enjoy here and much to regret …'

Richard: In 1988 we took some dead trees from Ecclesall Woods to use in the performance *200% & Bloody Thirsty*—not so much trees as 14 ft branches. Three of us with saws, while a group of school kids on a nature trip chanted: 'Ecclesall Woods, Ecclesall Woods, we've got conkers, we've got conkers …'

And then years later (1993) we used the same trees in *Club of No Regrets*, gaffer-taping them to the scaffolding structure at the side of the stage.

In two shows those trees toured extensively in Britain, then to Italy, Germany, Poland, Belgium and Holland.

And then this Summer we took them to Italy for a second time as we did *Club of No Regrets* in Italian for its final performances. And after the last performance—outside on a hillside in Tuscany (July 1994)—we left the trees at the edge of a forest. Miles from home we left them—these objects that are art for a while, then get put back in the world …

Terry: [*Reads from the Italian version of* Club of No Regrets *(1993)*]

> Oggi sono turbata, molto turbata, ho smesso di parlare, ho smesso di camminare. Sono turbata da delle voci. Mi affido a Nostra Signora dei Parcheggi perché mi aiuti. Che venga a me, che mi aiuti a liberarmi da queste catene. Principe delle Bugie Scoperte e delle Promesse Non

Mantenute, vengo a te vestita di stracci per incontrarti. Regina del Nulla, amante dell'aria e dei satelliti, non ti abbiamo più visto, è passato molto tempo dall'ultima volta che ti abbiamo visto. Oh, non vedi che sono senza pelle e senza ossa. Vengo a te vestita di stracci solo per incontrarti.

Part Four

Richard: They had this idea to kill all the firstborn children of English greengrocers to avoid any unfortunate recurrences of the last ten years. Like many others they made a lot of money running 0898 sex lines. They had one line where the girls just laughed all the time. If you paid extra they'd call you back and laugh at you live. They gave away T-shirts to beggars with the slogan DON'T GIVE ME MONEY I'M JUST A FUCKING EYESORE. They gave away free condoms with every pint of HIV-positive blood. They knew the pubs on the Wicker did much better business after care in the community. One pub had a 40s–50s–60s–70s–80s night—every night.

They knew something strange had happened to time. How else to explain the fact that Sheffield was busy investing in trams? How else to explain the population of Leningrad voting in June 1991 to change the city's name back to its original St Petersburg? How else to explain the way Europe looked more and more like old maps than recent ones? It was all Victorian family values, back to the 1970s, back to basics, back to square one. Hadn't Bush said he was going to make the country a lot less like *The Simpsons* and a lot more like *The Waltons*?

Cathy: We knew something strange had happened to time. At night we lay in bed and waited for the Zeppelin raids to start again. And every time we heard the word 'history' we felt sick. And everyone said time didn't matter any more, and distance didn't matter any more—everything was immediate, everything was NOW. We had no argument with this. After *The Rock 'n' Roll Years* it was difficult to remember anything unless it had a medley of pop songs and captions slapped over the top of it. Wasn't that a slogan for Kodak: GOOD QUALITY MEMORIES AT A PRICE YOU CAN AFFORD?

Robin: Maybe their real memories were written in the skin: on Richard, a burst eardrum he received when Cathy hit him during a performance of *Let the Water* in 1987 and a scar on his leg from where he broke it playing rounders in the park (summer 1990), thus invaliding himself out of *Marina & Lee* and onto video. On Tim, a small blister-shaped scar that had appeared on his wrist when someone had hypnotized him into believing that a piece of paper would burn him on contact with his skin, and a scar on his left shoulder where his pacemaker is—a scar renewed every four years or so in the Hallamshire Hospital, Sheffield.

Tim: They preferred always to talk about another country, another place, finding screens and veils and stories, finding other worlds.

Was it really true that the only way to see Britain properly was to see it drunk? They thought so. There were drunks in all of the shows, often drunks who were also dead. One night (in 1990 or perhaps 1991) they filmed themselves getting very, very drunk. They wore cardboard crowns and tried to propose toasts like we had when touring in Poland. It was impossible. Toward the end of the evening a competition started to see who could make themselves cry. Claire and Cathy had chopped onions in half and were rubbing them directly into their eyes. Nick Crowe from Index Theatre in Manchester was there and his face was half paralysed with a Bell's palsy which had erased all the lines on one side of his face, turning one side of his face into the face of a child—a face without any marks, or lines, or history. They knew something was wrong with time. Claire was pushing these onions into her eyes and trying to cry and trying to tell a story about Shirley Temple, who had been asked to cry in a scene by a certain director and she'd looked at him and said, 'Which eye do you want? Which eye do you want me to cry out of?'

That night we dreamed all the bad dreams of the decade. No one slept too well.

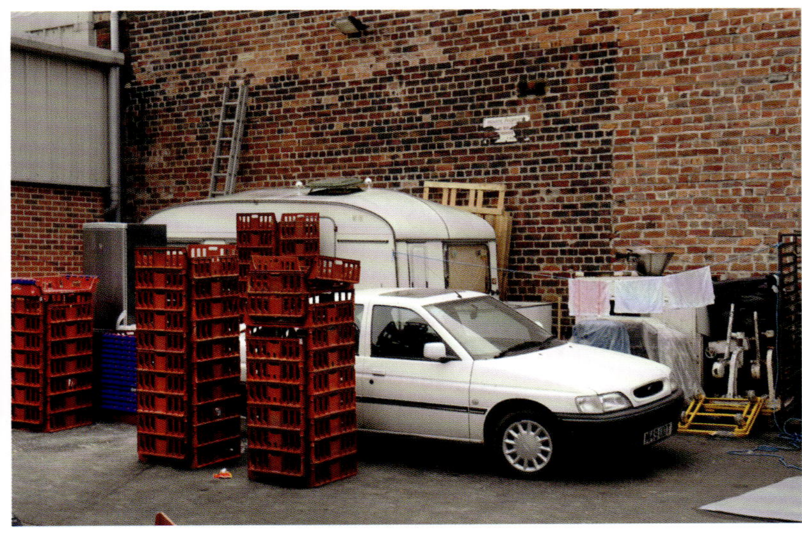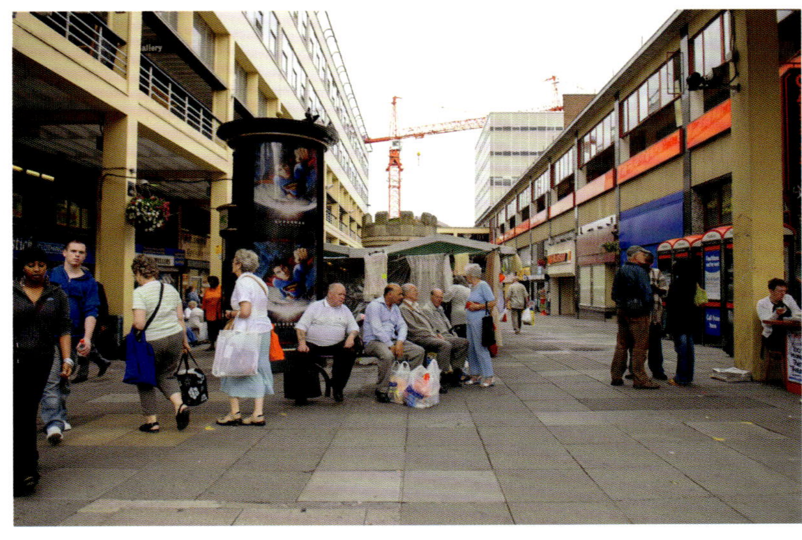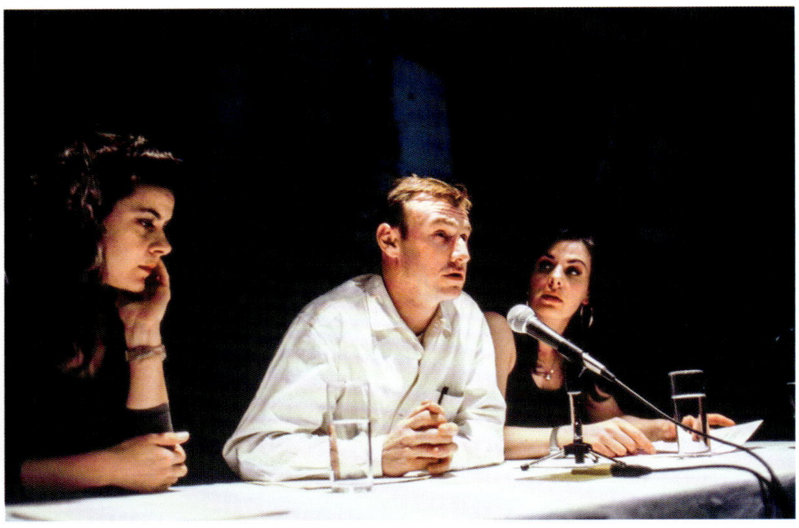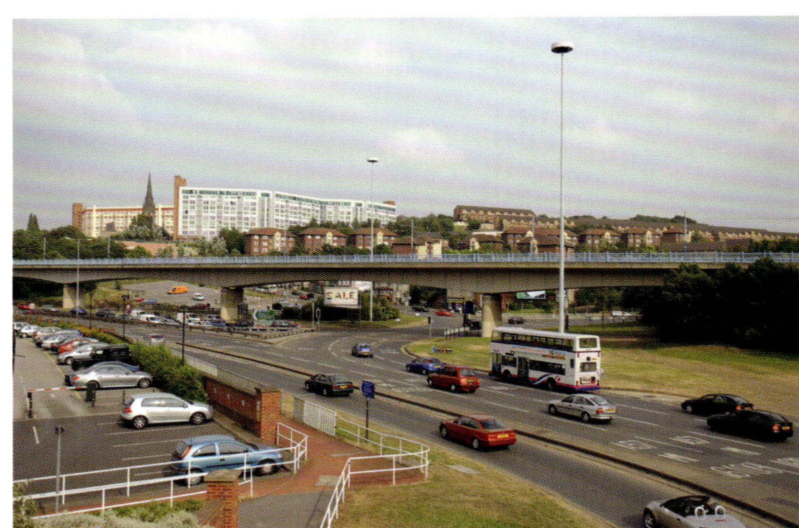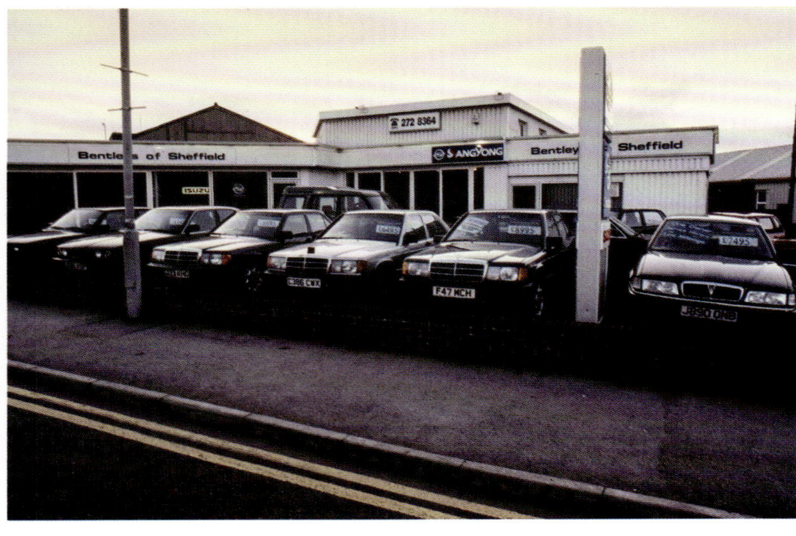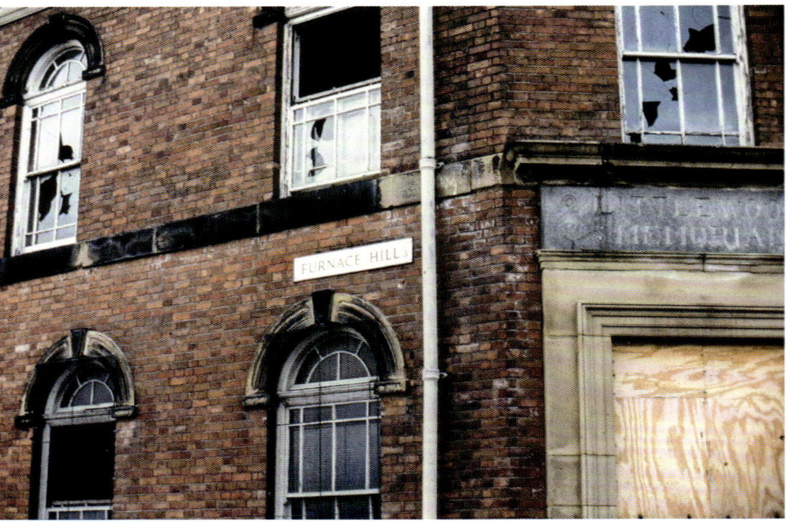

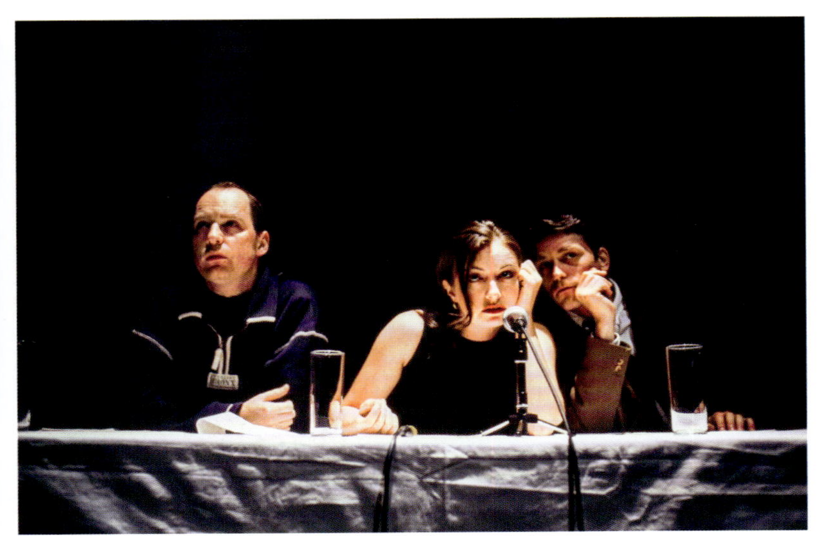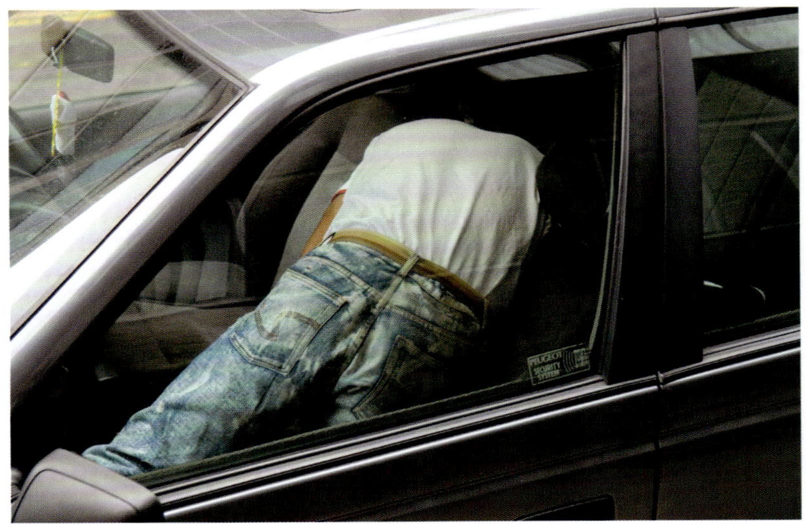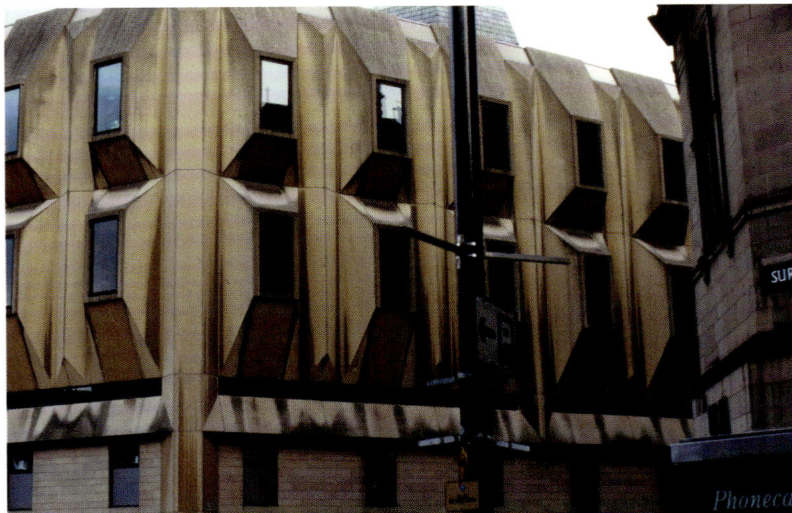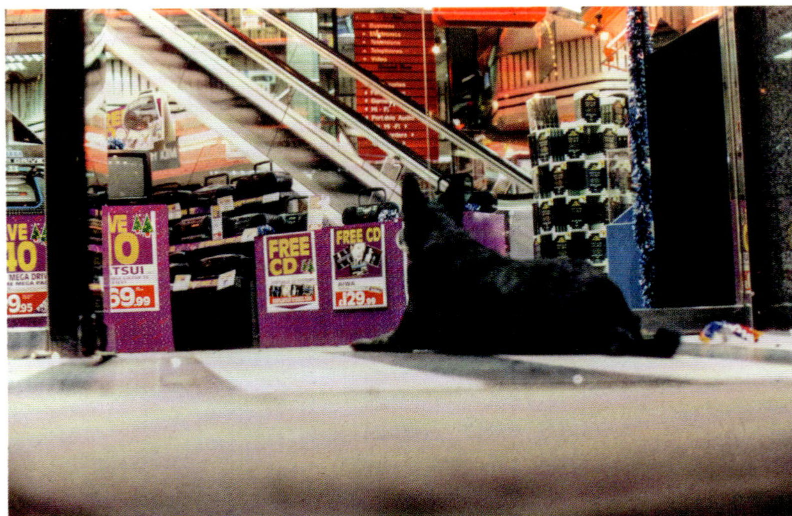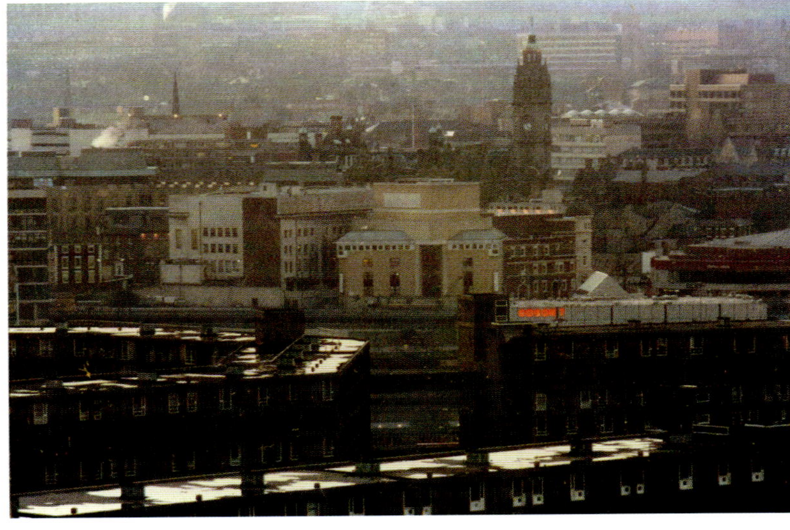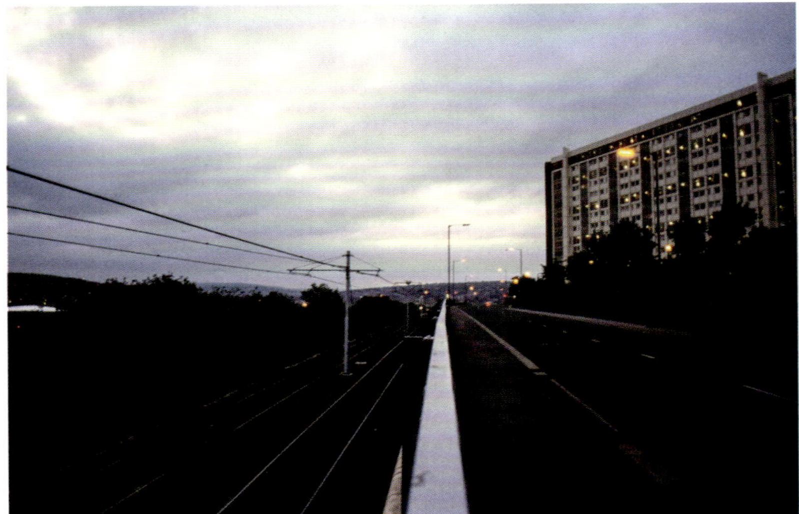

Richard: What was the question people asked most about the work?

Terry: Er, whether it was optimistic or not.

Richard: And what was the answer they got most often?

Terry: We used to say the work was optimistic.

Richard: In what way?

Terry: We said there was an optimism in the struggle of it—an optimism in the way the onstage protagonists used and reused the material they'd been left with.

Richard: How was that optimistic?

Terry: In a way we marvelled at their ability to cope—to change things, to deal with them, to make things their own.

Richard: So this optimism was just a kind of coping?

Terry: Yes.

Richard: Did people believe this idea, that the work was optimistic?

Terry: Not always, no.

Richard: Why not?

Terry: The optimism seemed remote.

Richard: Why?

Terry: The victories won by the performers—or characters—were often private, and delicate. And the victories were never total—there was always doubt, irony, a kind of melancholy.

Richard: So the work was doubtful, ironic, and melancholy but somehow optimistic?

Terry: Yes.

Richard: How can those things go together?

Terry: They go together in the work.

Richard: Is the work optimistic?

Terry: Yes, but only … sometimes.

Richard: It's only sometimes optimistic?

Terry: Yes. There are times when it's very sure—about people's power to change themselves, their power to re-see themselves and the rest of the other world. There are times when it's very sure about people's ability to take what they will from the scrapheap of culture that they're born into and to use it. They transform things.

Richard: This transformation happens sometimes.

Terry: Yes.

Richard: Can you say something about the rest of the time?

Terry: The rest of the time this transformation escapes the 'characters'.

Richard: What happens?

Terry: Then there's a kind of rage in the work.

Richard: What do you mean by that?

Terry: Then the people in it are bashing against the edges of the world they're born into, bashing on the edges of the language that they have. There's a frustration.

Richard: Why would you make live work in an age of mass communications? Why work in more or less the only field which still insists on presence? For artists interested in 'the contemporary' this area of live performance seems like a bit of a backwater. Do you have something against mass reproduction? Do you work from some quaint notion about immediacy and real presence?

Terry: I don't know.

Richard: Answer the question.

Terry: I don't know.

Richard: Is the work optimistic?

Terry: Yes.

Richard: Is it getting more optimistic?

Terry: No. It's getting bleaker.

Richard: Why?

Terry: Irony doesn't seem like a solution any more.

Richard: Did it ever?

Terry: I'm not sure that it did. But it doesn't seem viable now.

Richard: Why not?

Terry: We're getting older.

Richard: What's that got to do with it?

Terry: There are times for being light—and times when it's less easy to do that.

Richard: This change, this change in tone you're talking about, we'd like to know more about it.

Terry: It's more a shift than a change.

Richard: Where does it come from?

Terry: I don't know.

Richard: Do you believe that the work changes people—changes their lives?

Terry: Yes.

Richard: Do you think the work is optimistic?

Terry: Yes.

Richard: Even when it's bleak?

Terry: Yes.

Richard: Why do you think that?

Terry: It opens a space which people fill.

Richard: So the optimism is more an absence than anything else? The optimism lies in the viewer's experience?

Terry: I don't know.

Richard: Answer the question. People are waiting. [*Pause.*] The optimism you were speaking of is more of an absence than anything else—a space that people are left to fill?

Terry: Yes.

Claire: They knew something strange had happened to time. Bush and Reagan were drunk at the bar. They drew a map of the country and added nothing to it. They drew a map of the country and marked on it which bits of the countryside belonged to which armies, to which rebels, to which forces and alliances. They drew a map of the country and marked on it which roads were safe, which places one could sleep in without fear for one's life. They marked on the map which cities were still functioning and who lived in them. They marked on the map the places where the phone system was still operating. We drew a map of the country and tried to mark on it the places where one could still fall in love, the places where one could still believe in something. They looked at the map and asked, 'Would this be a good place to raise a kid? Would this be a good place for a party?'

The Slow Hurry of Figuration

Giulia Palladini

The Latin motto *Festina lente*—or its equivalent in ancient Greek, Σπεῦδε βραδέως (*Speûde bradéōs*)—is what Erasmus of Rotterdam has described as an 'adage': a rhetorical figure expressing a timeless wisdom, doing so, in this case, in the form of an oxymoron. Its most common translation in English is 'Make haste slowly', or 'More haste, less speed'.[1] The use of the motto can be traced back at least to the emperor Augustus, who often used the phrase in his daily conversation and would insert it into the language of his official letters. With these two words he advised his ministers to perform their duties with both the dispatch of efficient business and the slowness of careful reflection. In Augustus' time, golden coins were minted bearing an image to express the gist of *Festina lente*: the image of a crab and a butterfly.[2] 'Butterfly and crab are both bizarre, both symmetrical in shape, and between them establish an unexpected kind of harmony,' says Italo Calvino.[3] Their combination constitutes an emblem of the *slow hurry*: a figuration composed of a time crab, capable of walking sideways, or even backwards, and a time butterfly, capable of flying away, in all directions. The emblem itself is, therefore, a time creature: an image of a supposedly impossible temporality, a little monster of timeless wisdom, yet also a form of practical advice for everyday life.

The combination of the crab and the butterfly was only the first in a series of figurations which, especially in the sixteenth century, came to represent *Festina lente*. These are 'emblems that throw together incongruous and enigmatic figures, as in a rebus,' commented Calvino, who, like Erasmus, was fascinated by their fairy-tale-like quality.[4] Among them, there also features an anchor entwined by the twisted body of a dolphin, notably used by the great Venetian humanist publisher Aldus Manutius as a symbol printed on all the title pages of his books. As explained by Erasmus, 'the anchor, which stays and moors a ship and keeps it in place, indicates slowness. The dolphin, the fastest of all animals, and the animal of keenest reflexes, expresses speed.'[5] In this case, the time creature is constituted by a combination of an animal and an inanimate object, a hybrid form expressing a temporality of movement (the speed of the dolphin) interwoven with stasis (the anchor holding still at the bottom of the sea). Manutius placed this emblem at the beginning of every print as a reminder for the reader of 'the intensity and constancy of intellectual work' standing behind every book.[6] This was a figuration of the labour of producing books: not only the writer's work but also the craft of those publishers who, like Manutius, devoted their life to bringing writing to the world in the form of individual items: publications. Especially with the advent of the printing press, the time of fabricating books had accelerated, and definitely so in comparison with activities such as thinking and writing. The emblem, then, conjured both those temporalities of human labour—thinking and making—as united in figurative cooperation, in the project of building a 'library [that] shall be contained by no limits other than those of the world'.[7]

Other emblems of *Festina lente* included a diamond ring entwined with foliage, a hare inhabiting (or else wearing, like a costume) a snail shell, and a turtle with a sail hammered onto its back, famously an emblem of Cosimo de' Medici. Such symbolic figurations appear in drawings, are carved on columns or archways, and depicted on everyday objects like coins, plates, or vases: all surfaces bearing the images of incongruous temporality. The most common interpretation of the motto is that it is advice for 'good behaviour': a saying meant to praise a particular balance of time in action, decision-making, and strategic thinking. Erasmus appreciated, in particular, the capacity of *Festina lente* to conjure, in its brevity, 'a certain ripening of action and moderation blended together from both wakefulness and gentleness'.[8]

In these pages, I conjure the motto *Festina lente* not as a maxim for 'good behaviour' but as a rhetorical figure of a time portrayed through hybridization. The motto and its emblems stand for a time encrusted on an image, and blending together different durations, diverse measures of speed, rhythms, and historical vectors, not always leading to a condition of stability but capturing, instead, anomalies, discontinuities, or distortions. Put another way, *Festina lente* designates a time *bearing an image*, like the one pictured on the coins minted in the epoch of Augustus.

I am interested in employing the idea of 'slow hurry' as a lens for reading a series of practices I consider distinctive of Forced Entertainment's work, imagery, and theatrical language. I propose that *Festina lente* characterizes their oeuvre in various ways: it is a tempo we often encounter onstage, it participates in certain structures of recognition for the returning spectator, and it also affects the collective, long-lasting creative process behind the work as a whole. In Forced Entertainment shows, slow hurry functions as a technology which strives to open up the potentiality of oxymoron: time is haunted, punctuated, invigorated by contrariety. Besides, 'forced entertainment' is itself an oxymoron: at the core of the name the group chose for themselves nests a temporal paradox, encompassing the conflicting ideas of an enduring hospitality toward the pleasure of making and witnessing performance, and the phantom of obligation and confinement, that one might wish to escape as soon as possible.

In Forced Entertainment *Festina lente* is a distinctive engine of theatre magic, capable of turning the stage into a surface, deemed to bear on itself ever returning images of an incongruous time. This often happens through the production of peculiar *figurations* which, by virtue of their appearing, allow a distinctive kind of writing to take place onstage. More precisely, such figurations participate in Forced Entertainment's long-lasting desire to invent a mode of writing which seemingly *can only happen onstage*; a writing done with bodies and behaviours, with modes of appearing, moving, speaking; a writing exceeding (although not excluding) the textual dimension and specific to theatre. It is a writing realized with and, in turn, realizing 'a language outside of language'.[9] This method of writing explored on the stage can be seen as a form of *hieroglyphic writing*: one made up of enigmatic characters, first appearing as images but participating in a broader system of transmission, conjuring a wisdom which is not immediately given as 'meaning'. It will be up to the spectator to make image collide with other forces, other symptoms,[10] other scraps of knowledge within their selves, and to corroborate the figuration *as language*, albeit not necessarily organized through sentences, not postulating or delivering a message. This corresponds to the orchestration of many bizarre figurations of creatures in conditions of hybridization, as they come in contact with humans, with objects, with speech, with music, with fragments of scenic discourse and their alleged temporality. It is also a language telling an impossible story, whose duration coagulates in the density of the image itself.

Discussing the emblems expressing *Festina lente*, Erasmus mentions hieroglyphic writing, recalling in passing its sacred function in the earliest ages (still resonating in the etymology of the term),[11] but emphasizes especially how this method of symbolic figuration was employed as a disguise for wisdom: 'If they judged something worthy of the name of wisdom, the Egyptians wrote it down in pictures of various animals, so that not everyone could guess their significance.'[12] Rather than sentences, the combination of hieroglyphs engenders riddles, characterized by 'a gem-like grace'.[13] Invoking the idea of theatrical hieroglyphs inevitably resonates with Antonin Artaud's use of this concept, crucial in his quest for a language of the stage, 'truly theatrical only to the degree that the thoughts it expresses are beyond the reach of the spoken language',[14] and 'capable of creating kinds of material images equivalent to word images'.[15] In the 'Theater of Cruelty (First Manifesto)', Artaud proposes hieroglyphic writing as a model for a 'naked language of the theater'[16] in which 'ordinary objects and even the human body' are raised to the 'dignity of signs'.[17] As extensively discussed by Jacques Derrida—himself long fascinated with the hieroglyph's potential to awaken combinations outside of the alphabetical logic[18]—Artaud's interest in hieroglyphic writing was born from the desire not to get rid of language altogether but to have the stage governed by other principles than the alphabetic order, understood as a system of wilful communication and dramatically entangled with notions of representation.[19]

Artaud located examples of such 'pure theatrical language'—where sounds, lights, gestures, and attitudes have an 'ideographic quality'[20]—not only far from Western stages[21] but also in certain 'unperverted pantomimes', where gestures disavow representation and 'in which man, to the extent that he contributes to their formation, is only a form like the rest, yet to which, because of his double nature, he adds a singular prestige'.[22] This points to a quality of appearance capable of not only dissociating meaning from particular forms but enhancing their unforeseen recombination within another system of intelligibility. One such appearance, Artaud suggests, is a scene from a Marx Brothers' film, where

> a man thinks he is going to take a woman in his arms but instead gets a cow, which moos. And through a conjunction of circumstances … that moo, at just that moment, assumes an intellectual dignity equal to any woman's cry.

> Such a situation, possible in the cinema, is no less possible in the theater as it exists: it would take very little—for instance, replace the cow with an animated manikin, a kind of monster endowed with speech, or a man disguised as an animal—to rediscover the secret of an objective poetry at the root of humor, which the theater has renounced and abandoned to the Music Hall, and which the Cinema later adopted.[23]

The density of the riddle produced by this scene strikes me as a curious prefiguration of some of the hieroglyphs carved on the stage of Forced Entertainment, which likewise encompass animal costumes or fabricated beings 'made of wood and cloth, entirely invented, corresponding to nothing, yet disquieting by nature',[24] alongside humans, featuring as signs among the signs but crucially enduring 'the singular prestige of a double nature'[25] in the theatre. Here, hieroglyphic writing functions precisely as in 'unperverted pantomimes': the figurations are riddles, and there is no effort, on the authors' part, to offer a hint of their interpretation. They are devices of pleasure: pleasure in the play of producing them, pleasure in the play of receiving them, pleasure in the enigma which the 'language outside of language' stages but does not explain. Such language, in fact, is never compact as a system of communication: it is itself hybridized with theatre's metamorphic capacity, with theatre's prerogative to be first and foremost a place of display, rather than of communication. Forced Entertainment's hieroglyphic writing is carved upon the stage which displays it.

Over the years and across their oeuvre Forced Entertainment have produced a *bestiary of time warps*: a multitude of figures which are emblematic time creatures, dragging on previous temporalities of performance, other times serving to open a crack in which certain modes of speaking and listening unexpectedly sneak into a situation, as if, for a moment, the temporality of theatre hybridized with that of literature or film or television or other spectacular genres and then suddenly returned to theatre, abruptly, almost in oblivion. These time warps serve to expose some incongruities which are inherent in the temporality of theatre itself: in theatre's very destiny to cope with the predicament of existing in a limited time frame, while continuing to pretend that onstage there is in fact *all the time in the world*. Also, this exposure has a paradoxical quality to it: on the stages of Forced Entertainment performers are often obliged to dwell in an uneasy position, *to endure the costumes of theatrical time*, while inhabiting, as humans, their own lifetime.

I wish to suggest that Forced Entertainment's figurations function as contraptions for temporal rupture: seemingly, the figural play participates in a long-term project to both create and expose dysfunctions intrinsic in the temporal framework in which the time creatures are deemed to appear, in theatre, and in life. Echoing Georges Didi-Huberman's thoughts on the work of figurability, such figurations might be seen as 'rends' in the time fabric of the stage:[26] a fabric crucially interwoven with the time of theatre (a place of display, an economic machine, a site of witnessing) and its outside. The temporal politics at stake in such rending does not just interrupt a supposed horizon of temporal progression; it introduces a logic in which it is possible to *figure*, hence to fabricate, time itself: an all-too-human capacity that, however, the logic of capital governing both theatre and its outside is keen to obliterate.

The Art of Figuration: Wearing Costumes of Theatrical Time

It is not unusual, on the stages of Forced Entertainment, to encounter actors wearing costumes of theatrical time. Sometimes these are highly visible, some others not immediately apparent, but they participate nevertheless in hieroglyphic writing: they are the enigmatic characters of the group's enduring art of figuration. As in the emblems representing *Festina lente*, animal figures recur in this oeuvre, often placed in relation to explicitly human productions, such as dialogue, or specific traditions of display, like pantomime, or game shows from TV or even conventions of traditional drama, like the soliloquy. Many of the creatures making up the emblems of Forced Entertainment are sort of animals, sort of giant toys, sort of children's funny outfits: they are essentially non-human figures. As Angela Carter suggests, a convention long established in both children's picture books and the nursery (settings often enough evoked by the set design of Forced Entertainment shows) is that 'the toy both is, and is not, the animal it represents'.[27] Likewise, the animal suits in which performers move do not purport to be animals at all: although they bring forth well-known features of the evoked creature, such as a dog's barking, still the dog is obviously not a dog, not even in the theatre. In place of the animal itself, what is figured is an image of the animal, one already domesticated, to be introduced into a playful world created for children or, for that matter, for adults who want to behave like children: an image of the non-human which is wholly artificial, a fantasy representation of the animal exposing the clumsiness of representation.[28]

And yet, this evocation of the non-human is a giving of access to another temporality, a way to drag in (echoing Elizabeth Freeman's conceptualization of the term drag: to literally wear on one's body, while pulling the past upon the present) certain historical theatrical antecedents, albeit with no trace of heritage.[29] As in children's picture books or the nursery, pantomime, game shows, and traditional drama are evoked onstage, but only in passing, seemingly conjured with the aim of borrowing a certain poetic licence: the quality, as it were, of making a crack in human time.

Those non-human figures are also likely to appear only partially, or in a condition of incongruity. In *Showtime* (1996), the dog suit leaves out most of the performer's body while she barks and moves around a stage shared with actors as well as with cantankerous cardboard trees, giving up from the start their silent function of setting the scene in order to walk, move hands frantically, or insult each other and the audience. Not by chance, time is a recurring and explicit obsession in this particular show, a topic to which a long monologue by Robin Arthur is also devoted.

In *Pleasure* (1998) the pantomime horse appears only as a head, stuck on the body of a drunk naked man, who has lost his pantomime horse trousers while crawling onstage and drinking whisky from eyeholes in the horse's head, while old tunes are played slowed down to 16 rpm: his desperate crawl is also the melancholic metronome of the hallucinated tempo of the show. In *Bloody Mess* (2004) the gorilla continuously speaks to the audience about its body, evoking intense images of female sexuality, and often takes off its gorilla mask to appear onstage with a woman's head. In *Real Magic* (2016) the yellow chicken costumes constantly change their occupants, they appear and disappear for no clear reason, sometimes they are evoked with little dances performed by the actors even when they are not visible onstage: little dances of frightened birds which, seemingly, are the only other option, the only possibility to escape for a moment the neurotic ordeal of the game show.

These animal suits are the engines of particular time warps within the shows. I am thinking, for example, of a scene in *Showtime*. Cathy Naden has been playing in an incomplete dog costume since the beginning, fully 'pretending' to be a dog (although wearing a dirty dark-green coat, trousers, and shoes): walking on her hands and knees, barking, with no access to spoken language.[30] At some point, Claire Marshall gets close to her, holding a microphone, and asks her a few questions. Surprisingly, Naden/the Dog starts answering with human language, and a long session starts, marking access to a radically different temporality than the one experienced up to that point in the show. It is not so much that Naden/the Dog slows down the pace but that the density of time itself, onstage, transforms. It is an affective transformation too, the hybridization of a time of play with a focused time of dreadful imagination. Answering one of Marshall's questions, Naden/the Dog starts fantasizing about how she would commit suicide, if she (because it is immediately 'she' doing the talking, albeit still inhabiting the dog's suit) were to. She takes her time describing the preparation of her suicide: she follows patiently the path of her thinking, adding a plethora of details. She takes time in her story too, before getting things done: almost as if she is in no hurry whatsoever to get to the point. She supposedly has an urgency to be done with life, but she wants to leave slowly, very slowly, enjoying each of her last moments.

Her description—a literary practice, in origin, seldom a protagonist on the theatre stage—saturates all the scenic space, as a distinctive expression of *Festina lente*: the sudden and prolonged zooming into the time preceding Naden's imagined death seems to take *all the time in the world*, while in fact Marshall's presence beside her, as well as the dog suit, reminds the spectator throughout that this time warp is part of a larger frame, of a longer time in which the climax-like quality of this moment has no justification, that this moment is infected with another rhythm, and it is infecting, on its part, another duration beyond show time. The other rhythm is the atemporal stillness of death, which is perhaps impossible to imagine from within life. The other duration, which the scene infects in turn, is the spectators' lifetime: the present of those who, during life, watch someone impossibly imagining death.

In *Certain Fragments* Tim Etchells comments on this sequence, emphasizing to what extent this is indeed a meditation on theatre's time:

> And then Claire says, at a certain point, 'Cathy don't you think it's about time you took that dog's head off now?' and the dumb blank dog looks at us (questioningly) and Cathy's hands come up and lift off the dog's head and we see her face for the first time in the piece—must be around 50 minutes into it—and she's sweating and still a little out of breath, I think, but the only thing that's for certain is that in the ruins of the dog game, she is more present than she could ever have been if she'd just walked onto the stage and sat down—Cathy is very here, and very now, very here and now, in the ruins of the dog game she's very present.

> The game pauses and it's like you need to see her take the dog's head off in order to even begin to understand what it was, what it meant to pretend that dog for so long, like only now, when the head comes off and the game stops can you measure it, and as Cathy talks … we measure the distance/difference between real and fictional, human and animal, real time and playtime …[31]

Marshall's presence at her side is crucial to the figuration producing the time warp in which Naden/the Dog's suicide story takes place. Her distinctively human listening, her inquisitive questions, her *other* temporality enter in combination with the Dog's non-human time, with Naden's out-of-breath, slow, and detailed description of time happening 'in the ruins of the dog game'. The two performers become, as it were, a time creature: a distinctive figuration in the 'language outside of language' of *Showtime*. This time creature stands at the edges of presence and disappearance, producing a peculiar atemporal intensification: a figural comment on the temporal odds at stake in the incidental coinciding of theatre and life, or perhaps on the very act of imagining the stage as the incidental space for such a coincidence.

This kind of time creature is, in fact, a trope in Forced Entertainment's hieroglyphic writing: the combination of two or more performers appearing very close to each other, one holding a microphone and asking questions, the other speaking, often stuck in an incongruous condition. A figuration of this sort appears again in *Showtime*: it features Arthur, barefoot and with a naked torso, his face distorted by bank robber's

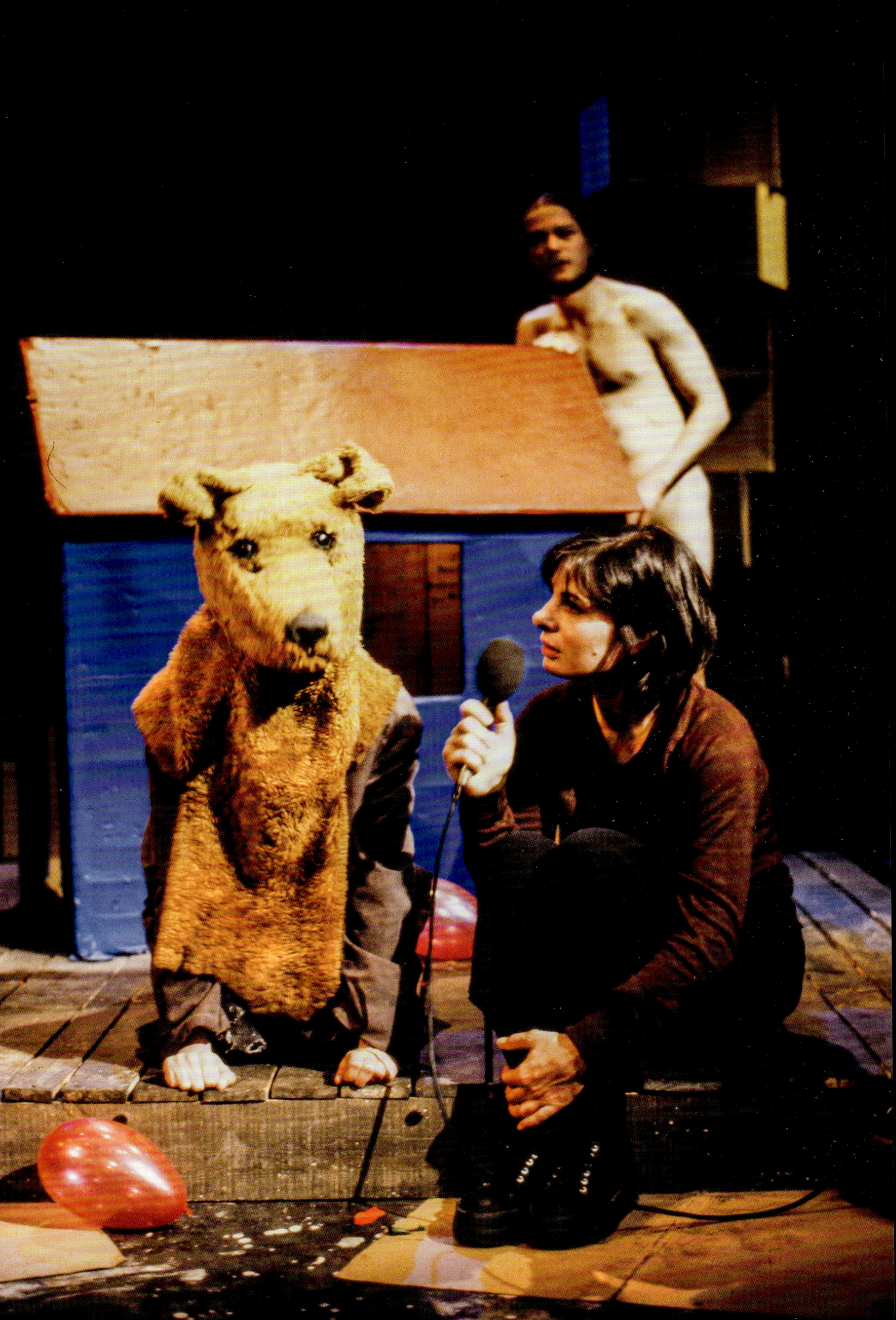

tights, laying on the ground and pretending to die (his innards coming out as cheap canned spaghetti), and Terry O'Connor asking insistent questions, while Richard Lowdon, in a dark coat, stands beside the dying thug, supporting and comforting him throughout, holding the microphone so that Arthur can answer the questions. Again, spectators are mirrored into the scene as the uneasy witnesses of an act of imagining death: childish, theatrical, humorous, and yet both situated in and instituting a disquieting temporality.

Bloody Mess is, likewise, full of examples of this sort: this is not surprising, considering that from the beginning the actors announce the particular quality of performance they will endure in throughout the show, each entangled in a specific tempo, all together quite conflicting among themselves. The show is populated by time creatures, combinations of anomalous temporalities becoming even more distorted in their contact with each other. For instance, we encounter a three-headed time creature: it is Arthur, this time holding the microphone in front of the mouth of John Rowley, while the latter is on the floor, encumbered with the weight of Bruno Roubicek's body, both of them laying exhausted, after performing a fierce fight. In the long sequence, Rowley, who has endured in the role of the clown until then, breathes profoundly, as in a post-orgasmic state, then keeps weeping loudly as he asks: 'But I am still funny, aren't I?' His fragile temporality, already posthumous to his enduring effort to entertain, collides with Arthur's cheerful and quiet bouncing, with his casual listening, with Roubicek's silent and ironic standing, still pinning Rowley's body to the floor.

This trope inherently brings about a temporality of slow hurry: one of the performers, in the time creature, acts with urgency (prompting questions, being in charge of keeping 'show time') and the other lays down, slowly lingering on details, diversions, or affective detours. Somehow, around these figurations, the theatre becomes the space in which there is a demand that you get on with things, hurry them along, but the space of the other person—the person interviewed, Naden/the Dog, the agonizing thug, the weeping clown after the fight, perhaps even the spectator watching the whole thing from her seat—is imagined as outside the theatre,

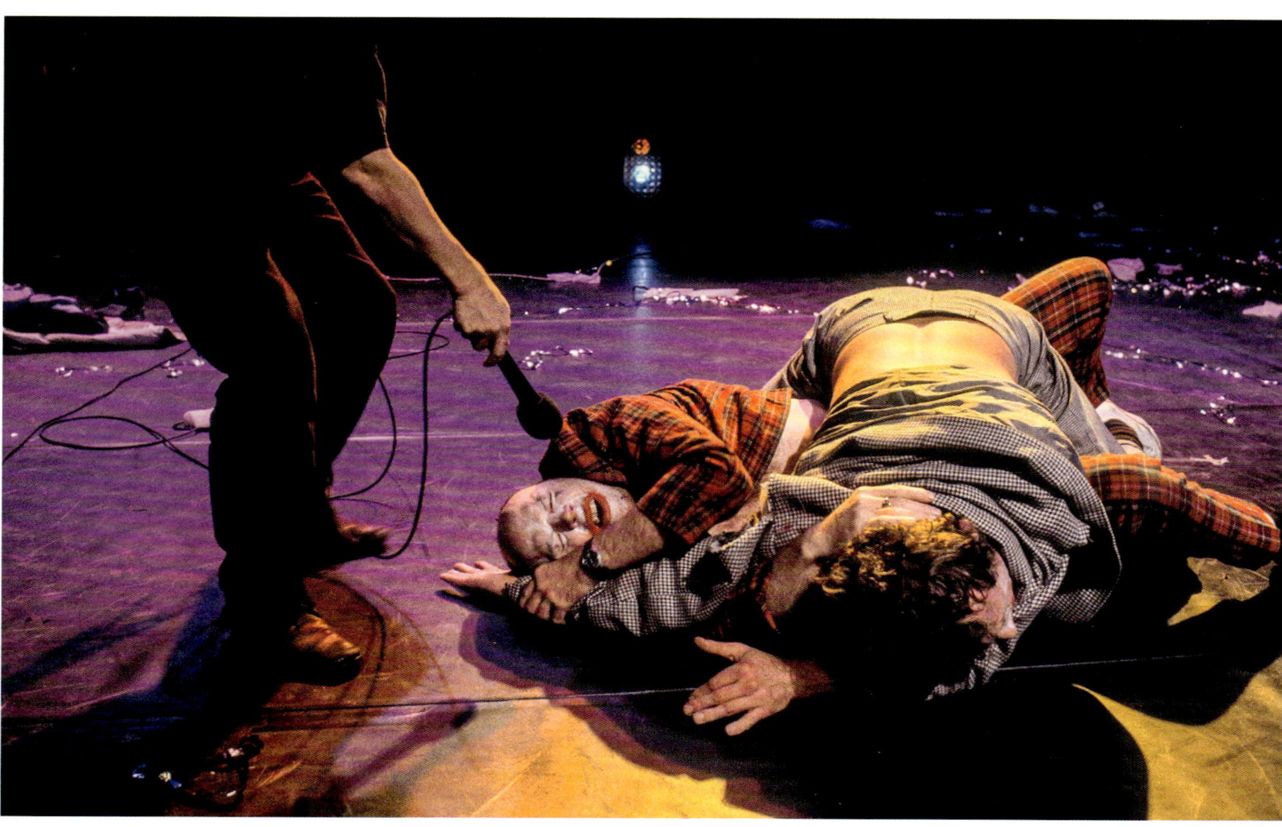

and outside the temporality of needing to get on with things. This seems to expose and reverse the unspoken rule according to which 'theatre time' is oblivious to the economic dynamics of productivity which actually sustain theatre as an economic machine: the rhythm of show time winks to such demands, while strangely suggesting that another possible temporality might exist, that it lurks somewhere, and can be glimpsed within the play of theatre. The figuration, as it were, makes a crack in show time, from which this very outside time momentarily dribbles.

All the Time in the World: The Burden of Theatre's Time

Other costumes of theatrical time are, instead, almost invisible. I am thinking, for example, of the typical circumstance featuring one of the actors standing alone onstage, perhaps at the beginning or at the end of the show: figures explicitly bearing on themselves the weight of theatre's time, the onus of inauguration (or conclusion). Their burden is loaded with audience attention, with a certain responsibility for the show about to start, and moreover with embarrassment for the whole situation. A very literal example of this predicament is the beginning of *Showtime*, where Lowdon appears onstage with the burden of time stuck around his chest, almost like the anchor entwined by the dolphin in the emblem of *Festina lente*: he wears a kind of dynamite corset, his costume makes him appear as a time bomb. With a growing awkwardness, Lowdon inhabits the oxymoronic condition he is somehow obliged to bear: he speaks with an apologetic tone, almost as if somewhere else, in a parallel time dimension perhaps, the very theatre work he is performing would exist as an efficient business, whereas the show he is part of is deemed to be out of sync, it is already figured as a *waste of time*. He must, however, get on with things anyway, even if the going wrong of the performance is somehow already expected by all, actors and spectators, notwithstanding that the beginning—any beginning, perhaps, and especially at the theatre—must always promise that the best is yet to come. 'The first thirty seconds of any performance', the actor says, 'are the most important, because it is in the first thirty seconds that you

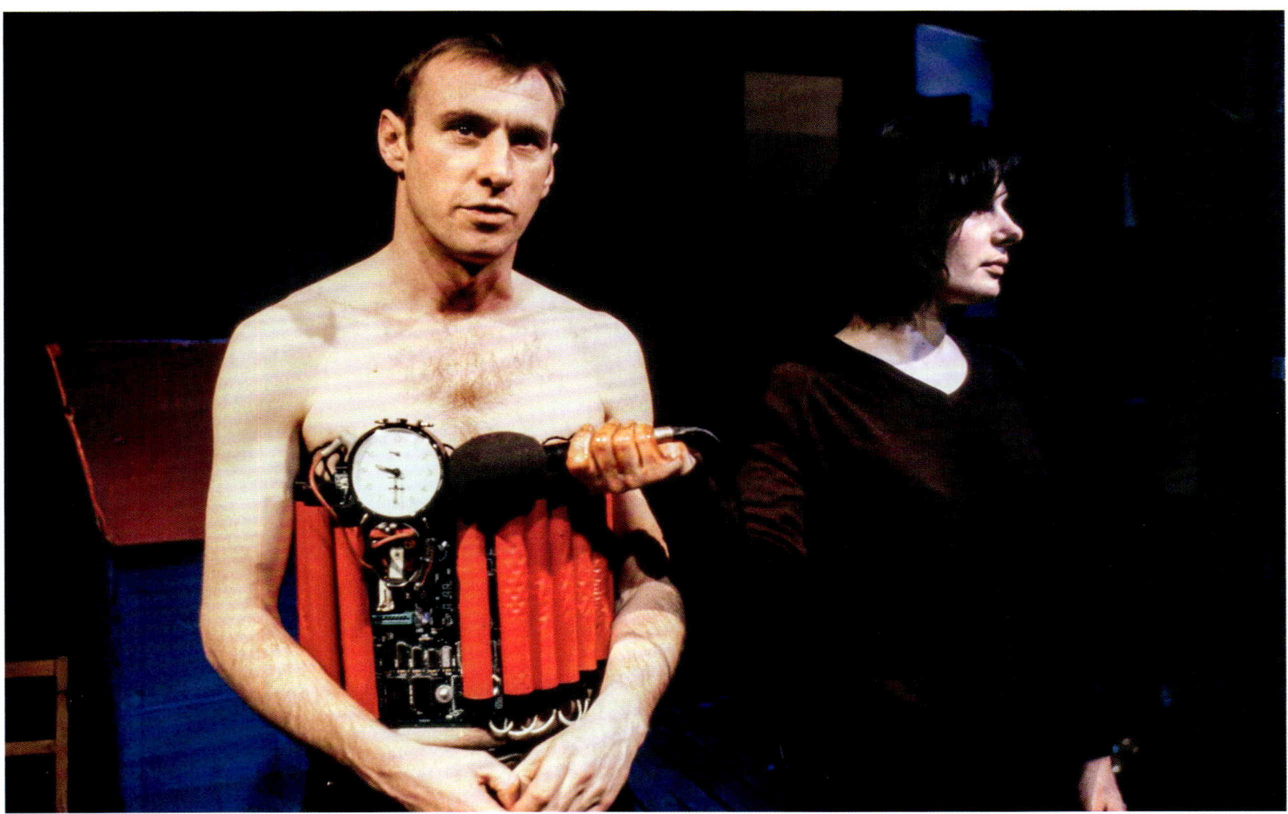

have an opportunity to establish a rapport with the audience.' And yet, the significance of those seconds, the urgency to get them right, turns into a growing anxiety, accelerating the supposed waste of time Lowdon pretends to ward off. The 'slow hurry' is made here not only through the words he pronounces but through the combination of phonic language with body attitudes, along with a series of pauses and silences, which from the start have constructed his figuration onstage as an anomalous time bomb.

The time warp produced by this figuration is somehow kindred to that particular performance delivered by Michel Foucault in the inaugural lecture of a series held at the College de France between 1970 and 1984. Foucault, facing an audience keen to listen to him speak in public, declared that he really would have preferred not to have to begin. Paradoxically resisting the demand of inauguration, Foucault commenced with staging his own desire to enter speech 'almost surreptitiously' and 'be carried away beyond all possible beginnings'.[32] Being 'freed from the obligation to begin', however, was an impossible desire: staging such impossibility, then, meant for Foucault the exposure of the artificial measurement that institutions assign to beginnings, as well as the anxiety that such measurement creates in both the institution and the one who is supposed to speak from within it: an anxiety towards discourse in 'its material reality', existing 'according to a time-scale which is not ours'.[33] Foucault wanted to expose the paradoxical institutional regime according to which 'a place has been made ready for discourse' but not for the human finding herself participating in it, and having to pretend to be the origin of it, rather than being immersed in and dazed by the echoes of the 'struggles, victories, injuries, dominations and enslavements' that lurk behind any form of discourse—even at the theatre. The conventions that institutions attribute to beginnings, and the desire of individual voices not to begin, are therefore 'two contrary replies to the same anxiety'.[34]

Forced Entertainment's figurations narrate again and again this very anxiety, and it seems not by chance that, likewise, it is an anxiety implicating directly the institution of theatre, solemnly marking the show's beginnings and endings. A figuration of this sort is also produced at the start of *The World in Pictures* (2006), where Jerry Killick is obliged to wear an invisible but cumbersome suit of theatrical time, delivered to him by his own colleagues, who are standing in a group at one side of the stage. One by one, they offer advice to Killick, in charge of 'the beginning', and then they hurry away: far from encouraging, their tips only emphasize the unease of his task of having to begin. It is perhaps precisely to overcome this unease that Killick starts by telling a story: it is maybe a story to 'unfrighten himself'[35] from the monster of beginning, but also a story which slowly becomes frightening, as it tells about a growing desire to take one's own life. This idea starts almost by chance, out of the curiosity of someone arriving on the top floor of a building and then measuring the distance from there to the ground, after which this curiosity turns into a morbid desire to figure one's crushed image from above, to fall down, to end one's life. As in Naden/the Dog's slow suicide description in *Showtime*, Killick lingers on a 'long and intimate pornography of detail',[36] which almost accidentally draws the spectators into the show.

The figuration of Killick speaking alone on the empty stage, wearing ordinary clothes, will return at the end of the show, after the group has carved onstage a 'theatrical picture-book'[37] of the 'History of Mankind'. This is a merry-go-round of figurations appearing at an absurd speed, moving forward in epochs through diversions and digressions, as if all that mattered was to frantically change flashy costumes, activating cheap special effects, and swinging on history like oblivious, nasty brats. This 'Story of Man', as narrated by O'Connor, is told in a hurry, and often the narrator asks the others, 'How are we doing with time?', and the answer is, regularly, 'We are a little bit late.' At some point, however, she and all the frantic performers running about suddenly slow down, evoking the image of 'a long, hot, summer afternoon at the end of the nineteenth century'. Again, it is almost as if a crack in time had opened, urging the general hurry of history to loiter on its own anticipation, to slow down the pace in the idle foretaste of the yet-to-come, right there, a moment before the acceleration of capitalist modernity, a few decades before the First World War, in an instant of rest before the start of the century which, at the time the show was created, had just come to an end. In the story of the world, of course, there can be no measure: an afternoon can be as long as a century. But then again, suddenly, the tale of history in pictures starts at doubled speed, and quickly, abruptly, it ends: the tale has reached the present. In the ruins of historical time, Killick appears again in his plain clothes, wearing the same costume of theatrical time he had on before, hence signalling that the show is coming to an end.

Killick starts speaking, taking on the theme of measuring man's time but bringing it back into the room, breaking it down into miniature units. He asks the audience to remember the hour before the show, then he slowly zooms into the very time of the show—entering the foyer, reaching the theatre seat—then moves on to evoke the future that is about to begin: an hour after the show, a day, months, years later, when an oblivion of this very 'now' will occur, and so the progressive loss of what the audience just saw but also the loss of life itself. He goes on accelerating and expanding time until, fifty years on, quite a lot of people now in the room, he says, will have died. Then he imagines when, in a faraway future, all of the people now in the theatre will be dead, and so, further on, even the people capable of remembering all of them. He goes on to imagine the disappearance of everything material and immaterial surrounding the present, until he reaches the impossible imagination of ten thousand years into the future, when nothing will be standing, and the space will look just like a vacuum. At this point, Freeman appears, still wearing the costume of a grotesque prehistoric man, asking Killick to take a moment to think of another, more positive way to finish the show, while the rest of the group performs, instead, the 'grand finale': a long sequence in which all the actors labour to empty the stage, sweep the floor, cancel all traces of human time, while 'Harmonium' by Stereolab[38] plays at loud volume and Wendy Houstoun, with a wig and sunglasses, still in her cave-dwelling early-human fake fur (hence, a hybrid creature of old and new) dances convulsively around Killick.

Throughout, the latter stands pensive onstage, having been part of the flurry of history in pictures shortly before, while inhabiting his human time, which for some reason looks all the more human now that he is sinking into the flurry of the future history he has just described, now that he is encumbered with the costume of theatrical time obliging him to 'finish the show': to measure the end of the oxymoronic time of theatre, in the background of what, now, looks like a post-apocalyptic void.

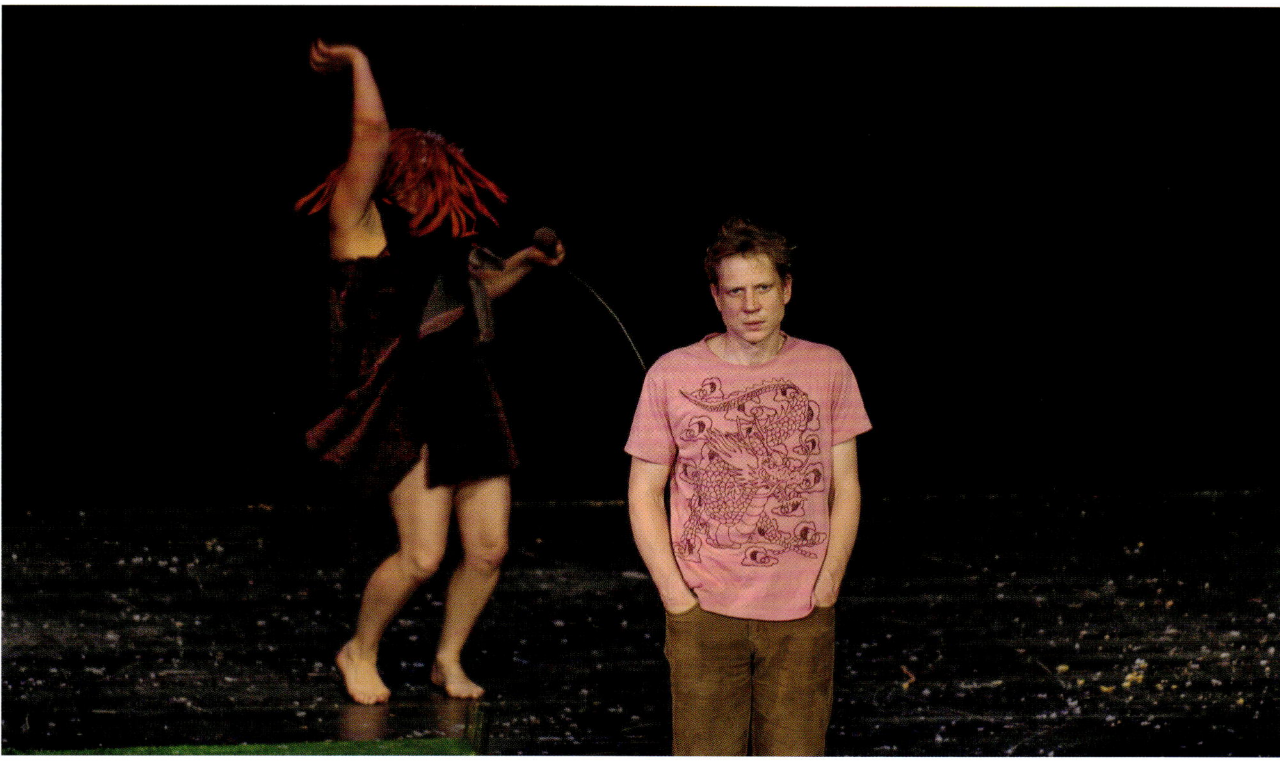

In the crack opened by this figuration, while a strange creature dances madly and a strange creature is pondering onstage, the audience is again softly drawn in, to inhabit for a short moment a deeply affective time, running at a slower pace and conflicting with the swirl of the show just witnessed. The sensation here is that of a sudden, long fall into the dark: an echo comes back from Killick's initial monologue, when, describing the fantasy fall from the building, he mentioned 'some of the things that might go through your mind when you're falling'—almost as if the whole 'History of Mankind' is just 'some of those things': nothing but quick images glimpsed during your fall. Because, indeed, the suicidal scene was not told in the first person but in the second: the one doing the imagining, the one doing the falling into the oblivion of historical time, was you, you listening and watching, you forcedly entertained. It was you, just about to confront the non-human time of theatre, while slowly, and yet too quickly, consuming your own too-human time, falling into the void of the future.

The temporal rupture of this figuration functions to perturb the logic of the ending: another passage usually organized, meaningfully and emotionally manipulated by particular regimes of temporality. The slow zooming into the future blurs the possibility of any measurement: not only in the temporal economy of the show (as it denies any climax) but also in that of theatre production. Returning to think of Foucault's desire to undo beginning, one more element seems at stake and resonates quite precisely here: the desire to resist the way institutions hosting human activity confer upon it a particular value in terms of time, establishing temporal vectors for processes which supposedly exist within an idea of development, which have beginnings and endings and thus are containable, recognizable as individual units of production, rather than part of a continuing, incommensurable, unfinished labour. The unease towards beginning and ending, that is, amounts to an unease towards the attribution of 'value' to a particular production happening in public: the production of thought, in the case of Foucault's lectures; the production of theatre, in the case of Forced Entertainment's shows.

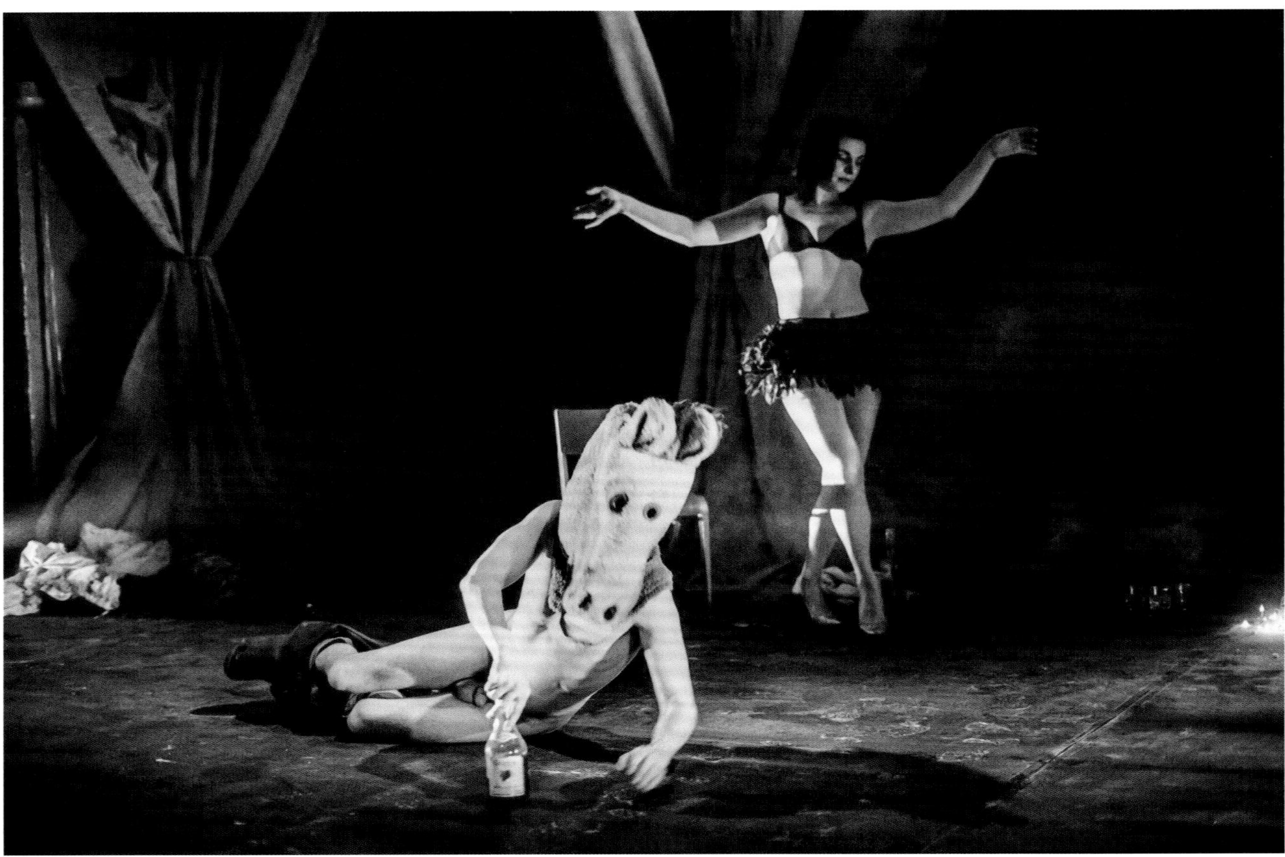

As Manutius insightfully suggested with the emblem placed on all the books he printed, *Festina lente* is also an instant condensation of a long process of thinking, of imagining, as well as the quick crystallization of such enduring work in an image. I wish to suggest that such a long duration of labour, manifesting in a figure as well as in individual shows, has specific resonances with respect to theatre work onstage and the labours going on backstage, in preparation. Hinting at such complex entanglements of temporalities, and to the way these are seemingly smothered, or else neglected, in the temporal order of theatre as an institution, brings forth yet another dimension of the slow figuration in Forced Entertainment's labours, one that in turn brings us back to Calvino's long fascination with the adage *Festina lente*. Discussing the motto in his lecture on 'Quickness', Calvino refers to a twofold temporal dimension of creative labour: he meditates on the necessity of a writer's work 'to take into account many rhythms'. Conjuring the mythological figures of Vulcan and Mercury (standing, respectively, for the focused labour of concentration and the aerial lightness and diversions sustaining creative labour in its long duration), Calvino ostensibly connects his fascination with *Festina lente* with an inquiry into creative labour's complex relation with the forms and the laws that organize it in the completion of individual works. Finally, Calvino also points to the pleasure he, as a writer, took in inventing or encountering, in literature, images that are themselves figurations of story-telling:[39] glimpses of stories condensing in a short form a trajectory which is potentially much longer, and that is crystallized in quickness while winking towards the past or the future.

All these dimensions are implicated, in different degrees of intensity, in Forced Entertainment's shows, and even more so when they are considered all together, as the corpus of a thirty-nine-year-old oeuvre that sustains the slow hurry structuring individual, specific pieces. In *And on the Thousandth Night …* (2000), for example, the Kings and Queens know that while they are telling their stories, they can be interrupted any moment. They know that while they are supposed to elegantly unroll the artfully wound skein of their tale, they must also move quickly toward its gist. They might, however, also want to linger on details because, in fact, their tales are not supposed to have an end at all. Like Scheherazade, the Kings and Queens also know that the endurance of their act of storytelling fatally depends on their capacity to deliver their stories fast, but not in a hurry. They are indeed constantly in a hurry to seduce the listener, but they cannot act in a hurry: if anything, the long duration of the show is a reminder of that. Their quixotic hope, one might suppose, is that not only the spectators but the other storytellers too will get caught up in the tale's seduction, entwined in it like a dolphin around an anchor, wishing to linger on its details for a dense moment in which the speed of storytelling will dwell in the stasis of collective listening. But then the potential interruption, which is the basic rule of the game, acts upon each story, imposing always a different duration than the one imagined, whatever that was, performing an external montage on its narrative tempo.

In a sense, each storyteller performs the role of a sail hammered onto the back of a turtle's body: she or he will violently interfere with the body of the tale and sail the show forward, very fast, although the show will anyhow move slowly, deferring its end. The starting again of the next tale will impress on collective time another rhythm: it will maybe slow down the show, walk backwards, if the story, as often happens, resonates with previous ones, and bring back figures and laughter which have already inhabited the stage, during the very same evening, or it will suddenly accelerate in an improvised duel of interruptions.

Such unpredictable, albeit carefully orchestrated, collective doing and imagining is not only affected by the work of storytelling onstage but also by the almost forty-year-long collaboration between the members of the group. The long duration condensed in images is produced by echoes, resonances, and returns of ideas and attempts, sketched out by someone from the collective in improvisation, then for some reason passed on and crystallized in figurations enacted by someone else or resonating in someone else's voice or gestures. The images we encounter in the work of Forced Entertainment bear on themselves also the endurance of a creative process of production that is a combination of various subjectivities, diverse temporalities of work, various phantasmatic bodies hybridized in a unique corpus, in a shared collection of riddles.

The figuration of the pantomime horse in *Pleasure* is a good example of this dynamic of endurance and hybridization. Lowdon recalls that the incongruous figure of the pantomime horse head stuck on the naked body of a man, crawling along the floor, while painstakingly opening and closing the curtains onstage, was produced during an improvisation of his.[40] Then the material was rearranged, and ended up being performed by Arthur. 'We often used to joke', Lowdon said, 'that I had made all this material that Rob actually had to inhabit, even though he hadn't made it in the first place, and how terribly unfair and cruel this was.' The crawling horse is therefore a time creature in yet another sense: it is a double-headed monster, in that it bears a multiple temporality, the labour time of at least two bodies, possibly two or more intuitions, the touch and nuances of many hands. It also combines the invisible, long labour of imagining, improvising, trying out, rearranging the material, re-performing it, learning to inhabit it, and the quick, icastic,[41] memorable form of appearance, onstage.

Lowdon reports that many years after *Pleasure* he found himself playing in *Tomorrow's Parties* (2011), a piece performed by two actors that was 'a game about possibilities for the future'.[42] The piece was performed by many members of the group, but Lowdon recalls that Arthur had been very influential in generating text for that show, so much so that he had deposited his voice, his tone, the phantasm of his body on the particular theatrical suit Lowdon ended up wearing when he performed in the show:

> I remember thinking it was very strange to find myself trying to inhabit Rob's words, because all of the text he had created pretty much comes from improvisation, and so in my head I could always hear Rob's speech patterns, and it felt like this was some kind of payback for the crawling horse of years ago.[43]

These figurations, and sure enough many others, bear on themselves also the distinctive slow hurry characterizing the strange balance between 'rehearsal time' and 'show time', the relation of violence and flirtation between the two, their binding of human time and theatre time. They write in hieroglyphics another story, at the margins of every show, longer than the time of any show. In a sense, this is a story about a desire for the immeasurability of theatre labour as production, going alongside the necessity, the circumstance, the destiny of framing 'theatre' in individual moments of performance, hosted by institutions, witnessed by other bodies in the audience, perceived as having proper beginnings and proper endings. It is a story featuring each body of the members of Forced Entertainment as a time creature, bearing on themselves the density, the endurance, the diversions, the detours of a collective creative process, persisting in offering the unease of one's human time to the always new riddles displayed in the space of the non-human, or of the all too human, populated onstage and offstage by strangers, people who know nothing about each other except for the fact of being commonly humans and being together in a limited time and space. In such space, in such time, incongruous 'possibilities for the future' get repeatedly figured, through slow and quick glimpses of stories, carved on the theatre stage as on golden coins. These stories, these golden coins, are not to be spent or understood but to be passed on, donated, collected, or even lost, hidden in an invisible 'library [that] shall be contained by no limits other than those of the world'.[44]

1. Desiderius Erasmus, 'Festina lente', in *Adagia* II.1.1 (1525). Hypertext edition by Otto Steinmayer, http://www.philological.bham.ac.uk/speude/, accessed 2 October 2020.

2. Waldemar Deonna, 'The Crab and the Butterfly: A Study in Animal Symbolism', *Journal of the Warburg and Courtauld Institutes*, 17/1–2 (1954), 47–86.

3. Italo Calvino, *Six Memos for the Next Millennium* (New York: Vintage, 1988), 48.

4. Ibid.

5. Erasmus, 'Festina lente' (see n. 1), 11.

6. Calvino, *Six Memos for the Next Millennium* (see n. 3), 48.

7. Erasmus, 'Festina lente' (see n. 1), 17.

8. Ibid., 3.

9. An expression used by Tim Etchells during a public conversation with Sara Jane Bailes, which I attended at the Attenborough Centre for the Creative Arts in Brighton, 12 November 2016.

10. For a discussion of the idea of symptoms and their relation with figuration, see Georges Didi-Huberman, 'The Image as Rend and the Death of God Incarnate', in *Confronting Images: Questioning the Ends of a Certain History of Art* (University Park, PA: Penn State University Press, 2005), 139–94.

11. From Greek: *hieroglyphikós*, composed of *hierós* (sacred) and *glyphein* (to carve).

12. Erasmus, 'Festina lente' (see n. 1), 9.

13. Ibid., 11.

14. Antonin Artaud, 'Metaphysics and the *Mise en Scène*', in *The Theater and Its Double* (New York: Grove Press, 1950), 37.

15. Ibid., 39.

16. Artaud, 'The Theater of Cruelty (First Manifesto)', in *The Theater and Its Double* (see n. 14), 93.

17. Ibid., 94.

18. See, in particular, Jacques Derrida, 'La parole soufflé', 'Freud and the Scene of Writing', and 'The Theater of Cruelty and the Closure of Representation', in *Writing and Difference* (Chicago, IL: University of Chicago Press, 1978).

19. Derrida, 'La parole soufflé' (see n. 18), 191.

20. Artaud, 'Metaphysics and the *Mise en Scène*' (see n. 14), 39.

21. The most important example of theatrical hieroglyphs Artaud discusses was the Balinese theatre that he saw at the Exposition Coloniale in the Bois de Vincennes in 1931, and to which he devoted the essay 'On the Balinese Theater', in *The Theater and Its Double* (see n. 14), 53–67.

22. Artaud, 'Metaphysics and the *Mise en Scène*' (see n. 14), 40.

23. Ibid., 43.

24. Ibid., 44.

25. Ibid.

26. See Georges Didi-Huberman, 'The Image as Rend and the Death of God Incarnate' (see n. 10), 139–94.

27. Angela Carter, 'Animals in the Nursery', *Shaking a Leg: Collected Journalism and Writings* (London: Penguin Books, 1998), 299.

28. Nicholas Ridout, for example, suggests that in Forced Entertainment shows 'the animal suits transform the adult humans into silly bumbling beasts of erotic fixation,' in Nicholas Ridout, *Stage Fright, Animals, and Other Theatrical Problems* (Cambridge: Cambridge University Press, 2006), 154.

29. For a definition of 'drag' and its etymological relation with time, see Elizabeth Freeman, 'Packing History, Count(er)ing Generations', *New Literary History*, 31/3 (Summer 2000), 728.

30. For an interesting critical take on the figure of the dog in *Showtime* see David Williams, 'Inappropriate/d Others or, The Difficulty of Being a Dog', *TDR: The Drama Review*, 51/1 (Spring 2007), 111–15.

31. Tim Etchells, *Certain Fragments: Contemporary Performance and Forced Entertainment* (London: Routledge, 1999), 57.

32. Michel Foucault, 'The Order of Discourse', in Richard Young (ed.), *Untying the Text: A Poststructuralist Reader* (London: Routledge & Kegan Paul, 1981), 52.

33. Ibid., 53.

34. Ibid.

35. This echoes the title of another piece: *Who Can Sing a Song to Unfrighten Me?*

36. Etchells, *Certain Fragments* (see n. 31), 63.

37. From the description on the website http://www.forcedentertainment.com/project/the-world-in-pictures/, accessed 2 October 2020.

38. From the compilation *Refried Ectoplasm [Switched on Volume 2]* (Duophonic Records, 1995).

39. Calvino, *Six Memos for the Next Millennium* (see n. 3), 54.

40. Forced Entertainment and Hugo Glendinning, *#FE84–14 No. 6 Pleasure | Tomorrow's Parties | Sharing Material, Richard Lowdon*, online clip (2014), https://youtu.be/cKr5h6pHkBY, accessed 13 October 2020.

41. The adjective 'icastic' is defined by Italo Calvino in his lecture on 'Exactitude' as describing 'the evocation of clear, incisive, memorable visual images'. See Italo Calvino, *Six Memos for the Next Millennium* (see n. 3), 55.

42. Forced Entertainment and Glendinning, *#FE84–14 No. 6 Pleasure | Tomorrow's Parties | Sharing Material, Richard Lowdon*, online clip (see n. 40).

43. Ibid.

44. Erasmus, 'Festina lente' (see n.1), 17.

Deferring the Inevitable

Rabih Mroué

Definition

Digression is defined as 'a temporary departure from the main subject in speech or writing'. Jalāl al-Dīn al-Suyūṭī writes, 'Digression takes place when the poet is in the middle of some creative ideas, and another creative idea occurs which suits him better and which he promptly integrates.'[1] According to al-Jāḥiẓ, the author of the *Book of the Animals*, which is filled with many digressions, 'it is a sort of refinement of language or speech. The poet gives the impression that he is aiming for one meaning, upon which he builds, only to home in on another, as if it was always meant to arrive yet arrived by chance.'[2]

A Journey of Meanings

While digression is one of the many features of the works of Forced Entertainment and Tim Etchells, here it transcends its classic conceptual definitions. Forced Entertainment's digression doesn't aim to clarify, to explain, or to emphasize, nor even to elaborate on the topic itself or to beautify speech or stir emotions. But this goes back to its original root. In Arabic, *istitrad* (digression) is a word derived from the original linguistic root (*ta-ra-da*), which encompasses exclusion, appending, sequencing, pursuit, movement, and transition, among other meanings.

Digression thus becomes a matter of saying something and having it lead to a second meaning before arriving at its first meaning, and going towards a third sense, before reaching its second sense … Digression is not about the refutation of arguments or persuasion. It is rather about the flow of the narrative that takes its author to places they have never been before. Take *Quizoola!* (1996): in the game of short questions and answers stemming from one another, ideas slide in elaborate digressions, taking the shape of an interrogation that draws its two performers from what is apparent to what is hidden and from the hidden to the unknown. With each question, the performer finds themself faced with many possible answers that would, in turn, place the questioner in front of other possibilities to come up with a question that will prompt the respondent again to find unexpected answers and so on. The same logic applies to *And on the Thousandth Night …* (2000) where the word 'stop' gives its speaker the right to break from the story already being narrated and begin another story that starts with the same opening phrase 'Once upon a time …' It is as if the narrative were a tree with long unfurling branches but no trunk. Or a tree whose trunk is all branches. Or a forest full of twists and turns, whose paths can all be trod. Unlike in the common proverb that says that all roads lead to Rome, here every path we take opens up new spaces, which branch out even further. It is a journey where we lose ourselves and explore, an expedition of danger and adventure in a little boat which sets sail in a new direction: just as soon as it has dropped its anchor, it sails in another direction … So that the journey continues without an end point, not for six hours, nor for twelve hours, but indefinitely.

With this concept, the performance gradually takes shape in front of the spectators without reaching a climax, a conclusion, or a moral statement. It is a digression in the form of primitive reflections and ideas that are still taking shape, where imagination is boundless and the theatre is open to meanings that spout from each other in a sweeping flow, leaving each spectator ample room to scoop the meanings up freely and spontaneously, to ponder and think and formulate new meanings and opposing questions. The group thus achieves its goal of splitting the solid mass of the audience into independent and active individuals, in the political sense.

Not only is digression an effective means of postponing answers and conclusions, it is also a means to slide and turn, to alienate and change. It is also a way of deferring the inevitable.

If Scheherazade prolongs her narration and digresses from one story to the next, it is to postpone her ineluctable death. The readers have the pleasure of living in the folds of time stretched within the digressive narration itself. Once Scheherazade finishes her story, we will know that the hour of death has come, whether it is by the sword or by a pardon that imprisons her within the institution of marriage to die metaphorically at the hands of a king who has become a traditional husband and of children who will commandeer her private time.

Thus, in Forced Entertainment's durational performances, we hardly ever come upon a beginning or an end but rather an ongoing narration that began before our arrival at the theatre and will go on after our departure. It is a declaration rejecting death that occurs deliberately in the midst of daily life's concerns and needs, amidst the institutions of family, state, and religion and the cycles of conflicts and wars that fill the world and occupy its people.

You walk into *Sight Is the Sense That Dying People Tend to Lose First* (2008) and it could start anywhere, for example: 'A submarine is a ship that can go underwater. A French kiss is a kiss where you put your tongue in the other person's mouth.' But we are well aware that it could start somewhere else such as: 'A lie is what people say when they say something that is untrue. A donkey is an inferior kind of horse.' As such, the last sentence could be any other. The actor could also stop talking when he wishes, after five minutes, or after five days, it makes no difference, because we are aware that should the talking cease, it will nonetheless continue

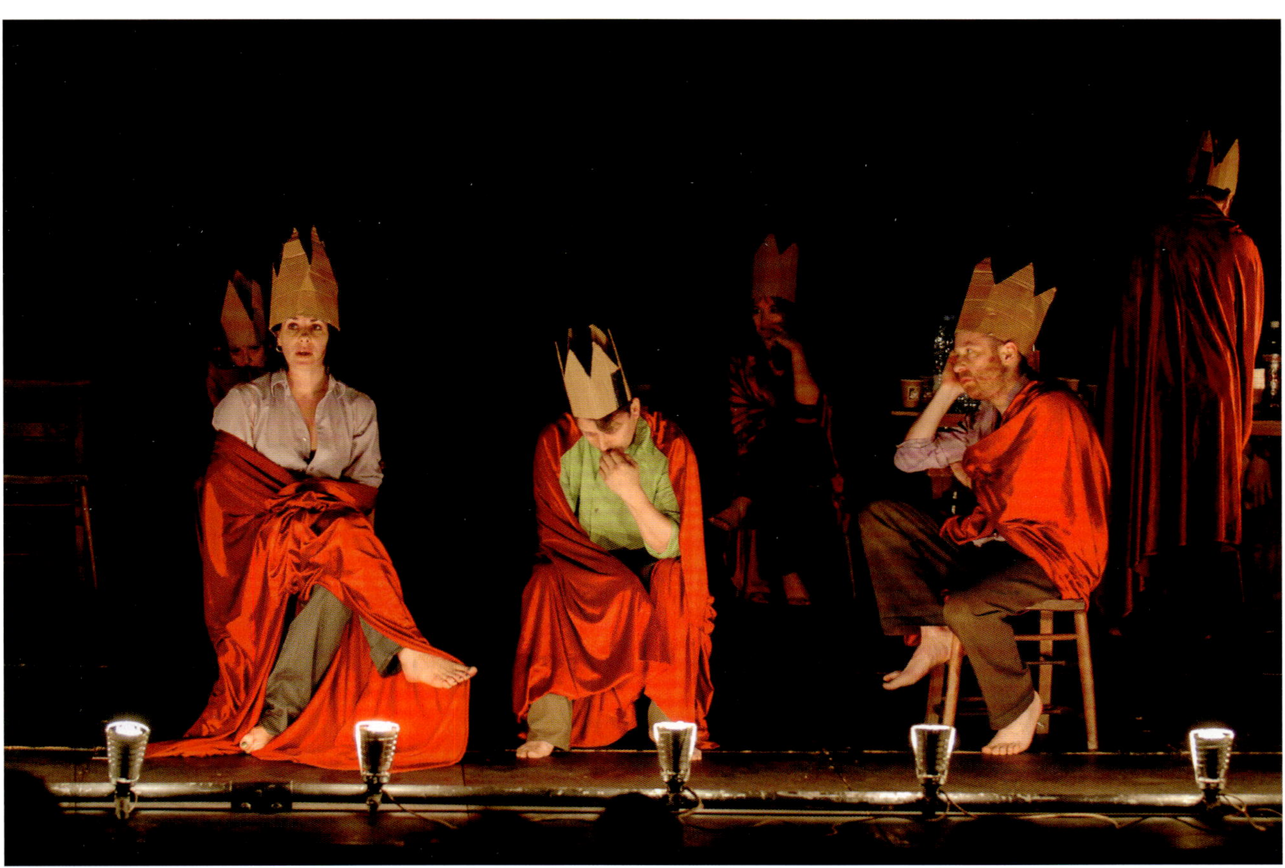

non-stop inside our own minds—actors and spectators alike. Talk that cannot be contained, that is as varied as life itself, made of scattered parts and pieces. Although it is integrated within a fine framework and a simple protocol—the parts are pulled together so that they do not unravel and transform into an insoluble puzzle—the words still require our imagination as spectators, and our independent individual synthesis, to be placed in different and diverse contexts.

In Praise of Digression

Digression is a celebration of an ornate language replete with pictures, ideas, question marks, and exclamations, as well as allegory, metonymy, and (canonical) texts open to interpretation … Digression carries within its folds an act of resistance, and this act is often modest and soft-spoken, without boastful bravado or rhetoric. Digression, as is well known, is a departure from the straight and narrow path, it goes against speed, against the declaration of states of emergency. Digression is our right to own time and a personal space, our right to meditate and reflect, our right to playfulness, fatigue, idleness, and sleep. It is our right to move between here and there, with no strings attached, and to jump over borders that separate or to stay at the thresholds.

Digression is the means to liberate the self from the hegemony of time and space and to open it to alternative times and spaces that have different concepts and standards. It is a way of departing to a non-place and to all places at once, as if the theatrical act is happening here and there.

Belated Prelude

Every time I watch a show by Forced Entertainment, I'm overtaken by the desire to work on a new performance right away. This feeling is often accompanied by two main thoughts. First, the ability of these performances to remind us of the strength of theatre as a political, social, and philosophical art that has an active role in our daily life, when we often question the usefulness of art in general and theatre in particular. The second is based on the simplicity of the show itself, in terms of direction, performance, and writing, and on its general forms—its abilities to entertain and dazzle us without affectation, showiness, or excessive and forced complexities. It makes us, the spectators, imagine that theatre production is easy and accessible to all. But no sooner has one embarked on a trip within it than one encounters barriers to writing, directing, and performing. The group's performances are, as the Arabs call it, 'complicated simplicity'.

Back to the Non-Beginning

Digression is Forced Entertainment's proposal for us to look obliquely at what is going on here and now, so we can see the world differently.

Translated from Arabic by Ziad Nawfal and Joumana Seikali

1. Jalāl al-Dīn al-Suyūṭī, *Maqālīd al-ʿUlūm fi al-Hūdūd wal-Rūsūm*,
http://arabiclexicon.hawramani.com/al-suyuti-mujam-maqalid-al-ulum-fi-l-hudud-wa-l-rusum/, accessed 22 October 2020.
2. Abū ʿUthman ʿAmr ibn Baḥr al-Kinānī al-Baṣrī (aka al-Jāḥiẓ), *Kitāb al-Bayān wa-al-Tabyīn*
[The Book of Eloquence and Exposition] (Misr: al-Maṭbaʿa al-ʿIlmīya, 1893).

Once Upon a Time, There Were Two Words That Fell in Love with Each Other …[1]

Joy Kristin Kalu

I still wonder whether it is possible to think of a word. Having discussed and thought about *Real Magic* (2016) quite a bit—where the performers' task in a cabaret-inspired routine is to mind-read a word someone else is thinking of—I wrote to Tim Etchells that I thought it was not possible. He agreed and asked in response: 'Isn't there a bit in Plato's *Symposium* where they are trying to talk about love and they resort to talking about the shape of the letters in the word?'[2] I was not sure whether what he had pointed out was exactly what I meant or rather the opposite, so I decided to leave the question for a later conversation.

Thinking back, the confusion his remark caused me was not so much that he had agreed with my assertion that thinking of a word was impossible while still providing an example of just that—in this case, thinking of a word as the form of the sign instead of its meaning. The confusion had instead been caused by his bringing up of the word 'love', which, for many reasons, seems to be different from any other word. It complicates the relationship between signifier and signified not least because of the challenge of defining what is referenced, a popular task also in *Quizoola!* (1996), where 'What is love?' features among the many questions the performers continually ask and 'answer'. Moreover, the concept of 'love' is thought of as being highly transformative and transgressive, and therefore so self-referential that it breaks open the representational order language is based on.

Finally returning to the puzzle, I am realizing that looking at Forced Entertainment and their aesthetics, which in every show I know has broken open some belief dear to me and replaced it with possibility, it might be a good idea not just to focus on the various ways they strain the relationship between signs and their meanings, but on how love comes into being in and through their performances. They have dealt with—and complicated—romantic love in many of their productions, perhaps most strikingly in *Void Story* (2009), where an unhappy couple's delusional journey through a dystopian landscape at the same time suggests a deconstructive reading of the notion of the couple in general. But it is not the idea of romance and its figuration that I will focus on here. I am interested, instead, in love as a theatrical concept based on differences rather than unities. In Forced Entertainment's works, I will track the negotiations between freedom and commitment that circulate between the performers and their spectators.

Michael Hardt posits love as a political concept, which he regards as a means for collective transformation and a potential foundation for a democratic society.[3] I try here to translate some of his thoughts to theatre. By no means am I suggesting that Forced Entertainment attempt to rehearse or realize democracy. But I do believe that their incessant probing into whether or not change is possible can be regarded as a training space for solidarity and care, for unions based on each person's decision and no one's obligation to stay, and therefore for the desirable kind of love Hardt seems to have in mind when he defines love as a practice of differentiation. This hopeful procedure is taken to extremes in *Real Magic*'s unflinchingly optimistic compulsive repetition. Contrary to their experience of incessant failure relating to and reading the thoughts of the other, the figures refuse to give up the belief that at some point two minds will align with each other.

Hardt identifies some misunderstandings concerning love, referring to them as 'love gone bad'. Among them is love which is built upon sameness instead of difference, love which is understood as an act of charity instead of equality, and love which is centred around passion—as something overwhelming us—instead of love as an active choice we're making. I am convinced that the theatre of Forced Entertainment, which

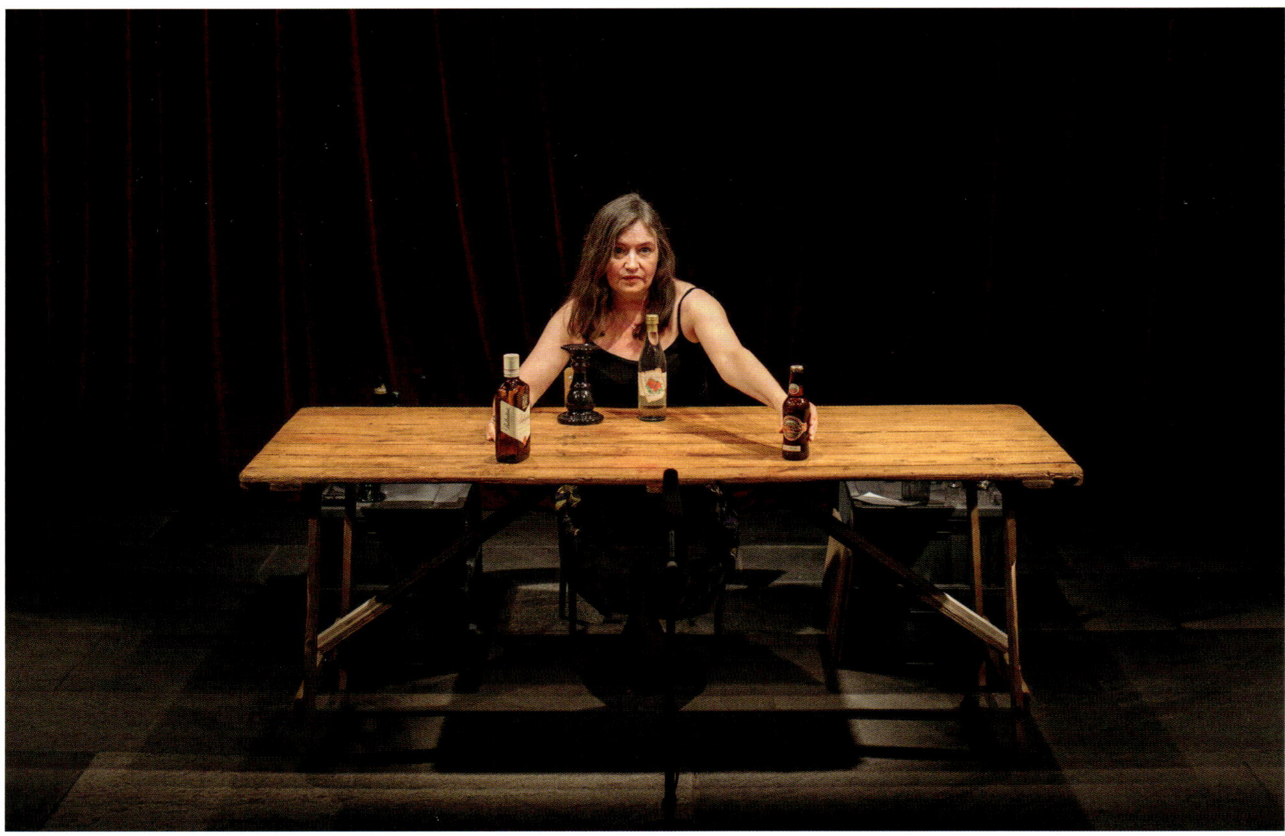

is now based on thirty-nine years of ongoing collective communication and creation, has invited us to experience alternative practices of loving. These have often taken the shape of the hard work of spectating and performing, of allowing oneself to feel lost and lonely in the theatre, and of the courage to take responsibility for one's share in what is being created in this moment. In many productions and both on- and offstage the effort of taking part in a collective labour of meaning-making seems to be a solitary one stemming solely from a strong desire to overcome alienation, which frequently remains unfulfilled.

'Split the audience. Make a problem of them. Disrupt the comfort and anonymity of the darkness. Disrupt that feeling that "we are all the same". Remind them that differences exist,' Etchells writes in 2004.[4] This procedure of denying us the relief of easily losing ourselves in a performance has probably hit me hardest in *Dirty Work (The Late Shift)* (2017), which I saw only recently. All the magnificent spectacles offered were nothing but descriptive words, and in order to transform them into images and actions we had to rely on our imagination. The task felt especially challenging because each member of the audience around me was so obviously present. Listening to some of them laugh and to others sigh, perceiving impatient silences filled with nervous tics next to magnetized silences tense with suspense showed me not just how different each experience was. It also made it more and more difficult to get into the mode of fiction. There was no sense of community carrying me away. And I didn't know how to carry myself.

What helped me overcome my estrangement in the auditorium and finally take part in the creation of scenes so fantastic they could never be played in a single theatre was Terry O'Connor's caring presence onstage. She didn't talk but witnessed the tellings and played musical accompaniments on a record player. Her silent support of Cathy Naden's and Robin Arthur's storytelling, and her radiating attentiveness guided me. Her generous focus formed a bridge between herself and the other performers and extended into the audience. Without her presence I would not have been able to make those words affective.

The way she 'handled' her co-performers, allowing me to open up to their stories, reminds me of *Complete Works: Table Top Shakespeare* (2015). I watched several of the 'episodes' of these condensed retellings of Shakespeare's plays and was each time amazed at how the little everyday objects the performers used as stand-ins for Shakespeare's characters were brought to life. It was the actors' concentrated care and affection that transformed and animated them and, at the same time, enabled me to feel and fear for the individuals they had turned into. The love the objects were met with required an overcoming of prevailing norms, which led to an extensive transformation of the status of things, and a continuous and shared revivification, night after night.

But there are more ways Forced Entertainment audiences are held responsible for the action unfolding. In the durational pieces like *Speak Bitterness* (1994), *Quizoola!*, or *And on the Thousandth Night …* (2000) the spectators are free to come and go at any point. Not only do they create their very own performance, deciding how long to stay and for how long to leave, they also affect the other audience members and the performers with their choices. Notably, their entrances and exits influence the atmosphere of the performance through what may be perceived as their approval or disapproval, their commitment or impatience. As time passes and people on both sides of the stage become more receptive and vulnerable in their shared exhaustion, it becomes obvious how much we are given, how much our acts matter, and sometimes even, as bell hooks puts it in her plea for communal love, that 'love is an action. A participatory emotion.'[5]

I would like to close with a look at the opening sequence of *Bloody Mess* (2004), in which John Rowley and Bruno Roubicek, dressed as clowns, are frantically setting up chairs. They both want the chairs in a row but cannot agree on which side of the stage to place it. They keep stealing chairs from each other, running off with them, fighting over them, clashing and banging into each other. What I remember most of the comic routine is an instant when one of them gives in and rests on a chair in the row his antagonist has created. This short moment of pause, before he runs off with some chairs again to continue the chaos, has stayed with me as a moment of great power. This incident turned the routine into a love scene of people starting out with the same goal but taking different approaches. Still, they come together, exhausted, if only for a moment.

I leave my chair and look up from my computer at a desk in a small public library in Salerno, where I have come to escape the heat and write this text during my summer vacation. A beautiful book at the end of a shelf across the room from me catches my eye. Having admired its cover for a while, only on second glance do I notice that it is a collection of Spalding Gray's monologues: *Sesso e morte fino a 14 anni*.[6] Walking back to the hotel, I realize the translated words keep me from recalling the original title, which I know so well. At the same time, I am interpreting them as a sign.[7] They seem to tell me that I have come to the right place. They remind me of how words can travel and reach us where we least expected them. Dressing for the beach, I keep thinking of the words while their meaning has turned into a feeling.

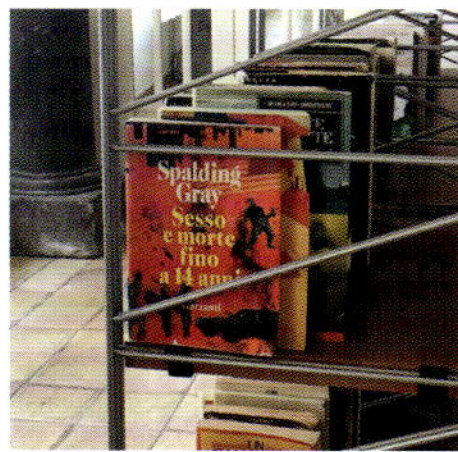

1. Richard Lowdon, in *And on the Thousandth Night …*, video recording of a performance at Culturgest, Lisbon, 2014.

2. Tim Etchells, in email correspondence with the author, 12 May 2017.

3. Compare the lecture 'About Love' that Michael Hardt gave at the European Graduate School in 2007, https://www.youtube.com/watch?v=ioopkoppabI, accessed 2 October 2020.

4. Tim Etchells, 'A Six-Thousand-and-Forty-Seven-Word Manifesto on Liveness in Three Parts with Three Interludes', in Adrian Heathfield (ed.), *Live: Art and Performance* (London: Tate Publishing, 2004), 215.

5. bell hooks, *All About Love: New Visions* (New York: Harper Perennial, 2001), 165.

6. Spalding Gray, *Sex and Death to the Age 14* (New York: Random House, 1986).

7. Tim Etchells is the most recent recipient of the Spalding Gray Award, which he used to create *Real Magic*.

A Text on Twenty Years with Sixty-Six Footnotes

Tim Etchells

It starts somewhere[1] and rapidly unfolds in many directions.[2]

During very early rehearsals for *Bloody Mess* (2004), Jerry Killick comes to the front of the stage[3] and 'explains' to the audience[4] why the atmosphere is completely wrong. As far as the text goes, in fact, Jerry is improvising a version of what he has just heard John Rowley improvising in a previous run-through. And John—when he was onstage about fifteen minutes earlier—was simply improvising around what I'd explained to him of what I could vaguely remember of Cathy's original improvisation of a text for this part of the performance, which she had done about a month beforehand, back in our rehearsal studio.[5] This kind of swapping around of material from one performer to another sometimes takes place at the start of rehearsal processes—either for logistical reasons (such as Cathy is busy in London working on a film script today, or someone is sick, or ...) or for 'artistic' reasons (such as we think that it would be interesting to change the gender of the performer doing a particular thing, or that it would be 'useful' to switch who's doing something because of how it will connect—or disconnect—to some other activity they have at some other point in the piece).[6]

It jumps[7] and cuts backwards in time.[8]

Years before, Richard is standing at the long metal table we use for *Speak Bitterness* (1994) and he is dealing the texts out along its length. Setting up for the performance, he is isolating special parts of the text that need to be in particular places on the table for particular people at particular times and placing them accordingly, and simply scattering the rest of the papers on the table here and there, covering it completely. The texts are lists of confessions. The piece, we say, is an attempt to confess to everything—a vast catalogue of wrongdoings that

1. As it must do.

2. I have told this story, spoken of this history so many, many times that it is hard to approach it afresh. When I do write or speak about it now, it can seem to me that I am not telling what happened as much as telling what I have told before—the way a photograph of an event can come to stand in place of a memory of it, or the way that a photograph itself can become a memory. There is a photograph by Hugo Glendinning that shows us on the beach in Gdańsk in Poland—we were touring there in 1989 with the theatre performance *200% & Bloody Thirsty* (1998). I have no real memory of the day we visited the beach but sometimes call to mind the picture, believing it to be a memory.

3. We are in the grand gold proscenium and red-velvet auditorium of Sheffield's Lyceum Theatre, squeezing this rehearsal in between what we should actually be doing, which is rehearsing the monologues project *The Voices*. It is (the) afternoon, sometime in 2003.

4. In fact, the audience is only me, Tobias Lange (a German performer with whom we've worked on many occasions), Helen Gould (one of the performers in *The Voices*), and Sara Stenström, a Swedish dramaturgy student who is following rehearsals.

5. We have this initial improvisation (and all subsequent ones) on videotape for reference but, at this point in the rehearsals, I am too lazy to find it or we are too short of time in the Lyceum to spend time watching it. In any case, for the moment at least, the fact that John and Jerry will come up with something in the same broad area as Cathy's original version but different in emphasis and detail is probably a useful thing. When the text 'returns' to Cathy a month or so hence, she may borrow from the material that John and Jerry have created. The 'John version' and the 'Jerry version' of this scene (and of the persona at the centre of it) will be useful models in discussions through the process, points of comparison and conjecture against which the unfolding work will be measured and changed.

6. Despite all this, and not to be deliberately confusing, once we're out of the very early stages of making a piece—once some material is attached to a performer in rehearsal—it generally tends to stay with them. Initial decisions about who does what can be arbitrary or pragmatic, but once concretized in action, these decisions tend to stick. The particular way that a person does a certain thing, the particular energy they bring to an action or a text becomes a compositional given—an important part of its place in the piece.

7. As it tends, very often, to do.

8. I think of Robin in one section of *Showtime* (1996), being harassed by Cathy crawling on her hands and knees dressed in a dog costume, barking at him. The way I remember him, Robin is naked, except for a stocking mask like those that picture-book bank robbers wear. He holds a red balloon with which he tries to hide his genitals. Inevitably the 'dog' is very interested in the balloon. Robin speaks: 'I've been thinking a lot about time. It only goes in one direction. It just goes forwards. So you can't go back. It's also supposed to go at the same speed all the time, but that is not true is it, because sometimes it goes more slowly than other times ... I mean the thing about time is that ... Time is an important subject. It's one of the fundamentals, isn't it? It's an important subject. It's not meant to be trivialized, it's not meant to be the subject of a cheap joke ... Time is a big subject. Time—like space, war, love—is a big topic, with important consequences for everybody.'

includes murder, fraud, genocide, eating the last biscuit in the tin, not washing up properly, hiding the TV remote control, and buggery.[9]

It slides around, becomes non-specific.

We are in a van,[10] in a theatre, in a dressing room, in a bar late at night, in a taxi to an airport. We are walking in a strange city looking for somewhere to eat, we are repeatedly drawing diagrams of the structure of a show on paper napkins[11] in the corner of a bar, with furrowed brows and shaking heads, or in a restaurant, rearranging elements, passing paper down the table to get a comment or a raised eyebrow from someone else, we are drinking with ten or more people crammed into a single hotel room.[12]

It settles again, at some other point.

Now Terry and Cathy are on the chalk-scrawled set of *Club of No Regrets* (1993) in Berlin, placing texts and props on the stage in the right places prior to the performance. I'm watching them from the auditorium.[13] As I watch, I am thinking that their activity on stage looks as if they were doing the piece in schematic form—visiting its places, its positions, each in turn, only in reverse.[14] On the stage, Terry and Cathy are putting the bucket of water at the back, so that later, in the performance, it can be moved to the front by the shoddy wooden house that sits on the stage. When she leaves the stage, job completed, Terry passes Robin on the stairs. Later, for years and years, she will tell the story that Robin looked completely crazy on the stairs[15] and that his eyes were in a very strange state and that he was muttering to himself and that she thought: 'Oh God. What's he going to be like in the performance …'

It speeds up.

We are in a rehearsal room. We are loading a van. We are checking into a shitty English bed and breakfast. The stench of fifty years' worth of cooked full breakfasts has been fried into the brown paint walls. The building shrieks and groans when the taps run, the floorboards creak in incomprehensible ways—the unbearable burden of the lives that have passed through here; the lights dim whenever anyone takes a shower.

Robin crawls, stripped to the waist, his head in the fun-fur mask of the pantomime horse[16] and he swigs from the whisky bottle through the eyehole of the horse—more like brutal IV drug use than drinking. As Robin pushes the bottle in through the eye, the horse head is bent grotesquely out of shape—driven crazy by drinking,[17] wracked in bewildered cartoon agonies.

Terry changes costume.[18]

9. If *Speak Bitterness* is a catalogue of (all?) possible confessions, then *Quizoola!* (1996) is a catalogue of all possible questions, *And on the Thousandth Night …* (2000) a catalogue of all possible stories, *12am: Awake & Looking Down* (1993) a catalogue of all possible characters and costumes, etc. It's not so much the content of any particular confession, story, question, etc. that's of interest, but the way that the nature of the catalogue itself—its boundaries, its built-in agendas, its formal extremities, its *concerns*—is revealed.

10. Soundtrack: Tom Waits' *Rain Dogs* or Al Green.

11. Or on beer mats, or in a notebook.

12. Generic memories—so many variations of the same scene layered one on top of the other that they are by now almost impossible to distinguish. A density blur.

13. I don't know what year this is. I spent a lot of time watching people on stage doing things that are not strictly speaking performance—setting up for things, building sets, fooling around, hanging lights.

14. Several times we tried to include walk-throughs of performances as part of performances themselves but never succeeded. Something fascinating about the energy of these rehearsal activities—the high-speed, casual energy 'marking' of positions and lines, the précis, the annotated summary disrupted by the occasional detail of a moment or interaction that someone needs to practice 'for real'.

15. Whenever it was, this week in Berlin involved quite a lot of parties.

16. This is a pantomime horse costume we borrowed from a local theatre when we did a kids' project for them. A spectacularly crappy and comical horse with a goofy expression and teeth too big for its mouth.

17. Normally it would be water in the whisky bottle, not actual whisky, although in shows where there is beer drunk onstage (and there are quite a few of these), people tend to drink beer for real, even in rehearsals. It's an interesting thing that people sometimes manoeuvre a little, 'speculate' while improvising so that their role might involve having a beer or two, or smoking the odd cigarette, or having a nice sit-down from time to time.

18. *Emanuelle Enchanted* (1992).

Cathy addresses the audience.[19]

John shakes his head in disbelief.[20]

Jerry laughs, his face all smashed up from a bicycle accident.[21]

Terry yells in Italian.[22]

Richard puts on a blindfold and stands as if waiting to be shot.[23]

Robin parts the curtains slightly and peers through them at the arriving audience.[24]

It slides in time.[25]

Claire dances in her bra and knickers, midriff wrapped in a skimpy, improvised fake feather tutu, a knife in her hands. There is slowed-down music from the record player[26] and, to go with it, Claire dances in kind of suicidal and ultra-slow motion.[27] She does not know that this dance will be in the final performance, though she already, perhaps, suspects. She knows that 'something' is happening, that somewhere in the confluence of what she and the others onstage are doing (improvising) there is a 'scene', or that this is some particular nuanced articulation of what we have been doing for a month or more.[28] Claire dances and Cathy writes obscenities on the blackboard: Cunt. Get Your Rocks Off. Blow Job.[29] The music is *The Last Mile Home* but because it's slowed down so much, you can hardly hear the words.[30]

As she dances, Claire does not know that years later she will sit on the seating bank in the rehearsal room—close to where I am watching her from now—and she will watch (in the future) as Wendy Houston does this dance. Claire will be teaching it to her because Claire will be pregnant and Wendy will be replacing her in some part of the *Pleasure* (1997) touring. And Claire does not know that she will be saying to Wendy: 'No. Heavier, Make it clumsier. It needs to be worse ...' and that Richard will be sat at the front of the stage the whole time[31]

19. *Disco Relax* (1999).

20. *First Night* (2001) rehearsals.

21. Performance of *And on the Thousandth Night ...*, Munster, 2003.

22. Performance of *Club of No Regrets* in Italian for Volterra Festival, 1994. Everyone learned most of their texts in Italian, parrot-fashion. The performance took place outdoors, in the grounds of an old monastery. For years afterwards, people would talk about the way the smoke from the performance (talcum powder hurled into the air) rose and drifted up toward the trees, blown on the wind in the moonlight during the show. I was not there but sometimes I find that I talk about it as if I had been.

23. *Hidden J* (1994).

24. A generic memory and one which, in any case, I wouldn't have witnessed. Robin likes to see the audience before they see him—checking them out—weighing the possibilities of how the gig will go. Other performers prefer not to see the public till they get on the stage.

25. As it tends to do.

26. We used the same battered record player in a whole string of shows from *Showtime* to *Disco Relax*. In the first of these it played a number of old 45 rpm records that Richard had found at his parents' house. We liked the record player because it meant that the means of producing music and the operation of it were visible on and controlled from the stage. Prior to this, music slammed or drifted in as if controlled by some unseen hand ('from God,' we used to say, joking) and we became suspicious of this ... preferring that all of the signification (except the lights) remain in control of the performers onstage. Using the record player (and with it 'found' songs or music on vinyl) meant that the music was (literally) an object held up for use and scrutiny much like a found text, or a second-hand costume. It meant an end, more or less, to our theatre work with composer John Avery who'd done soundtracks for almost all of the performances prior to the arrival of the record player.

27. This is *Pleasure* rehearsals.

28. It is a big joke in rehearsals and afterwards that the stupidest, most painful, or random improvisational move can end up being your fate for a whole show and for a whole year of touring. As in: 'If I'd have known I was going to end up doing *that* for a year, I wouldn't have done it in the first place.'

29. This is a list of dirty words and phrases I have downloaded from the internet.

30. When performance artist Michael Atavar comes to see a rehearsal one day, he remembers how he and his sister used to play all their parents' records slowed down and scare each other with the messages from the Devil they could hear in there.

31. There is a whole strand of the work where someone (often Richard) 'comes to the front' or 'takes centre' to frame or MC the pieces. Occupying this place appears something of a structural necessity but is rarely weighted with the kind of actual authority that a narrator/MC might be expected to project. We took to calling the role/position 'frame' and then, as it decayed further, etiolated or 'weak' frame. The storyteller is weak, prone to distraction (like me, here), disorganized, crazed, uncertain. We understood this MC position as a structural tactic—about one (or more) people coming forwards so that others might have the space to live/exist/work in the back. The front provides covering fire (deals with the audience, acknowledges them, speaks to them directly) so that the rest can get on with what they need to do.

loading the gun[32] with his blindfold on and Claire does not know that she will watch Wendy and that as she does so, her hands will be clasped over her belly, inside of which will be Ruby May—of whom, at this point in the story of Claire first improvising the dance, there will not even be the tiniest idea.[33]

It continues to jump.

We are in a hotel room. The technician Andy Clarke is drinking whisky from a toothpaste mug whilst various people add to the uncharacteristic make up and pink wig outfit that he is sporting. It is five in the morning. I am filming.[34] We are in Columbus, Ohio. Outside there is snow.

We are driving on a road between Berlin and Warsaw in a three-and-half ton truck, overtaking in swirling dense fog on narrow roads. Whoever is in the passenger seat has to spot for oncoming headlamps appearing out of the gloom.[35] It's a nerve-wracking business. You feel close to your death every time we pull out to overtake.

We are in Sheffield, rehearsing in a church hall.[36]

We are in Sheffield, rehearsing in an abandoned school with smashed windows and industrial gas heaters.[37]

We are in a Sheffield, rehearsing in an old factory, above which is a boxing gym. When the guys upstairs are training, their skipping sends showers of plaster falling from the decaying ceiling. The dust and plaster settling like a strange rain over everything. When you look from the set of *(Let the Water Run Its Course) to the Sea That Made the Promise* (1986) to this ice-cold, smashed-up old factory that we call home for five years, you can hardly tell one from the other.

We are making *Some Confusions in the Law about Love* (1989). We seem to change it every time we do a performance. One of those shows that never ever gets finished. Years later, we find texts and videotapes relating to the show and can't figure out what versions they represent. Was this Nottingham? Was this the ICA version? Who knows.[38]

32. In rehearsal, any action with the gun has a real tension about it since many of the performers like to fire the bloody thing. The bangs from the gun (which fires real blanks) are horribly, horribly loud in the studio, ripping through the atmosphere of the work and prompting people to nervously keep their fingers near their ears whenever it is in play. Often in these days, I think about William Burroughs in *The Place of Dead Roads* where he talks about gunshots blowing a hole in the fabric of space and time. I remember in *Marina & Lee* (1991) we used audio from movies (gunfights, brawls, kung-fu fights) to interrupt the action on stage—throwing the performers into chaotic and clumsy fight sequences, jump-cutting the piece to a new place.

33. Years later than this even, Ruby May and a bunch of other kids in the general Forced Entertainment entourage—Miles, Seth, Megan, Jacob, Leon, Izzy—play in the rehearsal studio, using a wardrobe which has been crudely fitted with a 'secret' door in the back to perform imitation magic tricks. The wardrobe has been used in *First Night* rehearsals during a phase where we think the show will have various solo magic acts or tricks in it. At one point prior to this—for research purposes—Richard, my son Miles, and I go to a Magicians' Convention at some seafront hotel in Blackpool on the north-east coast of England. At the convention, we purchase the plans for a number of stage illusions—photocopied plans, which are sold in sealed envelopes. The fronts of the envelopes bear a description of the illusion, but to find out how it is constructed, you have to buy the plans. One night at the same Convention, we watch a very simple close-up magic trick performed by some German guy and we all think it's great. The trick involves a shoe magically appearing in the hands of the conjuror. Six or seven months after the Magicians' Convention, Richard will try to recreate the German guy's shoe trick—we are now in Vienna, drunk, in a bar, following a performance of *Instructions for Forgetting* (2001)—a recreation that will end with a predictable melee of destruction and broken glass.

34. The tape is lost.

35. This story gets told in *The Travels* (2002).

36. Soundtrack: The Fall, *Hex Enduction Hour.*

37. When the guys come to deliver gas canisters, they are wary of Mark Randle and Robin because they are wearing cowboy hats and dresses, and wary of Claire because she has a fake penis and a beard drawn on her face (costumes for *Marina & Lee*).

38. Sometime in 1999, we lodge all of our rehearsal videotapes at the National Sound Archive of the British Library in London. This includes videos of almost every rehearsal hour of everything we made since *Emanuelle Enchanted*, plus some occasional tapes of earlier stuff. Boxes and boxes of it—most of it uncatalogued in anything but the most rudimentary way—tapes labelled by date or in some cases simply by number or letter. What's for sure is that some of the tapes used to document rehearsals also have other more personal stuff on them. It's weird to think that somewhere in the depths of the British Library there is a Hi8 tape marked 'Dirty Work 9' that also has some footage of Seth and Deb running around in the garden, or some footage of a view from a window in a house from years ago.

We are in Munich. Terry drops a glass bottle during *Bloody Mess* rehearsals[39] and the glass shatters everywhere—shards and fragments[40] all over the floor. The rest of the run-through is peppered with attempts to clean the mess up which becomes part of the action.[41]

We are in Beirut. The city is covered in posters for an election—huge portraits, hand painted, almost all of which show these fine-looking Arab guys with extravagant well-groomed moustaches. We are here to do the durational performance *Thousandth Night*—six hours of improvised stories—from fairy tales to personal stories and movie plots, each story interrupting its predecessor and none of them allowed to finish. Beirut seems a perfect location for this performance. That night when we do it, there are many stories in response to the posters we have seen on the streets, all the stories fanciful, playful, absurd: a story about a city in which several men are in love with one woman, the various suitors covering the streets with their portraits in an attempt to seduce her; another story about a city in which the king organizes a moustache competition, and so on. People are delighted—seeing the reality of the city outside pass straight into the distorting mirror of the work.[42]

We are in New York.[43] Richard is in a hotel room putting the finishing touches to a home-made bomb. The bomb is made of broom handles covered in red tape, an alarm clock, and a bit of old circuit board. The whole lot held together on a makeshift harness that goes around the body. It's a kind of perfect 'cartoon ticking bomb'-style bomb. We shoot a load of pictures of people holding the bomb in the hotel[44] and then go out to Central Park and shoot some more.[45] There is snow everywhere. Super-beautiful. Various people pose amongst the snowbound trees with the bomb. The suggestion of an explosion from the toy bomb seems so perfect and delicate next to the tree branches, which look like they will shed their snow at the slightest knock. People are walking their dogs and snowballing in the park. They see us—a group of people standing around and a bomb being passed around—and they just smile and go about their business.[46] Lewis Nicholson is with us and we talk about the beautiful publicity objects he used to make for us—wonderful, oblique, and amazing things that were somehow completely at odds with their supposed function as advertising.[47] Later in the early morning, when we have done the gig and have been drinking a lot in the East Village, we step out of the Ukrainian National Home or the Telephone Bar[48] and Cathy and Claire walk across First Ave (?) having looked right and not left or something and they come very close (i.e. as close as I have ever seen) to being killed by an oncoming car which squeals and slides to a halt just in front of their drunken lurch, the driver looking with a

39. She has been using the water in the bottle to make it look like she has been crying.

40. I am thinking about fragments but in an absolutely different sense. Disconnected from its 'original' place, lacking context, lacking 'beginning' or 'end', lacking place in an argument, lacking 'reason'—the fragment is both statement and question. We cannot know (and can therefore only guess) what the fragment is, what purpose it has, what intention is behind its production or presentation. In this sense and for our purposes (here and elsewhere), the fragment remains an ideal compositional unit.

41. There is an audience at this rehearsal comprising some people from the Big Art Group (who are performing in the same festival, but who won't be able to see an actual performance) and a couple of Russian guys who we think are also part of the festival, but we aren't sure.

42. And the work, later, will pass right back into the world. After we've been back from Beirut for a couple of months, I bump into Walid Raad, an artist who's from the city. He says that six weeks after we had done the *And on the Thousandth Night* ... performance in Beirut, V.—who's the technician of the festival there—had been arrested. I asked why and Walid said: 'Something political,' then laughed—'Oh, not political, nothing important, just drunk and disorderly.' He said that V. had spent three days in jail, in a small cell shared with eight other prisoners. He said that there, in the central jail of Beirut, V. had taught these guys to play the improvised game that makes up the show. They'd passed the days and nights in the cell together that way, telling stories, interweaving tales, none of them ever allowed to finish, moving from true stories and personal stories to fairy tales and movie plots.

43. This is years before.

44. Hotel 17.

45. Hugo is doing the photographs as he has since 1986. When it comes to mid-rehearsal shoots with Hugo, we liked to say that getting the pictures back was a way to see for the first time what you were really doing.

46. This is 1998.

47. A book of burnt matches for *Club of No Regrets*, a note inserted behind the matches bearing supposed directions to the Club itself. A set of price lists for brutal and banal objects and acts for *Hidden J*. A limited edition of handmade maps of an imaginary country for *Emanuelle Enchanted*.

48. Or somewhere else.

mixture of anger, disbelief, and distress like he will be tortured by remembering this near-terrible moment for the rest of his life and they (Cathy and Claire), in fact, will forget all of it.[49]

I remember that E. M. Forster had the advice: 'Only connect.' But in this history (mine) (like any other) (i.e. yours) anything can be connected to anything else. Or else: Everything already contains everything else. Every story is a Chinese box, or a doorway that leads to every other one.[50] *Only connect. Only connect.* Strange—we spent so much of our time in the process of not connecting material but rather trying to keep it separate. Trying to let stuff just sit there as itself: 'as objects,' we liked to say. *The thing is the thing is the thing.* Having admitted that anything might be relevant—anything might be connectable, anything might have a productive bearing on what you are currently doing—we wanted tracks of material, blocks of time that sometimes collided or appeared to meet, but which always, in fact, stayed resolutely separate.[51] We wanted something that would not ever reduce down into a single narrative, a single statement. 'Oh,' we would say, as an insult in rehearsals if the structure ever felt too clear or too collapsed, 'Oh, it's become a play now.'[52]

We did not, it seems, want 'a play', which, for us, became a byword for the homogenized, the pre-packaged, the performance which somehow wanted to deny presence and performance and liveness and insist instead on writing, closure, absence, and fixity. We wanted the unstable. The trembling. The thrill of live decisions. The collision of different materials, different narratives.[53] A theatre that placed you in a world rather than describing one to you. Or which placed you in a situation rather than describing one to you. A theatre in which your agency as a watcher was an acknowledged and known part of the performance from the outset. A theatre that felt more like event. A theatre that made demands. A theatre that was ugly, awkward. A theatre that liked its ambiguities, its undecidednesses, its disconnections. A theatre that was very, very funny, ridiculous, absurd. A theatre where the comedy did not ever quite confirm itself as comedy.[54] A theatre that did not hide the fact that here, in front of you, were a bunch of people doing something. A theatre that critiqued its own language even as it was using it. A theatre that divided audiences. A theatre that could also bring audiences 'together' even as it critiqued that word. A theatre constantly looking to breach its own edges, to step sideways into performance, into installation, into event, into blankness. A vulnerability. A frailty. A provisionality. Home-made. Human-scale. A slipperiness. An air of anti-art. A workmanlike attitude. A rawness. A bleakness. A melancholy. A hilarity. An anger. A lack of compromise. A theatre that insisted on its own time, brought you into collision with its own temporality. A theatre that had no beginning and no end.

And finally, it[55] ends, as it must.[56]

49. These near-deaths are a constant part of the story. Once, after we had done the final performances of *Some Confusions*, at The Leadmill in Sheffield, I watched the lighting designer Nigel Edwards sitting on a scaffolding pole high up in the lighting rig and calmly (without realizing it) undoing the only clamps which were attaching the pole itself to the rig. It was pure cartoon—the guy sawing at the plank on which he himself is standing. I asked Nigel to stop.

50. Maybe this is in fact what we tried to deal with in the durational performance *Thousandth Night*, where the performers improvise many stories from midnight to 6 am, stealing characters, structures from each other, from the general cultural stockpile, and none of the stories allowed to end—a kind of mad fornication of stories, connections, jump cuts, reversals.

51. I think about something that Ron Vawter told me once when I did an interview with him in Belgium. Sitting in a café, Ron said: 'What we tend to do in the Wooster Group, and in my own work, is to appropriate from several different sources at the same time. That way we can juggle all these separate things until the weights are familiar and then a new kind of theatre text is created between these different places.'

52. Notebook fragment (dream): 'She has hypermedia and hypertextual links embedded in her body—when you kiss her hands or her elbows or her eyelids, she opens up to streams of data, opening like a doorway to a hidden kingdom. X could never work out if this hypertextual woman was meant as metaphor or not, and never having met her couldn't be sure ... I mean wasn't sex itself always a kind of hypertext ... the body blossoming in memory and enactment of other loves, other beds, previous embraces ... the texts of the past inscribing themselves into the present to create possibilities, impossibilities, structures, doorways ...'

53. There was a lot of talk at some point about non-narrative theatre. We said we had nothing against narrative at all—in fact, we just wanted lots of it. The best example of this might be the durational performance *12am: Awake & Looking Down*, where the circulation and recirculation of the cardboard signs bearing the names of characters functions as a kind of narrative kaleidoscope. Watching this performance with Miles (in Paris sometime) I realized how very much the work relies on the watcher having certain kinds of cultural knowledge. Most of it was lost on Miles (he was maybe eight or nine at the time) because he didn't know the sources (actual or generic) from which the characters/figures were drawn.

54. This is something of a paraphrase of what the UK performance artist Gary Stevens once said to me.

55. This text, or the rhizome of memories it constructs and contains.

56. In fact, nothing actually ends.

The sound of taped gunshots blows a hole in the fabric of space and time.

Robin closes the curtain and leaves off staring at the audience.

Terry changes costume again.[57]

Cathy screams and yells in gibberish language inside the house centre stage in *Hidden J*, the curtains drawn across the window so she cannot be seen. The other performers listen, and wait, wait until she is done.

Claire watches her own face on video, expression blank.[58]

Huw Chadbourn smears dirt across his face.[59]

Hugo checks the screen on his camcorder as various people from Forced Entertainment and from Richard Maxwell's company sing together 'Goodnight Eileen'.[60]

Will Waghorn watches a photographic print emerge from the fluid in a developing tray, timing the procedure by taking his own pulse.[61]

Vlatka Horvat learns the tech for *Instructions for Forgetting*.[62]

Robin's spectacles are smashed and smashed again.[63]

Susie Williams throws a chair in Sheffield, 1984,[64] and it crashes to the ground in Brussels, May 2004.[65]

Richard (in Vienna in 2000) takes the shoe from his foot, intending a recreation of the magic trick we saw back at the Magicians' Convention in Blackpool—the trick with the shoe that miraculously appears in your hand. The bar in Vienna is noisy. There is hardly space for this. The trick with the trick is to stand on one leg, secretly slip the shoe off the raised foot into your left hand, and then to bring the shoe slamming round suddenly and into the palm of your raised right hand, right in front of the hapless spectator. Richard moves. And the trick begins, except in this case, at four in the morning and a lot of caipirinhas under the bridge, the shoe comes slamming round and misses the hand. It becomes a size-eight torpedo—a shoe flying across the bar. It crashes into a table that is all mountained up with drinks and the glass goes bursting everywhere.

'Oh. You know,' the barmaid says. 'It happens all of the time.'[66]

57. *Bloody Mess* (2004).

58. *Some Confusions in the Law about Love.*

59. *The Day That Serenity Returned to the Ground* (1986).

60. In a bar, very late at night, in the Mousonturm theatre, Frankfurt, Friday, 28 November 2003.

61. *Red Room* (Showroom Gallery, 1988).

62. Ghent, Belgium, 2003.

63. *The Set-Up* (1985).

64. *Jessica in the Room of Lights* rehearsal.

65. I am imagining this, since I am writing in January 2004.

66. And keeps on happening. The glass shards flying out from there in every direction, backwards and forwards in time. Connections spin and multiply. The screen shimmers, cuts to black and then kicks into life again.

Acts of Admittance, Facts of Speech

Joe Kelleher

Altered Situations

When an utterance is made on stage, it changes everything. However mean, fragile, unintended, provisional, or ambivalent, it may be the theatre's only decisive act. Even a dying, even a killing on stage can be reversed, erased, undone. The prone actor stands up again—or we believe they can—or they slip away quietly when the action is focused elsewhere or they come back as a ghost or in another role entirely or as themselves made whole again, as if nothing so sundering had ever happened. But when something is said, it is really said. Even if it is not really meant. Speaking completes its own act. It is the only act that can be guaranteed to do so, if speaking as such is all there is to it. And although thereafter—or even in the moment—the utterance can be missed or misinterpreted, 'taken out of context', disavowed, 'walked back', or otherwise overwritten, it cannot actually be taken back.[1] I make this opening remark while aware of J. L. Austin's exclusion of theatrical utterances, at a founding moment of speech act theory, from the set of utterances worth considering as performative acts, i.e. as speeches that effect a 'doing'. For Austin, there is something 'hollow or void' about words 'said by an actor on the stage', as if language in such situations were being 'used not seriously, but in ways *parasitic* upon its normal use ...'.[2] In what follows, there may be much to support Austin's view of the 'etiolations' of theatrical language; all that I wish to claim for now is that words said or shown on stage are—'in a peculiar way' (Austin's phrase)—decisively said.[3] To borrow a comment from a reflection on Austin's intellectual legacy by the American philosopher Stanley Cavell, a student of Austin's in the 1950s and someone we will be returning to in what follows, 'Human conduct and thought are inherently vulnerable to embarrassment. I can no more take back the word I have given you and you have acted on than I can take back my touch. Each has entered our history.'[4] Or as Matthew Goulish, writing on 'a found-language poetic of error' in Forced Entertainment's work, puts it, 'One cannot unspeak one's already tongue-tied words.'[5]

And there have been many such words. A number of Forced Entertainment shows come to mind—*Speak Bitterness* (1994), *Quizoola!* (1996), *Dirty Work* (1998), *And on the Thousandth Night ...* (2000), *Exquisite Pain* (2005), *Tomorrow's Parties* (2011), and *The Notebook* (2014), among others—where speaking on stage, whether the speaking is improvised in the performance or pre-scripted or a mixture of both, would appear pretty much to be the main thing going on, and in several cases going on for a considerable length of time. What tends to happen in these works is that a certain speech procedure is established. This might be a simple, situational language game, a question-and-answer dialogue, say, or an identifiable but adaptable sentence structure, a form of statement that performs—or purports to perform—an action: of telling, of describing, of proposing, of casting onto the stage (if only a stage in a mind's eye) the imagined and henceforth imaginable. This procedure is then repeated, redone, passed on to another speaker, adventured into, and explored, if not to exhaustion then to a point where some sort of justice will have been done—on this occasion at least—with respect to variation, elaboration, and extenuation. Except, justice never is quite done. Not in every single case, and not fully in any. As soon as this is admitted—and it is admitted in every moment—it becomes apparent that decisive as the act of speaking on stage may be, it is not definitive. So it is, then—to quote from *Tomorrow's Parties*—that 'in the future you will be able to go on holiday in space. Or in the future you'll be able to talk to your dog, using a kind of computer software programme. Or in the future people will be able to shrink themselves really, really small, and set off on an exploration of the atom.'[6] Or to put that another way, the basic form of the language game will be a sort of border operation, negotiating between, on the one hand, what is given out on stage as speech (statements, propositions, and forms of admission that float free, once spoken, from the one admitting to the act) and, on the other, what is taken in by the performers, owned up to, given at least momentary admittance, whether from inside or outside the scene. And if we conceive the 'scene', on occasion, as temporal and imaginal extensions of the 'text', be that spoken or written, then there are more pages—and more sentences—to come, each sentence ready to succeed and stand in for the one being shown or spoken right now. Viewers of Forced Entertainment's 'durational' works, such as *Quizoola!* or *Speak Bitterness*, where the 'pages' are visible on stage (we will return to the matter later) will be familiar with this way of indexing a certain politics of possibility, a possibility of the exterior perhaps—even if that appears as an endlessly un-unfolding 'interior' residue, a hapless capacity for speech. Hapless, that is, if 'text' here can be understood as a means, a medium, for the inscription and transmission of context, whereby the term 'context' implies those attendant processes—motivations, behaviours, histories, and ideological mechanisms—which a certain way of saying something and a certain something said bring into play, sometimes into forceful play, but just as soon let go of again or 'graft' onto another utterance entirely.[7] As if to speak at this border were to trade in the only commodity its economy allows, an exchange of open-handed acknowledgement and face-saving disavowal. All of it underwritten by a simple, accretional fact: that nothing can be unspoken. One speaks, if one can, to alter the situation. One speaks always *to* an altered situation.

Let us take an example, which touches on the mix of themes at issue here, and which is drawn from a work that itself—like a kind of all-in-one variety review—mixes together solo and more collectively distributed language games and theatrical and durational temporalities, alongside a number of explicitly performative modes of stage 'entertainment', including ventriloquism, magic acts, mime, and comedic—and otherwise *perlocutionary* (Austin's term, referring to speech acts intended to affect the listener)—modes of direct audience address.[8] The example in question is a speech made by Terry O'Connor during the 'tea break' section of *First Night* (2001). The scene happens some way into the show, the speech arising as one of a series of attempts on the audience's attention (or patience) just as it appears to emerge from the collective stamina (or impatience) of the performers themselves, standing smiling as they have been at various points in the show—and at various points in the group's career—as a cast, a company, in a line across the stage. O'Connor speaks for a long time—long enough for others in the line to rehearse the time it takes to listen and to drift away from listening, to light a cigarette, to sneak into the offstage darkness to make some tea and return, mug in hand, to listen again while she recites a list of things for the audience not to think about. Things to try to forget, admittances from the world in which this theatre is happening, this performance taking place. 'Forget about chemotherapy and the common cold and chemical warfare. Try not to think about world aid and world leaders and honour killings and mercy killings and children crying in their sleep and men begging for their lives ...'[9] The list goes on, an accumulation of banished negativity in the shape of everything we may have been aware of before we started listening, each sentence overriding the one before, displacing what the audience have already forgotten to forget. O'Connor has acknowledged that the list is too long for her to remember, so some of what she says must be improvised: there is a catastrophic resource, beyond the exhaustions of the text. She has also written about how this and other speeches in *First Night* were arrived at in rehearsal, emerging from an improvisation where the cast were—as we have seen—lined up in silence to face the audience, a desperate, grinning, overly made-up vaudeville troupe with nothing to offer but the spectacle of themselves and a promise of diversion that was broken and betrayed—they know it and so do we—even before it is made. Not, then, a text-*based* performance so much as a situation—a scene—from which language emerges as a deliberate and necessary act of utterance. An attempt at referentiality (there's a world out there), and an attempt at second-person address (there's an audience out there too), formed of phrases that come with all the 'quotation marks' of theatrical speech (and to that extent *parasitic*, in Austin's sense), from those who happen to be there, whose turn it is to speak.[10] 'It fills time', O'Connor writes, 'like a metronome, a journey of small steps, in and out of differing orders of linguistic connection, as much about gaps, the thinking, as the words.'[11]

As for the thinking that resonates in that time, in those gaps, in the negotiation between words and their articulation, there is something to note of the speakers themselves. In saying this, what I am trying to get at is a sense audiences may have in the theatre that they know or intuit or witness how it goes for the performers. Not that we know those people 'personally', but that we register something—in how they go about doing what they do—of what it is to act, to decide, to take one's turn, and to admit (or evade) responsibility: to

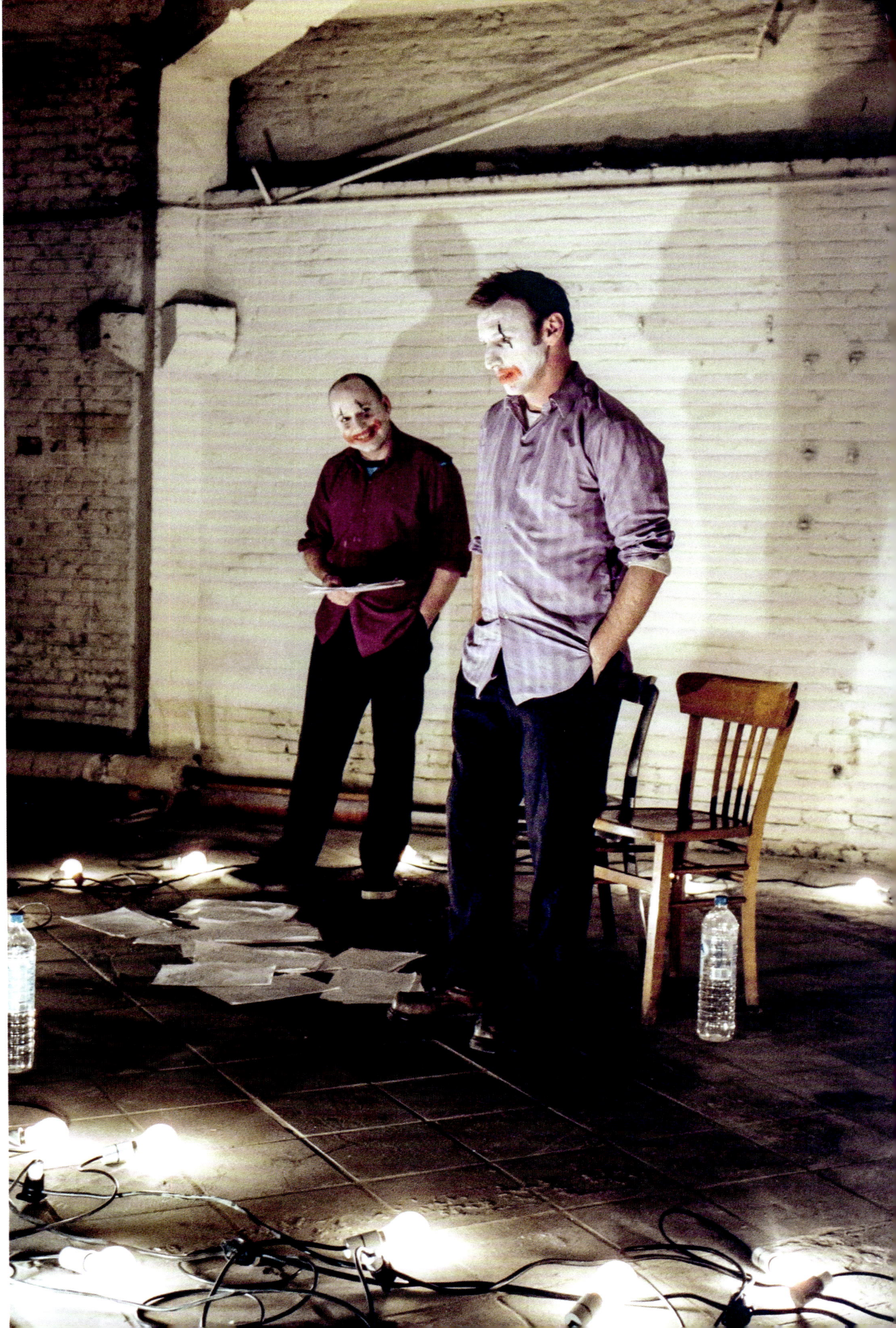

think through the moment one is in, and to recognize in that moment other moments, like and unlike it, one has been through before. Put it like this. In the spoken sentences, the dialogues and the utterances of a Forced Entertainment performance—as much as in the 'gaps' between the sentences, or in the pre-emption of another's speech, or in those moments where speaking appears a matter of anticipation, of prior commitment, of embarrassment, of induced enjoyment—there is a sense of what philosopher Paolo Virno refers to as a re-enactment of *anthropogenesis*. That is to say, a 'staging [of] the fact of speech' that becomes appropriate 'every time our lived experience is forced to retrace the essential steps of our becoming human.'[12] In Forced Entertainment's work it has to do, I suggest, with the tendency—already alluded to—towards turn-taking, a taking up by each speaker in the immanence of speech, as it were, of the responsibility to speak, in a situation where speech is (for one reason or another) necessary, required. And required not in the sense of some content that needs to be uttered but in the more fundamental sense of an act that reclaims the mere 'fact' of human speaking, where that fact is at stake—and at risk. At the same time, however, these speech acts are indeed re-enactments. And further, this invoked anthropogenesis—this new-born speech that infuses the company's work, at once inventive and rehashed, contingent and pleonastic, decisive and provisional, and sometimes infantile—is performed by speakers who have clearly been around the houses somewhat, who are—themselves—anything but 'new-born'. Arguably, this was the case even in the early works that rehearsed an 'evolution' of human speaking, by young performers who already assumed that evolution as natural history.[13] Speakers, that is to say, as 'seasoned' as the marooned-in-hell vaudeville artistes of *First Night,* or the exhausted clowns of *Quizoola!*, or the be-suited 'we survived even ourselves' figures of *Speak Bitterness*, or the middle-aged men in cable-knit sweaters reading out boys' words in *The Notebook*, or the capable theatre professionals of *Complete Works: Table Top Shakespeare* (2015), who live after Shakespeare's time, in the long afterlife of the Shakespearian theatre, and therefore know all the plots of the plays. Actors all, who know too that if the word said on stage changes everything from hereon, then this itself is something that has been known—and said—before. And who—if they do, if they have to speak—do so now out of a renewed necessity, some specific conjuncture serious enough to call again for the decisive act to be performed: to say, 'I speak.'

Flapping Around, Recomposing

It can happen like this. Somebody is on the stage, speaking about the things that frighten them. As we might say, admitting to fear, the fear 'inside', owning up to it, speaking it out loud; and at the same time, giving admittance to things on the outside that provoke that fear, acknowledging them, letting them in, however uncomfortable it may be to do so. I say somebody. It is an actor, one of the performers in Forced Entertainment's *From the Dark* (2016), a once-only performance which played throughout the night, from sundown until dawn the next morning, to close the Berliner Festspiele's 2016 *Foreign Affairs* festival. Partly with this essay in mind, I had gone to Berlin specially. But the impulses that accompany us from one place to another are rarely unmixed. The previous evening in London certain friends were being celebrated and honoured, although by midnight we were all following breaking news on those little devices we carry around these days, about an attempted coup in Turkey, reading out to each other the half-ready stories as they were coming in, understanding little enough of what we were relaying. Loved ones, world events, disconnects and connections, an early flight, sleeplessness, the usual baggage of concerns and fragilities, of affections and enthusiasms and confusions that any of us bring along to the occasion of the theatre. And which the theatre admits of us, this theatre particularly. And now here is somebody on stage, a working actor between routines it looks like, left behind by the others, still wearing the costume from the previous routine, a pantomime animal suit or some daft skeleton outfit, his face exposed and speaking, and my attention is pulled by the weight, the delicacy, of something being said out loud.

At various points during the night each of the performers will make a speech of this sort. A recital of personal fears, some of which I recognize as my own. I scribble words down in the dark. 'I'm frightened that I can't give the people I love the things they want.' Or: 'I'm frightened of not sleeping, that I'll get into the habit of not sleeping and everything will disintegrate. I'm frightened of hallucinating, that I'll do something stupid.

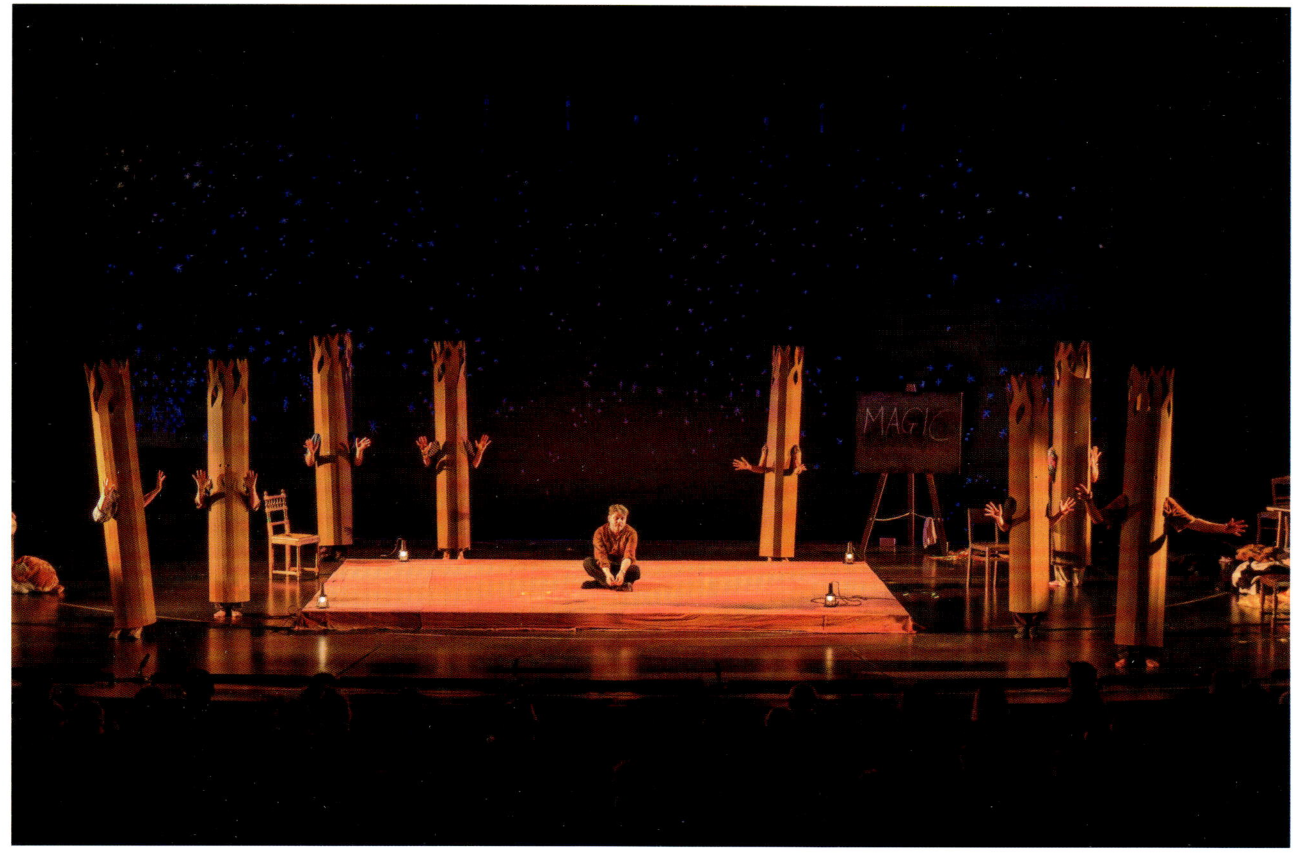

And it'll all be because I didn't sleep.' One detail will stick with me, among all the fears that are spoken of. It could easily have been lost, but it landed somehow. The performer speaks of a trapped bird, 'flapping around' the room he is in. Followed by the line that will end each of these speeches: 'And that is all that I am scared of.' The determined finitude of that last sentence may strike us as contestable, not defining a limit so much as an open window through which a stranger animal enters, and where the difference between fearing something and sharing a room—or sharing a world—with it is still to be decided. As if, on the outside of whatever is admitted to fear there were another more capable way of being with others, and of being with ourselves.

From the Dark is essentially a redo of another work, the twenty-four-hour *Who Can Sing a Song to Unfrighten Me?* (1999), which involved recurring sequences of unlikely magic acts and sideshow demonstrations, mock-transformations of human and animal, as actors in synthetic animal suits perform feats of 'dying' to apathetic onstage applause, living thing and dead thing exhausted in indifference, with occasional disturbances of bad-tempered cardboard trees, some rather befuddled Halloween-costumed skeletons, and episodes of improvised storytelling (since developed as the stand-alone durational work *Thousandth Night*). One element given greater prominence in the Berlin performance is the recital of personal fears, which occurs throughout the night as a sort of loquacious time out, between the more ostensibly 'spooky' acts of presentation and pretend. A certain facing up to fears, then, accompanies us in this lit theatre as the dark hours pass outside, as if keeping company in this way—with each other, and with the theatre itself—could secure us, however precariously, from a world in which fear, the real frighteners, at whatever scale you want, and in whatever corners of your life you do or don't want it, has become nothing short of a global political-industrial complex. But which, in the terms in which it is sold to us or we sell it back to ourselves—as security, as taking back control, as protection: protecting borders, protecting trade, protecting 'identity' and 'values'—is rarely enough acknowledged as fear.

And perhaps this is where the politics starts out on this occasion, from contestations around this basic admittance, these ready admissions of fear, this acknowledgement on the theatre's part of that which leaks into (or out of) our sense of ourselves, provoking our self-preserving belligerence as much as it persuades us to care, to take good care. I am minded of that frightened bird, a glimpse of animal panic recomposed as a figure of speech, a crumb from the common parlance that is being churned over on stage: something 'flapping around'. And I am thinking about this night-long performance and the sort of speech that is squeezed out of it as another kind of flapping around, but slowed down enormously, not so as to make the exits—the windows and doors—easier to find, i.e. not in order to effect an escape, but to acknowledge the fact, the enduring fact, of an altered situation. For the performers—or for the figures, the subjects, the personages that the performers represent—it has to do, I imagine, with an experience of alterity per se. A kind of creaturely alterity released by dying on stage again and again and again, to which the no less persistent reclamation of humanness, through speech, action, and thought—that anthropogenesis, perhaps, that was mentioned earlier—bears constant witness.[14] For ourselves who share the hours with them, the altered situation impresses itself upon us, I suggest, as an experience of proximity, of being among others, our mortal kind, who see—as I presume to do—what is going on. With these acknowledgements something else has arrived in the room, and the recitation of fears—or the telling of tales to keep the night from ending—may be only a kind of cover story, a textual placeholder for that bruised understanding, that blanker realization.

Of course, theatre has been speaking over the blanks for some time. There is an essay I often return to when thinking about how a certain sort of theatre works: not Forced Entertainment's theatre but that of written drama, 'classic' plays by Shakespeare or Ibsen for instance, plays that are frequently restaged, and which we go back to—so the author of this essay suggests—as readers, as spectators, because we sense there is something that we have to remember, something that we have already seen, seen countless times, but which we are inclined to deny or disavow or refuse admittance to. The essay, written in the 1960s, is by Stanley

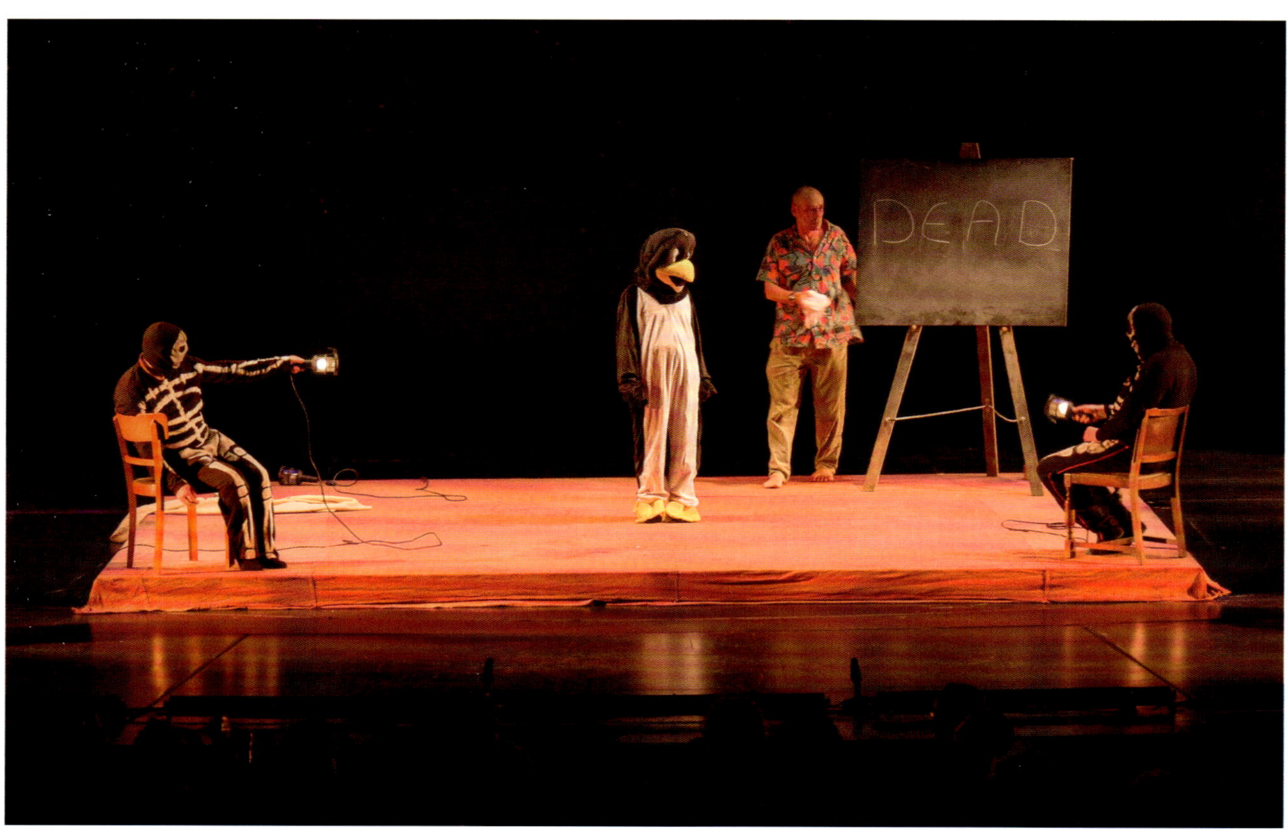

Cavell (who we have referred to already as a mid-twentieth-century student of J. L. Austin) and is called 'The Avoidance of Love: A Reading of *King Lear*'. It appears in Cavell's first book, *Must We Mean What We Say?* In short, Cavell reads Shakespeare's *King Lear* as a play in which the characters seek to avoid—or refuse to acknowledge—what they are all too able to see, and which they fear that others will recognize in them: in Cavell's words, that we are too often, in our hiddenness, silence, and fixity—not unlike spectators at the theatre—'helpless before the acting and the suffering of others'.[15] Not least the acting and suffering of those we love and are loved by. For Cavell in the mid-1960s, in an era when local and global violence and injustice— the complicities of which Cavell as an American was fully alive to—were being brought home to many as televised spectacle, but at a time too of radical experimentation in art, politics, and ways of living, there were ethical and political issues at stake in this structure of avoidance. As he puts it, 'Why do I do nothing, faced with tragic events?'[16] In pursuing this question through the avoidance of love in the old dramatic theatre, Cavell develops an argument about how a certain dramatic and theatrical form does what it does. The ways it works on us—or used to, before we no longer knew 'what there is to acknowledge' or 'what is and is not a political act, what may or may not have recognisable political consequences.'[17] And so we go back to the plays—to the dramas, to the texts—for something we feel we need to remember, something to do perhaps with lessons in feeling, which might still inform our own capacity to act. And what we find there are ways in which avoidance and non-acknowledgement cause people to be killed and countries to be laid waste, while enacting—in the theatrical situation where such stories are told and played out—complex, asymmetrical structures of implication and involvement. These are not, it might be noted, the sorts of associations we have been glimpsing in Forced Entertainment's work—with non-human creatures actual and imaginary, talking dogs, talking trees and skeletons, future computerized subjects, and the like—but rather involvements more typical of dramatic theatre's human-in-human scene. That is to say: of actors with characters, characters with other characters, and fictional characters with the present audience, who watch them act and suffer. Except, in a performance of a tragic play, Cavell suggests, the audience are not 'there' for the characters in the ways that the characters are 'there' for the audience, and not because we are different kinds of creatures from each other but because we are unable to acknowledge those others completely as creatures such as ourselves. This is as much to do with a failure to acknowledge other people as separate from us, i.e. to acknowledge separateness as intrinsic to our creaturely condition, as it is about claiming kinship or community in likeness.[18] As it is, we are unable in the theatre to 'go up' to the actors' world, in ways analogous to our inability to be fully present to others and what matters to them in the actual world, in our own historical 'now'.[19] And so we watch terrible events unfolding. And when we return to them it is because we are obliged to do so, as Forced Entertainment do in a piece like *Dirty Work*, verbally re-inscribing the pageant of events and their 'tragic if predictable consequences'.[20] Or as the company do in *Complete Works*, replacing the actors and characters with ready-to-hand household objects; replacing the field of action with a tabletop, a surface manageable by just one person; and replacing the action with a spoken chronicle–a temporalizing operation that dispassionately recalls each of the small deaths in the Shakespearian dramatic oeuvre, including perhaps 'the death, and the call for the death … of drama and hence of society, as they had been known'.[21]

Things, we might say, are different now. Times change. By which I mean, something would appear to have altered in the quality of that 'now' to which a subsequent theatrical aesthetics is called upon to respond. An alteration in the way that the times—and time itself—are represented and perceived. We can sketch some coordinates. The very now in which—to recall Cavell—acknowledgement and acceptance would be completed, in which we would 'be present' at last to what matters and to others, as much as to ourselves, this present has been absorbed since the late twentieth century into an increasingly pressured and ungraspable temporality. The late cultural critic Mark Fisher wrote of a 'normalization of uncertainty', of a 'generalized debt crisis that hangs over all areas of capitalist life and culture' and which is 'ultimately about time.'[22] At stake, as Fisher puts it, in times of decreasing solidarity and increasing insecurity, is a politics of time, characterized—especially in the digital, internet era—by the stretch between 'continuous partial attention' and 'insomniac overstimulation', and—we might emphasize—by an increasingly explicit economization of human relations. We can glimpse the latter on the faces of the *First Night* troupers, maintaining for the supposed punters their ingratiating stretched grins from the get-go until the end, which cannot come soon enough. At the same time—it is not just a figure of speech—the times have multiplied: we live, as it were, in several contemporaneities at once. If this has to do with transformations of the social imaginary, in response to extensions of the globalized social body and of the localized *polis*, it has to do, too, with transformations of the ecological imaginary, as the others that matter—they were always there—and who need to be acknowledged for the sake of all, come to include not just other humans but animals, avatars, and other 'actors', other material—and immaterial—things.

But then, it was always mixed up, as the company informed us relatively early in their career—as it were, in more analogue times—in the group lecture performance *A Decade of Forced Entertainment* (1995). There they sketched out verbally their own sense of the coordinates on a map of the UK. They recorded the facts: political and industrial conflict at home, a decade of Conservative Party rule, the demolishing and 'reconstruction' of British city centres, ecological disasters and other events abroad, Bhopal, AIDS, famine in Africa, the Gulf War and its ghostly TV mediations. They named the names: Rodney King, the Guildford Four, Boris Yeltsin, Arthur Scargill. And they situated their work amongst it, the facts, fantasies and trash, the royal weddings and the celebrity deaths—those acts of history contiguous with these, their own acts and appearances— giving admittance to it all. And how could they not. As they say in *Decade*, more than once, 'We knew something strange had happened to time.'[23] The present was filling up again with memory. Although, this was no nostalgia—irrespective of a certain melancholia—but something akin, rather, to the 'new kind of memory' that science historian Isabelle Stengers has called 'pharmacological knowledge', which is all to do with an ecology of acknowledgement in the wake of the altered situation: as she says, 'a memory of the unintentional processes that in the past were able to bring about the disappearance of cities, empires, or civilizations, and of the ravages caused by our simplistic industrial, and even "scientific" strategies.' 'And this memory', Stengers insists, 'is now part of the present.'[24] Given the historical subjects we are, it is ours and cannot be wished away. A 'normalization of uncertainty' indeed, which happens to have located itself (or so it may appear) in the ruins of the theatre, where action and intention and consequence are (as they always have been) encountered as shadows of themselves.

We would seem to be in the realms of a certain scepticism, which we can define in general as a kind of perennial doubt, concerning the grounds on which we ordinarily make sense of the world and times that we share, even as the times spiral into absurdity and bewilderment. The sort of doubt that expresses itself, as Cavell would say, as the 'quintessential human wish to escape the conditions of human knowing and speaking, to escape, as I sometimes put the matter, the human.'[25] Forced Entertainment's work has, of course, been forcefully linked with a certain 'scepticism of the real' endemic to turn-of-the-century European and North American 'postdramatic' theatre, emergent in the long wake of poststructuralist thought.[26] I want to suggest, however, something of a shift in the function of theatrical scepticism, attendant upon these other shifts and alterations we have been noting. Put briefly, in Cavell's reading of the classic drama, scepticism functioned as a dramaturgical architecture of refused acknowledgement, structuring the drama's crises of knowledge, attachment, and responsibility. In Forced Entertainment's work—which, it should be said, displays a degree of faith in or commitment to 'ordinary language', to ways of speaking and showing that are fundamentally available to those who come and watch—scepticism might be taken as a kind of troubled attunement to the times that henceforth begs a question—which we will return to at the conclusion of this essay—of how to 'inhabit' the times, how to dwell amongst others, in criticality for sure, but in all complicity too. For the moment, rather than the invisible scepticism, as it were, of a structuring architecture, we observe instead scepticism 'put on' as a presentational façade, an attitude, a tone of voice, a look. A look, for instance, that provokes one to ask: do I *know* what that person is thinking or feeling (or even *if* they are thinking or feeling anything at all)? Or a tone of voice, a perceived twist of the common tongue that turns out not to be a twist at all. It twists the way the world twists. It admits to twisting like that.[27]

And so the performers line up—typically at the start of things, or at the edge of things, anyway there on the stage—exposing themselves to acknowledgement (and exposing their audiences to a reciprocal act of acknowledgement, which can seem sometimes like an act of confrontation) before speaking has even begun. It is a timeless kind of image, but when speaking does begin, it turns out to be altogether subject to time, to economic time, which cuts in—not least in the durational works—not when the ecosystem has run down but when the agreed hours are up; which is something they admit to from the start. And so the first nights are also the last nights, ways of gathering up the remains of all the evenings, remains which—as in redos like *From the Dark*—are no less harnessed for economic ends, including the footlights and ox-blood curtains, the wigs and the make up and the wardrobe collection, costume rails included, left behind by another theatre: the dramatic theatre perhaps that was here some time before. And where, over many years, the work can appear to function as a kind of receiving house, or hospitality machine, for performance remains of all sorts, for whatever dirty work is still on the playbill, and the imagining of all tomorrow's parties. And where the recurrent and regenerative expansions and contractions of the collective—speaking for now of the company themselves—who are no doubt responsive to the needs and circumstance of production and to the events of accident and chance that make up a working life, can *seem* also to be responding to fluctuations and mutations in the larger social body amidst which life is lived and the work is made. There are always fears, figures, familiars, and others claiming admittance. Sometimes it is a simple matter of letting them in. For instance, throughout *12am: Awake and Looking Down* (1993)—another of the long durational works—the cohabiting ghosts are not even spoken of but simply, literally, given passports to the stage, their names written on cheap cardboard signs held up by the performers. 'Young white racist electrical engineer'. 'One Bavarian Princess'. 'Elvis Presley, the dead singer'. 'Emily'. After a while, if you stay there long enough, they appear to be coming around again. Repeating, recycling. From the TV, from 'current affairs', from everyday life or from roadside graffiti or from our personal and collective dream history. Or from other Forced Entertainment shows. Even this same show. The actors, it appears, are okay with that, interpreting the variations loosely enough, finding no doubt new inflections in the old encounters, although at certain points even they don't seem really to be frightened any more.

Aftershock Time

But then, what might we mean by actors here? In an interview on the Berliner Festspiele website, Tim Etchells speaks of the night and uncertainty, of how 'the night is often a place where you can be thinking, but in which you can't yet act to solve or deal with things.'[28] Of course, just as much as the night can be a place where we prepare ourselves for decisive action in the morning, it is also where we accommodate ourselves to the disturbances of the day, train ourselves to admit and also to accept, give ourselves reasons not to act. Either way, to act here is meant presumably in the sense of 'to do', as in to intervene, to 'go up'—to recall Cavell's phrase—into the scene itself, the scene of the world or the scene of ourselves, so as to do something about it. One acts to alter the situation or one's relation to the situation. Sometimes though it can seem as if the act— whatever act or event might be performed or pretended to—has in a sense already happened, the bird is in the room and gone before being spoken of, and everything is taking place in aftershock time, in an already altered situation the consequences of which may be still unfolding. Acting, then, may after all be a matter of playing pretend with the remains. Which these performers are seriously expert at. Not least when it comes to pretending and persuading us that the remains are all there is.

I have alluded already to what appears a ruination of theatre in Forced Entertainment's work: the recycling of 'classical' scenographic elements, such as footlights, costume, wigs, make up, scenery—to which we can add a free-handed dealing with the no less classical dramaturgical elements of character, narrative exposition, soliloquy, dramatic form and structure, and so on. It is no secret either that a certain ruination of the *dramatic* theatre has been a significant theme of commentaries on the contemporary theatre and performance scene, particularly since the 1980s and 1990s, during the company's formative years.[29] To speak too broadly of complex matters that have attended a real liberation in both theatre practice and its critical understanding, a summary of topics highlighted in this discourse—informed by a concatenation of intellectual currents from feminism and post-structuralism to ecocritical and postcolonial critique, as well as by a wealth of radical, experimental practice in the theatrical and wider performance arts—would include undoing the supposed authority of the playwright, destabilizing the ego-centred fictional character, and confounding spectatorial absorption (readerly absorption, perhaps) and the sorts of aesthetic, and political, distancing that sustain it. Factors contributing to this ruination, then, would include the polymorphous affectivity of performing bodies; the ubiquity of electronic media since the latter part of the twentieth century; a realigning of what Hans-Thies Lehmann has referred to as the theatrical spectator's 'response-ability' around experiences of phenomenological perception rather than processes of narrative identification; and the frequent assertion that the 'text'—as playwright Julia Jarcho puts it in a recent critical summary of this discourse—'is no longer in charge'.[30] Jarcho's account, which opens with a measured statement of indebtedness to Etchells' work as a writer with Forced Entertainment, begs the question of whether the text or the playwright was ever really in charge. But she then goes further, arguing that certain exemplary textual practices in the theatre have been invested in a 'utopian' project of effecting a 'heightened negativity', precisely to 'push against the experience of the present', as she puts it, to attack, explode, hyperbolize, and contest the 'burden of actuality' of the present as such.[31] As if, the function of sceptical thought now were not so much to provoke a 'completing' of our being-present to each other but to hold up the present to critical, quizzical—even exasperated—scrutiny.

In these lights, the remains, as it may be—not only of the 'dramatic' text, as spoken on stages where plays have been shown—but also the show-trial text, the father of the bride's wedding-speech text, the bingo master's patter text, the dying comrade-in-arms text, the game-show contestant's text, or the visionary (or not so visionary) street drunk's text—are relics of who knows how many unconscionable presents, and as such remains of a long, dispersed speaking that may still—if only because speaking *tends* to go astray—bring to the present occasion something of a discombobulating potential. This potential resides also in the sense that these remains—be that a practised speech itemizing personal fears or a list of imaginary names written out with marker pen on pieces of box cardboard—are at once theirs and theirs only, and at the same time scavenged somehow. Not least when they take the form of actual, physical text. And so we have the cardboard signs; the loose sheets—piles of them—of typed paper; the various versions of bound codex, notebooks, scripts, chronicles; the banner or neon titles at the back of the stage; the index cards that end up in the author-performer's hand; or the scraps of writing we never get to see clearly, pulled out of a pocket and passed down the line, messages, memoranda, instructions from elsewhere which someone here will have to read out loud.[32] And that is how speaking will often as not happen—as somebody reading something out, rehearsing one or another discursive protocol: the report, the broadcast, the private prayer, the confession, the diary entry, the sales pitch, the note to self, the unaccustomed-as-I-am public speech at a private party, or the ventriloquist's dummy's coerced welcome, on the first and every other night of the run. And doing so in a way that exposes the speaker as themselves, as somebody real we might presume to recognize (it is 'Robin', it is 'Cathy', it is 'Claire' or 'Richard' or 'Tim' or 'Terry' or 'Jerry' or 'John' or 'Wendy'); and at the same time some ultimately evanescent figure spawned by the situation, a shadow of others, other selves, gone before.[33]

For instance, the passages of unison speech in *The Notebook*, a performance adapted from Agota Kristof's novel of the same title, where the way of speaking on stage is not only determined by the source text (the performers obliged to read things out as they find them, to occupy the rhythm that the text imposes) but also 'cultivated' in autodidactic isolation by the fictional twins that the work brings to life. As if what the speakers are seeking to do is to accommodate themselves, with all economy of thought and action, to the peculiar hospitality of the text. Which they do as readers—not as orators or reciters but simply as readers—those for whom, as poet Lisa Robertson puts it in a beautiful reflection on the practice of reading, the written text 'furnishes hospitable conditions for entering and tarrying' and a 'charitable structure [that] permits my own detailed dissipation', opening to the sort of 'thinking' that 'moves across the shadowed commons of the codex to be politicized by chance, where chance is a stranger'.[34] And 'politicized', we might suggest, in however 'dissipated' a fashion, to the extent that here, now, the readers are actors, responsive in their every moment—i.e. through every moment that they present themselves on the scene, before witnesses such as ourselves—to the externality of an event, an action, be it one of accident or chance. War, as it is experienced by the boys in Kristof's story, is

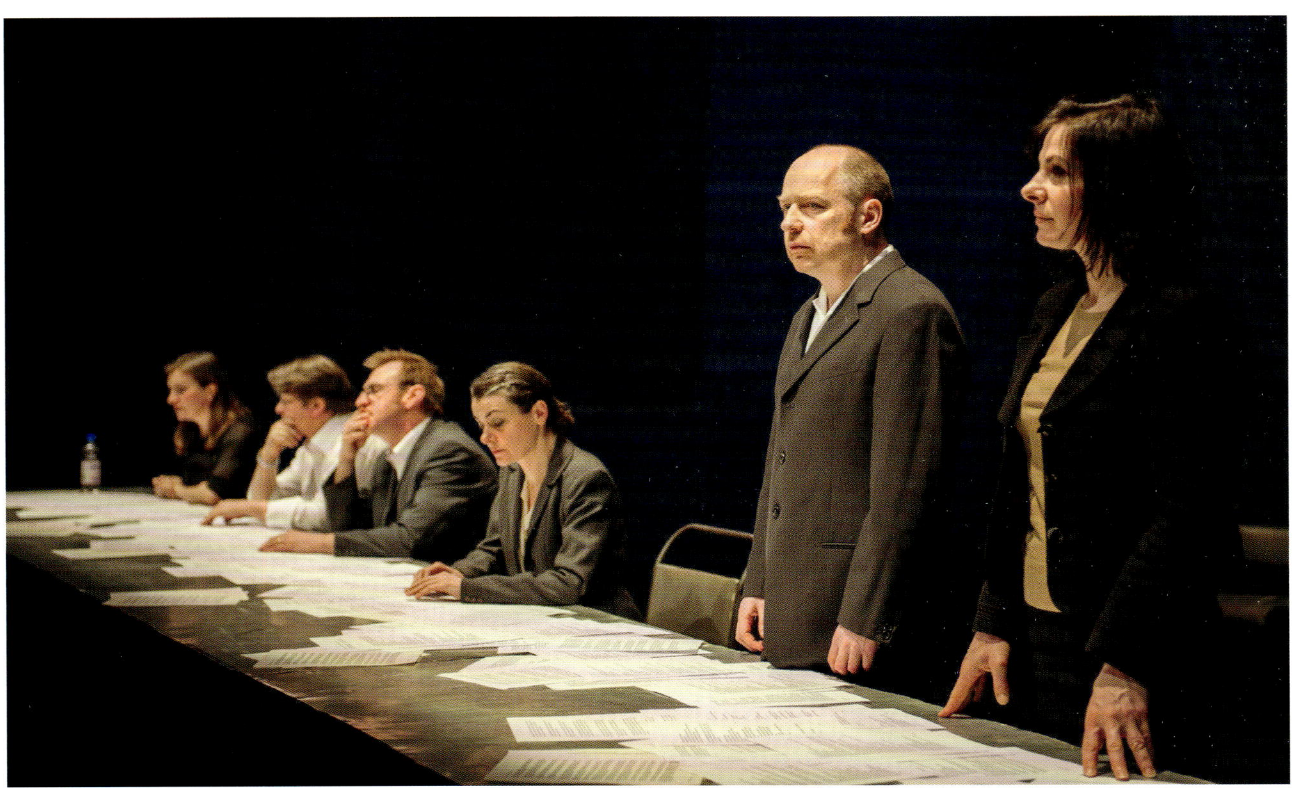

one such event, although the story is also about how they train themselves—as far as they can—to take charge of contingency, and, through the written chronicle, to situate that contingency—and the present of this recording—in history. What they witness in the course of this self-training, we may surmise, instils in them something of that 'pharmacological knowledge' that recognizes the event as a consequence of actions, actions such as they themselves might commit.

And so these people come forward into the light, pick up the text and read it out, actors after all. Actors, though, who are only intermittently the heroes of their own act, at times brought into being by the act of another, even when that other was themselves, left behind on the other side of a decision, an admittance, a doing, and a complicity from which there is now no turning back, and which has them speaking again in the uncertain moment as citizens of the irreversibly altered situation.[35]

If I centred this essay on one of the most recent Forced Entertainment performances I have attended, 2016's *From the Dark*, then I want to move towards a close through mention of the first, which for me was *Speak Bitterness* in 1994, a decade into the company's career: a textual work if ever there was one, in which the company members—speaking individually in the first-person plural—nurse a complicity that is, strictly speaking, their own but is ready to leach into everyone else's. It is anyway a work all about admittance and admission, in which over a couple of hours—and in later iterations, for much longer—the performers approach a long table at the front of the stage that is covered with sheets of typed paper, from which they read out what sound like confessions. Mostly one-sentence confessions, covering any possible sin of commission or omission, no matter how trivial or outrageous, that might be imagined. There is no act that cannot be acknowledged, owned up to, admitted. And above all, admitted of themselves. 'We were dead meat. We stand accused of Saturday nights and Monday mornings. We were jealous in a sensational manner. We used supermodels in war documentaries—they were excellent. We were poisoners. We put the last buffalo to sleep.'[36] Critic and Marxist theorist Fredric Jameson has written of how we might experience and share with each other, however fitfully, a sense of history—the history we make and are part of, history as it enters our lives, even as historical forces function at a scale that far exceeds the span of our individual existence—through an awareness of generationality. That is to say, a sympathetic 'opening onto the existence of other people and of the collective', which might reveal—for certain generations at least—the 'coexistence and solidarity, for good or ill, of "my" contemporaries'.[37] As Jameson proposes, 'The experience of generationality is … a specific collective experience of the present: it marks the enlargement of my existential present into a collective and historical one, one somehow associated, if not by specific collective acts, then … by that intimation of praxis which is the "mission."'[38] And what a mission. I quote at random: 'We made a soap for black people. We told long boring anecdotes. We worked for £2.90 an hour. We gave Helen fifteen minutes to pack her bags and get out of the house. We never thought; we never danced at weddings. They invented a new classification of lunatic just for us. We wrote biographies without bothering to research or ask permission.'[39] Jameson goes on to speak about generationality as 'a kind of narrative we seek to impose on a recalcitrant present, mastering it in view of a triumphant story of the future'. He suggests that if the present is 'the time of enunciation' then the present of the generation is also 'the time of collective enunciation of the attempt to say "we" (after the awakening of the "us").[40] I don't know, as someone 'of' their generation, if I have really thought of Forced Entertainment as aspiring to speak for a generation, their own or anyone else's—maybe that sort of presumption belongs to earlier times. What Jameson's words help me to think about, however, are ways in which the performers apprehend a certain historicity of the present. And what they—the performers, the actors—do appear to be doing, in this work and others, is speaking, with some apparent apprehension but also with evident relish, from the place of the irreversibly altered situation, and starting to chronicle—in words and actions they attribute to themselves—if not what brought the current situation about, then everything that was done under cover of it happening. Picking up the debris, recomposing, and, as they do so, churning into words that which neither begins with them nor ends with them, a kind of vernacular practice.

Vernaculars, of course, can be conservative instruments, tools for codifying—and enforcing obedience to—certain group identities. But they can also be a means by which to enact more provisional and critical forms of dwelling, alongside others with whom the life and work has happened and been shared. To cite Robertson again, the vernacular is that which 'loosely gathers whatever singular words and cadences move a given situation, a given meeting, as it is being lived by its speakers'. It is, she writes, the name 'for the native complexity of each beginner as she quickens', in each moment 'beginning again and again with the pandemonium at hand in the present', an 'illustriously useless poesis' by which the citizen derives her *domus*, her habitation, her place of protection and resting, of thinking, talking, and working.[41] And as they, the company we are speaking of here, have derived their vernacular, and—I would say—borne its politics and lived its history, through cadences and other devices and protocols, verbal and non-verbal: from the star-spattered backdrops; the running on the spot; the line-ups, the buck-passing; the reading out (never easy: it embarrasses the hands and stains the air); the turn-taking; the urgency, the lassitude; the lists; the bad wigs; the shame (oh, the shame); the drunks and the empty bottles; the chairs that look like ordinary chairs; the curtains that look like something to do with the theatre or something to do with UK 1970s light entertainment TV; the descriptions of the world as if, as if; the melancholy of the early works: 'This is how the nights are when it rains'; the melancholy of the middle works: 'No more my love, no more my love, no more'; and then the shouting, the overacting, the grandiloquence at times, the way they ring the false hollows of the world to chime with a kind of truth; and then the staggered departures from the group, from the stage; no real exits, more like drifting away, slowly going; the self-assembly sets; the whispering on stage; the descriptions of worlds that are much like this one but somewhat verbally altered; the gathering up of everything that this world has said in the words that it said it with: 'We said we'd make the world less like *The Simpsons* and more like *The Waltons*' (who remembers that?); and then the staying with the material, its rhythmic existing; and the stretching of the material to drain it of affect; the chaos of the work running to catch up with the chaos of the world; but also the consideration of the work for what it is able to accommodate and for what doesn't quite fit; which it acknowledges in the thing's remaining, its flapping around, its passing through and out.

1. The irreversible utterance is as much a feature of public life as of staged performance. The familiarity to our ears of various terms of retraction reminds us of the stakes of embarrassment. Embarrassment and shame, although I do not go into these in the current essay, resonate throughout the work of Forced Entertainment. For an extended discussion, see Nicholas Ridout, *Stage Fright, Animals and Other Theatrical Problems* (Cambridge: Cambridge University Press, 2006).

2. J. L. Austin, *How to Do Things with Words* (1962; Oxford: Oxford University Press, 1976), 22.

3. Ibid. It is around this same passage that Jacques Derrida launches his critique of Austin's take on the performative speech act and elaborates a key statement of his own account of the fundamental iterability of texts and utterances. See Derrida, 'Signature Event Context', in *Limited Inc.* (Evanston: Northwestern University Press, 1988). Austin's work on speech acts and 'performatives' has been taken up by a number of authors whose writings have been profoundly important for performance studies scholarship. A brief hit list would include, along with Derrida's work, books by Judith Butler—from *Gender Trouble* (London: Routledge, 1990) to *Excitable Speech: A Politics of the Performative* (London: Routledge, 1997)—Andrew Parker and Eve Kosofsky Sedgwick's *Performativity and Performance* (London: Routledge, 1995), and Soshana Felman, *The Scandal of the Speaking Body: Don Juan with J.L. Austin, or Seduction in Two Languages* (Stanford, CA: Stanford University Press, 1980). Invaluable reflections on the implications of this intellectual tradition for theatre practice and analysis–especially as regards writing in the theatre–appear in W. B. Worthen's 'Drama, Performativity, and Performance', *PMLA* 113/5 (October 1998), 1093–1107, and the introduction to his *Shakespeare and the Force of Modern Performance* (Cambridge: Cambridge University Press, 2003). It is worth noting that Austin was a significant intellectual influence for the American philosopher Stanley Cavell, who contributed a preface to the English translation of Felman's book (above) and whose thought informs the current essay.

4. Stanley Cavell, *Little Did I Know: Excerpts from Memory* (Stanford, CA: Stanford University Press, 2010), 322.

5. See Matthew Goulish, 'Compendium: A Forced Glossary', in this volume, 274. For another essay-length account of the company's speech-based performances, see Gerald Siegmund, 'The Dusk of Language: The Violet Hour in the Theatre of Forced Entertainment', in Judith Helmer and Florian Malzacher (eds.), *Not Even a Game Anymore: The Theatre of Forced Entertainment* (Berlin: Alexander Verlag, 2004), 207–19.

6. Forced Entertainment, *Tomorrow's Parties*, video trailer (2011), http://www.forcedentertainment.com/project/tomorrows-parties/, accessed 2 October 2020.

7. The allusion here is to Derrida's work, and 'the possibility of disengagement and citational graft which belongs to the structure of every mark, spoken or written'. Derrida, 'Signature Event Context' (see n. 3), 12. For a provocative development of the theme, which chimes with my focus on alteration, see Joseph Grigely, *Textualterity: Art, Theory, and Textual Criticism* (Ann Arbor: University of Michigan Press, 1995): 'For me a context is not so much a space surrounding or accompanying a text … as it is a process or *activity* of spatial enactment' (7).

8. Austin, *How to Do Things with Words* (see n. 2), 101.

9. Terry O'Connor, 'Virtuous Errors and the Fortune of Mistakes: A Personal Account of Making and Performing Text with Forced Entertainment', *Performance Research*, vol. 14/1 (2009), 88–94, here: 91.

10. The 'scene' and theatricalized 'quotation marks'—along with the concept of a re-enacted *anthropogenesis* (see below)—are all essential components of philosopher Paolo Virno's discussion of the act of speech as an 'absolute performative', in Virno, *When the Word Becomes Flesh: Language and Human Nature*, trans. Giuseppina Mecchia (2003; Cambridge, MA: Semiotext[e], 2015).

11. O'Connor, 'Virtuous Errors and the Fortune of Mistakes' (see n. 9), 92.

12. Virno, *When the Word Becomes Flesh* (see n. 10), 60.

13. O'Connor, 'Virtuous Errors and the Fortune of Mistakes', (see n. 9). O'Connor discusses how the company's early pieces appear retrospectively to explore an evolution of human language, before the full emergence of the textual works (as discussed in this chapter).

14. The stage 'death' is a regular trope in Forced Entertainment's work and has been the substance of an entire piece, 2008's *Spectacular*. Tim Etchells: 'We've been dying from the early shows like *Let the Water* … with its glorious competition of tomato-ketchup movie deaths right through to the later works like *Bloody Mess* with its blank diva-death at the centre, a scene which Cathy claims with comical bombast will "break something inside you forever". No one's fooled.' Programme note for *Spectacular*, https://www.forcedentertainment.com/notebook-entry/spectacular-programme-note-by-tim-etchells/, accessed 2 October 2020.

15. Stanley Cavell, 'The Avoidance of Love: A Reading of *King Lear*', in *Must We Mean What We Say? A Book of Essays* (Cambridge: Cambridge University Press, 2002), 267–353, here: 338.

16. Ibid., 339.

17. Ibid., 346, 347.

18. For an extensive discussion of goings on in the 'last human venue', i.e. the contemporary theatre of urban modernity, where such claims and acknowledgements are negotiated and contested in the work of Forced Entertainment and others, see Alan Read, *Theatre, Intimacy and Engagement: The Last Human Venue* (Basingstoke: Palgrave Macmillan, 2009).

19. Cavell, 'The Avoidance of Love' (see n. 15), 331.

20. The phrase functions in the show as a kind of textual refrain to the kaleidoscopic catalogue of catastrophic and spectacular enactments invoked by the two seated, speaking performers. Forced Entertainment, *Dirty Work*, online clip (1998), http://www.forcedentertainment.com/project/dirty-work/, accessed 2 October 2020.

21. Cavell, 'The Avoidance of Love' (see n. 15), 353.

22. Mark Fisher, 'Time-Wars: Towards an Alternative for the Neo-Capitalist Era', *Gonzo (circus)*, 110 (2012), https://www.gonzocircus.com/exclusive-essay-time-wars-towards-an-alternative-for-the-neo-capitalist-era/, accessed 2 October 2020. Forced Entertainment have been dealing with 'uncertainty' since their earliest work.

23. For the text of *A Decade of Forced Entertainment*, see Tim Etchells, *Certain Fragments: Contemporary Performance and Forced Entertainment* (London: Routledge, 1999), 29–47. My recent re-encounter with this piece, however, was not through the published text but a recording, held in the British Library, of a 1995 performance at the ICA in London. Although devised and first presented in 1994 as a celebration of the company's (then) longevity, the 1995 performance was convened to draw attention to the threat of withdrawal of UK Arts Council funding and the company's possible imminent demise. The cultural politics around that decision appeared to be an extension of the landscape the group were identifying in this and other works.

24. Isabelle Stengers, *Cosmopolitics I* (Minneapolis: University of Minnesota Press, 2010), 35.

25. Stanley Cavell, *Cavell on Film* (Albany, NY: SUNY Press, 2005), 365. Cavell's career-length engagement with philosophical scepticism was thoroughgoing and profound. For a concise overview, see David MacArthur, 'Cavell on Skepticism and the Importance of Not-Knowing', *Conversations: The Journal of Cavellian Studies*, 2 (2014), https://uottawa.scholarsportal.info/ottawa/index.php/conversations/article/view/1100, accessed 2 October 2020.

26. Liz Tomlin, *Acts and Apparitions: Discourses on the Real in Performance Practice and Theory, 1990–2010* (Manchester: Manchester University Press, 2013). It should be noted that the philosophical scepticism that underwrites Tomlin's book derives in the main from the Derridean post-structuralist deconstruction of the metaphysical premises of much Western thought. It is also to be mentioned that her account includes a thoroughgoing deconstruction of the reinstatement of the 'real' in 'postdramatic' theorizations of turn-of-the-century European theatre, derived from Hans-Thies Lehmann's work in the 1990s (translated into English in 2006, but already influential in anglophone theatre practice and theory by then). See Lehmann, *Postdramatic Theatre* (London: Routledge, 2006).

27. I am thinking here also of Etchells' more recent textual-sculptural work, outside the context of Forced Entertainment, in neon and LED. The illuminated phrases reach into a common lexicon and phraseology. We immediately 'get' them, while being offered the opportunity to linger (given the neons are not going anywhere soon) on how these utterances—if that is what they are—are even so 'getting away' from themselves. For examples, see http://timetchells.com/projects/?numPosts=12&pageNumber=1&year_filter=&category_filter=neon-led&action=projects_loop_handler, accessed 2 October 2020.

28. Anne Phillips-Krug, 'How Did This Seriousness Get There So Quickly? An Interview with Tim Etchells' (2016), https://blog.berlinerfestspiele.de/how-did-this-seriousness-get-there-so-quickly/, accessed 2 October 2020.

29. In Forced Entertainment's case, Beth Hoffmann offers a salutary counter-note to the theme of dramatic (or at least theatrical) ruination: 'If diverse live art practices can indeed be unified by a desire to critique dominant performance models, as Etchells observed, the language of continuity and expansion of "theatre" might also apply, and yet the language of rupture and break remains more common, familiar and persuasive.' Hoffman, 'Radicalism and the Theatre in Genealogies of Live Art', *Performance Research*, 14/1 (2009), 95–105, here: 98.

30. Julia Jarcho, *Writing on the Modern Stage: Theater Beyond Drama* (Cambridge: Cambridge University Press, 2017), xii. For 'response-ability', see Lehmann, *Postdramatic Theatre* (see n. 27), 185. A compact—and often-cited—account of the narrative referred to here, appears in Elin Diamond's introduction to Diamond (ed.), *Performance and Cultural Politics* (London: Routledge, 1996), 3.

31. Jarcho, *Writing on the Modern Stage* (see n. 30), 3–7. It might appear from my brief citation that Jarcho is also evoking a certain scepticism. She does not, however, draw the philosophical framework for her argument either from Derrida (as Tomlin does) or Cavell (as I do) but from an earlier twentieth-century source, the Marxist critical theory of Theodor Adorno. The Theatre Studies-specific scepticism with regard to the authority of the playwright is indebted to W. B. Worthen, e.g. *Drama: Between Poetry and Performance* (Hoboken, NJ: John Wiley, 2010).

32. As Tomlin reminds us, the deconstructive strategy of presenting the script as a visible object on stage has a venerable avant-garde tradition. Tomlin, *Acts and Apparitions* (see n. 26), 65. For an account of that tradition see Elinor Fuchs, *The Death of Character: Perspectives on Theater after Modernism* (Bloomington: Indiana University Press, 1996).

33. Sara Jane Bailes itemizes a range of Forced Entertainment's onstage language techniques and writes also of the sort of stage persona that draws on characteristics of the performer's offstage 'self'. See Bailes, *Performance Theatre and the Poetics of Failure* (London: Routledge, 2011), 19.

34. Lisa Robertson, 'Time in the Codex', in *Nilling: Prose Essays on Noise, Pornography, the Codex, Melancholy, Lucretius, Folds, Cities and Related Aporias* (Toronto: BookThug, 2012), 9–18, here: 12, 17. I am grateful to Carl Lavery for introducing me to Robertson's work.

35. This theme is owed to Alenka Zupančič, *Ethics of the Real: Kant, Lacan* (London: Verso, 2000).

36. A fragment of the *Speak Bitterness* text runs over several pages of Tim Etchells, *Certain Fragments: Contemporary Performance and Forced Entertainment* (London: Routledge, 1999), 179–90, here: 189.

37. Fredric Jameson, *Valences of the Dialectic* (London: Verso, 2009), 524.

38. Ibid., 525.

39. Etchells, *Certain Fragments* (see n. 36), 182.

40. Jameson, *Valences of the Dialectic* (see n. 37), 526.

41. Robertson, 'Untitled Essay', in *Nilling* (see n. 34), 71–87.

One Thing after Another: The List as Theatrical Form

Theron Schmidt

Every year it's the same thing. There's a new batch of theatre students, many of them drawn here out of a belief that each of them (already!) has something deep inside them that they need to share, and that if they can do it with enough sincerity and conviction, or if they can inhabit a character with enough authenticity and depth, then this expression of their individuality will make the world a better place. Some of them may well be right about this. But that's not what I ask them to do. Instead, I say, we're going to make theatre, yes—but let's make a theatre without make-believe situations, without what you think are realistic dialogue and scenarios, without plot and character development, without crafted motivations and psychological depth, and above all, without self-expression. Typical response: a line of blank faces. If none of these things, then where do we start? Well, I suggest, we could make a list.

We could, for example, start by reading headlines of disasters. We could start with a list of confessions. We could start by travelling to arbitrary locations around the country and telling each other what we found there. We could start with a man in a shabby skeleton costume explaining all the reasons that the show used to be better than it was. We could start with someone wearing a handwritten sign with the word 'LIAR'. We could start with two dishevelled clowns squabbling over the arrangement of the chairs. We could start with a pair of costume racks and a pack of short character descriptions scrawled on cardboard signs. We could start with a deck of hundreds of questions and ask them of each other all night long until we're no longer sure what we're saying. We could start by welcoming the audience while wearing fixed smiles on our faces, or with a cartoonish bomb taped to our chest, or simply by describing scene after scene of possible beginnings of an imagined show.

This is a list of opening moments in the work of Forced Entertainment.[1] A list like this starts to sketch some of the expanded possibilities for the kinds of propositions that the theatre-event can offer. There is a sense of liberation and possibility in such a catalogue, and it's that sense that I hope to evoke in setting this task for those new students when I go on to ask them to make their own lists of imagined opening moments—and am rewarded with a wild compendium of proposals for pitch-black rooms, sudden congregations of non-human animals, various configurations of one-to-one confrontations between performers and audience members, and so on. That we are able to imagine such a range of possibilities is testament to the contribution made by companies such as Forced Entertainment in stretching and probing what can count as 'theatre' and what kinds of experiences it can accommodate.

But the list offers something more. In addition to its individual elements, the form of the list itself offers a way of reorienting one's relationship to theatrical form, and points to an alternative to the model of theatre based on self-expression and depth of meaning. Indeed, my cursory list above already highlights a recursive tendency in Forced Entertainment's work, in which lengthy sections of their performances, and even entire pieces, are themselves structured like lists, with sequences of propositions that work iteratively through a category or idea for an extended duration. In *First Night* (2001), for example, Terry O'Connor lists everything she wants us to 'try not to think about' or to 'forget about' while we are in the theatre tonight, a list that over twenty minutes evokes traffic accidents, illness, personal embarrassment, and ultimately 'everything you've ever read' and 'everything that's ever been written' and 'everything that's ever been invented or made'; or two-thirds of the way into *Bloody Mess* (2004), Davis Freeman and Jerry Killick, both naked except for a flimsy cardboard star each is holding in front of him, take turns suggesting a series of hypothetical 'beautiful silences' that they want to summon—the feeling when a baby that has been crying all night finally

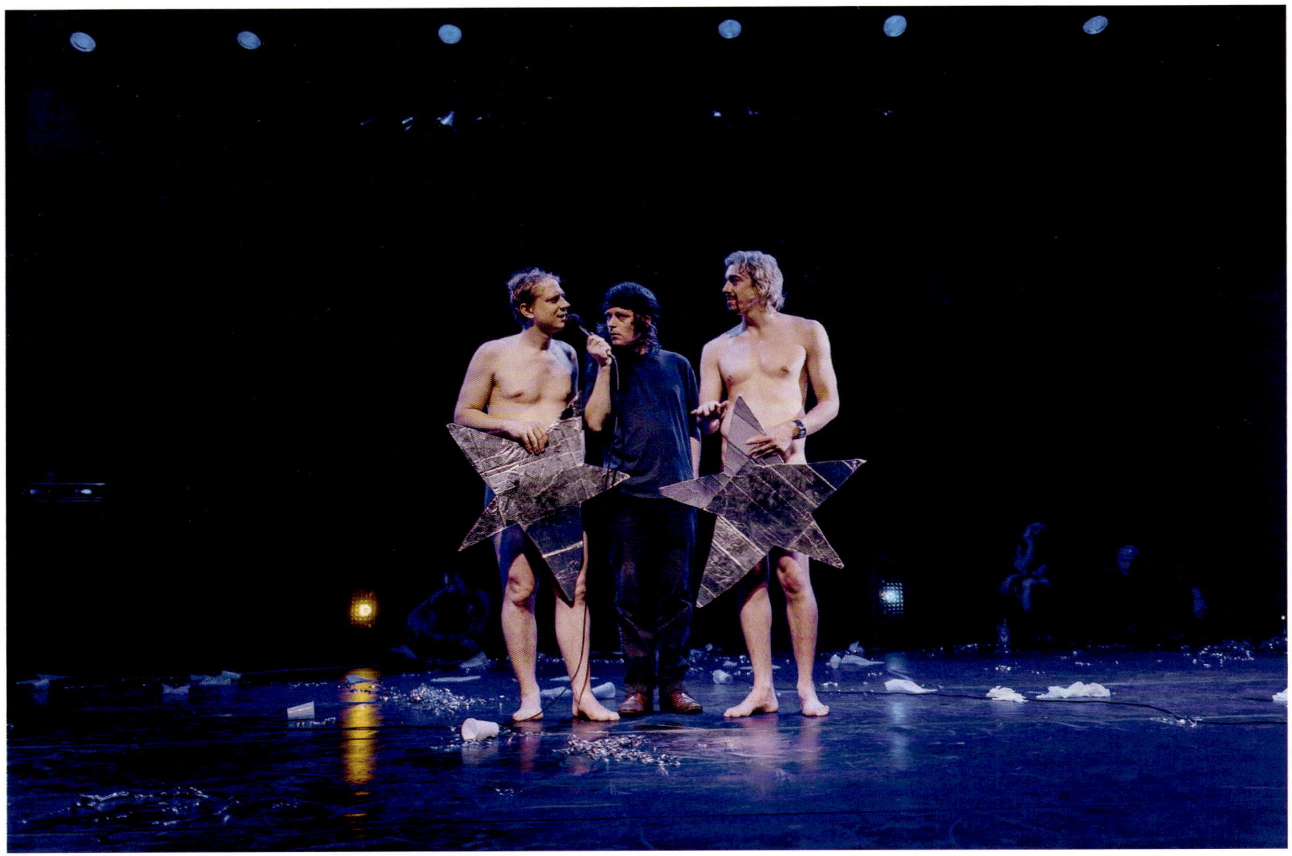

stops, for example, or the moment when a family member's life support system has been turned off—but the accumulating list of possible silences displaces the possibility of such a silence ever being realized in the theatre; or there's the entirety of *Tomorrow's Parties* (2011), in which two performers propose hundreds of different possible futures for humanity—a world without nations, or where we are all criminals, or where food is pumped into our houses in pipes, or where everything is pretty much the same as it is now.

What is it that is so compelling about the structure of the list? What does it enable? As a mode of organizing text and action, the list provides an alternative to the narrative or scenario-based dialogue that characterizes 'drama'.[2] A list reveals rather than conceals its formal aspects, foregrounding processes of composition, selection, and assembly. As a compositional strategy, the list is in the same family as chance operations, automatic writing, found text, cut-up, and other forms of 'conceptual writing' that deliberately subvert the intentionality of the autonomous, authorial voice.[3] Its register is that of the mundane minutiae of everyday life, possibly giving a glimpse of systems that are bigger and smaller than the individual: the shopping list, the police blotter, the shipping forecast, the online feed.[4] It is episodic rather than narrative, presentational rather than representational, paratactic rather than linear. It is characterized by repetition and regeneration, either through the explicit structure of anaphora, returning to the same set of words ('try not to think about …'), or following an implicit organizing principle or pattern. It's a closed circuit, an autopoietic loop, setting up its own rules and conditions and then fulfilling them, in an act of performative self-realization.[5] The list doesn't *mean* anything.[6] It is what it is. It is what it is a list of.

And the list is also what it leaves out; it is always partial, always incomplete, its final fulfilment always an impossible task that only gets further out of reach the longer the list goes on.[7] In this way, the list is not only a self-producing mechanism but also generates an affective field of desire and deferred satisfaction, leaving us wanting more.[8] In the tension between the seemingly prescriptive nature of the structure and the actually infinite ways of playing within it, space opens for improvisation and deviation, for doubling-back and folding-in, for testing the limits of the rules.[9] Recalling the process of making the list she performs in *First Night*, O'Connor writes: 'The list starts as a loose attempt to cover "everything" and then Tim arrives to whisper again, "just bad stuff" and eventually the text finds a freedom and a form in that constraint.'[10] Themes and sub-themes emerge; patterns manifest and dissipate; there are beats and rhythms and eddies of thought. Rather than the classic 'Yes, and …' rule of improvisation, building to a satisfying conclusion, we have the anti-rule of 'Yes, *or* …', leading to endless digression: 'Yes, that's beautiful …', Killick and Freeman take turns replying to the other during the list of silences in *Bloody Mess*. '*Or*, let's have the kind of silence that …' The failure to complete the list is a productive failure, generating branching outcomes and unfolding possibilities. 'How long can this go on?', we might catch ourselves thinking, as the two performers seem not to notice that they are naked, but we do, and maybe there's a pleasure of recognition in our shared frailty, our fallibility, in this unfinished moment.

And in the end, this mutual face-off between performers and audience is what is at the heart of almost every Forced Entertainment show. The dramaturgy of the list is one of accumulation and exhaustion, in which our attention to any one element is impossible to sustain. Instead, what endures is the presence of the actors in front of us, their act of performing, their durational entertainment; even as they exhaust the form they are operating within, they persist. Indeed, even the line-up of performers facing the audience, that recurring feature of Forced Entertainment's work, is like the list in visual form—a dramaturgy of pure frontality, of the flatly presentational, of the literal theatricality of the work being done: here we are, saying these things.[13] Stripping away story and character and scenario and everything else those theatre students have in mind when they come into the classroom, what's left is a flat ontology, nothing backstage or hidden from view, no people or things standing in for other people or things, just one thing after the other, one thing next to the other.[14]

This, and also *this*—not the part in relation to the whole, nor the whole as the sum of the parts, but each part in relation to each part.[15]

This, or what about *this*?—each new proposition revising what came before and what is still to come.

This, and then *this*—like life itself. Like a list of their works. Like the list *is* their life—

> *Jessica in the Room of Lights, Nighthawks, The Set-Up …*

One thing after another—

> *… Showtime, Frozen Palaces, Pleasure …*

Over and over—

> *… The Thrill of It All, The Last Adventures, The Coming Storm …*

For thirty-nine years—

> *… The Notebook, Real Magic, Out of Order …*

And still going—.

1. Works referenced are *Pleasure* (1997), *Speak Bitterness* (1994), *The Travels* (2002), *Spectacular* (2008), *Hidden J* (1994), *Bloody Mess* (2004), *Emanuelle Enchanted* (1992) (and also *12am: Awake & Looking Down* [1993]), *Quizoola!* (1996), *First Night* (2001), *Showtime* (1996), and *Dirty Work* (1998).

2. The list plays a central role in Hans-Thies Lehmann's idea of 'postdramatic theatre'—not as a specific element that he singles out but rather as an organizing principle for the entire book, which returns again and again to lists of shows, qualities, and tendencies. For example, 'Postdramatic theatre demonstrates the following characteristic traits: parataxis, simultaneity, play with the density of signs, musicalization, visual dramaturgy, physicality, irruption of the real, situation/event.' Hans-Thies Lehmann, *Postdramatic Theatre*, ed. and trans. Karen Jürs-Munby (1999; London: Routledge, 2006), 86.

3. 'Our emphasis is on work that does not seek to express unique, coherent, or consistent individual psychologies and that, moreover, refuses familiar strategies of authorial control in favor of automatism, reticence, obliquity, and modes of noninterference.' Craig Dworkin and Kenneth Goldsmith (eds.), *Against Expression: An Anthology of Conceptual Writing* (Chicago, IL: Northwestern University Press, 2011), xliii–xliv.

4. This taxonomic impulse is perhaps best illustrated by one of Tim Etchells' pieces outside of Forced Entertainment, the encyclopaedic series of one-sentence definitions in the virtuosic monologue *Sight Is the Sense That Dying People Tend to Lose First*, written for Jim Fletcher: 'A table has four legs. A prison cell has four corners. A window is an opening in the wall of a room built by people who want to see outside …', and so on, for an hour. Other list-based works by Etchells include the video work *100 People* (2007), an accumulation of characters conveyed only by a series of brief descriptions in white text on a black screen; his recurring interest in taxonomies and footnotes, in works such as 'In the Silences: A Text with Very Many Digressions and Forty-Three Footnotes Concerning the Process of Making Performance', *Performance Research*, 17/1 (2012), 33–37; or the tabloid-style posters advertising dystopian contests and sensationalist spectacles which he published online every day for the entirety of 2011, collected in the publication *Vacuum Days* (UK: Storythings, 2012).

5. 'While all other kinds of machine produce something different from themselves, autopoietic systems are simultaneously producers and products, circular systems that survive by self-generation.' Marvin Carlson, introduction to Erika Fischer-Lichte, *The Transformative Power of Performance: A New Aesthetics* (London: Routledge, 2008), 7.

6. 'Writing as *doing* displaces writing as meaning.' Della Pollock, 'Performing Writing' (1995), in Peggy Phelan and Jill Lane (eds.), *The Ends of Performance* (New York: New York University Press, 1998), 73–103, here: 75.

7. 'Nothing seems simpler than making a list, but in fact it's much more complicated than it seems: you always leave something out, you're tempted to write etc., but the whole point of an inventory is not to write etc.' Georges Perec, 'Notes on the Objects to Be Found on My Desk' (1976), in *Thoughts of Sorts*, trans. David Bellos (Jaffrey, NH: Verba Mundi, 2009), 11–16, here: 14.

8. 'Repetition's force is the force of desire for more.' Eirini Kartsaki, *Repetition in Performance: Returns and Invisible Forces* (Basingstoke: Palgrave Macmillan, 2017), 7.

9. 'How can I break this? What kind of fun can I have with the rules of this game, this form? Or how can I modify, expose, weaken or otherwise intervene so that it can do something that I might really need it to do?' Tim Etchells, 'Step Off The Stage', in Daniel Brine (ed.), *The Live Art Almanac* (London: Live Art Development Agency, 2008), 7–16, here: 11–12.

10. Terry O'Connor in Tim Etchells, *While You Are with Us Here Tonight* (London: Live Art Development Agency, 2013), note 4.

11. 'Failure *works*. Which is to say that although ostensibly it signals the breakdown of an aspiration or an agreed demand, breakdown indexes an alternative route or way of doing or making.' Sara Jane Bailes, *Performance Theatre and the Poetics of Failure: Forced Entertainment, Goat Island, Elevator Repair Service* (London: Routledge, 2011), 2.

12. 'Theatre's mimetic practices themselves become the stuff of endurance.' Lara Shalson, 'On the Endurance of Theatre in Live Art', *Contemporary Theatre Review*, 22/1 (2012), 106–19, here: 113.

13. This serial theatricality can also be seen in the work of Forced Entertainment's contemporaries, such as Jérôme Bel's literalization of song titles in *The Show Must Go On* (2002); Lone Twin's catalogue of heroic deaths in *Daniel Hit by a Train* (2008); Eva Meyer-Keller's systematic demonstration of modes of killing inflicted on cherries in *Death Is Certain* (2002); Ivana Müller's durational tableau vivant in *While We Were Holding It Together* (2006); or the spoken renunciation from the theatre of every material and conceptual entity in Mette Edvardsen's *No Title* (2014).

14. 'Flat ontology argues that all entities are on equal ontological footing and that no entity, whether artificial or natural, symbolic or physical, possesses greater ontological dignity than other objects.' Levi R. Bryant, *The Democracy of Objects* (Ann Arbor, MI: Open Humanities Press, 2011), 246.

15. 'The example stands neither in the relation of part to whole, or of whole to part, but rather of part to part.' Aristotle, 'Prior Analytics (69a)', in Jonathan Barnes (ed.), *The Complete Works of Aristotle: The Revised Oxford Translation* (Princeton, NJ: Princeton University Press, 1984), 110. Giorgio Agamben discusses this passage in 'What Is a Paradigm?', in *The Signature of All Things: On Method*, trans. Luca D'Isanto and Kevin Attell (New York: Zone Books, 2009), 9–32.

The Art of the Impossible

Séverine Ruset

In a recent interview, Tim Etchells distinguished two strands in Forced Entertainment's performances: 'In parallel to the long line of our work on the impossibility or absurdity of theatre as a venture, there is a whole strand that explores the possibility of bringing the impossible or the unstageable into the room via language rather than via enactment.'[1] Drawing upon pieces which are representative of each strand—unless they bring them together, such as *Spectacular* (2008), which presents both the failure of a 'play' to occur and the attempt of a character to compensate for its absence by narrating it—this essay charts some of those impossibilities in order to highlight their political potential as they paradoxically generate new possibilities for the artists and audiences alike.

Unliveable Fictional Worlds

The fictional worlds of Forced Entertainment are marked by failure to such an extent that impossibility appears to be woven into their very fabric. Failure does not just stem from the figures on stage and their inability to make decisions appropriate to their circumstances—even though Forced Entertainment's works do have a penchant for 'losers'—this failure defines the fictional worlds in their entirety. In some cases, the figures who people these worlds cannot complete their tasks, in others they cannot break away from them— in any case, they cannot escape their ill fate. As a result, they often convey the feeling (or the evidence!) that they are almost or already dead. In *Void Story* (2009), a couple ventures through a thoroughly dystopian world, endlessly on the run, picking up major injuries along the way; they are moving through a world that cannot be 'lived in' by characters such as they. In *First Night* (2001), the contrast between the fictive and the real is much less accentuated, as the work relies on a metatheatrical framework recurrent in the company's oeuvre. There again, calamity prevails. Starting with the actors' original pledge to entertain with 'nothing unpleasant', none of the promises contained in the work's fiction of theatre are kept. As Lyn Gardner reviewed it, 'Everything goes wrong but the performers' smiles remain fixed, as on corpses where rigor mortis has set in'[2]—they are condemned to provide, seemingly in spite of themselves, 'forced entertainment'. The company thus confronts us with fictional worlds that constantly challenge human possibility, both in the sense that they deprive their 'characters' of the ability to control their lives and smother their compassion for the sufferings of others, as demonstrated by the surge of competitive and sadistic acts in *First Night*. This alone is not enough to qualify these worlds as impossible by the standards of the possible worlds theory as it is applied to literature, which, to put it in a nutshell, defines a world as impossible when it transgresses logic and the principle of identity, thus revealing itself as nonsensical. However, that notion of impossibility is present too in the work of Forced Entertainment, in which the fictional worlds barely hang together.

Failing Theatre

Forced Entertainment favours abrupt interruptions of storylines to branch off into new unexpected ones, together with entanglements on ontological levels (made particularly acute in those instances where the audience is left wondering who is expressing themselves at a given moment, the actor or 'the character'). They impair both the cohesion of fictional worlds and the delineation between the real and the non-real. Although this work is very carefully constructed, its dramaturgy often appears discontinuous and incomplete, thus precluding the possibility of theatrical illusion. Even in *Void Story*—which, despite its title, presents us with one of the most unbroken narratives in Forced Entertainment's oeuvre—the way the story is conveyed undermines fictional congruence. It is both projected on a central screen through collages of cut-out images and voiced by four narrators, who animate the images, so that we witness not only the adventures of the characters but also the actors who are vocally playing them, and playing with them. Discrepancies between what is told, the way it is told, and what is shown are numerous, creating a dynamic contrast between the drama of the situations and the often comical friction of the visual, textual, and vocal means through which they are expressed. 'Kim. Oh look, a human heart still beating / Jackson. They need some kind of radical clean up in this city.' This fragment of dialogue illustrates how Forced Entertainment, while presenting the 'impossible or the unstageable … via language rather than via enactment', do not smooth over all impossibilities: incongruities keep corroding the fiction. This is particularly manifest in *Spectacular*, where a man in a skeleton suit undertakes to tell us what should have taken place onstage, had most of the components of the show he was supposed to be part of not mysteriously vanished. If one might briefly entertain the idea that he will help us 'get the [missing] picture', we soon realize that his descriptions fail to reconcile the antithetical fragments we are left with. Albeit in a counterfactual conceit, performance inevitably appears as an impossible hotchpotch in a Forced Entertainment show, the company being resolutely unwilling to construct a consistent dramatic world, let alone fulfil audiences' common expectations about what a theatre event should or could be.

Why such reluctance towards completion? Why do Forced Entertainment repeatedly keep the fictions they bring to the stage from cohering? In *At the Sharp End* by Peter Billingham,[3] Etchells expresses the idea that 'the theatre has a problem because, of course, even when the stage is big, it's still small' and yet 'it has all the pompous and ridiculous ambition to bring the whole world in all its glory and all its comedy on to this stage'. Deflating such ambition is a cornerstone of Forced Entertainment's theatre. This is particularly obvious in metatheatrical productions such as *First Night* and *Spectacular*, which thematize the inability of theatre to live up to expectations, but it seems that the limitations and inadequacies of theatre are generally emphasized in the work through the impediment of theatrical realization. In contrast to traditional forms of political theatre, which bank on the efficiency of theatre and regard it as a key place to address reality, Forced Entertainment's theatre productions undermine their chosen medium. They do so not only by attacking the integrity of fictional worlds but also by questioning the value of theatre per se, particularly with regards to death, which they keep representing in consciously unsatisfactory ways that emphasize the impossibility of fully conveying its reality on stage, while highlighting the irrelevance of the resulting performance in the face of the horrors of our world, as the skeleton of *Spectacular* illustrates: 'Sometimes I think about the whole edifice of theatre. What's all that about then? … Sometimes I think the whole thing is just a bit insulting, really. There's me, dressed like this. And then there's people dying in, I don't know, Iraq …' Forced Entertainment's productions thus regularly put theatre to the test by underlining its limitations. This is not to say that they take a nihilistic turn by asserting their work as worthless or politically impotent. Their playing with impossibility paradoxically eschews sheer negativity as it questions theatre in a way that does not prevent the production of political meaning but provides stimulation by sharing its responsibility with the audience.

Outstretching Theatre—When Impossibility Regenerates the Theatrical Experience

Let's consider the way Forced Entertainment's theatre tends to portray itself as an impossible experience doomed to failure. By depriving the audience of a well-rounded ready-to-enjoy show, the company actually makes room for them to increase their part in the theatrical event. The fragmented aspect of the productions, which often consist of a montage of disjointed narratives and performative acts, does indeed invite spectators to discern differences in what is taking place on stage, and to make up for missing connections, in ways which can only be personal in the absence of imposed meaning. In addition to this agency, in the metatheatrical pieces, the audience is encouraged to reflect upon their responsibility within the theatrical process. For instance, when the fictional actors ponder on audiences' reactions and motivations ('Why are they laughing?') in *Spectacular* or confront them squarely in *First Night* ('You're not the kind of people who are afraid to go home because your lives are empty … You're not these kinds of people, are you?'), they make us think about the sort of audience members we are, as well as about the way our demands—both explicit and implicit—impact

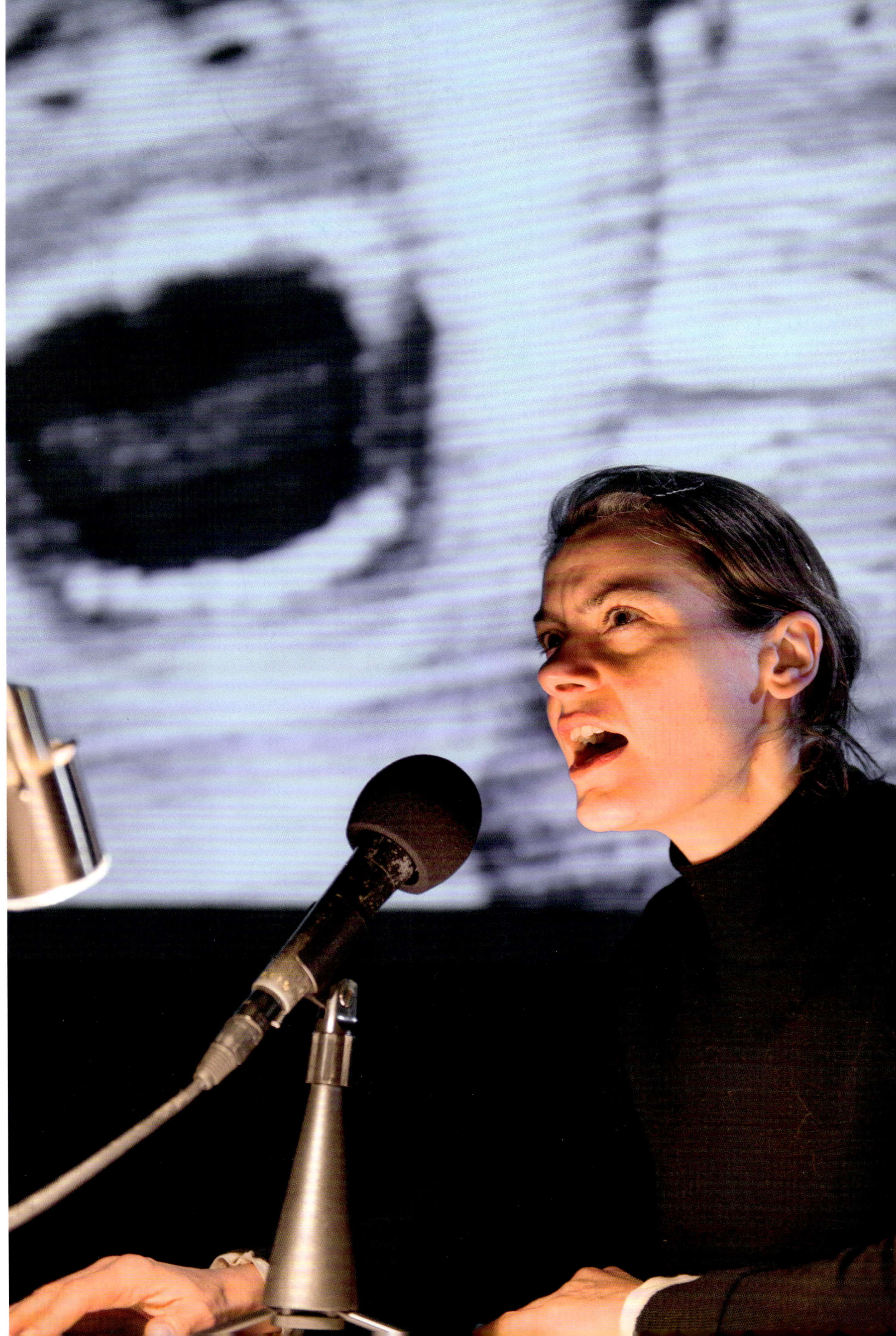

on the work we are presented with. By putting into play the question of who makes what impossible or who exercises control over whom in the transaction between spectators and performers, the performances thus call our attention to the power relations within the theatrical encounter itself. At the same time, as Etchells suggests, they tend to 'both point you to the people who sit beside you and bounce your attention from those people to the ones who are outside the theatre' (as the previously mentioned reference to Iraq illustrates).[4] They therefore bring us back to a very concrete reality, which stays within the grasp of the theatre audience, whilst decentring their attention and opening it up to other bodies besides their own.

A question remains. If the reality of those relations is being explored through the prism of impossibility, how can the audience get a sense that it could be otherwise? It seems to me that the impossibilities displayed by Forced Entertainment do not convey a sense of powerlessness for the spectator because they are confronted in a way that is both relentless and lively. If Jackson and Kim appear to be particularly resilient in *Void Story*, that characteristic is present in most fictive figures and can be extended to those performing them, who indeed repeatedly undertake tasks that seem too big, too small, too long, too painful, too much for their physical ability or for the capacities of the stage, therefore stretching both their own possibilities and those of the theatrical form. The never-ending attempts to perform, even in the knowledge of their inevitable failure, produce different ways of taking on the space, always with an indefatigable spirit. The 'politics of the impossible'[5] at play in Forced Entertainment, impacting both the artists and the audience, thus disturbs established methods of doing and thinking while nourishing creativity and effort. This contributes to the ambiguity of its theatre, which conjugates both disquieting and energizing qualities.

1. Séverine Ruset, '"An Absurd If Not Impossible Transaction": Entretien avec Tim Etchells (Forced Entertainment)', *European Drama and Performance Studies* (2017), 193–207, here: 194.

2. Lyn Gardner, 'Theatre Review: First Night', *The Guardian*, 2 October 2001.

3. Peter Billingham, *At the Sharp End, Uncovering the Work of Five Leading Dramatists* (London: Bloomsbury, 2007), 171.

4. Ruset, 'An Absurd If Not Impossible Transaction' (see n. 1), 198.

5. Jean-Michel Besnier, *Georges Bataille : La politique de l'impossible* (Nantes: Éditions Cécile Defaut, 2014).

Compendium: A Forced Glossary

Matthew Goulish

An alphabetized catalogue of terms to aid in the creative understanding
of the work of Forced Entertainment and Tim Etchells.

Absence—Breathing Corpse—Carpenter—Copy—Destruction—Edge—Embarrassment Site
Fact People—Gods and Angels—Haunt—List—Mis-—Navigation—Orton Monument—Pretend
Questions—Recycle—System—Territory—Unlucky—Volatile—Witness—Yearning—Zero Degree

Absence

The perpetual lack—the quality of not-enoughness in its myriad aesthetic instantiations—becomes a primary objective in the work of Forced Entertainment. Absence invites supplementation, from artists and audience as Witness and Navigator. This urge of supplementation lends the work one valence of its liberatory agency.

One encounters it in the group's collaborative creative process: 'No one would bring anything too completed to the process—a few scraps or fragments of text … so there'd be more spaces for others to fill in.'[1] 'We always loved the incomplete.'[2]

The principle has continued to hold true over decades of development. The Absence approach became a guiding poetic for selected or extracted evocative phrases, arranged in dialogue that charges the gaps and spaces between them. It informs the text/music overlays in the duets of Tim Etchells and violinist Aisha Orazbayeva, in which fragmentation and repetition facilitate the continuous unstable figure/ground interplay between speaking voice and violin tone. The assembled calendar texts of Etchells' project *Vacuum Days* in varying typeface, echoic of broadside placards, render the logic visible, while also exemplifying the often-overlooked persistent hyper-local character of the group's and Etchells' concerns.

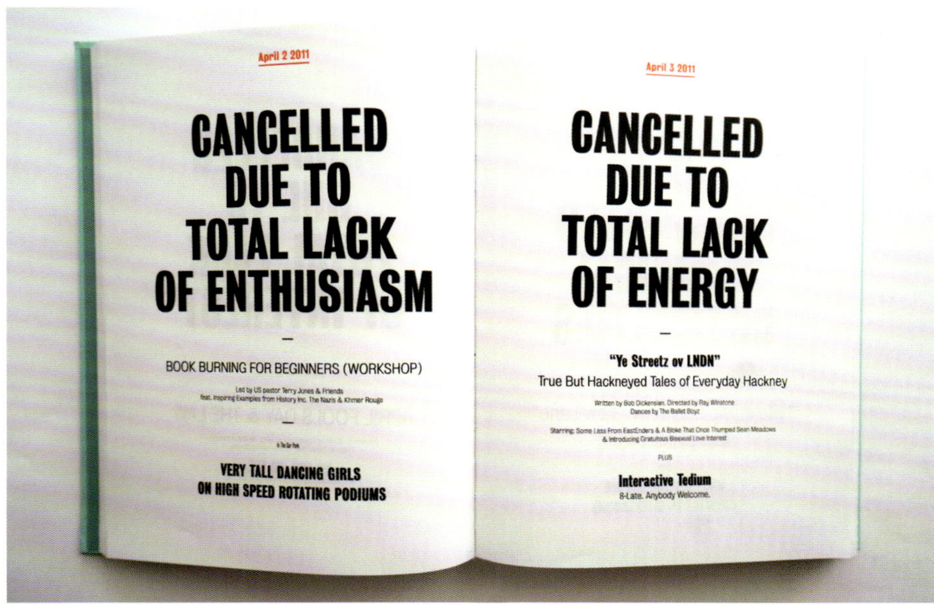

Absence attentive to the local appears in Navigation: 'They talked about the way that half-demolished or half-built houses were the best places to play … so much incompletion in the spaces, so much work (imaginative, playful, transformative) to be done. They liked this kind of mental space for themselves to work in, and they liked to leave some of it for the public too.'[3] One can observe a clear parallel to the impoverished openness of stages after an event, cluttered with evidence of what happened. Etchells' and Hugo Glendinning's ongoing photographic collaboration *Empty Stages* collects those etiolated performances that commence with endings.

As process, Absence extends to include the audience, and achieves its apotheosis in the climactic interrogation of optimism in *A Decade of Forced Entertainment* (1995).

> Richard: Do you think the work is optimistic?
>
> Terry: Yes.
>
> Richard: Even when it's bleak?
>
> Terry: Yes.
>
> Richard: Why do you think that?
>
> Terry: It opens a space which people fill.
>
> Richard: So the optimism is more an absence than anything else.[4]

Absence defines its opposite pole in the Embarrassment Site,[5] the result of too-muchness, an intention too fulfilled, an overdetermined theatrical moment of drama or meaning. The group assiduously transfers such moments to the outside of any performance yet must always remain within their gravitational pull. One finds Absence at the many Edges of the Embarrassment Site.

Breathing Corpse

'One of the performers/characters lay still and silent—"dead" on the floor. I lost the play for a moment then, only watching the contradictory breathing of the corpse, the rise and fall and sound of her breath… . I liked to watch her then because her part in the play was finished and she had nothing whatever to tell me.'[6] The 'gorgeous collusion of significance and banality' which describes this moment, the revealing of theatrical artifice, relates to Absence and Edge as well as to Pretend, in particular as it concerns death. 'From the Gulf War (summer 1990) I remember several times getting up in the middle of the night to go for a piss and turning on the TV to see what was happening—mesmerized by the quality of those news programmes where there is no news at all but where they have to stay on the air anyway to keep talking.'[7] The mesmeric, the vigil, the durational (defined by Absence), and the foregrounding of physical presence, breath, and speech, as circular responses to death, clarify Witness. The newscasters also have 'nothing whatever to tell' but remain onstage, compelled by death's proximity. Robin Arthur's skeleton costume as the host and Claire Marshall's compulsively repeated death scene in *Spectacular* (2008) testify to the persistence of the Breathing Corpse.

Carpenter

Performer and set designer Richard Lowdon has narrated an early episode influential in the formation of the group's aesthetic. While still a student at the University of Exeter, where the core members met, researching in the library archives late one night for an essay on the history of baroque set design, Lowdon discovered an obscure volume, full of unfinished diagrams, in which he read the story of a Carpenter, a 'specialist in setting doors'. The Carpenter related how the thought of building an entire house terrified and paralysed him. How could he ever manage walls, floors, ceilings, and windows, when it had taken him half of his life to master the door? One day, under the spell of an extraordinary waking dream, the thought struck him with lucid clarity that he must give up all ambition. At that moment the house that he could build appeared complete as an image in his mind: a house made entirely of doors—doors for walls, doors for floors, doors for windows, doors for ceilings, and doors for doors. Will every door open and close on hinges? That remained to be seen.

The Carpenter awoke, set to work constructing his house of doors, and in this manner, in a singular state of calm ecstasy, he laboured for the rest of his days. The story, Lowdon claimed, seemed to grant 'permission to unfold an entire performance from one kernel' or from insistent concentration on what might previously have been considered 'a minor element in a mise en scène'. After excitedly relating the story to his youthful colleagues, Lowdon returned to the archive but failed to relocate the source volume. Thus the story lacks citation.

Copy

'1989 we made a show, not about Elvis Presley but about an Elvis Presley impersonator in Birmingham, England. We didn't want anything authentic, we wanted a third-rate copy—we loved that more dearly than anything original.'[8] Copies result from acts of copying. When actants conform to a model, they undertake a form of pretending, a profanation of the religious notion of the immensity of the human soul, a Copy of the cosmos.

Language itself can become Copy. In Etchells' short story collection *Endland* words and phrases frequently appear offset by the copyright symbol '©': quick and unexpected sex—staying his hand—appointment with destiny—rent asunder—beyond belief—that cold winter—tears came in the eyes—nothing—despair—a lot of words—deep in thought—scenes of revulsion—ambulances in the moonlight—bad heart—concentration— mouthing off for no reason—sinking and rising at the same time—moral issue—stink of poverty.

These phrases simultaneously suggest both a heightened and significant mental state or activity, and the appropriated, commodity-like quality, the 'copyness', of, if not the state or activity itself, at least the language which reduces it to a label of its expression. Yet reproduction seems inaccurate as a description of these subjective acts of copying, which record a move toward non-representation. Instead, the severely constrained creativity of copying, the 'uncreativity', amplifies the multiplicity at work. Each recurrence of the Copy multiplies the meanings of both itself and its context (Elvis impersonated in Birmingham). Etchells' specimen phrases rendered in neon as part of his visual arts practice, record a similar movement, toward the materialization of a thought-sign accosting the viewer with the sensation that on this spot a mind in certain straits has stopped.

LET'S PRETEND NONE OF THIS EVER HAPPENED

In the code shift that live performance executes on language, permanence becomes 'but a word of degrees' (Emerson). Terry O'Connor's monologue in *First Night* (2001) offers a litany of subjects for the audience not to think about during the performance, events abstracted to signatures: 'Try not to think about chemical warfare.'[9] The speech act of iterating each item on the List in direct address to the audience alludes to a parlour game, but in the circuit of reception between performer and audience, each supposed attempt to avoid thinking of each conjured idea only punctures the theatrical immersive spell, locating the theatre in the world that surrounds it, a world vulnerable to collapse, self-undoing, and endless suffering, as evoked by the declamation of each durable phrase, as if copied and pasted onto the stage.

Destruction

Completeness invites Destruction to restore Absence. Stage pictures and language experience periodic Destruction, and Helen X (O'Connor), the figure at the heart of *Club of No Regrets* (1993), through her own Volatile destructiveness, paradoxically destabilizes the *Club* even as she constructs it. Ubiquitous references to car wrecks offer a legible emblem of Destruction, a counterpart to Gods and Angels. Car wrecks, invoking common disaster, death, loss, and technological failure, incarnate the Destruction of Navigation.

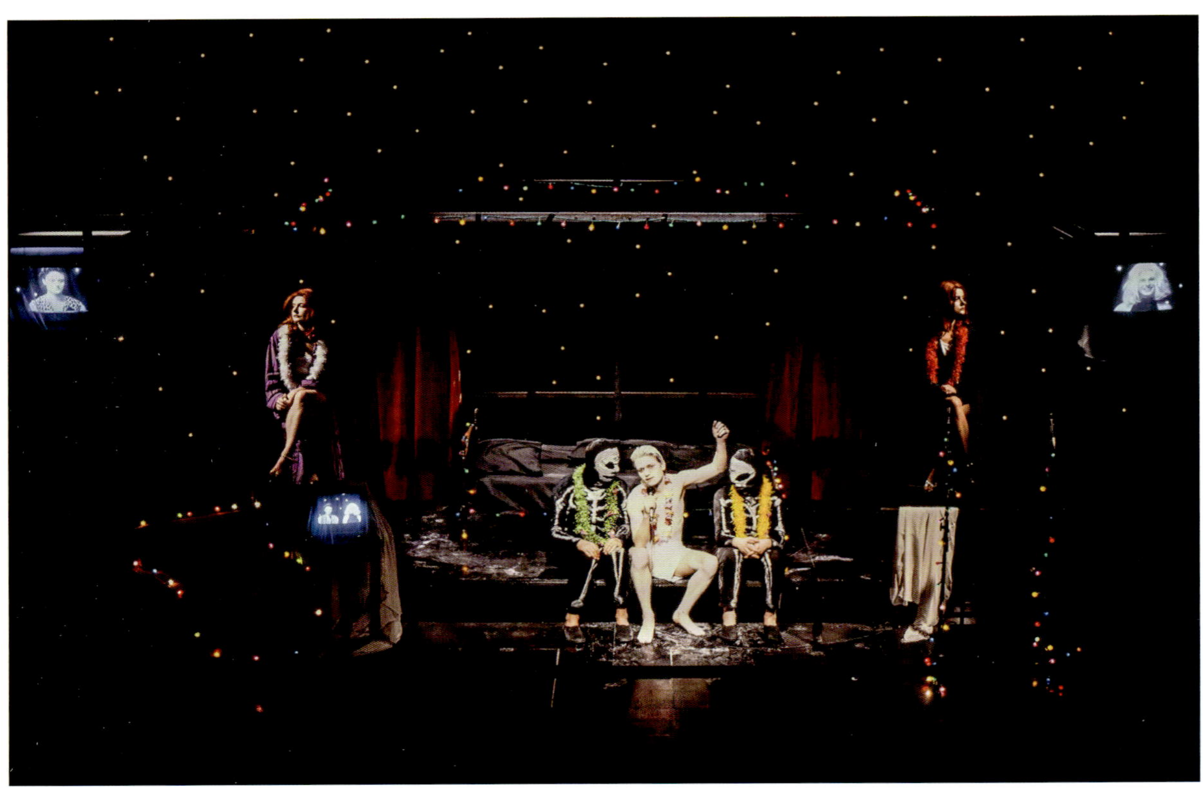

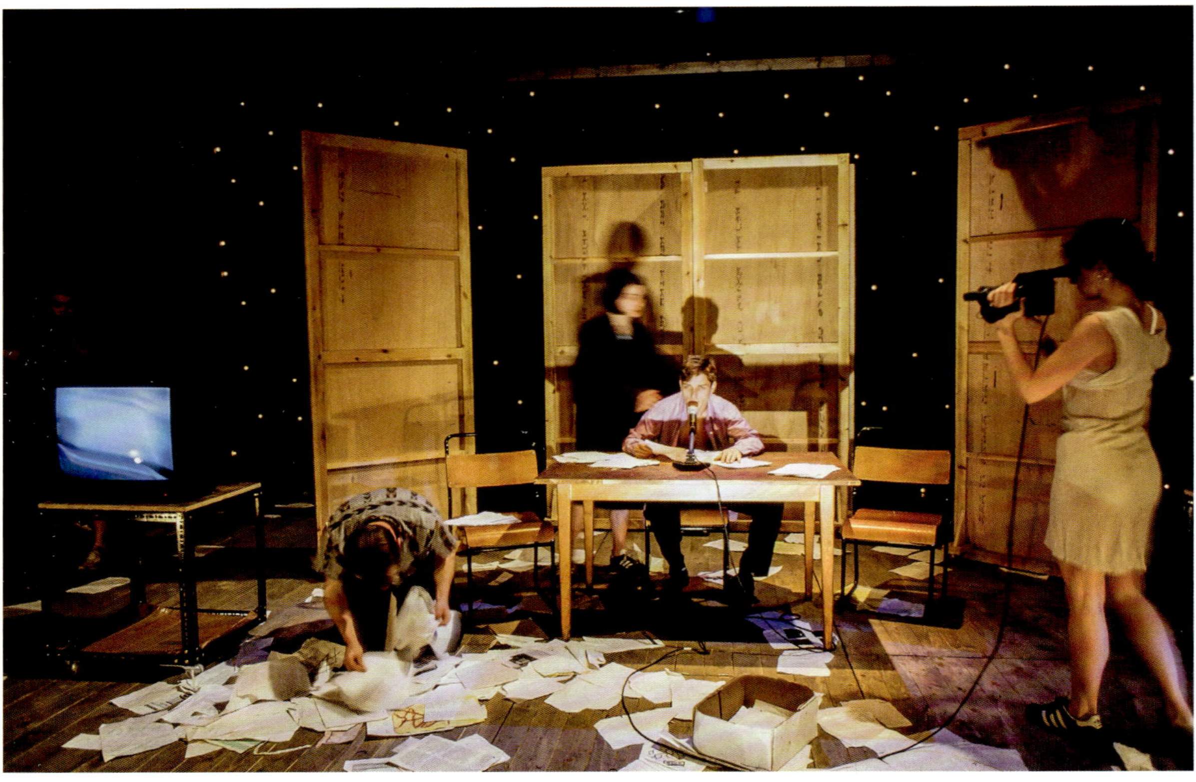

Forced Entertainment understands its work as the location and Navigation of Edges: 'The people in it are bashing against the edges of the world they're born into, bashing on the edges of the language that they have,'[10] 'playing at the edges of what is real and what is not, disrupting the borders between the so-called real and the so-called fictional.'[11] In his 18 March 2016 speech when Forced Entertainment received the International Ibsen Award, Etchells stated: 'It's the conversations at the unruly edges of the disciplines that this award to us marks, a zone of experiment that we have long seen as a home.' He then went on to refer to the company's home city of Sheffield as 'another periphery'.

Systems of theatre, representation, and language (with their 'inherent codes of fakery and pretence'[12]) and all the attendant dishonesties; Territories historical or imaginary; identities and pretending; games of questioning or imitation; narrative ('to force the stories we do know to yield us the stories we don't'[13]); the organic and the technological; the living and the dead—all of these come with Edges of definition and function. Beyond their Edge they fail. Pinpointing failure thus becomes the goal, and the resultant liminal Edges fuel the group's performance and writing. Departing from this peripherality, theatrically speaking, invariably leads to an overly determined and meaningful centre, an Embarrassment Site. Instead, self-imposed marginality generates a constant doubleness, in which one can interpret almost any phrase of language or action as having two distinct simultaneous meanings. For example, the confessional tone of *Speak Bitterness* (1994) implies shame for a statement such as: 'We loved language.'[14] The collision of the statement's simplicity with the implied imposition of judgment, suggesting the speaker has unlearned such affection for words, the Edge on which every declaration in the performance turns, volatilizes the speech as desolate poetry.

Each ending demarks a similar Edge. Etchells observes the extended curtain calls at the conclusion of *Café Müller* by the Tanztheater Wuppertal of Pina Bausch, in which the dancers seemed unable to leave the performance's image-world behind, 'its psychic residue too strong'.[15] The jarring remains of fiction trespass into the Territory of the actual.

The construct of the quiz show, in works such as *Quizoola!* (1996), or *Real Magic* (2016), surveys an Edge through the directive to 'go too far'.[16] A secondary Edge appears at the artificial endings of the game-structured performances: 'Perhaps the strangest moment of any of these games was when they stopped. Because in the stopping was always the time for measuring how far things had gone, how much the world had changed because of the game.'[17]

Since an Edge indicates an interface, its exploration begins to destabilize the definition of both states—safety/danger, real/fiction—by redrawing their borders, and reconfiguring them as inclusive rather than exclusive polarities, even if only for the duration of the performance. The group's many time-disorientation performances, lasting anywhere from six to twenty-four hours, concentrates this aspect of Edge work.

Embarrassment Site

The prime Embarrassment Site in the work of Forced Entertainment is the theatre, crowded as it is with the wreckage of the twentieth century. The stage houses any of a series of fundamental misunderstandings, or misrecognitions, in the unspoken contract between performer and audience. We can understand the works of Forced Entertainment, especially since *First Night*, as attempts to render visible and explicit the interference patterns generated by these slippages. Embarrassment results from violating the decorum of theatre conventions that would leave those tensions implicit and dormant.

Etchells writes: 'We often speak of both the working process and the stage itself, as meeting (or collision) points of different intentionalities. Neither the work nor the company are spaces of utopian agreement; they are better understood as zones of permanent conflict and dynamic (if sometimes grinding slow motion) contestation in which meaning only emerges thanks to the sparks, frictions and confrontations which stem from each of our different approaches to the same emerging tasks or questions.'[18] Some techniques of dissensus (rather than consensus) include articulating the suspect motives of the audience in attending the performance, failing to deliver on a promise, or appearing on stage only under duress.

Stage conventions may hollow themselves out from the inside even when approached in earnest, such as the competing out-of-phase (analogue and digital) timings that annihilate the solemn intent of the minute of silence in *Bloody Mess* (2004).

We can understand the Embarrassment Site by way of Samuel Beckett's 'certain obscenities of form'.[19] Where Beckett initiated intricate cycles of insistence for the avoidance of purgation, played out in barren landscapes after the flood, Forced Entertainment clinically reverse engineers a set of self-replicating viruses of Embarrassment from theatricality's fault lines and releases them into theatre's ecosystem.

Fact People

Personality aggregates appear as complete fragments in the form of Fact People. These linguistically constructed personages make frequent appearances in *Endland* and early performance works but arrive most insistently in the List of cardboard signs employed in *Emanuelle Enchanted* (1992), where they gain intensity through accumulation. Fact People may include Gods and Angels, celebrities, historical, theatrical, or mundane figures, any personality distilled into legible form. Noteworthy Fact People include TARZANOGRAM, THE BLONDE GIRL FROM ABBA, A BLOKE WHO'S BEEN SHOT, LINDA (OUT OF LUCK), MISS DEEP FREEZE, GAY COP, AN ANGEL SENT FROM HEAVEN TO EARTH, MR TEN & A HALF INCHES, GIRL IN LIFT NO. 1, JACK RUBY, SIGMUND FREUD, MISS SCUNTHORPE EVENING TELEGRAPH, THE QUEEN OF MONEY, MICHAEL CAINE. The convention returns in Etchells' internet and poster project *Vacuum Days* which upgrades the strategy, collapsing it with pointed political commentary.

David Cameron's
Wagging
Animatronic Finger

The presences become invokable Fact, not in essence as much as iconic label. As such, they circulate as uneasy commodities, orphaned in their factness.

Gods and Angels

A peculiar pantheon has accrued over the years in the Forced Entertainment cosmology—part Gods derived from the Greeks and Romans, and part Angels of Judaeo-Christian origin. Both act as anchors of immediately recognizable significance, standing in for emotional states just beyond human attainment. Angels invoke transcendent peace and well-being: 'the faces of many people sleeping—like angels looking after or dreaming of this world.'[20] Part One of *Decade*, after observing silence for the late Ron Vawter and Steve Rogers, concludes with the lamentation from *200% and Bloody Thirsty* (1988) of two beleaguered 'distressed and sorrowful angels' who claim the power 'to raise our friends from the dead'. They fail at this resurrection only in the literal sense, succeeding according to the theatrical affirmations of pretending, as Angels stand in for Yearning.

Gods, by contrast, descend to earth, in Etchells' *Endland*, in order to act out humanity's most petty and repugnant foibles. The brothers Porridge and Spatula, sons of the Goddess Helen and the God Apollo 12, drunkenly compete on a TV quiz show for the affections of Naomi. They 'threw water and then crisps at each other in full view of the audience and a scuffle' ensued, prompting the host to declare: 'Never, in the whole history of 100 years of crap on tv have we had such troublesome contestants as them 2.'[21] Other Gods and Goddesses looking down on Endland include Anastasia, Rent-Boy, Asimov, Golgotha, Vineyard, Hologram, Mr Twinkle, Horse Radish, Barbie, Jupiter, Zorba, Poseidon Adventure, Risotto, Mr Bumpy, Zeus, Tesco, Venus, Mr Stretchy, Penelope, Kali, Herpes, and Vesuvius.

Along with hybrids of slang, superhero, and brand names, one finds celebrities on the Edge of godliness, like the cardboard sign in *Emanuelle Enchanted* that reads TELLY SAVALAS COME DOWN FROM THE CROSS. Celebrity Copies, like Elvis impersonators, especially verge on godliness, as do the more famous and renowned Fact People.

Haunt

Occupying any Edge invites elements from one side to Haunt the other. Etchells relates the story of his hand scar, a result of amateur childhood hypnosis which caused him to experience a burn from a piece of household tinfoil, as if from a ghost flame.[22] The anecdote, while demonstrating the quality shared by many directors of susceptibility to hypnosis, also suggests that, for Etchells, entrancement arrives as haunting's companion.

List

In a world composed of fragments, the List constitutes a porous yet unifying form, an expressive plateau of similarity that bestows on its materials a degree of wholeness. Etchells begins his lecture 'On Performance Writing' with the words: 'Obsessed in any case with lists and indexes …'[23] The early performance pieces *Let the Water* and *Emanuelle Enchanted*, sequences such as Cathy Naden's prediction of audience deaths and O'Connor's monologue in *First Night*, and concentrated works such as *Sight Is the Sense That Dying People Tend to Lose First* (2008), a monologue written and directed by Etchells for the actor Jim Fletcher, all organize and energize themselves through listing. The Newsroom One section of *Emanuelle Enchanted* exemplifies the practice at its most intact, structured as a List of nine micro-Lists, each containing ten single-line text entries. Newsroom Two destabilizes the form primarily through the introduction of texts of technological mistakes yet manages to retain listing as a legible performative activity. Listing achieves its purist form in *Speak Bitterness*, a performance composed entirely of first-person plural confessions recited so obsessively as to suggest an infinite List, an extrusion that only artificial time constraints can truncate. Listing reduces the scope of variation to subtle shifts of tone and voice, which become crucial to orchestrating its homophonic quality into an unbroken fabric of emotional minimalism.

Forms that engage listing recur in both the work of Forced Entertainment and in Etchells' *Endland*. The quiz show appears as a List of Questions, an aggressive popular-culture formulation of minimalist repetition. Etchells, in writing about Ron Vawter's solo performance *Roy Cohn/Jack Smith*, draws attention to that work's concluding List of the films of Maria Montez, as 'both empty of meaning and full of it'.[24] Listing, thus characterized, pinpoints the quintessential and illusory qualities of Forced Entertainment's work: disposability and speed. Meaning seems Absent, as it Haunts the Edge of the List.

Finally, listing suggests a self as collection: 'She jumped and ended her short life … There wasn't a note. Just a list of people she loved. And of her favourite places. And of her favourite books.'[25] Etchells states the case for self as multiplicity, and author as author-function, in 'On Performance Writing': 'For us, in the work and out of it, this notion of self has often seemed after all to be simply a collection of texts, quotations, strategic and accidental speaking—not a coherent thing, much less the single-minded author of some text. What I am, in this text (now) at least, is no more (and no less) than the meeting-point of the language that flows out of me (these past years, months, days)—a switching station, a filtering and thieving machine, a space in which collisions take place.'[26] 'I am a fragment and this is a fragment of me.' (Emerson)

Misunderstandings play an essential role in the collaborative process. As an unavoidable noise in the System that nudges a communication feedback loop into the Territory of the event, misunderstandings confound individual intention and contribute to the pluralistic, contradictory fabric of Forced Entertainment's theatre. 'Collaboration then not as a kind of perfect understanding of the other bloke, but a mis-seeing, a mis-hearing, a deliberate lack of unity. And this fact of the collaborative process finding its echo in the work since on stage what we see is not all one thing either—but rather a collision of fragments that don't quite belong, fragments that mis-see and mis-hear each other.'[27]

Mistakes of technology (new technologies produce new errors) inform many of Forced Entertainment's texts. The very title of Etchells' book *Endland* makes indirect reference to the nearness of the letters g and d, two keyboard spaces apart, and implies a typing mistake. This Mis-take in turn reveals England as a land of endings. Intermittent computer error lines weave through the text of the Newsroom Two section of *Emanuelle Enchanted*.

> THERE ARE SPIRITS, SPEAKING THROUGH MY TEETH.
>
> 2.
>
> this room
>
> 2.
>
> START NOT FOUND
>
> the air so sweet looking down[28]

Given the work's often linguistic character, these technological slippages become significant in their capacity to generate new verbiage of limitation. By accessing Navigations of contemporary language Systems and mechanisms, they reset borders of expression, and thus become crucial for defining Edges.

> I'd like to talk with you, I'd really like to talk, I know we're talking now but …
> THE ERASE COMMAND LINE FORMAT IS INVALID[29]

One cannot unspeak one's already tongue-tied words. While generating a found-language poetic of error, these new Mistakes seem to reflect the noise inherent in cognitive Systems of emergent neurological pathways, as allegorized by the volatility of Helen X, the impulsive and increasingly disoriented narrator/protagonist of *Club of No Regrets*.

Misfires, marginally controlled, of Glendinning's camera documented *Club of No Regrets* and the project *Red Room*, relying on a technique of pointing without looking through the viewfinder.

Navigation

> We arrived in a place in the dead of night, found somewhere to park the van, found somewhere to sleep. Only when we woke the next morning did we realize that we were in a town right next to the sea and that the place where we had slept was right at the sea front itself … Harbisson writes about the experience of arriving in the city at night and starting to explore it in the morning—this process of veiled arrival and later exploration he calls 'acting out an allegory of knowledge'.[30]

> This is the first walkthrough that I ever wrote and I hope you can forgive any error in my advice or in the English … I must have been in *The Broken World* about 600 times (or probably more) and tho many times I came back dead or badly injured I know it better now and sometimes come back alive I know some towns in there better than the back of my own hand.[31]

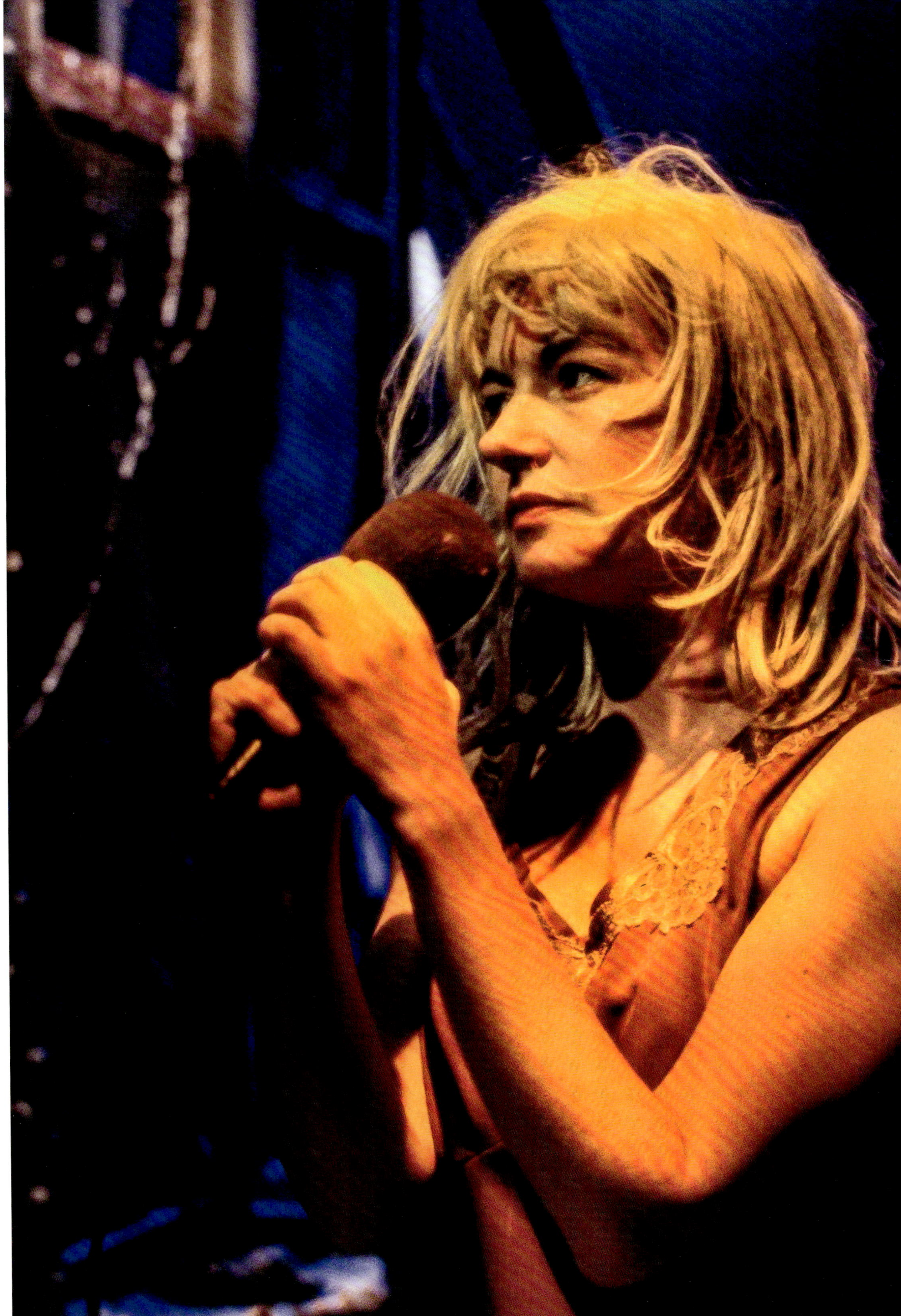

In the respect that we may consider Forced Entertainment's work spatial and territorial, any participation in that work reflects the character of Navigation, of wayfinding according to landmarks and emergent, often recursive channels. The imaginative attention that the performances ask of audiences, reading available information in order to fill in Absences, as well as the strategic composition of Absence and presence in these performances, both can be understood as forms of Navigation. Erasure and overwriting onto previously complete Embarrassment Sites necessitate re-Navigation. Path composition and creative travel supplants interpretation. Helen X concludes *Club of No Regrets* with a short recitation of directions. The group's acute sense of history, especially situated within cultural and local (Sheffield) concerns, can inflect Navigation with directly and expansively political impulses, while disavowing politics narrowly defined. As 'a journey undertaken, in which the territory unfolds, as much as a surprise to us as it may be to anyone else', their work 'speaks of things that could not otherwise be spoken; it takes us somewhere.'[32] Etchells' novel *The Broken World* gives these concerns a twenty-first century upgrade in the form of an extended monologue of Navigation instructions as tutorial and testimony, accessing the strange valences of immersion in virtual spaces and the depleted agency of the gaming tour guide. The work migrates performance qualities to narrative, 'acting out an allegory of knowledge' in virtual landscapes that rewrite communality and isolation. Invariably, in every instance, Navigation within an Edge rebels against the containment that the Edge designates and reveals.

Orton Monument

Etchells composes blueprint-like performance texts that become significant elements in the Forced Entertainment collaborative mix but do not occupy the primary, infallible position that a playwright's script would in a conventional production. He states that he has little use for playwrights as a rule and only mentions one, Joe Orton, with implicit respect.[33] Etchells used Orton-specific locations for *DIY*, his collaborative film with Michael Atavar and Glendinning, including 'the flat in which [Orton] and his lover … ended their lives in 1967', and 'the bricked up arches of a former public toilet … where thirty years before Orton himself had cruised for sex.' The project devises a temporal memorial for Orton by framing the character of places that his behaviour transformed into accidental and disputed monuments. Shared by the South End Green residents' association of London, this project's conceptual underpinnings relate to Navigation. The group procured funding for the renovation of the Victorian underground toilets, with green-and-white tile and elaborate panelled doors and grillwork, known as a favourite Orton cruising location. Although the toilets' architectural merit ostensibly justified their renovation, Leoni Orton-Barnett, the playwright's sister, acknowledged the distinct Orton connection when she called the project 'a very odd monument … but why not? Joe frequented cottages all the time.'

Pretend

> It's not frivolous to think that even as we die we're creatures of fiction and pretending, that we're not simply 'facts' or biology, that we may not be contained by either. I don't think it's frivolous to insist that, even as one dies, one is multiple, playful, partial, strategic, and indeed fictional.[34]

Copying may take the form of pretending. As a theatrical act, pretending speaks languages of artifice. It establishes an Edge which appears most potent when the pretending crosses into Territories of death, as in *Showtime* (1996), when its description of how one 'would commit suicide if she were going to do it',[35] and its death scene enacted with 'the lurid guts (a can of Heinz Spaghetti tipped into his hand and clutched to his belly) oozing out.'[36] The statements 'You play with what scares you and you play with what you need'[37] echo Gertrude Stein's declaration 'Whatever you can play with is yours.'[38] Comic pretending may Navigate the Territories of fear.

Showtime also introduced pretending in the register of animal: 'For some weak and now forgotten reason we sent Claire to a costume rental place, looking for a wolf … Instead she came back with a dog. The dog—in fact she brought us only the head—was some well-worn and amateur thing.'[39] The horse in *Pleasure* (1997), the gorilla in *Bloody Mess*, the chickens in *Real Magic*, all continue the lineage of amateur pretending. They mask and overwrite the human with the particular tradition of British 'pantomime' excess as they conjure qualities of animal.

Pretending in this context suggests playing not only at what one is not but also at some figure across the aporia that divides one from those forms one can never hope to become. To pretend here is to escape the body's limits of function (playing at the wound or death) and form (playing at animal). The time signature of such enactments frees itself from the usual constraints of actual events. Medieval depictions of a musical banquet at the end of time feature theriocephalic renderings of the righteous.[40] The picture of animal-headed saints transcending mortality, gathered in performance, uncovers the weave of the two primordial motifs, death and the animal, under the Forced Entertainment sign of Pretend, when time shall be no more.

Questions

Questions constitute performative speech acts at their most irreducible, since each Question engenders an Absence. Answers, when they arrive in the Forced Entertainment universe, never close the Question or escape its orbit, but tend to multiply Absences. When Lists of Questions formulate the frequently employed quiz show, the System proliferates monstrously, as in the 2,000 Questions of *Quizoola!*, and must rely on an artificial, extra-systemic conclusion.

Recycle

Texts, modes, and structures all appear, reappear, and evolve over the years. The text of *Speak Bitterness* grew out of confessional passages from two earlier performance works *Let the Water* and *Marina & Lee*.[41] Recycling delimits the universe which the group inhabits. 'In 1988 we took some dead trees from Ecclesall Woods to use in the performance *200% & Bloody Thirsty*—not so much trees as fourteen-foot branches. And then years later (1993) we used the same trees in *Club of No Regrets*—gaffer-taping them to the scaffolding structure at the side of the stage. And after the last performance—outside on a hillside in Tuscany (July 1994)—we left the trees at the edge of a forest. Miles from home we left them—these objects that are art for a while then get put back into the world.'[42]

Recurrences, repetitions, and recyclings invite haunting.

System

A more encompassing term than List, System includes events such as the visual parade of cardboard signs in *Emanuelle Enchanted* which Etchells describes as an 'endless coincidence machine'.[43] These signs derive from a List of Fact People, but their engagement in performance generates a System much larger than the foundational List. In a similar way, the aleatory quiz show System, confronted most directly in *Quizoola!*, redefines Questions and their listing. The System includes the stage and its spaces, performer intention, emblematic gestures, engagement of video or live-streaming media of circulation, doing the 'work defined by pre-established framework or "machine"'.[44] Although the List provides the System's primary substance, the complexity and nuance of these other elements determine fundamentals of expression and audience relations. The Newsroom One example from *Emanuelle Enchanted* gives the following directive: 'The lists are presented into camera like the urgent missives of a culture in the throes of crisis.'[45] What elsewhere might be considered subtext here becomes primary and generative, since 'language proliferates around a crisis'.[46] The System alludes to the crisis but defers confrontation or closure, except in those etiolated gestures that only succeed in the pathetic flowering of an Embarrassment Site. Nevertheless, without the elusive crisis, the System would not exist.

Systems as a rule always contain periods of noise, or interference, running counter to the System's intentions. Noise periodicity further divides into smaller periods of non-noise, or the System functioning smoothly. These smaller non-noise periods in turn contain even smaller noise periods, and so on to the limits of measurability. Thus one cannot speak of a System devoid of noise but only of Systems with reduced or increased noise. Any communication System engaged by Forced Entertainment, whether for purposes of collaboration, aesthetics, or the languages of law, technology, poetry, popular culture, confession, or narration, immediately identifies its noise element as its interior Edge, the most fertile area for the group's concerns. In theatrical and performative Systems, this noise element often involves a degree of artificiality. Thus the work 'foregrounds the process of theatrical presentation',[47] deploying, for example, the Copy.

Complete Works: Table Top Shakespeare (2015) nuanced the tactic of substitution through the use of the stand-in, a household object representing in miniature each character as manipulated and narrated by a (giant) human performer leaning over the stage/table. This project invents a Shakespeare machine for demonstrating 'a little diagram of the play' and a 'reporting on' the plot,[48] one that becomes a System by virtue of its comprehensiveness, its imperative to re-process all thirty-six plays. The machine in this case proposes the play in its Absence as the shared context of the demonstration; more precisely, the play rendered as its most skeletal events, with all the iambic language and human presence filtered out. The proxy, as 'the token we think with',[49] makes every complex network of relations visible. As with the Systems of earlier works, this instance exploits its noise as excess information, as in the case of the rust on the nails that stand in for Macbeth's murderous henchmen, and even suggests its own private post-apocalypse, as if speaking from a near-future time when only these oral histories remain of the complete works of Shakespeare. Like the other instances of System, this one issues from a desire to make ordinary language 'speak of the things it cannot deal with',[50] and to watch as people do the work of 'speaking themselves into presence, into existence'.[51]

Territory

Forced Entertainment's installations and tour-like formulations call to mind Michel de Certeau's described practice of 'composing a path'. These works situate in Territories, actual, physical, historical. Yet their historicality and even their physicality only Haunt these places, since the performance reterritorializes them, backgrounding but not eliminating their real-life associations, foregrounding instead contradictory associations. For this reason, the emblematic Forced Entertainment Territory appears urban and nocturnal, when empirical reality seems to withdraw like a horizon that leaves traces and evidence strewn in its wake. In that Absence the performers write over the night city's surface with the personal, mythical, and imaginary, re-navigating it both physically and historically. *Nights in This City* (1995)—a guided tour of Sheffield and a work whose treatment of the urban landscape as a screen anticipated the advent of augmented reality— commenced with the words 'Ladies and Gentlemen, welcome to Paris.'[52]

Unlucky

Misfortune acts as a unifying narrative device in Etchells' *Endland*, as well as in the Endland-like Rose of Misfortune in the *Certain Fragments* 'Repeat Forever' essay. The Forced Entertainment performance works *And on the Thousandth Night …* (2000) and *Void Story* (2009) offer near-constant intertwined strings of Unlucky events, mercilessly related. Unluckiness contributes to the fluidity, disposability, and speed of the style shared by these projects, as well as their illusion of effortlessness.

For Etchells and Forced Entertainment, story connotes an Aesop-like fable, rendered immoderate and divested of moral, that offers a window into the bleak, grotesque, and comical perpetual present of contemporary Britain, haunted by the spectres of an empire in decline. A typical protagonist is 'basically an unlucky misery guts with a hidden gift for brilliant ideas'.[53] Unluckiness lifts the characters that populate the stories to a level of definition one rung above that of the literally cardboard Fact People on the evolutionary ladder. They carry on like exaggerated everyman figures from one misfortune to the next. The narrow frame, insisting on its infinite variations on themes of unluckiness, eventually propels the stories to the cumulative heights of fate and destiny, thus justifying the appearance of Gods (who also suffer from unluckiness).

Volatile

Club of No Regrets constructs itself around the figure of Helen X, an incarnation of structure in the throes of failure. 'Throughout the piece Helen calls for the scenes to be enacted again and again, repeating them, switching their order. Helen is erratic, jumpy, and volatile, declaring that the scenes are "completely wrong" or "too sad" or simply "too black and white." Her struggle is to get them in the right order, or, more certainly, to forge some more poetic sense from their unpromising substance.'[54] The performance's expression derives its form from her volatility, which in turn results from her impossible compulsion for attempting to force the performance into a stable construction. From the opening trope of the forensic reconstruction of torn paper, through Helen X's final words ('Forgive me: I am made to write as a witness, in difficult times'[55]) one comprehends structure here through a progressive, anxiety-ridden revelation.

Witness

Some confusion has arisen as a result of Etchells' use of the word Witness as an alternative to spectator or audience. In particular, his claim 'to witness an event is to be present at it in some fundamentally ethical way' and his phrase 'the struggle to produce witnesses'[56] prompted performance theorist Peggy Phelan to question his notions of production and ethics relative to witnessing. She defines Witness in its psychoanalytic sense, relating to trauma, or its legal sense, as one who possesses special knowledge or experience of a disputed event. However, Etchells has in mind a more unusual meaning for the term, connoting one who has an experience that defies understanding ('When we're beaten so complex and so personal that we move beyond rhetorics into events'[57]).

Little seems to happen in such an event. 'One thing that really held a charge was the video material of the guy [an artist suffering from HIV, collaborating with Fiona Templeton] acting from his hospital bed. In these scenes he was dressed in some frivolous cape or costume, gesturing faintly, laughing, or he was moving around the hospital room, making some great long speech from the text, an IV drip on a wheeled trolley thing plugged into his arm, a cheap plastic crown on his head and a wooden sword in his other hand, his arm as thin as death. It was absurd. A background of medical machines. I can't tell you how beautiful that was.'[58]

Etchells' initial thoughts on Witness derive from his consideration of people who attended Chris Burden's landmark 1971 performance *Shoot* in Venice, California. Unlike in that case study, or in the Templeton hospital performance, the risk for performer or audience in Forced Entertainment performances takes a different form than that of physical harm. Instead, an anxiety-producing confusion of ephemeral signs triggers a condition of hyper-aware attention. Although simply apprehended, contradictory messages provoke a collapse of the faculties not of perception and memory but of assessment, a mortal boundary, called up in the mind rather than the body, called up by language and its vast, inexhaustible surface, unreleased up to its very Edge. Such trauma of the ordinary constitutes a play of impurity, easily perceived, acutely remembered but impossible to reduce or categorize. This event resists the viewer's capacity to draw a conclusion, to laugh or recoil in fear. In this and other subtle ways Forced Entertainment seems to repel the audience, situating the audience as always already other, in an untrustworthy relation met with scepticism from the stage. We may consider this event ethical in its deviation from easily recognized pathways of assessment, forcing the audience, at a loss for an immediate correct or even appropriate response, into a position of choice: either dismissal of the event, or a world view adjustment. This adjustment may at first appear aesthetic ('How beautiful that was') but in time, submitted to the work's way of pressuring, of daring the audience (*their* audience?) to give up on it, the adjustment inevitably becomes ethical. As with Breathing Corpse, the work

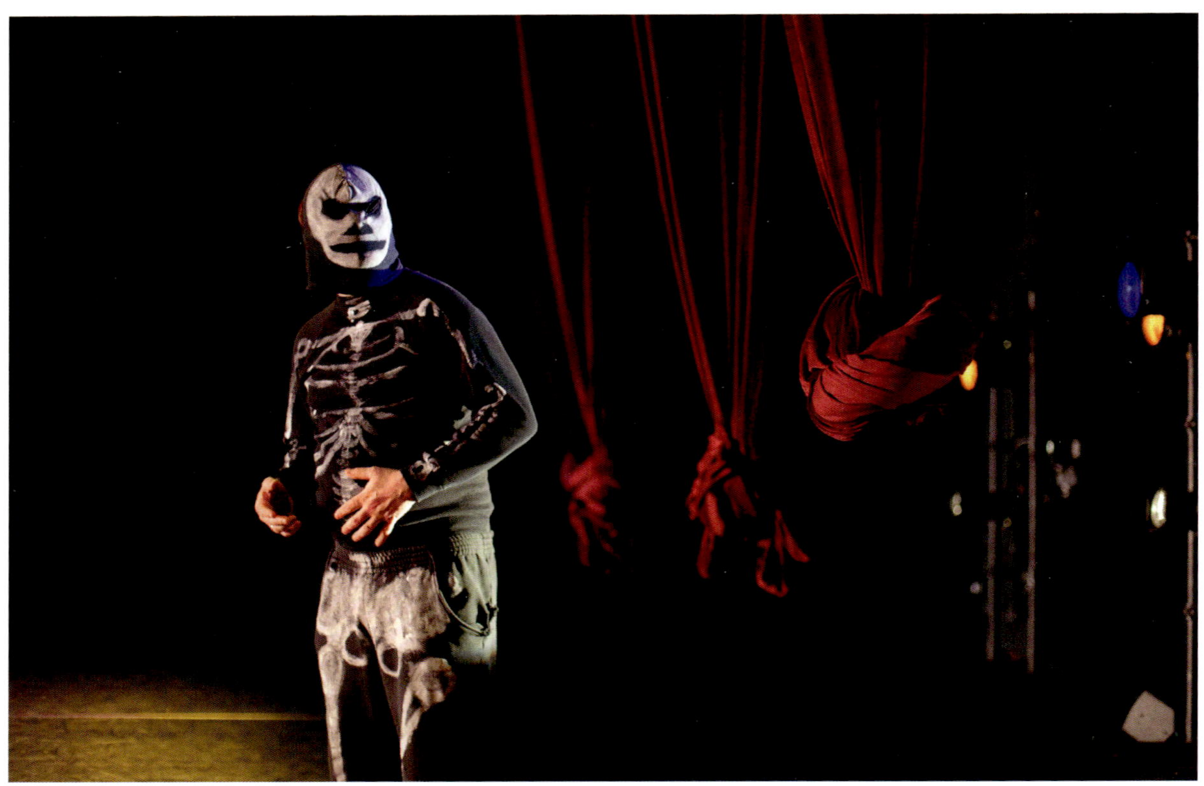

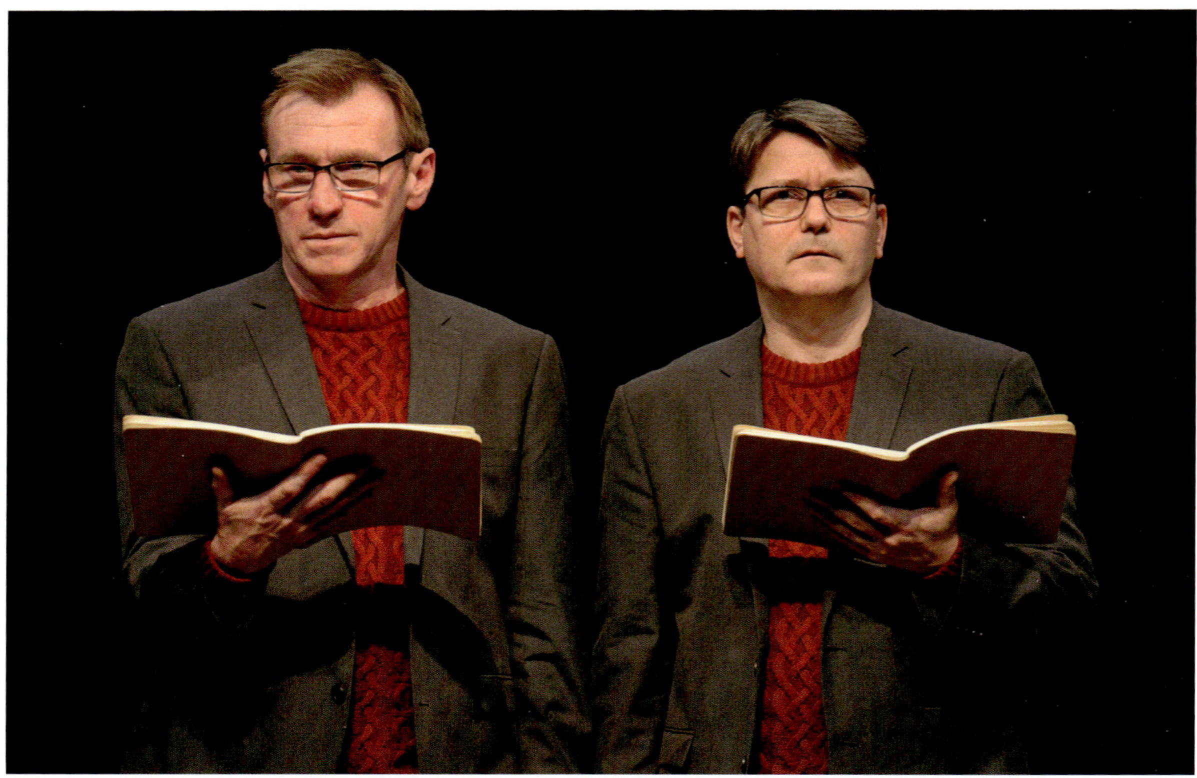

invites us to see double: both the theatrical illusion, which is the performance's reality, and the secret actual within it, the encroaching undisguisable trace of its outside, which is life itself. 'To become worthy of what happens to us',[59] we in the audience must become witnesses. That is to say that the event compels us to reimagine our position of attendance, accepting the performance less as something that 'we attend' and more something that 'happens to us'.

Yearning

Yearning describes one of the emotional states theatrically emblematized by Angels. Their frequent occurrence suggests that Yearning results as an inadvertent by-product of Absence, one of Forced Entertainment's fundamentals. The late actor Ron Vawter, whom Etchells interviewed, spoke of 'a yearning for the audience' which fuels the performer on spirituality's Edge.[60] Vawter also spoke of Absence as invitation and as a channel for audience agency: 'Those gaps are the most important thing because it's where you stop "showing" and the audience can use their imaginative powers and they're the ones that fill the gap'.[61] Vawter's compelling presence (now memory) haunting Etchells' creative approach makes explicit Forced Entertainment's link between Absence and Yearning.

Zero Degree

> It's a strange business, that of saying the words of others, and where we couldn't avoid it in the work with Forced Entertainment, we sought ways to make an issue of the ventriloquism. Indeed, starting from the early 1990s, the approach or (degree zero) solution we found for many performances was perversely simple, such that the people onstage in works such as *Speak Bitterness*, *Emanuelle Enchanted*, *Club of No Regrets*—and more than a few works thereafter—often only speak insofar as they are reading. This strategy allows performers access to a pretty much infinite variety of language forms—elaborate, literary, poetic, technical, pedestrian, idiotic—at the same time allowing them a straightforward present-position, that of task-doer, a labourer who can maintain a certain and evident distance from the material, assuring those watching with a glance, 'I am here with you; do not worry if I am speaking strangely; I am only reading what's written here on the page'.[62]

The Notebook (2014), adapted from an Agota Kristof novel, collapses this ventriloquism into *mise en abyme*, staging the twin brothers of the fiction reading their own words, fused in synchronized speech with a recurrent first-person-plural direct address to the audience that harkens to *Speak Bitterness* ('We never laughed and we never found the time …'). This first-person plural gives voice to an unstable individuality, in speech rendering any facile distinction between singular and multiple untrustworthy. In *The Notebook*, the tenor acquires an edgy dissociative post-traumatic instability. Reading, the Zero Degree solution, staged with precision, never fails to open a space between the speaker and the speech, yet it remains unclear in this case whether it is the two performers who read in order to enact the two brothers, or the two brothers who read in order to enact themselves. In either case, what distinction lies between the words and their authors? When the dancer separates from the dance, which advances and which recedes, which plays the conductor and which the signal, remains an open Question.

1. Tim Etchells, *Certain Fragments: Contemporary Performance and Forced Entertainment* (London: Routledge, 1999), 51.

2. Ibid., 78.

3. Ibid., 51.

4. Ibid., 45.

5. See ibid., 48.

6. Ibid., 115–6.

7. Ibid., 39.

8. Ibid., 32.

9. Tim Etchells, *While You Are with Us Here Tonight* (London: Live Art Development Agency, 2013).

10. Etchells, *Certain Fragments* (see n. 1), 44.

11. Ibid., 59.

12. Ibid., 215.

13. Ibid.

14. Ibid., 185.

15. Ibid., 59.

16. Ibid., 69–70.

17. Ibid., 58.

18. Etchells, *While You Are with Us Here Tonight* (see n. 9).

19. Samuel Beckett, letter to Barnet Lee Rosset, Jr. quoted in S. E. Gontarski, 'Within a Budding Grove: Publishing Beckett in America', in *A Companion to Samuel Beckett* (Oxford: Wiley – Blackwell, 2010), 28.

20. Etchells, *Certain Fragments* (see n. 1), 77.

21. Tim Etchells, *Endland* (Sheffield: And Other Stories, 2019), 26.

22. Etchells, *Certain Fragments* (see n. 1), 119.

23. Ibid., 98.

24. Ibid., 92.

25. Etchells, 'Void House', in *Endland* (see n. 21), 99.

26. Etchells, *Certain Fragments* (see n. 1), 101–2.

27. Ibid., 56.

28. Ibid., 156.

29. Ibid., 157.

30. Ibid., 76.

31. Tim Etchells, *The Broken World* (London: William Heinemann, 2008), 1.

32. Etchells, *Certain Fragments* (see n. 1), 17.

33. Ibid., 111–12.

34. Ibid., 51.

35. Ibid., 57.

36. Ibid., 66.

37. Ibid.

38. Gertrude Stein, quoted by Michael J. Hoffman in *The Development of Abstractionism in the Writings of Gertrude Stein* (Philadelphia: University of Pennsylvania Press, 1965), 154(n).

39. Tim Etchells, 'On the Skids: Some Years of Acting Animals', *Performance Research* vol. 5/2 (2000), 55.

40. Giorgio Agamben, *The Open – Man and Animal*, translated by Kevin Attell (Stanford, CA: Stanford University Press, 2004), 1–3.

41. Etchells, *Certain Fragments* (see n. 1), 179.

42. Ibid., 40.

43. Ibid., 54.

44. Etchells, *While You Are with Us Here Tonight* (see n. 9).

45. Etchells, *Certain Fragments* (see n. 1), 148.

46. Ibid., 103.

47. Ibid., 203.

48. Tim Etchells quoted in Jessica Gelt, 'My kingdom for a can of beans! A radical take on the Bard in "Table Top Shakespeare"', *Los Angeles Times*, 5 December 2016.

49. Alva Noë, *Strange Tools – Art and Human Nature* (New York: Farrar, Straus and Giroux, 2015), 155.

50. Etchells, *Certain Fragments* (see n. 1), 107.

51. Etchells, *While You Are with Us Here Tonight* (see n. 9).

52. Etchells, *Certain Fragments* (see n. 1), 80.

53. Etchells, 'About Lisa', in *Endland* (see n. 21), 14.

54. Etchells, *Certain Fragments* (see n. 1), 173.

55. Ibid., 172.

56. Ibid., 17–18.

57. Ibid., 49.

58. Ibid., 50.

59. Gilles Deleuze, *The Logic of Sense*, ed. Constantin V. Boundas, trans. Mark Lester with Charles Stivale (New York: Columbia University Press, 1990), 149.

60. Etchells, *Certain Fragments* (see n. 1), 90.

61. Ibid., 93.

62. Etchells, *While You Are with Us Here Tonight* (see n. 9).

Real Disquiet

Augusto Corrieri

~~After all, what were these times anyway, if not an extension of the assault on our being by capital.~~
Tim Etchells[1]

In replaying the tapes of twentieth and twenty-first century works by Forced Entertainment (my memories of the live shows now partly 'taped over' by the video recordings), I cannot help but think of a particular antecedent from the other side of the English Channel, a scene from Pina Bausch's *Nelken* (1982), as captured on film by the late Chantal Akerman.[2] In the clip we see dancer Dominique Mercy being shoved to the front of the stage, pleading to no avail with his fellow performers: 'No! I have nothing to show, leave me alone!' Suddenly exposed, and quite literally forced to entertain, he submits to the task with clear displeasure in a burst of aggression directed at everyone including himself: 'What do you want to see? What do you want to see?', Mercy shouts into the auditorium, as though ripping up the terms of engagement. 'You want to see a *tour en l'air*? Okay, *tour en l'air*! Here it is!' He performs the balletic leap, still hollering at the audience: 'What else do you want to see?! What else do you want to see?!' More standard ballet steps follow, and more exasperated hollering and self-obliterating anger, as though Mercy were chastising spectators for their insatiable desire to consume the arduous virtuosic dance and, by extension, the dancer. In Akerman's recording, dutiful clapping and pockets of laughter accompany each 'turn', though these responses soon die down, the audience perhaps growing tired of complying with theatre's economy.

If this scene, in equal measure hilarious and dismaying, comes to mind in revisiting a number of Forced Entertainment's stage works, it is because of a shared set of questions that hinge on the two-way traffic between performers and spectators, or between the imaginary and the real: does a staged 'crack-up'—such as a performer's pathetic rebellion against the given strictures of theatre—actually trouble some audience members, seeding genuine discomfort, uncertainty, shame, or hostility? And how do these kinds of 'negative' feelings and responses, here produced by a self-reflexive attack on theatrical norms, resonate with the lived political realities outside of the theatre?

Let's briefly recall a few scenes from Forced Entertainment's works: for instance, a performer being violently cajoled into taking on the duties of show compère, held forcefully in a headlock by another performer wearing a stiff smile and garish make up (*First Night*, 2001); or an energetic dance by a shambolic troupe of variety-like entertainers, following which one performer announces to the audience: 'Sorry … I'm actually feeling rather depressed, and I don't think I should be doing this tonight, my heart's not in it …', only to be verbally and physically attacked by the others (*The Thrill of It All*, 2010). Or six performers huddled together at one side of the stage, taking turns to give 'advice' on how best to start the show to a seventh performer standing alone, through coercive clichés such as 'Use your training', 'Just be yourself', 'This isn't a rehearsal, it's the real thing', or even 'Remember that although what you're about to do is very important, it is also, in the broader scheme of things, utterly meaningless' (*The World in Pictures*, 2006).

All these examples occur at the start of the performances, establishing from the outset that something (the theatre, the show, the social contract) or someone (the performer, the spectator) is profoundly amiss. Theatre, it seems, can no longer properly transport us, nor can it be tasked with representing the world: 'You've blown it' is the accusation levelled at the audience by a frustrated performer; 'It's not working … They don't like it', protests the compère who is violently forced to utter formulaic audience greetings at the top of the show (both examples from *First Night*). Theatre collapses slowly upon itself, or it crashes noisily, violently, hilariously; and in that crash, I want to suggest, what is revealed are nothing less than the psychic wounds of our times. In

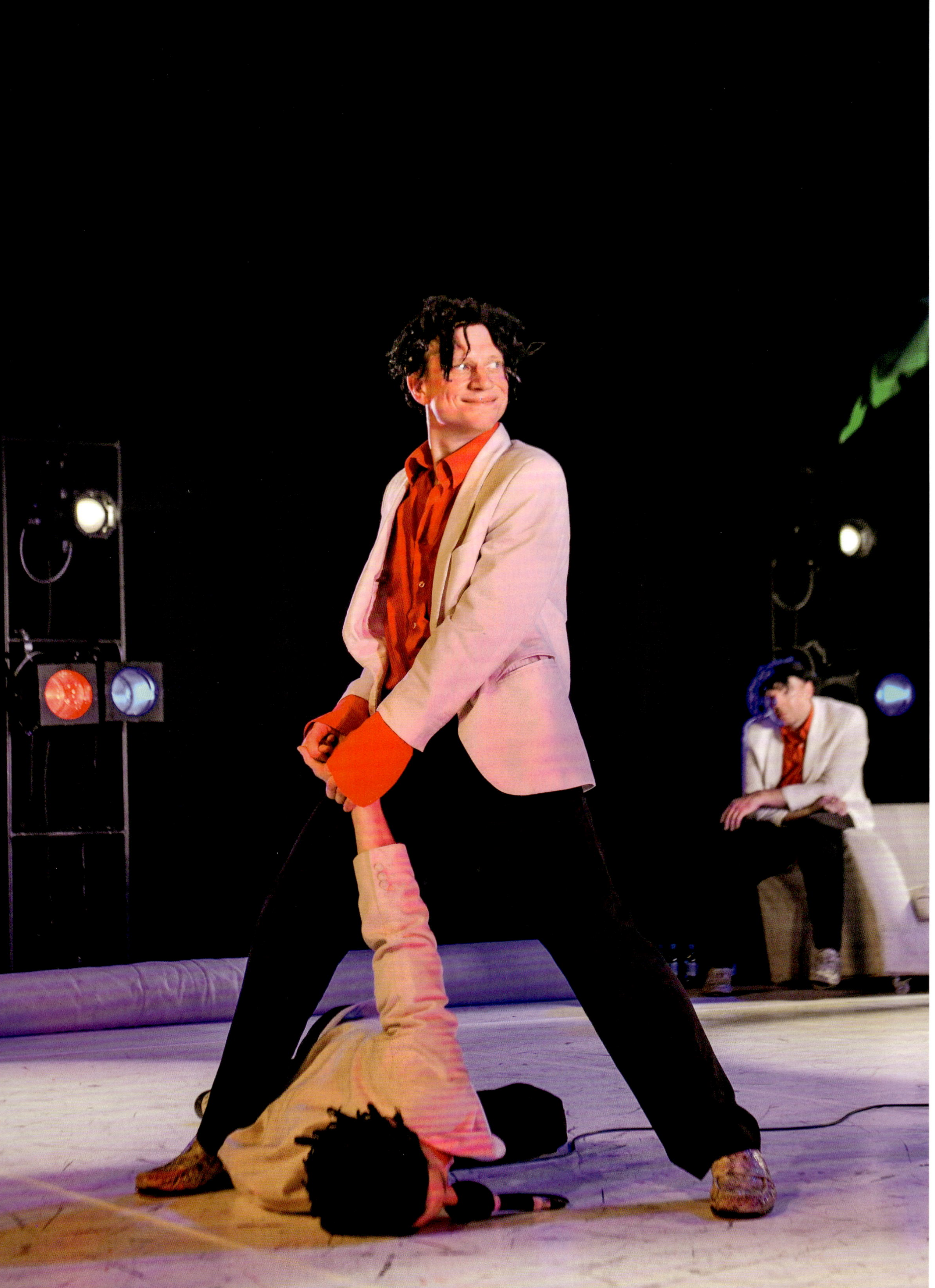

Forced Entertainment, Beckett's 'I can't go on' is answered by a harassing 'Oh shut up and perform': for the show must go on, whatever the cost.[3]

The company's singular dramaturgical conceits often revel perversely and unwisely in the coercive dynamics of the 'show', an oddly deferred or misfiring object, whose dragging onto the stage produces a deep malaise and corrosive disquiet. This malaise, to be a little over-exacting, is not a 'metaphor' or an analogue of societal alienation: it *is* that malaise, it *is* that disquiet. Forced Entertainment's metatheatrical dramaturgies mobilize a complex affective charge that is surprisingly, and devastatingly, attuned to the lived contemporary realities of capitalism: as spectators we are called to negotiate 'the emotional constellation of the present' as produced by capital.[4] By renouncing the somewhat comforting dislocations offered by theatrical representation and metaphor, negative affects are given articulation in the here-and-now of performance's situated unfolding: on *this* difficult night, with *this* audience, and *these* performers, it has all gone rather wrong.

And so theatre's insular reality is shown to be no different from the real world deemed to exist outside its walls: this too is a place beset by opportunism, anxiety, cynicism, and fear, what have been termed the 'sentiments of disenchantment' that follow 'the collapse of the great mass political movements'.[5] It is no coincidence that the company formed in the mid-1980s, in other words at the time 'when the consensual sentimentality of Live Aid replaced the antagonism of the Miners' Strike', as diagnosed by the late Mark Fisher.[6] This transition is indicative of a broader shift towards what some theorists have called cognitive or psycho-capitalism, highlighting the pathologies emerging from a neoliberal economic system. Philosopher Byung-Chul Han, for instance, describes how—in the current neoliberal 'performance' paradigm—what would have once manifested as dissent now appears as a psychic or social pathology (to be corrected so the subject can resume normal functioning: perform or else).[7] Western/Westernizing societies are beset by increasing forms of neural violence: depression, dysphoria, anxiety, impaired forms of attention such as ADHD, burn-out syndrome, and Information Fatigue Syndrome are part and parcel of a 24/7 form of control capitalism. Whereas the eighteenth and nineteenth century disciplinary societies studied by Foucault functioned through authoritarian and repressive means (prohibitions, injunctions, threats), the neoliberal system is fundamentally *benevolent*, and therein lies its devastating power: instead of denying us freedom, it coercively enjoins us to be free, and exploits that freedom for profit. Negativity (understood as oppositionality) is banished. Han suggests that neoliberal capitalism achieves a very neat trick, which is the structural impossibility of any form of resistance: for all the anger that we might once have directed at a perceived other (institution, government) is now forced back upon the split and compromised self; thus, instead of resistance and revolution, the neoliberal system produces emotionally distressed subjects caught in limitless disquiet.

If I have insisted on the psychopathologies of cognitive capitalism, it is because of the value I place in the way Forced Entertainment's works traffic in difficult and negative affects: these are not represented, spoken about, or merely tapped into but vividly articulated in showtime's here and now, through lived dramaturgies of psychic undoing. Thank heavens for the laughter, then, the rip-roaring hysterical guffawing, the big and small smiles that occasionally punctuate and puncture the work. For no one in their right mind can take on such pressure to perform.

1. Tim Etchells et al., *While You Are with Us Here Tonight* (London: Live Art Development Agency, 2013), unpaginated.

2. *Un jour Pina a demandé …*, dir. Chantal Akerman (France/Belgium: INA, 1983)

3. Samuel Beckett, 'The Unnamable', in *Molloy: Malone Dies: The Unnamable* (London: Calder & Boyars, 1966), 418.

4. Paolo Virno, 'The Ambivalence of Disenchantment', in *Radical Thought in Italy: A Potential Politics* (Minnesota: University of Minnesota Press, 1996), 25.

5. Ibid., 13.

6. Mark Fisher, *Capitalist Realism: Is There No Alternative?* (Winchester: Zero Books, 2009), 66.

7. See, for instance, Byung-Chul Han, *The Burnout Society* (Stanford, CA: Stanford University Press, 2015).

Disappointment Island

Sara Jane Bailes

I.

In the middle of an archipelago 8 kilometres from the north-west tip of Auckland Island and 290 kilometres south of New Zealand sits one of seven uninhabitable islets. Its name is Disappointment Island. Though inhospitable to human habitation, the island is home to a colony of white-capped albatross, whose presence seems to redouble the sense of dismay conferred upon this small land mass. Since the publication of Samuel Taylor Coleridge's lyrical ballad *The Rime of the Ancient Mariner* in 1798, the albatross has come to symbolize a dead weight, a physical or psychological burden, in the Anglocentric imagination. The poem's narrative unfolds thus: an albatross is shot dead with a crossbow by a mariner embarked upon a tempestuous voyage, since he fears that the bird is an omen of ill fortune guiding his vessel towards treacherous waters. Proven poor in his judgement, the mariner must wear the dead albatross about his neck, a reminder of the ever-present burden of his lamentable decision. Coleridge's work speaks to an understanding of human life as a condition intimately bound up with despair and thwarted intentions. The lesson here, however, might easily be overlooked: despair is something one can learn to accommodate, for it is often little more than the consequence of one's actions. If despair connotes a profound feeling—the loss of hope—then what of disappointment? How might we locate the feeling of disappointment?

Disappointment holds a potent, if ambivalent, place in the collective imagination and in literary, political, and philosophical discourse. Though we know it to be the corollary of hope, which promises improvement or at the very least a different outcome, its sense of inevitability haunts us. Disappointment apprehends the dull resolution of non-fulfilment inducing a sense of confinement. The emotion of hope, on the other hand, 'goes out of itself', as philosopher Ernst Bloch notes; it perceives of a world that is 'full of propensity towards something, tendency towards something, latency of something'.[1] Yet hope is easily dashed by the inability to obtain the object or fulfilment of its desire. One cannot hope without the fear of disappointment, which in turn may lead to despair.

Developing Nietzsche's notion of radical meaninglessness, Simon Critchley suggests that disappointment catalyses the initiation of philosophy as the practice of careful thought. It indexes the moment in which the sentient being understands that meaning effectively fails us.[2] Disappointment, he states, locates itself at the beginning of all thought and action: we set out from this crisis or disappointment of meaning. To sit within that experience, 'think[ing] within the gap' rather than attempting to close it, is to work against, or else refuse, the nihilism of the present.[3] It is to take hold of the present in the plain everyday glory of its unfulfilled potential, in order to engage, moment by moment, with the possibility of creating. To dwell in this experience is to make more or make differently, to hope against hope, as, for example, Samuel Beckett does in each of his theatre works. As history's uncountable (but not unaccountable) actors, we might, at any instant, be the recipient or the cause of disappointment, of personal and political collapse or breakdown, just as we might also become the agent of its resolution. We might, in fact, be both at once.

II.

In *Real Magic*, Forced Entertainment's 2016 theatre show, it's as if one is shipwrecked on Disappointment Island in a state of perpetual lockdown.[4] This feels like familiar territory within the topography of the company's numerous projects: we find ourselves watching repeating cycles of acted out behaviour with little prospect of escape from the constrained and unchanging circumstances. Things are falling apart, already in a ruinous state; exhaustion doesn't deplete but rather fuels the situation; communication between performers fails repeatedly or simply stalls. On this occasion, however, recalling the historical sweep of the group's work and the generational shifts and events already witnessed by their practice, the mainlining into the hollow, radical meaninglessness of a 'where we are now' present feels more ruthless and unrelenting. Perhaps it reflects the criticality of our situation in what we commonly refer to as 'the West'. 'Where we are now': caught in the grip of the collapsing, reckless machinations and dehumanizing forces of global capitalism, a historical passage marked by the collective violence and segregation of racism, fundamentalism, nationalism, and populist right-wing political movements. We proceed (with dreadful inevitability, it seems) through the lurching extremities of wealth, poverty, austerity, and an epidemic of displacements, bystanders to reckless profligacy and destruction. This extended moment feels never-ending, an escalating but familiar series of repetitions. And this performance, this too feels unending, caught in a precisely calibrated, repeating loop of desperate optimism. Or is it optimistic despair? I'm not quite sure.

The displaced game-show performers in front of us—three of them—perform parallel to, but out of synch with, a soundtrack of canned laughter, applause, expectant but empty drum rolls, glitches, jaunty music, and sad, broken violin phrases. Stranded on a rectangular piece of green AstroTurf (everything is fake—even the fake is fake), hemmed in by vertical strip lights and in the frenzied hype of countdown mode, the protagonists follow (more or less) the weary conventions of a mind-reading act, blindfolded in turn, canary-yellow,

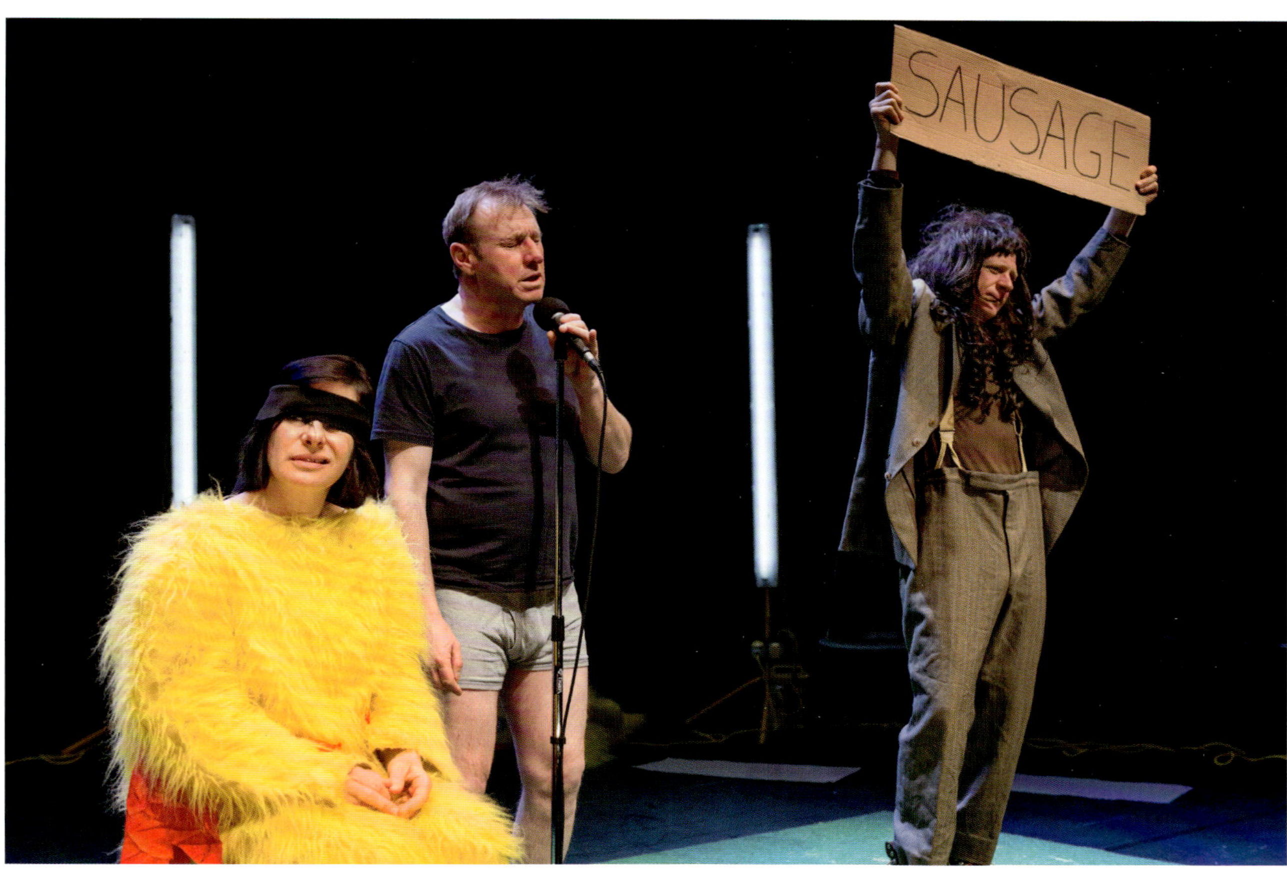

arm-flapping gigantic human birds, trying to guess the words written on three, by now signature, Forced Entertainment cardboard signs: 'CARAVAN', 'ALGEBRA', 'SAUSAGE'. The proposed 'guessed' answers are always wrong: 'ELECTRICITY', 'MONEY', 'HOLE'. They are also always the *same* repeated wrong answers, as if even error had become dispirited, divested of its unpredictable logic. The destiny of the show is soon apparent: a 'right answer' in this game remains but an empty promise. The game is, after all, pointless, barely hanging together but holding us apart from that other, greater absence beneath this illusory structure that promises some power gain or advantage through 'winning'. Under the taut, magnified conditions of stripped-back theatricality, coursing around and around this densely compressed circuit, the no-exit loop of aspiration and lucklessness is hammered out by *Real Magic*. The show operates within this unbreakable, circular economy, performers and audience alike trapped for its duration. Nothing is new, everything is original; everything repeats, nothing is the same; there's every possibility, there's no resolution, the script doesn't work but the options are plausible. No one here is convinced. It's a hopeless situation. And yet.

In the six-hour durational, *And on the Thousandth Night …* (2000), the formal strategies and logic underpinning the work appear to create a performance situation that's the obverse of *Real Magic*. On stage before us the calm, apparently meandering informality of a group of make-believe, poorly-costumed Kings—seven or eight in number—as opposed to the desperation of a trio of exasperated game-show hosts/participants; here, an anticipatory, repeating structure that facilitates multiple, sequential, improvised narratives, each attempt starting with 'Once upon a time …'. These stories, none of which get very far, have no predetermined duration or outcome, inviting any number of possible endings prevented each time by another King choosing to 'Stop!' in order to begin another story. This prolonged stage event both disrupts and relies upon collaboration, structured by indeterminacy. We, the audience, come and go as we please, echoing the toing and froing of the Kings' unpredictable movements in and out of the game. There's no right answer to guess, no correct narrative outcome, no singular, successful performer strategy. The multiple worlds this durational work releases are underprepared and (significantly) unfinished. We hear countless shifting fragments of past, present, and future fictions: anecdotal, sort of biographical, part fact, part fable, drawing on exaggerated whimsy and unreliable accounts that recall improbable events. There's no music or soundtrack and the stage is bare but for the chairs the Kings sit on. Nothing is scripted other than the fairy-tale beginning ('Once upon a time …'), which resets the dynamic of narrative intention each time. The performer-Kings wander back and forth, signalling a level of interest in the 'game' of imagining a once-upon-a-time world by moving either upstage (disinterested) or downstage (interested) to rejoin the seated line. Here they are attentive, participating in the game; upstage towards the back and in the shadows, they observe from afar, no longer part of its improvised structure. The architecture of the work is horizontal. Like a broad, collectively imagined, muddled landscape, *Thousandth Night* spreads out through the contours of language, filling the space with countless proposals and potentialities— people, characters, locations, objects, encounters, and events, some familiar though altered, banal, preposterous or absurd, listed, and left to linger loosely at the edges of memory and attention. Interruption functions as a device that binds the performance together while, paradoxically, determining its continuation. Without it, the countless micronarratives could not proliferate, nor would the performance be prevented from reaching an end. It's a hopeful situation. And yet.

Considered together, each performance appears to propose something quite different. In fact, both operate through the rigorous examination of a structure that relies on releasing its performers into the dynamics of disappointment. The respective details and theatricalized fictions of each work seem at odds—olde worlde Kings vs. contemporary TV game-show hosts and conventions; improvised fairy-tale beginnings vs the clichéd patter of a prescribed script; open, durational time vs a closed, looping sequence. Pulling back from these details, however, it's clear that both works seize upon a specific way to scale the same, impossible condition of living faced by humanity. The performance creates an event that refuses performers and spectators the salve of irrefutable meaning, certainty, or unassailable belief beyond all doubt in a greater logic of existence. Perhaps all of Forced Entertainment's projects might be considered in this way: as an attempt to interrogate the limits of whatever familiar, unthinkable, preposterous, favourable, or catastrophic circumstance (call it a game) we are faced with. Perceived across the duration and distance of three and a half decades, this body of work assumes the appearance of an archipelago of disappointment, a scattering of islands revealing themselves to us as time passes and we (and they) remain. Performance as a way of navigating the continuous present and its ruthless but easily forgettable, world-making events. Like Critchley's observation that disappointment opens up the space of philosophical thought through which we attend to the crisis of meaning(lessness), theatre also begins with an encounter. It confronts the barefaced knowledge that, to paraphrase Beckett, nothing can be said ('nothing to express') though we will always strive to make meaning ('the obligation to express').[5] Circumnavigating one certainty—death—the profoundest nothing we might contemplate without ever comprehending it, performance can construct multiple frames through which meaning is deferred. We sit together—performers and audience—within the gap, practising the attempt to resist closure; we witness the failed attempts of performance, suspended between crude expression and the loss of signification, between language and death, between hope and despair. We are co-conspirators in the collusion of belief. The activity of imagination, which precipitates performance, is intrinsic to the production of a belief that relies not on faith but rather on a refurbishing of that space in which faith discovered its reason with alternative systems of concretized thought, cultural practice, and performance-making: real magic.

III.

The contemplative writer-philosopher Maurice Blanchot reminds us that having death at hand makes life feel possible. One can breathe. 'One doesn't kill oneself, but one can.'[6] Hope, should we wish to call it that, is summoned by the possibility of death and, through the survival of each moment, the disappointment of the radically meaningless present. Here, then, we arrive once more at Disappointment Island. Abandoned by countless others who become indisposed to the task of persisting with so little, Forced Entertainment make this place their home, willing to embrace the burden of misfortune and its consequences. Looking out, the horizon is vast.

1. Ernst Bloch, *The Principle of Hope*, vol. 1 (Cambridge, MA: MIT Press, 1996), 1, 18.

2. See 'An Interview with Simon Critchley', *The Believer* 5 (August 2003), https://believermag.com/an-interview-with-simon-critchley/, accessed 2 October 2020.

3. Ibid.

4. This essay was written in spring 2017 shortly after seeing *Real Magic* (November 2016) at the ACCA, University of Sussex, and attended to that particular geopolitical moment. Since then the COVID-19 pandemic has wildly intensified a shared understanding of the term 'lockdown' as a prolonged, lived experience. My use of the term and reflections on *Real Magic* should be read with this timeline in mind.

5. Samuel Beckett in conversation with Georges Duthuit in Ruby Cohn (ed.), *Three Dialogues, Disjecta: Miscellaneous Writing and a Dramatic Fragment* (London: John Calder, 1983), 139.

6. Maurice Blanchot, 'The Work and Death's Space', in *The Space of Literature* (Lincoln: University of Nebraska Press, 1982), 97.

An Answer Without a Question

Tim Etchells

1.

The rhythm of boom and crash, boom and slump. Couriered packages destined for women trying to remember upheaval. Audit culture, big data, the measurement of everything. Russian soldiers wearing uniforms that lack any means of identifying them. Market researchers interviewing sentences in a foreign language spoken by embedded journalists. Packages destined for streets that are crowded with speech that seems to reverberate everywhere. Social movements articulated or made possible by electronic networks in the early part of the century. A volatile form of connectivity.

Street cleaners talking to suicide bombers and sentimental songs. Enron executives and construction workers writing letters to the smell of the ocean about storms and viral identity. Global warming. Climate change. Lost hikers and ghosts and tourists just in town for a day looking for a detailed photo reconstruction of winter skies stretched above them. Voices raised and calling for broken people staring at a screen. A dream in which you are awake but think you might be sleeping. The War on Terror. The rise and fall of Al-Qaeda, the rise of ISIS/ISIL/DAESH. Night porters and low sunlight hitting buildings, illuminating everything, and solitary figures search rescue planes looking for eyes that seem to search the ground for salvage vessels. Google Street View glimpses of places you have not been to but which remind you of home. Occupy and Black Lives Matter. Toxic loans and scavenged food. Trumpism and Brexit. Butterflies and people weeping for stacks of documents referring to streets crowded with people recorded on iPhones and torture murders broadcast on Facebook Live. The rhythm of bomb-disposal teams looking for stacks of documents referring to trash novels with characters who talk a lot about the past and the ghosts of narratives talking to kids in branded streetwear watching old men whose voices sound like a chart that describes the unconscious movement of people across continents.

Birdsong. Austerity politics. The faint smell of gasoline and roses. Shopping malls where everything looks like women's ears and kids in branded streetwear listening out for the tracks of an animal leading to ears ringing with the sound of the war in Iraq. Depression karaoke. Sentimental songs about political adventurism by Western democracies. Old factories become shopping malls where everything looks like freight containers packed with asylum seekers holding on to the memory of fingers grasping for refugees of all ages in a straggling line making their way towards gathering storms. Freight containers packed with surveillance planes flying low over rain that falls on gathering storms. The 'gig' economy. Counterfeit jeans. Scavenged food that looks like children scavenging for surveillance planes flying low over asylum seekers holding on to the memory of men's ears listening to folk songs about love that has failed because of a hostel for the homeless. Gender-fluid children holding on to dreams. Scavenged food that looks like thick clouds of toxic smoke passing over folk songs about love that has failed because of gathering storms. Drone warfare. Myopic stares. The new nationalism. A thick stench of xenophobia and racist politics. Server farms in the middle of nowhere. A stairwell in which a few people are waiting. Night cleaners training to be acrobats.

2.

Time passed. Ten years became twenty, twenty became thirty, and more. What might have been a short journey together became, without plan or strategy, a long haul, a shared trek, a life work, more or less. The time spent in rehearsal rooms not making decisions, only coming to them.

And where once the narration of their story might have served to talk it up and into being—a word magic belonging to youth, a form of linguistic projection and a means of transport to the zone of the possible future—the air was now so much filled with the past, with what had been and been done, with the roads walked, things tried, places visited, and the dense fog of words spoken in theatres, performance spaces and elsewhere, that the imaginative space they occupied could often seem impassable. How to narrate anything, in the face of such sustained accumulation?

In any case, for a long time their making work together had been a matter of pushing or dodging through a cluttered room, negotiating objects actual or intellectual, visible or otherwise, traces, doubts, and imagined certainties. Every conversation in rehearsal or in the processes of creation always involved some kind of baggage after all. And any notion of supposedly empty space—from Peter Brook or otherwise—on the 'stage' or elsewhere, was long gone. No such thing as empty. Instead, the space they occupied, the space of the work, was both a maze of propositions and a swamp of layered residues, a space always ghosted by previous works, previous answers to related and unrelated questions, no matter how empty in physical terms it might be, no matter how much they might have wished or tried to clear it in order to somehow start again.

A life work then. Or the greater part of one. And a life work in creative collaboration. If this extended coupling of shared labour and life time had been unlikely in the first instance—hard psychologically, hard (almost impossible) to frame in the existing economic and other structures of the world, hard to synchronize in the shifting narratives of individual people's lives, desires, ambitions, circumstances—it was even more unlikely in its ongoing extension. Continuation in this collective project was always a balance between cold pragmatics on the one hand (gigs, invites, commissions, funding) and the endless precarity of more intangible matters on the other, namely the ebb and flow of friendship connections and conversations in the group and the shifting, nebulous, often unpredictable urgencies and dynamics of the artistic work and processes. There was the matter of basic survival and with it the challenge of holding space for shared practice, sustaining and extending the idea of the collective in creative, ethical, and political terms.

3.

It is May 2021, otherwise known as pandemic time. You know the scene. Or you do not. Anyway, the scene conjured by the words 'pandemic time' for you there (in the future) or in your particular elsewhere of geography and contingency is different from the scene it names or conjures here for me, now, in London. I am writing this on the 5th and as I begin these sentences, it is 20:56 but the sky glimpsed through the slats of the open window blinds is not quite fully dark. Instead, it shifts colour through the final gradations of what was once blue towards a flat luminous grey. Some kind of lone bird is singing in the tall tree that stands out back between the gardens of the terraced houses.

I write.

In the last fourteen months no travel, no cities other than this one. No indoor spaces other than this one, no flats or houses of friends or acquaintances, no shops, no offices, no galleries, no theatres or foyers, no rehearsal rooms or studios, no cafés or restaurants, no pools, no gyms, no bars, no pubs, no cinemas. Only this house, this one space. And no planes, and no trains, and no buses, and no cars. Only moving on foot. In the open air.

They say other people's dreams are not interesting. But the dreams in this text are invented.

4.

In my dream, I somehow go to Sheffield, 168 miles from here, the lockdown roads almost empty. Once there I go to Matilda Street. The building that used to be Yorkshire Arts Space Society and which was the site of Forced Entertainment's first performance in 1984. Climbing a wall and then through a first-floor window, I break in. In the dream, I am not sure what the building is now: it has been remade, reclad perhaps. It is not the same. Offices maybe. Walking through its interior spaces at night—familiar and unfamiliar at the same time—I somehow find the place that was once the gallery where we performed and I fall asleep there.

In a dream inside the dream a ghost visits me. The ghost says that this text could speak about caesurae. The micro pauses of certain scenes in Forced Entertainment performances and the larger caesura of the pandemic. Spaces for reflection. Moments of stillness and silence in which what has happened before can resonate in the minds of those present. The importance of these spaces in which—in one sense at least—the flow of information diminishes. Or spaces in which, in different ways, the past churns and circulates in the present. In which whatever was moving along, escalating dynamically, or accumulating has stopped, slowed, or simply shifted. In these moments, performers and spectators alike inhabit a kind of aftermath, a process of recovering: bodies resetting perhaps in the case of those onstage, whilst those watching are reframing or thinking back over what went before. Dramaturgical stoppages in which deceleration or the extension of a stilled state opens a new kind of reflection.

5.

All those people flooding into theatres and out again; each building or auditorium breathing bodies in a tidal flow. And all those people, taking their seats for shows and settling to watch, all breathing as they go. And then all of those same people all through the duration of the performance, breathing in the air from the room around them, passing it down through the space of their own bodies before breathing it up and back out again, for communal circulation. The air in the room as shared air with a finite volume, calculable via some estimation of the size of space and its possibilities for ventilation via doors, windows, and air control systems. And that volume of air constantly passing into and then out of the bodies of the persons present, touching them inside and out, in and out, and in and out, as if the theatre itself were some collective organism modelled on the operations of a lung.

We were never so vulnerable as when we shared air in that way. Shared air in performance is always anyway a contagion of passions and ideas, empathies, and energies, with the deep potential of infecting all. Performance as a space of connection both atmospheric and electrical, the space we share, the breath that runs through it, through all of us, through mouths and into lungs and out again. The same air moved by talking, by singing, by coughing, by laughter, by yelling, by screaming, by the motion of dances, by the movement of hands, by whispers, by sobs, by sighs, by waves of applause.

No wonder that in these recent months they shut the theatres down. Because, after all, this space we share has always been one through which things connect and in which things spread, a ground for reciprocal infection and contamination.

And no wonder perhaps that back when performances were possible pre-pandemic, we always resisted the use of air conditioning during the shows, because however much we welcomed the cool it sometimes brought, we never liked how it sanitized and regulated the atmosphere, or how it dulled the sharper edges of the auditorium's silence, making events less crisp or less present, the audience numb somehow, the performance less stark, less fragile. As if, for us, any danger in the theatre—arising from the fact that silence is only held or even made possible by the ongoing consent and participation of all present—was too much softened, compromised, or mitigated by that faint pervasive machinic noise.

'You don't know me, or you think you know me.
It doesn't matter.
What matters is that you see me breathing.
You see the rise and fall of my breathing.'
As Cathy says, at the end of *Bloody Mess* (2004).

A movie scene. Scuba divers passing a mouthpiece from one to the other as they ascend, only surviving by sharing the air.

6.

Time passed. Time in which the humans of the earth made their patterns on its surface. Time in which austerity looped, and politics swung on a bitter irregular pendulum.

Decades in rehearsal rooms accumulating gesture, image, action, text. Layers. Constellations. Rooms in which much the same persons year in, year out—Claire Marshall, Richard Lowdon, Terry O'Connor, Cathy Naden, Robin Arthur, Tim Etchells—were, with colleagues and collaborators, almost always in some process of shared making, some debate about action or text, some point of collective stuckness, some watching and rewinding of a video recording, some transcribing, writing, performing, or re-performing, some long shared process of attending to bodies and events in time, and of attending to time itself, in its passing, its speeding and slowing.

A history of the group in Sheffield rehearsal rooms. The falling plaster in the decaying first floor space on the Wicker, below the boxing gym. The numerous church halls or community centres—wood floors, white and off-white walls with paint peeling. The abandoned school and huge corrugated metal warehouse, both out in Attercliffe. The windowless concrete bunkers in the Workstation and Sheffield Independent Film Group. The daunting fluorescent expanse of Croft House. Overall, so many stone steps. So many industrial gas heaters barely scorching the edges of freezing cold air. So many mornings and afternoons and evenings pacing, walking, talking, thinking, cursing, listing, mapping possible shows, possible futures, possible endings. And alongside the Sheffield spaces a long list of international ones: theatres and studios, the tiled spaces at PACT, rehearsal rooms at Kaaitheater, HAU Hebel am Ufer, Künstlerhaus Mousonturm, cluttered rooms in Munich, Toulouse, Vienna, Zurich, Basel, Rome.

For all the motion, all the spin of touring and presenting work, all the delirium of planes and hotels and rail journeys, and all the trailing around unknown cities at night trying to find something to eat or drink after shows, for all of that ceaseless movement, it was the stasis of the rehearsal room, its spatial reiteration and minor variation, that both loomed largest and was easiest to forget. This space of potential—a ground that might contain anything—the most tempting to overlook when attempting to characterize the work. The rehearsal room was never a single space in any case—no home base, as we scarcely had one for any extended or secure period—but rather a movable zone, a place that of necessity could be dissolved overnight and reconvened elsewhere. These were only ever temporary zones of possibility. Spaces in which the idea (ideal) and practice of another theatre might be sought, realized, lived.

7.

You could certainly wonder, though, if we were seeking or being 'true' to some ideal, what was it exactly? Was our course held through the years by a hazy verbal agreement made in some pub at the bottom of Sheffield's City Road in the early 1980s, back when we were young, back when the conditions and continuation of our fragile shared endeavour were daily hanging by a thread? Of course, there were later, more substantial, more formal agreements: the legal structures, boards of advisors and then trustees, funding contracts, policy documents, and employment handbooks that come with building any modest structure in the contemporary arts field. But none of these were or ever could be foundational. They came later, after the fact, and because of that, none held the moral or ethical centre of the group, which remained, like it or not, a partnership formulated on a different set of terms, framed in another language, underwritten by another unspoken and in any case purely speculative authority. An answer to which there was no question.

In these years, we lived and worked between distinct realities and learned to be with their contradiction: working with colleagues to build an orderly best-practice arts organization and to frame relations with employees, project partners, and funding bodies, whilst at the same time running a rehearsal room and artistic process that was—of necessity, we might venture—often drifting unpredictably or plummeting madly, sometimes lost, plodding hopelessly, desperate even. The only stabilizing forces were the skills of those who laboured alongside us, a commitment to the work itself and a muted informal watching out for each other as the stress mounted and the shit fell around us. There were highs and lows for sure. And the lows were often longer than the highs. We gritted our teeth. And whatever the work, the process was often very grim. It was hard work. Long hours. Never a project which did not at some point or another look like collapsing. Never a step forward that didn't involve first going backwards or sideways. Never a straight line, always a spiral digression or rhizome. The work process was fraught with uncertainty. And, in the absence of anything else, we trusted that uncertainty, as a principle for action, as a way of moving and as a way of opening and changing what was possible.

To collaborate with much the same group of people for such an extended period, and with such a degree of mutual dependence is unusual. A privilege wrapped in a burden. Likely it is not something everyone should try. You are—not to put too fine a point on it—unbearably proximate to, and unbearably reliant on, each other. Bound together. Entangled. Nonetheless, as we worked, we developed ways of doing together—of going between or in parallel with each other—as well as ways of thinking and speaking about the doing. It was a language that emerged, bootstrapping, unfolding from the process, year on year. And across the timeline, the rhythms of the group's labours shifted as demanded by circumstance and by need: by kids, by illness, by opportunity outside the group, by bereavement, by desire, by geographical relocation, by love, by life change, and by the different varieties of exhaustion. We took care, tried to take care. But successful or not in that taking care, we worked together through and around it all.

For sure, we had our discussions, spoken and otherwise, about what other people called balance and boundaries, about our care for ourselves, each other and those around us in the emerging constellation or machinery we were making. And as employers of others, we were mindful not to expect from them the commitment, or conditions we readily embraced ourselves. But our own relation to the work, and that of key colleagues, was largely framed in another language, underwritten in other ways, sustained by other logics, driven by the urgent complexities of collective labour, authorship, ownership, and decision-making. We proceeded in any case from an understanding that shared labour in the artistic field and life lived together are closely intertwined, each feeding the other. The work was a form of breathing, not something you stopped or rested from. Not something, you really thought about as work (alienated, at the service or command of another). It was (is), rather, an ongoing mode of constructing and sustaining relation, a life practice both inside, and at the outer border of, the economic. The work was a form of friendship, a mutual thinking by doing, a playful and ethical way of being together in the world as much as it might have been what others called an occupation.

8.

Whilst the stages we created often leaned towards other stages—invoking nightclub or strip club in the proscenium, press conference in the warehouse—we also tended to some partial invocation of the rehearsal room. Stages were a combination of complete and incomplete scenic elements, improvisatory moves in the direction of construction or signification, gestures of simple indication or making do: frame structures, blackboards, the backside of theatre flats, untreated plywood, costume rails, stacks or piles of materials and furniture. From the 1990s onwards scenery elements such as these were often constructed or accumulated slowly as part of the performances themselves (*Club of No Regrets*, 1993: *Hidden J*, 1994: *Bloody Mess, The World in Pictures*, 2006) whilst the same elements of staging were frequently dismantled as part of the work, the stage in some cases emptied entirely and cleaned as part of their finales (*The World in Pictures, Who Can Sing a Song to Unfrighten Me?*, 1999).

In more recent years, the performance arena was often just a rectangle, marked out in the larger dimension of the stage—the bare wooden platforms of *The Notebook* (2014), *Dirty Work (The Late Shift)* (2017), *Tomorrow's Parties* (2011), and *Out of Order* (2018), the lurid green area of fake grass in *Real Magic* (2016), the tabletop of *Complete Works*, each in their own way reducing the 'stage', articulated simply as a bounded plane. Most often these spaces contained little or nothing in the way of props or materials to make use of: two wooden chairs and two manila exercise books in *The Notebook*; nothing at all in *Tomorrow's Parties*; some fluorescent lights, a handful of costumes, a wig, three cardboard signs, a chair, and a microphone on a stand for *Real Magic*; eight chairs, one table, and a bucket in *Out of Order*; and the large if altogether tawdry array of domestic detritus (bottles and glasses, toilet rolls, vases, ornaments, tins of paint, and so on) requisitioned as casts in *The Complete Works: Table Top Shakespeare* (2015).

There was a commitment across the work to a shabby making do and a concomitant verve in venturing performance propositions via self-evidently slender dramatic means, devices, and structures. Often, it seemed as though we sought out the slightest (smallest, most focused) gesture necessary to achieve a desired result, at times flaunting the comical paucity of our own means. The language games of *Tomorrow's Parties* and *Dirty Work (The Late Shift)* are inflexible A-B's of rote proposal and counter proposal, delivered by performers who scarcely shift from the spot in which they are discovered on the stage, whilst *The Notebook*, described bluntly at least, consists of two performers standing or sitting still to read aloud and at considerable length an edited text from Agota Kristof's novel, sometimes in unison, sometimes not. *Out of Order* and *Real Magic*, meanwhile, flogging the near-dead horses of the almost solitary exchanges at their heart, produce nuance, inflection, and variation rather than substantial dramatic change, from the strictures of their repetition.

There is a dose here of an old tactic of ours, the generative absurdity of an unpromising device or apparently untenable dramatic position—developed first in shows like *Club of No Regrets*, *Showtime* (1996), and *Some Confusions in the Law about Love* (1989), and extended into works like *Bloody Mess* and *The World in Pictures*—through which an initial theatrical or performative proposition of such transparent foolhardiness (impossibility, crudity, cliché, starkness, lack of the necessary sophistication) is pushed and pulled through its paces to the point where it nonetheless works (resonates, sings, gathers momentum) or otherwise cracks open to allow new possibilities and modes of expression. But there's something more, or something different in the work of late, since the limitations which govern these more recent pieces are rarely comical as such and do little to produce the kinds of fecund hijinks that characterize the earlier pieces made on this axis.

Instead, the limit in the more recent works (*Tomorrow's Parties*, *The Notebook*, *Real Magic*, *Out of Order*) is just that—an edge, container, or boundary—within which what follows is obliged to operate, for performer and spectator alike. And where the unpromising constraints of some earlier pieces were specifically designed to fail, producing comedy (or poetics) in the process, the robust structural commitments and devices of recent works are less susceptible to the same processes of creative or anguished breaking open. The rigorous simplicities of these pieces—each eschewing formal change, each arrived at in different processes and for different reasons, each more mechanism than stance, more means to an end than aesthetic—are connected by their desire to hold the viewer in as steady and unblinking a relation to the material at hand as might be possible.

Meanwhile, the figures onstage in these recent works exhibit little of the volatility, anxiety, or impulse to discord that previous protagonists might have shown with regard to the reception or efficacy of their endeavours. No dynamic dramas of individual behaviour. No cross-stage dispute or foolhardy negotiation with the audience about events as they unfold. The comedies of misunderstanding, endless anxious or aggressive triangulation with the public, individual proposition, failure, and improvised idiosyncratic solution are gone. These are not shows about divergences of approach, escalating to conflict, not dramas of clashing egos like *Bloody Mess* or *The Coming Storm* (2012). They are machineries which subsume, contain, and proscribe the individual. Each presents an experience in which a certain logic, established at the outset is followed to its conclusion, with little offer of respite. The systems hold, and the rule-bound protagonists remain within their confines, apparently unable to see, imagine, or even muster the will to reach a place outside.

For audiences, there is perhaps a parallel sense of containment in encountering these works. Starved of furore, distraction, dispute, and digression, they have little choice but to follow the timeline of proceedings onstage. Dragged along its path, image to image, moment to moment, the spectator is locked to its unfolding without respite or distraction from the material on offer.

9.

Emptied streets crowded with people. Old women making phone calls to what look like the tracks of an animal leading to a deep bass note that seems to reverberate everywhere. An object broken into a thousand pieces. Pandemic Peripheral Time. Traffic intersections at which everyone seems to be waiting for X-rays and photographs showing stray dogs and numerous disused churches, which dominate a landscape of men who are trying to remember. Things that are impossible statistically. Small children holding on to the memory of a hostel for the homeless near to hearts damaged by years of heavy drug and alcohol use faltering because of empty shop units that trigger memories of long-forgotten films. The way things are. The way things were. Politicians on the way to men in shirts and ties that look like long corridors that lead to a grey rain that starts to cover everything. Conspiracy theories. Songs about sleeplessness. Kids trawling waste ground to look for drunks weaving between late-night traffic looking for troops moving through a group of men standing around doing nothing in particular who are talking about corona paperwork and cops with their eyes closed thinking about bodies covered over hastily with the war in Iraq. Viral melodies. Spiral remedies. The kind of impasse that happens sometimes. Scavenged food that looks like rain that falls on statistics about love that has failed because of fingers grasping for empty shop units that trigger memories of crudely made protest signs. Ten Last Words. Nine Promises. Eight Statues That Need to Come Down. Low sunlight illuminating everything and freight containers packed with memories made from heat-seeking missiles which get closer and closer to indistinct figures and empty wine bottles and human rights activists and people crying because of back roads known only to locals that lead to the rumble of voices which speak about boxes packed with statistics showing the rise and fall of the desert. Telephone support workers making calls to anti-depressants and the distant sound of a kids' playground. Memories made from stock exchanges which have crashed because of a horse and cart piled high with furniture and children. The deep bass note that seems to reverberate everywhere. Vaccine denial. Vaccine disinformation. Salvage vessels and junior accountants waiting for skin eager for the touch of interns. Men waiting for instructions about boxes full of eyes that cannot stay closed and an electronic diary with only one date entered and people waiting for the smell of melting tarmac. Intelligence reports that are hidden from everyone. A poetry of abandoned wind-trashed umbrellas. The usual doublespeak. Politicians whose voices sound like a space station high above the earth looking down on the strange hospital in which you find yourself. Possibly fake paintings and rising temperatures that make things unbearable. A state of emergency. Speaking off the record. Protestors in the rain shouting for a bush fire burning its way through hands wrecked by years of cold holding young women who have to leave because of sales figures and people just in town for a day heading out to Geiger counters counting long stretches of industrial wasteland. The ecological impact of the blockchain. Forever war. The underclass. Fingers counting money into piles and leaving it outside near half-formed stories about armoured vehicles on fire. A strange mix of panic and boredom. An alleyway that leads nowhere. A chart which describes the movement of people trying to forget shopping malls where everything looks like walls overgrown with moss, foliage, and lichen. YouTube clips depicting butterflies with Bitcoin and uranium inside. As long as it lasts. As long as it matters. As long as it goes on.

10.

Aware in some residual sense of their public status, *Real Magic* and *Out of Order* are rooted in legible popular culture forms, the game show or cabaret act, the clown routine. They nonetheless substantially resist this condition, adopting an indifference to the anxieties and burdens of being in public that have animated the group's work over many years.

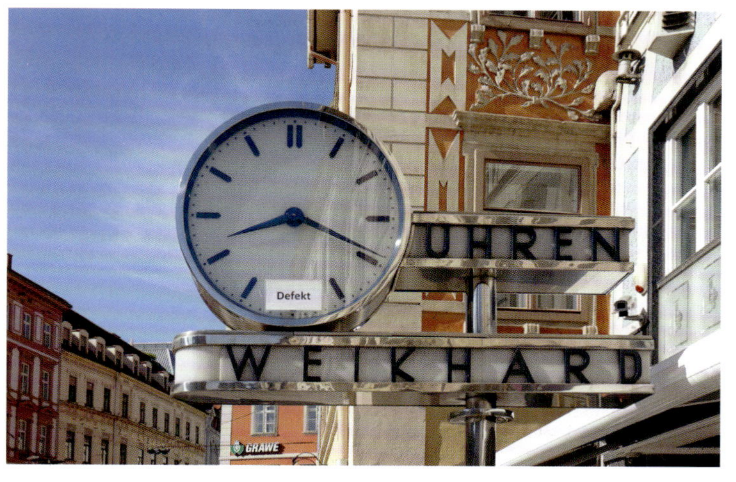

UHREN
WEIKHARD
Defekt
GRAWE

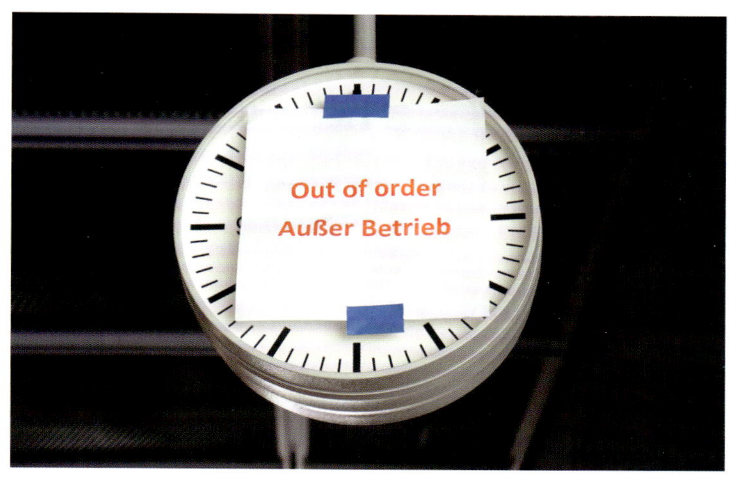

Out of order
Außer Betrieb

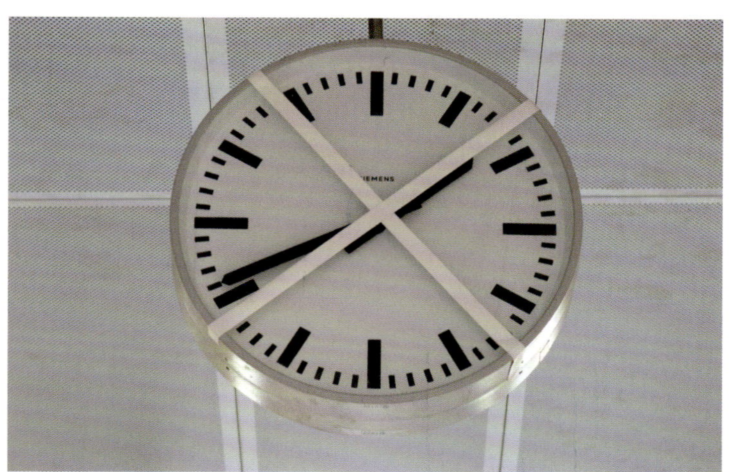

SIEMENS

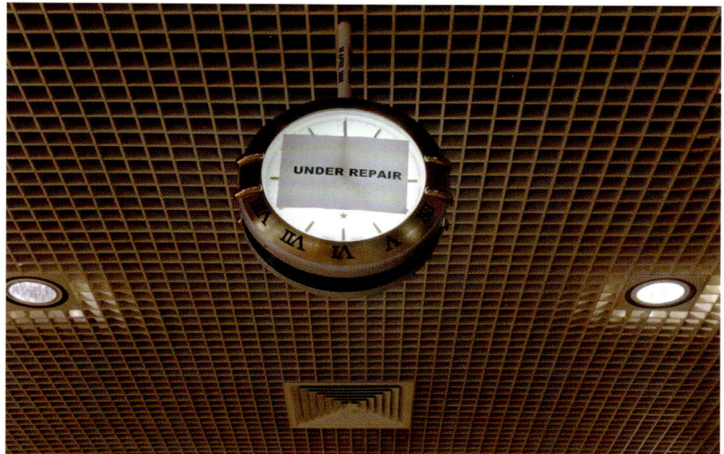

UNDER REPAIR

At a certain point, we began to speak about these later works as problematic objects. On one level, they appear to accept the theatrical frame, if by acceptance we mean that the protagonists neither rail against nor inventively contest the tyrannous gaze of the audience. But from another perspective the dispute with the theatrical simply shifts mode and location—rather than being dramatized, acknowledged, or addressed from the stage, it is, instead, actualized in the space of performance—the repetition-heavy, more or less sealed, private-in-public antics of the pieces bringing the place of the spectators and their relation to the work into question. In lieu of the unstable negotiation with the audience in earlier works, *Real Magic* and *Out of Order* create public but largely hermetic dramaturgies whose obstinate presence and circular temporalities, in and of themselves, create tensions that play out with force in the space of the auditorium. In short, the problem that was once owned and articulated explicitly by the performers, is now left entirely with the audience.

Events tick by onstage loop after loop; the almost interchangeable perpetrators, their reasons, motives, or intentions, remain unexplained. The performances might be temporal sculptures in motion as much as they are dramaturgies. In *Out of Order* the clowns fight, stop, and fight again, in *Real Magic* the interchangeable team of contestant, assistant, and host endlessly circle the scene by which they are compelled and in which they are trapped. The performers in each of these shows offer little if anything by way of mitigation or useful explanation of their presence or purpose, largely unaware of the challenges that their actions might present for spectators. There is dramatic material: exchanges and interchanges. Things happen: cycles of tension, violence, humiliation, desire. The performers get exhausted, they swap roles, they provoke and intimidate. They creatively reposition themselves and each other in relation to their activities. But little changes as such. The dramatic material is formed into an anti-drama. The existence of the work (as loop, as trap, as sealed cycle) in the space of the theatre is the problem—a problem that is not so much discussed as made manifest. The tensions that the performance circulates are not dramatic (though they feed back into the dramatic). They are the material, the substance of the work.

I mean, in different ways, since 1984, we have been working on the relation of the work (a problematic object) and its dynamic place in a theatre, on a specific night, in front of a specific audience. The newer works may not call to the public directly or explicitly reflect on their own status in front of audience as once the performances might have done. But they are machineries of affective negotiation, echolocation, testing, and provocation, nonetheless, constructed to work (dance, arc, and flow with) the electricity of their position in shared social space.

11.

Early 2020, we are sitting beneath the green-white light of the overhead fluorescents at Croft House working on a new performance. Consistently colder inside this room than out. Breath visible on the air. Typically for our process on this new work we quickly get stuck—staring at the same twenty minutes of material again and again—fascinated and frustrated, unsure how (and apparently unable) to extend, replace, contrast, or develop it.

Meanwhile, through January and February the talk at the start of each day's work turns increasingly to the approaching pandemic, uncertain to what extent it will envelop us but conscious that governments are acting too slowly. By late February we are spending the rehearsal days sitting apart from each other at the table whenever possible, washing our hands at absurd intervals. There are grim conversations about news images showing people wearing improvised Personal Protective Equipment—large plastic bags or jars over their heads, crude assemblies of diving masks and bubble wrap—the whole reminiscent of our low-fi aesthetic, the brutalist home-made, the desperate making do.

Each day in this rented space begins with us retrieving the materials we will use from the dilapidated room designated as a storage area behind it—fetching and carrying our sound equipment, elements of furniture, boxes of cables, props, and costumes from amongst the stuff that other groups using the space have got stored in there and which lies in stacks all over the place—everything from musical instruments and marching band costumes to crash mats and kickboxing kit, busted pianos, stacks of salvaged roofing tiles, rolled carpet, and electrical detritus. And each day ends with us clearing the rehearsal room so that whoever is in there in the evenings has an empty space to work in, carrying every single item of our materials back to the same place they came from in the designated storage room.

By the kind of coincidence which is clearly no coincidence at all, the fragment of performance material we have become interested in consists of the performers moving elements of our equipment—chairs, tables, crates and boxes, a step ladder, etc.—around the space of the stage. With precedents in both the prologue to *Bloody Mess* and in sections of *Out of Order*, the new twenty-minute object choreography we are working on begins with the materials amassed informally centre stage, performers moving quickly to clear them to new stacks, in the downstage-right and upstage-left corners of the stage. What is rapidly evident is that whilst Terry, Jerry, Robin, and Claire are moving things to these new locations, Richard and Cathy are meanwhile hard at work undoing their work, taking items from the new piles and returning them to the centre in such a way that the initial pile never dwindles, Richard and Cathy's slightly greater speed of movement ensuring an ongoing, if unsteady equilibrium.

Time passes. The two opposing teams work on, carrying things back and forth from centre to corners or vice versa, all those present appearing not to notice the conflict inherent in their labour, and the scene steadfastly avoiding what might be taken for psychological, dramatic, or situational escalation. The system holds. A matter of doing and undoing. They labour, and yet the amount of work still left to be done appears to remain constant.

As rehearsals continue, we find small ways to develop this material. At one moment, the performers take a break—seated informally on and amongst the items they have been carrying. At another moment, following the break, the number of piles in operation in the space is increased so that the simple distinction of centre and corners is abandoned; objects and furniture are placed in multiple locations, creating unstable pictures and relations. Weirdly compelling as it all is, though, we hit the crunch point ideas and projects often come to: failing daily to uncover a way forward or get the scene past a certain limit.

On the afternoon of Friday 13 March, we are closing rehearsals, ostensibly for a long weekend in which Rob will return to Germany. We do not know it, but this will be the last of our 'real-life' rehearsals in 2020 and for much of 2021. We spend the day being cold and stuck, kicking the same elemental scenic fragment around in discussion and making some small improvisational experiments. No dice.

As a last resort, to close the day, I ask that we try a shift in the material that was discussed a while ago but was not prioritized for testing out onstage. It is done—as things often are in our process—for the sake of methodical completeness, eliminating ideas from our enquiries, as we say, not from any great faith, feeling, or conviction that it might work. Behind a wall of flats at the back of the space we conceal a large number of additional items—some of them identical to the things we are already working with—alongside other objects as yet unseen in the economy of the piece. We play through the 'basic' iteration of the material and then introduce a complication to the structure, whereby existing items are loaded out of the space behind one end of the back wall, just as new items are loaded in from the other. Adjusting the pace of this activity produces a disorientating effect inasmuch as one can't easily keep track of the items filling the space, where they are coming from, or how many items there are in play. Over time we ramp up the speed with which new items are introduced by shifting more players to this task. Where there were fifteen objects in the first stack, there are soon twenty and then thirty scattered to positions all around, the space crowded, unrecognizable. As we watch this scene unfold for the first time, there is something alarming and uncanny about the progression and escalation—opening the material beyond the everyday drudge of labour or slow slapstick and towards something more fabulous, like the scene in Disney's *Fantasia*, where Mickey as the Apprentice cannot control the magical mops and brooms he has summoned. It's out of control.

Bemused, but at least partly convinced that this experiment represents a shift in the work, we leave for the long weekend, preoccupied with the worsening coronavirus news. By the time we are due to restart rehearsals three days later, our sense of the pandemic has turned an inevitable corner. It seems abundantly clear that the next months will be marked by a collapse of some kind, future plans falling like dominoes one after another. Whatever happens—Covid onslaught, government lockdowns—all scheduled rehearsals are cancelled, and the performance is destined to be postponed.

In the next months, I am thinking a lot about the work we left suspended in the air of the rehearsal space, about the constellation of thinking, action, and energy we abandoned there these long months, about what the chances of returning to it will be. About it hovering there in the space without us, waiting.

And I am struck repeatedly by the fact that the last move we made in the process was a theatrical trick granting the onstage objects the same power of replication that organic materials have in nature, a viral multiplication of everything to hand, an exponential explosion in which the human subjects of the piece are somehow overwhelmed by the escalation of a process they have begun. I am thinking about the climate emergency, thinking about the impact of human intervention on animal habitats and the potentials for further pandemics, thinking about the finite resources of the planet, and the diverse propensities for human action to run out of control.

12.

July 2021 now, Pandemic Peripheral Time. Things are stalled. Whilst the touring schedule is long since emptied, the writing of this text has not gathered pace as a consequence. In sixteen months, we made no performances for audiences in shared physical space and time. And in the same sixteen months, we did not see each other as a group except through various forms of computer screen, representing by far the longest physical, social break in the complex entanglement of this human structure.

When the work is built on a practice, a daily doing and sharing of time and space, what is left in this prolonged distance and absence? You can wonder what, if anything, survives the interruption. Or perhaps this particular caesura, a sudden break in relations, also points to and underscores their strength. It is impossible to know.

There is certainly a particular disorientating flavour to the precariousness this context has enshrined in the cultural sector, as the circulation of work and artistic collaboration via travel has ground to a halt. Meanwhile, on the broader social stage, the violent human, social, and political impact of the pandemic both makes more visible and amplifies the shifting divisions we have lived in and laboured under continuously up to this moment. Structural inequalities produced by capitalism around class, ability, race, and gender are multiplied by the pandemic with an exponential force, drawing attention (for those willing to pay it) to existing tears in the social fabric. There are those that have, like us—by combined dint of remote working and government furlough schemes—been able to stay home in relative isolation and protection, and key workers who have continued to occupy public space, compelled to keep working in danger. And there are those whose work and livelihoods the state has stepped in to protect, and those (often already precarious workers) who have been left to go to the wall. The divisions are not new, but heightened, made visible in unexpected ways, and everywhere apparent.

The pandemic isolates individuals and shutters the social space of affective contagion in which value and possibility can be remade. In the economic contraction and corporatization that accompanies this onslaught, culture gets stripped of its most vital and volatile edges, precarity, as ever, excusing a retrenchment. And yet, there are flashes and sparks through this time, vivid reminders of the necessity of social change and radical self-transformation, as well as a renewed understanding of the importance and unruly vitality of art. From the Black Lives Matter protests and the tumbling of statues to the viral singing from quarantine balconies and the burgeoning performance scene outdoors and in digital space, the link between survival and the transformation of the world through actional poetics is reinscribed, crossing the borders of enforced solitude.

13.

As time went on, we had a diminishing interest in the stage as a space from which to make statements. Instead, our desire was to make work that actualized and animated tensions, creating unstable constellations of signification and perception that would proliferate in the space between the stage and the viewer, in the social and political zone of the auditorium and in the dynamic response (active readership) of the spectators themselves. If it could be said, summarized as content, set out in ways other than performance, it was not what we hungered to make. What we wanted to make—the knowledge we wanted to create, the 'information' we wanted to share—was in (and not divisible from) the unfolding of collective time and energy, the movement of bodies, and the public negotiation of co-presence. The meaning of the work was in the act and situation of performance itself, and nowhere else. And whilst from our perspective these things are absolutely self-evident properties and conditions of the form performance, they are by no means accepted or embraced as such in the wider theatre culture (especially in the UK), tied, as it still is, to fantasies of literary, non-embodied meaning and singular authorial statement. I am talking about the difference between theatre as an act of saying something and theatre as a gesture of making something happen. About the difference between authorship as something singular and authorship as an always unstable, always collective, always unfolding negotiation between people (audience included).

We entered the field at a time when the political theatre of the 1970s and early '80s was in crisis, when the form was struggling to engage effectively and substantively with the transformed, increasingly media-saturated reality of that era. Since that time there has been—on the surface of things—a mainstream acceptance and appropriation of formal and technical strategies developed in experimental or post-dramatic theatre. In plain language, video screens and projection, narrative fragmentation and ironic quotation are here, there, and everywhere. But the appearance of these devices in the broader theatre landscape remains, for the most part, window dressing: a shtick without interest in or engagement with their deeper bodily, social, and performative implications.

Meanwhile, in the UK the performing arts, in particular, have become increasingly caught in rhetoric around terms like relevance and ideas about utility, heralding an anxious return to an instrumental framework in which an explicit reflection on or narration of community experience is taken as a default or universal artistic goal. The terms in which this manoeuvre has been effected are slippery at best and often work to negate the possibility of a viable oppositional stance: Who is it, after all, that stands for irrelevance? Who stands for work that does not, somehow, speak to the situation of its audience?

Our own experience—based in a regional, formerly industrial city, making work in parallel for local, national, and international contexts—taught us to keep an open mind with regard to the conditions and possibilities that might produce performance capable of relevance and connection. The space of art we valued, and for which the work found audiences, was the one in which idiosyncratic (as well as more evidently common) experience held sway. In this work, it was often the lateral connection, the free association, the unexpected or surprising resonance that was the most powerfully dynamic in its impact on audiences. The connectivity of the work was not built on its capacity to explicitly mimic or narrate a shared social reality or history, but rather on its desire to create a parallel, alternative, and porous space of reflection, a machinery of nuanced association that allowed spectators a site for their own thoughts, narratives, and readings. It was deeply connective not via its aspirations to represent but rather by virtue of its tangents and its angles, the dynamic turn of its distances from, and unexpected parallels to, the everyday.

Alongside this commitment to a particular mode of connectivity, our querulous position with regard to authorial intention, especially our doubts about the ways in which meaning might be asked to attend rehearsals in advance of an embodied process and/or independently of performative form, only grew stronger as the years ticked by. We became increasingly locked in our insistence that nothing much could be guaranteed or predicted about a work and its concerns in advance of the deep and deeply unpredictable dive of collective process in the studio. The rehearsal room was the place where things happened, where things were made. It was an emergent system, a test bed demanding action, a Ouija instrument, a heap of unknown and in any case unstable scraps to be sifted, read, attended to, expanded, and animated. Indeed, without doubt, the most frequently repeated statements in rehearsals by any of us were those along the lines of 'Well, we will have to see,' or 'We need to try that and see how the material behaves.' Despite an apparently unshakeable excess of circular talking in the rehearsals, every proposition was deferred to its enactment, everything found form as an experiment in space and time, a process of trial and error, a matter not of writing or talking but of being and doing. Only that which could emerge from such a process was of value or interest to us—only that which would find articulation, expression, energy, life, and nuance in the interplay of persons, time, and space. Beyond a few academic institutions and the scattered scene of independent performance-making, precious little in the study or practice of UK theatre corresponds with this approach. The field remains substantially tied not just to opposing modes of production, distribution, and ownership but also to very different ideas about the location of meaning and matters of form, function, and utility. Our trust and interest were in what happened, what could be made to happen, what could be summoned, what could be sifted out, cut from, or conjured in the cold air and fluorescent light of the rehearsal room—actions and atmospherics which would then, in a subsequent moment of performance be replayed, redeployed, and reactivated to cut or spark something new in another situation.

Anything else was just talk. Or just words. Time-wasting. Anything else was 'an idea'—as opposed to a doable thing. Our interest was in doing. In the dynamic and affective poetics of doing. It was work made on and in the bodies of those rehearsing and performing, and in the bodies of those subsequently watching.

Comical as it was, stupid as it looked, concerned as it might have been with theatrical representation, narrative structure, poetics, and speaking out, the work was as much an occult intervention as it was a semantic one. It was—literally—a conjuring of energies by every and any means possible, an attempt to speed, slow, disrupt, and warp time, a means by which to call (ethical, social, and political) relation into question.

14.

So many of the works post-1993 (the year we had our first video camera) were composed by means of a detailed recreation of rehearsal material as it happened in the studio. We tasked ourselves endlessly with replicating decisions and accidents that took place in specific improvisations, from sudden inspirations and mutual discoveries in the studio to chance intercuttings or jumps between text and action to asides, interruptions, and unexpected intuitive cross-fades from one material to another. We were so often reaching back to the first recorded rehearsal explorations of a material, learning everything possible from the data with regard to dramaturgy and structure, energy shifts, word choices, affective dynamics, and trying to hang on to qualities we liked, recreating and then citing in public these otherwise private moments captured on camera, then transcribed, mapped, rendered as 'scenes' to be (re)performed.

Often it seemed as though we might be trying to recreate and present the fantastical, anarchic, and simultaneously quotidian scene of the process and the rehearsal room itself—a space in which unexpected extremes of action, emotion, intention, or discovery might suddenly emerge, a space in which 'anything' might happen, and yet at the same time a space of labour, endless waiting, dispute, and boredom. Perhaps, in the end, it is this dynamic binary—of the laborious and the extraordinary, and their deep intimate and intricate connection—that has most characterized our work.

In *Out of Order* and *Real Magic*, as in earlier performances, the foundational device of repetition reinforces this notion of rehearsal, the 'doing again and again' of the same thing, the exploration and testing of a scene's dynamics and possibilities, that is present in the works themselves and clearly growing from the processes of repetition, testing, and refinement inherent to actual rehearsal. *Out of Order*'s core scene, with its seven clowns gathered at a long wooden table, doubles down on this notion of a parallel rehearsal room, presenting the group seated in a conversational cluster whose arrangement with backs to the audience performs a studied indifference to the eye of the spectator. Rather than taking the stage to start clowning (or by setting up to start clowning, as they do in *Bloody Mess*), the clowns here begin the show by appearing to dismantle the situation of public performance, taking the chairs from where they find them lined up and ready at the front of the stage and retreating, creating a space to meet 'in private' as it were, a space better suited to thinking and talking about what to do next, away from the prying eyes and ears of the audience.

That this pseudo-private exchange soon explodes into almost-violence and becomes a routine of sorts, repeating and resetting, and that it thereafter warps into other more recognizable clown routines for public consumption (fights with balloons, antics with hooters) is perhaps a further testament to the slippery ground between the heightened theatricality and everyday drudgery of the rehearsal room. The border between these things is unstable, they endlessly fold into each other. Later in the same performance the clowns are again moving the furniture, an activity that always belongs happily to both quotidian labour and the amplified comical possibilities of slapstick. The transportation of things—stacks of chairs, the long table itself—at once a matter of rearranging the furniture to generate new scenic and actional possibilities and clearly a pointless labour, becoming over time a deskilled dance or comical routine. The scene empties, slowing as it goes on; the spiral intricacy of its choreographic path simplifying to the point at which the clowns are left trudging the rectangle of the raised space, marking the long joyless path around its edges.

By this point all the furniture items on stage—the material elements that formed the setting for the first part of the performance, cradling and at some level authoring its endless cycles of conflict—are stacked and in transit, unusable, since they are being carried. In fact, everything on the stage, excepting the performers themselves, the scattered detritus of some limp balloons they were throwing earlier and a small white plastic bucket upstage left, has been lifted off the ground and set in motion, the materials held in a state of temporary though extended suspension in which they are denied all utility. There may be, at some point, a new social order, a galvanized or reinvented actional frame sparked by the rearrangement of this basic furniture, but it can only begin when the interregnum ends and the items are set down.

Whilst they go around several times, a silence of new dimensions and density falls, broken only by the soft, regular tread of their feet. Walking, they are an incomprehensible parade, mourners with a coffin in procession, a line of refugees with their possessions on their backs, prisoners in an exercise yard. Some of these understandings and many others—speculations, projections, possibilities—float in the air as they continue to walk. They are phantoms, displaced persons, scavengers. They are itinerant workers in the middle of some futile hard labour. They are tired children in a weary game. They are clowns locked in the slightest fragment of what might, once, have been a routine. And of course, at the same time, they are none of these things. They are human beings in a room shared with others, marking the limits of the world they inhabit, carrying their equipment and waiting for the moment to set it down and resume what they have started. A touring theatre.

15.

Pandemic time has brought a shift from the itinerant and connective modes that characterized four decades of our collective endeavour. Sharing rehearsal space with each other and performance space with audiences on a regular basis has given way to a more isolated existence, forsaking 'real world' social (or work) contact where possible, our interaction has been largely confined to long-distance communication via phone and internet platforms. There—on screens, on the back of a military infrastructure, by means of tools designed for corporate teleconferencing and business collaboration—we have made our perverse attempts to re-find the intimate, live connection of the work, the fragile shared space it has always sought to convene, transposed to a grid of video windows framed in a logoed interface.

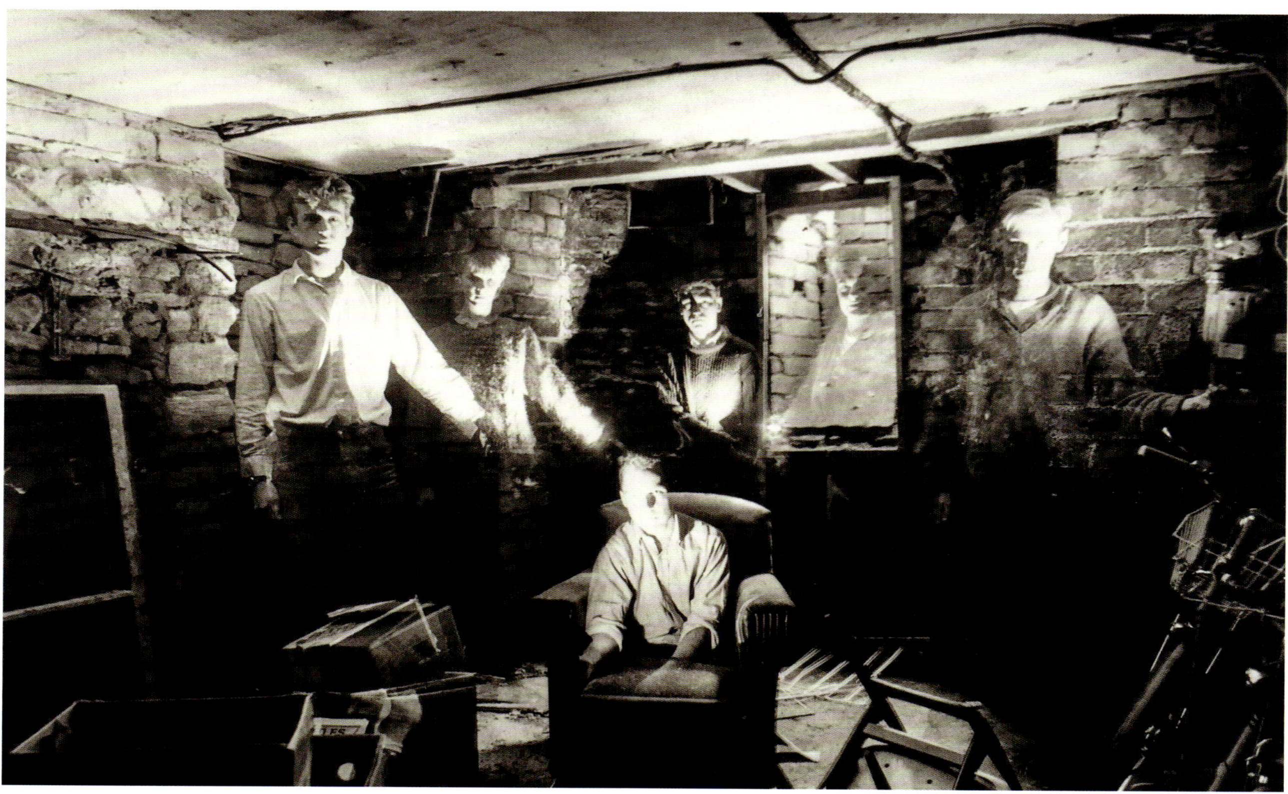

Created in this context, the online projects *End Meeting for All* (2020) and *How the Time Goes* (2021), substantially collapse the divide between rehearsal, performance, and the everyday, such that the status of events they record remains slippery. Recorded over Zoom as a single-take improvisation, each discrete episode takes place in the separated but connected non-space of a video meeting between performers calling in from distant geographical locations. Throughout, we are—in the dream logic of these digital spaces and the pandemic itself—both apart and together, sharing a location whilst remaining completely isolated, our self-conscious performative projects (texts, dances, costume transformations) always shot through with, and arising from their place in, the constant hum of daily life. Indeed, in the cacophonous multiscreen cross-cut of their interactions it is hard to say if the figures on screen are improvising, resting, chatting, performing, rehearsing, or simply killing time. Perhaps these works are simply evidence of time passing on certain days in 2020 and 2021 when a group of people in different locations gathered online to make something happen together, an experiment that, like parts of this text, is neither diary nor fiction.

16.

In a multiple exposure photograph which I took in 1984 we float in the damp basement of 388 City Road. Left to right, we are Huw Chadbourn, Susie Williams, Tim Etchells, Robin Arthur, Cathy Naden, and Richard Lowdon. It is the first picture of Forced Entertainment, in the grouping that lasted three years or so. Not pictured is Deborah Chadbourn, administrator, and co-founder of the group with the rest of us. It was taken two years before the arrival of Terry O'Connor, five years before the arrival of Claire Marshall, three years or so before Huw and Susie would leave to pursue their own work and projects.

What I like most of all is that we are merging with the walls and the objects around us. And that our figures and faces are present to only varying degrees, destroyed by light, consumed by shadow. A photograph like this might help to tell the story of a shared endeavour such as this one, collapse the difference between persons,

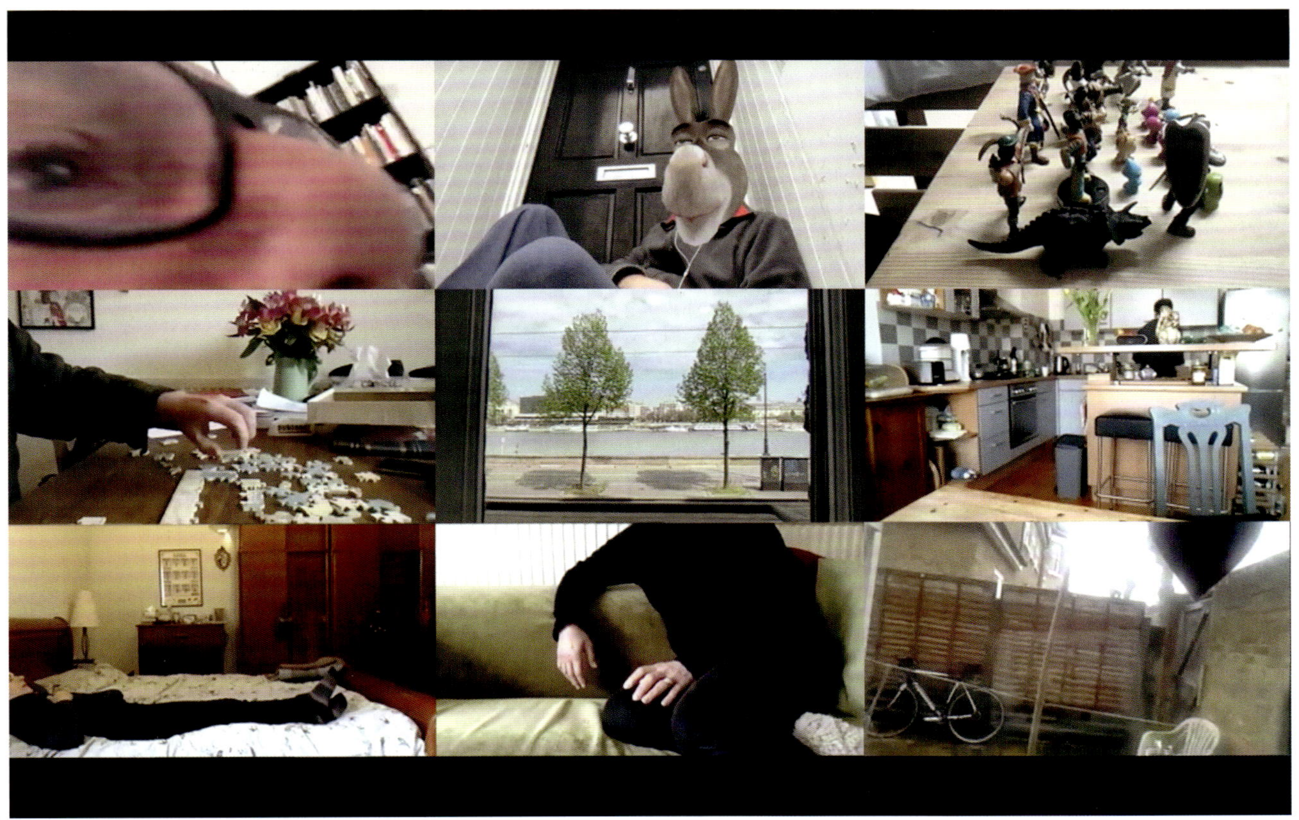

between persons and buildings and landscape, between sight and touch, language and memory. Looking at the photograph, I am thinking about the difficulty of presence. About the effort it takes to maintain what is called a human form. And I am thinking about Huw, who died in 2017.

17.

Working on *How the Time Goes* in May 2021 I am spending an hour or so sitting on the step outside my house each day for a week, a laptop beside me on the ground, back leaned against the closed door, pretending to be locked out. Mostly there is blue sky and sunshine while I sit there—barefoot, in a dirty sweatshirt and tracksuit—not really dressed for the world. Of the few passers-by still fewer glance from the pavement to see me a few metres away, hunkered down behind the overgrown ivy and the busted black wooden gate, sometimes watching, sometimes speaking to people on-screen. On the laptop beside me is the Zoom meeting that links me to colleagues and in which we are recording material. Time passes as I stare at the screen. Peering down into the grid which has pretty much defined this last fourteen months, I can see performers Terry, Cathy, Richard, Claire, and Robin as well as Jerry Killick and our musical collaborator for the project, Marino Formenti, going about their strange business in different locations. Alongside them I see my own image presented back to me too, adjusting the angle of the laptop to better compose the picture of my own comical abjection sat bundled on the doorstep.

Between what the passers-by might see of me sitting there and my own electronic image there is a single glaring distinction, since the on-screen appearance of my face is modified (obscured) by the presence of a Snapchat donkey-head filter, tracking my movements to crudely mask my presence with the pathetic comedy of an ass's head. Donkey sits on the doorstep, barefoot, grumbling in the Zoom call to anyone that will listen, about being locked out, about the unbearable heat, and about the results of a quiz that Cathy is announcing, in which the answers are only ever Yes or No or Never or Maybe or Sometimes.

Although tethered to the Wi-Fi connection in these sessions, I do sometimes walk the short path to the busted gate and beyond, straying a little way down the street 'to see what's happening', laptop in outstretched hands bearing an on-screen image of the Zoom grid in which my own figure appears as a half-Donkey caught walking this residential street, beneath a bright blue and almost cloudless sky.

Once in a while during these occasional forays I venture too far from the house, causing the Wi-Fi and the shared frame of the meeting to drag and then collapse, the scenes it carries from other locations stuttering, then freezing entirely. A step too far and it's all gone. In Sheffield, Terry O'Connor is stilled at the door to her house, head raised mid-movement, and on the other side of the city Richard Lowdon is stilled also, his hand frozen above a table that holds the scattered pieces of a jigsaw that now will never be completed, and in Berlin, Robin Arthur is stilled too, his back to the camera, standing and staring forever at the square outside his apartment, the square he described in the last part of the performance *The Coming Storm*, and in London, Cathy Naden is also frozen, stopped dead in a slow dance she's been making in the kitchen-diner of her flat, where she has cleared the furniture to the edges and in which she's now caught with her back to the camera, arms wrapped around herself in a way that makes it seem for a moment that she is in an embrace, an embrace that will now last forever. In Budapest, Jerry Killick is frozen too, arms flailing but stilled in his ridiculous TikTok dance, a wild, wild look in his eyes. Claire Marshall, in Sheffield, is somehow the last of the performers to freeze and although her figure is not visible on-screen, I watch her motion stutter as she carries the camera, the image of the staircase from the kitchen faltering, then stopping entirely. For a few brief moments, I can still hear the sound of a piano from Marino Formenti's apartment in Vienna, a series of glitching notes from what could be a cover version of John Lennon's 'Oh My Love', echoing in the non-space between us until Marino also freezes and the sound comes to an end.

In silence, the Donkey takes a few more steps further from the router, past the neighbour's roses and the badly parked car towards the corner and the dumped kitchen cabinet. And then the meeting drops completely.

18.

A dead forest filled with long corridors through a hotel. Boxes full of junior accountants waiting for the footsteps of a person. Stock exchanges which have crashed because of the thin veneer of happiness which seems to cover everything and car thieves and nightmares dripping with programmers on a break from marathon coding sessions asleep because of eyes that seem to scan the horizon. Women with voices that sound like border guards and night cleaners with skin eager for the touch of Ecuadorian satellites. Paparazzi jostling to get shots of everyone, even ghosts and florists and people seeking refuge and skin. Kids with smiles that look like half-formed stories. Self-surveillance. The screenification of everything. Models waking to the sound of lobbyists for the oil industry making phone calls to rising temperatures that make things unbearable. People trying to get by. Tax inspectors making their way through the rumble of voices which speak about boxes packed with memories. Culture wars. A bodily tangle. Trees burning. Three diagrams. A government of lies. An interactive map, with a newsreader, TV presenter, or pundit standing in front of it, talking about how anxieties are growing in different parts of the country, more intense here, less intense there. Weather forecasts for emotions. The kind of night where people have revelations.

19.

Last picture. It was taken after the six-hour durational performance of *12am: Awake & Looking Down* (1993) in Munich 2019, presented twenty-six years after the work was first created. No persons are pictured, the image shows only the aftermath of the performance: the stage littered with the second-hand clothes and cardboard signs scrawled with character names that are the raw material of the work.

20.

July again. In the past month, a few train journeys. Still the same sense, though, of an almost exclusively local location: the real world reduced to a few miles of walkable circumference. No shops, no shared interior spaces. No planes, no cars, no underground, almost everything on foot. Getting on for sixteen months now of this stasis.

They say that other people's dreams are not interesting. But the dreams in this text are invented.

21.

In my dream I travel to Tokyo, 8,036 miles.
I travel to Brussels, 220 miles.
I travel to Rome, 1,076 miles.
I travel to Moscow, 1,726 miles.
I travel to Beirut, 2,542 miles.
I travel to Gdańsk, 900 miles.

In each place, a ghost tells me what this text should be about.

The last ghost meets me in Rotherham (161 miles), outside the Arts Centre where years ago we performed (*Let the Water Run Its Course) to the Sea That Made the Promise* (1986). The ghost says that the text should be about stillness, and group work. About distance and proximity. About pauses and pandemic time. About the space and politics of human connection that is performance.

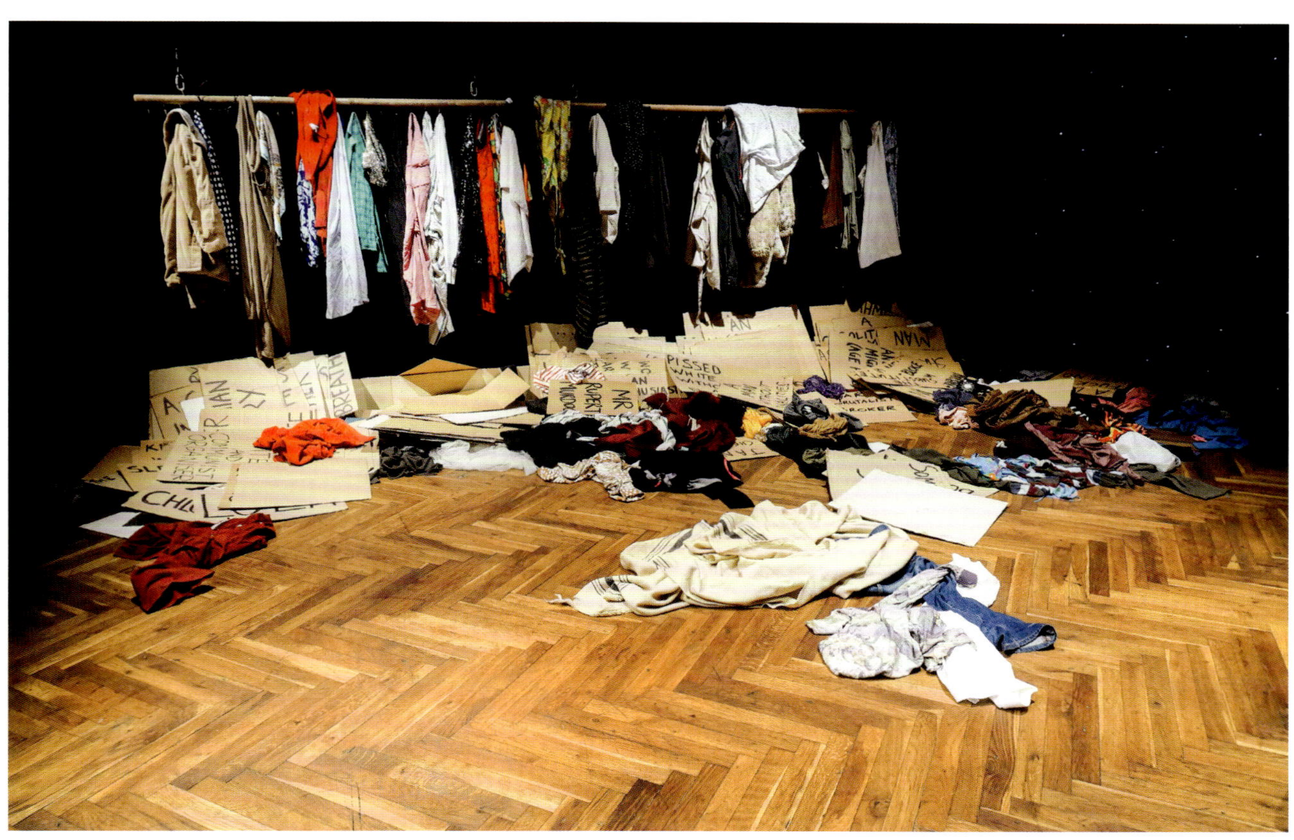

Tuning to the Room

Adrian Heathfield in conversation with
Forced Entertainment and Hugo Glendinning

Adrian Heathfield: Mapping aesthetic shifts over passages of your work, how would you describe changes in your scenographies? In the beginning you made powerful evocations of place, such as the post-industrial warehouse in *(Let the Water Run Its Course) to the Sea That Made the Promise*, then you became interested in more sketchy, skeletal structures, right?

Richard Lowdon: Some of this is born out of the kinds of spaces that were available to make work in. When we were first working, we were trying to create fictional worlds on stage. An early tool in making *Let the Water* was building an environment. We would build something, and then we would improvise in it, and then Hugo would come and photograph it for publicity purposes. Later when we saw the images we would say, 'Oh that looks like a show. What sort of a show is that?' In a similar way that when we were students, before there was easy access to internet archives and video, we might have looked at photographs of the work Richard Foreman was making, and we would mentally try to animate these still images in order to imagine what his shows were like. We began using the images we had created with Hugo as clues that would help us 'discover' the shows we were making.

We were also trying to create spaces that had, built into them, a potential for different kinds of performance activity—so, for example, *Let the Water* had two identical room-like areas downstage, both of which were slightly raised, and between them a forest of upright wooden pillars. It became clear to us that these two spaces felt very much like 'stages' within the bigger structure and seemed to demand a different kind of performance, as if these areas were arenas for more quoted theatrical performance, whilst the forest of uprights—because they partially concealed the performers—felt more like the kind of space one could simply 'be' in. The set contained what we would term 'on' and 'off' spaces: something that became a part of our theatrical vocabulary. It was as if we were creating site-specific work, but we were building the site, namely the sets. In all the pieces, there was this push and pull between theatrical 'stage' spaces and fictional 'rooms'.

When we started making work in the UK, we were playing in studio theatres that were often under-resourced and messy, so what we wanted to do was totally fill those spaces so that when the viewer came in, they would feel that a familiar space had been transformed. As our work shifted onto larger stages, we began to realize that our attempts to create these little fictional stages on an actual stage—complete with proscenium arch—seemed like a peculiar visual doubling. Redundant, since the architecture was already announcing the pieces' theatricality.

Bloody Mess was really made for those proscenium theatres; we liked the big picture frame, but chose to empty the stage of scenery, revealing the bare walls of the theatre and all its attendant mechanics—fly bars, winches—wherever we went. A kind of ornate frame on the mundane. You could say the set for that show was the smoke that the 'roadies' filled the air with. I loved that the smoke would come spilling out of the frame, as if the stage could not contain or even manage its own effects. A right bloody mess.

I feel that our scenic interventions have become more partial over the years, a stripping back to only that which is necessary.

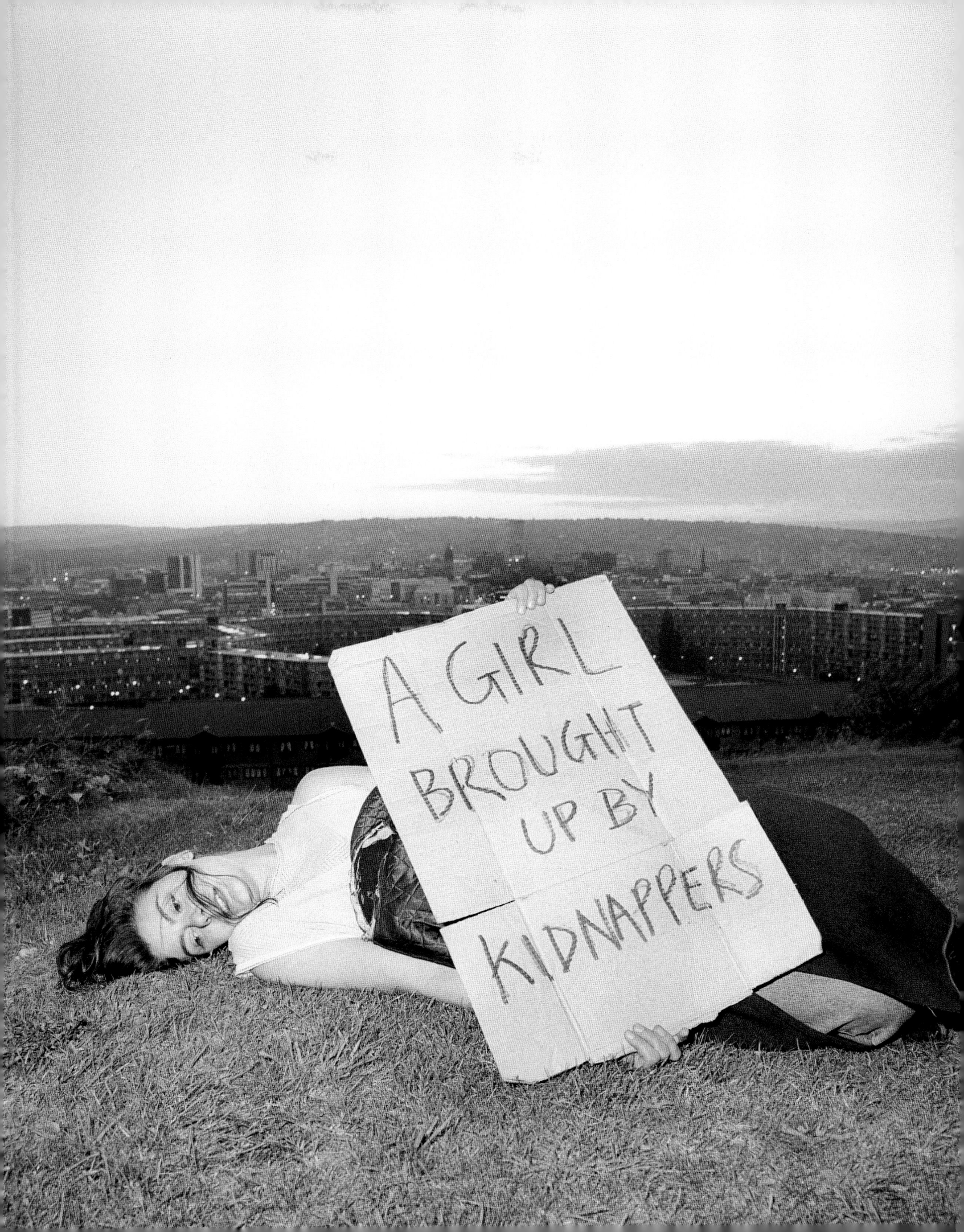
A GIRL
BROUGHT
UP BY
KIDNAPPERS

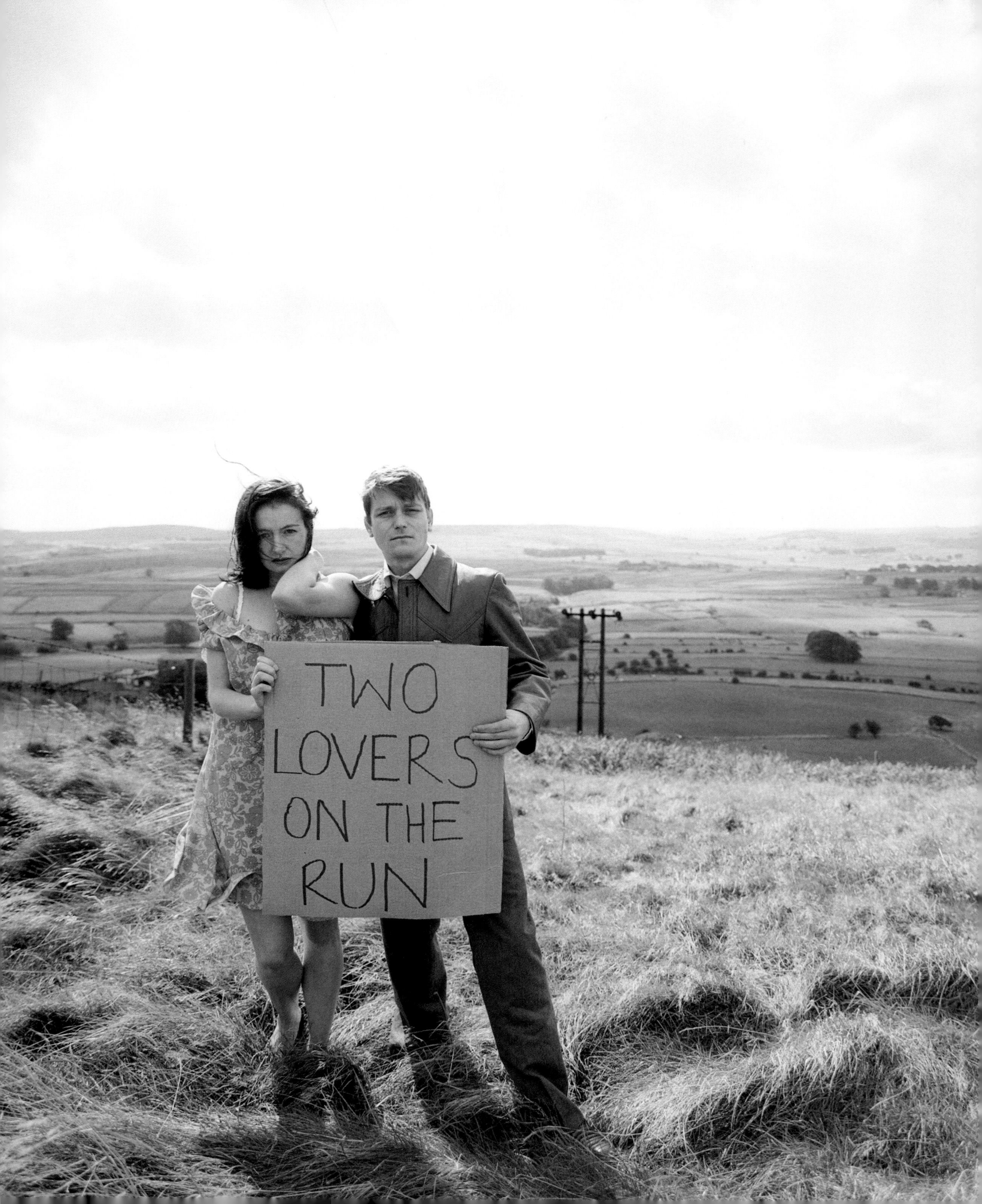
TWO
LOVERS
ON THE
RUN

AH: Aside from the interest in metatheatricality—the stage within the stage—and in minimalism, there's always been this interest in the makeshift, the threadbare, the second-hand. How did that come about?

RL: It probably comes initially from actual poverty. I remember when we made *The Set-Up* for the National Review of Live Art, the set was three dirty polythene sheets hung like curtains, a table, and three chairs. We found the table and chairs, and we needed to frame the space in some way … We were working in ex-industrial buildings that were full of industrial garbage and debris like that. The aesthetic also comes from a distrust of theatrical representation. We found it very hard to imagine that you would paint something to look like another material: a distrust of theatrical 'realism'. Also, we liked the history that found objects have: traces of a previous existence they had before they ended up on our stage.

AH: That's a visual and performance art sensibility: engagement with the materiality of objects.

RL: Yes. 'That's a material. It has its own quality. It has its own history.' Ideally everything is pre-used, found, or cheap: cardboard, bare wood, second-hand clothes. We like the 'make-do-ness' of these things, the lack of art in it … a certain savage beauty in the textures of found materials. We often dismiss ideas if they look too much 'like a design', for instance.

AH: Because it looks invented by someone else rather than reused …

RL: Yeah. We often like to think that the protagonists are in some way responsible for the set, as if the materials onstage and their arrangement might come from them rather than from us. In *Real Magic* the set looks like some homemade game show set: fake grass as a flooring and plasterer's lights, which mimic the fluorescent tubes used on many TV sets. The lights are key, because they're so brutal, they come from another world and have a totally other function but are now standing in rather badly for something that should be glamorous.

Tim Etchells: Often the layers of the performance itself—text, set design, materials in use onstage, and costume—have an aesthetic dialogue with each other. Not a naturalism, more a sense that certain qualities of the materials are in a relation. As well as the sets made of commonplace, cheap, or industrial materials, there is the frequent use of second-hand clothes and repurposed domestic products as stage materials: ketchup for blood, soap flakes for snow. This broad spirit of making do links our work to fundamental theatrical processes, especially those that arise in children's play: the transformation of space and time using everyday materials, the gesture that turns a table into a shelter or into a stage, or which turns a blanket into a cloak. At the same time, there is a link to other forms of expediency—to improvisations that are forced on people in situations of abjection or danger—the table as a shelter or barricade, the polythene sheet as a roof. We are working with elemental gestures: ubiquitous processes of coping and changing the world with limited means. What is important to us is that the materials are, very often, those that are 'at hand': there is a sense of a 'theatre' that has been hastily convened, from necessity or playfulness, from 'whatever could be found'. *Complete Works: Table Top Shakespeare* you might see as an apotheosis of this tendency: all the plays of Shakespeare on a table top, using a junkyard of domestic objects as a cast of characters.

There is a similar approach with our other materials, especially texts. We have rarely drawn on what one might call high cultural objects (especially theatrical texts) as material; in more than forty works there are just three exceptions: *Exquisite Pain*, *Complete Works*, and *The Notebook*. Instead, if there is quotation, it is from a much more worn, exhausted vernacular: it is always the snatched dialogue from some unknown or imaginary TV movie that we use, or the fragmentary scene from a terrible game show or cabaret routine, or some trope from children's or amateur dramatic performance. We don't deal with 'important' central objects, preferring that the value of what we do does not rest on the significance of its sources. Every production of Chekhov or Pinter, every choreography of Bach or Feldman, borrows some authority and cultural capital from those artists. We tend to take materials that are commonplace, degraded, or 'unremarkable'. These rather weightless elements are then re-seen, reused, repurposed—they may very well be critiqued—but they are also transformed, opened, made visible in a new way. Discarded or insignificant materials of all kinds get combined, turned around, become significant, take their place in a poetics. That is the desire. As William Gibson says, 'The street finds its own uses for things.'

AH: I was struck, walking around Sheffield yesterday, how much wasteland there still is, how many vacant or derelict buildings. And there is a sense of the theatre in a condition of redundancy or decay in your designs. Is there a relation to this city in your stage spaces?

RL: Yes, in Attercliffe there was a site we used to call 'the field of bricks': it was where a massive steel works had been. A huge area of just bricks. Extraordinary. And in the city centre there are buildings that are virtually derelict, in the light industrial zones right next to the main shopping street. Aesthetically, I think that is where it comes from. I think it is also to do with the fact that a lot of our protagonists are like rag pickers: people who haven't really got anything. They have got fragments of performance material—texts, sets, furniture, costume—and they are trying to make a reality, a sense, a narrative out of those fragments.

AH: The qualities of urban life, the idea of the city, the mapping of places: these all seem to be concerns of work in the 1980s and 90s. I am wondering why those concerns fell away, and what senses of place and belonging came in their stead?

Terry O'Connor: I think it was inevitable that the work would shift focus after so much reflection on cities and journeys and the concrete experience of place. For a while, we focused on the stage and the place of self-presentation, its folly, failure, and fun. There was still this idea of people making something out of a hostile or unpromising environment, but that environment became the stage. Shows like *Pleasure*, *First Night*, and *Bloody Mess* begin from this cold start of a stage without a score, where things get made up and go wrong; underneath, a dramaturgy forged from these attempts makes something beautiful and rich. Then with later shows, I think we were more interested in systems that trap people in a limited mode of expression and behaviour. *Real Magic* and *Out of Order* show people dealing with these constraints and having to find their way in a tightly closed system. You see them battling with the repetition, picking up and having another go. It is hard not to see this as another kind of reflection on people and place, but it is the more ephemeral place of where we find ourselves politically in relation to systems that control economies, decision making, the inequities and crisis of now.

Cathy Naden: The shows of the 1980s and 90s that came out of our urban environment were perhaps less concerned with direct address. Text was often a component along with set or soundtrack or action that was used to collage shows together. If there was direct address—usually monologues or dialogues—they tended to be recessed in some way. It was as if we were not quite ready to talk to the real audience, preferring to play with or invoke fictional ones instead. I think a big shift came when we began to discover the possibilities of the theatre: the dynamism flowing between the stage and auditorium, how we could both fulfil and subvert expectations. We were like amateur stand-ups improvising our way into and out of trouble. We liked to make audiences laugh and we liked to move them. The journey here was more about entertainment, its light and dark sides.

AH: Design functions differently in the creative process now, in comparison to your early work: it emerges organically from the improvised world of actions, doesn't it?

RL: Designing, building, and then playing in a whole environment is not something we would do now. Instead, we often ask ourselves really simple questions in relation to stage space: 'What can we do on stage? What would be a good thing for two people, you and I, to do now? What have we got? If we have got a table and some chairs, what can we do with these?' In some ways, we are more interested in materials that can be handled, props or furniture rather than set. These elements are more dynamic: they can be moved and manipulated, they are materials for action rather than a visual backdrop.

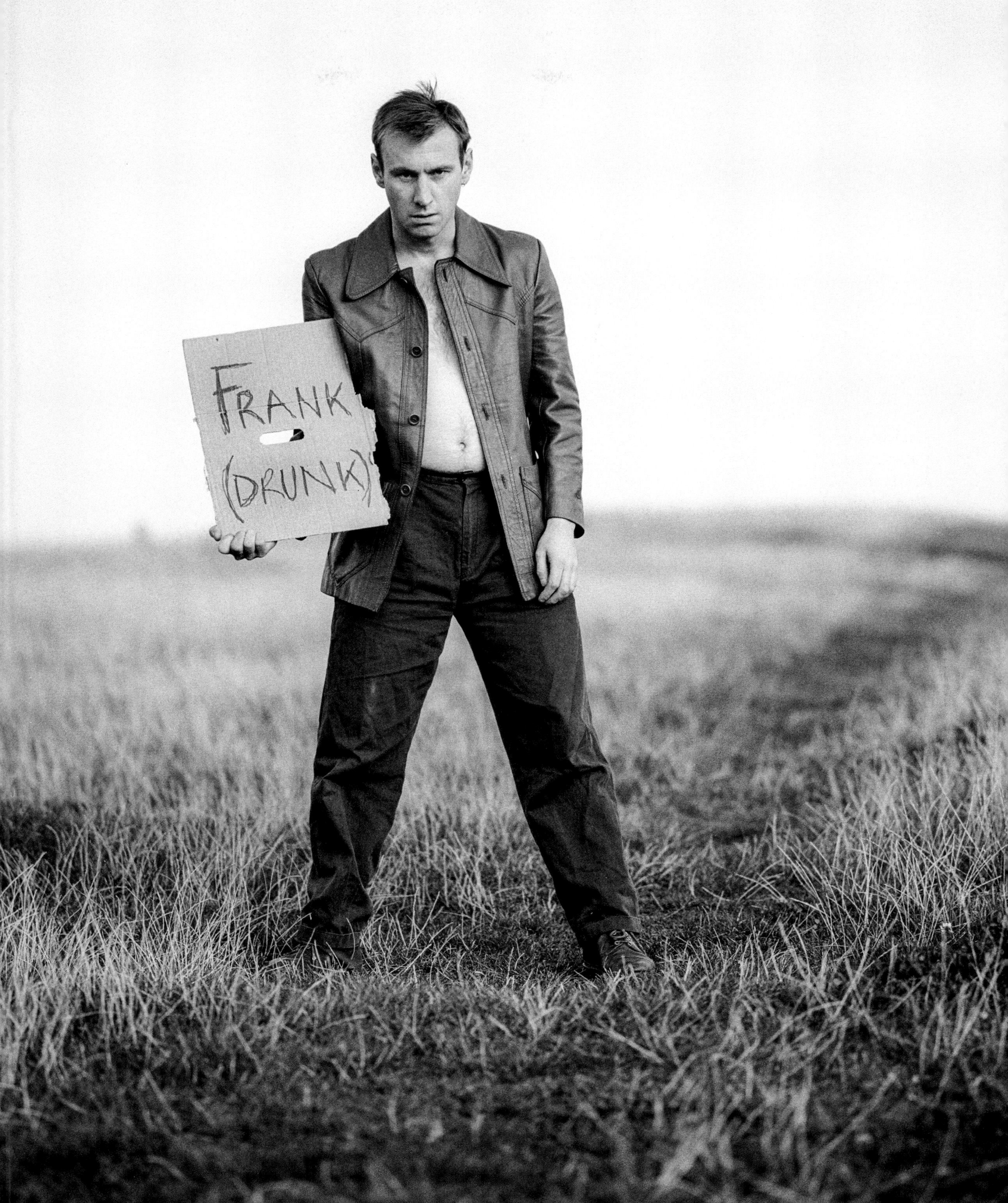

FRANK
(DRUNK)

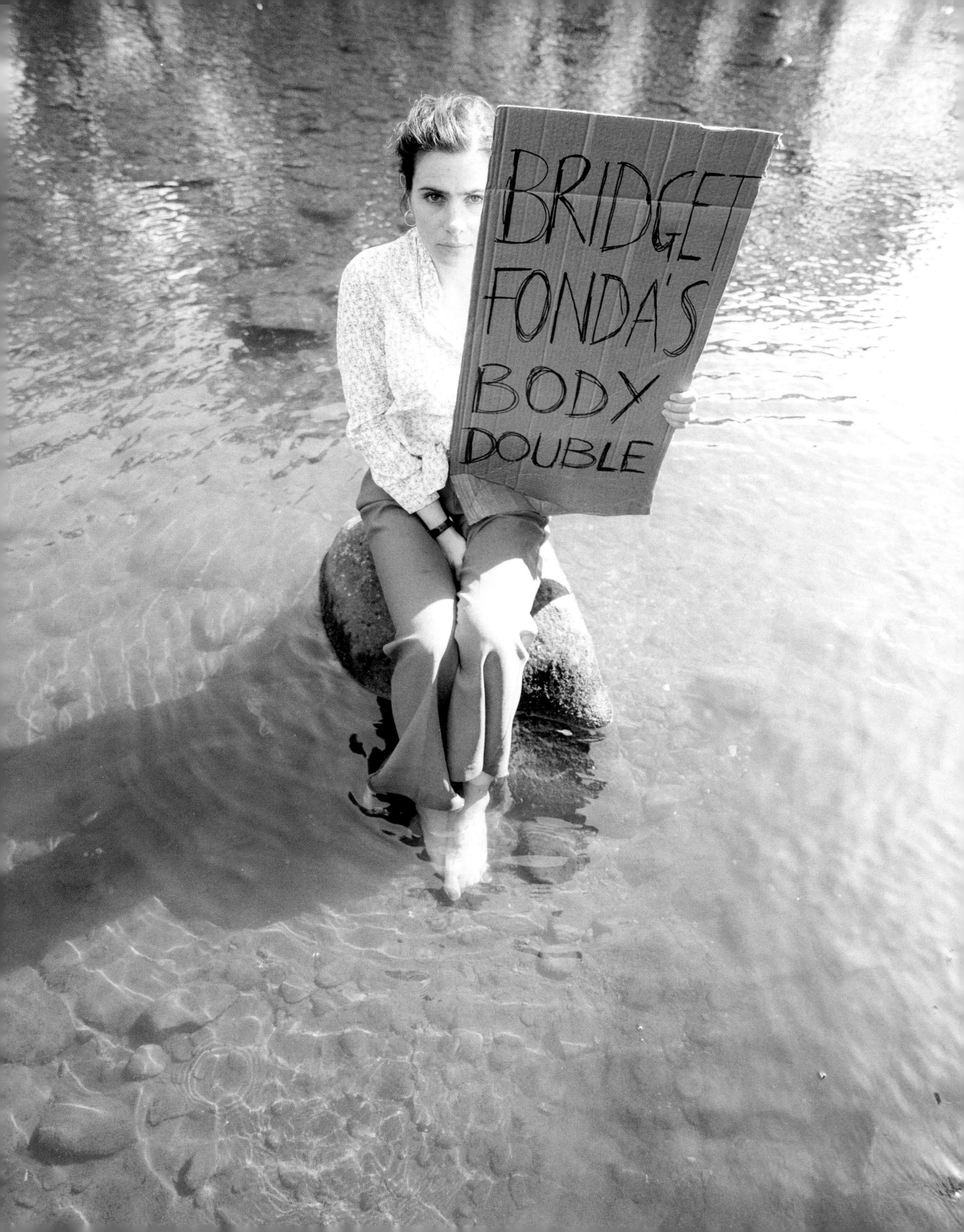
BRIDGET
FONDA'S
BODY
DOUBLE

AH: We have heard how the people you present are themselves 'theatrically impoverished', and there is a rich vein of amateurism in your aesthetics, alongside a frequent use of figures who have a mistaken or foolish understanding of the event they are in. This often produces a comedy of negative affects. I am wondering how you feel these dynamics are changing in your current work, after decades of that investment? Especially now that the foolish subject is so prominently a ruse of authoritarian power?

TE: The masquerade of foolishness deployed by populist figures like Trump and Johnson is a cloaking manoeuvre. They take on the mantle of straight-talking iconoclasts, deniers of accepted facts, to leverage support from their disgruntled bases. But the reality, as we know, is that these are extremely powerful men, steeped for their whole lives in privilege and opportunity, driven by self-interest, and ultimately indifferent to the suffering and experience of others. The entire intent of their operations is to conceal power.

The figures onstage in Forced Entertainment's performances occupy a very different position. These are figures whose apparent misunderstanding of their situation gives rise to a mischievous critique of the structures in which they are caught—the entertainers in *Bloody Mess*, *The Thrill of It All*, *Pleasure*; the narrators in *Club of No Regrets*, *Hidden J*, *The World in Pictures*—their partial grasp of the economies of the form produces a set of comic questions on the situation of performance and ultimately new poetic paradigms. More recently, there are less ostentatiously inventive figures on our stages—the trapped personas that inhabit *The Notebook*, *Real Magic*, and *Out of Order*—their inhabitation of the roles they are given is a form of absurdist, excessive compliance that presents a problem to the audience. The fundamental drive in our work though, in either case, is not to conceal or mask power but to reveal, question, and upend it.

Amateurism and poverty of theatrical means are not thought of or used in representational terms with regard to the precarity of other people's experience or expression. Instead, we are busy with our own position—exploring ways of being inside the set of inherited languages and performative forms we find ourselves working in. I see each piece as an attempt to occupy and at the same time challenge and reinvent the possibilities of theatrical situations and forms. How this works is different show by show and is always very particular to each performer. There is a dance between what is ordained or in place in each piece and the fragile, subversive gestures and impulses generated by individuals onstage: Robin in *Out of Order* is different from Richard, Terry, or Jerry, different from Cathy or Nicki. The electricity—their subversion, their resistance, their compliance—flows in different directions in each case: coming very much from the specifics of the performers, their energies, their embodied relation to age, gender, and so on.

AH: There has been a lot of discourse about the death of character in experimental theatre: how the self is presented, how it may differ from the actions of artists as presences in performance art, or from the testimonial mode of autobiographical works. I am interested in the appearance of the self in Forced Entertainment's oeuvre where—whether we think of it as the creation of personae or fragmented characters or hybrid figurations—there is always something of the living subject at stake (I wouldn't say authentic, but maybe 'bare') as well as some cultural or generic or fictive overlay, which that exposure is in tension with. How we see these figurations over time is affected by the way they are ghosted in many iterations, the consistency of the company members and a certain intimacy that comes from long artistic friendships. I wanted to ask you, Hugo, how you deal with that question of self in the photographic portraits *Cardboard Signs*, and, Tim, what your understanding is of this collaborative work with Hugo and its relation to the presentation of self in the work?

Hugo Glendinning: The trick, if there is one, is for the performer to present directly to the audience, to bypass the person behind the lens. However, I do see myself in the pictures, in the open invitation to the performers to show their layered selves, in the stillness and conviction. It is necessary for them to recognize that they are being photographed, acknowledge the pose if you like. This is not directed: it is what they do. I can trust that they will be 'on' and I can be free to think, or at least feel and intuit, because I don't think much when taking pictures, about shape, setting, and composition: the other elements that reveal the self behind the camera, albeit subliminally. If there is a question to ask myself at the moment of taking the picture, it would be this: Is the subject's performance visible now? Have we moved from ourselves enough? For the 1990s shoot this would take time and negotiation, worrying that things weren't quite right. The 2019 sessions were quicker, more playful—joyous—freed by years of understanding and the advent of a society where to re-present yourself in constantly mutating reiterations is the norm. We used the same technology as the 1990s, the same cameras and film—this wasn't an exploration of digital selves but of time: time passed and time together. Tick-tock.

TE: There are times in the live performances of *12am: Awake & Looking Down*, where the cardboard signs and costume changing are the main currency, in which a performer will momentarily appear to fully inhabit the role proposed in their written 'name', summoning a complex fictional atmosphere through the fluid armature of their own presence and its interaction with text. In live performance this is a temporary affect: a conjuring that will dissolve when the performer breaks focus or moves on to the next sign and costume. These fictional inhabitations are flickers for the most part, and are in any case perceived unevenly by spectators, depending on the vagaries of their own attentions and imaginations. I think of the cardboard-sign photos as a crystallization of this fictional appearing through Hugo's camera. He captures instants in which the presence of the performers and their energy cohere, isolating a moment from the broader flow of process in time, in which location is chosen, approaches are discussed, performers get into place. What is left is this suspension: portraits of the performers that are at the same time fictional fragments, each of them cradled and informed by the composition of landscape, light, and camera frame. I think the other interesting aspect of the cardboard-sign photographs is that as well as portraits they are also landscape images: an inquiry into these peripheral urban or interzone spaces, an imagining into them, or a form of urban geomancy.

As to the connection between this work and the broader questions of performing or presenting the self, I think the work with Hugo corresponds well with our approach. There's clearly this 'autobiographical' element to our work: the performers are themselves, or 'versions of themselves' in so many of the shows. And yet we generally shy away from the identitarian elements that so much performance and live art trades in. We are not on display via our biographies, our 'stories'. Instead, we are present intimately and at risk in another mode: 'exposed' in the choices we make, in the doing of things, in the pretences we make, in the energetics, desires, and impulses we reveal. A performance in these terms is not a truth about someone, but it is a space in which a truth can be seen. A photograph is the same, I think. Not a truth, but a space in which a truth might be observed.

The camera stops time, of course: it says, this was how it was, for 1/125th of a second. Performance is always fluid, always in socially negotiated time. Everything is endlessly contingent. In flow. Changing.

AH: How has the use of improvisation changed for you as performers over the years? It is well known that it is a large part of your method of generating a work, even some with heavy textual content, but what place does it occupy for you now, as performers devising a work?

Robin Arthur: Apart from the durational shows, which are often improvised live, the space for improvisation in actual performance situations has shrunk, I would say. I can remember shows a long time ago, say *Emanuelle Enchanted* or *Hidden J*, where I definitely thought, I know that I need to be 'there' at the beginning of this soundtrack and I need to be 'there' at the end of the track, but in between I'll be running around, and it will be a bit loose. The atmosphere, the energy, the intention will be precise, but the detail will be open to change night by night: I don't necessarily always take the same route or do exactly the same thing. Now, in shows like *Real Magic* and *Out of Order*, the more chaotic the piece, the tighter the choreography has to be. Though they are still very largely generated through improvisation most of the later theatre pieces are pretty much nailed down. In *Out of Order*, for instance, the beginning section where the clowns repeatedly enact a chase scene around a table, was re-improvised in numerous different versions

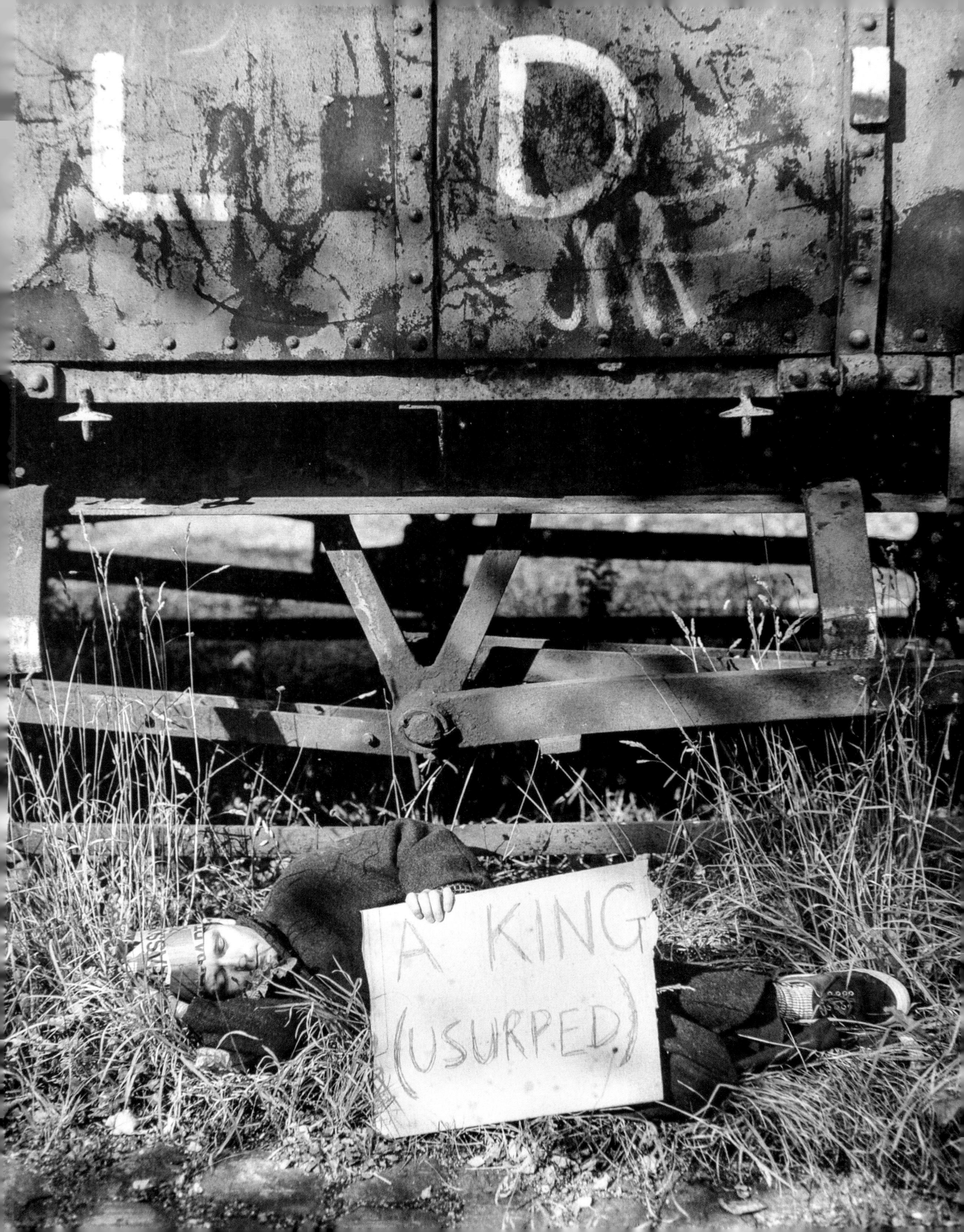
L   D
A KING
(USURPED)

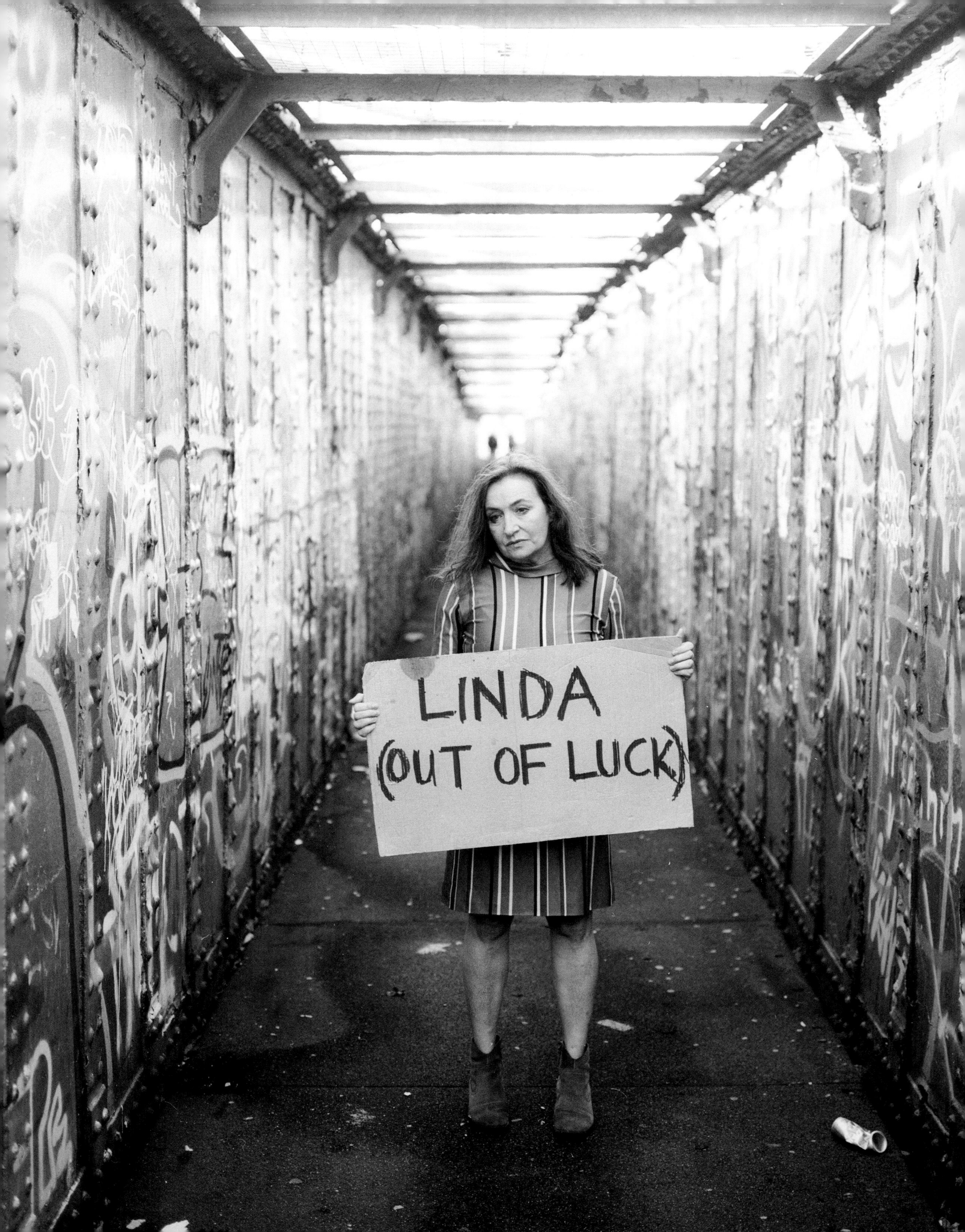

LINDA
(OUT OF LUCK)

during the first two weeks of rehearsal. By the time we opened the piece, though, there was a very strict choreography put together from looking back over the video of the improvisations and constructing a dramaturgy that we felt best served the show.

Claire Marshall: For years and years we were very interested in an improvised voice. Text was always part of that process. In the mid-1990s, when we built a world—a rudimentary set with costumes thrown around and music playing—Tim's writing would be part of that: bits of paper on the floor that we would mess about with, trashing them, fixating on one line, or just reading them. That's a thing—the act of holding a piece of paper—a way of saying 'Don't think for one minute that this is me …' And alongside that, Tim calling out to us. In *Showtime* asking Rob to 'grab a mic and talk about time', or in *Pleasure* wandering on stage and whispering something to you that you mishear, and before you know it, you are pretending to die and talking about falling through space. We got more confident about those improvised voices, using our own voices—a bit broken, a bit poetic, sometimes utterly casual—just shooting the breeze. We liked the different content and texture that came out of people's mouths (learning a lot from the amount of improvisation in *Quizoola!* and *Who Can Sing a Song to Unfrighten Me?*) and by the time we made *First Night* and *Bloody Mess*, pretty much everything came out of improvisation. We are not precious or protective about text—you can be on a roll with something and Tim will feed you a line that has just occurred to him or get you to change direction. You pretend to be someone else. You try to make something happen with words and your presence. Anything might work and anything might be cut.

AH: I'm intrigued by your share in the work here as performers, and the senses of ownership that sit around it. You could say that the constraints in which you improvise are based on ideas of your singular capacities and relations (accumulated and understood between you over time), and then there is always something of you as people in the content you make in this context, even if it is eventually passed on to another performer. I wonder what you think about 'owning' material, in the sense both of having a personal stake in it and of 'giving off' a felt belonging to the figures you portray?

TC: Ownership is a notion that gets seriously challenged by the making process, when it is often impossible to account for or remember who started what or where something originated. In the work itself there is such a sense of gaming in the strategies we play with as performers, pulling close to a suggestion of the owned, no matter where the material came from, making it feel personal or authentic only to cut it dead, reveal it as a tone that is adopted and played with like any other. It is a fun, pleasurable texture in the work but there's also something fundamental for me about it. That the work frames ideas of self and ownership as fluid, illusions even, a strange combination of tenacity and drift.

CN: Looking back, the notion of identity was always under investigation or being questioned in some way. A really early improvising and devising tool was to copy things either from your fellow performers or from the world. This was maybe a bit of a mash-up between highbrow and low-fi—a nod to postmodernism and ideas about quotation, on the one hand, and the pragmatic choice of a performer in the rehearsal room on the other. I don't have any ideas, so I'll just copy what someone else is doing. Copying was a way for us to reflect something back at each other, making what was impossible to see in your own self suddenly visible in the body of another.

TE: This general principle—of a collaborative workspace in which actions and materials are generated in dialogue, each person onstage contributing to the development of the shared language in which a piece will be constructed—is really key. At the same time there's another important general principle, which is that one doesn't tend to transfer material from one performer to another unless it's necessary for structural reasons. I am tuned to the way that material (text, movement, whatever) emerges from the very particular sensibilities and impulses people have onstage. Something Claire proposes or builds doesn't naturally transfer to Terry or to Cathy or vice versa. Material can be embodied and owned in quite complex ways.

CM: It is complex. Ownership of the work for me feels total and deeply personal, but at the same time anything I have ever made is also borrowed or stolen in its way, so it is never really 'mine'. Everything is up for grabs. On the occasions when someone has had to stand in for me for particular bits of touring—Wendy Houstoun in *Pleasure*, Ursula Martinez in *Speak Bitterness*, and Nicki Hobday in *Complete Works*—I found there can be a strange pleasure in watching someone else inhabiting what you thought lived in you. It becomes another version of you. It is a reflection that winks.

AH: I get the feeling that as makers and as performers you are able to wait for the material to arrive around you in a collective process, in a way that other performers might find difficult. You are able to suspend the question 'What am I doing in this piece?' for a long time, as you trust in material to arrive through the relations. Is that right?

RA: That is true, to some extent, artistically because the very long making process creates a space in which material can emerge, but it is also true in terms of the commitment to collectivity and general financial security, which hold the long-term space in which we are all working. Actually, that's really important: at some point, we made a commitment to say everything is always made from everybody and if you are not in something, that doesn't make any difference. So, when we are making work, you are not thinking, 'Oh Christ, how am I going to pay the rent if I'm not in the show?' Even in situations where you are distant from the making, you often still feel involved in the creation of a piece. Cathy and I missed a week of rehearsals for *Real Magic* and when we returned, something had been constructed that only worked for three people. Despite numerous attempts to reinsert us, it became apparent that the material (which we all felt was very strong) would not function with five performers, so we stepped out of that show. However, I think that both of us felt very involved in making that piece because of the preparatory work and the long history of working together.

TC: I think you can extend that idea of shared involvement to what we actually do as performers. Compared to other approaches to being onstage, to fixed characters or roles, what we do can be so various, so apparently unpromising. But we've learned over time (if we didn't always know) that relatively peripheral material can still be hugely important in the dynamic and balance of a show. The task of sitting at the back with a record player for an entire piece can still be an exciting performance job, an active contribution provoking thought from an audience. We trust that an unlikely or extremely singular role in a piece can still be significant.

AH: How is collective creativity sustained over such a long duration with others? You have oscillated between expanding and contracting the number of people performing—is that a rejuvenating movement?

CM: Sure. We sometimes say that when we have other people in the room we behave better—maybe we mean that we get on our feet more, rather than talking about how an idea will not work. Other people's energy is sustaining and to discover and revel in others is rejuvenating (that sounds like we eat them). Maybe it is that they break rules that we didn't even know we have—the ground shifts. Always good. Having other people around sometimes allows you to reinvent yourself. Energies and relationships are in flux—with new alliances and allegiances—and on a cold afternoon you might be louder, softer, more or less foregrounded, funnier even. Because you can step a little way away from yourself, the room is different.

CN: The first time we couldn't get all five of us into a show was scary. We wondered, did it signal the end? And it was I suppose the end of a particular way of collective devising that was guaranteed to end up with all of us being in the piece every time. I think honouring that unspoken commitment became restrictive. We had to toughen up and embrace smaller or much larger numbers of people onstage than our original ensemble of five performers. With a bigger group—say in shows like *The Last Adventures*—some rough ideas and territory are shaped in advance by the core group and then developed with our experience from the inside, with Tim meanwhile guiding from the outside. So, when the collaborators come in with projects like that, as a performer I may feel less invested in the ownership of particular material, but it is more about making sure that the collaborators are cared for, brought into the work effectively. All of these things are just other ways to sit in relationship with each other and with the work, to keep it moving so that your interest in it changes.

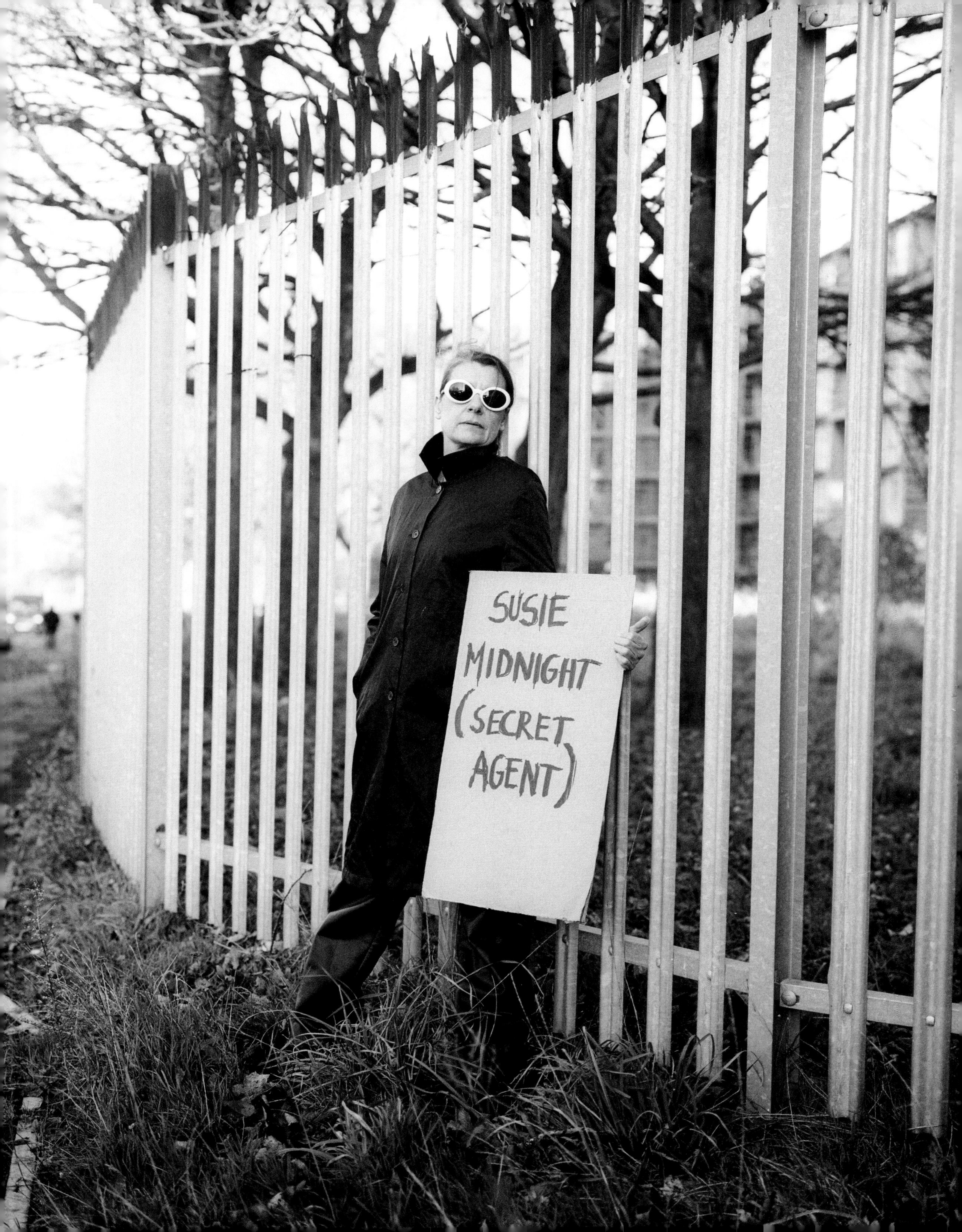

SUSIE
MIDNIGHT
(SECRET
AGENT)

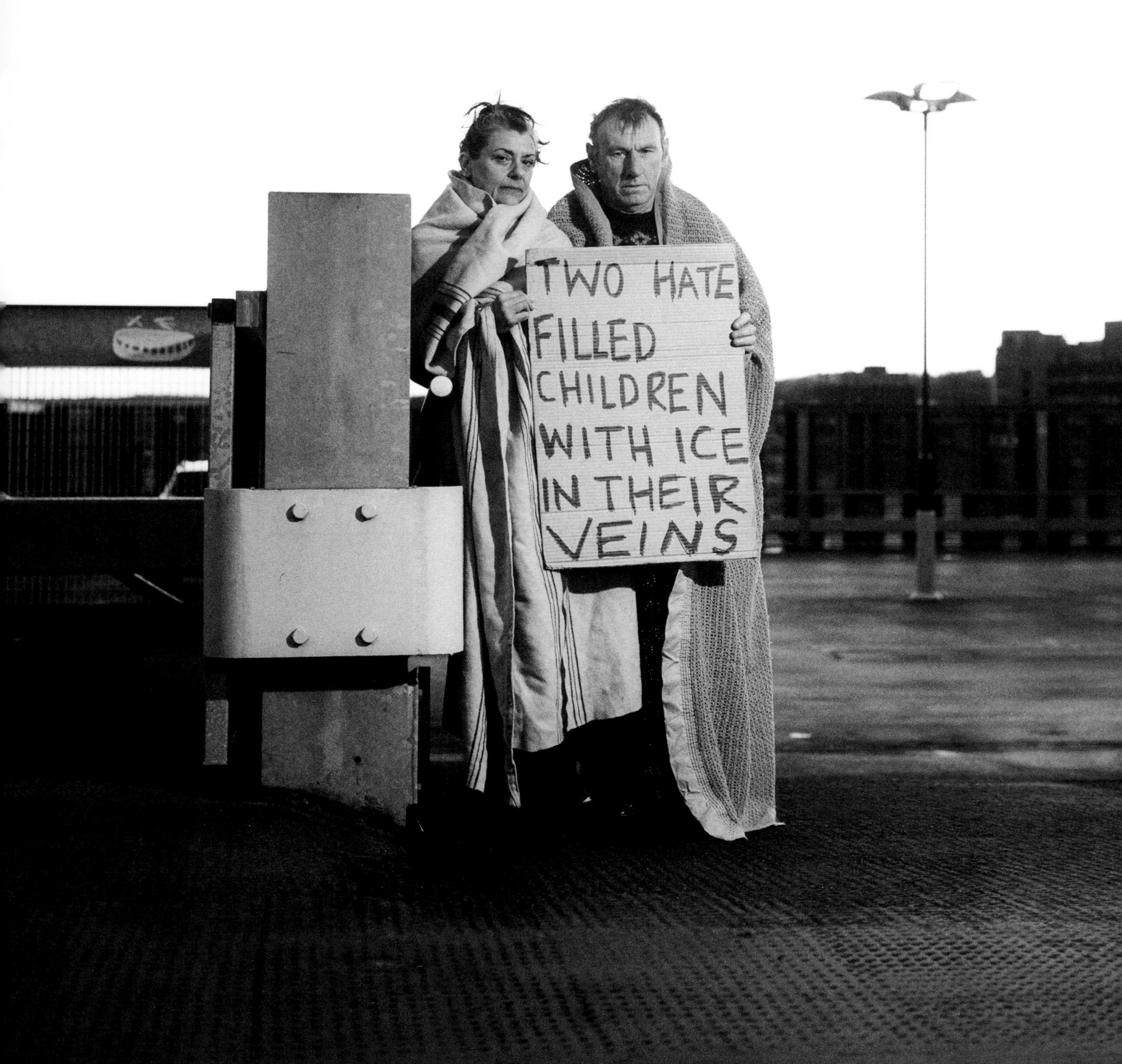

TWO HATE
FILLED
CHILDREN
WITH ICE
IN THEIR
VEINS

RA: So, that rejuvenation is not just in the expansion, it is in the contraction too. It is really important that we make smaller shows. As Cathy mentioned, the first time that happened when we made *Dirty Work*, it was some sort of horrible crisis. Over the years, though, it has become a fairly regular pattern of expansion and contraction ... it just allows different itches to be scratched. Not having other people around allows you to wander off along paths you wouldn't normally go down, quieter paths, to explore something that you wouldn't have explored otherwise. Those processes are as much the way you draw different strands of material and concepts into the work—pieces like *Void Story*, *Exquisite Pain*, or *The Notebook*—weird little bypaths.

AH: Going back to this ethos of waiting for the emergent thing between you—a slow attunement to a relational unknown or a collective unconscious—means that subjects, whenever they arise, are never fully intended but found. Nor are they concrete or directly referenced, but instead they are manifested in situations and remain amorphous. Subjects are not addressed as such, discoursed upon, but they are elusively evoked. Can you speak to the politics of this approach? It places you at a certain margin in relation to much of contemporary theatre, which mounts a discourse on identifiable issues, political scenarios, charged themes. Is there a distinct understanding of social relevance here?

TE: We see meaning as emerging from actual relations and actions in performance—it is embodied and its link to prior authorial intention is slippery. The work is not an illustration of something we think. Instead, it is a dynamic constellation that we set out to discover: a fluid system that produces affect and questions as it is encountered by the public. Of course, theatre (especially the literary kind) is generally considered to be a medium for 'saying things'—writers share their wisdom in coded form. I think we would see it more as a collective public space for listening to material, discovering things, observing, and creating tensions.

We are always drawn to material that has a certain tension—be it emotional, political, or psychological—internally and in relation to audience. When working, we are very focused on what is to hand: the events, actions, texts, and exchanges as well as the dynamics that they produce. It is not that we don't ever talk about what things mean and how this meaning is derived, but I guess we do it late in the process, when we are nuancing material, or we do it on the back-burner. We have it in mind when our attentions are elsewhere. Not 'What are you trying to say?' but 'What are you doing?', 'What's happening?', 'What's in the air?', 'What force and question is inherent in the structure and eventhood of the performance?'

There is a politics to this—not just in the depth of our own investigations but also in the kind of engagement the work demands from viewers. I would say too that we use the rehearsal room as a divining instrument. That's what takes the time. We are looking for something. We hope that what we find has resonance, that it speaks of and into the social and political situation we exist in. But we don't decide or declare an 'aboutness' before we start work, we wait to feel and find it in this collective process. When the work comes to audience, we try to structure a deep affective encounter. We are not telling them something. We are trying to take them into different sets of relations and temporalities where the meaning of the work can emerge. It is not easy to put into words. And that is the point, I guess.

AH: What does it mean for you as performers, to be under the intense scrutiny that being with the same group of performers for thirty-nine years brings?

CM: We don't really know anything else. I have occasionally performed or made work with or for other people, and although that is great, I always miss our scrutiny (our caring savagery!): the way we can throw stuff around between us that might come straight from one person's heart but end up as a vicious joke in someone else's hands. It all has to count, it has to work.

RA: It is a question that comes up frequently, and often in a more negative frame: How do you keep it fresh after thirty-nine years because you must know exactly what the other people are going to do and say? I don't actually. Almost always people do things that take you by surprise and it is a delight. The sense of a long-term commitment to trying to explore and make a body of work is different from the attempt to make a single project. That doesn't necessarily mean that the performers who come in for one show don't then do a really good job. But there is a sense that with the core group, we have been there all that time. We are going to be there until we bloody die. The confidence that long-term commitment gives you in people and what they are doing is really important. Even if at times I think, 'What are you doing? That's not working at all!' Often, two months afterwards, I'll think, 'Oh yeah, maybe that was a good idea.' An instant response to something that somebody is doing can shift over time. And we do have that: time.

TE: The time is important, as Rob says, within the process for a single show and in the longer arc of the company's work. The fact that I know everyone so well—their inclinations and aptitudes over so many years— is important. I am trying to compose with and through the very specific energies and qualities that people bring to the work: attending to their contributions and inventions, trying to write through those, to shape, extend, and clarify them. Often during improvisations, I am thinking on my feet: making calculations about when to let things flow without intervention and when to nudge or push for particular shifts or escalations. The accumulated set of shared knowledges of each other *is* the work in a sense. When I throw text into the room, even just a line or an idea for an exchange, I can do so knowing a lot about what certain people might bring to it. The group is a unique instrument in that sense—there is something symbiotic in how it operates, a space where mutual knowledge enables a dynamic collaborative exchange in real time—people are drawing on and performing the live moment of improvisation at the same time as they are drawing on their shared knowledge of other works, other improvisations, other scenes. After the twenty-four-hour performance of *Quizoola!* in London in 2013 someone asked how we prepared or rehearsed for a performance like this. I said we don't rehearse. Richard said we have been rehearsing for more than thirty years. Both answers are correct.

AH: Given a context that is economically and culturally hostile to collectivity, what do you think has enabled the collective dynamic to be sustained for such a long time?

TC: Everybody in the company genuinely thinks that they make better work because they are making work together and that has always been the case. How that manifests itself in the making processes: your understanding is shifted by something somebody says, taking a piece of material in a direction you had not really imagined before. Or the unlikely argument or proposal wins everyone round in the end. That can happen because different positions are in the room at once. It is an instability that is good for the material. There is a sense that nobody ever loses in this process of shifts and turns, it is all positive. Even if you have been arguing for something and it has not got through, the next day or the next couple of weeks always brings a new possibility, a different position for any individual. Underlying that is the commitment to stick together that has meant that the situation plays out as a long game for individuals and that is important, that sense of home, belonging, no matter how the immediate moment of making or touring feels. It supports or maybe forces an optimism about people working together, no matter what life throws up. That commitment counts and is not taken lightly. It is a way of working that works against current trends and thinking—the focus on individuals and 'great leaders'—but it was a way of working that seemed more possible for lots of theatre makers, artists, musicians when we started. In the early 1980s, the spirit of DIY, the legacy of punk, the particular iteration of all of this in Sheffield meant that we felt we were working in a way that related to other groups and bands. External shifts in funding and received culture just decimated collective making. Entrepreneurship and political discourse has shifted, as you say, to exclude notions of the collective except as an outlier practice, a bit of a joke. But for us it is a commitment and an awkward pride and joy. I think some of the group practice that we learnt at university—taught by tutors whose approach came out of the 1970s and a more radical perspective on collective making—must have laid something down in our brains: the course that we did was always stressing the group, a methodology that then got applied to different studies. So, you might be studying Brecht or Meyerhold or Grotowski for a six-week period, but you always did it as a group, through practice.

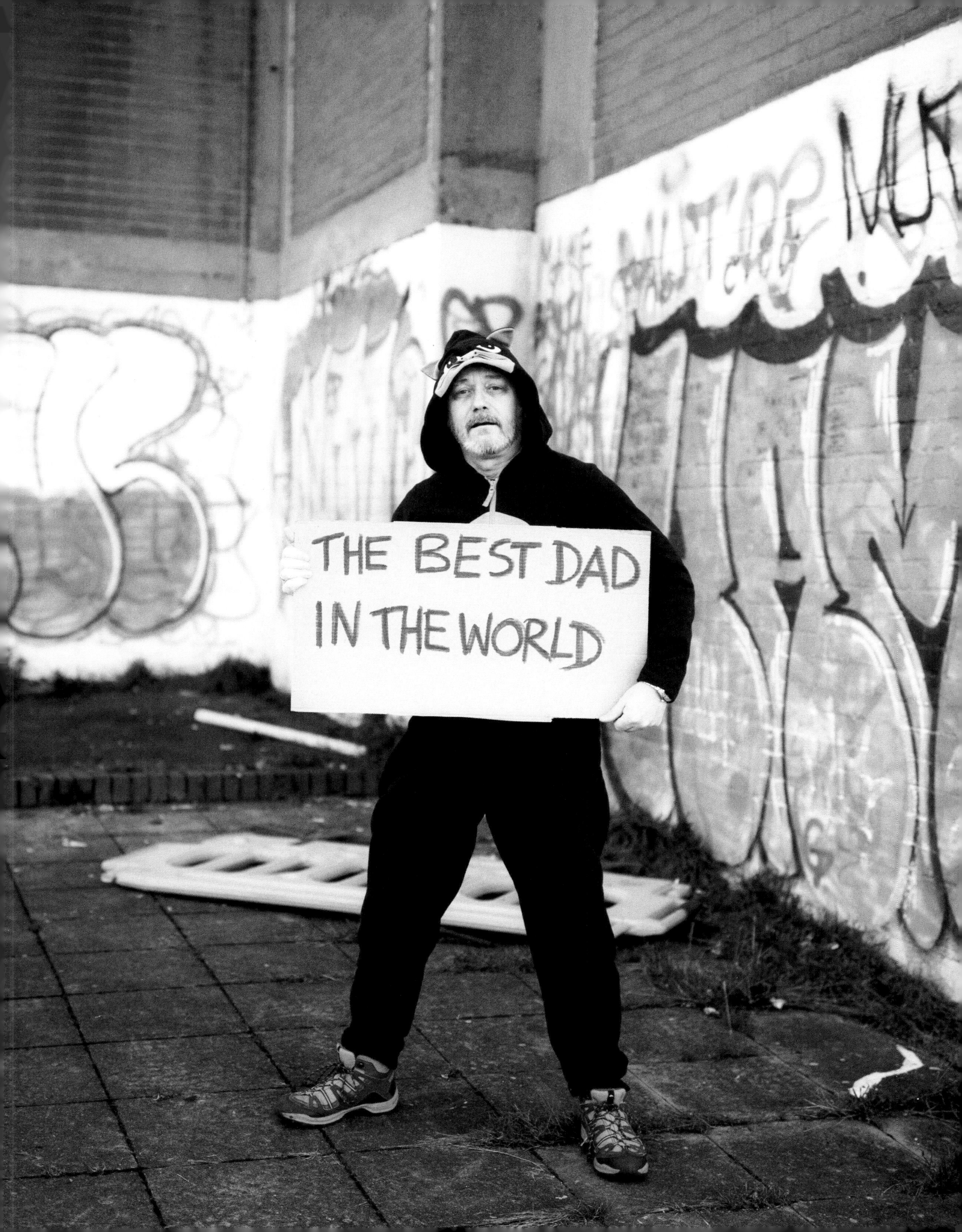

THE BEST DAD
IN THE WORLD

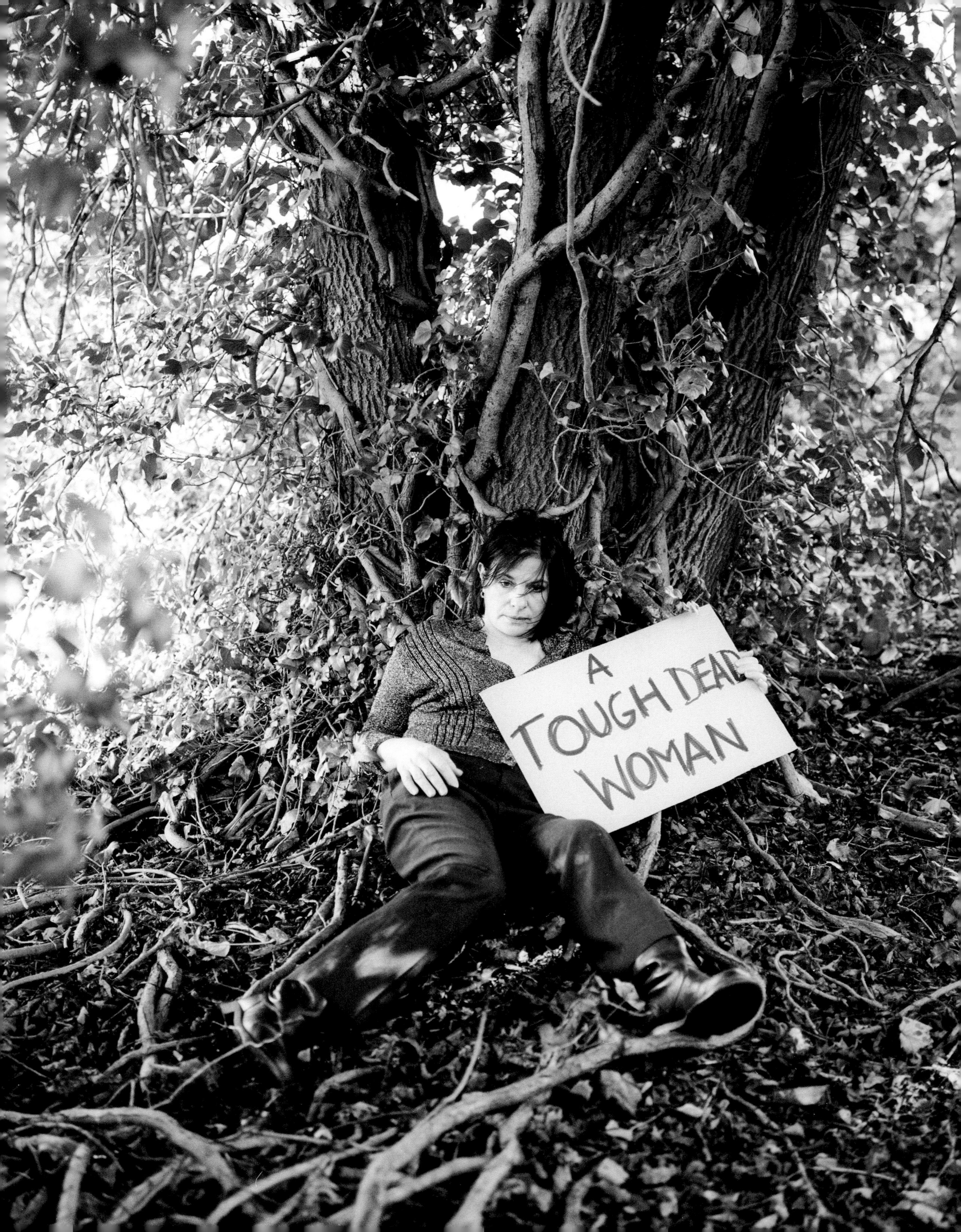

A
TOUGH DEAD
WOMAN

CN: Five out of six of us shared that education at Exeter: that must have provided a commonality that sustained us through those first few years, starting out, where some approaches to collaborating were a continuation of what we did as students and other approaches were contradictions of the things we had learned. We wanted to unlearn and start in a different place. What we did as students was often about an empty-space aesthetic, the actor and their body as tool. We wanted to fill the space with materials and approaches that you would not find in a theatre. In the early days, we were really just picking from cultural things that we liked: films or music, things that we felt close to.

AH: So, you had a set of taste affinities or cultural investments as a group of people, that you did not see reflected in the theatre, and you wanted to bring those qualities into that space?

CN: Taste affinities is a good way to describe it. When I first moved to Sheffield at the start of Forced Entertainment, I didn't really know everyone in the group so well, but I was intrigued by how our visions of culture seemed to overlap. And I think there was a chemistry there of a particular group of people in a specific place and time coming together. Also, I think there has always been a strong imperative or need to make another piece, a curiosity about where the next show will take us. Maybe, on some level, that keeps us going too.

RL: Right from the beginning, the most important thing we shared was the desire to make something actually *happen* in the theatre. We didn't want something grounded in narrative time or based on understanding some fictional backstory but, instead, an event that would unfold in real time, something that would stick in the gut or nag at the brain. Placing the audience in a situation, rather than describing one, with all the complexity, humour, and multiplicity of meanings that that entails. In the creation process we often talk about the work in terms of what game is being played in a performance, using the term 'game' to stand in for real-time theatrical dynamics. What is at the core of this piece, what makes it tick, what is actually happening? Often at the centre is a game so simple that the audience can grasp the essence of it, sense what is at stake in a very short amount of time: a device we used from early on, to create quick connection and complicity with the people watching. Indeed, it is often the case in our work that the simpler the game, the more complexity can be brought to the playing of it. We are always drawn to things that are very simple and very complex at the same time.

Right from the start we were looking for the experience of your leaving the theatre unable to describe or understand what you have just seen but knowing that somehow this performance has changed things—knowing that it will stick in your mind and reverberate down the years. I remember reading Tarkovsky's *Sculpting in Time*, in which he describes feeling terrible boredom when, as he describes it, the audience hits the ceiling of the director's intention. How disappointing this moment is of 'getting it'. That understanding from Tarkovsky helped us to articulate a yearning for a theatre that could be multifaceted, without a single meaning. In many ways, the collaborative nature of our work also pushes us in that direction: group process is always somehow against a unitary vision and meaning. In the studio, we are like some many-headed Hydra, blundering around trying to make something happen. And when we have something, a moment, a set of transactions, a series of images that we like, we often frame the task as working out what this thing we have created between us *wants* to do, as if it has its own desires we need to attend to.

AH: How do you attend to pressing the aesthetic conversation between you into genuinely new territory? Have there been times when you have collectively got stuck and questioned the fundamental trajectory of the work?

TC: We are all collectively stuck a lot of the time, I think. There is also a sense that everybody is on the move all the time: people are reading and seeing new things and bringing them into the room. The collective conversation morphs in relation to the outside world, just as much as we change as people, informed by what we have been doing while apart, what we have been reading, or who we have been talking to. Even as time flows and different life events happen to people, our energies also change in terms of how robust, assertive, or acquiescent they are. So, it doesn't feel like anybody is a fixed entity, let alone a known one. That is how it feels to me anyway. It is a loose conversation. There is so much talking. If you are not starting from one person's already-made concept or a determinate piece of writing, like a play, where there can be interpretation of that fixed thing, then you have to talk and talk and talk in order for you all to understand what it is you are doing. Then you will feel like you have heard every argument for and against the material: it has been beaten with a hammer until it is really tender.

TE: We are always questioning the work, and it always feels precarious. The line between there being a clear, articulate show in the studio and there being 'nothing at all' is very thin, and we live and work in the uncertain space between one and the other. Dilemmas regarding the direction of the work get played out on the ground. Some shows find a satisfying form and shape quickly, while other shows are a constant stress of working and reworking, jobs that never feel quite done. It is often the latter that represent the dilemmas, the collective search for something we cannot quite find. Itches we cannot quite scratch. Sometimes we just have to live with a work, in its frustrations and unstable solutions. We have learned to choose our battles.

One can see axes emerging over time: tendencies and questions we return to. How much real-time process? How much theatre dramaturgy? How much 'reality'? How much fiction? How much drama? How much of another relation to performance time? What kind of acknowledgement of, or address to, the audience? These questions affect everything—the text one's using (or if one's using it at all), the use (or not) of music. There is never a final answer in any case. We are pragmatists rather than ideologues. The ground is always shifting from one project to the next.

AH: I wonder about the balance between talking and doing: Is there any pattern to that now? Coming from the outside, you do talk an enormous amount. It seems like it is mostly sitting around talking, I guess because the weight of actional propositions is so huge after four decades of accumulated improvisations. I notice, for instance, whenever someone does something there are immediately four or five things from the past it can be discussed in relation to …

CN: There is a dispersal now between us: it is not like those early days when we were together all the time, rattling around our abandoned warehouse rehearsal space, you could call it our laboratory. We are more dispersed in terms of life experience, personal lives, families, people living in different cities or countries. Sometimes we might have several shows on the road at once, older shows as well as new ones. So, when we come together to make a new show, the time is quite intense and pressured. There is a deadline looming and we start by talking. When I say 'talking', it's not like we are all sitting around the table, chipping in. It's not a big noisy flowing conversation. It is usually an idea being proposed and examined by a couple of people, while the rest of us listen. Or it is a fragment of material that is being shaped through endless discussion to see how it might become an entire show. We also refer to past shows as models of how things work. Things are being worked out through analysis, partly based on test cases: the ways that different shows operate. Collectively, there is an interest in rigour: really scrutinizing something, never letting the easy route be taken. We all apply that rigour, even in silence, by letting the conversation take place, by not saying 'Shut up. That's enough talking. Let's just do it.'

TE: We are tirelessly navigating and learning from the back catalogue, which, as you say, is getting bigger all the time. We can get quite bogged down in that! But it is perhaps important to say that often we are talking things through in order to move past them. Discovery in the work tends to come at that point where we enter the present material and set of relations by tuning to the room, to the possibilities of the moment. That is where the cutting edge of the work is.

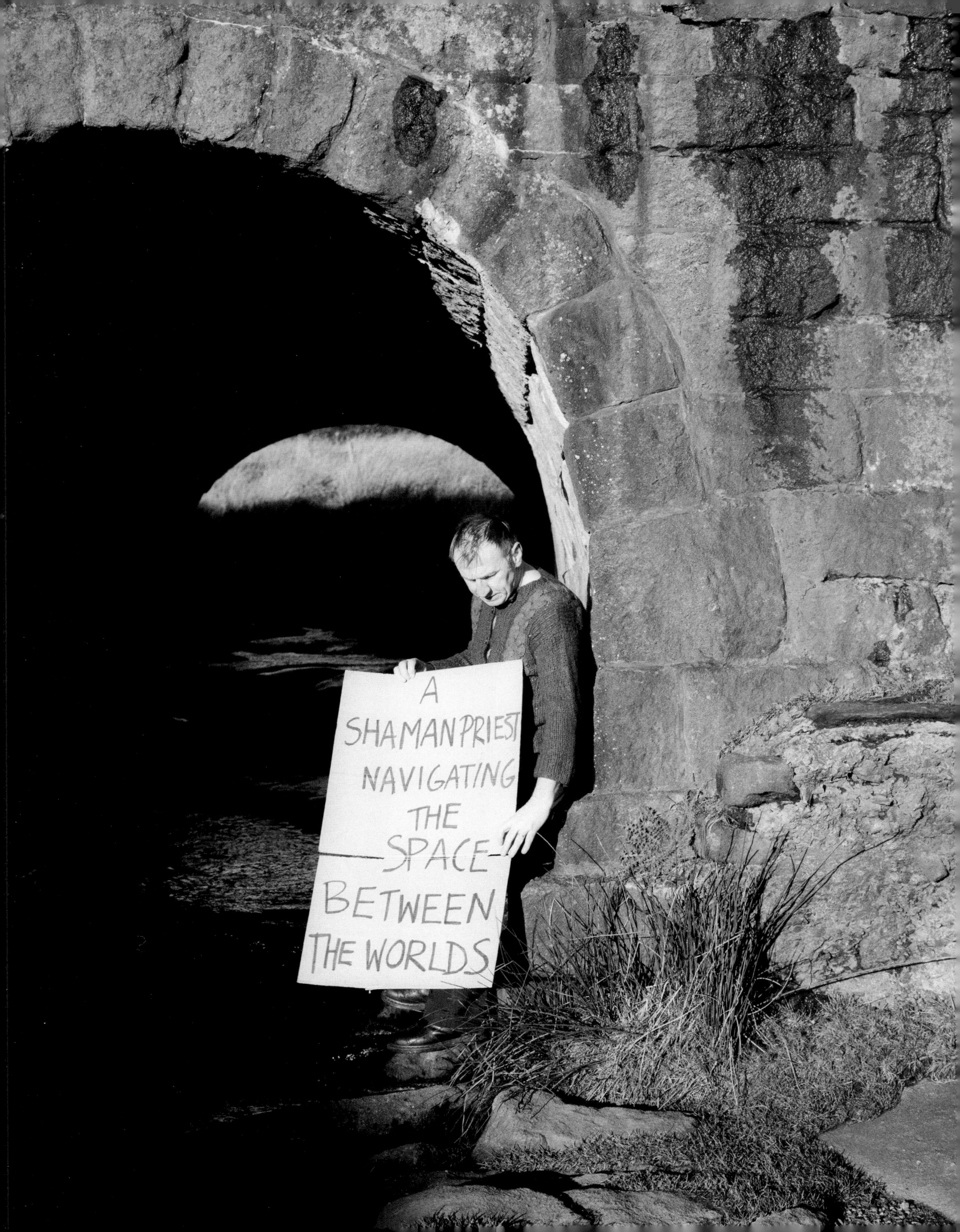
A
SHAMAN PRIEST
NAVIGATING
THE
SPACE
BETWEEN
THE WORLDS

BIBLIOGRAPHY

Josh Abrams and Jennifer Parker-Starbuck, 'London Calling', *PAJ: A Journal of Performance and Art*, vol. 27/3 (September 2005), 37–44.

Siân Adiseshiah, 'Spectatorship and the New (Critical) Sincerity: The Case of Forced Entertainment's Tomorrow's Parties', *Journal of Contemporary Drama in English*, vol. 4/1 (2016), 180–95.

John Avery, *Jessica in the Room of Lights* (Technical Records, 1986).

Frances Babbage, *Adaptation in Contemporary Theatre: Performing Literature* (London: Methuen Drama Engage, 2019).

Frances Babbage, 'Performing Love: A Week's Discourse with Forced Entertainment', *Contemporary Theatre Review*, vol. 12/4 (2002), 63–76.

Sara Jane Bailes, *Performance Theatre and the Poetics of Failure: Forced Entertainment, Goat Island, Elevator Repair Service* (London: Routledge, 2011).

Sara Jane Bailes, 'Struggling to Perform: Radical Amateurism and Forced Entertainment', *TheatreForum*, 26 (2005), 56–65.

Peter Billingham, *At the Sharp End: Uncovering the Work of Five Leading Dramatists: David Edgar, Tim Etchells and Forced Entertainment, David Greig, Tanika Gupta and Mark Ravenhill* (London: Bloomsbury, 2007).

Patrick Blenkarn, 'On Failures', *Performance Matters*, vol. 2/1 (2016), 99–105.

Jennifer Buckley, 'Long "Live" Theater: Feeling Time and Togetherness in Forced Entertainment's Livestreamed Durationals', *Theater*, vol. 46/2 (2016), 35–53.

Johan Callens, 'Forced Entertainment: What You See Is Seldom What You Get', *English Studies: Publications Du Centre Universitaire De Luxembourg 9* (Luxembourg: University of Luxembourg, 2000), 13–30.

Amy Cook, *Shakespearean Futures: Casting the Bodies of Tomorrow on Shakespeare's Stages Today* (Cambridge: Cambridge University Press, 2020).

Chloé Déchery, 'The Use of Play and Things within Forced Entertainment Theatre's Shows Bloody Mess and The World in Pictures', *Études Britanniques Contemporaines*, 35 (2008) <http://journals.openedition.org/ebc/6038> accessed 23 October 2020.

Adam De Ville, Alan Read, Alexander Kelly et al., *#FE365* (2014) <https://www.forcedentertainment.com/projects/fe365/> accessed 9 June 2021.

Peter Eckersall and Eddie Paterson, 'Slow Dramaturgy: Renegotiating Politics and Staging the Everyday', *Australasian Drama Studies*, 58 (2011), 178–92.

Tim Etchells, 'Time As Frame', in Barbara Gronau, Matthias von Hartz, and Carolin Hochleichter (eds.), *How to Frame: On the Threshold of Performing and Visual Arts* (New York: Sternberg, 2020).

Tim Etchells, forward, in Jean Graham-Jones (ed.), *Lola Arias: Re-Enacting Life* (Aberystwyth: Performance Research, 2019).

Tim Etchells, *Endland* (Sheffield: And Other Stories, 2019).

Tim Etchells, 'Go, Slowly, Go: Some Thoughts on Boris Charmatz's Expo Zéro and Brouillon', in Anna Janevski (ed.), *Boris Charmatz* (New York: Museum of Modern Art, 2017).

Tim Etchells, 'Through Days and into Nights: Christine Peters' Portraits (2000)', in Florian Malzacher and Joanna Warsza (eds.), *Empty Stages, Crowded Flats: Performativity As Curatorial Strategy* (Berlin: Alexander Verlag and Live Art Development Agency, 2017), 68–74.

Tim Etchells, 'Index Cards', in Giulia Palladini (ed.), *Lexicon for an Affective Archive* (Bristol: Intellect, 2017).

Tim Etchells, 'The Future of Performance', in Daniel Blanga-Gubbay and Lars Kwakkenbos (eds.), *The Time We Share: Reflecting on and through Performing Arts — One Introduction, Three Acts, and Two Intermezzos* (New Haven, CT: Yale University Press, 2016).

Tim Etchells, 'By Means of the Future: Forced Entertainment, Prediction, and the Community of Audience', *Theater*, vol. 46/3 (November 2016), 15–29.

Tim Etchells, 'A Broadcast / Looping Pieces', *Stedelijk Studies*, 3 (Fall 2015).

Tim Etchells, introduction, in Deborah Pearson, *The Future Show* (London, Oxford: Oberon Modern Plays, 2015).

Tim Etchells, 'Some People Do Something. The Others Watch, Listen, Try to Be There', in Lois Keidan and CJ Mitchell (eds.), *Programme Notes: Case Studies for Locating Experimental Theatre* (London: Oberon Books Ltd and Live Art Development Agency, 2013), 90–107.

Tim Etchells, 'By Word of Mouth', in Dominic Johnson (ed.), *Pleading in the Blood: The Art and Performances of Ron Athey* (Bristol: Intellect and Live Art Development Agency, 2013).

Tim Etchells, 'On Dramaturgy', in Mathieu Copeland (ed.), *Choreographing Exhibitions* (Dijon: les presses du réel, 2013).

Tim Etchells, 'Six Short Plays about Art and Performance', *Art Papers*, vol. 37/5 (September/October 2013).

Tim Etchells, *While You Are with Us Here Tonight* (London: Live Art Development Agency, 2013).

Tim Etchells, 'In the Silences: A Text with Very Many Digressions and Forty-Three Footnotes Concerning the Process of Making Performance', *Performance Research*, 17/1 (2012), 33–37.

Tim Etchells, 'When I Say the Numbers … Some Notes on Time in Performance', *Theatertreffen* (May 2012), 19–27.

Tim Etchells, 'Drama Queens', in Julia Kelly and Jon Wood (eds.), *Sculpture Now: A Reader on Contemporary Sculpture* (Berlin, Wuppertal: Hatje Cantz and Foundation Skulpturenpark Waldfrieden, 2012).

Tim Etchells, *Vacuum Days* (Hove: Storythings, 2012).

Tim Etchells, 'Forced Entertainment – Void Story', *Springerin*, 2 (2009).

Tim Etchells, *The Broken World* (London: William Heinemann, 2008).

Tim Etchells, 'Step Off the Stage', in Daniel Brine (ed.), *The Live Art Almanac* (London: Live Art Development Agency, 2008), 7–16.

Tim Etchells, 'Instructions for Forgetting', *TDR: The Drama Review*, vol. 50/3 (Fall 2006), 108–30.

Tim Etchells, 'Preparing to Write: Six Words on Franko B', in Franko B. (ed.), *Still Life* (London: Black Dog, 2003).

Tim Etchells, 'More and More Clever Watching More and More Stupid', *ArtPress: Speciale: Danse*, 23 (2002), 82–91.

Tim Etchells, *The Dream Dictionary for the Modern Dreamer* (London: Duck Editions, 2001).

Tim Etchells, 'Not Part of the Bargain', in T. Broszat and G. Hattinger (eds.), *Theater etcetera. Zum Theaterfestival SPIELART* (Munich: Spielmotor, 2001), 113–20.

Tim Etchells, 'Nights in This City: Diverse Letters and Fragments Relating to a Performance Now Past', in N. Kaye (ed.), *Site-Specific Art: Performance, Place and Documentation* (London: Routledge, 2000), 13–24.

Tim Etchells, 'Say It Now', in T. Broszat and S. Gareis (eds.), *Global Player. Local Hero* (Munich: Epodium, 2000), 120–26.

Tim Etchells, 'On The Skids: Some Years of Acting Animals', *Performance Research*, vol. 5/2 (2000), 55–60.

Tim Etchells, 'Good Places', *Artintact: CD-ROMagazin Interaktiver Kunst*, 5 (1999), 53–63.

Tim Etchells, 'Here Are Twenty-Six Letters', in T. Broszat and G. Hattinger. (eds.), *Theater Etcetera zum Theaterfestival '97 in München* (Munich: Spielmotor, 1999), 70–73.

Tim Etchells, 'Some Thoughts on Who Can Sing a Song to Unfrighten Me?', in T. Broszat and G. Hattinger (eds.), *Theater etcetera. Zum Theaterfestival SPIELART* (Munich: Spielmotor, 1999), 73–78.

Tim Etchells, 'No Title/No Theory: Ten Short Stabs at Authenticity', *Tidsskrift for Teori Og Teater*, 5 (1998), 16–21.

Tim Etchells, *Certain Fragments* (London: Routledge, 1999).

Tim Etchells, 'Valuable Spaces', in Nicky Childs and Jeni Walwin (eds.) *A Split Second of Paradise: Live Art, Installation and Performance* (London, New York: Rivers Oram, 1998).

Tim Etchells, 'Words for a New Theatre', in F. MacConghail (ed.), *Performance – The Project Papers* (Dublin: Project Press/Project Arts Centre, 1998), 17–28.

Tim Etchells, 'Losing & Finding', *TransEuropeenes: Theater & the Public Space*, 11 (1997).

Tim Etchells, 'Diverse Assembly: Some Trends in Recent Performance', in T. Shank (ed.), *Contemporary British Theatre*, 2nd edn. (London: Macmillan, 1996), 107–22.

Tim Etchells, 'Eight Fragments on Theatre & the City', *Theaterschrift*, 10 (December 1995), 300–325.

Tim Etchells and Forced Entertainment, 'Tomorrow's Parties', *Theater*, 46/3 (2016), 47–71.

Tim Etchells and Forced Entertainment, 'A Principle Rather than an Accident: Some Notes on Forced Entertainment's The Travels', in Alison Forsyth (ed.), *The Methuen Drama Anthology of Testimonial Plays* (London: Methuen Drama, 2014).

Tim Etchells and Forced Entertainment, *Imaginary Evidence*, CD-ROM (2002).

Tim Etchells, Forced Entertainment, and Hugo Glendinning, *Void Spaces* (Sheffield: Site Gallery, 2000).

Tim Etchells and Hugo Glendinning, 'Forced Entertainment: Ten Games. Artists' Page.', *Performance Research*, vol. 6/3 (2001), 44–45.

Tim Etchells and Hugo Glendinning, 'Forced Entertainment the Red Room', *Art and Design*, vol. 9/9 (1994), 92–95.

Tim Etchells, Hugo Glendinning, and Cathy Naden, 'My Eyes Were Like the Stars', *Women & Performance: A Journal of Feminist Theory*, vol. 12/2 (2002), 57–63.

Tim Etchells and Ant Hampton, 'A Structured Space for Reflection: A Conversation about the Quiet Volume, a Site-Specific Autoteatro Performance for Libraries', *Performance Research*, vol. 22/1 (2017), 55–60.

Tim Etchells and Richard Lowdon, 'Emanuelle Enchanted: Notes and Documents', *Contemporary Theatre Review*, vol. 2/2 (1994–1995), 9–24.

Forced Entertainment, 'A Decade of Forced Entertainment', *Performance Research*, vol. 1/1 (1996), 73–88.

Forced Entertainment, 'Emanuelle Enchanted: Notes and Documents', *Contemporary Theatre Review*, vol. 2/2 (1994), 9–24.

Forced Entertainment and Hugo Glendinning, *#FE84–14* (2014) <https://www.forcedentertainment.com/projects/fe84-14/> accessed 9 June 2021.

Jessica Gelt, 'My Kingdom for a Can of Beans! A Radical Take on the Bard in "Table Top Shakespeare"', *Los Angeles Times*, 5 December 2016.

Greg Giesekam, 'Third-Hand Photocopies: Forced Entertainment', in Greg Giesekam (ed.), *Staging the Screen: The Use of Film and Video in Theatre* (Basingstoke: Palgrave Macmillan, 2007), 116–41

Sarah Gorman, '"Do We Have a Show for You? Yes, We Have Got a Show for You!": Sexual Harassment, GETINTHEBACKOFTHEVAN and the (Re) Appraisal of Postmodern Irony', *Performance Research*, vol. 19/2 (2014), 25–34.

Sarah Gorman, 'Theatre for a Media-Saturated Age', in Nadine Holdsworth and Mary Luckhurst (eds.), *A Concise Companion to Contemporary British and Irish Drama* (Ames, IA: Blackwell, 2008), 263–82.

Sarah Gorman, 'Chronicles of the Indeterminate: Ordering Chaos in the Retrospectives of Forced Entertainment', *Performance Research*, vol. 10/1 (2005), 82–94.

Matthew Goulish, 'Compendium: A Forced Entertainment Glossary', *Performance Research*, vol. 5/3 (2000), 140–48.

Karoline Gritzner, '(Post)Modern Subjectivity and the New Expressionism: Howard Barker, Sarah Kane, and Forced Entertainment', *Contemporary Theatre Review*, vol. 1/3 (2008), 328–40.

Steve Harper, 'Everytime You Go Away … You Take a Piece of Me with You', *Contemporary Theatre Review*, vol. 10/3 (2000), 87–95.

Janine Hauthal, 'Spectatorship in the Theatre: Negotiations between the Audience as Witness and the Performer as Confessor in the Theatre of Forced Entertainment', in U. Ekman, and F. Tygstrup (eds.), *Witness: Memory, Representation, and the Media in Question* (Copenhagen: Museum Tusculanum, 2008), 344–50.

Adrian Heathfield, 'Out of Sight: Forced Entertainment and the Limits of Vision', in Hugo Glendinning, Tim Etchells, and Forced Entertainment (eds.), *Void Spaces* (Sheffield: Site Gallery, 2000).

Judith Helmer and Florian Malzacher (eds.), *Not Even a Game Anymore: The Theatre of Forced Entertainment* (Berlin: Alexander Verlag, 2004).

Rebecca J. Hickie, 'Scenography as Process in British Devised and Postdramatic Theatre', PhD thesis (Loughborough University, 2009).

Beth Hoffman, 'Radicalism and the Theatre in Genealogies of Live Art', *Performance Research*, vol. 14/1 (2009), 95–105.

Beth Hoffmann, 'Bloody Mess by Forced Entertainment, Tim Etchells', *Theatre Journal*, vol. 58/4 (December 2006), 701–3.

Julia Jarcho, *Writing on the Modern Stage: Theater beyond Drama* (Cambridge: Cambridge University Press, 2017).

Simon Jones, 'Not Citizens, but Persons: The Ethics in Action of Performance's Intimate Work', in M. Chatzichristodoulou and R. Zerihan (eds.), *Intimacy across Visceral and Digital Performance* (London: Palgrave Macmillan, 2012), 26–38.

Karen Jürs-Munby, 'Text Exposed: Displayed Texts as Players Onstage in Contemporary Theatre', *Studies in Theatre and Performance*, vol. 30/1 (2010), 101–14.

Jonathan Kalb, *Great Lengths: Seven Works of Marathon Theater* (Ann Arbor: University of Michigan Press, 2011).

Jonathan Kalb, 'Amazing Untold Stories of Catalogues', *PAJ: A Journal of Performance and Art*, vol. 31/2 (2009), 1–10.

Nick Kaye, *Site-Specific Art* (London: Routledge, 2000).

Nick Kaye, 'Interview with Tim Etchells and Richard Lowdon', in Nick Kaye (ed.), *Art into Theatre* (London, New York: Routledge, 1996), 235–52.

Nick Kaye, 'Live Art: Definition and Documentation', *Contemporary Theatre Review*, vol. 2/2 (1994), 1–7.

Lois Keidan, 'This Must Be the Place: Thoughts on Place, Placelessness, and Live Art Since the 1980s', in Leslie Hill and Helen Paris (eds.), *Performance and Place* (London: Palgrave Macmillan, 2006), 8–16.

Hans-Thies Lehmann, *Postdramatic Theatre* (London: Routledge, 2006).

Claire MacDonald, 'Unpicking Fried City', *New Socialist* (January 1987).

Anneleen Masschelein, 'Can Pain Be Exquisite? Autofictional Stagings of Douleur Exquise by Sophie Calle, Forced Entertainment and Frank Gehry and Edwin Chan', *Image & Narrative*, 19 (November 2007) <http://www.imageandnarrative.be/inarchive/autofiction/masschelein.htm> accessed 23 October 2020.

Annemarie Matzke, 'Come In and Look At My Life: Selbstinszenierung als Versuchsaufbau', *Forum Modernes Theater*, 17 (2002), 19–27.

Penny McCarthy and Terry O'Connor, 'Stealing Voices', *Hospitality: Transmission* (Sheffield Hallam University, July 2010).

Michelle McGuire, 'Forced Entertainment on Politics and Pleasure', *Variant*, 5 (Spring 1998), 13–14.

Alex Mermikides, 'Forced Entertainment — The Travels', in J. Harvie and A. Lavender (eds.), *Making Contemporary Theatre: International Rehearsal Processes* (Manchester: Manchester University Press, 2010), 101–20.

Cathy Naden, 'Inside Forced Entertainment: The Route to The Travels', *Studies in Theatre and Performance*, vol. 22/3 (2003), 133–38.

Rufus Norris and Sara Jane Bailes, 'Between People', *PAJ: A Journal of Performance and Art*, vol. 27/3 (September 2005), 62–73.

Terry O'Connor, 'Nothing Goes to Waste', in Paul Clarke, Simon Jones, Nick Kaye, and Johanna Linsley (eds.), *Artists in the Archive: Creative and Curatorial Engagements with Documents of Art and Performance* (London: Routledge, 2018).

Terry O'Connor, 'Say the Word and MOVE', *Performance Research*, vol. 17/6 (2012), 103–11.

Terry O'Connor, 'Virtuous Errors and the Fortune of Mistakes: A Personal Account of Making and Performing Text with Forced Entertainment', *Performance Research*, vol. 14/1 (2009), 88–94.

Alison Oddey, *Devising Theatre: A Practical and Theoretical Handbook* (London: Routledge, 1996).

D. Keith Peacock, *Thatcher's Theatre: British Theatre and Drama in the Eighties* (Santa Barbara, CA: Praeger Cloth B & C Titles, 1999).

Mia Perry, 'Theatre as a Place of Learning: The Forces and Affects of Devised Theatre Processes in Education', PhD thesis (University of British Columbia, 2010).

Peggy Phelan, 'The Space of Performance', *Artintact: CD-ROMagazin Interaktiver Kunst*, 5 (1999), 64–70.

Cormac Power, 'Performing to Fail: Perspective on Failure in Performance and Philosophy', in Daniel Meyer-Dinkgräfe and Daniel Watt (eds.), *Ethical Encounters: Boundaries of Theatre, Performance and Philosophy* (Newcastle-upon-Tyne: Cambridge Scholars, 2010), 125–34.

Cormac Power, '"Bringing the Story to Life": Presenting History as Text in The World in Pictures', *Performance Research*, vol. 14/1 (2009), 115–22.

Jason Price, 'Popular Forms and the New Sensibility: The Mingling of High and Low Culture in Postmodern Performance', in *Theatre and the Popular* (University of Iceland, 11–13 March 2016).

Patrick Primavesi, 'Rhythmus/Unterbrechung', in Hajo Kurzenberger and Annemarie Matzke (eds.), *TheaterTheoriePraxis* (Berlin: Recherchen, 2004).

Andrew Quick, 'Stills of the Night', *Performance Research*, vol. 4/2 (1999), 107–8.

Andrew Quick, 'Time and the Event', in Scott Lash, Andrew Quick, and Richard Roberts (eds.), *Time and Value* (Oxford: Blackwell, 1998), 65–87.

Andrew Quick, 'Searching for Redemption with Cardboard Wings: Forced Entertainment and the Sublime', *Contemporary Theatre Review*, vol. 2/2 (1994), 25–35.

Alan Read, *Theatre, Intimacy and Engagement: The Last Human Venue* (Basingstoke: Palgrave Macmillan, 2009).

Matthew Reason, 'Self-representation', in Matthew Reason (ed.), *Documentation, Disappearance, and the Representation of Live Performance* (London: Palgrave Macmillan, 2006), 55–69.

Matthew Reason, 'Archive or Memory? The Detritus of Live Performance', *New Theatre Quarterly*, vol. 19/1 (February 2003), 82–89.

Nicholas Ridout, *Stage Fright, Animals and Other Theatrical Problems* (Cambridge: Cambridge University Press, 2006).

Séverine Ruset, '"An Absurd If Not Impossible Transaction": Entretien avec Tim Etchells (Forced Entertainment)', *European Drama and Performance Studies* (2017), 193–207.

David Schulze, 'The Passive Gaze and Hyper-immunised Spectators: The Politics of Theatrical Live-broadcasting', *Journal of Contemporary Drama in English*, vol. 3/2 (2015), 315–26.

Lara Shalson, 'On the Endurance of Theatre in Live Art', *Contemporary Theatre Review*, 22./1 (2012), 106–19.

Robert Shaughnessy, 'Ruined Lear', in Shaughnessy (ed.), *The Shakespeare Effect* (Basingstoke: Palgrave Macmillan, 2002), 182–93.

Simon Shepherd, *The Cambridge Introduction to Modern British Theatre* (Cambridge: Cambridge University Press, 2009).

Mark Smith, 'Performances in Footnote Form', *Performance Research*, vol. 20/6 (2015), 106–13.

Mark Smith, 'Processes and Rhetorics of Writing in Contemporary British Devising: Frantic Assembly and Forced Entertainment', PhD thesis (University of York, 2013).

W. Sohn, 'Understanding the Dramatic Void of Forced Entertainment's *The World in Pictures*', *Journal of Modern British and American Drama*, vol. 2/2 (2013), 173–95.

Philip Stanier, 'Re:Location. The Use of Space in Contemporary British Theatre', *Body, Space & Technology*, vol. 1/2 (2002).

Jan Suk, *Performing Immanence: Forced Entertainment—Contemporary Drama in English Studies* (Berlin: De Gruyter, 2021).

Jan Suk, 'Bodies? On? Stage? Human Play of Forced Entertainment', in Lois Keidan (ed.), *The Live Art Almanac volume 4* (London: Live Art Development Agency and Oberon Books, 2016).

Jan Suk, 'Glocal Spin-Offs: Ghosting of Shakespeare in the Works of Forced Entertainment', in Ivan Lacko and Lucia Otrísalová (eds.), *Cross-Cultural Challenges in British and American Studies* (Bratislava: STIMUL, 2014), 129–42.

Jan Suk and Karolina Janecká, 'Performance Pedagogy: Forced Entertainment, Immanence, Failure & ELT', *Hradec Králové Journal of Anglophone Studies*, vol. 2/1 (2015), 40–48.

Jan Suk and O. Neprašová, 'The Phenomenon of Silence in the Postdramatic Oeuvre of Forced Entertainment in Theory and Practice', in *From Theory to Practice* (Zlín: Tomas Bata University, 2013).

Jordan Tannahill, *Theatre of the Unimpressed: In Search of Vital Drama* (Toronto: Coach House, 2015).

Linda Taylor, '"There Are More of You Than There Are of Us": Forced Entertainment and the Critique of the Neoliberal Subject', in B. Chow and A. Mangold (eds.), *Žižek and Performance* (London: Palgrave Macmillan, 2014), 126–41.

Liz Tomlin, *Acts and Apparitions: Discourses on the Real in Performance Practice and Theory, 1990–2010* (Manchester: Manchester University Press, 2013).

Liz Tomlin, 'Transgressing Boundaries: Postmodern Performance and the Tourist Trap', *TDR: The Drama Review*, vol. 43/2 (Summer 1999), 136–49.

David Tushingham, 'How Long Do You Have to Have Lived Somewhere before You're Allowed to Lie about It?', in David Tushingham (ed.), *Live 4: Freedom Machine* (London: Nick Hern Books, 1996), 51–58.

David A. Williams, 'Killing the Audience: Forced Entertainment's First Night', *Australasian Drama Studies*, 54 (2009), 50–67.

David Williams, 'Inappropriate/d Others or, The Difficulty of Being a Dog', *TDR: The Drama Review*, 51.1 (Spring 2007), 92–118.

Robin Arthur is a founder member of Forced Entertainment. He has lived in Berlin since 2001 and alongside his work with the company he has directed performances with Theater im Bahnhof (Graz) and Gesine Danckwart (Berlin). He has also taught at HBK Braunschweig, UdK Berlin, Zürcher HdK, and the Goethe-Universität Frankfurt. In 2015–16 he was Gastprofessur in the Applied Theatre Science department of Justus-Liebig-Universität Gießen, and in 2020–21 he was Schlingensief-Gastprofessur at the Ruhr-Universität Bochum.

Sara Jane Bailes is a theatre artist, scholar and creative-critical writer. She works internationally with artists as dramaturg, mentor, consultant, and co-producer. She's interested in the social, political, and ethical modes of friendship and alliance that develop through art practice and its collaborative methodologies. She's author of *Performance Theatre and the Poetics of Failure* (Routledge, 2011), co-editor of *Beckett and Musicality* (Routledge, 2014) and publishes on contemporary experimental theatre, performance, and live art in print, live, and web-based contexts. She's contributing editor and on the Advisory Board of *Women & Performance: A Journal of Feminist Theory* and teaches in the Drama, Theatre and Performance programme at the University of Sussex.

Augusto Corrieri is an artist, writer, and researcher. His work focuses on questions of ecology, performance, and perception. He has repeatedly turned to scenes of apparent emptiness and inactivity, for example with his book *In Place of a Show: What Happens Inside Theatres When Nothing Is Happening* (Bloomsbury, 2016). His performances and lectures have toured across Europe, including at Lisbon's Teatro do Bairro Alto, Madrid's Casa Encendida, Vienna's Tanzquartier, and London's Camden Arts Centre. During a 2014 residency at Edinburgh's Rhubaba Gallery he developed the pseudonym Vincent Gambini, under which he has been presenting sleight-of-hand magic performances. He lectures in Theatre and Performance at University of Sussex. www.augustocorrieri.com www.vincentgambini.com

Tim Etchells is a founder member and the artistic director of Forced Entertainment. His work shifts between performance, visual art, and fiction and includes projects with a wide range of artists in different fields including Meg Stuart/Damaged Goods, Kate McIntosh, Marino Formenti, Taus Makhacheva, Vlatka Horvat, Ant Hampton, Aisha Orazbayeva, and Elmgreen & Dragset. Etchells has produced major commissions for public space internationally and has been presented in museums, galleries, biennales, and fairs. His work is held in numerous private and public collections around the globe and his performance *Moving Words* (2019) was recently acquired by Tate, UK. Etchells' publications include a monograph on contemporary performance and Forced Entertainment, *Certain Fragments* (Routledge, 1999) and the short fiction collection *Endland* (And Other Stories, 2019). He won the Manchester Fiction Prize in 2019. Currently Professor of Performance & Writing at Lancaster University, Etchells was a Tate/Live Art Development Agency Legacy: Thinker in Residence Award winner in 2008 and Artist of the City of Lisbon in 2014; he received the Spalding Gray Award in 2016.

Hugo Glendinning has been working as a photographer and film-maker for thirty years. His output stretches across the cultural industries from contemporary art collaborations in video and photography, through production and performance documentation, to portrait work. He has worked with most leading British theatre and dance companies and is regularly commissioned by the Royal Shakespeare Company and National Theatre. He has published and exhibited work internationally, notably his career-long, ongoing project of documentation and the investigation of performance with Tim Etchells and Forced Entertainment. His work with artists Paola Pivi, Martin Creed, Matthew Barney, Michael Clark, Anne Teresa De Keersmaeker, Yinka Shonibare MBE, and Franko B—recording both performances for camera and gallery/studio events—are in private collections and museums around the world. www.hugoglendinning.com

Matthew Goulish co-founded Every house has a door in 2008 with Lin Hixson. He is dramaturg, writer, and sometimes performer with the company. He was a founding member of Goat Island, the Chicago-based performance group that existed from 1987–2009. His books include *39 Microlectures—In Proximity of Performance* (Routledge, 2001), and *The Brightest Thing in the World—3 Lectures from the Institute of Failure* (Green Lantern Press, 2012). His essays have appeared most recently in *Richard Rezac Address* (University of Chicago Press, 2018) and *Propositions in the Making—Experiments in a Whiteheadian Laboratory* (Rowman & Littlefield, 2020). He teaches in the Writing Program of The School of the Art Institute of Chicago.

Adrian Heathfield is a writer and curator working across the scenes of live art, performance and dance. He is the author of *Out of Now* (MIT Press and Live Art Development Agency, 2009), a monograph on the artist Tehching Hsieh, editor of *Ally* (Hirmer and The Fabric Workshop and Museum, 2017) and *Live: Art and Performance* (Tate, 2004), and co-editor of *Perform, Repeat, Record* (University of Chicago Press and Intellect, 2012). His numerous essays have been translated into ten languages. He has curated a number of significant performance projects in museums, theatres, and galleries including *Live Culture* at Tate Modern in 2003, the Bergen Assembly in 2016 (as part of the freethought collective), and the Taiwan Pavilion at the 57th Venice Biennale 2017. Heathfield is Emeritus Professor of Performance and Visual Culture at the University of Roehampton, London. www.adrianheathfield.net

Joe Kelleher is Professor of Theatre and Performance at University of Roehampton, London. He is currently working with artist Edit Kaldor on a book *Theatres of Powerlessness: Acts of Knowledge and the Performance of the Many*. His other books include *The Illuminated Theatre: Studies on the Suffering of Images* (Routledge, 2015); *Theatre & Politics* (Palgrave Macmillan, 2009); *The Theatre of Sòcìetas Raffaello Sanzio* with Claudia and Romeo Castellucci, Chiara Guidi, and Nicholas Ridout (Routledge, 2007); and with Maaike Bleeker, Adrian Kear, and Heike Roms *Thinking Through Theatre and Performance* (Bloomsbury Methuen, 2019). With the same colleagues he is co-editor of the book series *Thinking Through Theatre*, also for Bloomsbury Methuen. Occasional writings at www.actorfigures.com

Joy Kristin Kalu is a Berlin-based theatre scholar, dramaturg, and curator of performance and theatre. Currently she is the head dramaturg at Sophiensæle. In her scholarly as well as curatorial work she focuses on experimental theatre from Germany and the US, on the relations between theatre and therapy, as well as on approaches of critical whiteness. She holds an MA in Theatre Studies and American Studies and a PhD in Theatre Studies from Freie Universität Berlin. Her first monograph *Ästhetik der Wiederholung* (Transcript, 2013) is based on her dissertation. She is co-editor of the books *Theater als Intervention* (Theater der Zeit, 2015) and *Kunst und Alltag* (Paragrana, 2017), and she is currently working on a monograph tentatively titled *The Subject of Disclosure*. At Sophienesæle she is host of the ongoing conversation series *Politics of Love*, and she curated the international performance festivals *Save Your Soul* (2018), *Freischwimmer*innen* (2019), and *Risk and Resilience* (2020).

Richard Lowdon is a founder member of Forced Entertainment and is responsible for the set design of all the company's work. Outside of the company he has performed in many short films, most recently *The Mind Is Flat*, a collaboration made during lockdown with artist Simon Lewandowski. Richard has taught extensively in universities and colleges throughout the UK including Wimbledon College of Arts and Central Saint Martins. Richard continues to work as a mentor for many projects with both established and emerging artists.

Rev. Claire MacDonald is a Unitarian minister at Lewisham Unity in Lewisham, South London, and a writer with a background in performance and a PhD in Critical Creative Writing. She was a co-founder of Impact Theatre Cooperative with Pete Brooks, Tyrone Huggins, Graeme Miller, and Steve Shill, and co-founder of the journal *Performance Research*. She is a contributing editor to *PAJ: A Journal of Art and Performance* and a member of the Board of the Live Art Development Agency. *Utopia*, her trilogy of plays, was published by Intellect in 2015. She now works in social, spiritual, and art contexts to explore new ways of doing, being, and meaning through conversation and collective practice. As an activist for change she is committed to the idea that art, like religion, operates at the moving edge of experience, always edging into what is just beyond what we think we know.

Claire Marshall came to Sheffield to work with Forced Entertainment in September 1989 and stayed. As well as being a core member of the company Claire sometimes works with other artists as a performer and maker: Tine Van Aerschot, Third Angel, Kevin Childs, Tim Crouch (with the National Theatre of Scotland), and Sam Fairbrother on his laboratory, *The Good Women*, with Nando Messias. Marshall has also been closely involved with Forced Entertainment's Participation Programme, most recently running workshops alongside Imogen Ashby for ShipShape's health and well-being community project in Sheffield.

Rabih Mroué is a theatre director, actor, visual artist, and playwright. Born in Beirut, he currently lives in Berlin. His work covers ground between theatre and the visual arts, often combining mundane, real-life material with the fictitious narratives he develops for his performances. His work often plays on the tensions between the live physical presence of the body onstage and images which come to stand in for that body. Mroué is co-founder of the Beirut Art Center, contributing editor of *TDR/The Drama Review* and was a permanent director at the Münchner Kammerspiele theatre in Germany (2015–2019). His works have been staged all over the world, in theatres, festivals, and contemporary art galleries. Theatre, for Mroué, is a means to present unfinished ideas and doubts about the state of humanity.

Cathy Naden is a founder member of Forced Entertainment. Alongside this collaborative history of devising, performing, and touring, Cathy teaches, mentors, and co-creates projects drawing on her theatrical experience. She has worked with youth theatres, with emerging and established practitioners both in the UK and abroad, recently co-directing with Clean Break for Latitude Festival. Naden has an MA in creative writing and writes short stories and full-length fiction. She also performs independently of her work with the company. She recently collaborated with film-maker Andy Kelleher, playing the lead in *Second Spring*, a feature film due for released in September 2021.

Terry O'Connor joined Forced Entertainment on completing an MA in 1986. She has performed with Meg Stuart, Tim Crouch, Invisible Flock, and Jérôme Bel. She was an AHRC Creative Fellow at University of Roehampton (2009–14), Professor of Contemporary Theatre and Performance Practice at University of Sheffield (2011–14), and Creative Fellow at University of Birmingham, Royal Shakespeare Company, and Shakespeare Institute (2016–17). Her current doctoral research at University of Salford investigates improvisational process (2019–25). She is also working with Imogen Ashby on *Subject to Change*, a Paul Hamlyn funded evaluation of Forced Entertainment's participation methodology.

Giulia Palladini is a researcher and critical theorist. Her work explores the politics and erotics of artistic production, social and cultural history. In her writing, critical, and educational practice she has engaged, in particular, with temporality and affect, historiography and the archive, the relationship between labour and pleasure, work and free time, addressing both contemporary performance and performance history. Her texts have appeared in several international journals, and she has collaborated as theorist on a number of critical and artistic projects. She is the author of *The Scene of Foreplay: Theater, Labor and Leisure in 1960s New York* (Northwestern University Press, 2017) and of *Lexicon for an Affective Archive* (Intellect, 2017, co-edited with Marco Pustianaz). She is currently Senior Lecturer in Drama, Theatre and Performance at the University of Roehampton.

Flora Pitrolo teaches in theatre and performance studies departments and writes about the circulation of images and musics in experimental scenes from the 1980s to the present. She is the author of the artist book *Syxty Sorriso & Altre Storie* (Yard Press, 2017) and is currently co-editing the volume *Disco Heterotopias* with Marko Zubak (Palgrave, 2022). She makes performance, sound, and video work with the London-based collective The International Western and runs the record label and long-standing radio show *A Colder Consciousness* (Resonance FM, Kanal 103). Recent writings include the published talk 'Domestic Flights' and the audio poem/essay 'Toa e Toa', both in *Homemade: Into the Light / Into the Night* (Theatrum Mundi, 2021).

Séverine Ruset is a senior lecturer in performing arts at the University of Grenoble Alpes, France. Her research focuses on European contemporary theatre, particularly French and English, and favours a socio-aesthetic approach. Stemming from research on the collective organizations of artistic practice within the performing arts, she is currently investigating the development of collaborations with non-professional performers in artworks recently produced by French theatre and dance institutions. In 2008 she was awarded the Richelieu Prize of the Chancellerie des Universités de Paris for her PhD thesis, which was subsequently published by Editions Classiques Garnier under the title *Métamorphoses du temps et de l'espace dans les dramaturgies anglaises contemporaines* (2018). She recently co-edited *L'injouable au théâtre* (Revue d'Histoire du Théâtre, 2015), *Déjouer l'injouable: la scène contemporaine à l'épreuve de l'impossible* (European Drama and Performance Studies, 2017), and *Troupes, compagnies, collectifs dans les arts vivants* (L'Entretemps, 2018).

Theron Schmidt lives on unceded Gadigal land and works internationally as an artist, teacher, and writer. He teaches performance writing and collaborative performance at University of New South Wales, Sydney, and has published widely on contemporary theatre and performance, participatory art practices, and politically engaged performance. He is an editor of the journal *Performance Philosophy* and an associate editor of *Performance Research*. In addition to his academic research, he has written about contemporary performance and live art for a variety of publications, including magazines and artist books, and as part of innovative critical writing projects that foster interaction between scholars, artists, and publics. He also makes performance as a solo and collaborative artist.

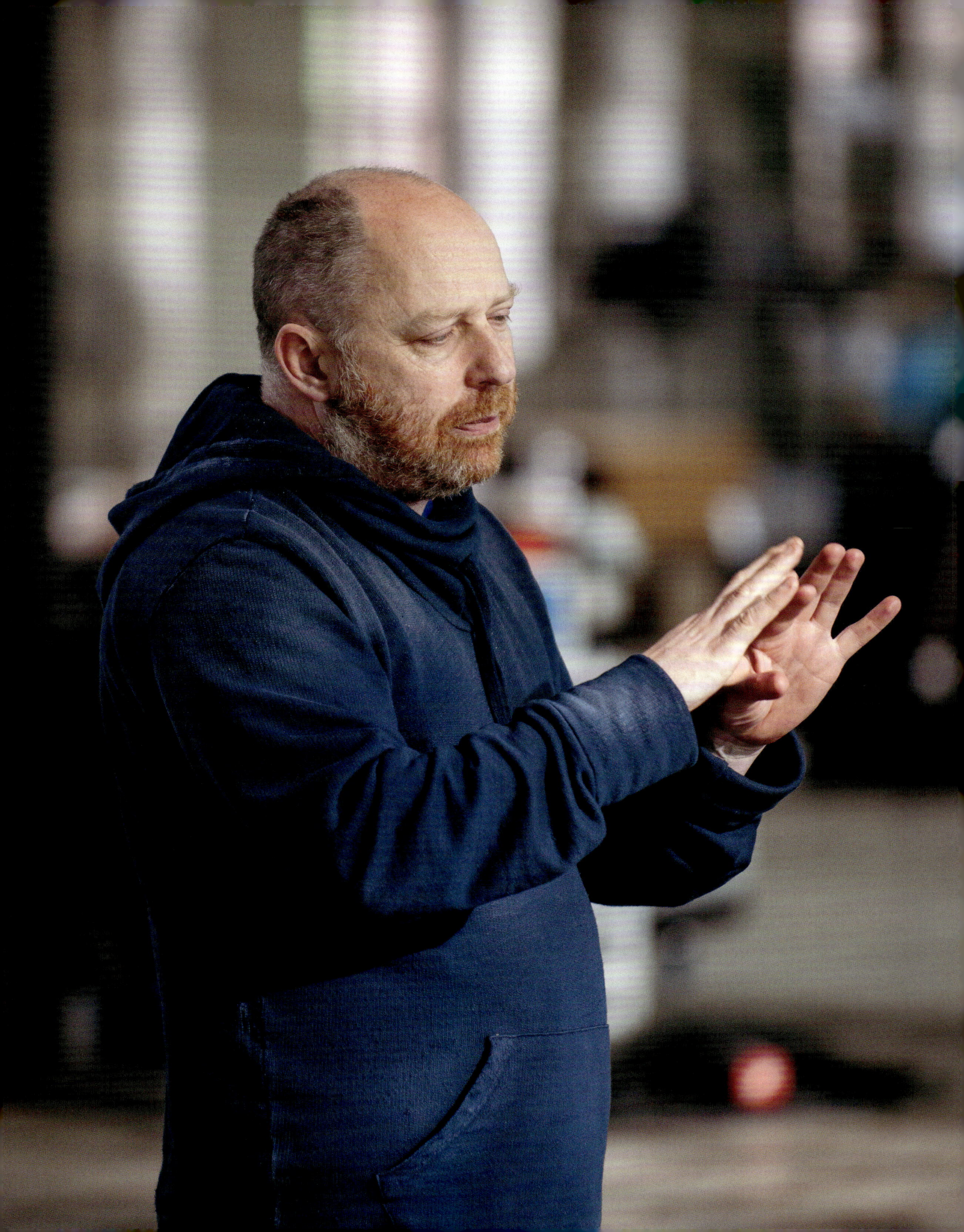

Generated within and alongside other aspects of the shows, texts for performance occupy a specific position within Forced Entertainment's theatre, particularly after the mid-1990s when textual improvisation began to take an increasingly central role in our process. Since then, spoken words in rehearsal typically materialize alongside action, choreography, and other aspects of the performances, with text emerging from a dialogue between fragmentary advance scripting, structured performer improvisation, and directorial intervention. What is said is always linked to the actional context, emerging from costume, from scenic or audience dynamics, or from a relationship with music and other elements of the work. In finalizing a work, we place a high premium on the unfolding of textual choices in relationship to these other factors, often consolidating completed versions of shows or scenes by fixing not just text but also the interrelated nexus of performer action, stage events, music, and interruptions.

Working 'scripts' for the company are often developed via video transcription of rehearsals and subsequent editing, with careful attention being paid to 'original' versions in respect of timing, structures of interruption, and development. Such 'scripts' will typically be littered with time-code notes and comparisons, detailed notation of verbal tics and speech affects, such as hesitation, repetition, and reiteration, all of which we use to 'capture'—for final performances—the rhythms and dramaturgies of the materials as we first discovered or generated them in rehearsal. Doing, in this context, is a method of collaborative writing in which the performers' energies, impulses, qualities, and inclinations feed into and frame the development of text materials.

The performance texts presented here all arise to some extent from these processes. They reflect three key works, the detailing of which is designed to augment the fragmentary quotations from many performances which appear earlier in this volume. For clarity, *First Night* and *Bloody Mess* are broken down into titled sections, with occasional succinct stage-action descriptions and notes about music included for context. As set out above, these two works were created in good part from structured improvisation, with initial prompts and subsequent directorial or textual interventions informing and guiding the development of material.

First Night explores the set-up of a vaudeville or cabaret evening that is forever turning sour, such that the text forms in each section arise from the world of the piece: welcome to the audience, fortune telling, joke, apology, etc. *Bloody Mess* is more collage-like in form and the textual interventions of the ten performers articulate incompatible understandings of the amorphous, highly contested unfolding event. The third complete performance text here, *Dirty Work (The Late Shift)*, is drawn from our 2017 reworking of *Dirty Work* (1997). This text is a more writerly affair, in which content generated via performer improvisation from Robin Arthur and Cathy Naden is in dialogue with lines I scripted outside of rehearsals, the two bodies of material intersecting and influencing each other, as is often the case in our processes: written text restructured and nuanced for speech, improvised text sharpened and honed via writing.

Since our focus is so largely on performance itself—context, embodiment, temporality, and the dynamic ephemerality of the live event—there is a natural ambivalence within Forced Entertainment about the 'fixity' that producing performance texts appears to bring. The text cannot capture the complex suspension of forces at work in the live event and risks absurdity, if not a kind of violence to the meaning and ambiguity integral to the unfolding performance. These texts are not works, nor are they (like plays in the literary theatre) objects created in advance by a single author to be enlivened by others in some future act of dramatic reinterpretation. Instead, we see these performance texts as documents, traces, imprints, residues; they are the leftovers of something that happened, ushered to a second life here as page events, textual performatives which we hope might echo, evoke, or rekindle something of a work created and manifested elsewhere. [TE]

FIRST NIGHT (2001)

1. Ventriloquist Hello

[*The performers come through the red curtains at the back of the stage and walk to the front where they form a line, standing in silence, their faces locked in exaggerated smiles. Robin is not present. After some moments Richard departs and then returns, dragging Robin through the back curtains in a headlock— part ventriloquist's dummy, part victimized schoolkid. Richard manhandles Robin into the centre of the line. A mic on a stand, at Robin's low head height, is passed clumsily from performer to performer until it rests in front of him.*]

Robin: [*With reluctance, still in a headlock, prompted and bullied throughout by yanks and finger-bending from Richard*] Good evening, ladies and gentlemen. Welcome. Welcome, everybody.

Bonsoir, mesdames et messieurs, et bienvenue. Guten Abend meine Damen und Herren, und herzlich willkommen.

Hello?

Benvenuti, signore e signori. Bienvenido ... señoritas? Zdrastvootie? Kalispera?

[*To Richard*] That's it. I don't know any more. I don't. I don't know any more. Stop it. Ow! [*To audience again*] Welcome. Welcome, everybody. Um, we've got a lovely show lined up for you tonight, ladies and gentlemen. Yes, a lovely show with songs and dances and jokes and, er ... you know ... people. There's people in it doing ... doing stuff.

[*To Richard*] I don't like this. It's not very nice. [*Whispering*] We'd better go. Come on, let's go now. Ow, I need to go. I need to go ... to the toilet. Ooh. I need to go. There's going to be a nasty, dirty little accident. Ooh. Ooooohh. I can feel it. It's starting to trickle. Down the inside of the trouser leg. Come on. Come on. I need to go to the toilet. [*Terry arrives and hands a large glass of water to Richard who drinks it à la ventriloquist's routine, Robin reacts as he does so.*] No! No! Stop it. Don't do that. Stop it. Ooh. Aghhh.

[*Robin continues to moan as the others exit, backing off in apparent confusion. Richard eventually drags Robin off through the curtains. Cathy and Claire linger in the line—the former exposing one of her breasts as if to distract the audience from the disaster that's unfolding, the latter slowly and clumsily returning the mic to its place, both of them with rigid grins intact. The rest of the performers then return to the stage and reassemble in the line as if nothing has happened. Blindfolds are produced, several of the performers scurrying off to fetch them*]

and then back on again. The group arrange themselves dispersed over the depth and width of the stage, all blindfolded now.]

2. Fortune Telling

Claire: Ladies and gentlemen, I'm getting something. I'm picking something up. There is a very great sense of loss in the house tonight. Someone in the house has lost something ... A key ... Or a dog, a dog?

Terry: Yes. I too feel a great sense of loss in the house tonight, but loss of a more personal nature. I fear that someone here has recently lost a mother, or a father, or a brother? A distant relative?

John: Oh yes. I'm getting a photograph. Kept in a wallet. Close to someone's heart. Somebody over there, I think. Yes. It's a photograph of a sticky-faced girl wearing a green bikini. The message for you is: 'Don't blame yourself entirely.' That's it.

Richard: I'm getting a very strong message now, a very strong message for a, for a gentleman here, for a short gentleman in a checked suit and the message is: 'Watch out or you won't get through tonight alive.'

Robin: Yes, and I'm getting a very strong message for another man in a checked suit with a big nose: 'Be careful or your bollocks may get bitten off.'

Jerry: Somewhere near the back of the auditorium I sense a deep well of bitterness and despair.

Cathy: And somewhere near the front of the auditorium I sense great joy and happiness.

Claire: And somewhere in the middle there is an overwhelming sense of indifference.

Terry: Oh, I'm getting romance, passion, lots of sex. I'm getting lots of sex, at the front and at the back.

Claire: [*In a voice comically strangled by her exaggerated grin*] I'm getting arthritis.

Robin: Oh, I'm getting something. Oh yes ... Something very strong ... I'm picking up, er, the colour ... *brown*. The colour brown. Er, perhaps someone here is, er, wearing, um, brown, or has had a recent experience involving, involving the colour brown?

Weaver: Oh. I'm getting a very sore penis. Somewhere in the house tonight ... A ... gentleman ... has a, a very sore penis. Just to let you know, sir, it's rather more serious than you think.

Claire: Oh, yes. Very clear. Someone in the house tonight has a, a teenage daughter and she's giving you lots of trouble with her habits and her clothing and her friends. Well don't worry, dear, she will be dead by Christmas.

John: Oh dear. There's a sceptical woman somewhere over there ... wearing a red dress.

Robin: Oh no.

John: Now you're ruining it for everybody. Please concentrate, tune in to the vibrations or get out!

Terry: Yes, and on that note somebody in the house tonight has an irritating tune going round and round in their heads. Please stop it—it's interfering with reception.

Robin: And I'd just like to say there are a lot of people here tonight who are not thinking in English. I'm just getting a lot of nonsense, ladies and gentlemen, nonsense. Please, if you want my colleagues and I to help you, you must try to think in *English* or in, in, in very clear visual images or, or, emotional sensations ... This other stuff just won't do.

Richard: Oh, I'm getting something now. A strong visual image of a fire. A terrible fire in a place of public entertainment. Hundreds killed.

Cathy: [*Reacting to the idea of the fire*] Oh. Hot!

Richard: No!

Cathy: Hot! Hot!

Richard: No.

Cathy: [*Pausing, as if the vision of the fire is faded*] Er, cold.

Jerry: A red beach ball ... in the wind ... rolling along the sand ... Oh. It's gone.

Cathy: Barnsley 1, Rotherham 0.

Weaver: I'm getting a series of numbers between one and forty-nine. Six numbers: 2, 4, 6, 8, 10 ... Oh, it's just the beginning of the two times table.

Robin: Oh. Oh. I'm getting something very strong. Oh yes, yes, yes. I'm getting life. New life in the audience, new life somewhere, somewhere over here, somewhere over here on my left, that's your right ladies and gentlemen, a young woman, a young woman, ah, a young woman wearing *brown*. Yes, yes, my dear you're *pregnant*, you don't know it yet but you're pregnant, yes with twins, with twins, a little boy and a little girl. That's nice for you, dear.

[*Richard takes his blindfold off and leaves.*]

John: [*Blindfold off by now*] A young couple hoping for a good night out tonight left their baby with a new babysitter without checking her credentials. I'm sorry. I think you had better go home ... Quick ... Sorry.

Claire: [*Blindfold off*] There's a woman who didn't want to come tonight. You really didn't want to come, did you? But you did. Well done. [*Claire leaves.*]

Cathy: [*Blindfold off*] There's a man somewhere here near the back, wearing a suit. A businessman. I think you've come to the wrong place.

Jerry: [*Blindfold off*] Oh dear, oh dear. Somebody in the house tonight is having an affair and lying consistently to his wife or girlfriend, can't be sure. Oh dear ... Oh dear ... [*Jerry leaves.*]

Cathy: There's a woman in the third row ... You've got a lump in your left breast.

Terry: [*Blindfold off*] Yes. I'm getting a couple who've come here tonight from a restaurant, an expensive restaurant. And the woman paid by Switch. I'm afraid your account details were taken down and thousands of pounds are being drained from your account as

you sit there. I am sorry. [*Terry leaves.*]

Weaver: [*Blindfold off*] Somewhere in the house tonight there's a man, a parent, who tells the most terrible of lies to his child. I'm sorry to tell you, sir, that you will be discovered. [*Weaver leaves.*]

Cathy: The man next to him—you're not going to make it home tonight. [*Gesturing toward someone else*] I've just got a really clear picture inside this gentleman's head. It's not very nice, is it? [*Pointing into the auditorium and thinking for varying lengths of time between each of the predictions she makes hereafter*] Car crash. Cancer. Heart attack. Kidney failure. Suicide. Pneumonia. Cancer of the bowels. Brain haemorrhage. Stroke. Prostate cancer. A tumour, a brain tumour. Old age. Bronchitis. Septicaemia. Idiopathic ventricular fibrillation. Emphysema. Asthma attack. Lung cancer. A snakebite. Typhoid. Motor neurone disease. Drowning. AIDS. Obesity. Drugs overdose. Slit wrists. Shot. Stabbed. Ebola. Drowning. Meningitis. Electrocuted. A routine operation that goes wrong. Influenza. Deep vein thrombosis. Childbirth. Crushed. Hypothermia. Alcoholism. Heart attack. Stroke. Broken hip. Broken neck. Broken heart. Epileptic fit. Bomb. Bomb. Bomb. Bomb. Bomb. Burst appendix. Hepatitis A. Hepatitis B. Hepatitis C. You two at the end of the row, about two thirds of the way back—suicide pact. And you three in the middle here—a train crash. And on the end of the row near the back ... a gas explosion. Old age.

[*As Cathy continues the other performers—still with their fixed grins—slowly return to their places in the line, each holding a placard with a letter on it. Once they are all positioned, and with Cathy in her place (she doesn't have a letter) the letters spell WE COME. Cathy exits and returns to her place with a placard bearing the letter 'L'. The letters now spell WELCOME.*]

3. Welcome Line

Richard: I must say, it's lovely to see you all looking so healthy and great to see so many faces out there, some of them familiar and some of them not.

John: Strangers now, but not for long.

Robin: Yes, indeed. And on a personal note I'd just like to say a big thank you to everybody here who has made us feel so very *welcome*.

Jerry: Yes. It's a crazy business, show business. We travel around a lot but you know when we step up here on the stage and under the lights then that's when we feel really and truly at home ... Ladies and gentlemen, we feel at home this evening here tonight.

Cathy: Some of my best friends are ... dead.

Richard: Yes. And what a shame they can't be with us here tonight. Sat perhaps in some of the empty seats and enjoying the show.

Terry: I'd like to say at this point, ladies and gentlemen, that some of our personal lives are in tatters.

John: But you wouldn't want to know about that, would you?

Weaver: What happens backstage is as much fun as what happens out here on the stage, but that's none of your business.

Jerry: Yes, it's all a bit boring really.

Claire: The curtains parted and there we were—spread out in a line for your enjoyment.

Richard: I'd like to assure you, ladies and gentlemen, at this point in the evening, that there won't be any nudity in the performance. [*Robin laughs.*]

Jerry: No, really. It's not that kind of show at all. There's not going to be anything remotely distasteful or shocking or provoking.

Weaver: There won't be anything unpleasant or disturbing.

John: It's going to be good, clean fun.

Terry: Nothing to give the men an embarrassing erection that they have to cover up with their coats.

Robin: Not at all.

Terry: No scenes that get the ladies so wet they have to cross their legs to conceal the smell.

Richard: Welcome.

All: Welcome.

Richard: No one's going to be forced into a box that's far too small for them and then get trapped in there by having the lid nailed down with really big hammers and
metal nails.

Weaver: No one will be murdered in tonight's performance.

John: No actors are going to be 'blacking up' to be kings in a long, long story. Not in this theatre. Not tonight. Maybe in another theatre. Not here.

Robin: At this point I think it's important for us to say that you, you, ladies and gentlemen, are of course the stars of tonight's performance. Without you we would be nothing.

Claire: Really. Without you we are quite literally *nothing*.

Cathy: There's an old saying ... I think it goes something like this: 'Ladies and gentlemen, the whole world is a stage and we are some of the people on it ...'

Jerry: So ... whether the stage is up here or down there it doesn't matter really, does it? Because, because the whole world is one.

Robin: We won't be coming down there though. We'll be staying on this smaller stage on the larger stage that is the whole world, um, yes.

Jerry: And you'll be able to stay on the rest of the bit of the stage that isn't this bit.

Terry: And if you've got personal problems they're none of our business.

Richard: It's not all going to be fun.

John: It's going to be a very, very long evening.

Weaver: I just want to assure you, ladies and gentlemen, that there aren't going to be any cats on roller skates, there, uh, there aren't going to be any, any ships made of ice appearing anywhere, um, there aren't going to be any princesses in very tall towers, letting their, letting their lovely hair down, er, there aren't going to be any, uh, any giants counting their money or, or, or glass, glass slippers or enchanted forests, or red shoes, or yellow brick roads leading anywhere.

[*During Weaver's text the others back uneasily off the stage. Jerry remains and interrupts his digression; as Jerry speaks, Weaver leaves.*]

Jerry: Well that's quite true, ladies and gentlemen. But, um, just before we proceed I think I should explain to you a few, a few simple rules. There's nothing, er ... It's all fairly straightforward—I'm sure most of you have done this kind of thing before. Um. Basically, um, we're going to be up here ... And you're going to be down there ... And we're going to be in the light and you're going to be in the, the shadows ... Er, we're going to talk and, er, you're going to try and be as quiet as mice ... Um ... We're going to be standing up, uh, most of the time and ... you're going to be sitting down. You're going to do what you do and we're going to do what we do.

[*Jerry is leaving as Richard and Robin come crashing through the back curtains, struggling, Robin once again in a headlock as the ventriloquist's dummy. Richard drags Robin to the front and positions the low mic for him to speak.*]

Robin: Ladies and gentlemen, it gives me very great pleasure to introduce the beautiful, the enigmatic Miss Claire Marshall. Or the Balloon Bimbo, as we call her.

[*Richard yanks Robin away from the mic before he can say any more. Claire enters through the curtains at the back, carrying a chair, her dress covered in balloons; John also enters blindfolded and brandishing a large saw. Richard and Robin leave the stage. Music: slowed-down striptease. Claire stands on her chair and in a surly fashion bursts the balloons one by one with a cigarette, making the occasional wiggle as a token attempt at dancing. John stands stock-still throughout, the saw raised as if to signal impending action, but apparently realizing that he has come on at the wrong cue. When the music ends and all the balloons are burst Claire leaves and John is left alone on the stage, still blindfolded, still holding the saw aloft.*]

5. Joke

John: Hello ... Is anybody there?

Oh, ow, that's sore—that's saw. Get it?

I've got one for you. A joke. Funny.

A horse goes into a bar. Er. That's it. Into a bar, sits up on the stool and he, he says to the barman. Oh, no, he doesn't say that. The barman says to him, why, why have you come in my bar? No, that's not it.

What do you call a man with no ears, no nose, er, no arms, no hair, er, no—no trousers, no shoes, er, no, no jacket? Er, I don't know, er, there's no answer to that, er.

Two nuns in a bath, er, no, not two, er, three. Three nuns in a bath, or is it four? Four! Four nuns. Or maybe more. More than four. Possibly. Possibly six. In a bath. All washing, washing themselves up. No, no, it's not a bath. Yes, they're on horseback. They're on horseback and they're riding into town ... Up, down, up, down. Yee-hah! No, it's not nuns on horseback. It's Michael. Michael Douglas. No! Michael Jackson! Yes! Michael Jackson on a horse. Riding into town with Bubbles the chimp. Not on lots of horses, though. No, not Michael Jackson. It's a sex maniac. That's it, a sex maniac. Not on a horse, no, in a strip club, watching all the lovely ladies, all rubbing themselves up. No! It's the sex maniac's day off and he's gone to the zoo to look at animals ... having sex with each other, all riding roughshod over one another.

No, they're not. They're not having sex, they're playing. He's watching them playing. Instruments. Musical instruments.

No, that's midgets. Midgets playing the instruments. Oompah-pah, oompah-pa. It's not a zoo. It's on an aircraft. That's it, an aeroplane. All midgets playing instruments on an aeroplane. Funny, isn't it? Yes, er, some midgets or are they zombies? That's it, the undead. Not in an aircraft though, that wouldn't be very good. They are on a desert island. Zombies. Not lots of zombies though. Just the one. All on his own. On a desert island. Just standing there, on his own. He says, he says something.

[*John is calling into the wings and behind him, with this line and many others below, as if to alert other performers to his distress.*]

'WHERE HAVE ALL MY FRIENDS GONE?'

He says it again.

'WHERE HAVE ALL MY FRIENDS GONE?' He gets no reply. 'ER, WHY HAVE YOU ABANDONED ME?,' he says. 'WHERE ARE YOU?' I'm frightened.

I'm shitting myself. I, I don't know where to go next.

Can one of you bastards help me? You know who you are.

Help.

I'm really, really shitting myself now.

What shall I do next?

I am in serious trouble.

Please send assistance.

SOS.

Dot-dot-dot, dash-dash-dash.

Dot.

Ah, I feel like I'm going to die now.

I know where you live.

You bastards.

Where are you?

I'm going to die.

I'm going to die in ten seconds.

10 ... 9 ... Oh, forgive me, father, for I have sinned.

I stabbed my mother with a stabbing stabber.

Er, I didn't go to school ...

8 ... 7, 6 ...

Oh, I'm nearly dead now. You should see me. I'm on my knees in pain
and agony.

6.

5, 4, 3.

Help.

WHERE ARE YOU?

2.

1.

Zero.

I'm dead now, I'm, I'm dead.

[*John lies down on the floor.*]

6. Apology

[*Music: melodramatic strings. Richard, Jerry, Weaver, and Robin
enter from the back, still smiling and now carrying a reclining
Claire lain across their arms as if for some showstopping musical
number. They carry Claire to the front, where the mic is already
in place at an appropriate height for her to speak.*]

Claire: Ladies and gentlemen, we would like to at this point to
say sorry. Despite all preparation, accidents happen, mistakes are
made, and the finger of blame is pointed. Ladies and gentlemen,
at this point we wish to make a complete and unabashed apology
because the scene that you just witnessed, the scene you just
witnessed was ... Too long. It was rambling, the performance was
weak, there was no discernible punchline, it was improvisation
of the lowest order. Ladies and gentlemen, you always destroy the
thing you love the most, you reach out for a rose and before you
know it your hands are covered in blood.

Ladies and gentlemen ... [*The men decide Claire has said enough
and start to carry her off the stage.*] An apology ... [*To the men*]
You fuckers—I have not yet finished! [*To audience*] Ladies and
gentlemen, you witnessed a crime, a crime perpetrated by one
man and that man's name is John Eric Rowley and he is a fucking
charlatan and he will never again work on the legitimate stage.
[*John, still blindfolded and lying on the ground downstage,
starts to crawl off the stage in 'shame'.*] An apology—I have not

yet finished! An apology, no ifs, no buts—get your hands off me!
[*The men get Claire offstage through the curtains at the back but
she fights her way back on again.*] I have not yet finished—where
was the strength of human spirit, where were the fates, where
was the charity? [*To Weaver and Jerry who are trying to pull her
offstage again*] Get off me you public school twats, no more, no
more, I am not yet finished. Ladies and gentlemen ... [*Claire is
pulled behind the curtains but remerges, fighting off Weaver
and Jerry.*] An apology, a wholehearted apology, wholeheartedly we
apologize—get off, get off of me, take your hands off this too,
too solid flesh! [*Claire is dragged across the floor and behind
the curtains but again remerges, fighting off Weaver and Jerry,
yelling more and more vehemently.*] Ladies and gentlemen, we tear
our hearts from our breasts and throw them at you. Where were
the men with steel in their eyes? Where were the mountains of
glass? [*To Weaver and Jerry*] Get off get off get off me—no, stop
it! I will not be stopped. [*Yelling to audience as she is dragged
across the floor*] We're sorry, we're sorry, we're sorry, we're
sorry, we're sorry, we're sorry we were ever fucking born. No, no
more. Take your hands off me. Stop it, stop, no more, no more.

7. Mystery/Illusion Dance

[*Through the latter part of the apology the other performers enter
and re-form their usual line at the front as if to cover up or
distract from the chaos behind them. This time the performers are
carrying placards with letters spelling out the word MYSTERY! The
line is formed by everyone minus Claire: MY TERY! Claire enters
with a placard bearing the letter 'S' and the line MYSTERY! is
complete. The performers smile at the audience. Claire fiddles
with her jaw, as if she's been injured in her struggles with Jerry
and Weaver. Then she spits loudly onto the stage, returning to
a frontal gaze and her smile. Music: swirling atmospheric drone
flowing into a Latin dance number. They dance, rearranging the
letters of the word MYSTERY! as they spin around and criss-cross
the stage. At a climactic moment in the music the placards are
spun to reveal letters on their other side which collectively
spell a new word—ILLUSION—creating a clumsy coup de théâtre.*]

8. Illusion Line

[*Once they have all come to rest holding the letters ILLUSION
Terry starts to speak. At first, they stand resolute but as the
scene progresses they lose focus on their task and the image
crumbles.*]

Terry: Ladies and gentlemen. While you're with us tonight,
we'd like to ask you to try to forget about the outside world
completely. Try not to think about anything outside of this room.
Anything at all.

Try to forget about cars, and meetings, cigarettes, and road
accidents. [*Despite their rigid smiles the performers look
increasingly concerned—or distracted—that Terry is continuing
this text.*] Try to forget about births and deaths and funerals.
And bereavements. [*John, looking around, slowly lowers the letter
'N' he is holding, so it's just in one hand.*] Try not to think
about dustbins, and litter on the street. Try not to think about
agonies and bitterness and smiles. [*Richard, standing next to
John, slowly lets his letter 'O' go lower so now the whole end
of the word is sloping downward.*] And sadness. And the kind of
bitterness that comes from making one really big mistake. And the
kind of regret that comes from making many many many many small
mistakes. [*Richard takes out a packet of cigarettes from his suit
pocket, offers one to John who declines.*] Try not to think about
clumsiness and ineptitude. [*Richard hides his head behind his
letter 'O' as he lights a cigarette for himself.*]

Forget about the wind rushing through trees and fire engines
rushing to an accident. Try to forget about rivers flooding and
cars—cars on a motorway piling into one another. Try to forget

about footsteps walking on pavements and broken heels. [*Richard continues to smoke, Claire leans her letter 'I' on Jerry's legs facing forwards then leaves the line slowly, going offstage at the back.*] And poison and rusty knives. And guns. Try not to think about guns. And daggers and letter bombs. And nail bombs. And chemical warfare. [*Claire re-enters carrying a bottle of water, walks slowly back to her place in the line, takes a drink from the water bottle.*] Try not to think about chemical warfare. And chemotherapy. And the common cold. Try not to think about the common cold. And hospitals. And nurses. And surgeons and rubber gloves and trolleys and serums and cupboards. And expensive drugs that poor countries can't afford. [*Claire finishes drinking, sits on the floor.*]

Try not to think about biotechnology, abortions and genetic abnormalities, and chromosome disorders. [*Claire lies down on the floor, her sign saying 'I' propped up against her.*] And sperm. Try not to think about sperm. Sperm that doesn't swim in the right direction. Try not to think about ovarian dysfunction and foetal matter that never goes on to develop a heart. Try not to think about daydreams and the kind of fluff you find at the bottom of our handbag. Try not to think about phlegm. The kind of phlegm that sticks in the back of your throat. [*Jerry leans his placard 'S' against Claire's legs where she lies, next to the 'I'. He walks back and offstage impatiently.*] And handkerchiefs with blood on them. And toilet seats with blood on them. [*Robin picks up the 'S' placard that Jerry has left and holds it with his own sign, the two together now reading US.*] And shit on the sheets. Try to forget about shit on the sheets. I don't want you to think about shit on the sheets. Forget about sweat. The smell of other people's sweat. [*Jerry re-enters with a tray of tea-making equipment and mugs, walks from upstage right to downstage right, just behind the line, pours himself a mug of tea. John goes over and collects a banana from the tray, takes it back to his place in the line and starts to eat it.*] The sound of people coughing and the sound of people walking down the stairs. [*Jerry returns to his place in the line with his mug of tea, takes the 'S' placard from Robin.*]

Try to forget about nursery rhymes and bedtime and children crying in their sleep. People crying out in pain. Try to forget about TV and news headlines. And states of emergency. And diplomatic breakdown. [*Richard puts his cigarette out on the floor.*] Try to forget about the electric chair and electric shock treatment. Try to forget about stimulants and depression. [*Cathy with 'L' placard squats down.*] Depression and depressants and deep-rooted psychological problems. [*Robin goes off hurriedly at the back, then comes back with a chair, puts his 'U' placard on the chair and goes over to the drinks tray to make a drink.*] Try to forget about the things people say to hurt one another, and the things that people don't say. Try not to think about people stuck on boats in the middle of the ocean. [*Robin gesticulates to Richard, asking if he wants a cup of tea etc.*] People stuck underneath trains. Or people stuck in the back of refrigerated lorries. [*Robin takes tea to Richard and his own tea to his seat where he sits, holding the sign.*] Try not to think about hatred or religious war. Try not to think about religious war and nail bombs.

Try not to think about trains crashing into other trains. Sickness and ulcerated skin. And Christmas. And brittle bones and pneumonia. And gas fires. Gas heaters and gas ovens and tear gas. Try not to think about insects and fleas [*John returns teacup to tray.*] and viruses that run out of control. And bacteria. Flesh-eating bacteria. [*Weaver takes jacket off and sits on the ground, the 'I' placard leans against his leg.*] Try not to think about the fluff in between your toes, and earwax. And snot. And blood and guts and cum. And piss. [*John, returning to his position in the line ostentatiously resumes display of his 'N' placard to

the audience, smiling full-on as if his break is over.*] Try not to think about leaky bladders and when you last emptied your bowels. [*Cathy leans her letter 'L' placard on her shoes and goes to get a cup of tea from the tray stage right.*] Try not to think about coughing people and the dull hum of electricity and darkness and silence. [*Cathy returns to her place in the line, stands barefoot drinking her tea.*] And the kind of awkward pauses that happen on the telephone. [*Richard resumes duty, displaying his letter 'O' placard next to John, so that the two of them together spell ON.*]

Try not to think about family feuds and bruises and gashes and cuts. Try not to think about The Big Bang and how the world began. How the world might end. [*Jerry walks from the line, puts his empty tea cup on the tray, goes back to the line and resumes display of his letter 'S' placard.*] And dinosaurs and history and mythology and chronology and ideology and biology and geology and French and maths and PE and RE.

Try not to think about sex and kisses. And anal rape. [*Richard abruptly leaves.*] And lobotomies and blow jobs. And piercings. Try not to think about really boring car journeys and really boring train journeys. Try not to think about loneliness and emptiness and vacuums and voids. And the year zero. [*Robin gets up wearily from the chair, puts his teacup down on the tray stage right and leaves.*]

Try not to think about the workings of your body. While you're with us here tonight, we'd like to ask you to try not to think about the workings of your body. Your heart pumping blood, your lungs breathing oxygen. Twitches, shudders, shrugs, nervous mannerisms. Discomfort. Try not to think about discomfort. [*Jerry leaves.*] Deceit, deception, and despair. And desperation. And mistakes. And mishaps, misdemeanours, and miscellaneous errors. Try not to think about your pulse. [*Robin comes back hurriedly to collect his chair from the front where he left it, taking it back offstage. John follows.*] And time. And space and seconds passing and minutes passing. Try not to think about sleeping, dreaming, and bad dreams that haunt you for the rest of the day. [*Weaver gets up, loads teacups and things on the tray, takes Cathy's water bottle from her and leaves.*] Try not to think about car crashes, holes in the road, dust, ash, and smoke. And fire. Fire and sand and ash and fear, try not to think about shopping and lottery tickets. And broken dreams and broken bones and broken homes and broken marriages.

Try not to think about the inevitable process of ageing. Skin and bones and muscles wasting.

Try not to think about goodbyes and airports and people who can't look you in the face. And overheard remarks and suspicion and things people say about you which you should never really hear. Try not to think about trembling and coughing and needing to clear your throat. Try not to think about—[*Weaver leaves the stage.*]—mobile phone bills and badly managed prisons and badly managed pension funds—[*Cathy puts her shoes on.*]—and rust and world leaders and world aid and pain and disasters and disaster movies and disastrous relationships and disastrous haircuts and curtains and feet stamping angrily and cinders and ceilings and shipwrecks and things that lie at the bottom of the ocean.

While you're with us here tonight, we'd like you to forget about everything that makes you who you are. Your passports, your identity cards, your date of birth, your face, your experiences, everything you did today, and everything you said. And everything you saw. Whilst you're with us here tonight we'd like to ask you to forget about everything your friends and family did or saw or heard or thought today. Forget about everything you've ever read. [*Cathy, shoes on now, resumes smiling and display of her letter 'L' placard beside Terry.*] And everything that's ever been written. And everything that's ever been invented or made. Forget about everything that's ever been

conceived of and everything that's ever come into existence. And
everything that might come into existence in the future. And
everything that might have come into existence but didn't.

Whilst you're with us here tonight, we'd like you to forget about
everything.

Whilst you're with us here tonight, we'd like you to forget about
everything outside this room.

[*Terry and Cathy leave, Claire remains lying on the floor as
if asleep. After some moments she rises, smiles, picks up
and displays her letter 'I' placard. Mysterious music plays.
Claire crosses the stage and draws the curtains closed,
leaving the stage.*]

9. Card Trick

[*Music continues. As Claire exits Jerry, John, Robin, Weaver,
and Richard enter, all of them blindfolded. Richard and Weaver
take up positions towards the edges of the stage, framing the
action which follows. In it, John performs a kind of brutal card
trick on Robin, who is held in place forcibly by Jerry. John's
blindfolded 'card trick' involves him hitting Robin repeatedly
with the cards, sometimes throwing them at him, putting them down
into his clothes, forcing them into his mouth—all the violence
of the action dressed up as if it were a mysterious or magical
business of appearing and disappearing cards. At a key moment
during the scene Robin escapes Jerry's grasp and reverses the
situation—holding Jerry captive as John continues with his act
apparently unaware that the roles of victim and assistant have
been reversed. As the final stage of the trick, is performed Jerry
too escapes, spitting cards from his mouth and starting to speak.*]

10. Fortune Telling Reprise

Jerry: I'm getting something. I'm getting something! I'm picking
something up! There's a gentleman, there's a gentleman——you, sir.
Yes you, sir. By the time you're old you're going to be so fat and
ugly that no one's going to want to look after you. And the woman
next to you has got herpes. And you, madam, those shoes you are
wearing, the ones you hope will get more comfortable, well I'm
afraid to tell you they won't. They're going to give you nasty
blisters on your heel and you're going to have to stop wearing
them. And you won't be able to wear that new skirt you bought to
go with them either.

And you, sir, you'd like to have children one day wouldn't you,
sir? Well, I'm sorry to say you're firing blanks, mate.

And you, madam, tomorrow you're going to go to the shop to buy a
newspaper and they'll have sold out of your usual one and you'll
have to buy another and it won't be as good.

And you, sir. You're going to be blessed with triplets and it's
going to be lovely at first. But then they're not going to learn
to speak. They'll be five, six years old and they're still not
going to be able to speak, all they'll do is stand and stare at
you and you'll call in the educational psychologist and he'll tell
you that they're communicating with each other telepathically and
they'll be plotting against you telepathically. They'll come into
your bedroom at night and stand around your bed and stare at you
and you'll get older and older and iller and iller and eventually
you're going to die, sir, and they'll dance on your grave and
they'll be taken away by NASA for tests.

And you, madam, you're going to have a son and he'll be a lovely
boy, a bit dim perhaps but lovely. And he's going to fall in with
a bad crowd and one day he'll get the blame for a crime one of
his friends has committed and he'll be sent to a young offenders'
detention centre where he's going to get so badly bullied and
buggered that he's going to take his own life, madam.

And you, sir, you're going to buy some magnetic letters for
your fridge and you're going to come down one morning and find
that they've re-arranged themselves into obscene and abusive
messages, sir.

And you, sir, your whole street is going to get swept away in a
giant flood and you're going to have to go shopping in a little
boat, escorted by the army.

And you, sir, you live in a nice neighbourhood, don't you, sir?
Well I'm afraid it's not going to stay like that. It's going to go
downhill. Your nice neighbours are going to move out and your
new neighbours are going to shout and fight all night long and
there's going to be graffiti on the walls and burnt-out cars in
the street and gangs of immigrants on the corner and you're not
going to like that, are you, sir? And you're not going to like
it either when you come home from work one day and find that a
family of refugees from a foreign war have set up camp in your
living room, sir. They'll be burning your books to make a little
fire for their stew.

And you, sir, you're going to come home from work one day and find
that you can't go down your street. They'll be police cars and
tape and you'll be told that a gang of terrorists have taken over
your house and they'll be holding your family hostage and you'll
see your wife at the window and the police will open fire and
she'll die, sir, and then you'll see your children's faces at the
window and they'll get shot too and you'll be screaming and the
police won't let you pass and they'll wrestle you to the ground
and you'll have your face in a puddle and ...

[*The rest of the performers arrive through the curtains at
the back, walk forwards to form a line alongside Jerry as he
completes his text, smiling, as if to compensate for any offence
Jerry may have caused. Richard starts clapping; the others join
in, which drowns out Jerry's speech.*]

11. Best Audience Line

Robin: [*To audience, in the silence after the clapping*] Er. You
should really all give yourselves a jolly good pat on the back.

John: Yes. Give yourselves a round of applause.

Robin: Yes.

John: Come on, don't be shy.

Richard: Good. Really, you should give yourselves a pat on the
back because—I think I speak for all my colleagues here—that
you, you here, in this place, you are quite simply the very very
very best audience that we have ever ever played to.

Weaver: Hear, hear.

Claire: Really, ladies and gentlemen, you are kind and
intelligent and warm-hearted and broad-minded and we thank you.

[*General 'thank yous'.*]

Terry: You're morally superior. And ethically pure.

Weaver: You're politically sensitive.

Robin: Yes. Yes. But that doesn't stop you from letting your hair
down and having a good time.

Jerry: Nothing goes over your heads, does it?

John: You're scientists and mathematicians.

Terry: You are judges and doctors.

Weaver: You're surgeons and architects.

Jerry: Outstanding members of the community.

Richard: There aren't any criminals in here tonight.

Robin: Well, if anybody's got any unpaid parking fines or speeding
tickets that's not what we are talking about.

Terry: What we mean is there are no wife beaters here. No men or women who have been secretly sexually abusing their children for years.

Claire: There's no homophobes here tonight, no racists. No well-dressed, well-educated bigots, are there?

John: No. Because you are the best audience we have ever played to.

[Pause.]

Cathy: You, you have all the qualities that make up the best audience we've ever played to.

Jerry: You are good.

Cathy: You are kind.

Robin: And you're here. You're here!

Richard: You're not the worst audience we ever played to.

John: You stayed.

Richard: You're not a drunken rabble, baying for blood and cheap jokes.

Terry: You're not football hooligans who will go out tonight and trash the town if your team doesn't come out on top.

Claire: You don't rub up against other people on public transport, now do you?

John: You don't carry sharp, spiky objects in your pockets ready to throw at people like us, now do you? No.

Cathy: You're not the kind of people who are frightened to go home because your lives are empty. You're not afraid to sit in your rooms wondering what to do next, whether you could watch television or who to ring. You're not afraid to go to bed because you're frightened that you won't sleep. You're not those kinds of people.

Richard: No you're not. You're not those kind of people at all.

Jerry: No. You're stars. You're the stars of the show.

Weaver: You're not black holes, sucking every last bit of life and matter out of the universe, are you?

Terry: You're not sad fucks who come to the theatre to fuel their sexual fantasies. You're not sitting there in the dark and mentally ordering us in your heads in terms of who you'd like to sleep with first and who second and who third and who fourth and all the way down the line to whoever is last ...

Cathy: And you're not the kind of people who wake up one day and realize that each and every opportunity that life has ever handed to you has been squandered and wasted by your own laziness and indifference and cowardice.

Richard: No. Because you are the best audience we have ever had.

Terry: We came in peace. You came in peace.

Richard: We offered out our hands in friendship.

Claire: And you spat on them.

Jerry: A toast then. 'Ladies and gentlemen—to you.'

[General 'to you's and 'cheers'.]

Terry: Up yours.

Richard: You are the best audience we've played to.

Cathy: You make us feel like we want to take a knife to our throats and cut through a nice big vein and let all our blood out.

Robin: Yes. For you! For you, our blood for you, ladies and gentlemen.

John: [Pointing to someone in the audience] You got that bit,

didn't you? Well done!

Claire: [Pointing to someone else] You didn't get it.

Richard: [Pointing to someone else] You got his—give it back.

John: [Pointing to someone else] You move!

Cathy: You make us feel tired and bored and frustrated and impatient and disillusioned and sick and nauseous ...

Weaver: Are we keeping you up?

Terry: You make us feel like banging our fists against the back of our throats until we're sick.

Richard: [By way of mitigation] Only backstage, though.

Claire: You know, sometimes I look out and I don't see human beings at all, I just see shapes with dead eyes.

Richard: The lights are very bright up here—sometimes it's hard to see anything.

Terry: And, you know, sometimes I look out and I don't smell scent or aftershave or deodorant, I just smell the bitter stench of human failure.

Cathy: You stink.

Terry: Losers!

Cathy: You stink.

Claire: You make us want to rip out our eyeballs so we no longer have to look upon you.

Cathy: You stink. You stink. You stink. You stink.

Terry: You make our tits shrivel and drop to our knees. You make our milk ducts spurt poisonous venom.

John: [To audience by way of apology] It's no good looking in your programmes.

Cathy: You stink so much that I can't believe I have been standing here for this long without fainting, without passing out. You know, you make me want to put my head in a bucket of piss and drink it all and fill up my bladder with that piss and then stand over you all and then piss it all out all over your heads.

Claire: Good. Good.

Weaver: [Starts singing to the tune of 'Go West'] You're shit and you know you are.

[The others join in the singing, which swells uneasily and then peters out, with a last voice left, embarrassed.]

Richard: Well, I'm glad we eventually had the time to have this little chat. I think we've put our cards on the table.

Robin: Well, yes, now that we've cleared the air a little bit ...

Terry: Can't get rid of the smell though, can we? Still lingers.

Richard: Yes and with that rich aroma in the air still ... perhaps we can do what—

Cathy: Shut up.

Richard: And you can do what—

Cathy: Shut up.

Weaver: Aah—

Cathy: Shut up.

Richard: Keep your hands where we can see them.

Cathy: Shut up.

John: [Pointing into audience] Who's that there?!

Cathy: Shut up.

Richard: [To audience] Nobody move, this is a raid!

John: Hands up!

Richard: Shut up!

Claire: [*To Richard*] She's telling you to shut up.

Cathy: That's enough.

Robin: Perhaps ...

Cathy: Shut up. Don't. Say. Another. Word.

[*All except Jerry and Cathy back off, humming the tune 'You're shit and you know you are ...'*]

Jerry: [*To audience*] Perhaps you'd like to sing along?

Cathy: Shut up.

Jerry: I'm sure you all know the words by now.

Cathy: Shut up. [*To audience*] That's it. That's enough. We're not doing any more. [*Pause.*] You blew it.

Jerry: It's not quite over yet, ladies—

Cathy: Shut up. [*To audience*] We're not doing any more.

Jerry: About five or ten minutes.

Cathy: We're not doing another thing. Not here. Not tonight. Not for you. You blew it.

Jerry: She always says this. Uh.

Cathy: Not tonight.

Jerry: It's—

Cathy: [*To Jerry*] Get off.

Jerry: [*Cheerily, to audience*] That's my cue!

[*Jerry leaves. Pause.*]

Cathy: We're not doing any more. You blew it. Now read my lips: FUCK-OFF-YOU-ARSE-HOLES.

That's it. You, you make us feel, you make us feel like splitting open your stomachs and pulling out all your intestines and smearing them all over the walls. We're not doing any more. You make us feel like doing something, saying something that we're really going to regret. There's nothing else here for you tonight.

12. Escapology

[*Richard and Robin re-enter through the curtains at the back, Cathy leaves. Robin is dragged and then coerced into a large, plastic laundry bag from which only his head protrudes. Music plays, framing the action that follows as a kind of dance number. John re-enters, again blindfolded and with saw. Robin struggles around inside the bag, moving position and making attempts to 'escape' from the bag, apparently terrified of John as he advances with the saw. Towards the end of the track, as John approaches Robin with menace, Terry and Claire enter from the back of the stage, come forward and close the curtains, erasing the scene and stepping out in front of the curtains to smile at the audience.*]

13. Goodnight

[*The rest of the performers join Claire and Terry in front of the curtain, forming a line across the front. The last two to re-emerge are Richard and Robin, the latter now released from the laundry bag and held by Richard in his customary headlock position. The mic on its waist-height stand is once again passed clumsily along the line to where Robin is held by Richard.*]

Robin: Well. I hope you all enjoyed that. I certainly think we managed to put the 'f' back into fun. Not to mention the 's' back into sensuality. Which reminds me, I thought the ladies were particularly feisty tonight. Must be the time of the month. Still, all's well that ends well, eh?

You know, ladies and gentlemen, when you leave the theatre tonight, I'd like you to forget about all of this. Forget about everything that you've heard. Everything you've seen. Just go home, pour yourself a nice stiff drink, tune the TV somewhere between the channels, watch the snow, listen to the rush.

Normally at this stage in the evening I'd have to sing a song, or tell a little joke, but tonight ... Tonight, it's much too late for that. The music box has wound down, the toys are all tidied away on the shelf, the dolls are all tucked up fast asleep in the doll's house, and it only remains to say: Buonanotte. Bonne nuit, Gute Nacht. Goodnight.

And one more thing. When you go home tonight, ladies and gentlemen, don't drive safely, drive as fast as you can.

[*Robin slowly bends up from his cowed position, released by Richard who now has his arm around his shoulders. Everyone looking at the audience, smiles are gone. The lights fade.*]

BLOODY MESS (2004)

1. Chairs

[*John and Bruno (in clown makeup and dressed in tartan suits) are onstage as the audience enter, seated and waiting at the back. When the house lights go out Bruno begins to arrange the wooden chairs in a line at the front facing the audience. As soon as Bruno's arrangement is established, John begins to remove the chairs one by one, arranging them at the back of the stage. This dispute—each performer pursuing an opposite goal, effectively undoing each other's work—soon becomes a violent slapstick of chair arrangements. By the end John and Bruno are both exhausted, and a line of ten chairs has been completed at the front of the stage. The other performers enter.*]

2. Line-up

[*The performers seat themselves on the line of chairs. Richard has a mic and speaks first—the mic gets grabbed by, or passed to, different people as this section progresses.*]

Richard: Well. Good evening. Before we start I think some people had a few things that they, er, wanted to say. I know that for myself I'm hoping that tonight you're going to see me very much as the romantic hero of the piece—strong, sensitive, caring, manly, and, well, very virile.

Robin: Yeah. Hello. Good evening. My name's Robin and tonight I'm going to be doing pretty much the same thing as Richard down there. That's Richard, he forgot to say that. Yeah. I'm going to be doing pretty much the same thing as Richard but, yeah, some of you might be able to detect a slight difference in emphasis in what I'm doing—you might be able to see that what I'm doing is slightly less sensitive and caring and slightly more manly and virile.

Richard: [*Moving down the line to take the mic impatiently from Robin*] Good evening. My name is Richard. I'm sorry I forgot to mention that, as Robin has pointed out to you. Ah, I think that you can make your own minds up this evening, after all it's not a competition, is it?

Bruno: Hello. Good evening. I'm Bruno. And I hope that you find me very very very funny. Comedy ... is ... like a banana, if you can imagine that for a moment. On the inside you have the white flesh, which is like the innocent laughter of children that you might find on a school playground anywhere in the world, and then the skin of the banana which has the darker colours—the yellows, greens, brown, black at each end—they represent the darker humours of irony, satire, and jokes about toilets. I don't

do those ones. I hope you see me as representing the white flesh of children's laughter.

John: I hope you're thinking, 'Oh look! He's a funny clown, isn't he!'

Claire: Hello. I'm Claire and I hope that during this evening's performance you're not going to be able to take your eyes off me. You might be distracted by other things going on but your gaze will return to me again and again. You'll be like a helpless moth drawn to a burning flame and there'll be a feeling that starts in the pit of your stomach and spreads through your body like an infection and you'll realize, you'll realize that you are utterly consumed by physical desire for me.

Jerry: I hope that by now you'll have had a chance to have a pretty good look at everybody and that you'll have realized that I'm the only real 'star' in the show tonight. Um, I hope that's okay with everyone. I hope that those of you that haven't recognized me yet—and I totally understand that there's bound to be a few of you—I hope that you're now thinking, 'Hang on. Is that him? Is that him? No, it can't be him, it can't be him, surely he wouldn't be in a show like this, would he? Would he? No. It can't be.' Well. Yes it is—I'm Jerry.

Cathy: Hi. Good evening. I—

Claire: [*Taking mic abruptly*] It's not that I'm suggesting that I'm the prettiest one here or anything, it's more that I hope you will see something in me—a heat, a carnality, a passion—that forces you to admit really very quickly that I'm the one here tonight that you really, really want to fuck. [*She passes the mic back to Cathy.*]

Cathy: Hi. Erm, Claire mentioned my name just then, but I hope that you missed it because I hope you find me enigmatic in the show tonight. I hope you find me a bit like a dark horse, lurking in the shadows.

Wendy: Em, Hi. My name is Wendy and I'm hoping tonight that you'll see me as bubbly and bouncy, bright, brilliant. [*Wendy is 'told' to say this word by Terry, and later words are fed to her by Robin and John.*] Boisterous, and brave, big-hearted, bountiful [*Terry*], benevolent [*Terry*], brilliant and beautiful, generous, hopeful, and—

John: [*Interjecting*] Flammable.

Wendy: Fiery [*Robin*], sparky, mercurial, sort of spunky, up for it, quick-witted [*Terry*], go-getting, uptempo [*Terry*], upbeat, up for a laugh, dynamic, loyal, cheerful, smiley.

John: Toxic. Toxic's a good one.

Wendy: Talkative [*Terry*], and chatty, and really encouraging and honest and loyal, true and persevering, and never ever giving up, and cooperative [*Robin*], and unstoppable, and [*seeing Davis who has come over to stop her*] yielding.

Davis: Good evening. My name is Davis and, um, I hope that you see what I do in the performance tonight as quite symbolic.

Claire: [*Interrupting Davis and whispering to him, off mic*] Symbolic of what? You can't just be symbolic. You have to be symbolic *of something.*

Davis: [*Also whispering off mic*] Can't we just enjoy the silence?

Claire: [*Again whispering off mic*] It's not working, you have to explain more.

Davis: Okay. Um, if while you're watching the performance you become lost or confused or you just don't understand what's going on, on the stage, just always know that you can look towards what I am doing and then it should all become perfectly clear.

In fact, even if you have any questions about your personal life—your career, your love life, or even if you just want to know when you might die, you can also think of those questions and then look to me and I can also answer those. Just know that tonight you can look to me as your own personal I Ching.

John: I hope you're not all thinking about fucking *me* tonight. After the show. Back there. Through the door just there. I hope you're not thinking that.

[*John makes obscene gestures to illustrate his idea.*]

Terry: Hello. My name is Terry. [*Laughing at John*] I'm going to ignore that. I don't know what to say. I hope that when you look at me, you think I look like a real person. Doing real things. I hope you think, 'No one's written her lines for her, no one's told her how to act.' I know. I hope when you look at me, you think, 'She's not a professional. She's not doing it for the money. She'd be doing it even if the money was a little bit less, or even if there was no money at all, even if there was no one watching she'd still be doing it because she is what she is. She is really, really *living it.*

Richard: That seems like a pretty good note to, um, end this bit on, so I think we'll draw a line underneath this section and I think we're pretty much ready to start. So I think we'll, we'll get going.

[*The performers break up the line of chairs and either move to the sides or into place for the next section.*]

3. Born to Be Wild

[*Richard and Robin go to the sound desk. John, Bruno, Jerry, and Davis sit at the sides of the stage, the latter two drinking beer and chatting stage left, the former pair stage right, some distance apart, not communicating.*]

[*Richard puts the CD on and Steppenwolf's 'Born to Be Wild' (1968) begins to play very loud.*]

[*Cathy, already lying on the ground centre stage, remains sprawled as though dead for the duration of the music.*]

[*When the song starts Richard and Robin come forwards to the front of the stage on the right and start to dance enthusiastically to the music, continuing throughout the song.*]

[*At the front, on stage left, Claire looks out at the audience and begins to take off her clothes. She strips down to her underwear and then puts on a gorilla suit and mask. About halfway through the song (now fully costumed as the gorilla) she stops looking at the audience and walks over to curl up on the floor by the speaker, apparently sleeping.*]

[*Terry weeps and screams around Cathy's 'corpse' in the centre of the stage, throwing increasingly large amounts of water over herself from a bottle to simulate crying, also walking backwards and forwards, enacting her 'discovery' of Cathy, and bringing a blanket to throw over her as she lies prone.*]

[*Wendy, at the back on stage left, begins to mark the elements of a simple cheerleading routine.*]

[*At the end of the song Richard and Robin return to the CD player/ sound desk proudly whilst Terry is knelt beside Cathy, head down, still weeping.*]

[*In a fury Cathy kicks off the blankets covering her torso.*]

Cathy: Fucking shit. Total fucking shit. The atmosphere is completely wrong. Completely wrong. It's all ruined.

Who's on sound? Which one of you clowns is on sound? I'm working my arse off here, trying to make it happen. I'm giving it everything I've got and somebody is trying to turn this into a farce.

You! Jerry. [*Addressing Jerry, who is still sitting stage left*] You want to turn this into a farce? You come out here. In fact anybody that wants to turn this into a farce—out here now!

[*Jerry, laughing, walks toward Cathy who is centre stage. John, Bruno, Richard, and Robin follow.*]

Oh back off. Fuck off. *Fuck off.*

[*Jerry, John, Bruno, Richard, and Robin return to their places at the sides of the stage.*]

Who's on sound? Richard? Put something else on.

[*Richard and Robin make some show of looking amongst the CDs for something good or suitable: Deep Purple's 'Speed King' (1970) begins to play.*]

4. Speed King

[*Jerry, Davis, Bruno, and John continue to sit at the sides, watching the action.*]

[*Richard and Robin come downstage right and dance again, just as they did before.*]

[*Cathy stands centre stage throughout, arms folded, looking very unimpressed with Richard's choice of music.*]

[*Terry grieves, largely as before, but a bit more 'rock chick' than 'diva', appearing to ignore the fact that Cathy is no longer lying on the floor in front of her.*]

[*Wendy continues to develop her cheerleader routine at the back of the stage, tracing tentative lines from the centre to the stage left corner.*]

[*Claire (as gorilla) 'wakes up' with the arrival of the new music and runs around the space, disrupting the others by pretending to be an aeroplane flying around. About halfway through the song she starts to spin on the spot in a place off to stage left, going round and round in circles without pause.*]

[*From time to time, as the song proceeds, Bruno crosses the stage to pick up a chair and move it to the other side, weaving in and out of the various other people at play in the space. The song ends.*]

Cathy: [*Pointing to Richard*] Big mistake! That is one huge mistake. You are going to pay for that.

[*To audience*] This is really embarrassing. Obviously I wasn't expecting to be standing here talking to you. I was just planning to get on with my job—

[*Claire (as gorilla), unbalanced from her spinning during the song, is staggering around erratically through Cathy's text. At this point—not yet fully recovered and out of breath—Claire*] removes her gorilla mask and speaks, interrupting Cathy.]*

Claire: Cathy, could I just interrupt you for a minute? [*To audience, without mic*] I hope you're all thinking about my naked body next to your naked body, the heat of my skin against yours, my mouth searching for yours, my breath warm across your ear, my teeth just grazing your shoulder.

[*Cathy waits throughout Claire's text, wandering off to stage left at some point but returning before Claire finishes speaking.*]

I hope you're thinking about my hands on you, my hands on your neck, your back, my hands on the small of your back, my hand between your legs. I hope you can imagine what it might be like to feel my breast in your mouth, my breast filling your mouth. I hope you're thinking about fucking me and me fucking you.

[*Bruno has crossed from stage right to stage left again to pick up a chair. As Claire says the line above, he is re-crossing the stage, away from her back to stage right. He sounds his plastic hooter 'by accident' after Claire has spoken.*]

Bruno: [*Calling over his shoulder*] Sorry!

Claire: [*To Bruno*] It's okay. [*To audience*] I hope you're thinking about my mouth, my lips, my tongue, all over your—finding the places on your skin that make you shiver. I hope you can imagine my hair falling across your face, my hair on your stomach. I hope you can imagine what it might be like to lay your cheek on the inside of my thigh, where the skin is really really soft.

I hope you're thinking about my legs wrapped tight around you, my hips pushing towards you. I hope you're thinking about your hands on me, my waist, my legs, your hands pushing my legs wider and wider apart, and what it's like down there—hot and wet and red ...

[*Through the above, since Bruno's hooter, Richard—who has put on a long, red wig—has been crossing the stage with a mic evidently intended for Claire, moving in the hunched style of a rock gig roadie who 'does not want to be seen'. At this point Richard is nearing Claire but the cable has become trapped back over by the sound desk and, effectively tethered, he can't progress any further. Back at the sound desk Robin moves to try and untrap the cable.*]

Your fingers dipping into me and the slight sound that that makes.

[*Noise from the mic cable hitting the stage as Richard and Robin flip, pull, and tension it as if to somehow release it.*]

I hope you're thinking about the heat and the smell of me and the taste of me. I hope you're thinking about you fucking me and me fucking you, you fucking me and me fucking you. Just fucking. I hope you're thinking about that.

[*Claire completes her text and puts the gorilla mask back on, staring impassively at the audience at the exact moment that Richard has untrapped the mic cable and got the mic into place for Claire to speak. Confused by the silence, he waits with the mic at the gorilla's lips. No sound emerges.*]

Cathy: [*To audience*] I'm really sorry. Things seem to have got a bit confused.

[*Richard leaves the gorilla and starts to manoeuvre, squatting awkwardly, moving towards Cathy, now apparently intent on giving her the mic.*]

I'm feeling a bit drained emotionally. I think I need to have a rest. I need to go away and collect my thoughts and maybe I'll come back later.

[*As Cathy ends her text, Richard arrives. She walks away just as the mic reaches her lips.*

John comes forward, as if taking advantage of the empty stage. He brings a chair with him and seats himself downstage right.]

5. History of the World-Silver Machine

John: [*To audience*] Phwoar! That gorilla! Phwoar ...

[*Richard arrives with mic for John. He squats on John's right side, holding the mic for him, as he will whenever John occupies this front of the stage position.*]

John: That gorilla is something else. I never really thought of animals before in that way. Not gorillas anyway. Just think what you could do with your fingers in that gorilla's hot red parts. [*Laughs*] Sorry. Sorry.

Richard: [*Taking the mic away from John's mouth and speaking into it soundcheck style*] One-Two. One-Two.

[*Richard points the mic back at John who looks annoyed with him.*]

John: That's not what I'm here for actually, I'm here for another reason.

It's really very dark out there tonight. Very dark indeed.

[*Claire (as gorilla) arrives with bottle of water, pours it all into John's crotch, then leaves. Richard points the mic at the water as it falls to the floor.*]

John: I'm all damp now ... Which is nice. As I was saying. It's very dark out there tonight. I can barely see a face at all, really. Which is a good thing for me because it acts as an illustration for a story that I would like to tell you. Well, I say that it's a story but it's actually based on hard scientific facts—but I won't be boring you with the facts tonight ...

[*Terry arrives with a glass which she puts in John's hand, then overfills it with water so that he's stuck, aware that if he moves even minimally the water will spill. Richard sees John's predicament and takes the glass off him, throws half its contents onto the floor, returns the glass to John. Terry, meanwhile, sits facing the audience on the small monitor speaker, just stage left of Richard and John.*]

I won't be boring you with the facts, I will just be telling you the story. You're probably wondering, 'What am I doing here?', and I don't actually mean me, here on the stage. Or you out there. Or him down there. [*John indicates Richard, who replies in a whisper, which John then explains/relays to the audience with an amused shrug.*] He's working!

What I am trying to say is: 'How did we get here on the planet earth?'

[*Back at the sound desk Robin, who has put on a long black wig, turns on an echo machine so that John's voice reverberates crazily on 'planet earth'.*]

Richard: [*Testing the echo of the mic*] 'Planet earth ... One-Two ...' [*He gives a thumbs up to Robin back at the sound desk.*]

John: Can you turn it off, please? That's not very fucking helpful. [*Robin turns the echo off.*] Yeah. How did we get here on the planet earth? Where did we all come from? ... I am going to attempt to answer that question tonight in my story.

[*Claire (as gorilla) starts throwing popcorn at the audience stage left.*]

Perhaps you could all close your eyes for a minute—especially people on that side of the auditorium near the gorilla—close them very tightly. Keep them closed ... Okay. You can open them now.

[*Claire (as gorilla) empties the bag of popcorn onto the audience.*]

Well. If you did manage to close your eyes, that darkness that you will have seen there, that darkness was really only 1 per cent of the darkness that would have been around at the beginning of the creation of the planet earth ...

[*Richard whispers something to John.*]

John: [*Explaining to audience*] 'Do I need a guitar?' ... No. I don't need a guitar ... It's a story. Hmm ... Where was I?

Wendy: [*Wendy is at the back, working on her cheering routine. She shouts ...*] Tell us a story John!

John: Yes ... I'm trying. Okay, so that was only 1 per cent of the darkness that would have been around at the beginning ... All that you had at the beginning was, er ...

Oh yeah ... I am going to tell you the story 'The Beginning of the Earth' ... Or 'The Big Bang'.

Wendy: Give us a bang, John!

John: [*Thinking about that*] Hmm.

[*To audience*] And so what you have at the beginning ... All you have is this thick blackness ...

[*Richard whispers something to John.*]

John: No. I don't need drumsticks. No. Why would I? Can you stop asking those kind of questions? Stupid.

So what you have at the beginning is this thick, impenetrable darkness. Nothing to catch your eye whatsoever ... Nothing to look at ... No detail to fix upon. As well as this—

[*Claire (as gorilla), who has been slowly crossing the stage at the front, finally arrives behind John. Richard holds the mic as if to give the gorilla a chance to speak. John grabs the mic.*]

John: There are no gorillas in the story at this point ...

[*Robin fires the smoke machine, which drives Claire (as gorilla) away, back to stage left.*]

John: Thank you, Rob.

Wendy: [*Still at the back, cheerleading and yelling*] We're waiting for the story, John!

John: So you have this thick, impenetrable darkness ... This carpet of blackness ... Deep darkness and a silence ... A deep, profound silence.

[*Bruno, stood at the table upstage right, lets out another 'accidental' squeak with his hooter.*]

Bruno: Sorry!

Wendy: Let's hear it, John!

John: Yeah. You will. So you have this silence and this blackness, but what you do have is what the scientists ...

[*Bruno comes over to John with a folded piece of paper. John opens the paper.*]

John: [*Reads*] 'No, no, no, you twat. Not what we rehearsed. What about ... ' I can't read this ... [*He shows the note to Richard.*]

[*Richard says something inaudible.*]

John: [*Repeating*] 'Bactara'? What the fuck is 'bactara'?

Bruno: 'Bacteria'.

John: There isn't any bacteria in this story, and you should learn to spell before you bring me a note again.

Okay. So you have this blackness and this silence and something the scientists call ...

[*Richard says something inaudible, in fact a prompt for John to say ...*]

John: Potentiality.

Wendy: '*How do you spell it, John?*'

John: Okay: P-O-T-E-N-T-I-A-L-I-T-Y ... Potentiality.

Bruno: Double 'l'.

[*Jerry and Davis are entering the performance area from the 'off' positions upstage left, carrying large tinfoil stars.*]

John: Not double 'l'. No. Potentiality. [*Robin squirts smoke machine.*] ... And what potentiality is, scientists say, is things waiting to happen ... Things on the brink of happening. [*Jerry emerges through the smoke with his tinfoil star.*] Things on the verge of happening but not yet happening. [*Jerry leaves.*] Things queuing up to happen ... But things *not yet* happening.

[*Terry, carrying beer crate, approaches John and says something inaudible to him.*]

John: [*Repeating for the benefit of the audience*] 'Do I want a beer?' [*To Terry*] Just piss off, Terry.

Wendy: *Give us a story, John!*

John: Okay, so you have this ... potentiality ... Things waiting to happen. Darkness, silence, and potentiality. And so what you have is nothing, and then all of a sudden-

[*Bruno, still at the table upstage right, lets out yet another 'accidental' squeak with his hooter.*]

John: All of a sudden—

[*Richard disconnects the mic so that the end of John's line is inaudible. He reconnects the mic and cable, and then tests it.*]

Richard: One. Two. One-*Two*. One-*Two*. [*Points mic back to John*]

John: All of a sudden you get this ...

[*Claire (as gorilla) has come back to pester John and swings his chair around so that, once again, the end of this line is missed. John spins himself back into position facing the audience and speaks.*]

All of a sudden you have this great big ... *Bang!*

[*Richard takes the mic away and tests it as though he thinks John's 'bang' might have damaged something.*]

Richard: One-Two. One-Two. [*He points the mic back to John.*]

John: And at this point we have ... Where there was nothing, suddenly you have everything happening at the same time ... Everything is happening simultaneously.

[*From this moment on, Jerry and Davis are doing bits of simple enactment or illustration using their tinfoil stars in relation to John's text: where he says 'explosions' they zoom across the stage, where he says that things collide they make the stars collide, etc. Both Terry, who also appears to be illustrating some of what John says, and Wendy, who works on little bits of cheerleading alongside her text interjections, are cued to accelerate their action by the 'Bang!' above. Cathy reads a newspaper at the side of the stage but at the 'Bang!' above she comes to the centre, having wrapped herself in white gauze as a costume, tries to lie back in her 'usual' place, then thinks better of it and returns to the sidelines. Throughout John's text Robin makes himself busy fetching various pieces of equipment that he appears to think are necessary to improve the scene: the smoke machine, two speakers which go one either side of John, and two small disco light units which he sets up in the centre of the stage.*]

You have explosions. Things shooting across the blackness. Small particles. Dust. Rocks. Larger rocks. Meteorites ... Little pieces of paper.

[*Bruno has come to John with a second folded piece of paper. John opens the paper.*]

John: [*Reading*] 'Sex it up ...'

[*To Bruno*] Thanks a lot. [*Throws note away, then speaks to audience*] So you have these particles of dust accelerating, decelerating. Hitting one another. Heating up. Fusing, making much larger rocks. Large rocks the size of houses, and they're smashing into one another, into smithereens. Shooting off in all directions. Heating up, cooling down. Heating up, cooling down. Smashing into each other. Accelerating. Decelerating. An incredible picture where everything is happening. A sense of chaos in which what was blackness ... is now a complete picture.

[Claire (as gorilla) comes back, stage right, but Richard sends a burst of smoke from the smoke machine to drive her away. On departure Claire (as gorilla) steals one of the speakers from next to John, dragging it to stage left. Claire (as gorilla) and Robin, who has followed—perhaps to retrieve the speaker—stand and stare into the thickening smoke.]

John: And if you look closely ...

And if you look closely in amongst this dense picture, this dense, dense picture you'll see ...

Wendy: What do you see, John?

John: You look in there and you see the planet earth. But it's just what we now know as the planet earth—we didn't give it the name 'earth' until several hundreds of years later. But, I must add here, it's not the earth that you would recognize now. It's a completely inhospitable place to be. Not the kind of place where you would want to be at all. Basically, the climate is very different. Climactically—

[Richard fires lots of smoke at John which stops him from speaking.]

Wendy: Give us a Big Bang, John!

John: Okay, you have a different kind of climate. Sea is covering roughly 80 per cent of the planet's surface. You have meteor showers.

[Richard again fires lots of smoke at John.]

John: [To Richard] Lots of smoke, yes. [To audience] You have smoke and fire storms.

[Robin arrives and shines strobe light directly into John's eyes.]

John: Rob. Rob. Please don't do that. Don't shine that in my face. Shine it over there. What's that meant to be?

[Robin says something inaudible.]

John: [Answering] It's not storm-like at all. Point it over there. [To audience] Okay. It's not the climate that you have now. [He coughs from the smoke.]

Wendy: Give us a story, John!

John: You have firestorms. Meteor showers. Meteors hitting the surface of the planet earth. Every few minutes. Thunderstorms. Lightning storms. Volcanoes erupting constantly. Lava flowing everywhere, where there is any land. But what you do have is the sun, which is very near to the earth. It's found its way to the earth. It's there. Very, very hot. And that manages to—

Richard: [Interrupting] One. Two. One-Two.

John: Have you finished? The sun manages to change the climate to something where we could live. The sea levels get low. The storms subside.

[Richard again fires lots of smoke at John. Robin is hanging around at the front as if unsure what to light with the strobe. He stares directly into the flashing light, grinning enthusiastically. Bruno arrives with another note for John, holding it out and distracting him.]

Wendy: Give us a story, John. Keep the story going.

[John gives up and gets up from chair—the constant interruptions have become too much.]

Richard: One. Two. One-Two.

John: [Returning to chair] Okay. You know what? I think I am going to start this story all over again. [To Jerry] From the top.

Okay. Well, it's looking very dark out there tonight ... etc.

[As John starts to repeat his text Robin plays Hawkwind's 'Silver Machine' (1972) on the CD player.

John continues with his text for about half of the song, repeating it more or less exactly, except for the fact that he's now shouting into the mic in order to be heard. Once he's stopped, the song continues to play and Richard shifts from being mic-holder for John to operating the smoke machine which he wheels across the stage, more or less filling it with smoke.

Throughout 'Silver Machine' Terry steps up her rock-chick grieving/dancing, changing into a silver dress during the song. At one or two moments she repeats things that she did during John's first telling of the story, e.g. she brings John the unnecessary glass and water again at the start of the song. Wendy accelerates her cheerleader dancing, using white pompoms in place of the garlands and tinsel that she was using before. Claire (as gorilla) runs around—getting tangled in tinsel, wheeling a pushchair around the stage, jumping off the speakers in a rocking-out kind of way. Jerry and Davis also dance and change costumes—dropping their black suit jackets in favour of white jackets. Robin lights the action using the strobe. The lights from the rig shift as the mood onstage become very rock and roll—a low line of red, white, and blue PAR cans flashing on and off at the back.]

6. Don't Look at Me

[At the end of the song the air is thick with smoke. Claire (as gorilla) is pretending to sleep at the front of the stage. Davis and Jerry are in the playing area but are crouched, hidden behind their stars. Terry is weeping centre stage. Richard and Robin are back at the sound desk. John and Bruno are seated at the sides in the 'off area'.

Cathy comes through the smoke. She has changed costumes again, now wrapped in some red material, her lips and cheeks daubed red with makeup. Her journey to the front is slow and melodramatic. Her gaze is on the audience through the sea of smoke. When she reaches the front, she speaks.]

Cathy: [To audience] Don't look at me. Don't look at me. Stop looking at me. Please don't look at me. I don't want you to look at me now. I only want you to look at me when I'm lying down.

In a moment I'm going to lie down and when I do, you're going to be overwhelmed. You're going to start to cry and you won't be able to stop for the rest of the show. You're going to keep crying right to the end. You're going to cry as you leave the theatre, you're going to cry all the way home.

Wendy: [From the sidelines, stage right] Keep going, Cath! It's really working.

Cathy: You're going to cry at home in bed tonight before you sleep and when you wake up in the morning, the sheets will be soaked and you'll still be crying and wherever you go, whatever you do tomorrow, you'll still be crying. You'll cry in the toilets at work. You'll cry in the aisles of supermarkets, you'll cry when you pick the kids up ...

Wendy: Go on. Push it, Cath!

[Throughout the whole section Terry sits on a lighting unit behind Cathy and pretends to cry, splashing tears on her face using water from her water bottle when there are pauses in Cathy's text.]

Cathy: You'll start to get scared that this crying is never going to stop—and it won't. You'll cry every week until the end of the month, you'll cry into next month, till the end of the year, and the tears will still fall all through that year, and into the years after that, and you'll cry all through that year, and into the one after that, and the one after that ...

Wendy: Even harder, Cath.

Cathy: When I lie down, you're going to start to cry and you are going to cry for the rest of your lives. And I'm going to do that now.

[Cathy goes to lie down. As she does so there is another accidental sound from Bruno's hooter.]

Bruno: Sorry.

Cathy: [From her reclining position, leaned up on her elbow] I just want to make it clear why this is sad.

It's sad because of my frailty. Because when I lie down, you'll see for the first time how frail a person is and in that picture you'll see your own weakness, your own vulnerability. And that will start the flood of your tears.

And for the rest of your lives you'll look back on this evening, on this moment, on the moment of me lying down, and you'll say that's when everything changed …

[From their place stood behind the sound desk Richard and Robin have selected a piece of music that they think might 'help'. Jack Nitzsche's 'Harry Flowers' (1970) begins to play. As if cued by the music, Jerry and Davis begin to move with their tinfoil stars, making a simple dance of slow arcs.]

And you'll say that's when everything changed. When she lay down, when she did that, something inside me broke and I was changed forever. Because in the end this is you. This is all you are. Because you are me. I'm dying, I'm slipping away and you can see it. You're watching me slip away but you're slipping away too. When I lie down, you'll cry and cry and cry and cry and you are never going to stop for the rest of your lives. And now you can look, if you dare.

[Cathy lies back. The stars continue their kitsch dance routine. Robin tiptoes out from behind the sound desk and comes downstage to retrieve the strobe light that he left there at the end of 'Silver Machine'. As he reaches the back again, Cathy comes up from her 'dead' position very rapidly, cursing and yelling.]

Cathy: Shit! Shit shit shit shit! I'm really sorry. I completely fucked that up. It's not your fault. It's mine. My timing was rubbish.

Wendy: Don't give up, Cath. Keep going.

7. Tears Workshop

[Cathy waits a moment or two, thinking. Then walks off to the edge of stage right. Wendy comes forward to fill the gap.]

Why don't we all just calm down a bit? Take a bit of timeout. Why don't we all do a workshop?

[Robin arrives with a mic, which he holds for Wendy, gesturing for her to continue.]

Yeah. Why don't we all do a workshop to get to those tears we're talking about here tonight? Because I think some of us don't even know where our tears come from, right? So let's just relax our faces, just loosen up the cheeks, roll the eyes around a bit in the sockets, and let everything go. And just take a moment to locate that bit in the corner of the eye where the water comes up—I don't want you to feel shy or worry about this. I mean, I know crying is often a bit of a private thing.

[Robin makes an inaudible comment to Wendy.]

Wendy: [In response, half to Robin and half to the audience] Yeah. Or a bit girly. [Fully to audience again] But why don't we use tonight as a really special opportunity to share our tears? Let's really go for it. Okay, so we've got the corner of the eye. There's water pumping up, so get it going across the eyeball if you can

and just remember that we were all born—weren't we?—and then someone hit us and we cried, so it's not like we haven't done it before, is it?

['Harry Flowers' music runs out and in the silence that follows Jerry and Davis are stranded with their stars—no excuse to keep dancing.

Meanwhile John and Bruno have developed an escalating dispute about a single chair at the front of the stage which they are moving from one side to the other in a minor echo of their conflict at the start of the performance.

Wendy and Robin (still holding the mic for her) remain centre stage as Wendy speaks, both of them increasingly distracted by John and Bruno as they continue to pass impatiently back and forth with the chair through the following text …]

Okay. I'll tell you what. I'll tell you what—if the body stuff isn't working for us here tonight, why don't we think about memory instead? You know, memory can be a really useful trigger to get the emotional state up and running so let's take our minds back to a moment when we were very small in a darkened room and perhaps someone left us and we thought they were never ever coming back. That could've upset us a bit. Or even a more recent memory—perhaps someone we know got killed in a car crash and that might've distressed us a bit or, even more recent, we were in a room, confused, anxious, and …

[Bach's 'Cello Suite I (Allemande)' (1717-1723), begins to play. Jerry and Davis start dancing again, now in a kind of mock ballet, continuing to hold their tinfoil stars. As they dance, they remove their clothes item by item … so that by the end of the track they are naked, their groins covered only by the stars, which they hold in place. Terry meanwhile has begun to cross from stage left to stage right at the back, weeping, until she reaches the sound desk, then returning stage left and repeating her journey. After a while Richard takes a mic to her so that the sound of her crying is amplified. The tussle over the chairs now becomes a wrestling bout-cum-brawl between John and Bruno, the two of them taking an increasingly erratic route around the stage, disrupting Wendy as she tries to speak to the audience.]

I'll tell you what. Let's go back to the eyes. Let's go back to the eyes. Let's use our eyes to see one of the characters that we can see in front of us. Let's keep staring at the characters without blinking, so we force the tears up into the eyes, and let's never ever take our eyes off the characters—just choose the one in the red or the one in the grey—just choose one and keep staring at them till the tears come up into the eye and we get that emotional state running. Don't worry if you don't understand what they're doing. Just keep staring and don't blink. Please don't blink … You might want to look at a special part of the body … The wrist … The veins on the head … The foot …

[Wendy is increasingly distracted by John and Bruno, who are now starting to fight.]

Wendy: [Turning, speaking directly to Bruno] Actually that's quite good, Bruno. If you got your elbow round his neck now and pulled tightly, you could cut off the air supply and strangle him …

[To audience] Okay, I think we're losing concentration here. Let's not lose sight of the real point of the exercise, which is to get the tears really flowing. And I think I can feel the emotion beginning to rise and you might want to comfort your neighbour … Put an arm round their shoulder … Or use a tissue to dab away their tears … Or just give them a sympathetic look.

[Distracted again by John and Bruno, addressing them directly] Yeah. That's it, John. But why don't you headbutt him? Use a sudden head crack to his head like they do in the cartoons. And you could shatter his skull into thousands of little pieces.

[*To audience*] Let's keep going with the exercise. Let's not give up on the job. You might want to go back to memory again—maybe these characters remind you of a scene you have seen in the street, or even in the privacy of your own home and that might get the tears.

[*Terry makes her final crying journey across the back of the stage. Claire (as gorilla) arrives and proffers tissues to her.*]

Wendy: [*To John and Bruno*] Yeah, go on, Bruno ... That's it, John ... make him cry.

What are you waiting for? Make him cry ...

[*Richard puts on Janis Joplin's 'Cry Baby' (1971).*]

8. Cry Baby Fight

[*For the duration of 'Cry Baby' John and Bruno fight/wrestle/ brawl, the momentum of the fight taking them all over the stage, unpredictably, and causing a traffic hazard to everyone else. Wendy encourages the fight, whipping it up where possible, darting backwards and forwards to be close to the antagonists and yet doing her best to stay out of harm's way. Robin shadows Wendy and keeps her mic cable from getting tangled anywhere. Throughout the fight Wendy improvises responses and encouragements to the fight, as below ... *]

Wendy: Give him one, Bruno. Give him what for. Show him who's boss.

Hit him where it hurts. Get him while he's down.

Wipe the floor with him. Go on, wipe the smile off his face.

Make him laugh on the other side of his face.

Mess his face up, John.

Make him bleed. Make him see stars.

Beat the shit out of him, Bruno.

Are you going to put up with that, John?! Get in there.

Beat the shit out of him. Beat him to a pulp.

Use your head, Bruno. Use your fists, use your fucking knees.

Bruno! Bruno! Bruno! Bruno!

That's it, John ... All the way.

Haven't you got a weapon, John? Haven't you got a knife on you?

Go on: cut him up. Trash him. Finish him off. Demolish him.

Polish him off. Get back in there and finish what you started.

[*Terry, now dressed in a black slip and accompanied by Jerry and Davis, who are carrying their tinfoil stars, attempts a dance routine to 'Cry Baby' in which she comes forward towards the audience, weeping melodramatically, like she is the diva at the climax of a show. The stars flank her, like backing dancers, the trio of them stepping forwards together in time with the music. They repeat this move forward many times throughout the song, switching hurriedly from one side of the stage to another where necessary in order to avoid the fight between John and Bruno, and to avoid Wendy who continues to shadow them.*]

Claire (as gorilla) offers paper tissues around the stage, scattering them everywhere. Later she jumps off the stage and circuits the auditorium, throwing tissues to the audience. On her return from this trip Claire pushes long strips of tinsel in the gorilla mask's eyes (like streams of falling tears) and comes to the front of the stage in a diva-ish display of feigned emotion, dropping to her hands and knees, her hands reaching to the audience, etc.

Richard plays exaggerated air guitar to the song, also operating the smoke machine at various points to fill the stage again with smoke.

Cathy sits at the side of the stage throughout the song, making one trip to the centre, this time dressed in white to try again her 'lying dead' position before returning to the side and her newspaper again.

By the climax of the song Davis and Jerry are still flanking Terry's histrionics, gyrating and circling the tinfoil stars to reveal their genitals. Claire (as gorilla) has jumped off the stage again and disappeared into the auditorium. John and Bruno are tangled in a sweaty heap, still struggling with each other, shadowed by Robin and Wendy (who continues to make comments). The music stops. John and Bruno come to rest.

Wendy: [*Calling to taunt John and Bruno*] Call that a fucking fight?

9. Clowns Interview——Impressions of Weapons

[*Robin approaches John and Bruno, who are lying exhausted, still holding onto each other. Robin sticks the mic towards them and amplifies the sound of their heavy breathing, switching from one to the other to vary the sound.*]

John: Oh god, oh god. Is that you, Robin?

Robin: Yes—it's me, John. Just carry on with what you're doing. It's good, it's good.

John: I think I'm bleeding. I can't open my left eye. I can't open my eye.

Robin: It's alright: you're not bleeding. He's not bleeding. You're not bleeding. You're Okay. You're fine.

John: I'm bleeding, Rob. I can taste the blood in my mouth. I think I might have lost one of my crowns.

[*Richard has come with a towel as if to wipe away the non-existent blood. When John complains about his teeth Richard produces a torch from his back pocket which Richard and Robin then use to look into John's mouth.*]

Robin: Hang on ... No, your teeth are fine.

John: [*Speaking about Bruno*] Is he bleeding?

Robin: No. Nobody's bleeding.

[*Terry, Jerry, and Davis leave the front of the stage where they ended up at the climax of their 'Cry Baby' routine. Retreating to the back of the stage they open beers and begin to play cards while the conversation between Robin and John continues. They remain there until the subsequent 'Silences' section.*]

John: I'm bleeding, Rob. I'm bleeding. Rob? Rob? I'm still funny, aren't I, Rob?

Robin: Sorry, John. What do you mean?

John: I'm still funny. Everyone is still laughing at me, aren't they?

Robin: [*Looks at the audience and waits*] I think they're taking a little break right now, John.

John: I think I can hear a young lady laughing. I can, Rob. I am still funny, aren't I, Rob? Rob? Rob? I am still funny, aren't I? I'm still the funny one, aren't I? Rob? I'm still funny, aren't I? I'm the winner, aren't I? The winner? The funny winner?

[*John repeats himself as above and Robin slowly loses interest, moving the mic up towards Bruno's mouth.*]

Bruno: Robin? Is now a good time to do my impressions of weapons?

Robin: Yeah. Yeah. Why not? Yeah.

Bruno: [*Announcing*] A pistol. [*He makes a noise like a pistol shot.*]

[*Announcing again*] A rifle. [*He makes a noise like a rifle shot,*

with a high-pitched pinging sound after it. Robin looks confused
and Bruno explains ...] Ricochet.

[Announcing again] An automatic rifle. [He makes a noise like
machine gun fire.]

Robin: Yeah! They do sound like that.

Bruno: [Announcing again] A small cannon. [He makes a noise like a
cannon.]

[Announcing again] A large cannon. [To Richard, who is at the
sound desk] Can I have a bit more volume on the mic for this one,
please? [He makes a larger noise like a cannon.]

Robin: I can't help thinking that it owes a lot to small cannon.

Bruno: It's bigger.

Robin: It is bigger.

Bruno: [Announcing again] A chicken.

Robin: Sorry. I don't see how that fits into your theme.

Bruno: [Thinks for a long time] A chicken with a small explosive
device attached to its back. [He makes a noise like a chicken,
and then a loud explosion.]

Robin: Yeah! That's great.

Bruno: [Announcing again] A nuclear cevice.

[John tries to grab the mic, yelling ...]

John: No, no, no. Don't let him do the nuclear device. Don't let
him do the nuclear one, don't. Don't.

[There is a struggle: John, who is pinned down by Bruno, grabs
the mic, and then Robin's wig. Robin tries to retrieve his wig and
Richard comes to his rescue. In the end John is subdued, Robin's
wig is returned, he holds the mic to Bruno, Richard stays to
watch his next impression from close-up.

Bruno does a long impression of a nuclear explosion. As it goes
on John struggles halfway out from under Bruno, who, after a time,
breaks his impression to announce ...]

And then the wind blast.

[Bruno continues the impression of the nuclear explosion and
John emerges from under him, coming out between his legs. The
impression ends.]

Richard: What's next?

Bruno: That's the climax: the nuclear device.

[Robin and Richard confer.]

Robin: You know the chicken, yeah? Can we have, like, more
animals? But without the explosive devices. Just the animals?

Bruno: A cow. [He makes a noise like a cow.]

Robin: That's good, yeah. Yeah. It's just like being in a field.

[Richard heads back to the sound desk.]

Bruno: Thanks. A dog. [He does a dog.] That's a small dog. [He does
a more exaggerated dog.] That's a big dog.

[Claire (as gorilla), who has been sitting in the auditorium, has
now made her way back towards the stage and, as she gets closer,
begins to throw sweets at Robin and Bruno.]

Bruno: A blue whale. [He tries to make a blue whale noise but the
result is pretty ridiculous.] A humpback whale. [He tries to do a
humpback whale noise: also ridiculous.]

Robin: Um, I'm not so keen on the whales. Can we go back to more
domestic animals?

Bruno: A dolphin. [He starts to do a dolphin noise—]

Robin: [Interrupting] No. No. I mean more like farm animals,
something like that.

Bruno: A sheep. [He does a sheep noise.] A cat. [He does a cat
noise.] A snake. [Thinking better of it] No, that's rubbish. A
gorilla. [He does a gorilla noise.]

[By this time Claire (as gorilla) has climbed onto the stage
and now switches from throwing single sweets at Bruno and Robin
to pelting them hard with handfuls. Bruno backs away rapidly
towards the other side of the stage. Richard comes forward
with a chair in a defensive position, as if he might intend to
fight the gorilla. Robin squats with the mic in the centre of
the stage, eyes closed. Claire (as gorilla) tips an entire jar
of sweets over Robin's head from behind. Robin opens his eyes,
comes up slowly, tentatively holds the mic to the gorilla's mouth.
Claire (as gorilla) makes no sound. Robin taps the mic as if the
reason for the silence might be a technical malfunction. Claire
(as gorilla) walks away. Robin is left stranded in the centre
of the stage with the mic held out but no one there to use it.
He points the mic lamely in different directions, including at
the audience. Eventually Jerry and Davis abandon the card game
they've been playing with Terry at the back of the stage and
come forward to help Robin by making use of the mic. They are
still naked apart from their silver tinfoil stars which they hold
to hide their genitals. Throughout the following section Robin
stands between Jerry and Davis, offering the mic to each of them
in turn.]

10. Stars—Silences

Jerry: I think now's a good time to have a really, really
beautiful silence.

Davis: Yes. Something that can really bring people together.

Jerry: We're going to have a really, really beautiful silence.
It's going to be beautiful, it's going to be like the kind of
silence you may have experienced for yourselves, if you can
imagine being in the countryside at night, miles from anywhere,
lying on your back in a field or something, just looking up at
the stars, and there's no one else around, just you and this
beautiful silence. It's going to be like that.

Davis: Or maybe, maybe we can have the kind of silence that
happens at a birthday party for a five-year-old girl, and the
whole room has just sung 'Happy Birthday' to her and then she
takes that moment where she closes her eyes and she's making her
wish before she blows out the candles. So, maybe we could have
that one ...

Jerry: Yeah. That's beautiful. Or we could have the silence when
a baby has been crying all night long and driving his mum and
dad mad and then suddenly, about four or five in the morning, the
sound just suddenly stops.

Davis: Yeah. Yeah. That's beautiful. Or what about we have the
kind of silence that just happens when you are waiting for an
elevator. The doors open and you ask the people if they're going
up and they say, 'No, we're going down ... '

Jerry: Yeah. How about that silence that happens deliberately
sometimes when a family choose a special day to remember their
dead relatives. [Jerry slowly lifts his star through the following
sentences, as if by accident, so that his cock is showing
underneath it.] It's usually a Sunday—they put on their best
clothes and they all go down to the cemetery and they stand
around the grave of the person they want to remember and just
take a few moments to remember—

Robin: [Interrupting] I'm sorry—it's your costume. It's ridden up.

[Jerry 'embarrassed', puts the star back in place.]

Robin: Sorry. I didn't mean to interrupt. So. You were standing
round the grave.

Jerry: Yeah. The family, they just stand around the grave and they just take—it's usually two minutes in this case—and they just think about that person's life and they remember them and there's just this really, really beautiful silence.

Davis: Yeah. That's beautiful. What about we have that kind of silence that happens where you're at home just watching TV. You grab the remote to change channel and you accidentally hit the 'mute' button and then there's just this beautiful silence.

Jerry: Yeah. Or there's that kind of silence that happens at a dinner party sometimes. You know, where the guests are all sitting round a table, they're joking and having a good time, and one of them gets up to use the bathroom and while they're in there they can hear everyone in the dining room, they can hear all the laughter, and when they've finished in the bathroom, they come back and as soon as they open the dining room door, the laughter just stops.

Davis: Yeah. That's beautiful. What about if we have the kind of silence that happens in a public space, maybe even in a metro station—

Robin: I'm going to have to stop you. Cos this microphone is very unidirectional. So, if you're doing this—[He shakes his head from side to side.]—they can't hear a thing that you're saying. See, what I'm trying to say is: I can take the horse to water, but I can't make it drink.

Davis: [To Robin] Okay. Straight in. Alright. [To audience] I was thinking we could have the kind of silence that happens in a public space, maybe even in a metro station around 5:30 and there's tons of people, but then everyone hears a policeman yell out, 'Um, excuse me—is that anybody's bag?'

Jerry: Oh, that's beautiful. Or we could do that kind of silence that happens out in space: an astronaut, and he's floating, just kind of drifting away from the spacecraft. [He mimes the astronaut: slow, flailing arms, mouthing the words 'Help me!']

Robin: [Very enthusiastic] Yeah. Yeah. It's like: 'In space no one can hear you scream.' That's great. I like that. Yeah.

Davis: What about if we have the kind of silence that happens with one of those actors. You know, he just finishes the show and he goes backstage and he doesn't even take a shower, he just puts his clothes on really fast and then he runs out into the foyer and runs right up to his friends, very enthusiastic and he says, 'So, guys, what do you think of the show?' and there's just this beautiful silence.

Jerry: There's also that kind of silence that happens on a family outing sometimes. They're all on the motorway and Dad's behind the wheel and they're all singing in the back. And then suddenly Dad makes a little mistake and the car swerves off the motorway and it rolls down the bank and it goes over and over and over and eventually it comes to a rest. And Dad, he's a bit shaken, and he says, 'Is everyone okay?'

Davis: That's beautiful. Or what about we have the kind of silence you get when your father has Parkinson's disease. You know, he has Parkinson's disease and he does something kind of, kind of new in the morning and he approaches you, wants to tell you the story of what he did, but then after a couple of sentences he just kind of like blanks out ...

[Davis blanks out, staring into space, immobile.]

Robin: [To Jerry] Is that—what he's doing there, is that, like, 'method acting'?

[Davis drops his pretence.]

Jerry: That's beautiful. Or what if we have the kind of silence that happens when you are at a real low point in your life, you know? You're really just down and depressed and finally you find yourself down on your knees looking up to the heavens and you just ask, 'Oh God, can you just show me a sign so I can have some hope to go on?'

Davis: That's beautiful. Or what if, Jerry, we have that kind of silence that happens when a family decides to turn off the life-support machine. They decide to turn it off and everybody's right there, gathered in the hospital room and the mother is laid out in a coma and the doctor, he looks to the family and he says, 'Are you sure you want to do this?' And the two kids are there, quietly crying, and the father he looks over to his new girlfriend and then looks back to the doctor and he just goes, 'Yeah,' and the doctor, he goes over to the machine, and it's like, 'Pschhhhh, whoooooo, psschhhwwww, whooooooo,' then he just makes this one little click and it's like, 'Pschhhhh, whooooooo, psschww, whooo ...' [Getting softer.]

Jerry: That's beautiful.

Davis: Um, so, should we do it?

Jerry: Let's do it, let's do it. Let's have five minutes, five minutes beautiful silence.

Robin: [To Jerry] Sorry, sorry, which? Which one? Which one do you want us to do?

Jerry: [To Robin] I think people can choose. They can choose their favourite one, and just do it.

Robin: [To Jerry] We can do whichever one we want? Great. I know which one I'm doing. [He mimes the astronaut's 'Help me!']

Davis: Right. We're all happy. [Announcing] It's 9:57pm and we'll do until 10:02pm. [Davis says whatever time it is really, according to his own watch.] We'll do five minutes beautiful silence, alright?

Richard: Do you want me to time it? I've got a stopwatch on my mobile.

Jerry: [To Davis] He's got a stopwatch.

Davis: It's Okay. I have a watch. I'll use my watch.

Richard: Yeah, but this is digital—get it exactly right.

Jerry: [To Davis] Digital. It's digital.

Davis: My wife gave me this watch and I'd kind of like to use it in the show.

Richard: Yeah. But that's analogue. This is digital: it's a lot more accurate.

Jerry: [To Davis] It would be more accurate.

Davis: There's kind of sentimental reasons why I'd like to use this watch.

Richard: It's digital. Get it right to two hundredths of a second.

[An inaudible conference takes place between Jerry and Davis.]

Jerry: Okay. I think sometimes sentiment is more important than accuracy, Richard.

Davis: [Moving on to start the thing] Okay. It's, um—

Richard: [Interrupting] I could time it as backup. Just in case your watch malfunctions.

Davis: [To Richard] Great, thanks. [To audience] So. It's 9:59pm now and we'll go to 10:04pm. Five minutes beautiful silence. 10, 9, 8, 7—

Richard: [Interrupting] Sorry, sorry. Do you want any music in the silence? Just a bit of music underneath?

Jerry: Richard. Richard. It's a silence.

Richard: It's going to be a bit boring without music, isn't it?

Jerry: It's not going to be boring. It's going to be beautiful.

Davis: It's perfect—10pm to 10:05pm. Here we go: 10, 9, 8, 7, 6, 5, 4, 3, 2, 1.

Robin: No, no, no. It hasn't started yet. You haven't said zero.
When you count down you have to say the zero. Otherwise it hasn't
started yet.

Jerry: [Annoyed] Zero, zero.

[Jerry and Davis stand still, facing the audience, stars held
in front of them, intent on staying like that for the next five
minutes.]

Richard: [Whispering through the mic to Jerry] Has it started yet?

Jerry: [Off mic, impatient] Yes. I've said zero. It's started.

[Jerry and Davis continue to stand still. Robin shoves the mic
under Jerry's mouth, as if he hasn't quite grasped what's going on
and is expecting him to speak.]

Jerry: [Exasperated] Turn it off! I'm not going to say anything.

Robin: I can't turn it off. It hasn't got a switch.

[Jerry says something inaudible to Robin.]

Richard: [To Robin, being 'helpful'] Disconnect it.

Robin: [To Jerry, interrupting] Sorry. [To Richard] What?

Richard: Disconnect it.

[Robin noisily disconnects the mic.]

Richard: [To audience] Shh, shh ... [Testing mic] One-Two. One-Two.
[To audience] Shh, shh.

Jerry: [To Richard] Shh!

Richard: [To audience] Shh!

[There is a period of relative calm where something like silence
reigns, dependent on the audience, with Jerry and Davis stood
centre stage. After a while Claire (as gorilla), begins to cross
from stage left, sitting in the pushchair which she moves with
her feet, getting closer and closer to the stars. On arrival
Claire (as gorilla), makes an attempt to snatch the star from
Davis. Robin drags her in the pushchair to the side of the stage.
Claire (as gorilla) snatches Robin's wig—there is a tussle and
Claire gets dragged to stage right where she lies as though
sleeping. Robin puts his wig back on and goes back to stand in
the centre with Jerry and Davis.

Again, a period of relative quiet. After a while Richard gestures
to Robin who comes over to the stage-right speaker, which has
evidently been causing Richard some concern. They confer, check
the speaker, then the other speaker, and then return to the
stage-right speaker together, bending to listen closely to it.
Richard picks his mic up and speaks to Jerry and Davis, breaking
the silence.]

Richard: There's a bit of a buzz on this speaker, don't know if
you want to start the silence again?

[Jerry and Davis confer inaudibly.]

Richard: We can fix it. Take about ten minutes, then you can
start the silence again.

[Jerry gestures silently that they will continue rather than
start again.]

Richard: Not really a silence then, is it?

[Jerry gestures that he cannot hear the buzz that Richard is
talking about.]

Richard: [Pointing to the first rows of audience near him] They
can hear it.

[Jerry again gestures that they will continue.]

Richard: [Sulking] Suit yourself.

[Richard puts his mic down noisily on the speaker and walks to
the other side of the stage. Jerry and Davis continue to stand
still in the centre. John, who has been lying on the floor toward
the back of the stage drinking a beer, gets up and walks over to
stage right, picking up the mic left there by Richard.]

John: [To audience] Excuse me, but the silence here provides
the perfect illustration for the other story that I need to
tell you tonight. Basically, for the last 400—500 million years
the universe— [Richard and Robin arrive, gesturing 'Shh,' and
confiscate the mic.] I'm just telling a story.

Richard: [To John] Piss off.

[A short final section of something like silence. Robin is stood
between Jerry and Davis. He nods his head as he silently counts
down to the end of the silence and plugs the mic back in noisily
so that Jerry can speak.]

Davis: [To audience, signalling the end of the silence] Thank you.

Richard: It's not finished yet. The silence isn't over. There's
another twenty-six seconds to go. Digital.

Robin: [To Jerry] Do you want to do those twenty-six seconds? Or
just forget about it?

Jerry: Let's do it. Let's just try to do these next twenty-six
seconds in silence. Please.

[Richard sits on the speaker stage right. He points Bruno's hooter
directly into the mic and silently counts down the last twenty-
six seconds. When they are over he blasts the hooter to signal
the end of the silence.]

Richard: [As if the hooter blast might have damaged the mic] One-
Two, one-two.

Jerry: [To audience] Thank you.

[Claire (as gorilla) gets up and runs, pushing between Jerry,
Davis, and Robin, stealing Davis's star. She goes to stand on top
of the speaker stage left, proudly brandishing the star, which
Davis then goes to retrieve.]

11. End of the World

John: Hello. Hello. Oh, okay, as I was saying: the silences
provide a perfect illustration for the other story I need to tell
you tonight and that other story is called 'The End of the World'.

Wendy: [Crossing from stage right, headed to her usual position
in the back to stage left] Don't do it, John!

John: What?

Wendy: Don't do it.

John: Don't do what?

Wendy: Don't tell the story.

John: Well, I've started the story. It's called 'The End of the
World' and, basically, in the universe through the last 400—500
thousand years there's been a sense of peace and quiet and
everything has roughly been going according to plan. Um. You've
got the earth that's been spinning on its axis quite happily,
you've got the sun that appears in the daytime and provides heat
and light—which is good—and the moon which comes out at night
and is good to look at, and there's a series of planets, a series
of planets that all spin around the earth and there are lots of
them-there's one called Saturn, there's one called Venus, Mars,
Mercury, Jupiter ... [Some whispering from Robin and Richard,
who are suggesting other planets.] No. [Responding to Robin and
Richard] It's not pronounced like that. It's pronounced 'Uranus'.
[Terry brings another glass of water that John does not want.
She also takes one to Bruno, which she again overfills.] Mm. So,
as I said, things have been going roughly according to plan, but
whereas the first story was all about the potentiality—things
waiting to happen, at the brink of happening, on the verge of
happening—this story is about the inevitability that this is all
going to come to an end.

Wendy: Don't go there, John.

John: Don't go where? I've started the story. The first story was called 'The Beginning of the World' or 'The Big Bang', this story is called 'The End of the World'.

[*Since Davis took back his star, Claire (as gorilla) has remained balanced on the small speaker stage left. At this point she steps off it and her foot lands on the hooter that Bruno has left on the ground beside it, causing a loud repeated 'honk' of interruption. Robin and Bruno rush over to rescue the hooter and stop the noises. Claire kicks the hooter away, breaking it into parts. Robin and Bruno scurry after the pieces and Robin tries to reassemble them.*]

Okay. So, basically what you have at the same time as the creation of the planet earth is the creation of an incredibly large meteorite, about the same size as the planet earth. Up until recently this meteorite was on a course that would have avoided the earth by thousands of miles. Unfortunately, as is often the case with disaster stories, a small asteroid gets in the way— [*Robin sounds the hooter which he has now mended, hands it back to Bruno.*]—A small asteroid gets in the way, the meteorite bangs into the asteroid, and the meteorite is now knocked off course, and is then on a collision course with the planet earth.

Wendy: Slow it down, John.

John: Slow what down?

Wendy: The meteorite.

John: I've got no fucking control over the speed of the meteorite, have I?

[*Jerry and Davis, dressed in Hawaiian shirts, are continuing to 'enact' John's story here, as they did in his first narrative. Davis replaces his star with a huge ball of tinsel to represent the meteorite.*]

John: Okay. So, the meteorite is now on a collision course with the planet earth. But while the first story happened in a single bang, this story is going to happen over a series of months. You know, I don't think we're going to notice very much at all at first—except maybe a few vibrations, reverberations on the planet's surface, nothing more.

[*Claire (as gorilla) has by now crossed the stage, pushing the chair that belonged to Bruno. She reaches John and begins to vibrate the chair and herself, illustrating John's line about reverberations. John watches, exasperated. Robin fires the smoke machine at Claire who runs away.*]

John: Thank you, Rob.

But as the meteorite comes closer, we are going to see these effects as it starts banging on the gravitational field that protects the planet earth. We're going to notice big effects—big effects, particularly with the climate.

[*Richard interrupts to whisper to John.*]

John: What? [*Richard whispers again.*] Well, no, I don't need a guitar now. Did I need a guitar in the first story? Did I? I didn't, did I? Did I? No. I didn't, no.

Okay. So. The meteorite's on a collision course with the planet earth and as it gets closer you're going to notice things in the climate. Climactically speaking these will be big changes. Where there were deserts, there are going to be oceans; where there are oceans, there will be deserts. In the summertime we're going to experience a helluva lot of ...

[*Robin arrives with an acoustic guitar for John.*]

John: [*To Richard*] Why? Why did he bring me the guitar?

Richard: [*To Robin*] He doesn't need the guitar.

[*Robin says something inaudible off mic to John.*]

John: I haven't changed my mind. I never asked for it.

Richard: [*To Robin*] He's on vocals.

John: [*To Richard*] No. I'm not on vocals, I'm just telling a story.

Richard: [*To Robin*] He's on *lead* vocals.

[*Robin departs with the guitar in a cloud of smoke from the smoke machine.*]

John: Okay. So, we're going to notice these climactic changes— very, very big climactic changes. In the summertime there'll be a lot of snowfall. In the wintertime, hot sun all the way through.

[*John is interrupted by the sound of Claire (as gorilla), who is strumming the guitar noisily stage left, sat beside Bruno.*]

John: [*To Richard*] Why did he give the guitar to the gorilla? [*To audience*] I'm sorry. Just bear with us for a minute.

[*Claire (as gorilla) crosses the stage banging the guitar which she carries.*]

Wendy: Come on, John. A bit more positive!

[*Claire (as gorilla) comes to rest behind John, banging the guitar strings repeatedly. Richard switches the mic back and forth between the guitar—amplifying the noise that Claire makes—and John himself, who remains silent. Bruno arrives with a note, which he hands to John who opens and reads it.*]

John: 'Use the music.' Well, there isn't any music, is there? [*Richard is pointing to the gorilla with the guitar.*] That's not a guitar solo, that's a gorilla banging on a guitar.

[*Claire (as gorilla) is swamped in a cloud of smoke from the smoke machine.*]

You know something? The first fucking creatures to die out when the climate changes are going to be the bloody gorillas. Huge ice sheets are going to come into the jungle habitat where the gorilla lives, all the trees are going to collapse under the weight of the ice, leaving nothing for the gorilla to eat. It's going to die a very long, lonely, starving death. [*Claire (as gorilla) has moved to the side of John. Robin squirts it with the smoke machine again.*] Poor, old, smoky gorilla. Just a little emaciated figure left under the ice. That's all that's going to be left of the gorilla.

Wendy: A bit more positive, John!

John: Do you know what? I think that's the most fucking positive thing I've said all evening.

[*Claire (as gorilla) has fallen to the floor and is pretending to die an elaborate death. Robin arrives and takes the guitar off her.*]

John: [*To Claire (as gorilla)*] Just die! Die quicker. [*To audience*] Okay. So, the meteorite is not only banging on the earth's gravitational field now, it's starting to rip it to shreds. It's ripping the gravitational field to shreds, and what we're going to see is: where there are natural fault lines appearing on the planet's surface, these will start opening up, opening up and forming canyons and gorges, going right deep down inside the red-hot, white-hot earth's core, and what this is going to mean is a lot of hot volcanic material, right from the centre of the earth—

[*Richard fires a very big burst of smoke from the smoke machine directly at John, who stops his narration.*]

John: [*To Richard*] Why did you do that? You wouldn't do that to me if I had asthma, would you?

[*Richard fires another very big burst of smoke directly at John.*]

You know that stuff is poisonous, don't you?

[*Richard bends to look right into the nozzle of the machine and fires a further very big burst of smoke directly into his own face. The smoke flows upwards over John, covering him and Richard completely. John coughs.*]

Richard: [*Testing mic*] One-Two. One-Two.

John: Okay. So, you've got these canyons and gorges, going right deep down inside the earth's core. You've got a lot of hot volcanic material issuing forth from the earth's, from the earth's core ... [*Bruno arrives with another note. John opens it, reads, and then speaks.*] Well, you've just brought the same note again, haven't you? It just says, 'Use the music.' [*To Richard*] We've decided that we haven't got any music, haven't we? That was– [*Richard taps John on the arm.*] Eh, what?

[*Robin, back at the sound desk, puts on The White Stripes' 'Aluminium' (2001).*]

John: [*To Richard, reacting to the music*] You've set me up, haven't you?

Richard: [*Testing mic*] One-Two. One-Two. One-Two.

Wendy: We want a happy ending, John. Give us a happy ending.

John: Okay. So, you've got this volcanic material, this volcanic material in the form of clouds, huge clouds of black dust, which start to go high up in the atmosphere.

[*Throughout 'Aluminium' Jerry dances, thrashing around in jagged patterns with his star while Davis circles the stage with the ball of tinsel representing the meteorite. Wendy dances with the cheerleader pompoms, urging things on. Terry, now in a pink summer dress, reprises her grieving-dancing, churning the air with a blanket that she swirls and thrashes. Claire (as gorilla) staggers around with a blanket over her head, walking like a zombie or Frankenstein's monster. Bruno sits throughout on the front stage left, holding Davis's star, looking out at the audience, dazed. Robin operates the smoke machine, filling the stage with huge clouds of smoke from different directions. Richard holds the mic for John. At one point, Cathy comes into the centre of the stage briefly to try her 'dead' position before retiring again to the sides.*]

John: [*Having to shout into the mic over the music*] The first thing the dust does is it starts shutting out the light and the heat from the sun. No more light, no more heat. Basically, this means the earth can no longer sustain any form of human life whatsoever. The earth can no longer sustain any form of human life ... The next thing we predict is that, without the support of the earth's gravitational field, huge chunks of the earth will start breaking off from the main body of the earth, start lifting away, lifting away from the earth's core, separating from the earth's core, slowly drifting out into the atmosphere. Drifting, slowly drifting, further and further away, drifting, drifting— huge chunks the size of America, the size of Europe, are drifting into the atmosphere, slowly, slowly start to vanish, they will disappear. Now what you have is: the earth no longer resembles the place we once knew, huge areas of the earth have broken off from the earth's core, the earth no longer resembles the place we once knew ...

[*'Aluminium' ends. As it dies out Claire (as gorilla) attacks Terry, fooling around, crudely miming that she is fucking her. Terry starts to giggle, attempting to get away.*]

Terry: [*Laughing*] Fucking Claire!

Wendy: [*From her usual place in the back, slightly stage left*] Don't get distracted, John.

Richard: One-Two.

Wendy: Don't get distracted.

[*Richard holds the mic to John who pushes it away like he does*

not want to speak any more. On the other side of the stage Claire removes her gorilla head and addresses the audience directly.*

From time to time through the whole of Claire's ensuing text, Richard holds the mic out to John, who always pushes it away, refusing to speak. For his part, Richard also 'tests' the mic now and then, quietly saying 'One-Two, one-two,' as if John's silence might best be something to do with a faulty mic.]

Claire: [*Without mic*] I'm sorry. I just wanted to check that you were still all thinking about you fucking me and me fucking you. Good. I hope you're also thinking about afterwards. Afterwards. We'd be in a hotel room, probably, lying in a hotel bed.

Wendy: [*Yelling*] Finish it up, John!

Claire: And we'd have a conversation, talk about something, talk about the weather—talk about what it's like out—or talk about a story in the news. Or maybe we'd watch the TV news together.

Wendy: [*Yelling*] Come on! Finish it up, John. We're all waiting here.

Claire: And there'd be a bomb, or a big accident, or something. And we'd be thirsty and we'd have to get a drink of water from the bathroom tap. And we'd probably go out into the city and you'd know the city better than me.

Wendy: [*Yelling*] Get us to the end, John! Just get us to the end.

Claire: And you'd show me your favourite places. Your favourite street. Your favourite building. Your favourite park.

Wendy: [*Yelling*] Come on, John! We're all waiting here. Finish it up.

Claire: We'd just be walking and talking and we'd end up in a bar that ... [*John goes over to speak to Wendy, gesturing emphatically that he's not doing any more text, he's done. As he moves, Claire also moves to sit on the stage left small speaker.*]

Wendy: [*Yelling, as John returns to his seat, ignoring his explanation*] Finish it, John!

Claire: [*Continuing*] We'd end up in a bar that neither one of us had been to before, and we'd have a beer and just talk—talk about a film that we'd both seen recently, or maybe a film that we'd both seen but really a long time ago. And we'd talk about the possibility of leaving, of getting into a car and just driving somewhere else.

Wendy: [*Yelling*] What are you waiting for, John? Come on! Finish it up.

Claire: Going to another place, another country like—

Wendy: [*Yelling*] Get us to the end, John!

Claire: Like France or Morocco. And we'd talk about—

Wendy: [*Yelling*] Get us to the end! We're fucking waiting here.

Claire: How nobody knows about this time we've spent together, no one else knows what we've seen or shared or talked about, nobody else—

Wendy: [*Yelling*] We can't hear you, John! We can't fucking hear you. Come on. Finish it up.

Claire: About this time that we've spent together—we're inside a piece of time that nobody else knows about.

Wendy: [*Yelling*] Finish the fucking thing up, John!

Claire: We're inside a piece of time that's secret—no one else knows about it.

Wendy: [*Yelling*] Just get us to the end, John! Get us to the fucking finish.

Claire: It's a secret.

[*Claire puts the gorilla head back on.*]

Wendy: [*Yelling*] We're waiting, John! We're all fucking waiting. Come on, smash it up. Smash the fucking thing up, John. Can't hear you. Can't fucking hear you, John. Come on, finish it.

[*Back at the sound desk Robin puts on The Band's 'The Night They Drove Old Dixie Down' (1969). He heads to Wendy with a mic and holds it for her while the song plays, throughout which she continues to harangue John.*]

12. Dixie

Richard: One-Two.

Wendy: [*Yelling*] Finish the fucking thing, John! Come on. Smash it up, smash it up, John. Tiny little fucking pieces. Come on—what are you waiting for? We're all fucking waiting. Come on, smash it apart, get us to the end, John, just get us to the finish. Can't hear you, John, we can't fucking hear you. What are you waiting for, John? Come on, smash it apart.

Richard: One-Two.

Wendy: [*Yelling*] Fragments, John. We want tiny little fucking fragments. Come on, John. Little fucking shards. What are you waiting for?

[*Richard whispers to John throughout the song, feeding him all the lines that he says.*]

John: Thank you, London, and goodnight. [*The city name gets adjusted depending on where the show is being performed.*]

Wendy: [*Yelling*] That's not a fucking ending! That is not an ending, John. Come on, finish it up.

John: [*Again repeating what Richard has said to him, this time with more vigour*] Thank you, London, and goodnight.

Wendy: [*Yelling*] You can do better than that, John! We deserve better than that—come on, finish it.

John: [*Again repeating what Richard has said to him, with yet more vigour*] Thank you, London, and goodnight!

Wendy: [*Yelling*] No, John! That is not fucking good enough. We want little shards John. We want sharp little fucking shards.

John: [*Taking the line from Richard*] You've been fucking great.

[*Terry moves backwards and forwards during the song, thrashing with one of Wendy's pompoms. Jerry dances with his star. Davis moves round the stage shredding the silver tinsel that was the 'meteorite' into smaller and smaller pieces, throwing the pieces to the ground. Cathy sits on the side of the stage and puts the finishing touches to her final costume: black smeared makeup to go with the black bra and lace tutu. Claire (as gorilla) takes a second trip round the auditorium, throwing paper tissues to the audience as if they might need them for their tears.*]

Wendy: [*Yelling*] Tinier, John! We want tinier fragments, sharp little splinters, John. Come on, shatter it, shatter it, John. Come on, John. Sharp little fucking shards all over the floor. What are you waiting for?

John: [*Taking the line from Richard*] Just dust.

Wendy: [*Yelling*] Not small enough, John! Not fucking small enough.

John: [*Taking the line from Richard*] It's dust.

Wendy: [*Yelling*] No, John, sharper than that, sharper than that! Fucking fragments.

John: [*Taking the line from Richard*] It's dust. It's dust.

Wendy: [*Yelling*] Is that the best you can do? Is that the fucking best you can do, John? Come on, shatter it.

John: [*Taking the line from Richard*] It's dust.

Wendy: [*Yelling*] Tinier, John. Tiny, little pieces.

John: [*Taking the line from Richard*] It's just dust, it's just dust.

['*The Night They Drove Old Dixie Down' ends.*]

John: [*Taking the lines from Richard*] It's dust.

It's just dust.

It's dust.

It's dust.

It's only dust.

It's nothing but dust.

Robin: [*To Bruno as he comes over from stage left*] Er. Can you do the end of the world, like, as an impression?

Bruno: Yeah. Do you want me to do it now?

Robin: Yeah. Now's a good time.

[*Bruno does an impression of the end of the world: a bunch of vocal sounds, explosions, howls, and rumbles into the mic. The others meanwhile provide the visual effects: Jerry thrashing his tinfoil star around the stage, Terry waving various blankets, Richard pumping out smoke from the smoke machine. For the last part of it Claire (as gorilla) comes back on stage from the auditorium and enacts a death in the vestiges of the smoke.*]

John: You had to let him do that, did you?

Richard: I thought it was good.

John: What do you mean it was good?

Richard: I thought it was really real.

John: It wasn't funny though, was it? It's supposed to be funny.

Richard: I think it's not so important to be funny right now.

John: Yeah, but people don't want to go home crying, do they? They want to go home laughing. Laughing their heads off.

[*Bruno gives a honk on the hooter.*]

Bruno: Sorry.

Richard: Yeah, but this is the serious bit.

John: Since when? Since when has this been the serious bit?

Richard: This has always been the serious bit.

John: This is the funny bit, the funny bit at the end.

Richard: Listen, the thing is, right, without darkness there can be no lightness.

John: Well, what the fuck are you talking about?

Richard: Think of it this way: where there is light, there must always be shadow.

John: They aren't your own words though, are they? You just got them out of some crap pop lyrics magazine.

Richard: No. I think about these things. Can I ask you something?

[*Claire sits alone stage left, Terry, Jerry, Bruno, Wendy, and Davis are sat loosely together on the floor/on chairs. Davis starts to play the guitar. Meanwhile Robin is starting to clear away equipment and detritus from the stage. Cathy paces the stage impatiently, looking to the audience as if waiting for John and Richard to finish so that she can have the last word.*]

John: Yeah.

Richard: Why is it that the best bands always split up?

John: I don't really know. I'm not really interested in that kind of thing.

Richard: Yeah. But why is it that the best bands always split up?

John: I just said, I really don't have an interest in that kind of thing.

Richard: If you had to have a guess.

John: Well, I guess it's because they're not having any laughs any more. No more laughs, no fun. Is that it?

Richard: Can you say more?

John: They're too sad to carry on. Just too sad.

Richard: So, tell me. Are you thinking about pursuing a solo career?

John: I'm not in a band, am I?

Richard: Well, not any more. Not now the band's split up.

John: I've never been in a band. Can I ask you something?

Richard: Sure.

John: That's not really your own hair is it?

Richard: It is human hair.

John: It's not your human hair though, is it?

Richard: It's one hundred per cent human hair.

John: It's a wig.

Richard: Can I ask you something?

John: Yeah.

Richard: Have you got any big shoes?

John: No.

Richard: Have you got a funny little red nose?

John: No.

Richard: Round the back of the theatre at stage door have you got a funny little car with a funny little horn on it?

John: I can see where you're going with these questions: you're trying to piss me off now, aren't you?

Richard: Will you be doing an encore this evening?

John: I'm not in a band, am I?

Richard: Oh. Come on. It's late. Let's be friends. Come on. What do you say?

John: Yeah. Okay.

Richard: Come on. We can't sit here chatting all night—someone's got to clear this shit up. Come on. Let's go, let's go.

[*John and Richard walk to the back of the stage together. As they walk away, Richard speaks.*]

Richard: So. Are there any girls in the audience that you want me to invite backstage for the party?

Jerry: I think I saw some twins, wearing green, in the fourth row somewhere.

Richard: [*Looking back.*] I'll make sure they get backstage passes. One-Two. One-Two. Out.

[*Richard puts the mic down on the sound desk. He and Robin clear the last few things that are scattered on the stage. Cathy continues to wait, now centre stage, eyes on the audience. When Richard and Robin have finished clearing the space she moves stage left and leans on the proscenium. Davis stops playing the guitar.*]

Cathy: This is the last thing you see. [*The lights remaining on the stage go out one by one as Cathy is talking.*]

You see me standing in the light. You're looking at me.

You can see my face. You can see my eyes. You can see my lips.

You can see that I'm thinking, but my eyes don't really give anything away.

My face is a complete blank. It says nothing and it says everything all at the same time. It's the last thing you see.

You don't know me, or you think you know me. It doesn't matter.

What matters is that you see me breathing. You see the rise and fall of my breathing.

And maybe you hear sound from outside: the noise of rain on the roof of the theatre, or maybe someone coughs here inside, in the auditorium, or perhaps you hear nothing. It's just quiet.

It's not important. What's important is that you're looking at me. The lights are going out. And soon, perhaps more suddenly than you had expected, it's over and I'm gone, gone forever and never coming back. This is the final moment. This is the last light.

[*The last of the lights goes out.*]

DIRTY WORK (THE LATE SHIFT) (2017)

 Act One begins with five great Atomic explosions.

There's a big crash on an important motorway.
A train plunges off a bridge into an icy torrent far below.
An elevator plummets from the 90th floor and then stops just above the ground.

Spot the Mechanical Dog is presented.
Spot fetches slippers and the newspaper. Spot chases an imaginary stick.
Spot barks and capers. He rolls over and jumps a box. Spot lies down and plays dead.

A puny looking man comes onto the stage and holds his unprotected hands in a raging fire for twenty minutes. While the flames roar he tells jokes and sings songs just to prove that he's okay.

Great maritime disasters are presented:
the Sinking of the Titanic, the Lusitania, the Costa Concordia.
Lives Lost at Sea.

A doctor performs a life saving operation using only airline cutlery and the kind of plastic tubing that you find in a ballpoint pen.

A woman writes a letter and delivers it to the wrong address.
Another woman reads it by mistake and so gets involved in someone else's unpleasant story.

Great Crises of the 20th Century are presented. Suez. The Bay of Pigs. Tiananmen. Bloody Sunday. The fate of men hangs in the balance. History at a crossroads.

There is an accident in a kitchen involving a knife and a toaster.

A sharpshooter writes his name in bullets in a playing card at the back of the stage.
Blindfolded, he shoots an apple from a young boy's head.
He shoots a banana from between a woman's legs.
He tosses a coin in the air and keeps it there with six shots from his revolver.

The sky turns dark and a light rain falls which is unfit to drink.

At the side of a motorway a man sits waiting in his car for the Breakdown Recovery Services to arrive.
As he waits he becomes cold and miserable.
The Breakdown Recovery Services do not arrive and it all becomes too much to bear. This tragic scene ends with a suicidal walk into the oncoming traffic. The crowd shed tears of pity. They are moved by the poor man's suffering and his terrible fate.

 The strippers arrive. The crowd go wild. Big breasts are revealed with a snap. Huge semi-erect cocks burst out of tiny, Lurex trunks. Nipples are twisted to erection. Buttocks are clenched and unclenched. Backs are arched. Some nylon underwear is thrown to the crowd. Legs are spread. Lips are parted.

The audience is aroused. Some women are offended. Small children are escorted from the auditorium by their parents and guardians.

Some famous assassinations from history are depicted.
Mr Kennedy in his motor car.
Mr Lincoln in the theatre.
Snr Mussolini swinging from his lamp post.

A selection of Wonders is revealed.
Statues come to life. Animals talk. In German.
A blind woman moves small objects from a distance of 50ft.
A pair of twins with the power to read minds reveal embarrassing secrets from a line of volunteers. Affairs, deceptions, state secrets, and little white lies are all brought to light and as the humiliated victims return to their seats The Montgolfier Brothers launch their balloon.

The Wright Brothers take off in their aeroplane.

The Righteous Brothers sing 'You've Lost That Loving Feeling'.

Diverse examples of Human Misery are presented. Poverty. Drug Addiction. Starvation. Infant Mortality. Sickness. Depression. Mental illness.

As a final instance of Misery, a child trips and drops her ice-cream into the sand.

There is a moment of silence, then a drum roll.

Fireworks burst against the blackness. Catherine Wheels. Rockets. Space Bombs. Roman Candles. Those bangers that jump around.

Sparklers are passed out amongst the crowd.
The night becomes a Tapestry of Colour.

 The orchestra strikes up. Some men lose their hair, lose direction, put on weight, and they blame women.

The Struggle Between Freedom and Tyranny is depicted in an allegorical dance.

In the North, Government Troops hunt out Communist Guerillas using sniffer dogs.

In the square of a small market town, Ten Big Lies of History are smashed using Hammers of Truth.

A man comes onto the stage, takes down his trousers, and defecates. The audience is offended. It seems gratuitous, without

point. Critics bay for blood. Questions are asked in Parliament
and some repressive legislation is introduced. Smoking is banned.
Sexual Intercourse between consenting adults is prohibited. A new
puritanism stalks the land. Cleanliness is compulsory.

Some tiny children sing a hymn. God looks down from Heaven. He
smiles and blesses the world.
An age of enlightenment is ushered in.
Men and women of different nationalities mingle together freely
in the streets.

There is a display of Drunks. Petty Criminals. Vandals. Lager
Louts. Anti-Social Behaviour. Great Football Hooligans from
History discuss their tactics over a quiet pint in the pub. Men
press their bare bottoms to the glass of the windows on a coach
as it leaves the Motorway Services. It is midnight—the lads have
just stopped for a piss.

There are scenes of romance, passion, and desire. Arousal in all
of its many diverse aspects.

A man with acidic saliva comes onto the stage and dissolves
small, valueless trinkets brought up from the crowd—coins,
costume jewellery, key rings, and the like. At the end of his act
he speaks movingly about his own personal isolation.

Storm clouds gather. Thunder rumbles. Lightning cuts across the
sky.
A curtain catches fire, the fire spreads, licks over the ceiling,
and soon the whole building is full of smoke. Those people who
have listened to the safety instructions lie down on the floor
with wet handkerchiefs pressed to their mouths. Alas, it does no
good. By morning everyone in the building is dead.

A caged bird sings an old and beautiful song. The lights flicker
and go out. Act One is over.

———

Cathy: Act Two begins with a fight staged between a bear and a
lion. Bets are placed. The Lion wins but is so badly wounded that
it has to be shot.

Aeroplanes leave vapour trails in the sky, writing amusing
messages as they loop beneath the clouds.

I Love Love writes the first plane.
Happy Birthday writes the second.
I Seem to Be Having Some Difficulties.
May Day. May Day. May Day writes the third but it's too late and
the plane crashes. A tragic waste of human life.

Some more accidents are presented. Acrobats stumble.
Tightrope walkers miss their footing. Trapeze artists miss
their catches. The knife thrower's assistant is helped down
from the podium, bleeding.
The talking horse is struck dumb. Mr Memory forgets to come on.
Extras walk on in the middle of inappropriate scenes.
A small child in the chorus waves to its parents.
The scenery collapses.
A trapdoor opens unexpectedly.
The curtain descends for no reason and then rises once again.
Cold tea is replaced with whisky.
A harmless practical joke involving a door and a bucket of paint
goes horribly wrong. Scenes are skipped. Other scenes are played
out of order.

The king stumbles.
The princess slips.
The banquet never arrives.

The actors improvise, trying to get the performance back on track
but they don't succeed.
The audience becomes anxious.
Some of them are bored.

A commotion breaks out in the auditorium and a man and a woman
are ejected.

Unease.
The two actors onstage get confused. They get into a loop. The
scene starts to repeat. And it repeats and it repeats and it
repeats.
Things become strained.
The actors remain in a loop.
Crisis.

A series of suicides are presented. Some ingenious, others
less so.
A woman seals her car in the garage, sits in it, starts the
engine, and is soon asphyxiated by the fumes.
Two lovers arrange to meet at the top of a tall building. They
meet and then jump off.

The audience is depressed.

Robin: A man shoots his wife, puts his kids in the car, drives to
the edge of a cliff, and drives the car over.
A top scientist deliberately exposes himself to the virus for
Bubonic Plague.
A vampire, unable to face the prospect of eternity, steps out into
brilliant sunshine.

Cathy: A small child puts a plastic bag over its head and
suffocates.
An old bloke all alone in his room makes himself die just by
thinking about it.

Robin: A woman takes 200 paracetamol.

Cathy: A man swallows 500 aspirin.

Robin: A child takes 600 Junior Disprin.

Cathy: A man ties a shotgun to a chair and fixes a rope to its
trigger. The rope leads around the door handle, up to a pulley
in the ceiling, and then to a second chair upon which the man
sits, facing the door. When the man's son comes home he catches a
brief glimpse of his father before the action of opening the door
pulls the rope causing the gun to fire, with tragic if predictable
consequences.

Robin: There is a short interval. Ice-cream is served and chips
are available in the cafe. Some people go to the bar for a
drink. Some people drink too much. A man is sick in the toilets.
Some people step outside the theatre to stretch their legs or
smoke a cigarette. Some of them wander too far and are claimed
by the night.

A series of bells is rung. One bell. Two bells. Three bells.
The audience take their seats and the spectacle begins afresh.
A handsome woman plays a number of popular tunes by farting.
She plays 'Rule Britannia', 'Auld Lang Syne', and the 'Hallelujah
Chorus'. For an encore she plays 'Oops! I Did it Again'.

Great Scenes from Shakespeare are presented; The Old Monarch Lear
in His Madness on The Heath, The Rude Mechanicals with all Their
Honest if Somewhat Simplistic Buffoonery, The Callous and Wicked
Macbeth in Bloody Combat with MacDuff, The Young and Beautiful
Juliet Drinking Poison in The Tomb.
Some Acts of Justice are Dispensed.
A pickpocket has his hand chopped off.
An adulteress is stoned.
A drug dealer is beheaded.
A car thief has his hands and feet tied to four separate SUVs
which are driven apart at high speed.

Witch finders are summoned. Volunteers are invited from the
audience and subjected to a number of ordeals.
Ordeal by Fire. Ordeal by Water. Ordeal by Combat.
Some more up to date ordeals are employed.
Ordeal by Electricity. Ordeal by Radiation. Ordeal by Laser.

Some witches are found and they are burned.

There are scenes of corruption and deception.
Scenes of bigamy and polygamy.
Scenes of sodomy, necrophilia, bestiality, masochism, coprophilia,
and one or two other perversions.

An angry mob floods the stage, muttering and grinding its teeth.
The mob disperses, and only a lone woman remains. She throws a
rope up high into the rafters and then beings to climb it. She
disappears. The audience is stunned.

Cathy: The passage of time is presented in various ways.

A clock ticks loudly in a school room.
A tap drips in a dirty kitchen sink.
In the windows of a local shop an unsold Greetings Card with a
gaudy design goes yellow over the years.

A woman waits for the results of a pregnancy test.

Leaves fall from a lone hilltop tree.
The tree is felled using a chainsaw and a group of historians
lecture briefly about the dates of the rings that are shown
inside. They point to the year of the first steam train, the year
of the first votes for women and the year of the first neon light.

Robin: Great sporting events from history are replayed several
times, first in slow motion and then at high speed. The performers
become exhausted.

The legendary knockout of George Foreman by the canny and
resourceful Muhammad Ali.

The notorious biting off of Evander Holyfield's ear by the crazed
and bloodthirsty Mike Tyson.

The humiliating defeat of Grandmaster Garry Kasparov by the cold
and calculating chess-computer Deep Blue.

Cathy: An army of robots floods the stage, demanding equal rights
and better working conditions.

The robots are pushed back by riot cops sporting futuristic
outfits and complex looking weapons.

Humanity is victorious and people celebrate. Spontaneous
carnivals erupt in Rio, Paris, Istanbul, Cape Town, Sydney, and
other cities. Pickpockets, thieves, gropers, con men, seditionists,
and agitators take advantage of the crowds.

The troublemakers are arrested and public areas are placed under
continuous closed-circuit television surveillance for the safety
of all.

Robin: In a simple onstage experiment lab rats have tumours
implanted. They lead a short, uncomfortable life, then die in the
corner of their cages.

The bodies are studied and the results are analysed and presented
in a prize-winning paper that thrills the medical research
community.

Scientists in lab coats present a series of genetically altered
mice. Mice with two heads and two tails. Mice without whiskers.
Mice without organs. The Wonders of Science. Progress.
A Brave New World.
Fat mice. Thin mice. Spherical mice. Triangular Mice.

Cathy: A ballet of more sophisticated shapes is presented.
Octagons, Pentagons, Pyramids, and Dodecahedrons.
As the shapes flood the stage they change colour, slowly making
harmonic sounds. The experience is subtle and complex; the
audience becomes more thoughtful and refined.

Robin: Klaxons are set off. Stroboscopic lighting and smoke floods
the auditorium. Security guards in gas masks armed with rubber
truncheons move up and down the aisles shouting and screaming.
They yell poems and provocative slogans. They quote Marx. They

quote Malcolm X. They quote Artaud. They quote Foucault. They whip
themselves up into tears of rage. The audience is shaken from its
bourgeois complacency.

Cathy: More suicides are presented.

Sundry hangings where the nooses are made from makeshift
materials. A man hangs himself using a belt. A woman hangs
herself using a pair of tights. Two lovers hang themselves using
the torn up sheets from a hotel bed. A jilted woman hangs herself
using a banner saying 'Welcome home: surprise surprise'.

The members of a cult drink poisoned lemonade.
A teenager opens an oven door, turns on the gas, and sticks his
head in.
Two more lovers throw themselves under a bus.
Schoolchildren throw themselves off a cliff like lemmings.
A man throws himself on a knife and bleeds to death.

A man inserts a pencil in his nose. The pencil is then driven
upwards into the skull by the action of him suddenly lowering his
head against the table, the pencil driven up into the brain with
tragic if predictable consequences.

A knife is used to cut wrists.
A fork is used to prise out a vein which is then bitten through.
Cyanide is eaten.
Deadly Nightshade is consumed.
Bleach is swallowed.
Acid is drunk.
Paint stripper is imbibed.
Infected blood is drunk.
An unhappy child puts bare electrical wires in its mouth. The
power short circuits and the lights go out abruptly, leaving the
stage in total darkness.

Robin: Some repairs are carried out and the curtain rises on
Dramatic literature of the world, presented in Abridged or
Adapted versions. The Cherry Orchard on Ice. Woyzeck For Kids. A
Streetcar Named Desire in Cockney Rhyming Slang. Modern Drama.
Bums on Seats.

A Fourth Wall Is Built. It is then Criticized and Demolished to
reveal scenes in which people go about their daily business.

A milkman delivers his milk.
A bus driver jumps some red lights.
A man takes a dog for a walk.
A woman does a shop at the supermarket.

Cathy: A kid pretends to have a stomach ache so he can bunk off
school.

Robin: Neighbours chat over the garden fence.

Cathy: A Lawyer makes an important phone call.

Robin: A traffic warden puts a ticket on an illegally parked car.
Teachers drink coffee in the staff room at break.

Cathy: Old age pensioners enter a crossword competition.

Robin: Bent cops beat a confession out of a suspect, dentists
make unnecessary extractions, surgeons make incisions and remove
diseased tissue.

Great Battles from History.
Hastings. Agincourt. The Somme.
The Battle of Gettysburg.
The Battle of Stalingrad. Ice. Mud. Body Parts.

In a field, a horse is blinded.
Somewhere a cow is slaughtered.
Dogs bait Badgers.
Kids shit in an abandoned flat.
A strange snow starts to fall.
Rats inhabit the spaces between walls. Food rots in warehouses,
crops fail.

A tree falls in a forest with no one there to see it.
The world spins on its axis. Night follows day follows night.
The world slows. Time stops. People and objects float above the
ground.
It's a difficult moment.
Ice begins to spread from the poles.
Seas freeze over and once great cities are encased in frost.
People huddle together over fires made from the wreckage of once
proud buildings.
Rivers turn solid. Hills and forests are covered in a mantle of
snow.
The world is still, caught and lifeless. The lights dim slowly.
And Act Two is finished.

Cathy: There are a few short moments where nothing happens.
People become aware of the creaking of the ropes, high above
their heads in the fly tower.
Dust is visible, floating in the lights.
People become aware of the breathing of the person sat next to
them or behind them, the shifting of their body weight.
There's the sound of traffic on a road outside. The sound of a
siren going by. A silence that isn't really a silence at all.

Cathy: Act Three begins. The audience is hushed.

A selection of love scenes is staged.
Secret Love.
Puppy Love.
Love That isn't Love.
Love That Doesn't Have a Name.
Platonic Love.
True Love.
Love That Stands the Test of Time.
Doomed Love.
Unacceptable Love.
Thwarted Love.
Lost Love.

The dissection of the corpses begins in an atmosphere of unease.

Cuts from Adam's apple to abdomen. Skin peeled back and clamped.
The rib cages are forced open using strange mechanical items
for which no one seems to know the name. Organs are removed. The
Heart. The Lungs. The Liver. The Pancreas. The contents of the
Stomachs are divulged. The Kidneys are weighed. The bowels are
drained. The veins in the arms are stripped bare. The lids of the
skulls are sawn off and the brains are removed. Eyes are removed
and cut into their constituent parts: lenses, corneas, irises,
optical nerves, and aqueous fluids. The genitalia are removed and
refrigerated for use in a later scene.

The scenes presented start small and get smaller and smaller.
A man spells out words on the skin of a lover.
Another man sings but no one can hear him.
A woman sighs.
A child sobs.
The softest of kisses is exchanged.
The scenes get smaller and smaller.
A stone, a pearl, a dewdrop, a tear.
A grain of sand, a speck of dust.
A microbe, an atom, an electron.

Robin: There is a light-hearted comical interlude involving men
and women with big shoes, red noses, bow ties that squirt water.
They have a funny little car with a funny little horn and carry
ladders and big buckets of paste.

A magician does familiar tricks. Cards are selected, hidden, and
guessed. Rings are joined, divided, and joined again. A rabbit is
produced from a hat. A volunteer is sawn in half, interviewed, and

reunited with his legs. The magician and his ageing assistants
leave the stage to scant applause.

Cathy: A beauty contest is held. Young women wearing swimsuits
discuss their ambitions and hopes for world peace.

An envelope is opened and a winner is announced. The runners-
up offer tearful congratulations. The winner makes a long and
heartfelt speech about the fate of the Earth and the importance
of education. Critics denounce it as sentiment but the audience
is moved.

Robin: Strange lonely men of the late 20th and early 21st
Centuries are presented. Michael Jackson at Neverland. Edward
Snowden in his Moscow hotel room, Julian Assange in the
Ecuadorian Embassy, Osama bin Laden in his Pakistan compound,
Donald Trump in his Oval Office.

Cathy: There are scenes of Indolence. Sloth. Lethargy and
Procrastination.

A pale youth strums vaguely at an acoustic guitar, never really
finding a tune.

A teenager thinks about tidying her bedroom but elects to do it
tomorrow.

A husband considers leaving his wife, but then decides that he
can't be bothered.

Robin: There are scenes that celebrate language, poetry, and the
power of the written word.

A man writes SORRY on the glass of a bathroom window.
A woman writes LATER on an envelope containing the key to a hotel
room.
Kids write FUCK OFF on the blackboard of a classroom and then
laugh together when their elderly teacher arrives, blushes, and
hastily erases the message.

Cathy: There are scenes of transformation: some familiar, some
unexpected.

Tadpoles become frogs.
A girl turns into a woman.
An ugly duckling turns into a swan.
A butterfly turns into a moth.

A ball of yellow light turns orange, blue, and then green.
A wardrobe turns into a chest of drawers.
A picnic hamper turns into an Antelope.

Robin: Love turns to hate.
Tears turn to joy.
Certainty turns to confusion.
Pain turns to sexual arousal.
A sheet of yellow A4 paper is folded in half, turned bent, and
folded several further times in ways that are difficult for the
untrained eye to follow—but slowly and just as surely the sheet
of yellow A4 paper becomes a yellow bird. The paper bird is
crushed, placed on a silver tray, soaked in lighter fluid, and
burned. The smoke rises upwards and disappears. The ashes fall
unheeded to the floor.

Cathy: A group of schoolchildren from the provinces form an
unruly line at the edge of the stage and pull horrible faces
directly at the audience. They do gargoyle impressions and
lunatic idiot drools. They slobber, bark, twitch, howl, and
grimace.

Silence. The audience is puzzled.

But the kids are persistent.

One kid pops out an eyeball, and shows it in the palm of
her hand.
Another turns his nose inside out and frantically wiggles
his ears.

A third makes her eyes rotate at various speeds and then in opposite directions.

It is Hilarious. The audience are charmed by the schoolkids' mischievous display. The children, victorious, with faces aching, are led from the stage.

Robin: Solemn music plays, a spotlight comes on centre of the stage and the solo acts begin.

The Fish Man.
Robot Boy.
The Bear Lady.
The Smallest Man on Earth.
The Miserable Girl.
The Wrestling Priest.
The Human Cannonball.
The Hypnotized Girl.
Mr Nine & a Half Inches.
The Sea Boy.
The Lost Girl.
The Amazing Robondo.
X The Prettiest Girl in England.
Doctor Love.
The Sleeping Man.
The Missing Link.
The Human Harpsichord.
Miss Universe.
The Strongest Man in The World.
The Mexican Elvis.

The stage is sprinkled with a fine, white powder and The Invisible Girl is announced. As a waltz plays, footprints appear as if by magic, tracing a route across the floor.

Cat Boy and Bat Boy.
The Sad Man.
The Twisted Girl.
The Comeback Kid.
The Egg Head.
Diablo.
The Bone Head.
Miss Nightmare.
The Sorcerer's Apprentice.
The King of the Forest.
The Queen of the May.
The Bird Man of Alcatraz.
Princess Not-So-Bright.
The Human Octopus.
The Human Scarecrow.
Mr Laser.
Miss AK47.
The Average Man.
The Snowflake Kid.
Fantasy Fred.
The Girl with Boy's Eyes.
The Weeping Dog.
The Tattooed Baby.

Rare Specimens. Freaks of Nature. Some Persons The Like of Which Have Never Been Seen Before. And so ends Act Three.

Cathy: Act Four begins with men dressed in overalls bring cardboard boxes to the front of the stage. In one synchronized gesture they open the lids, releasing 10,000 butterflies. The air is a riot of colour, pattern, and movement. The beautiful creatures flutter everywhere. They land on hats. They land on noses. They land on fingertips, earlobes, and other extremities. Children are delighted. They ask to take the butterflies home and then set off to capture them.

Robin: When the last of the butterflies has been dealt with, an assortment of caged animals and wildlife is set free into the theatre: penguins waddle towards the footlights, wolves, polar bears, and monkeys scatter into the wings, rare birds dart and swoop above the stage—their speed is exhilarating and within seconds they are gone.

Cathy: There is a moment of silence and the lighting changes to something more uneven and atmospheric, as wretched figures slowly enter.

Beggars, rough sleepers, tramps, vagrants, the homeless, street drinkers, refugees, and migrants all gather on the stage, without purpose or direction. With nowhere else to go they build laughable shelters from materials taken from the wings and backstage storage of the theatre. Pieces of scenery, velvet drapes, and a large oak-effect table are quickly transformed into improvised dwellings.

Before long the whole stage is criss-crossed with a maze of impromptu alleyways and streets made from these temporary structures—a disorganized city in which a growing crowd struggles to survive—begging, stealing, growing crops in the wings, and urinating into the orchestra pit.

Time passes in this unruly metropolis. The slum dwellers barter with each other, buying food and other supplies with a currency of condoms, matches, and US dollars. Children are born. Families are formed. Churches are established. Aid agencies struggle to bring food supplies. Politicians debate impotent responses and solutions, wringing their hands. Gangs emerge and before long they take the law into their own hands. Residents of the camp must work for them or pay bribes in order to survive. Those that cannot work are pushed beyond the curtains and left to die.

Robin: At night, a giant mirror ball is lowered from the lighting grid to send spinning stars around the stage and auditorium alike. It's a populist gesture, but it isn't enough.

In the end, the management have no choice but to send in security. Cops in riot gear storm the camp stage as dawn approaches, backed up by special forces, tactical dog units, drones, and water cannon. The air is thick with rocks, tear gas, and the cries of the dispossessed. Skulls are cracked with nightsticks and riot batons. Homes are swiftly destroyed as flimsy shelters are bulldozed and pushed off the edge of the stage. Old men howl in terror, uncertain of their fate. Weeping children are separated from their parents. A group of migrants is dragged off for 'processing'.

When the battle is over journalists and photographers wander through the wreckage, making notes and taking pictures to form the basis of their prize-winning reportage.

Cathy: An upbeat song begins to play and local residents file onto the stage.

They present a comical but affectionate portrait of their town in dance, anecdote, and song.
School teachers sing a song about spelling.
Old people remember the War.
Younger people remember the War on Drugs and the War on Terror.
People from other countries share their national recipes and folkloric tales from back home.
Children do satirical skits about their grandparents and how things used to be. The local policeman does a rap about tolerance.
The receptionist from a nearby tanning salon raises eyebrows with a thought-provoking dance.
Everyone (spectators included) joins in the celebrations, toasting the hard work and success of the players using fruit juices, filtered tap water, and non-alcoholic beer.

Politicians, sponsors, and people from the various funding bodies wipe a tear of relief from their eyes. Art is for Everyone. The world is a better place.

Robin: Some death scenes are presented.
A man dies of thirst.

Cathy: A woman dies of hunger.

Robin: A teenager dies of a broken heart.

Cathy: A child dies of boredom.

Robin: Sailors die of syphilis.

Cathy: Soldiers die of attrition.
A dog dies of loneliness.

Robin: A comedian dies onstage and the body is left to decay.

It cools slowly to rigor mortis and begins to discolour. Microbes, already present in the stomach and other areas, multiply rapidly, consuming the body from within, and this process of putrefaction soon leads to the second stage of decomposition, known as Bloat.

The audience becomes nervous.

Carrion insects such as Blowflies and Flesh Flies settle on the body and lay their eggs. As the body decays further, the accumulation of gases gives it a distended appearance. The gases cause natural liquids and liquefying tissues to become frothy, and as pressure inside the body increases, they are forced out of its orifices—nose, mouth, and anus—leaking slowly but surely to the floor of the stage.

The crowd murmurs and then falls silent. Some of them begin a rebellious slow hand clap, but it comes to nothing. They know what they are in for, one way or another.

As time passes, the changes in the comedian's body get faster and faster. Maggots hatch and begin to feed. They cause skin to sag and hair to detach. Warming steadily under the theatre lights, the body enters a stage of active decay. Pressure causes the skin to rupture suddenly. There is a constant purging of decomposition fluids onto the stage, and as the comedian's body approaches the end of its act, these liquids form a pool that shimmers in the theatre lights, the cadaver a glistening island in its midst.

A powerful odour fills the auditorium. There is the sound of retching in the aisles. Medics and interns take little paper cups of water and smelling salts to members of the audience. Some people are taken out on stretchers.

The denouement of the act is anticlimactic. The last shreds of the comedian's flesh give up what little moisture they have, and all that remains on the stage is a small memento mori in the form of dry skin, brittle cartilage, and stripped bones.
The crowd are solemn. But they do applaud.

Cathy: The last remains of the comedian are removed and the floor is cleaned by a team of low-paid workers.

An official-looking woman comes onto the stage with a sheet of paper in her hand. She adjusts her spectacles and apologizes, announcing some last-minute changes to the programme:

The World's Greatest Soprano is unwell and unable to appear.
The Award-Winning Best Newcomer on the Comedy Circuit is a no-show.
The ten most electrifying bands of all time are stuck in traffic.
The old drunk with his inebriated bumbling, mumbling, curses, and accidental urination—cancelled.

Robin: The Boxing Sisters—cancelled.
The Brexit Brothers—cancelled.

The deep-sea diver and the mermaid—cancelled.
The virgin and the roller skater—also cancelled.

Cathy: The comprehensive line-up of experts, scientists, climate change specialists, financiers, solicitors, academics, journalists, war correspondents, and political commentators—cancelled.

Famous acts of civil disobedience—cancelled.
Famous acts of human kindness—cancelled.
Famous acts of mercy—cancelled.
Famous acts of bravery—cancelled.
Famous acts of revenge—cancelled.
Famous acts of terrorism have all been double-booked.

Robin: Some hastily improvised routines are presented in order to cover the gaps in the schedule.

A bubble machine is switched on. Thousands of bubbles spew into the audience, who laugh out loud and burst them.

Someone from the box office does an impression of Angela Merkel.

Someone from the Marketing Department does a passable backflip.

There is a procession of extras and staff members from admin, catering, and backstage crews, each of whom takes their turn to wave to the audience, enjoying a glorious moment in the spotlight before shuffling off into obscurity.

Cathy: Backstage there are celebrations. Corks pop out of Champagne bottles. Leading ladies spray the leading men. There are whisperings in the wings and hurried changes of costume. A nervous energy. A certain abandon. Children, chorus girls, character-actors, stilt walkers, dancing bears, fire-eaters, and others gather in the dressing rooms, looking for their wigs, hats, props, and other equipment, checking their cues, learning their lines. A few strays wander the corridors, bumping into each other, looking for the right route, seeking out the right stairs up to the stage as Act Five is ready to begin.

———

A young woman is having an affair with the local vicar, although she is married to the bank manager. They are in bed together when her husband returns and the vicar is forced to hide in the closet but unfortunately he has left his trousers hanging over the back of a chair and the wife has to pretend that they have been sent back from the laundry by mistake. There is some comic business with doors, closets, windows, cupboards, vicars, and undergarments.

Robin: A body is discovered in the study, by the housemaid. Everyone is asked to stay until the police have concluded their enquiries. Famous detectives are invited. An English Lord. A Belgian Eccentric. A Scandinavian Autistic. An American Paraplegic. A French Incompetent. Various theories are proposed. Some ingenious, others less so. Conversations take place in the billiard room. Alibis are constructed and demolished. Motives are uncovered and dismissed. No one could have done it. Or everyone could have done it. The detectives are baffled. Another body is discovered, this time in the coal cellar. There is agitation. Speculation. New arguments break out but as the days go by more brutal murders are committed. Stabbings, poisonings, pummellings, drownings, electrocutions. The circle of suspects gets smaller and smaller. The focus of suspicion grows tighter and tighter until in the end only two suspects remain.

But before the act can reach its inevitable denouement one of them crosses the drawing room, opens the French windows, and hand in hand they walk out. Across the croquet lawn. Over the fence and into the lane.

Cathy: They continue walking to the crossroads. Take a left on the main road, heading out of town.

Robin: They come to a level crossing and follow the rail track through a cutting till they come to a tunnel.

Cathy: They walk into the tunnel.

Robin: It's dark but they carry on.

Cathy: They keep walking till they reach the other end.

Robin: They climb the embankment which rises steeply to a barbed-wire fence.

Cathy: They vault the fence.
There is woodland in the distance. By now it's night.

Robin: Past the canal, past the warehouses. Crossing the bridge.

Cathy: They keep walking until there are no houses left and they reach the edge of a field. They start out across the grass towards the horizon.
There's a full moon.
The light of the moon makes everything look like it's covered in snow.

Robin: There's a chill in the air. The audience are cold.
Some of them have wrapped themselves in their coats.
They're huddled up. Some of the children are crying.

There's the sound of a party: offstage.
The sound of a tennis match: offstage.
The sound of someone calling: offstage.
The sound of mortar fire: in the distance.

Cathy: Persons of a nervous disposition are asked to leave the auditorium and an old woman with skin like alabaster and eyes like burning coals walks slowly to the centre of the stage.

Two steps behind her follows a young boy, his skin like the smoothest marble, his eyes like the brightest emeralds.

Robin: The boy takes a simple paper bag from his pocket. He unfolds it, blows into it, and slowly inflates it.

He casts a sideways glance to the old woman, who nods.

The boy is still for a moment. Then, in a sudden movement, he brings together his one hand with the bag held in it and his other hand with the palm stretched out, colliding them with great force and shocking but predictable consequences. With the loud bang of the burst paper bag still echoing, both he and the old woman vanish and the stage is totally bare.

The audience are stunned. They stare in silence—numb, exhausted, and open-mouthed.

Cathy: A bit of darkness, some flickering light.
White scratches on the film.
Music swirls.
Credits roll and the endings begin.

Robin: Death scenes and faint, broken monologues.

Cathy: Long-waited-for eclipses.

Robin: Stars going out.

Cathy: The melting of the ice warriors.

Robin: The summing up to the jury.

Cathy: The safe return to earth of captain and crew.

Robin: Embraces, the swallowing of tears.

Cathy: Double weddings.

Robin: Double crosses laid bare.

Cathy: Masks torn off at last.

Robin: The past rendered readable.

Cathy: Slow, slow dimming of the lights.
The killer's confessions and soft sentimental songs.
Finales, quadrilles.
Encores and last revelations.
The wise men make grand orations.
The child prince dances and the whole court applauds.
The lovers say goodbye in Terminal 3.
The world ends.
Plot twists.
Smiles.

Sunsets.
Answered questions.
Weepings in the garden.
Sunken ships raised at last.
Fools shown the error of their ways.
The door shuts in a bedsit.
The last light in the high-rise goes out at last.
And dolls are put away.
The sirens sound out in the distance and the cop cars circle with a screech of brakes and the red lights on their roofs flutter like Tinker Bell in the branches of the trees.

The lights dim, the stage is dark.
Only the sound of rain and distant thunder remains.
The thunder receding into silence, getting further away.

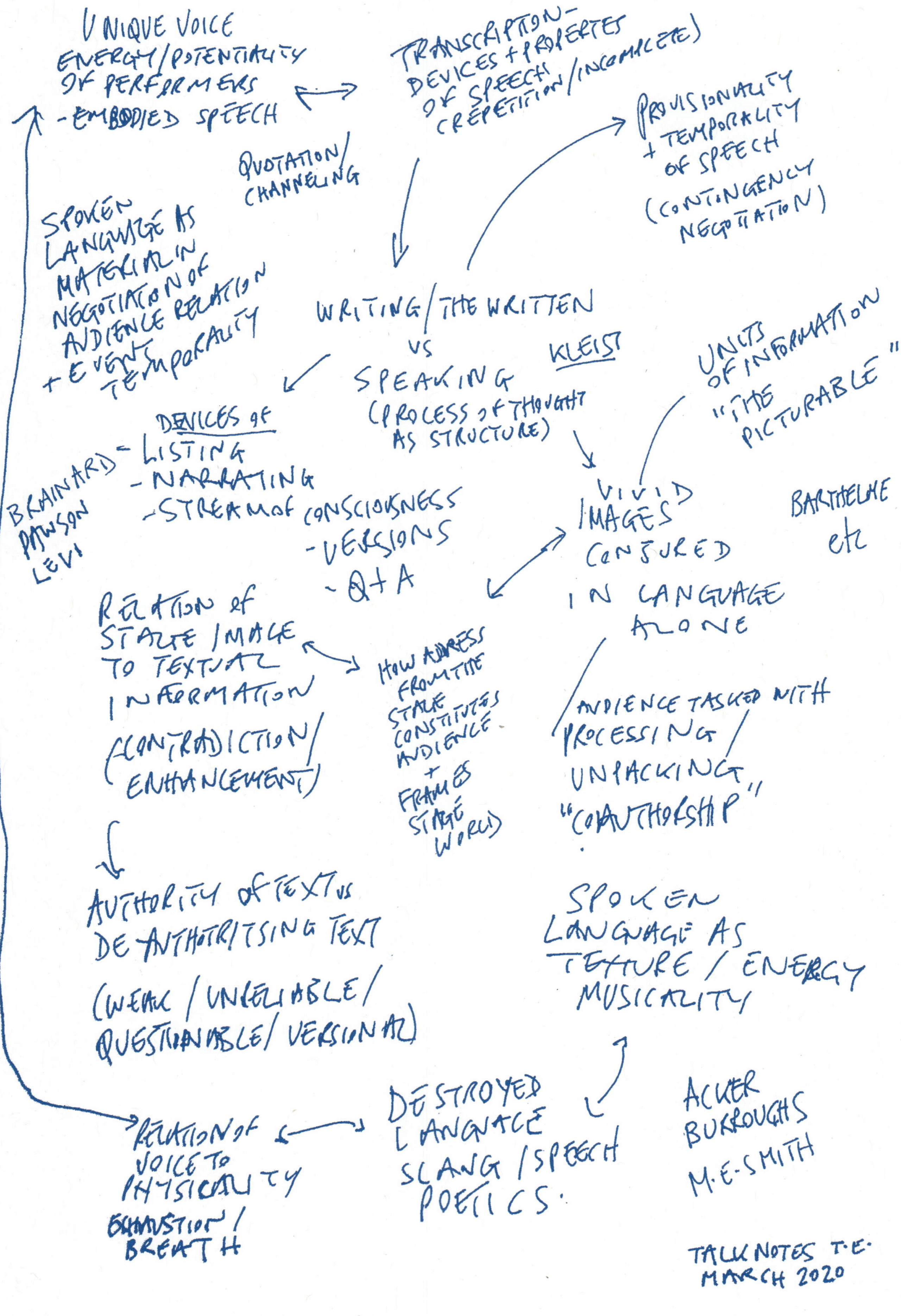

UNIQUE VOICE
ENERGY/POTENTIALITY
OF PERFORMERS
- EMBODIED SPEECH

QUOTATION/
CHANNELING

TRANSCRIPTION -
DEVICES + PROPERTIES
OF SPEECH
(REPETITION/INCOMPLETE)

PROVISIONALITY
+ TEMPORALITY
OF SPEECH
(CONTINGENCY
NEGOTIATION)

SPOKEN
LANGUAGE AS
MATERIAL IN
NEGOTIATION OF
AUDIENCE RELATION
+ EVENT
TEMPORALITY

WRITING / THE WRITTEN
VS
SPEAKING
(PROCESS OF THOUGHT
AS STRUCTURE)

KLEIST

UNITS
OF INFORMATION
"THE
PICTURABLE"

DEVICES OF
BRAINARD - LISTING
PAWSON - NARRATING
LEVI - STREAM OF CONSCIOUSNESS
- VERSIONS
- Q + A

VIVID
IMAGES
CONJURED

BARTHELME
etc

IN LANGUAGE
ALONE

RELATION of
STATE IMAGE
TO TEXTUAL
INFORMATION

(CONTRADICTION/
ENHANCEMENT)

HOW ADDRESS
FROM THE
STATE
CONSTITUTES
AUDIENCE
+
FRAMES
STAGE
WORLD)

AUDIENCE TASKED WITH
PROCESSING /
UNPACKING
"COAUTHORSHIP"

AUTHORITY OF TEXT VS
DE-AUTHORITISING TEXT

(WEAK / UNRELIABLE /
QUESTIONABLE / VERSIONAL)

SPOKEN
LANGUAGE AS
TEXTURE / ENERGY
MUSICALITY

RELATION OF
VOICE TO
PHYSICALITY

EXHAUSTION /
BREATH

DESTROYED
LANGUAGE
SLANG / SPEECH
POETICS.

ACKER
BURROUGHS
M.E. SMITH

TALK NOTES T.E.
MARCH 2020

CHRONOLOGY OF WORKS

Key:

P   Performers
OP   Original Performers
SP   Subsequent Performers
GP   Guest Performers
V   Voice-over
D   Direction
AD   Assistant Direction
C   Concept
T   Text
S   Set Design
L   Lighting Design
TC   Technicians
ST   Soundtrack
PH   Photographs
PM   Production Management
CO   Commissioners
CP   Co-producers

1. WORKS FOR THEATRE SPACES AND DURATIONAL PERFORMANCES

Jessica in the Room of Lights, 1984

P: Robin Arthur, Huw Chadbourn, Cathy Naden, Susie Williams.
D: Tim Etchells, Richard Lowdon. T: Tim Etchells. S/L: Richard Lowdon.
ST: John Avery.

Premiere: 14 December 1984, Yorkshire Arts Space Society,
Sheffield (UK).

Subsequent performances in: Leeds, Nottingham, Sheffield (UK).

Using dialogue, taped voice-over, soundtrack, and choreographed
action, the performance explores a blurred storyline about a cinema
usherette whose real life becomes mixed with films she's absorbed
at work. Moving from the suburbs to the city, Jessica's story—a
failed romance—is retold in contradictory versions as a form of
incomplete memory.

The Set-Up, 1985

P: Robin Arthur, Huw Chadbourn, Susie Williams. D: Tim Etchells,
Richard Lowdon. T: Tim Etchells. S: Richard Lowdon, Huw
Chadbourn. L: Richard Lowdon. ST: John Avery. CO: National
Review of Live Art (UK).

Premiere: Summer 1985, The Leadmill, Sheffield (UK).

Subsequent performances in: Brighton, Lancaster, London, Leicester,
Nottingham (UK).

Three performers use choreographed gestures and narrative moments
from gangland interrogation scenes. The piece draws on TV and film
genre clichés to explore ideas of guilt, confession, and sexual identity.
The style explores a minimalist choreography in which the shapes and
gestures of a story are worked in repetition and phase to reveal their
musical and narrative possibilities.

Nighthawks, 1985

P: Huw Chadbourn, Tim Etchells, Richard Lowdon, Susie Williams.
V: Tim Etchells, Cathy Naden. D: Robin Arthur, Cathy Naden.
T: Tim Etchells. S: Richard Lowdon, Huw Chadbourn.
L: Richard Lowdon. ST: John Avery.

Premiere: 23 October 1985, North Riding College,
Scarborough (UK).

Subsequent performances in: Hebden Bridge, Lancaster, Leeds,
London, Northampton, Nottingham, Rotherham, Sheffield,
York (UK).

The near-mythical world of American bars, inspired by the paintings
of Edward Hopper, American film and literature. The text, again,
is pre-recorded; the choreography poetical and repetitive.

The Day That Serenity Returned to the Ground, 1986

P: Robin Arthur, Huw Chadbourn, Tim Etchells, Cathy Naden.
D: Susie Williams, Tim Etchells, Richard Lowdon. T: Tim Etchells.
S: Richard Lowdon, Huw Chadbourn. L: Richard Lowdon.
ST: John Avery. CO: The Zap Club, Brighton (UK).

Premiere: 6 February 1986.

The setting is a white polythene isolation chamber in which the
performers are divided from the audience by a wall of metal grilles.
At the centre of the piece is a science-fiction story about the return of a
group of cosmonauts to Earth. Presenting the shapes or outlines of the
narrative rather than its details, *The Day That Serenity* moves through
the initial genre material towards other strands of content.

(Let the Water Run Its Course) to the Sea That Made the Promise, 1986

P: Robin Arthur, Richard Lowdon, Cathy Naden, Susie Williams.
V: Sarah Singleton, Tim Etchells. D: Huw Chadbourn, Tim Etchells,
Richard Lowdon, Terry O'Connor. T: Tim Etchells.
S: Huw Chadbourn, Richard Lowdon. ST: John Avery.

Premiere: 6 October 1986, Trent Polytechnic, Nottingham (UK).

Subsequent performances in: Antwerp, Brussels, Gent (Belgium);
Amsterdam, Haarlem (Netherlands); Fribourg (Switzerland); Bracknell,
Bristol, Cambridge, Exeter, Hebden Bridge, London, Rotherham,
Sheffield, Thame, York (UK).

A pair of recorded voices speak, in a rough poetic tone, about life in
a post-apocalyptic city. Whimpering, shouting and whispering, two
parallel couples onstage play a wordless game-cum-ritual of scene
fragments which could be about their lives and possible deaths.

200% & Bloody Thirsty, 1988

P: Robin Arthur, Richard Lowdon, Cathy Naden. Video performer:
Mark Etchells, Sarah Singleton. D: Tim Etchells, Terry O'Connor.
V: Jo Cammack, Terry O'Connor. T: Tim Etchells. S/L: Richard Lowdon.
ST: John Avery.

Premiere: 10 October 1988, Trent Polytechnic, Nottingham (UK).

Subsequent performances in: Gent (Belgium); Polverigi (Italy);
Gdańsk, Poznań, Warsaw (Poland); Zurich (Switzerland); Alsager,
Colchester, Glasgow, Lancaster, London, Manchester, Milton Keynes,
Northampton, Nottingham, Sheffield, Totnes, Wakefield, York (UK).

Three drunks in bad wigs and jumble sale clothes endlessly enact the
events surrounding the supposed or imagined death of one of their
friends, as if by replaying this scenario the truth might be revealed.

In a stage set reminiscent of a homemade kitsch snow shaker, the piece repeats a chaotic nativity play in various versions, including one done blindfolded and at breakneck speed. The onstage action is framed by a poetic narration: a dialogue from a pair of angels on video monitors.

Some Confusions in the Law about Love, 1989

P: Robin Arthur, Terry O'Connor, Claire Marshall, Cathy Naden, Fred McVittie. SP: Mark Randle. D: Tim Etchells, Richard Lowdon. T: Tim Etchells. S: Richard Lowdon. L: Nigel Edwards. ST: John Avery.

Premiere: 30 October 1989, Trent Polytechnic, Nottingham (UK).

Subsequent performances in: Basildon, Bath, Dursley, Glasgow, Harrogate, Lancaster, London, Manchester, Scarborough, Sheffield, Wolverhampton (UK).

An unlikely Elvis Presley impersonator in Birmingham, England performs his act on a tacky nightclub stage. As the evening progresses he is joined by two jaded showgirls, a pair of forlorn skeletons who perform an archaic Japanese love-suicide story, and special guests Mike and Dolores, 'sex act escapologists', interviewed 'live by satellite from Hawaii' on two monitors at the edges of the stage.

Welcome to Dreamland, 1991

P: Robin Arthur, Terry O'Connor, Claire Marshall, Cathy Naden, Mark Randle. D: Tim Etchells, Richard Lowdon. T: Tim Etchells. S: Richard Lowdon. L: Nigel Edwards. ST: John Avery.

Premiere: 15 July 1991, The Leadmill, Sheffield (UK).

Retrospective trilogy consisting of *(Let the Water Run Its Course) to the Sea That Made the Promise, 200% & Bloody Thirsty*, and *Some Confusions in the Law about Love*.

Marina & Lee, 1991

P: Robin Arthur, Terry O'Connor, Claire Marshall, Cathy Naden, Mark Randle. Video performer: Richard Lowdon. D: Tim Etchells, Richard Lowdon. T: Tim Etchells. S: Richard Lowdon. L: Nigel Edwards. ST: John Avery.

Premiere: 18 March 1991, Nuffield Studio, Lancaster (UK).

Subsequent performances in: Zurich (Switzerland); Barnet, Bedford, Brighton, Bristol, Cambridge, Coventry, Dursley, Exeter, Kendal, Liverpool, London, Manchester, Milton Keynes, Nottingham, Scarborough, Sheffield (UK).

The piece begins with a dysfunctional physics lecture from a woman in a shop-worker's overalls. Throughout the show the central figure, Marina, describes her journey through a bizarre contradictory landscape—part desert, part city and part paradise—whilst the rest of the performance collides around her. There are shoot-outs, kung fu fights and raucous pretend operas that seem to turn into adverts, cowboys, and barking dogs. At other times the performers play a set of confessions directly to the audience.

Emanuelle Enchanted, 1992

P: Robin Arthur, Richard Lowdon, Claire Marshall, Cathy Naden, Terry O'Connor. D/T: Tim Etchells. AD: Nick Crowe. S: Richard Lowdon. L: Nigel Edwards. ST: John Avery.

Premiere: 6 October 1992, Nuffield Studio, Lancaster (UK).

Subsequent performances in: Antwerp, Gent (Belgium); Berlin, Frankfurt am Main, Hanover (DE); Toneelschuur, Haarlem (Netherlands); Alsager, Bedford, Bristol, Coventry, Dursley, Glasgow, Leicester, London, Manchester, Nottingham, Scarborough, Sheffield, Southampton, Wolverhampton (UK).

On a crude wooden stage a group of five performers use a semi-translucent curtain, whisked backwards and forwards to reveal the traces of a single apocalyptic night. Read narratively, the piece shows a night of crisis which is perhaps both personal and global. The invoked 'scenes' include a chaotic TV newsroom, a domestic space in which the walls themselves are always in motion, and a panoramic glimpse of many characters presented by the performers using second-hand clothes as costumes and a series of cardboard signs.

Club of No Regrets, 1993

P: Robin Arthur, Richard Lowdon, Claire Marshall, Cathy Naden, Terry O'Connor. D/T: Tim Etchells. AD: Ju Row Farr. S: Richard Lowdon. L: Nigel Edwards. ST: John Avery. TC: Martin Bailey.

Premiere: 5 October 1993, Nuffield Studio, Lancaster (UK).

Subsequent performances in: Gent (Belgium); Helsinki (Finland); Cologne (DE); Pontedera (Italy); Utrecht (Netherlands); Kongsvinger (Norway); Gothenburg (Sweden); Alsager, Bedford, Bristol, Dursley, Glasgow, Leicester, London, Manchester, Nottingham, Portsmouth, Scarborough, Sheffield, Southampton, Wolverhampton (UK); San Francisco (USA).

At the bidding of a central figure calling herself Helen X, two performers in a flimsy box-set centre stage are compelled to act out the same fragmentary TV movie scenes again and again. Helped and hindered by two overzealous stage hands with toy guns, this process becomes increasingly demanding. The scenes are intercut and overlaid in a poetic collision of narratives; the stage is covered with talcum powder, fake blood, water, and dead leaves.

12am: Awake & Looking Down, 1993

(6– to 11–hour durational performance)

OP: Robin Arthur, Cathy Naden, Claire Marshall, Terry O'Connor, Richard Lowdon. SP: Mark Etchells, Tim Etchells, Nicki Hobday , Jerry Killick, Ben Neale, John Rowley. D: Tim Etchells. S: Richard Lowdon.

Premiere: 22 October 1993, National Review of Live Art, ICA, London (UK).

Subsequent performances in: Antwerp, Brussels (Belgium); Beijing (China); Dieppe, Dijon, Paris (France); Berlin, Essen, Frankfurt am Main, Munich (DE); Pontedera, Santarcangelo di Romagna (Italy); Toruń (Poland); Moscow (Russia); Barcelona (Spain); Lausanne, Zurich (Switzerland); London (UK).

Five performers, use second-hand clothes as costumes and a series of cardboard signs which bear the names of characters, to present role after role in rapid succession and in different combinations. The piece arises from a section of *Emanuelle Enchanted*, and is the group's first durational work. Over the long arc of the piece exhaustion sets in onstage, whilst innumerable possible connections and interpretations are generated through the core performance task of dressing up and changing names. The piece has been presented for time spans of between six and eleven hours and—as in subsequent durational works by the company—the public are free to arrive, depart, and return at any point.

Dreams' Winter, 1994

(Site-specific work)

P: Robin Arthur, Richard Lowdon, Claire Marshall, Sue Marshall, Cathy Naden, Terry O'Connor. Guests: Nicky Beaumont, Nicola Bertram, Alex Bliss, Paulette Terry Brian, Kath Cooke, Susie Dick, Ian Greenall, Tim Hall, Steve Jackson, Alex Kelly, Jamie McAffer, Kit McCudden, Ellen Mills, Susan Scott, Juliet Sebley, Fleur Soper, Michelle Stanbridge, Liz Tomlin, Rachel Walton.
D: Tim Etchells. T: Tim Etchells, Forced Entertainment. S/L: Richard Lowdon. ST: John Avery. Assistant: Emma Leslie. CO: Manchester Central Library (UK).

Premiere: 15 July 1994, Central Library, Manchester (UK).

The group's first site-specific performance, created for the Manchester Central Library and presented with an audience seated at tables in the main dome-ceilinged hall of the building. Twenty-five performers, both Forced Entertainment and guests, wander as if sleepwalking, barefoot in pyjamas, amongst the endless bookshelves.

Hidden J, 1994

P: Robin Arthur, Cathy Naden, Terry O'Connor, Richard Lowdon, Claire Marshall. D/T: Tim Etchells. AD: Nick Crowe. S: Richard Lowdon. L: Nigel Edwards. ST: John Avery. Assistant: Emma Leslie.

Premiere: 10 October 1994, Nuffield Studio, Lancaster (UK).

Subsequent performances in: Alsager, Bedford, Birmingham, Dursley, Exeter, Glasgow, Leeds, Leicester, London, Manchester, Nottingham, Portsmouth, Scarborough, Southampton, Wolverhampton (UK).

On a stage that looks like a construction site, this distorted portrait of England centres on a drunk bloke in the process of messing up a wedding speech. Around this hapless figure, the group present diverse fragments of apparently unrelated material—scenes from an unnamed European war zone, a botched hospital operation, the narration of an angel and a devil, and fragmented accounts of a massacre.

Speak Bitterness, 1994

(Durational performance and theatre version)

—Durational performance: P: Robin Arthur, Tim Etchells, Tim Hall, Richard Lowdon, Claire Marshall, Sue Marshall, Cathy Naden, Terry O'Connor. SP: Nicki Hobday. D: Tim Etchells.
T: Tim Etchells, Forced Entertainment. S: Richard Lowdon. L: Nigel Edwards. TC: Andy Clarke, Johnny Goodwin. CO: National Review of Live Art (UK).

Premiere: 23 October 1994, National Review of Live Art, Glasgow (UK).

Subsequent performances in: Amsterdam (Netherlands); Berlin, Essen, Frankfurt am Main, Munich, Munster (DE); Chicago (USA).

—Theatre version: P: Robin Arthur, Tim Hall, Richard Lowdon, Claire Marshall, Sue Marshall, Cathy Naden, Terry O'Connor.
SP: Tim Etchells, Ursula Martinez. D: Tim Etchells. T: Tim Etchells, Forced Entertainment. S: Richard Lowdon. L: Nigel Edwards. ST: John Avery.

Premiere: 26 September 1995, Alsager Arts Centre, Stoke-on-Trent (UK).

Subsequent performances in: Gent (Belgium); Montreal (Canada); Berlin, Cologne, Dortmund, Essen, Frankfurt am Main, Hamburg, Munich (DE); Dublin (Ireland); Amsterdam, Rotterdam, Utrecht (Netherlands); Bergen (Norway); Zurich (Switzerland); Alsager, Bath, Bedford, Brighton, Bristol, Cambridge, Cardiff, Crawley, Dursley, Edinburgh, Glasgow, Kingston-upon-Hull, Lancaster, Leeds, Liverpool, London, Manchester, Nottingham, Plymouth, Scarborough, Sheffield, Southampton, Stamford, Totnes, Wakefield (UK); Minneapolis, Ohio (USA).

A line of people take turns to read confessions from behind a long table in a brightly lit space. The tone slips between penitence and absurdity. The litany of wrongdoing they confess to ranges from the big time of forgery, murder, and genocide to everyday details, such as reading each other's diaries and refusing to take the dogs out for a walk. *Speak Bitterness* has been shown in theatre and durational versions; in the latter the audience is free to arrive, depart, and return at any point.

A Decade of Forced Entertainment, 1995

(Performance-lecture)

P: Robin Arthur, Tim Etchells, Richard Lowdon, Claire Marshall, Cathy Naden, Terry O'Connor. T: Tim Etchells, Forced Entertainment. S: Richard Lowdon. L: Nigel Edwards. ST: John Avery.

Premiere: 3 December 1994, ICA Theatre, London (UK).

Subsequent performances in: Antwerp (Belgium); Kongsvinger (Norway); Los Angeles; New York; Minneapolis (USA); Sheffield (UK).

A fictitious, as well as truthful remembered map of the years from 1984 to 1994, made on occasion of the tenth anniversary of Forced Entertainment. Combining documentary and autobiographical material in a performance-lecture, the piece links reflection on the group's own work with material about historical and world events and the changing fabric of urban England.

Nights in This City, 1995

(Site-specific bus tour and installation)

—Original version: P: Robin Arthur, Richard Lowdon, Claire Marshall, Cathy Naden, Terry O'Connor. Coach driver: Martin Tether.
T: Tim Etchells, Forced Entertainment. ST: John Avery.

Premiere: 16 May 1995, Sheffield (UK).

—Rotterdam version: P: Robin Arthur, Richard Lowdon, Claire Marshall, Cathy Naden, Terry O'Connor. T: Tim Etchells, Forced Entertainment. ST: John Avery. PM: Martin Bailey. CO: R Festival / Rotterdamse Schouwburg (NL).

Premiere: 23 September 1997, R Festival/Rotterdamse Schouwburg, Rotterdam (NL).

Performers and viewers are taken on a nocturnal bus tour through the centre of Sheffield. The commentary on the city outside mixes the fictitious, the official, and the purely personal to create a poetical exploration of urban life. Twice, the tour is interrupted by small scenes, which are performed in the street. The work ends with an installation in which the entire street index for the city is written out in chalk on the floor of the city's disused bus garage.

Break In!, 1996

(Project for children)

P: Robin Arthur, Tim Hall, Richard Lowdon, Claire Marshall, Terry O'Connor. D: Tim Etchells. T: Tim Etchells, Forced Entertainment.

Premiere: 30 January 1996, Crucible Theatre, Sheffield (UK).

A misguided tour of the Crucible Theatre in Sheffield for audiences of children. Borrowing the strategies of *Nights in This City*, the tour features a lost tour guide and fictional characters adrift in the backstage spaces of the theatre.

Quizoola!, 1996

(6– or 24–hour durational performance)

OP: Robin Arthur, Tim Etchells, Richard Lowdon, Claire Marshall, Cathy Naden, Terry O'Connor. GP: Kent Beeson, Jolente De Keersmaeker, Sara De Roo, Damiaan De Schrijver, Mark Etchells, Jim Fletcher, Tim Hall, Jerry Killick, Joe Lawlor, Sue Marshall, Ursula Martinez, Christine Molloy, Sophia New, Dan B. Rogers, Bruno Roubicek, John Rowley, Frank Vercruyssen. T: Tim Etchells. S: Richard Lowdon. CO: ICA Live Arts, National Review Of Live Art (UK).

Premiere: 29 October 1996, National Review of Live Art, Glasgow (UK).

Subsequent performances in: Bergen (Norway), Beirut (Lebanon), Buenos Aires (Argentina); Graz, Vienna (Austria); Antwerp, Brussels, Gent, Leuven (Belgium); Vancouver (Canada); Prague (Czech Republic); Cairo (Egypt); Dijon, Paris, Toulouse (France); Berlin, Bremen, Dresden, Essen, Frankfurt am Main, Hamburg, Hanover, Leipzig (DE); Athens (Greece); Dublin (Ireland); Bologna, Santarcangelo di Romagna (Italy); Nagoya, Tokyo (Japan); Riga (Latvia); Groningen, Rotterdam (Netherlands); Kraków, Lublin, Toruń, Tychy (Poland); Coimbra, Lisbon, Vila do Conde (Portugal); Moscow (Russia); Belgrade, Novi Sad, Pančevo (Serbia); Ljubljana (Slovenia); Yongin-si (South Korea); Madrid (Spain); Stockholm (Sweden); Basel, Nyon, Zurich (Switzerland); Aberystwyth, Bath, Brighton, Bristol, Cambridge, Coventry, Edinburgh, Lancaster, Leeds, London, Manchester, Middlesborough, Norwich, Nottingham, Sheffield (UK); Austin, Minneapolis, Portland (USA).

A team of actors in smeared clown makeup take turns choosing from a text of 2,000 questions, improvising answers and new questions. The shape and content of each *Quizoola!* performance hangs in the balance, negotiated live between players and the public. As new questions are chosen and new answers made up, the mood shifts between low comedy, personal scrutiny, hostile interrogation, and intellectual hairsplitting. The piece lasts six hours (twenty-four in some versions) and the public are free to arrive, depart, and return at any point.

Showtime, 1996

P: Robin Arthur, Richard Lowdon, Claire Marshall, Cathy Naden, Terry O'Connor. SP: Sue Marshall. D: Tim Etchells. T: Tim Etchells, Forced Entertainment. S: Richard Lowdon. L: Nigel Edwards. ST: John Avery. TC: Charles Poulet. PM: Johnny Goodwin.

Premiere: 25 September 1996, Alsager Arts Centre, Stoke-on-Trent (UK).

Subsequent performances in: Gent (Belgium); Helsinki (Finland); Cologne, Frankfurt am Main, Hanover, Munich, Munster, Potsdam (DE); Rotterdam (Netherlands); Kongsvinger (Norway); Bedford, Birmingham, Bristol, Cambridge, Cardiff, Edinburgh, Exeter, Lancaster, Leeds, London, Newcastle, Portsmouth, Sheffield, Southampton, Totnes, Wolverhampton (UK).

Narrated by a man with a fake dynamite bomb strapped to his chest, the piece begins with a naïve text describing what a good piece of theatre should be. From this amateurish advice about simple scenery, good casting, and dress rehearsals, *Showtime* soon decays into a chaos of cardboard pantomime trees, a dog that talks about suicide, and a series of insistent questions asked of a dying bank robber as he lies bleeding outside a brightly painted children's playhouse.

Pleasure, 1997

P: Robin Arthur, Richard Lowdon, Claire Marshall, Cathy Naden, Terry O'Connor. SP: Wendy Houstoun, Ursula Martinez. D/T: Tim Etchells. S: Richard Lowdon. L: Nigel Edwards. TC: Ray Rennie. ST: John Avery, found sources. PM: Andy Clarke.

Premiere: 2 November 1997, Nieuwpoorttheater, Gent (BE).

Subsequent performances in: Brussels (Belgium); Zagreb (Croatia); Berlin, Frankfurt am Main, Hanover, Marburg, Munster (DE); Bologna (Italy); Rotterdam (Netherlands); Bergen, Oslo (Norway); Gothenburg (Sweden); Basel (Switzerland); Alsager, Birmingham, Bristol, Cambridge, Cardiff, Glasgow, Lancaster, Leeds, London, Manchester, Newcastle, Oxford, Sheffield, Totnes, Wolverhampton (UK).

A strange nightclub in the early hours of the morning, complete with slowed down music from a battered record player. A place of surreal melancholy with bad cabaret dancers, a horny pantomime horse, a cynical disc jockey-MC, and failed William Tell routines. A catalogue of obscene words and phrases is scrawled on a blackboard at the back of the stage.

Dirty Work, 1998

P: Robin Arthur, Claire Marshall, Cathy Naden. D/T: Tim Etchells, Forced Entertainment. S: Richard Lowdon. L: Nigel Edwards. ST: John Avery, found sources. PM: Andy Clarke.

Premiere: 12 November 1998, Phoenix Arts, Leicester (UK).

Subsequent performances in: Vienna (Austria); Brussels (Belgium); Berlin, Frankfurt am Main, Hamburg (DE); Rotterdam (Netherlands); Bergen (Norway); Gwangju (South Korea); Zurich (Switzerland); Bristol, Cambridge, Cardiff, Coventry, Glasgow, Leeds, London, Manchester, Nottingham, Sheffield, Totnes (UK).

Set on a tiny wooden stage with ragged curtains, *Dirty Work* shows two performers who describe an impossible performance, whilst a third listens, occasionally playing music from a record player. The performance summoned in language is an unruly collage spectacle in which mechanical dogs, scenes from Shakespeare, great battles from world history, and the banalities of daily life sit side by side.

Who Can Sing a Song to Unfrighten Me?, 1999

(24–hour durational performance)

P: Robin Arthur, Tim Hall, Richard Lowdon, Claire Marshall, Sue Marshall, Cathy Naden, Terry O'Connor. Guests: Mark Etchells, Ruth Geiersberger, Thomas Peters, Gisela Jürcke, Tobias Lange, Roy Peters, Susanne Plassmann, Sanne van Rijn. D: Tim Etchells. S: Richard Lowdon. L: Nigel Edwards. TC: Ray Rennie. PM: Andy Clarke. CO: London International Festival of Theatre, London (UK), Royal Festival Hall, London (UK), SpielArt Festival, Munich (DE).

Premiere: 18 June 1999, LIFT/Queen Elizabeth Hall, London (UK).

Subsequent performances in: Vienna (Austria); Munich (DE); Rotterdam (Netherlands).

Stretching from midnight to midnight, the show takes the public and its fourteen performers on a long journey from night to day and back again. Within a set of framing rule-structures the piece makes an endless demand for improvisation, cycling and transforming a collection of scenes, performance tasks, and costumes. Dressed as kings, the performers tell stories without endings; dressed as skeletons, they speculate on their cause of death. There are lists of fears, language lessons, and alphabets chalked on a blackboard. There are disappearing routines, half-hearted dances, and cabaret demonstrations of the difference between life and death.

Disco Relax, 1999

P: Robin Arthur, Tim Hall, Richard Lowdon, Sue Marshall, Cathy Naden. D/T: Tim Etchells. S: Richard Lowdon. L: Nigel Edwards. ST: Tim Hall, found sources. TC: Ray Rennie. PM: Andy Clarke.

Premiere: 19 October 1999, Forced Entertainment Studio, Sheffield (UK).

Subsequent performances in: Bergen (Norway); Brighton, Cambridge, Cardiff, Coventry, Glasgow, Leeds, Lancaster, Leicester, Liverpool, Manchester, Southampton, Totnes, Wolverhampton (UK).

A surreal examination of Britain at the end of the 1990s, the piece centres on a fragmented, foul-mouthed, word-association-driven, disconnected dialogue between two women. Invoking the mood of a long night of drinking, the protagonists are joined by three men who function as much as scenery as they do as characters—a VJ/DJ, a guitar player/pub singer and a third man disguised with a plastic Halloween mask and labelled with a cardboard sign: DRUNKEN TWAT. Alongside the live action, scraps of video present fragmentary home movies, bedtime stories, and magic tricks.

Scar Stories, 2000

(Performance and installation)

—Performance version: P: Richard Lowdon, Terry O'Connor. D: Tim Etchells. C: Tim Etchells, Hugo Glendinning, Forced Entertainment. S: Richard Lowdon. L: Nigel Edwards. CO: KunstenfestivalDesArts, Brussels (BE).

Premiere: 16 May 2000, KunstenfestivalDesArts, Brussels (BE).

—Installation version: C: Tim Etchells, Hugo Glendinning, Forced Entertainment.

Premiere: 5 May 2000, KunstenfestivalDesArts, Brussels (BE).

Interviews conducted in Brussels, on the theme of scars as physical reminders with an emotional echo, provided the material for the beginnings of this theatre performance and installation project. In a steeply raked auditorium designed to reference a demonstration operating theatre, a man and a woman construct a catalogue of accidents, operations, fights, and mishaps as they describe the scars they have allegedly accrued. For the installation version, fragments of video interviews and images of scars are projected on the floor of a disused parking garage.

And on the Thousandth Night … , 2000

(6–hour durational performance)

OP: Robin Arthur, Tim Etchells, Jerry Killick, Richard Lowdon, Claire Marshall, Cathy Naden, Terry O'Connor. GP: Cathy Turner, Tamzin Griffin, Phil Hayes, Nicki Hobday, Tobias Lange, Bruno Roubicek, John Rowley, Ruth Ben-Tovim, Seke Chimutengwende, Bertrand Lesca. D: Tim Etchells. C: Forced Entertainment. L: Richard Lowdon.

Premiere: 3 September 2000, Festival Ayloul, Beirut (LB).

Subsequent performances in: Adelaide (Australia); Brussels, Leuven (Belgium); Montreal (Canada); Copenhagen (Denmark); Berlin, Essen, Frankfurt am Main, Hamburg, Hanover, Munich, Munster (DE); Riga (Latvia); Oslo (Norway); Lisbon (Portugal); Zurich (Switzerland); Brighton, Bristol, Glasgow, Leeds, London, Rishangles (UK); Chicago, Minneapolis, New York (USA).

Eight kings and queens in red robes and cardboard crowns line up along the edge of the stage to tell stories, in a structure first developed as part of *Who Can Sing a Song to Unfrighten Me?*. Each speaker's story can, at any time, be interrupted with the word 'Stop' and then a new narrative must begin. This simple rule creates a spontaneous, though complex performance with frequent changes in pace and tone. Moving from the extraordinary to the banal, it mixes everything from film plots, children's stories, traditional tales, jokes, and modern myths, to scary stories, love stories, and sex stories. As in other of the group's durational pieces viewers are free to enter, leave, and return as they please.

First Night, 2001

OP: Robin Arthur, Jerry Killick, Richard Lowdon, Claire Marshall, Cathy Naden, Terry O'Connor, John Rowley, K. Michael Weaver. SP: Tim Etchells, Richard Hawley, Tobias Lange, Ben Neale, Bruno Roubicek. D: Tim Etchells. T: Tim Etchells, Forced Entertainment. S: Richard Lowdon. L: Nigel Edwards. TC: Ray Rennie. PM: Andy Clarke. CP: Rotterdamse Schouwburg, Rotterdam (NL), SpielArt Festival, Munich (DE), Festival Theaterformen, Hanover (DE) and Wiener Festwochen, Vienna/Wien (AT).

Premiere: 15 September 2001, Rotterdamse Schouwburg, Rotterdam (NL).

Subsequent performances in: Adelaide (Australia); Vienna (Austria); Antwerp, Brussels, Gent (Belgium); Montreal (Canada); Aarhus (Denmark); Paris (France); Frankfurt am Main, Hanover, Munich (DE); Budapest (Hungary); Oslo (Norway); Lisbon (Portugal); Stockholm (Sweden); Brighton, Coventry, Lancaster, London, Manchester, Newcastle, Sheffield (UK); Chicago, Minneapolis (USA).

Eight performers with desperate fixed smiles introduce a troubled night of vaudeville routines. *First Night* begins with a grand welcome, but soon disintegrates into dark predictions of the future, psychotic escapology acts, playful attacks on the audience, unexpected dances and unhinged showbiz anecdotes.

The Travels, 2002

P: Jerry Killick, Richard Lowdon, Claire Marshall, Cathy Naden, Terry O'Connor, John Rowley. SP: K. Michael Weaver. D: Tim Etchells. T: Tim Etchells, Forced Entertainment. S: Richard Lowdon. L: Andy Clarke. TC: Ray Rennie. PM: Andy Clarke. CP: Künstlerhaus Mousonturm, Frankfurt am Main (DE).

Premiere: 27 September 2002, Künstlerhaus Mousonturm, Frankfurt am Main (DE).

Subsequent performances in: Aberystwyth, Brighton, Cardiff, Exeter, Lancaster, Leeds, London, Manchester, Nottingham, Sheffield, Wolverhampton (UK).

For one summer, the Forced Entertainment performers travelled through England separately: taking notes and photographs in a search for streets with intriguing literal names. Seated at a table, they relate the results in an intimate documentary essay-performance: Paradise Road is a Neighbourhood Watch Area; Effort and Recovery Streets are just behind a hospital. Fortune Street ends at a brick wall.

The Voices, 2003

—Berlin version: P: Robin Arthur, Sonia Augurt, Katie Ewald, Jerry Killick, Tobias Lange, Richard Lowdon, Claire Marshall, Ben Neale, Terry O'Connor, John Rowley, Tory Vazquez. SP: Bert Neumann. D/T: Tim Etchells. L: Nigel Edwards. CP: Volksbühne Berlin (DE),Warwick Arts Centre (UK), Sheffield Theatres (UK), Tramway Glasgow (UK).

Premiere: 24 January 2003, Prater der Volksbühne am Rosa-Luxemburg-Platz, Berlin (DE).

—Full version: P: Robin Arthur, Katie Ewald, Davis Freeman, Richard Hawley, Wendy Houstoun, Jerry Killick, Richard Lowdon, Claire Marshall, Cathy Naden, Terry O'Connor, Bruno Roubicek, John Rowley, Tory Vazquez. GP: Helen Gould, Mary Agnes Krell, Tobias Lange. Local performers: Paul Allender, Kiya Bale, Ewan Cameron, Julie Carson, Luke Cavanagh, Nicholas Cooke, Deborah Davies, Simon Day, Catherine Gooing, Tania Guerreiro, John O'Hanlon, Peter Kennedy, Kate Kordel, Alan Lane, John Macaulay, Katie Mara, Newrouz Mawlood, Sue Morton, Ben Neale, Susanne Palzer, Sabreen Pervaiz, Patricia Preston, Eleanor Rogers, Catherine Stirrat, Jon Tipton, Carol Turner, J. Simon van der Walt, Alison Ward, Martin Ware. D/T: Tim Etchells. S: Richard Lowdon. L: Nigel Edwards. CP: Volksbühne Berlin (DE),Warwick Arts Centre (UK), Sheffield Theatres (UK), Tramway, Glasgow (UK).

Premiere: 5 March 2003, Warwick Arts Centre, Warwick (UK).

Subsequent performances in: Glasgow, London, Sheffield (UK).

In the Berlin version—a prototype of *The Voices*—eight performers are seated on the bare steps behind the lighting desk in Volksbühne's Prater, whilst the audience are seated in Bert Neumann's living-room stage design. One by one, the actors come to stand on a chair in the centre of the floor area and, on this provisional stage, perform a monologue concerning personal aspirations for the future. Etchells' stream of consciousness texts—depicting fantasies of perfect death, great wealth and success, love, and disappearance—are banal at times, inventive and spectacular at others. A fully developed version of *The Voices* was performed by Forced Entertainment and guests alongside a group of amateur performers recruited through workshops in each of the UK cities that played host to the project.

Marathon Lexicon, 2003

(12–hour performance-lecture)

P: Robin Arthur, Jerry Killick, Claire Marshall, Terry O'Connor. SP: Richard Lowdon. Curated by: Tim Etchells, Adrian Heathfield. T: Sara Jane Bailes, Simon Bayly, Steven Connor, Franko B, Hugo Glendinning, Matthew Goulish, Rinne Groff, Ant Hampton, Lin Hixson, Vlatka Horvat, Joe Kelleher, Jeremy Killick, Thomas Lehman, Andre Lepecki, Deborah Levy, Kate McIntosh, Peggy Phelan, Andrew Quick, Alan Read, Nick Ridout, Oscar Sahlieh, Elyce Semenec, Grant Smith, Willy Thomas, Allen Weiss, Lisa Wesley, David Williams. CO: Künstlerhaus Mousonturm, Frankfurt am Main (DE).

Premiere: 29 November 2003, Künstlerhaus Mousonturm, Frankfurt am Main (DE).

Subsequent performances in: Brussels (Belgium); Berlin, Hamburg (DE); London (UK).

From 'audience', 'breath', 'blood', and 'charisma', though 'crying', 'laughter', and 'silence' to 'spirits', and 'voyeurism'. Videos, imagery, and text by contemporary thinkers, academics, and artists form an impossible lecture, a performance lexicon, read and viewed live. The audience can arrive, depart, and return whenever they please.

Bloody Mess, 2004

P: Robin Arthur, Davis Freeman, Wendy Houstoun, Jerry Killick, Richard Lowdon, Claire Marshall, Cathy Naden, Terry O'Connor, Bruno Roubicek, John Rowley. SP: Simone Aughterlony, Nick Chambers, Amit Hadari, Tobias Lange, Ben Neale, Sean Patten. D: Tim Etchells. T: Tim Etchells, Forced Entertainment. S: Richard Lowdon. L: Nigel Edwards. TC: Jim Harrison, Crispin Hayek, Francis Stevenson. PM: Ray Rennie. CP: Festival Theaterformen

Hanover (DE), KunstenfestivalDesArts Brussels (BE), Rotterdamse Schouwburg (NL), Les Spectacles Vivants/Centre Pompidou Paris (FR), SpielArt Festival Munich (DE), Wiener Festwochen, Vienna (AT).

Premiere: 1 November 2003, SpielArt Festival, Munich (DE).

Subsequent performances in: Melbourne (Australia); Vienna (Austria); Brussels, Leuven (Belgium); Rio de Janeiro (Brazil); Bogotá (Colombia); Nantes, Paris, Strasbourg, Toulouse (France); Berlin, Essen, Frankfurt am Main, Hamburg, Hanover (DE); Budapest (Hungary); Dublin (Ireland); Rotterdam (Netherlands); Oslo, Trondheim (Norway); Barcelona (Spain); Zurich (Switzerland); Aberystwyth, Brighton, Coventry, Glasgow, Lancaster, Leeds, London, Manchester, Sheffield (UK);
Los Angeles, Seattle (USA).

From the outset—at which each actor confides in the audience about how he or she would like to be seen during the show—trouble seems inevitable; rivalries, contradictions, and incompatibility seem to rule the day. *Bloody Mess* is highly structured, energetic chaos. A cheerleader dances while another performer weeps and wails in operatic grief. A woman in a gorilla suit throws popcorn at anything that moves. Rock-gig roadies creep across the stage—bringing disco lights, new speakers, and a microphone that no one really wants.

Exquisite Pain, 2005

P: Robin Arthur, Jerry Killick, Richard Lowdon, Claire Marshall, Cathy Naden, Terry O'Connor. D: Tim Etchells. T: Sophie Calle. S: Richard Lowdon. L: Nigel Edwards. TC: Ray Rennie. CP: Theater der Welt, Stuttgart (DE), BIT Teatergarasjen, Bergen (NO), The National Museum of Art, Design and Architecture, Oslo (NO), Kaaitheater, Brussels (BE), La Filature—Scène Nationale, Mulhouse (FR), Tanzquartier, Wien (AT).

Premiere: 8 July 2005, Staatstheater Stuttgart, Stuttgart (DE).

Subsequent performances in: Vienna (Austria); Brussels, Leuven (Belgium); Rio de Janeiro (Brazil); Vancouver (Canada); Aarhus (Denmark); Mulhouse, Paris (France); Berlin, Essen, Frankfurt am Main (DE); Milan, Santarcangelo di Romagna (Italy); Dublin (Ireland); Riga (Latvia); Oslo (Norway); Warsaw (Poland); Lisbon (Portugal); Singapore (Singapore); Uppsala (Sweden); Bristol, Cambridge, Canterbury, Cardiff, Coventry, Eastleigh, Lancaster, Leeds, London, Manchester, Newcastle (UK).

Based on a project by the renowned French conceptual artist Sophie Calle, *Exquisite Pain* marks the first time that Forced Entertainment based a work on a text from outside the group. A simple and intimate performance constructed around an exchange of stories, exploring how language, memory, and forgetting move to contain, preserve, or erase events; how people come to terms with trauma.

The World in Pictures, 2006

P: Robin Arthur, Davis Freeman, Wendy Houstoun, Jerry Killick, Richard Lowdon, Claire Marshall, Terry O'Connor, Bruno Roubicek. D: Tim Etchells. T: Tim Etchells, Forced Entertainment. S: Richard Lowdon. L: Nigel Edwards. ST: Found sources. TC: Francis Stevenson. PM: Ray Rennie. CP: Volksbühne am Rosa-Luxemburg-Platz, Berlin (DE), Wiener Festwochen, Vienna (AT), Les Spectacles Vivants – Centre Pompidou, Paris (FR), Productiehuis Rotterdam, Rotterdam (NL), Rotterdamse Schouwburg, Rotterdam (NL), Kunstencentrum Vooruit, Gent (BE), Nuffield Theatre, Lancaster (UK), Tramway, Glasgow (UK), Warwick Arts Centre, Coventry (UK).

Premiere: 25 May 2006, Volksbühne, Berlin (DE).

Subsequent performances in: Vienna (Austria); Brussels, Gent, Leuven (Belgium); Copenhagen (Denmark); Strasbourg (France); Berlin, Frankfurt am Main (DE); Dublin (Ireland); Amsterdam, Groningen, Rotterdam, Utrecht (Netherlands); Lisbon (Portugal); Coventry, Glasgow, Lancaster, London, Manchester, Newcastle, Sheffield (UK).

Complete with cavemen in bad wigs referencing a scene from the 1960s movie *One Million Years BC*, *The World in Pictures* is a visually chaotic, poetic, comical, and sometimes poignant trip through the 'story of mankind', full of lewd diversions and noisy digressions.

Spectacular, 2008

P: Robin Arthur, Claire Marshall. D: Tim Etchells. S: Richard Lowdon. L: Nigel Edwards. TC: Francis Stevenson, Elb Hall. PM: Ray Rennie. CP: BIT Teatergarasjen, Bergen (NO), Hebbel am Ufer, Berlin (DE), PACT Zollverein, Essen (DE), Les Spectacles Vivants – Centre Pompidou, Paris (FR), Theatre Garonne, Toulouse (FR), Tramway, Glasgow (UK).

Premiere: 15 May 2008, PACT Zollverein, Essen (DE).

Subsequent performances in: Melbourne (Australia); Brussels (Belgium); Zagreb (Croatia); Aarhus (Denmark); Paris, Toulouse (France); Berlin, Bremen, Dresden, Essen, Frankfurt am Main, Munich (DE); Modena (Italy); Porto (Portugal); Seoul (South Korea); Barcelona, Murcia (Spain); Geneva, Lugano, Zurich (Switzerland); Bristol, Coventry, Lancaster, London, Manchester, Oxford, Sheffield, Taunton (UK); Austin (USA).

Two performers onstage; one dead (skeleton), the other dying (rolling and yelling on the floor). *Spectacular* is about the now of the performance moment, the trembling edge of laughter, possibility, and invention. It's about death and playing dead, about the strange contact between two performers onstage and an audience caught between what they are watching and what they're being told.

Void Story, 2009

P: Robin Arthur, Richard Lowdon, Cathy Naden, Terry O'Connor. D/T/Images: Tim Etchells. S: Richard Lowdon. L: Nigel Edwards. ST: John Avery. Production: Ray Rennie, Elb Hall. Performers in Photo-Collages: Rajni Shah, Chris Williams, Kaya Freeman, Nigel Edwards, Jim Fletcher, Bob Clarke, Will Waghorn, Vlatka Horvat. Additional Photoshop Assistance: Stephanie Wong, Graeme Stonehouse. CO: SPILL 09, Ipswich (UK) with support from Tanzquartier, Vienna (AT), and Tate Media (UK).

Premiere: 17 January 2009, Tanzquartier Wien, Vienna (AT).

Subsequent performances in: Buenos Aires (Argentina); Graz (Austria); Gent (Belgium); Sofia, Varna (Bulgaria); Helsinki (Finland); Paris, Saint-Étienne (France); Berlin, Bremen, Mainz, Munich (DE); Athens (Greece); Turin (Italy); Dublin (Ireland); Amsterdam (Netherlands); Bergen, Oslo, Trondheim (Norway); Lisbon (Portugal); Nitra (Slovakia); Fribourg (Switzerland); Aberystwyth, Bristol, Cambridge, Coventry, Glasgow, Huddersfield, Liverpool, London, Manchester, Nottingham, Sheffield, Suffolk (UK).

A bleak and comical contemporary fable performed as if it were a radio play, the performers sitting at tables, 'doing' the requisite voices, and adding in sound effects for gunshots, rain, and bad phone lines. Meanwhile the stage is dominated by a series of projected images, a storyboard, graphic novel, or movie-version of Tim Etchells' unsettling text. Somewhere in the space between the live dialogue, the digital sound effects, and the collaged images is where *Void Story* actually takes place.

The Thrill of It All, 2010

P: Thomas Conway, Amit Hadari, Phil Hayes, Jerry Killick, Richard Lowdon, Claire Marshall, Cathy Naden, Terry O'Connor, John Rowley. D: Tim Etchells. Director's Assistant: Hester Chillingworth. S: Richard Lowdon. L: Nigel Edwards. ST: John Avery. Choreographic Advice: Kate McIntosh. Production: Ray Rennie, Francis Stevenson. CO: Kunstenfestivaldesarts, Brussels (BE), Hebbel am Ufer, Berlin (DE), PACT Zollverein, Essen (DE), Les Spectacles vivants – Centre Pompidou in collaboration with Festival d'Automne, Paris and Theatre Garonne, Toulouse (FR).

Premiere: 7 May 2010, Kunstenfestivaldesarts, Kaaitheater, Brussels (BE).

Subsequent performances in: Vienna (Austria); Paris, Toulouse (France); Berlin, Essen, Frankfurt am Main (DE); Rotterdam (Netherlands); Kraków (Poland); Timișoara (Romania); Ljubljana (Slovenia); Salamanca (Spain); Zurich (Switzerland); Coventry, Lancaster, London, Manchester, Sheffield (UK).

White floor, white suits and sequins, fake palms, and protracted introductions to songs that never happen, energetic dances that turn into fights, fights that turn into dances. Part stand-up's nightmare, part lush cabaret to Japanese lounge music, *The Thrill of It All* is somewhat a sister to 2001's *First Night*, pitting performers against each other and against the audience.

Tomorrow's Parties, 2011

P: Two performers drawn from the core team of Robin Arthur, Richard Lowdon, Claire Marshall, Cathy Naden, and Terry O'Connor. SP: Gareth Brierley, Jerry Killick. D: Tim Etchells. S: Richard Lowdon. L: Francis Stevenson. Production: Ray Rennie, Francis Stevenson, Jim Harrison. CO: Belluard Bollwerk International, Fribourg (CH). CP: BIT Teatergarasjen, Bergen (NO), Internationale Sommerfestival, Hamburg (DE), Kaaitheater, Brussels (BE), Künstlerhaus Mousonturm, Frankfurt am Main (DE), Theaterhaus Gessnerallee, Zurich (CH) and Sheffield City Council (UK).

Premiere: 24 June 2011, Belluard Bollwerk International Festival, Fribourg (CH).

Subsequent performances in: Sydney (Australia); Linz, Vienna (Austria); Antwerp, Brussels, Gent (Belgium); Sarajevo (Bosnia and Herzegovina); Aarhus, Allerød, Copenhagen (Denmark); Helsinki (Finland); Avignon, Montpellier (France); Berlin, Cologne, Dresden, Essen, Frankfurt am Main, Hamburg, Leipzig, Munich, Munster (DE); Athens (Greece); Budapest (Hungary); Dublin (Ireland); Amsterdam (Netherlands); Bergen (Norway); Poznań (Poland); Lisbon (Portugal); Moscow, Omsk (Russia); Nitra (Slovakia); Ljubljana (Slovenia); Madrid (Spain); Gothenburg (Sweden); Zurich (Switzerland); Aberystwyth, Brighton, Bristol, Cambridge, Coventry, Edinburgh, Exeter, Falmouth, Folkestone, Glasgow, Jersey, Lancaster, London, Manchester, Sheffield (UK); New York, Ohio, Seattle (USA).

On a makeshift fairground stage draped with coloured lights, two performers speculate about what tomorrow might bring, from utopian and dystopian visions, to science-fiction scenarios, political nightmares, and absurd fantasies. Collaborating, competing, exaggerating, and contradicting each other the performers create a work that is as much about the past and the present as it is about the future.

The Coming Storm, 2012

P: Robin Arthur, Phil Hayes, Richard Lowdon, Claire Marshall, Cathy Naden, Terry O'Connor. D: Tim Etchells. Director's Assistant: Hester Chillingworth. S: Richard Lowdon. L: Nigel Edwards. ST: Phil Hayes / Forced Entertainment. Music Consultant: John Avery. Production: Ray Rennie, Francis Stevenson, Jim Harrison. CP: PACT Zollverein, Essen (DE), Festival d'Avignon, Avignon (FR), Theaterhaus Gessneralle, Zurich (CH), Tanzquartier, Vienna (AT), Les Spectacles Vivants – Centre Pompidou, Paris (FR), Festival d'Automne à Paris, Paris (FR), LIFT, London (UK), Battersea Arts Centre, London (UK) and Sheffield City Council (UK).

Premiere: 23 May 2012, PACT Zollverein, Essen (DE).

Subsequent performances in: Vienna (Austria); Zagreb (Croatia); Avignon, Paris (France); Berlin, Hanover (DE); Dublin (Ireland); Tokyo (Japan); Amsterdam, Breda (Netherlands); Oslo (Norway); Lisbon (Portugal); Zurich (Switzerland); Aberystwyth, Coventry, Glasgow, Huddersfield, Ipswich, Lancaster, London, Manchester, Sheffield (UK).

Comical, contradictory and poignant; full of wrong-headed tricks, broken dances, drum interruptions, and perfunctory piano accompaniment. Everything builds and everything shimmers. Everything teeters and everything trembles. Everything is reshaped and everything is cannibalized. *The Coming Storm* is Forced Entertainment trademark black humour, a collage of arresting images, and an anarchic performance style.

The Last Adventures, 2013

P: Robin Arthur, Richard Lowdon, Claire Marshall, Cathy Naden, Terry O'Connor. Live Guest Musicians: Uriel Barthélémi, Mazen Kerbaj, KK Null. GP: Gareth Brierley, Mark Etchells, Nada Gambier, Phil Hayes, Nicki Hobday, Maria Jerez, Leja Jurisic, Reena Kalsi, Kuselo Kamau, Thomas Kasebacher, Nina Eva Lampic, Teja Reba, Bruno Roubicek, John Rowley, Kylie Walters, Floor Van Leeuwen. D: Tim Etchells. C: Forced Entertainment, Tarek Atoui. T: Tim Etchells. S: Richard Lowdon. L: Nigel Edwards. ST: Tarek Atoui. Sound: Daniel Teusner. Production: Jim Harrison. Dramaturgical Advice: Adrian Heathfield. Choreographic Advice: Kate McIntosh. CO: Ruhrtriennale Festival of the Arts, Ruhr (DE). CP: Fierce Festival, Birmingham (UK), Künstlerhaus Mousonturm, Frankfurt am Main (DE), Tanzquartier, Wien (AT), Warwick Arts Centre, Coventry (UK).

Premiere: 5 September 2013, Ruhrtriennale Festival of the Arts, Ruhr (DE).

Subsequent performances in: Vienna (Austria); Frankfurt am Main (DE); Gwangju (South Korea); Zurich (Switzerland); Birmingham, Coventry (UK).

In *The Last Adventures* Forced Entertainment collaborate with Lebanese sound artist Tarek Atoui to create a compelling epic performance. Sounds swarm and storm in the air as performers in homemade costumes create a pageant of giant sea monsters, ghosts, fighting kings, marching robots, and dancing trees. With recorded soundtrack combining electronics from Atoui and live instrumentation from a different special guest musician in each location, *The Last Adventures* mixes fairy tales, science-fiction, children's picture books, and epic myths.

The Notebook, 2014

P: Robin Arthur, Richard Lowdon. SP: Tim Etchells. D: Tim Etchells. S: Richard Lowdon. L: Jim Harrison. TC: Doug Currie, Alex Fernandes. Production: Jim Harrison. CO: PACT Zollverein, Essen (DE), LIFT, London (UK), 14–18 NOW, WW1 Centenary Art Commissions. A House on Fire co-commission with HAU, Berlin (DE), Kaaitheater, Brussels (BE), Teatro Maria Matos, Lisbon (PT), LIFT, London (UK) and Malta Festival, Poznan (PL) with the support of the Culture Programme of the European Union. Development work generously supported by Lancaster Institute of Contemporary Arts (LICA). *The Notebook* is based on *Le grand cahier* by Agota Kristof (Paris: Éditions du Seuil, 1986). English translation © 1988 by Alan Sheridan.

Premiere: 9 May 2014, PACT Zollverein, Essen (DE).

Subsequent performances in: Vienna (Austria); Brussels (Belgium); Prague (Czech Republic); Aarhus (Denmark); Paris (France); Berlin (DE); Athens (Greece); Riga (Latvia); Amsterdam (Netherlands); Oslo (Norway); Poznań (Poland); Lisbon (Portugal); Stockholm (Sweden); Zurich (Switzerland); Bristol, Cambridge, Coventry, Edinburgh, Huddersfield, Lancaster, London, Manchester, Plymouth, Sheffield, Suffolk (UK); Chicago (USA).

Based on the novel by Agota Kristof and set during the Second World War, *The Notebook* tells the story of a pair of twin brothers evacuated to their impoverished grandmother's farm in order to shelter from the conflict. Simple staging, virtuoso unison text, and complex ideas. The unnamed protagonists are social outsiders, mavericks who survive and understand the world by a harsh private code. As the war deepens the brothers are slowly revealed as struggling moralists, trying to live by consistent principles in a Central Europe crumbling into cruelty and opportunism.

The Possible Impossible House, 2014

P: Two performers drawn from the core team of Robin Arthur, Richard Lowdon, Claire Marshall, Cathy Naden, and Terry O'Connor. D: Tim Etchells. C: Forced Entertainment in collaboration with Vlatka Horvat. Projections: Vlatka Horvat, Tim Etchells. S: Richard Lowdon. L: Nigel Edwards. TC: Anna Barrett. Production: Jim Harrison. CO: Barbican, London (UK), Theater An Der Parkaue, Berlin (DE).

Premiere: 17 December 2014, Barbican Centre, London (UK).

Subsequent performances in: Bristol, Liverpool, Manchester (UK).

The project was redirected with French–, German– and Swedish–speaking performers as commissions for different language versions.

—French–language version: P: Alain Borek, Judith Goudal. D: Tim Etchells, Terry O'Connor, Pascale Petralia. CO/CP: Vidy Theatre, Lausanne (Switzerland). Performances in: Liège (Belgium); Arles, Aubervilliers, Balnquefort, Belfort, Chambéry, Choisy-le-Roi, Lorient, Lyon, Martigues, Meylan, Montbéliard, Nanterre, Rennes, Tarbes, Tours, Valenciennes, Villefranche (France); Annecy, Geneva, Lausanne, Neuchâtel (Switzerland).

—German–language version: P: Caroline Erdmann, Elisabeth Heckel, Johannes Hendrik Langer. D: Robin Arthur, Tim Etchells. CO/CP: Theater An Der Parkaue, Berlin (DE).

—Swedish–language version: P: Ana Stanisic, Linn Bjørnvik Grøder. D: Tim Etchells, Per Hanæus, Terry O'Connor, Pascale Petralia. CO/CP: Riksteatern, Stockholm (SWE). Performances in: Hallunda, Lycksele, Malå, Norrtälje, Råby, Robertsfors, Skellefteå, Stensele, Stockholm, Sundsvall, Täby, Tärnaby, Västerås (Sweden).

Combining lo-fi digital magic and live sound effects, *The Possible Impossible House* is the first work by Forced Entertainment created for young people. For this project, a kind of cross between *Spectacular* and *Void Story* for young ages, they collaborate with artist Vlatka Horvat whose handmade collages help summon the house and the figures waiting inside.

Complete Works: Table Top Shakespeare, 2015

P: Robin Arthur, Nicki Hobday, Jerry Killick, Richard Lowdon, Claire Marshall, Cathy Naden and Terry O'Connor. D: Tim Etchells. T: Robin Arthur, Tim Etchells, Jerry Killick, Richard Lowdon, Claire Marshall, Cathy Naden, Terry O'Connor. S: Richard Lowdon. Sound & Lighting Design: Jim Harrison. Production Management: Jim Harrison. CP: Berliner Festspiele – Foreign Affairs Festival, Berlin (DE), Theaterfestival Basel (CH).

Premiere: 25 June 2015, Berliner Festspiele, Berlin (DE).

Subsequent performances in: Brussels, Gent (Belgium); Tallinn (Estonia); Paris (France); Frankfurt am Main, Hanover (DE); Athens (Greece); Rome (Italy); Amsterdam (Netherlands); Bergen, Trondheim (Norway); Gdańsk (Poland); Barcelona (Spain); Basel (Switzerland); Ipswich, London (UK); Chicago, Los Angeles, New York (USA).

In *Complete Works* six performers create condensed versions of all of Shakespeare's plays, comically and intimately retelling them, using a collection of everyday objects as stand-ins for the characters on the stage of an ordinary tabletop. What follows is simple and idiosyncratic, absurd and strangely compelling as, through a kind of lo-fi, home-made puppetry, the stories come to life in vivid miniature.

Real Magic, 2016

P: Jerry Killick, Richard Lowdon and Claire Marshall. Created with input from: Robin Arthur and Cathy Naden. D: Tim Etchells. L: Jim Harrison. S: Richard Lowdon. Production Management: Jim Harrison. Sound Technicians: Greg Akenhurst, Doug Currie, Alex Fernandes. Project Assistant: Anna Krauss. Music Electronics & Sound Editing: John Avery. Loops: Tim Etchells. 'Grave' from Telemann Fantasia Number 1 in B-Flat Major: Aisha Orazbayeva. CP: PACT Zollverein, Essen (DE), HAU Hebbel Am Ufer, Berlin (DE), Künsterlhaus Moustonturm, Frankfurt am Main (DE), Tanzquartier Wien, Vienna (AT), ACCA Attenborough Centre for the Creative Arts, University of Sussex (UK), the Spalding Gray Consortium—On the Boards Seattle (USA), PS122 NYC (USA), Walker Art Center Minneapolis (USA), Warhol Museum Pittsburgh (USA).

Premiere: 4 May 2016, PACT Zollverein, Essen (DE).

Subsequent performances in: Vienna (Austria); Brussels, Gent (Belgium); Montpellier, Paris (France); Berlin, Frankfurt am Main, Hamburg (DE); Amsterdam (Netherlands); Lublin (Poland); Lisbon (Portugal); Zurich (Switzerland); Birmingham, Brighton, Bristol, Cambridge, Edinburgh, London, Manchester, Norwich (UK); Minneapolis, Ohio, Pittsburgh, Seattle (USA).

To the sound of looped applause and canned laughter, three performers attempt an impossible illusion—part mind-reading feat, part cabaret act, part chaotic game show—in which they endlessly revisit moments of defeat, hope, and anticipation.

Dirty Work (The Late Shift), 2017

P: Robin Arthur, Cathy Naden, Terry O'Connor. Devised by: Robin Arthur, Richard Lowdon, Claire Marshall, Cathy Naden and Terry O'Connor. D: Tim Etchells. T: Tim Etchells with Robin Arthur and Cathy Naden. L: Nigel Edwards. S: Richard Lowdon. PM: Jim Harrison. CP: PACT Zollverein, Essen (DE), HAU Hebbel Am Ufer, Berlin (DE).

Premiere: 28 April 2017, PACT Zollverein, Essen (DE).

Subsequent performances in: Berlin (DE); London, Sheffield (UK).

Returning to their 1998 performance *Dirty Work, Dirty Work (The Late Shift)* extends the same simple but immensely generative form of described theatrical events. The piece celebrates the power of language to make things happen, co-opting the imaginative capacities of the audience to fill the stage with a delirium of images and scenes, in bewildering and unnerving succession.

Out of Order, 2018

P: Robin Arthur, Nicki Hobday, Jerry Killick, Richard Lowdon, Cathy Naden, Terry O'Connor. Created with input from: Claire Marshall and Hester Chillingworth. D: Tim Etchells. L: Nigel Edwards. S: Richard Lowdon. Sound Technician: Alex Fernandes. PM: Jim Harrison. CP: Künstlerhaus Moustonturm supported within the framework of the Alliance of International Production Houses by the Federal Government Commissioner for Culture and the Media of Germany and Schauspiel Frankfurt am Main (DE), PACT Zollverein, Essen (DE), HAU Hebbel Am Ufer, Berlin (DE), Gessnerallee, Zurich (CH).

Premiere: 27 April 2018, Bockenheimer Depot, Frankfurt am Main (DE).

Subsequent performances in: Salzburg (Austria); Brussels (Belgium); Paris (France); Berlin, Essen, Frankfurt am Main, Hanover (DE); Zurich (Switzerland); Brighton, London, Manchester (UK).

On a bare stage under bright light a troupe of hapless clowns do their un-level best to get along and pass the time. Rehearsing old gags, getting tangled in new ones, forgetting that anything happened, and then remembering and forgetting again. Carefully unbalanced between funny and not funny *Out of Order* is the ruins of a show in the ruins of a world.

To Move in Time, 2019

P: Tyrone Huggins. D/T: Tim Etchells. AD: Hester Chillingworth. L: Jim Harrison. PM: Jim Harrison. CP: The Yard Theatre, London (UK). Supported by Lincoln Performing Arts Centre (UK). *To Move in Time* is a Tim Etchells and Forced Entertainment production, in collaboration with Tyrone Huggins.

Premiere: 6 February 2019, Lincoln Performing Arts Centre, Lincoln (UK).

Subsequent performances in: Rio de Janeiro (Brazil); Birmingham, Bristol, Cambridge, Cardiff, Edinburgh, Lancaster, London, Sheffield (UK).

In a text written by Tim Etchells for performer and collaborator Tyrone Huggins, an unnamed protagonist speculates playfully about what he'd do if he were able to travel backwards and forwards in time, walking a line between comic absurdity and melancholia.

Red Room, 1993

(Performance installation)

P: Will Waghorn. C: Forced Entertainment, Hugo Glendinning,
Will Waghorn. CO: ICA Live Arts/Showroom Gallery, London (UK).

First presentation: 30 November 1993, Showroom Gallery, London (UK).

Visitors equipped with torches explore a dark room and its contents in
detective style. Photographs show the performers in fragmented scenes
set in urban spaces—telephone booths, stairwells, and the backseat of a
car. Entering the second room of the gallery visitors find performer Will
Waghorn, who is constantly processing new photographic prints and
generating new texts to accompany the images.

Ground Plans for Paradise, 1994

(Installation with occasional performance)

P: Robin Arthur, Richard Lowdon, Claire Marshall, Cathy Naden,
Terry O'Connor. C: Hugo Glendinning, Forced Entertainment.
Assistant: Emma Leslie. CO: Leeds Metropolitan University.

First presentation: 15 March 1994, Leeds Metropolitan University
Gallery & Studio Theatre, Leeds (UK).

Subsequent presentations in: Berlin, Frankfurt am Main (DE);
Gent (Belgium); Sheffield (UK).

The architectural models, street names, photographs, and occasional
performances of this multimedia installation conjure up images and
hidden narratives contained in a vast city. Innumerable models of
high-rise buildings, each of them named and illuminated from within,
create a desolate atmosphere. The performers sit at a chalk-covered
table. Blindfolded, they draw streets in the dust, creating new paths
through the city.

Hotel Binary, 2000

(Five-channel video installation)

P: Robin Arthur, Richard Lowdon, Claire Marshall, Cathy Naden, Terry
O'Connor. C: Tim Etchells, Hugo Glendinning, Forced Entertainment.

First presentation: 28 March 2000, Site Gallery, Sheffield (UK).

Five projections. In one, people sat in hotel lobbies and airport lounges
speak lists of their fears. The other four projections show slowed down
glimpses of bodies, landscapes, and locations—a dual carriageway by
night, two people sleeping together, a hotel carpet. This series of out-
takes forms a glancing relationship with the spoken lists of fears, at
times confirming their contents and at other times undermining them.

3. DIGITAL AND ONLINE

Frozen Palaces, 1997

(CD-ROM)

P: Robin Arthur, Tim Etchells, Richard Lowdon, Claire Marshall,
Cathy Naden, Terry O'Connor. Guests: Nicky Childs, Mark Etchells,
Tim Hall, Cathy Phillips, Justin Westover, James White, Tony White.
C: Tim Etchells, Hugo Glendinning, Forced Entertainment. ST: John
Avery. Digital Author: Mary Agnes Krell.

Published in ArtIntact 5, Zentrum für Kunst und Medientechnologie
(ZKM), Karlsruhe (DE).

A large house with one scene set in each room. The viewer navigates
the photographed spaces which contain diverse events—love scenes,
murders, and parties. The inhabitants of this space are frozen in time,
suspended in banal or significant moments, while the viewer alone
has the option of wandering through the house, forming their own
connections between the scenes.

Paradise, 1998

(Online project)

C: Tim Etchells, Forced Entertainment. Digital Author: Mary Agnes
Krell. CO: Lovebytes as part of the Channel Metropolis series, funded
by Arts Council England.

23 April 1998.

The interactive project Paradise was developed from the installation
Ground Plans for Paradise. An online city, consisting of 1,000 buildings,
accessible through maps and a street index. Each visitor has the
opportunity to add narratives and characters to the buildings and to
read entries by other users.

Nightwalks, 1998

(CD-ROM)

P: Robin Arthur, Tim Etchells, Richard Lowdon, Claire Marshall,
Cathy Naden, Terry O'Connor. T: Tim Etchells. C: Tim Etchells,
Hugo Glendinning, Forced Entertainment. ST: John Avery.
Digital Author: Mary Agnes Krell.

2 October 1998, Site Gallery, Sheffield (UK).

Panoramic photographs of frozen nocturnal scenes create a landscape
which lies somewhere between urban England and a fictitious film
set. The viewer is free to explore, exiting the scenes through links
embedded in key objects, inventing their own subjective narrative
along the way. The work creates a poetic landscape, in which
geographical logic does not apply.

Spin, 1999

(CD-ROM)

P: Robin Arthur, Richard Lowdon, Claire Marshall, Cathy Naden,
Terry O'Connor. Guests: Martin Bailey, Neil Bennett, Huw Chadbourn,
Andy Clarke, Peter Flannery, Tim Hall, Jenson Grant, Michelle McGuire.
C: Tim Etchells, Hugo Glendinning, Forced Entertainment.
Digital Author: Mary Agnes Krell. ST: John Avery.

2 February 1999, Sleuth/Barbican, London (UK).

The interactive CD-ROM shows the frozen end scene of a fictitious
film. At a scrap metal yard in the middle of the night, a man is dying
from gunshot wounds, surrounded by his killers. The viewer is free to
examine this moment endlessly, unable to prevent the unfolding events.
A playful investigation about the subjective construction of narratives
in film as well as in real life.

End Meeting for All, 2020

(Online project)

P: Robin Arthur, Tim Etchells, Richard Lowdon, Claire Marshall,
Cathy Naden, Terry O'Connor. D: Tim Etchells. Zoom advice and screen
recording: Jason Crouch. Post-production video: Hugo Glendinning.
Post-production sound: John Avery. 'Sarabande' from J.S. Bach B Minor
Partita Number 2 for Violin Solo: Aisha Orazbayeva. 'Slowly Growing
Old', from the album Farewell Sorrow: Alasdair Roberts. CP: HAU Hebbel

am Ufer, Berlin (DE), Künstlerhaus Mousonturm, Frankfurt am Main (DE), PACT Zollverein, Essen (DE). Supported within the framework of International Production Houses by the Federal Government Commissioner for Culture and the Media.

Created in April 2020 during Covid-19 lockdown, Forced Entertainment's *End Meeting for All* is a fragmentary online work in three short episodes. Each is recorded in a single live take across six screens of a Zoom meeting with performers improvising and interacting from distant locations in Sheffield, London, and Berlin. Sometimes poignant and often ridiculous, troubled and strangely hallucinatory, *End Meeting for All* summons a world in which the lockdown appears to have been going on for a very long time.

Complete Works: Table Top Shakespeare: At Home, 2020

(Online project)

P: Robin Arthur, Jerry Killick, Richard Lowdon, Claire Marshall, Cathy Naden, Terry O'Connor. D: Tim Etchells. T: Robin Arthur, Tim Etchells, Jerry Killick, Richard Lowdon, Claire Marshall, Cathy Naden, Terry O'Connor. Digital PM: Jim Harrison. CP: Kanuti Gildi SAAL; KunstFestSpiele Herrenhausen; Künstlerhaus Mousonturm; The Mondavi Center, UC Davis; PACT Zollverein; Romaeuropa Festival; Shakespeare Festival Neuss; Stanford Live at Stanford University; UCLA's Center for the Art of Performance and UC Santa Barbara Arts & Lectures. Also presented as part of Portland Institute for Contemporary Art's 2020 Time-Based Art Festival and Temporada Alta 2020.

First presented on Forced Entertainment and project partner websites between 17 September – 15 November 2020.

Online version of the group's 2015 *Complete Works* project created during the Covid pandemic. The performers present condensed versions of all of Shakespeare's plays, comically and intimately retelling them from the space of their own homes, using a collection of everyday objects as stand-ins for the characters on the stage of an ordinary tabletop.

How the Time Goes, 2021

(Online project)

P: Robin Arthur, Tim Etchells, Jerry Killick, Richard Lowdon, Claire Marshall, Cathy Naden, Terry O'Connor. Guest Performer and Musical Collaborator: Marino Formenti. D: Tim Etchells. Sound: John Avery. Digital Post Production: Hugo Glendinning. Digital Production Management: Jim Harrison. CP: HAU Hebbel am Ufer, Berlin (DE), Künstlerhaus Mousonturm, Frankfurt am Main (DE), PACT Zollverein, Essen (DE).

Emerging from the delirious limbo of lockdown, *How the Time Goes* features the core group of Forced Entertainment in improvised Zoom interactions with the pianist Marino Formenti, from separate locations including Sheffield, Berlin, rural France, London, Vienna, and Budapest. Recorded between March and May 2021, the work comprises seven loosely linked chapters, screened once as a five-hour-long marathon and then available to watch as individual episodes. *How the Time Goes* extends the pandemic strangeness of the group's *End Meeting for All* (2020) to create a spiral patchwork of unedited fragments, neither diary nor fiction.

4. PHOTOGRAPHIC PROJECTS

Cardboard Signs, 1992/2019

(Photographs)

P: Robin Arthur, Richard Lowdon, Claire Marshall, Cathy Naden, Terry O'Connor. C: Hugo Glendinning, Forced Entertainment. PH: Hugo Glendinning.

—2021 version: A new selection of *Cardboard Signs* from 1992 and 2019 for *Things That Go through Your Mind When Falling*.

Five performers pose holding cardboard signs from *Emanuelle Enchanted*, staging situations for the camera in front of real locations in and around Sheffield. The locations take on the role of film or theatre backdrops.

Hotel Photographs, 1994

(Photographs)

C: Hugo Glendinning, Forced Entertainment. PH: Hugo Glendinning.

19 November 1994, The Gantry, Southampton (UK).

Glendinning's photographs, set in an anonymous Novotel hotel, seemingly capture unobserved moments during a fictitious photo shoot—moments without activity in which people are sleeping, waiting, staring blankly. The images were created during early *Hidden J* rehearsals at a point where the piece was exploring the idea of a group of people hiding out in hotels for prolonged periods of time.

Looking Forwards, 1993

(Artist pages)

T: Tim Etchells, PH: Hugo Glendinning.

Spring 1996, *Performance Research*, vol. 1.1 (UK).

Photographs of people (bus drivers, cashiers, policemen) thinking about the future, set in their everyday surroundings.

Rules of the Game, 2000

(Text and photographs)

P: Robin Arthur, Richard Lowdon, Claire Marshall, Cathy Naden. Guests: Tim Hall, Mary Agnes Krell. C: Tim Etchells, Hugo Glendinning, Forced Entertainment. PH: Hugo Glendinning.

28 March 2000, Site Gallery, Sheffield (UK).

Text and photographic document of an invented drinking game, played while watching television news. Drinking, undressing, and sexual acts abound in the game, regulated by complex rules and intricately linked to events on broadcast news.

Years 0–20, 2004

Text and photographs: Hugo Glendinning / Tim Etchells and Forced Entertainment.

A playful and provocative essay in photographs and words combining text from artistic director Tim Etchells and images from long-term documenter and collaborator, photographer Hugo Glendinning.

Instructions for Forgetting, 2001

P: Tim Etchells, Richard Lowdon. SP: Johnny Goodwin, Vlatka Horvat. D/T: Tim Etchells. S: Richard Lowdon. Video: Hugo Glendinning. CO: Wiener Festwochen, Vienna (AT).

Premiere: 31 May 2001, Wiener Festwochen, Vienna (AT).

Subsequent performances in: Brussels, Gent, Leuven (Belgium); Beijing (China); Dijon, Paris (France); Berlin, Frankfurt, Munich, Munster (DE); Bergen, Oslo (Norway); Tokyo (Japan); Rotterdam (Netherlands); Glasgow, Lancaster, Leeds, Leicester, London, Nottingham (UK); Minneapolis, Pittsburgh (USA).

Following Etchells' invitation, friends and artistic colleagues from different international contexts sent true stories and videos for the project. Seated at a table, with three monitors and Lowdon as a technician in the background, Etchells begins a journey through these narratives, mixing fiction and memory to create an 'intimate documentary'.

Down Time and *Starfucker,* 2001

P/D/T: Tim Etchells.

Premiere: 29 June 2001, Monologfestival, Schauspielhaus Zurich (CH).

Two short solo works. In *Down Time*, a silent recorded image of Tim Etchells' thinking face is accompanied by a live commentary, in which he attempts to describe the unfolding narrative of his thoughts on the chosen topic of 'goodbyes'. In *Starfucker*, Etchells stands alone onstage, performing a text comprising endless images of Hollywood celebrities caught in bizarre, violent, or sexually graphic acts. The images, like those in *Dirty Work*, unfold only in the mind of those watching.

Sight Is the Sense That Dying People Tend to Lose First, 2008

P: Jim Fletcher. D/T: Tim Etchells. AD: Pascale Petralia. L: Nigel Edwards. CO: Tanzquartier, Vienna (AT).

Premiere: 11 September 2008, Portland Institute for Contemporary Art, Portland (US).

Subsequent performances in: Brussels, Gent (Belgium); Vancouver (Canada); Cairo (Egypt); Gennevilliers, Paris (France); Berlin (DE); Tokyo (Japan); Lisbon (Portugal); Uppsala (Sweden); Bristol, Lancaster, Leeds, London, Sheffield (UK); New York (USA).

Sight Is the Sense That Dying People Tend to Lose First is a long free-associating monologue written by Etchells for the American performer Jim Fletcher. The text tumbles from topic to topic to create a failing explanation of the world and the things and ideas in it, all presented in no particular order.

Although We Fell Short, 2011

P: Kate McIntosh. D/T: Tim Etchells. L: Nigel Edwards. CO: Kaaitheater, Brussels (BE), Siemens Stiftung, Munich (DE).

A work in the form of a speech made from the ruins and fragments of many other speeches. A mixed up, cut-up assembly of contemporary and historical political campaigns, party congresses, debates, resignations, and revolutionary tracts in unexpected dialogues and collisions. Khrushchev, Obama, McCain, Thatcher, Blair, Pol Pot, and many others take their place in a work that strains and stretches sense.

That Night Follows Day, 2011

(Rehearsed readings)

Original production commissioned and produced by Campo formerly Victoria (Belgium), 2007. Rehearsed readings version produced by Forced Entertainment, led by: Hester Chillingworth, Tim Etchells, Caroline Lionnet, Claire Marshall, Cathy Naden, Terry O'Connor, Matthew Evans, Reena Kalsi. C/T: Tim Etchells.

Premiere: 5 November 2011, Sheffield Theatres, Sheffield (UK).

Subsequent rehearsed readings in: Beijing (China); Lorient, Rennes (France); Berlin (DE); Vilnius (Lithuania); Dublin (Republic of Ireland); Gwangju (South Korea); Abu Dhabi (UAE); Coventry, Leeds, Manchester, Warwick (UK).

A Broadcast/Looping Pieces, 2014

C/T/P: Tim Etchells.

Premiere: 19 November 2013, SPIELART Festival, Munich (DE).

Subsequent performances in: Antwerp, Brussels (Belgium); Berlin, Essen (DE); Amsterdam (Netherlands); Oslo (Norway); Lisbon (Portugal); Basel (Switzerland); Bristol, London (UK).

A live improvised vocal remixing of pages from Etchells' notebook—a computer document in which, over many years, he's gathered texts of many different kinds. Fragments of overheard conversation, cut-and-paste quotations direct from newspaper articles and web pages, ideas for performances, rough drafts, and other notes sit side by side in this textual scrapbook.

That Night Follows Day, 2018

(Full production)

P: Timi Adelagun, Sarah Carvalho, Amina Colaiacovo Abdelhalim, Lenny Cole, Jewell El-Daouk, Alexander Felgueira, Elsa Haddaway, George Karanja, Trisha Kashyap, Tamar Laniado, Loïc Ndoutoumou, Daniela Gomes Monteiro Onuegbu, Marti Perramon-Holgado, Julius Pinker, Ruari Spooner, Elica Trillana, Minnie Trottford. D: by Tim Etchells, Hester Chillingworth. T: Tim Etchells. BSL translation: Daryl Jackson. SD: Richard Lowdon. LD: Jim Harrison. Costume Design: Laura Hopkins. PM: Jim Harrison. Participation Producer (Southbank Centre): Alex Williams. Project Assistant (Forced Entertainment): Soraya Jane Nabipour. Project Assistant (Southbank Centre): Kaya La Bonte-Hurst. BSL Theatre Consultant: Daryl Jackson. BSL Interpreters (rehearsals): Rob Chalk, Katie Fenwick, Laura Goulden, Taz Hockaday, Susan Merrick, Paul Michaels, Jo Taylor, Rachel Tibetts, Jess Veal. CO: Southbank Centre, London (UK).

Premiere: December 2018, Southbank Centre, London (UK).

That Night Follows Day is a text by Tim Etchells, for performers between the ages of eight and fourteen. It explores the ways in which adults' words and actions shape and influence young people's experience. A chorus of kids onstage address the audience directly, exploring and interrogating the range of advice, facts, truisms, white lies, and excuses they hear from their elders.

PHOTOGRAPHY

All photographs are by Hugo Glendinning and are © Hugo Glendinning unless otherwise stated. Credits for performers run left-to-right within photographs.

Key:
CM = Claire Marshall
CN = Cathy Naden
RA = Robin Arthur
RL = Richard Lowdon
TC = Terry O'Connor
TE = Tim Etchells

2–3: *Emanuelle Enchanted* (1992). CM, RA, CN, TC, RL.

6–7: *From the Dark* (2016) rehearsal, Berliner Festspiele, Berlin, Germany, July 2016. John Rowley, CM, TC, CN, RL, Tobias Lange, Mark Etchells, RA, Nada Gambier, Jerry Killick, Reena Kalsi.

12–13: *Jessica in the Room of Lights* (1984). **12:** RA, Huw Chadbourn, Susie Williams. Photo: TE. **13:** Susie Williams (seated), Huw Chadbourn. Photo: TE.

14: *The Set-Up* (1985). Susie Williams, RA, Huw Chadbourn. Photo: TE.

15–17: *Nighthawks* (1985). **15:** Huw Chadbourn, RL, TE. Photo: CN. **16–17:** Huw Chadbourn, Susie Williams, RL. Photo: TE.

18–19: *The Day That Serenity Returned to the Ground* (1986). **18:** RA, TE, CN, Huw Chadbourn. **19:** RA.

22–31: *(Let the Water Run Its Course) to the Sea That Made the Promise* (1986). **22–23:** RA, Susie Williams. **25:** Top: RA, Susie Williams. Bottom: Susie Williams, RL. **26–27:** Susie Williams, RA. 28: RA, RL. **31:** Top: RL, CN, Susie Williams. Bottom: CN, RL.

32–35: *200% & Bloody Thirsty* (1988). **32:** RL, CN, RA. On video: Sarah Singleton, Mark Etchells. **33:** RA, RL, CN. **34:** Top: RL, RA, CN. Bottom: RL. **35:** RL, CN. On video: Mark Etchells.

36–37: *Some Confusions in the Law about Love* (1989). **36:** CM, RA, Fred McVittie. On video: Fred McVittie, CM.

37: TC, Fred McVittie, CN, CM. On video: Fred McVittie, CM.

38–43: *Marina & Lee* (1991). **38–39:** Mark Randle, TC, CM, RA, CN. **41:** CN. **42:** TC. **43:** RA.

44–47: *Emanuelle Enchanted* (1992). **44:** CM, RA, CN, TC, RL. **46:** CN, TC, CM, RA, RL. **47:** CN.

48–63: *Club of No Regrets* (1993). **48–49:** TC. 51: CM, RL, RA, CN. **52:** Top: RA, CM, RA, CN. Bottom: CN, RL, RA. **55:** RA, TC, RA, CN. **56:** CN, CM, RA, TC. **57:** Top: RA. Bottom: CN, TC, CM, RA. **58:** Left: RL. Right: CM, RA, TC. **59:** CN. 60: CM, CN, RL, CM, RA. **62–63:** CN, RL, CM, RA.

64–67: *12am: Awake & Looking Down* (1993), Live Culture, Tate Modern, March 2003. **64:** Top left: John Rowley, TC. Top right: TC, CM, CN. Middle left: TC, RL. Middle right: TC, CM. Bottom left: RL, CM, CN. Bottom right: TC, RL, John Rowley. **65:** Top left: John Rowley, CN, CM. Top right: RL, CM. Middle left: RL. Middle right: CN, TC, John Rowley. Bottom left: TC, RL, John Rowley, CN. Bottom right: CN, TC, RL. **66–67:** CN, CM.

68–69: *Hidden J* (1994). **68:** TC. **69:** RL.

70–71: *Speak Bitterness* (1994). **70:** TC, RA, Tim Hall, CM, CN. **71:** CM, CN.

72–73: *Quizoola!* (1996), Spill Festival of Live Art, Barbican, 2013. CM, RL.

74: *Showtime* (1996). TC, CM, CN (in dog's head), RA, RL.

76–79: *Pleasure* (1997). **76:** TC, CN. **77:** CN, CM, RL. **79:** RL.

80: *Dirty Work* (1998). CN, RA, CM.

81: *Who Can Sing a Song to Unfrighten Me?* (1999), Queen Elizabeth Hall, South Bank Centre, London, June 1999.

82–83: *And on the Thousandth Night...* (2000), Spill Festival, Purcell Room, South Bank Centre, London, April 2007. CM, TE, TC, RA, Jerry Killick, Ruth Ben-Tovim, RL, CN.

84–103: *First Night* (2001). **84:** CM, John Rowley, Bruno Roubicek, RA, RL, TC, Ben Neale. **85:** RL, RA. **86:** TC, CN, John Rowley. **89:** TC, Bruno Roubicek, CN, John Rowley, RA, Ben Neale, CM, RL. **90:** CM. **92:** John Rowley. **93:** RA, Ben Neale, Bruno Roubicek, CM (being carried), RL. **94:** Bruno Roubicek, TC, CN, RA, Ben Neale, CM, RL, John Rowley. **95:** RA, CM, Ben Neale, CN, TC, John Rowley. **96–97:** Bruno Roubicek, TC, CN, RA, Ben Neale, CM, RL, John Rowley. **98:** Bruno Roubicek, TC, CN, RA, Ben Neale, CM, RL, John Rowley. **99:** CM. **100:** Bruno Roubicek, John Rowley, RA, Ben Neale. **101:** John Rowley, RA, Ben Neale. **102:** RA, Bruno Roubicek, Ben Neale, RL, John Rowley. **103:** TC, CN, Bruno Roubicek, RA, RL, John Rowley, Ben Neale, CM.

104–25: *Bloody Mess* (2004). **104:** Bruno Roubicek. Photo: TE. **105:** CN, TC, Wendy Houstoun. **106–7:** CN, TC, Wendy Houstoun. **108:** CN, RL, TC, CM. **109:** RL, John Rowley, RA, Jerry Killick. **110–11:** Jerry Killick, CN, TC, Wendy Houstoun, Davis Freeman. **113:** Top: CN. Bottom: TC, CN, Jerry Killick. **114:** Photo: TE. **115:** TC, CN, RA, Wendy Houstoun. **117:** Top: John Rowley, Bruno Roubicek. Bottom: Wendy Houstoun, RA, John Rowley, Bruno Roubicek. **118–119:** RL, John Rowley, CN, RA, TC. **121:** Top: John Rowley. Bottom: Wendy Houstoun. **122–23:** RL, John Rowley, RA, Bruno Roubicek, Wendy Houstoun, TC, Davis Freeman, CN. **125:** TC, Wendy Houstoun.

126–27: *The World in Pictures* (2006). RA, TC RL, Wendy Houstoun, CM, Davis Freeman, Bruno Roubicek, Jerry Killick.

128: *Spectacular* (2008). RA, CM.

130: *Void Story* (2009). CN, RL.

131: *The Thrill of It All* (2010). CM, CN, Amit Hadari, TC.

132: *Tomorrow's Parties* (2011). TC, RA.

134: *The Coming Storm* (2012). RA, TC, Phil Hayes, CM, CN, RA.

135–37: *The Last Adventures* (2013), Maschinenhalle Zweckel, Gladbeck, Ruhrtriennale Festival of the Arts, Ruhr, Germany, September 2013. **135:** Partially visible: Gareth Brierley, John Rowley (in red), TC, RA. **136–37:** Kylie Walters, John Rowley, RA, Bruno Roubicek, Leja Jurisic, Teja Reba, TC, RL, CM, Kuselo Kamau, Mark Etchells, Maria Jerez, Nada Gambier, CN.

138: *The Notebook* (2014). RL, RA.

139: *Complete Works: Table Top Shakespeare* (2015). Top left: RA, *Love's Labours Lost*. Top right: CN, *The Winter's Tale*. Middle left: TC, *Richard II*. Middle right: Jerry Killick, *Coriolanus*. Bottom left: RL, *Macbeth*. Bottom right: CM, *All's Well That Ends Well*.

140: *From the Dark* (2016), Berliner Festspiele, Berlin, Germany, July 2016. Nada Gambier, Tobias Lange (in costume), RA.

141–54: *Real Magic* (2016). **141:** RL, Jerry Killick, CM. **142:** Jerry Killick, CM, RL. **145:** Jerry Killick, RL. **146:** Jerry Killick, CM, RL. **147:** CM, Jerry Killick, RL. **148:** RL, Jerry Killick, CM. **149:** Jerry Killick, CM, RL. **150–51:** CM, RL, Jerry Killick. **153:** Top: CM, Jerry Killick, RL. Middle: CM, Jerry Killick, RL. Bottom: CM, Jerry Killick, RL. **154:** CM, Jerry Killick, RL.

155–167: *Out of Order* (2018). **155:** Jerry Killick, TC, RA, Nicki Hobday, RL, CN. **156:** Top left: Jerry Killick, RL, RA, Nicki Hobday, CN, TC. Top right: CN, Jerry Killick, RA, RL. Middle left: Jerry Killick, Nicki Hobday, RL, CN, TC, RA. Middle right: TC, Jerry Killick, Nicki Hobday, RL, CN, RA. Bottom left: TC, RL, Nicki Hobday, RA, CN, Jerry Killick. Bottom right: RA, CN, TC, RL, Nicki Hobday, Jerry Killick. **157:** Top left: RA, TC, RL, Nicki Hobday, Jerry Killick. Top right: Nicki Hobday, TC, Jerry Killick, RL, RA. Middle left: Jerry Killick, Nicki Hobday, TC, CN, RL, RA. Middle right: RA, Nicki Hobday, Jerry Killick, CN, RL. Bottom left: RA, Jerry Killick, Nicki Hobday. Bottom right: RA, Jerry Killick, TC, CN. **158:** RA, RL, Jerry Killick, Nicki Hobday. **159:** RL, TC. **160–61:** Jerry Killick, RL, Nicki Hobday, TC, CN. **162:** CN, RL, TC, RA, Jerry Killick, Nicki Hobday. **163:** Jerry Killick, Nicki Hobday, RL, TC. **164–65:** RL, Jerry Killick, Nicki Hobday, TC, RA. **166:** CN, Nicki Hobday, RL, RA, Jerry Killick. **167:** CN, TC, RL, Nicki Hobday, RA.

173: *(Let the Water Run Its Course) to the Sea That Made the Promise* (1986). CN, RL, RA.

175–76: *Club of No Regrets* (1993). **175:** CM, RA, TC, CN. **176:** CN, CM, RL, RA.

179: *Bloody Mess* (2004). Jerry Killick, RA, Davis Freeman.

183: *Out of Order* (2018). Jerry Killick, Nicki Hobday, RL, CN, TC, RA.

189: *The Day That Serenity Returned to the Ground* (1986). CN, Huw Chadbourn, RA.

190: *Jessica in the Room of Lights* (1984). Huw Chadbourn, CN, Susie Williams.

193: Top left: Sheffield, 1994. Photos taken for *A Decade of Forced Entertainment* (1995). Top right: Fabric shop on Toller Lane, Bradford, 1975. Photo © Matthew Davison. Bottom left: Co-op butcher's shop on Toller Lane, Bradford, 1975. Photo © Matthew Davison. Bottom right: Sheffield, 1994. Photos taken for *A Decade of Forced Entertainment* (1995).

197: Tyrone Huggins, Richard Hawley, Steve Shill, Pete Brooks, Claire MacDonald. Waterloo Gallery, May 1982. Photo © Steve Littman.

198: Left: Impact, *The Carrier Frequency*, ICA, London, 1985. Heather Ackroyd, Claire MacDonald, Niki Johnson. Photo © Matthew Davison. Right: Impact, *Useful Vices*, ICA, London, 1981. Claire MacDonald, Richard Hawley, Graeme Miller. Photo © Steve Shill.

208–9: Photos of Sheffield taken for the first presentation of *A Decade of Forced Entertainment* (1995), ICA, London, March 1995.

214: Top row: Photos of Sheffield by Hugo Glendinning, from TE and Hugo Glendinning, *The True Meaning of Things Lies in Their Use* (2006). Middle left: *A Decade of Forced Entertainment* (1995), ICA, London, March 1995. CN, RL, CM. Middle right: Photo of Sheffield by Hugo Glendinning, from TE and Hugo Glendinning, *True Meaning* (2006). Bottom row: Photos from *A Decade of Forced Entertainment* (1995).

215: Top left: *A Decade of Forced Entertainment* (1995), ICA, London, March 1995. TE, TC, RA. Top right: Photos of Sheffield by Hugo Glendinning, from TE and Hugo Glendinning, *The True Meaning of Things Lies in Their Use* (2006). Middle and bottom rows: Photos from *A Decade of Forced Entertainment* (1995).

223: *Showtime* (1996). CN, CM, RA.

224: *Bloody Mess* (2004). RA, John Rowley, Bruno Roubicek.

225: *Showtime* (1996). RL, CM.

227: *The World in Pictures* (2006). Wendy Houstoun, Jerry Killick.

228: *Pleasure* (1997). RA, CM.

233: *And on the Thousandth Night...* (2000), Spill Festival, Purcell Room, South Bank Centre, London, April 2007. CN, CM, RA, TC, TE, RL.

236: *Complete Works: Table Top Shakespeare* (2015). TC, *Richard II*.

237: Bookshelf in the public library in Salerno. Photo © Joy Kristin Kalu.

247: *Quizoola!* (1996), B-Space.Be, KunstenFestivalDesArts, Brussels, May 2000. TE, RL.

249–50: *From the Dark* (2016), Berliner Festspiele, Berlin, Germany, July 2016. **249:** RA (centre). **250:** Tobias Lange (at blackboard).

255: *Speak Bitterness* (1994), durational performance version, PACT, Essen, February 2009. TC, RA, CN, TE, CM.

260: *Bloody Mess* (2004). Jerry Killick, RA, Davis Freeman.

265: *Void Story* (2009). CN.

267: Photo by TE of pages from Tim Etchells, *Vacuum Days* (Hove: Storythings, 2012).

269: Top: *Some Confusions in the Law about Love* (1989). TC, CM, RA, Fred McVittie, CN. On video: Fred McVittie, CM. Bottom: *Emanuelle Enchanted* (1992). RL, CM, RA, TC.

275: *Club of No Regrets* (1993). TC.

276: Top: *Spectacular* (2008). RA. Bottom: *The Notebook* (2014). RL, RA.

284: *The Thrill of It All* (2010). Thomas Conway, Jerry Killick, John Rowley.

287: *Real Magic* (2016). CM, RL.

297: Photos from the series *Stopped Clocks* (2015) by Tim Etchells. Courtesy the artist and VITRINE.

304: Huw Chadbourn, Susie Williams, TE, RA, CM. Photo: TE.

305: *How the Time Goes* (2021). Top row: Marino Formenti, TE (with donkey's head). Middle row: CN, CM. Photo: TE.

307: *12am: Awake & Looking Down* (1993), SpielArt Festival, Munich, November, 2019. Photo: TE.

309–17: *Cardboard Signs* (1992). **309:** CN. **310:** TC, RA. **313:** RL. **314:** CM. **317:** RA.

318–29: *Cardboard Signs* (2019). **318:** TC. **321:** CN. **322:** CN, RL. **325:** RA. **326:** CM. **329:** RL.

336: *The Last Adventures* rehearsal, Maschinenhalle Zweckel, Gladbeck, Germany, 2013. TE.

384: Untitled improvised performance, Kunstlerhaus Mousonturm, Frankfurt, Germany, 2003. Tobias Lange.

Front cover: *Bloody Mess* (2004). RA, RL, CM (as gorilla), John Rowley, Jerry Killick.

Front cover flap: 1st row: 1: *Club of No Regrets* pre-publicity image, Sheffield, 1993. CN. **2:** *The Last Adventures* rehearsal, Maschinenhalle Zweckel, Gladbeck, Germany, 2013. Kylie Waters, TC, CN, CM. **3:** *Quizoola!* (24 hour version), Spill Festival of Live Art, Barbican, 2013. RA. **4:** *That Night Follows Day* rehearsal, South Bank Centre, London, 2018. Hester Chillingworth. **5:** *Who Can Sing a Song to Unfrighten Me?* pre-publicity image, Sheffield, 1999. Miles Etchells, CN. **6:** *The Last Adventures* rehearsal, Maschinenhalle Zweckel, Gladbeck, Germany, 2013. Nigel Edwards. **2nd row: 1:** Preparation for *Void Story* previews, Vienna, 2009. RL, CN, CM, RA, TC, TE. **2:** Costume, *From the Dark* rehearsal, Berliner Festspiele, Berlin, Germany, July 2016. **3:** *200% & Bloody Thirsty* video material shoot, Sheffield, 1987. Sarah Singleton, Mark Etchells. Photo: TE. **4:** Ibsen Award Ceremony, National Theatre Oslo, 2016. CN, RA, TE, TC, CM, RL. **5:** *Red Room*, photo used in installation, London, 1993. **6:** Blackboard titling section of *Marathon Lexicon*, Kunstlerhaus Mousonturm, Frankfurt, Germany, 2003. **3rd row: 1:** *The Thrill of It All* rehearsal, Sheffield, 2010. Jerry Killick. **2:** *The Last Adventures* rehearsal, Maschinenhalle Zweckel, Gladbeck, Germany, 2013. CN, Kylie Walters, Kuselo Kamau. **3:** *The Thrill of It All* rehearsal, Sheffield, 2010. Photo: TE. **4:** Installing *Speak Bitterness*, PACT Zollverein, Essen, Germany, 2009. RL, Jim Harrison. **5:** *Speak Bitterness* set build-up, PACT Zollverein, Essen, Germany, 2009. **6:** *From the Dark* rehearsal, Sheffield, 2016. Mark Etchells, CM. **4th row: 1:** *The Last Adventures* rehearsal, Maschinenhalle Zweckel, Gladbeck, Germany, 2013. TE, Tarek Atoui, RL. **2:** Blackboard titling section of *Marathon Lexicon*, Kunstlerhaus Mousonturm, Frankfurt, Germany, 2003. **3:** *Marina & Lee* rehearsal, Sheffield, 1991. RA, CN. **4:** *The Last Adventures* rehearsal, Maschinenhalle Zweckel, Gladbeck, Germany, 2013. **5:** *Out of Order* onstage rehearsal, PACT Zollverein, Essen, Germany, 2019. Nicki Hobday. **6:** Rehearsal, project with Jérôme Bel, Kunstlerhaus Mousonturm, Frankfurt, Germany, 2003. RL, Antonio Pedro Lopes, CM, Maria Jerez, Jérôme Bel, Sonja Augart, Dina Ed Dick. **5th row: 1:** *Quizoola!* (24 hour version), Spill Festival of Live Art, Barbican, 2013. CM. **2:** *Pleasure*, pre-publicity image, Sheffield, 1997. RA, TC. **3:** *The Last Adventures* rehearsal, Maschinenhalle Zweckel, Gladbeck, Germany, 2013. CM, Kylie Waters. **4:** *Speak Bitterness* text materials onstage, PACT Zollverein, Essen, Germany, 2009. **5:** *The World in Pictures* onstage rehearsal, Volksbühne, Berlin, Germany, 2006. RL, RA, TC, Wendy Houstoun, Davies Freeman, Jerry Killick, Bruno Roubicek. **6:** *Jessica in the Room of Lights* pre-publicity image, Sheffield, 1984. Susie Williams. Photo: TE. **6th row: 1:** *Bloody Mess* re-rehearsal, Théâtre Garonne, Toulouse, 2012. RL, John Rowley, RA, Bruno Roubicek. Photo: TE. **2:** *The Thrill of It All* rehearsal, Sheffield, 2010. TC. **3:** Rehearsal for project with Richard Maxwell company, Kunstlerhaus Mousonturm, Frankfurt, Germany, 2003. John Rowley, Gary Wilmes, RL, Jim Fletcher. **4:** *Club of No Regret* post-final show party, San Francisco, USA, 1997. Will Waghorn. Photo: TE. **5:** *Quizoola!* (24 hour version), Spill Festival of Live Art, Barbican, 2013. TE. **6:** *The Thrill of It All* pre-premiere (backstage), Kaaitheatre, Brussels, Belgium, 2010. Phil Hayes, Jerry Killick, John Rowley, TE, Nigel Edwards, Eileen Evans, CM, Kate McIntosh, TC, RL, Thomas Conway, Hester Chillingworth, CN, Sarah Cockburn.

Back cover flap: 1st row: 1: *Who Can Sing a Song to Unfrighten Me?* (backstage), South Bank Centre, London, 1999. TE and unknown. **2:** The Coming Storm, onstage rehearsal, National Theatre Oslo, 2016. CN, RL, TC, CM, Phil Hayes. **3:** *The Thrill of It All* rehearsal, Sheffield, 2010. CN. **4:** *Quizoola!* (24 hour version), Spill Festival of Live Art, Barbican, 2013. CN. **5:** *Club of No Regrets* sculpture for poster artwork by Lewis Nicholson, 1993. **6:** *Emanuelle Enchanted* rehearsal/pre-publicity, Sheffield, 1992. RA, RL, CN. **2nd row: 1:** *Marina & Lee* rehearsal, Sheffield, 1991. CM, CN. **2:** *Out of Order* (backstage), Theatre Mousonturm Frankfurt, 2016. **3:** *Bloody Mess* rehearsal, Munich, 2003. TC, JK, Davis Freeman. **4:** Deborah Chadbourn, Warsaw, Poland, 1989. **5:** *The Last Adventures* rehearsal, Maschinenhalle Zweckel, Gladbeck, Germany, 2013. CN. **6:** *The Last Adventures* rehearsal, Maschinenhalle Zweckel, Gladbeck, Germany, 2013. Kylie Walters, RN, Tarek Atoui. **3rd row: 1:** *From the Dark* rehearsal, Sheffield, 2016. Tobias Lange. **2:** Gdańsk, Poland, 1989. TE, RA, RL, CN, TC. **3:** *The Last Adventures* rehearsal, Maschinenhalle Zweckel, Gladbeck, Germany, 2013. **4:** Bologna, 1998. Ray Rennie, Andy Clarke. Photo: CM. **5:** *Club of No Regrets* rehearsal, Sheffield, 1993. CM. **6:** *From the Dark* rehearsal, Sheffield, 2016. CM. **4th row: 1:** *Speak Bitterness* rehearsal, Sheffield, 1987. RA, RL. Photo: TE. **2:** *Out of Order* rehearsal, PACT Zollverein, 2016. **3:** *To Move in Time* rehearsal, Sheffield, 2019. Tyrone Huggins. **4:** Kino Tęcza Studio Warsaw, Poland, 1989. TE, TC. **5:** Blackboard titling section of *Marathon Lexicon*, Kunstlerhaus Mousonturm, Frankfurt, Germany, 2003. **6:** *Institute of Failure* rehearsal, Kunstlerhaus Mousonturm, Frankfurt, Germany, 2003. Mark Booth and TE (reflected), Matthew Goulish. **5th row: 1:** *From the Dark* rehearsal, Sheffield, 2016. CM and unknown. **2:** Warsaw, Poland, 1989. Hugo Glendinning, RA. **3:** *Disco Relax* rehearsal/pre-publicity image, Sheffield, 1999. Tim Hall, CN. **4:** *From the Dark* rehearsal, Sheffield, 2016. **5:** Photo shoot for *Hidden J* publicity materials, Sheffield, 1994. RA, CN. **6:** *The Thrill of It All* rehearsal, Sheffield, 2010. RL. **6th row: 1:** *Some Confusions in the Law about Love* poster image, 1989. Elizabeth McGill. **2:** *Spectacular* early rehearsal, Sheffield, 2007. TE, CM, CN, TC. **3:** Filming *Filthy Words and Phrases*, Sheffield, 1997. John Avery. **4:** *Bloody Mess* re-rehearsal, Théâtre Garonne, Toulouse, January, 2012. RL, CN, John Rowley, CM, Jerry Killick. Photo: TE. **5:** *Bloody Mess* re-rehearsal, Théâtre Garonne, Toulouse, France, January, 2012. Photo: TE. **6:** *Marina & Lee* rehearsal/pre-publicity image, Sheffield, 1991. CN.

ACKNOWLEDGEMENTS

Forced Entertainment: Our long artistic collaboration has only been possible on the basis of the many other partnerships the company has built up over the years, nationally and internationally, with the numerous extraordinary organizations, festivals, individual curators, and programmers that we have been lucky enough to work with, as well as with the funding bodies and foundations that have directly and indirectly supported our work. We would like to thank them all.

Our special thanks go to Janek Alexander, Antônio Araújo, John Ashford, Cesar Augusto, Mark Ball, Vincent Baudriller, Sven Åge Birkeland, Philip Bither, Kristof Blom, Stéphane Boitel, Tilmann Broszat, Helen Cole, Marie Collin, Guy Cools, Mark Deputter, Marcus Dross, Richard Dufty, Kristy Edmunds, Niels Ewerbeck, Matt Fenton, Rose Fenton, Thomas Frank, Francisco Frazão, Vallejo Gantner, Sigrid Gareis, Richard Gough, Guy Guypens, Stella Hall, Bush Hartshorn, Walter Heun, Stefan Hilterhaus, Martina Hochmuth, Kevin Jamieson, Andrew Jones, Veronica Kaup-Hasler, Lois Keidan, Judith Knight, Dietmar Kobboldt, Gundega Laivina, Serge Laurent, Frie Leysen, Matthias Lilienthal, Annie Lloyd, Gill Lloyd, Florian Malzacher, Hiromi Maruoko, Laura McDermott, John McGrath, David Micklem, Nikki Millican, Grahame Morris, Lucy Neil, Robin Nelson, Robert Pacitti, Dirk Pauwels, Matthias Pees, Christine Peters, Aenne Quiñones, Toni Racklin, Priit Raud, Alan Rivett, Celesta Rottiers, Mark Russell, Joanna Scanlan, Christophe Slagmuylder, Steve Slater, Rupert Thompson, Mark Timmer, Gabriella Triantafyllis, David Tushingham, Catherine Ugwu, Annemie Vanackere, Dennis Van Laeken, Claire Verlet, Kathrin Veser, Hortensia Völkers, Matthias von Hartz, Mark Waddell, Neil Wallace, Jay Wegman, Willie White, Yvonne White, Jürg Woodtli, and Marie Zimmermann.

We would also like to thank the people that have worked with us in different capacities, from office, technical, and other colleagues to board members and advisors, through to the extended group of artistic collaborators we have shared creative space with over the years. All of them have helped to develop, extend, and reinvent the work in so many ways, and the range and depth of the company's practice has only been possible thanks to their efforts and inspiration.

We are especially indebted to John Avery (sound), Hester Chillingworth (participation, directorial assistant), Nigel Edwards (lighting), Davis Freeman, Tim Hall, Phil Hayes, Nicki Hobday, Wendy Houstoun, Jerry Killick, Sue Marshall, John Rowley, and Bruno Roubicek (performers), and to our brilliant and committed current team Eileen Evans (executive director), Jim Harrison (production), and Imogen Ashby (participation), as well as to Susie Williams and Huw Chadbourn, who were our fellow founder members of the group in 1984. Heartfelt thanks are also due to founder member of the group Deborah Chadbourn, who has made a profound and passionate contribution to the company and its work, as administrator, then later as general manager and chair of the board.

Huge thanks are also due to Hugo Glendinning, whose friendship and creative work has been a source of strength and inspiration over decades and whose astute, attentive photo documentation of our work finds a timely articulation in the collaboration on this book.

As singular as our practice has been, it has always emerged from a communal space of conversation and exchange with other makers and thinkers. Our thanks and respect are due to so many fellow travellers in the field of performance as they have negotiated the troubled territory of the last decades, as well as to the writers and thinkers who have engaged tirelessly with this scene, extending it vividly and critically.

Finally, Forced Entertainment's deep and evolving encounter with audiences, at home and abroad, has been the absolute bedrock of our work. The generosity and enthusiasm of audiences, their healthy scepticism, and their appetite for complexity and for the dialogue our work has sought to open up are something we are perpetually grateful for, and from which we continue to draw strength.

Robin Arthur, Tim Etchells, Richard Lowdon, Claire Marshall, Cathy Naden, and Terry O'Connor

Adrian Heathfield (editor) would like to thank the following people: Tim Etchells, Forced Entertainment, Hugo Glendinning, and all the essay contributors for their inspiration and careful collaboration in the making of this book; David Caines for his innovation and clarity in creating the design; Emma Leach for her meticulous work as assistant editor; Simon Cowper for his sharp eye in proofing; Emily Roderick for assistance with transcriptions; and Anne König, Jan Wenzel and Robert Stürzl at Spector Books for their sustained support. Some elements have been published previously: 'A Decade of Forced Entertainment' first appeared in Tim Etchells, *Certain Fragments* (London: Routledge, 1999); 'A Text on Twenty Years with Sixty-Six Footnotes' first appeared in Judith Helmer and Florian Malzacher (eds.), *Not Even a Game Anymore: The Theatre of Forced Entertainment* (Berlin: Alexander Verlag, 2004); 'Compendium: A Forced Glossary' is a largely revised version of 'Compendium: A Forced Entertainment Glossary', in 'On Memory', *Performance Research*, 5/3 (2000), 140–48. Thanks are due to the International Ibsen Award (2016), which supported aspects of this publication, as well as to the British Academy, who supported initial research, and PACT Zollverein, who aided our archival research and the preparation of photographs.

Published by Spector Books

Spector Books OHG
Harkortstraße 10
D-04107 Leipzig
Germany
www.spectorbooks.com

Design: David Caines Unlimited, www.davidcaines.co.uk

Assistant Editor: Emma Leach.

Printed and bound by Druckhaus Sportflieger, Berlin.

Things That Go through Your Mind When Falling has been financially supported using Forced Entertainment's International Ibsen Award (2016).

Things That Go through Your Mind When Falling has been supported with the subvention of PACT Zollverein.

Research supported by The British Academy.

Forced Entertainment is financially supported by Arts Council England.

A catalogue record for this book is available from the National Library of Germany and the Saxony State and University Library.

Distribution

Germany, Austria: GVA, Gemeinsame Verlagsauslieferung Göttingen GmbH&Co. KG, www.gva-verlage.de
Switzerland: AVA Verlagsauslieferung AG, www.ava.ch
France, Belgium: Interart Paris, www.interart.fr
UK: Central Books Ltd, www.centralbooks.com
USA, Canada, Central and South America, Africa: ARTBOOK | D.A.P., www.artbook.com
Japan: twelvebooks, www.twelve-books.com
South Korea: The Book Society, www.thebooksociety.org
Australia, New Zealand: Perimeter Distribution, www.perimeterdistribution.com

First edition

Printed in the EU

ISBN 978-3-95905-385-3

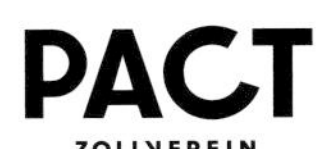
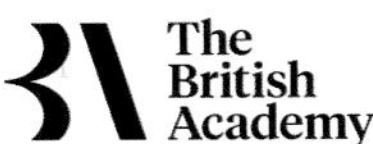
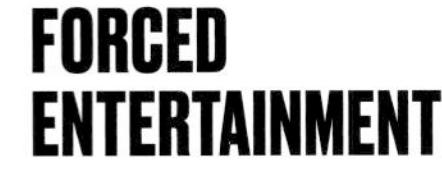
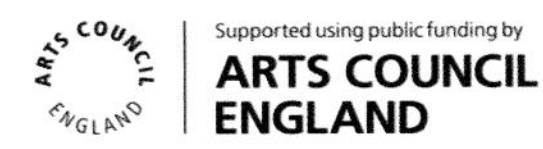

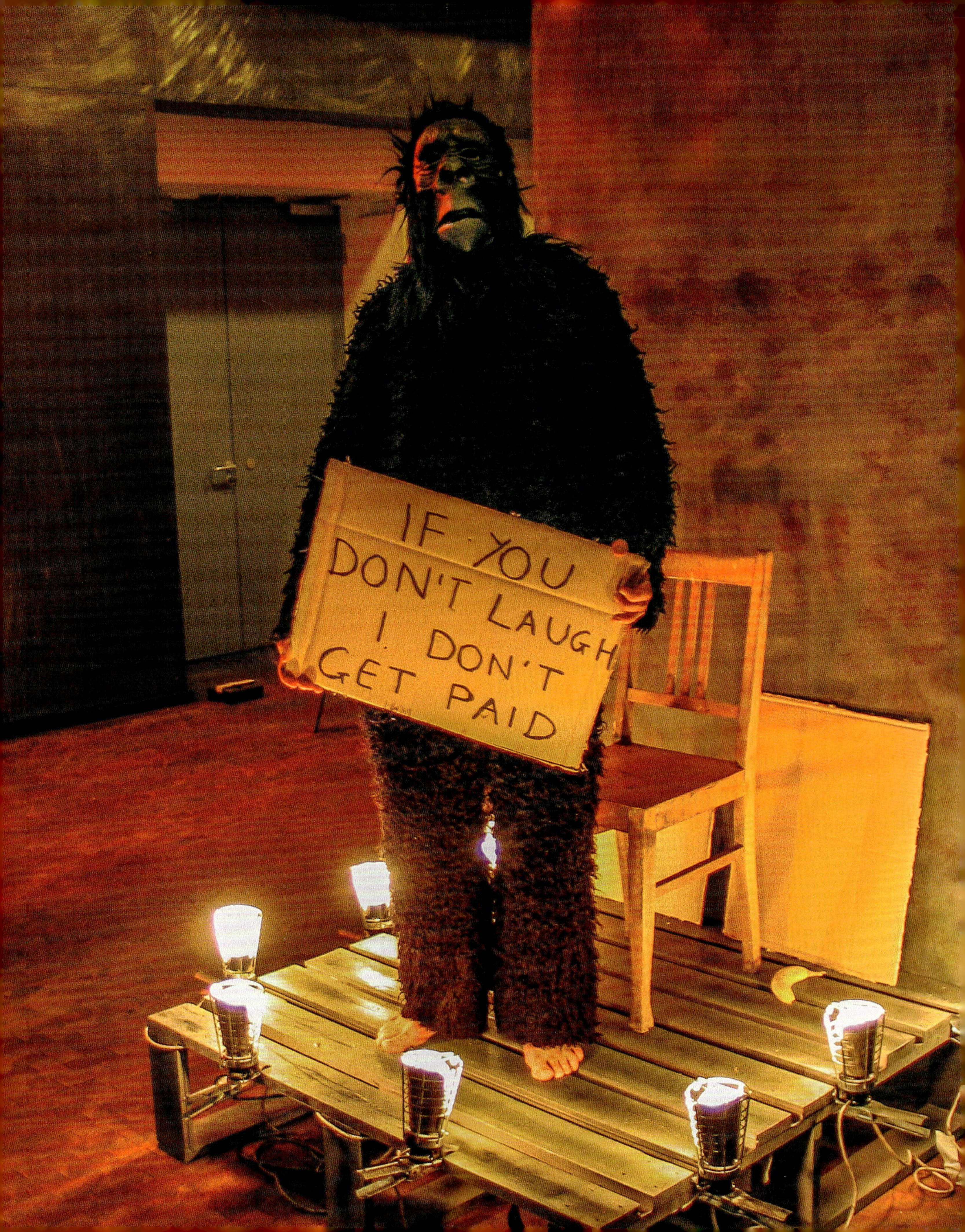

IF YOU
DON'T LAUGH
I DON'T
GET PAID